Lecture Notes in Computer Science 6627

Commenced Publication in 1973
Founding and Former Series Editors:
Gerhard Goos, Juris Hartmanis, and Jan van Leeuwen

Editorial Board

David Hutchison
  Lancaster University, UK
Takeo Kanade
  Carnegie Mellon University, Pittsburgh, PA, USA
Josef Kittler
  University of Surrey, Guildford, UK
Jon M. Kleinberg
  Cornell University, Ithaca, NY, USA
Alfred Kobsa
  University of California, Irvine, CA, USA
Friedemann Mattern
  ETH Zurich, Switzerland
John C. Mitchell
  Stanford University, CA, USA
Moni Naor
  Weizmann Institute of Science, Rehovot, Israel
Oscar Nierstrasz
  University of Bern, Switzerland
C. Pandu Rangan
  Indian Institute of Technology, Madras, India
Bernhard Steffen
  TU Dortmund University, Germany
Madhu Sudan
  Microsoft Research, Cambridge, MA, USA
Demetri Terzopoulos
  University of California, Los Angeles, CA, USA
Doug Tygar
  University of California, Berkeley, CA, USA
Gerhard Weikum
  Max Planck Institute for Informatics, Saarbruecken, Germany

Juergen Dingel   Arnor Solberg (Eds.)

Models in Software Engineering

Workshops and Symposia at MODELS 2010
Oslo, Norway, October 3-8, 2010
Reports and Revised Selected Papers

Volume Editors

Juergen Dingel
Queen's University, School of Computing
Goodwin Hall, 25 Union St, Kingston, ON K7L 3N6, Canada
E-mail: dingel@cs.queensu.ca

Arnor Solberg
SINTEF
Forskningsveien 1, Pb. Blindern, 0314 Oslo, Norway
E-mail: Arnor.Solberg@sintef.no

ISSN 0302-9743 e-ISSN 1611-3349
ISBN 978-3-642-21209-3 e-ISBN 978-3-642-21210-9
DOI 10.1007/978-3-642-21210-9
Springer Heidelberg Dordrecht London New York

Library of Congress Control Number: 2011927190

CR Subject Classification (1998): D.2, D.3, F.3, K.6, I.6

LNCS Sublibrary: SL 1 – Theoretical Computer Science and General Issues

© Springer-Verlag Berlin Heidelberg 2011
This work is subject to copyright. All rights are reserved, whether the whole or part of the material is
concerned, specifically the rights of translation, reprinting, re-use of illustrations, recitation, broadcasting,
reproduction on microfilms or in any other way, and storage in data banks. Duplication of this publication
or parts thereof is permitted only under the provisions of the German Copyright Law of September 9, 1965,
in its current version, and permission for use must always be obtained from Springer. Violations are liable
to prosecution under the German Copyright Law.
The use of general descriptive names, registered names, trademarks, etc. in this publication does not imply,
even in the absence of a specific statement, that such names are exempt from the relevant protective laws
and regulations and therefore free for general use.

Typesetting: Camera-ready by author, data conversion by Scientific Publishing Services, Chennai, India

Printed on acid-free paper

Springer is part of Springer Science+Business Media (www.springer.com)

Preface

The MODELS series of conferences is the premier venue for the exchange of innovative technical ideas and experiences relating to model-driven approaches in the development of software-based systems. Following the tradition of previous conferences, MODELS 2010 hosted several satellite events in Oslo during the three days before the main conference. There were two MODELS symposia and 12 MODELS workshops:

- Doctoral Symposium
- Educators' Symposium
- Model-Based Architecting and Construction of Embedded Systems (ACES-MB)
- Aspect-Oriented Modeling (AOM)
- Equation-Based Object-Oriented Modeling Languages and Tools (EOOLT)
- Model-Driven Interoperability (MDI)
- Models and Evolution (ME)
- Models@run.time
- Model-Driven Engineering, Verification and Validation (MoDeVVa)
- Multi-paradigm Modeling: Concepts and Tools (MPM)
- Non-functional System Properties in Domain-Specific Modeling Languages (NFPinDSML)
- OCL and Textual Modeling
- Quality of Service-Oriented Software Systems (QUASOSS)
- Model-Based Engineering for Robotics (RoSym)

In addition, the MODELS 2010 satellite event program included two industry-oriented events (*Project Presentations* and *Industry Track*), four Tutorials (*DSL1, DSL2, Methods and Tools*, and *Eclipse/EMF*), and one MODELS co-located event (*The 6th Workshop on System Analysis and Modelling (SAM 2010)*).

New this year was a more flexible organization of the satellite events which allowed and encouraged participants to move around and create their own customized MODELS 2010 satellite event program. For example, participants could follow a session of a workshop, then shift to another session of another workshop or participate in a tutorial or follow some presentations of the Industry Track or Project Track. During the satellite events there where up to eight parallel sessions. This flexibility was received very well, and we believe it helped create a setting which offered something interesting to attend for everybody at any point in time.

MODELS 2010 had a record number of more than 400 attendees, of which about 350 attended the satellite events. The workshops and symposia provided a collaborative forum for groups of participants to exchange recent and/or preliminary results, to conduct intensive discussions on a particular topic, or to coordinate efforts between representatives of a technical community. The discussions were lively and the attendance was high.

These proceedings include the selected best papers of the MODELS workshops and symposia. Fourteen MODELS workshop proposals were submitted. The selection of workshops was performed by the Workshop Committee which consisted of the following experts:

- Juergen Dingel, Queen's University, Canada (Co-chair)
- Arnor Solberg, SINTEF, Norway (Co-chair)
- James Bieman, Colorado State University, USA
- Jean-Marc Jézéquel, INRIA, France
- Alexander Pretschner, TU Kaiserslautern, Germany

The focus of the Educators' Symposium was on sharing experience related to teaching modeling techniques and on developing resources to support effective training of future practitioners of model-driven development.

The Doctoral Symposium provided a forum in which PhD students could present and get feedback on their work in progress. The symposium fostered the role of MODELS as a premier venue for research in model-driven engineering. The symposium provided the students with independent and constructive feedback about their already completed work and more importantly their planned research work.

The organizers of the 12 workshops and the two symposia invited the authors of the selected best papers to revise and extend their papers for publication in these proceedings. The selected papers went through two rounds of reviews before being included in the proceedings. Each workshop and symposium also provided a summary of the event; these summary reports are included in these proceedings.

We would like to thank everyone involved in making the satellite events highly successful, especially the organizers of the satellite events, the members of the Workshop Committee, the General Chair, Øystein Haugen, the chair of the MODELS Steering Committee Heinrich Hussmann and last, but not least, all the active participants.

February 2011

Juergen Dingel
Arnor Solberg

Organization

Sponsoring Institutions

ACM
IEEE
SINTEF
Department of Informatics, University of Oslo

Table of Contents

Doctoral Symposium

The Doctoral Symposium at MODELS 2010 1
    Bernhard Schätz and Brian Elvesæter

ReuseMe - Towards Aspect-Driven Reuse in Modelling Method
Development 4
    Alexander Bergmayr

A Model-Based Framework for Software Performance Feedback 19
    Catia Trubiani

Educators' Symposium

Software Modeling in Education: The 6th Educators' Symposium at
MODELS 2010 35
    Martina Seidl and Peter J. Clarke

Novel Communication Channels in Software Modeling Education 40
    Marion Brandsteidl, Konrad Wieland, and Christian Huemer

Implementation of the Concept-Driven Approach in an Object-Oriented
Analysis and Design Course 55
    Ven Yu Sien

Workshop – ACES-MB

Model Based Architecting and Construction of Embedded Systems
(ACES-MB 2010) 70
    Stefan Van Baelen, Iulian Ober, Huascar Espinoza,
    Thomas Weigert, Ileana Ober, and Sébastien Gérard

Virtual Verification of System Designs against System Requirements 75
    Wladimir Schamai, Philipp Helle, Peter Fritzson, and
    Christiaan J.J. Paredis

From Interaction Overview Diagrams to Temporal Logic 90
    Luciano Baresi, Angelo Morzenti, Alfredo Motta, and Matteo Rossi

Workshop – AOM

Report of the 15th International Workshop on Aspect-Oriented
Modeling 105
Jeff Gray, Dominik Stein, Jörg Kienzle, and Walter Cazzola

Aspect-Oriented Feature Models 110
*Marko Bošković, Gunter Mussbacher, Ebrahim Bagheri,
Daniel Amyot, Dragan Gašević, and Marek Hatala*

Mapping Aspect-Oriented Models to Aspect-Oriented Code 125
Max E. Kramer and Jörg Kienzle

Workshop – EOOLT

Equation-Based Object-Oriented Modeling Languages and Tools:
Report on the Workshop EOOLT 2010 at MODELS 2010 Oslo, Norway,
October 3, 2010 140
*Peter Fritzson, Edward A. Lee, François E. Cellier, and
David Broman*

Workshop – MDI

Model-Driven Interoperability: MDI 2010 145
Jean Bézivin, Richard M. Soley, and Antonio Vallecillo

From the Heterogeneity Jungle to Systematic Benchmarking........... 150
*M. Wimmer, G. Kappel, A. Kusel, W. Retschitzegger,
J. Schoenboeck, and W. Schwinger*

Specifying Overlaps of Heterogeneous Models for Global Consistency
Checking 165
Zinovy Diskin, Yingfei Xiong, and Krzysztof Czarnecki

Workshop – ME

Models and Evolution - ME2010 180
*Dirk Deridder, Alfonso Pierantonio, Bernhard Schätz, and
Dalila Tamzalit*

Conflicts as First-Class Entities: A UML Profile for Model Versioning... 184
*Petra Brosch, Horst Kargl, Philip Langer, Martina Seidl,
Konrad Wieland, Manuel Wimmer, and Gerti Kappel*

A Manifesto for Semantic Model Differencing 194
Shahar Maoz, Jan Oliver Ringert, and Bernhard Rumpe

Workshop – Models@run.time

Summary of the 5th International Workshop on Models@run.time 204
  Nelly Bencomo, Gordon Blair, Franck Fleurey, and Cédric Jeanneret

Meta-modeling Runtime Models 209
  Grzegorz Lehmann, Marco Blumendorf, Frank Trollmann, and Sahin Albayrak

The Role of Models and Megamodels at Runtime 224
  Thomas Vogel, Andreas Seibel, and Holger Giese

Workshop – MoDeVVA

MoDeVVa 2010 Workshop Summary 239
  Levi Lúcio, Elisangela Vieira, and Stephan Weißleder

Efficient Test Suite Reduction by Merging Pairs of Suitable Test Cases 244
  Harald Cichos and Thomas S. Heinze

Traceability for Mutation Analysis in Model Transformation 259
  Vincent Aranega, Jean-Marie Mottu, Anne Etien, and Jean-Luc Dekeyser

Workshop – MPM

Summary of the Workshop on Multi-Paradigm Modelling: Concepts and Tools 274
  Hans Vangheluwe, Vasco Amaral, Cécile Hardebolle, and László Lengyel

Model-Based System Verification: A Formal Framework for Relating Analyses, Requirements, and Tests 279
  Aleksandr A. Kerzhner and Christiaan J.J. Paredis

Simplifying Model Transformation Chains by Rule Composition 293
  Mark Asztalos, Eugene Syriani, Manuel Wimmer, and Marouane Kessentini

Workshop – NFPinDSML

The 3rd International Workshop on Non-functional System Properties in Domain Specific Modeling Languages (NFPinDSML2010) 308
  Marko Bošković, Daniela Cancila, Claus Pahl, and Bernhard Schätz

Integration of Component Fault Trees into the UML 312
  Rasmus Adler, Dominik Domis, Kai Höfig, Sören Kemmann, Thomas Kuhn, Jean-Pascal Schwinn, and Mario Trapp

QVTR^2: A Rational and Performance-Aware Extension to the
Relations Language 328
  Mauro Luigi Drago, Carlo Ghezzi, and Raffaela Mirandola

Workshop – OCL and Textual Modelling

Tenth International Workshop on OCL and Textual Modelling 329
  Jordi Cabot, Tony Clark, Manuel Clavel, and Martin Gogolla

A Specification-Based Test Case Generation Method for UML/OCL 334
  Achim D. Brucker, Matthias P. Krieger, Delphine Longuet, and Burkhart Wolff

Integrating OCL and Textual Modelling Languages 349
  Florian Heidenreich, Jendrik Johannes, Sven Karol, Mirko Seifert, Michael Thiele, Christian Wende, and Claas Wilke

Workshop – QUASSOS

Quality of Service-Oriented Software Systems (QUASOSS 2010) 364
  Heiko Koziolek, Steffen Becker, Jens Happe, and Paul Pettersson

An Accuracy Information Annotation Model for Validated Service
Behavior Specifications 369
  Henning Groenda

Focussing Multi-Objective Software Architecture Optimization Using
Quality of Service Bounds 384
  Anne Koziolek, Qais Noorshams, and Ralf Reussner

Workshop – RoSym

First International Workshop on Model Based Engineering for Robotics
(RoSym'10) 400
  Laurent Rioux, Davide Brugali, and Sébastien Gérard

Integrating Ontological Domain Knowledge into a Robotic DSL 401
  Gaëlle Lortal, Saadia Dhouib, and Sébastien Gérard

Author Index 415

The Doctoral Symposium at MODELS 2010

Bernhard Schätz[1] and Brian Elvesæter[2]

[1] Fortiss GmbH, Guerickestrasse 25, D-80805 München, Germany
schaetz@fortiss.org
[2] SINTEF ICT, P.O. Box 124 Blindern, N-0314 Oslo, Norway
brian.elvesater@sintef.no

Abstract. The research of 10 doctoral students was selected for presentation at the symposium from a total of 28 submissions. All submissions received detailed feedback via written reviews by three members of the program committee. At the symposium, the research described in the accepted submissions was presented, discussed, and additional, detailed feedback was provided. This summary provides a brief overview of the symposium.

Keywords: Doctoral Symposium, MODELS 2010.

1 Introduction

The Doctoral Symposium at the ACM/IEEE 13th International Conference on Model Driven Engineering Languages and Systems took place on October 4, 2010 in Oslo, Norway. The goal of the Doctoral Symposium is to provide a forum in which PhD students can present their work in progress and to foster the role of MODELS as a premier venue for research in model-driven engineering. The symposium aims to support students by providing independent and constructive feedback about their already completed and, more importantly, planned research work.

The symposium was preceded by the submission and review of 28 papers from 12 countries. Reviews were conducted by a program committee which consisted of the following international experts:

- Ruth Breu, Universität Innsbruck, Austria
- Betty Cheng, Michigan State University, USA
- Jürgen Dingel, Queens University, Canada
- Brian Elvesæter, SINTEF, Norway
- Gregor Engels, Universität Paderborn, Germany
- Robert France, Colorado State University, USA
- Jeff Gray, University of Alabama, USA
- Gerti Kappel, TU Wien, Austria
- Gabor Karsai, Vanderbilt University, USA
- Jost-Pieter Katoen, RWTH Aachen, Germany
- Ingolf Krüger, University of Californa at San Diego, USA
- Jochen Küster, IBM Research Zürich, Switzerland

- Peter Mosterman, The MathWorks, USA
- Ivan Porres, Åbo Akademi, Finland
- Alexander Pretschner, Fraunhofer IESE, Germany
- Bernhard Rumpe, RWTH Aachen, Germany
- Bernhard Schätz, fortiss GmbH, Germany
- Jonathan Sprinkle, University of Arizona, USA
- Friedrich Steimann, Fernuni Hagen, Germany
- Ketil Stølen, SINTEF, Norway
- Stefan Wagner, TU München, Germany

Each submission received three reviews and was evaluated with respect to the overall quality of the submission itself and the potential impact of the completed and proposed research. The committee decided to accept 10 papers for presentation in the symposium.

2 Summary of Presentations and Feedback

The following 10 papers, available online at [1], were accepted for presentation:

- *Towards the Verification of State Machine-to-Java Code Generators for Semantic Conformance*, Lukman Ab Rahim, Lancaster University, UK
- *Reuse in Modelling Method Development based on Meta-modelling*, Alexander Bergmayr, University of Vienna, Austria
- *Rearrange: Rational Model Transformations for Performance Adaptation*, Mauro Luigi Drago, Politecnico di Milano, Italy
- *A Model Driven Approach to Test Evolving Business Process based Systems*, Qurat-ul-ann Farooq, Technische Universitäat Ilmenau, Germany
- *A Transformational Approach for Component-Based Distributed Architectures*, Fabian Gilson, University of Namur, Belgium
- *Modeling Complex Situations in Enterprise Architecture*, Hyeonsook Kim, Thames Valley University, UK
- *Reference Modeling for Inter-organizational Systems*, Dieter Mayrhofer, Vienna University of Technology, Austria
- *Applying Architecture Modeling Methodology to the Naval Gunship Software Safety Domain*, Joey Rivera, US Naval Postgraduate School, USA
- *A Model-based Framework for Software Performance Feedback*, Catia Trubiani, University of L'Aquila, Italy
- *Scenario-based Analysis of UML Design Class Models*, Lijun Yu, Colorado State University, USA

Each presentation was about 20 minutes in length and followed by a 10-minute discussion, which included the program committee members present and the students.

During the lively and constructive discussion, feedback was provided by the fellow participants, the committee members Betty Cheng, Gregor Engels, Robert France, and Stefan Wagner, as well as the organizing chairs.

In the following, we will summarize some of the advice and suggestions that were given repeatedly and are also relevant to future participants of a Doctoral Symposium.

- **Focus your PhD topic and problem:** Often, comments indicated that the scope of thesis – and specifically the problem statement – was not defined clearly enough. More precisely, it was not clear exactly what kinds of problems the thesis work would address.
- **Be realistic about your intended achievements:** Being overambitious will necessarily lead to the frustration of non-achievement. Rather, try a "Think big – start small" approach. Specifically, also use this scoping to make clear, which kind of problems your thesis will not address.
- **Be conscious about your research method:** Upon scoping your problem and research questions, you need to design your research methodology. How do you intend to validate your research? Are the research methods chosen the correct ones?
- **Provide an illustrative example:** It is often helpful to provide an illustrative example when presenting your PhD topic. One often asked questions by the committee members were: "What is the killer app?"
- **Be clear about your own contributions:** It is important to be very clear on what contribution and improvement the work makes over existing research. Failure to do this will invite questions about the significance of the work.

During the feedback session it was suggested that a presentation template to help doctoral students to focus on key issues to present would have been beneficial.

After the symposium, the following two papers were selected for inclusion in the MODELS 2010 Workshop and Symposia Proceedings after additional review and revision cycles.

- *Reuse in Modelling Method Development based on Meta-modelling*, Alexander Bergmayr, University of Vienna, Austria
- *A Model-based Framework for Software Performance Feedback*, Catia Trubiani, University of L'Aquila, Italy

3 Conclusions

The Doctoral Symposium at MODELS 2010 continued the successful tradition of previous doctoral symposia. It featured high-quality presentations and mutually beneficial and enjoyable interaction. The chair would like to thank the members of the program committee for their excellent work, Jürgen Dingel for sharing his experience from the symposium in 2009, and the MODELS 2010 general chairs Øystein Haugen and Birger Møller-Pedersen for their support.

References

1. Schätz, B., Elvesæter, B. (eds.): Preliminary Proceedings of the MODELS 2010 Doctoral Symposium (2010), http://models2010.ifi.uio.no/papers/DocSymp2010 PrelimProceedings.pdf

ReuseMe - Towards Aspect-Driven Reuse in Modelling Method Development*

Alexander Bergmayr

Faculty of Computer Science, University of Vienna
Bruenner Strasse 72, 1210 Vienna, Austria
ab@dke.univie.ac.at

Abstract. Today, the construction of individual modelling methods is a commonly accepted practice in different application domains. Method engineers are, however, faced with complexity and high effort involved, especially during modelling language development, considered as one major task when developing methods. To alleviate this, one obvious step is to promote reuse, thereby increasing productivity and quality similar to what can be expected from reuse in software and information systems engineering. Although considerable progress in language modularization and composition is observable, the reuse principle is still rarely adopted in practice. Therefore, in this work, a research roadmap for *ReuseMe* (**Reuse Me**thods), a novel *aspect-oriented reuse approach* is proposed. By involving artefacts generated during a method's conceptualization down to its implementation and putting forth fundamental ingredients for a comprehensive method reuse process on top of an *Open Model Repository*, method reuse becomes leveraged. This paves the way for establishing a library, populated with potential reusable aspects that modularize method artefacts based on separating language concerns.

Keywords: Modelling Method Development, Reuse, Aspect-orientation.

1 Introduction

The construction of new modelling methods is one major challenge in Model-Driven Engineering (MDE) as they provide the necessary concepts capable of capturing the relevant knowledge of an application domain in terms of models. Assuming that a modelling method consists of three major building blocks, i.e., modelling language, process, and functionality (e.g., comparison, composition, translation etc.) [1,2], in this work the primary focus is on modelling languages. Although, likewise in research as well as practice the development of Domain-Specific Modelling Languages (DSMLs) has become a commodity, it is still a complex task and the effort involved is usually extensive [3,4].

One obvious step to mitigate this complexity and high effort is to emphasize *reuse* during method development. Systematic reuse in the development of

---

* This work has partly been supported by the EU project plugIT (ICT-231430) and the Austrian Federal Ministry of Science and Research (BMWF).

modelling methods is, however, rarely adopted, although Brinkkemper coined the notion of reusable fragments about 15 years ago [5]. Recent approaches (as further discussed in related work Section 4) that contribute to the reuse principle are indeed promising, particularly in the composition of different language modules. But still, there is a need for improving the way composition semantics is made explicit if at all and the support of composition directives, necessary to cope with more complicated reuse scenarios. Furthermore, lack of flexibility during language modularization restricts the composition of language modules to their exposed parts which is unfavorable when modules being composed hide potential composable elements. Finally, although language modules can be composed in various different ways (e.g., extending, interleaving, binding or overriding, cf. [6]) which may even include removing modularized language elements, current approaches do not provide the required flexibility to adapt the composition strategy to a particular situation in a feasible way.

As a consequence, method reuse is hardly applicable even though recent work on the investigation of modelling language support for the area of nuclear inspection [7], for instance, exposed that the availability and accessibility of a method reuse library would have beneficial effects on the language development. From a conceptual point of view, concerns addressed in the area of business process and organisational modelling (e.g., connected activities, roles and skills) were of interest to be composed with the specific language concerns core to the application domain. In general, the provisioning of a method reuse library, method engineers can draw on support during the development life-cycle is worthwhile. The fact that modelling methods may then become realized by considering existing ones that might partly or entirely be reused rather from scratch, enables similar to the software engineering area increase of productivity and higher quality results.

The goal is, thus, clearly to support the separation of potential reusable language concerns and their composition resulting in new modelling languages. To achieve this goal *ReuseMe* (**Reuse Me**thods), a novel *aspect-oriented* (AO) reuse approach is advocated and further discussed in Section 2 by exploring its conceptual grounding and providing insights into the process leveraging the proposed reuse approach. Developing a *method reuse process* is considered as the first main contribution while the second main contribution is *collecting reusable language aspects* in the form of a method reuse library. Aspects are considered as modular units of elements that satisfy language concerns while AO techniques provide the grounding for composing them. The provisioning of an *Open Model Repository (OMR)*, serving as the basis for operationalizing the reuse process and managing the reuse library is the third expected contribution. More detail is given in Section 3. Section 4 reports on work that is related to ReuseMe. Observing current efforts to establish an Open Model Initiative[1] with the vision of dealing with models in a way similar to how the open-source community is dealing with source-code, ReuseMe is discussed in the realm of such an environment to validate its feasibility and applicability as outlined in Section 5. Current status and next steps are summarized in Section 6.

---

[1] www.openmodels.at

2 Aspect-Driven Reuse in Method Development

When adopting the principle of reuse during development of new modelling methods, higher quality results with reasonable effort can be expected. Consequently, a novel aspect-oriented reuse approach is layed out that allows bringing together reusable language concerns of possibly different domains, resulting in a cohesive hybrid modelling method. Language concerns are codified through aspects, thereby separating modelling languages in different modules. Obviously, the provisioning of modules that tend to be generally useful, i.e., independent of their original application domain in an appropriate way is indeed worthwhile as known from the area of software development. Similar to programming libraries (e.g., Java Class Library) the idea is to promote libraries managing reusable crosscutting language concerns (e.g., identification, reflection or element naming) as well as non-crosscutting (e.g., organization, strategy, or process) ones. To beneficially apply such a reuse library during method development, clarification is required how the reuse principle can be incorporated in a language development life-cycle and what core tasks actually leverage the reuse of language concerns. The focus in this paper is on static descriptions of a modelling language's structure expressed through a meta-model. A conceptual overview of ReuseMe is given in Section 2.1, addressing the above raised questions. The concepts proposed are then applied for a simple example in Section 2.2.

2.1 Conceptual Overview of Method Reuse

A typical modelling language development life-cycle comprises different phases (cf. [8,3]) similar to engineering processes known from the software or information systems discipline (cf. [9]). *Language Conceptualization* is dedicated to capture fundamental concepts, relationships in between and properties adhering to them, usually obtained through the analysis of a selected domain [10]. On the basis of identified domain elements, the basic structure of a modelling language becomes derived and aligned to functional and non-functional requirements, or architecture and language anatomy relevant decisions (cf. [4]). Although explicit language conceptualizations are indeed desirable and vital for several application scenarios (cf. [11]), in practice they are most often created after the modelling language has already been released, i.e., reverse engineered from a language design, if at all. The actual realization of the designed language on a selected platform is part of the *Language Implementation* and again design relevant elements may be reverse engineered from a concrete implementation for the purpose of refactoring, for instance. Observing modern workbenches for modelling language development (cf. MDD-TIF07 workshop[2], introducing a list of commercial and research tools, or ADOxx, currently advocated by the Open Model Initiative [12,13]), reasonable support is provided for the last phase while the support becomes weaker when turning the focus towards language conceptualization. Nonetheless, from a theoretical viewpoint (at least) the assumption

---
[2] www.dsmforum.org/tools.html

ReuseMe - Towards Aspect-Driven Reuse in Modelling Method Development

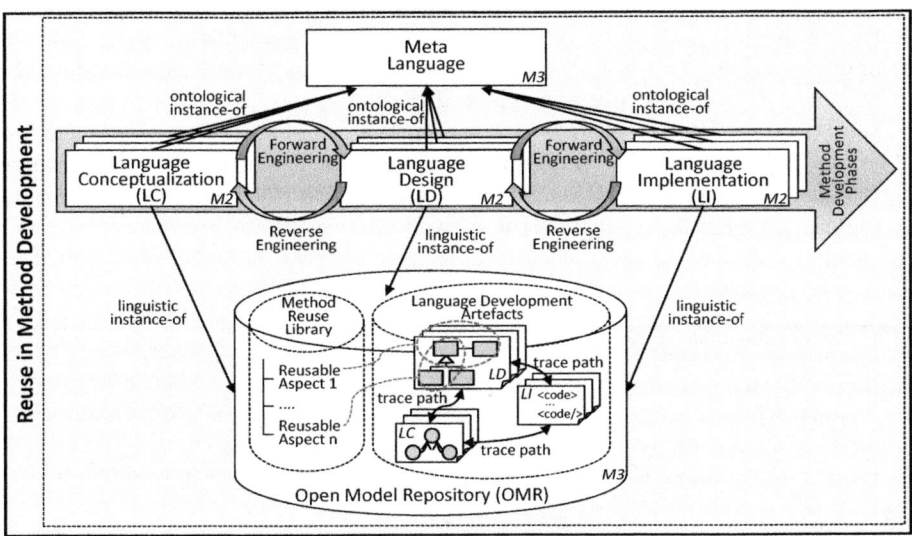

Fig. 1. Conceptual Overview of ReuseMe in Method Development

of a common language development formalism, i.e., a *Meta Language* allowing to express *Language Development Artefacts* of each phase is feasible. Although in the literature additional phases like, for instance, deployment, maintenance or evolution are discussed, in this work the spectrum from conceptualization to implementation as shown at the top of Figure 1 is primarily addressed.

Considering the incorporation of the reuse principle into the discussed life-cyle phases, the entry point for method engineers interested in drawing support on a reuse library is to explore and discover language concepts that fit the needs of domain experts. The management of language development artefacts is concerned by an *Open Model Repository*. Note, that the use of *ontological* and *linguistic* relationships is in line with the work of Atkinson & Kühne [14], allowing to address the structure of a repository independent of possibly various regarded ontological layers. This is indeed of relevance, since the repository provides the grounding for the advocated reuse approach. To retrieve a potential design artefact for a given conceptualization[3] such a repository needs to ensure the *traceability* between development artefacts constructed throughout different life-cycle phases. Having identified appropriate language designs, i.e., *Reusable Aspects* collected within a *Method Reuse Library* that allows accessing these modularized design elements, their composition is required to obtain a cohesive result. At the design level this means static composition of meta-model elements (cf. [15], discussing aspect composition of UML models) satisfying a structural language concern rather than program code weaving based on explicit join points in the execution of a

---

[3] In fact, a given language conceptualization may have several different designs that satisfy the needs of the former while similarly a particular design can be implemented in various ways [9].

program as typically supported by aspect-oriented programming (AOP). This static composition needs to be reflected on the implementation level, thereby bringing together concretely realized structural language concerns that form the hybrid character of a resulting modelling method.

Let's particularly concentrate on the composition of such concerns at the level of language design and vital prerequisites by addressing the major tasks involved, their input and output, relationships in-between, and roles involved as presented in Figure 2, targeting to outline the overall advocated method reuse process of ReuseMe.

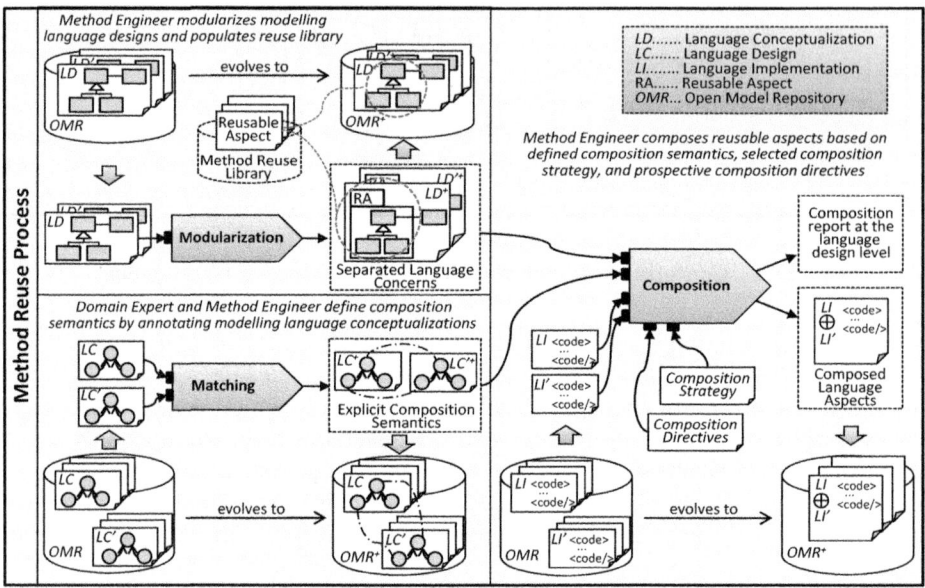

Fig. 2. Method Reuse Process

Modularization separates language concerns at the design level into reusable aspects (e.g., through selection, generalization, or filter [16]) and populates a method reuse library with logically connected language design elements. This separation preserves compatibility [17] if (instance) models conforming to a defined aspect still conform to the original language structure, i.e, its abstract syntax. Compatibility is, however, not always intended (e.g., deep inheritance hierarchies) hence, flexibility is required during the separation of language designs. The latter influence the parts of a language design actually considered during concern composition. In fact, arbitrary language artefacts may serve as composable parts, allowing to interleave reusable aspects at certain points, i.e., pointcuts as known from the AspectJ[4] AOP approach. These points are actually defined through a dedicated model, determining possible join points (e.g., class

---

[4] www.eclipse.org/aspectj/

or method). Thus, a join point model (cf. [18,19]) allows controlling possible model composition scenarios.

Another main prerequisite for concern composition is to determine the language elements potential for being composable by taking into account the intension to compose them when required. This task is subsumed under the term *Matching*, addressing generally the finding of corresponding language elements. Having identified a correspondence between language elements, the assumption is made that a binary equivalence relation, describing composable elements holds between matched elements, resulting in what is called explicit composition semantics. Obviously, this requires involving domain experts as they know the concepts underlying the elements of a language design. Turning the focus on the conceptualization level when describing composition semantics appears worthwhile and allows at the same time clearly separating it from language designs, thereby avoiding to unnecessarily expand them with details about concept correspondences across language designs.

Now, the way is paved to bring together reusable aspects selected during the development life-cycle. *Composition* addresses this task by producing a cohesive language implementation and reporting on composed language concerns at the design level. Modularized structural language concerns and explicitly defined composition semantics enable such a composition. To allow delegating composition results from the design level to the level of implementation, the corresponding language implementation details need to be provided to the composition as well. Combining the notions of these three core tasks involved, language concerns become considered by ReuseMe from three perspectives. This is in accordance with the development phases addressed in Figure 1. While the language conceptualization hides details about the composition semantics of language concerns from the design phase, the latter in turn hides the applied AO techniques from the composed language implementation. From the viewpoint of a modelling language's implementation it seems to be irrelevant how it has actually been produced. This consideration is similar to the way AspectJ produces Java Bytecode. The produced composition result of ReuseMe is influenced by possible *Composition Directives* (e.g., through composite pointcuts) in addition to the composition semantics and the selected *Composition Strategy*. Considering the literature in the area of aspect-orientation, symmetric and asymmetric concern composition is generally differentiated [20]. Roughly speaking, the latter requires a base in which aspects that crosscut the base are woven into. In contrast to the asymmetric view, the notion underlying the symmetric view does not explicitly separate concerns in crosscutting and non-crosscutting ones. Consequently, the symmetric view does not mandate the existence of a base for composing aspect. Their practical application is demonstrated in the following Section 2.2 for the purpose of composing reusable aspects involved by the example.

2.2 Method Reuse by Example

To promote a better understanding of the concepts underlying ReuseMe and the generic method reuse process presented, let's address a concrete method reuse scenario. The sample scenario considers a language's abstract syntax from the design point of view and the corresponding conceptualization while omitting implementation details since they naturally depend on a selected platform. Remember, the approach underlying ReuseMe primarily operates on a language's conceptualization and design and produces when applied to a specific platform composed language implementations that adhere to the internal platform format, i.e., the format of the language used express meta-models.

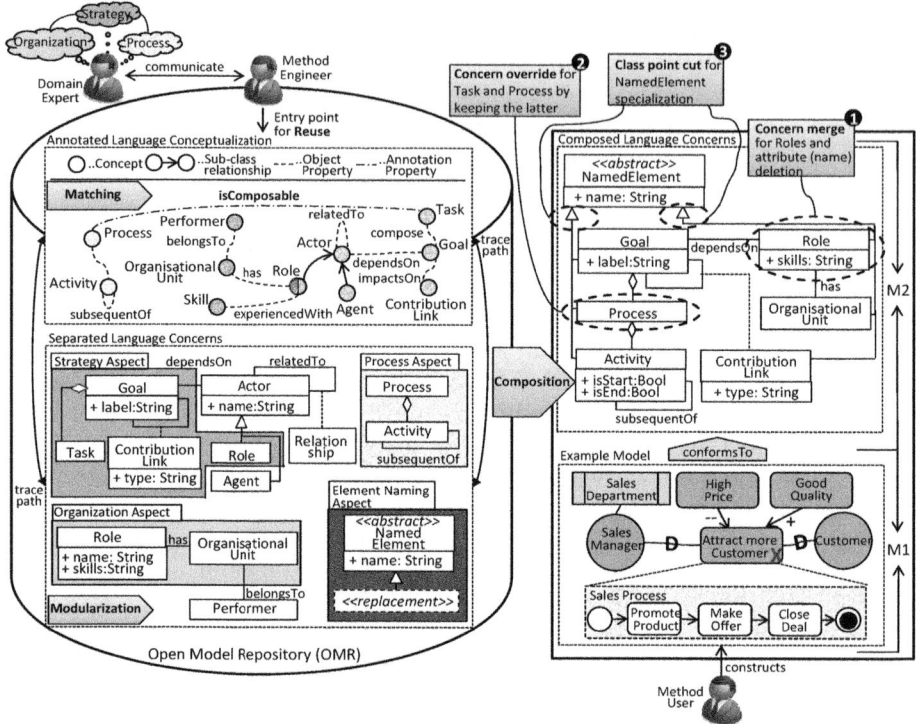

Fig. 3. Sample Scenario for Method Reuse

On the top-right part of Figure 3 the requested language design is depicted. It consists of *Composed Language Concerns* that allow constructing the *Example Model* given beneath to make the sample scenario more concrete. Let's incrementally identify the requirements for the requested modelling language based on the modelled situation which is about the intention of a sales manager to attract more customers and how a process could particularly support this goal. Clearly, this is a rather straightforward approach but the focus here is not on requirements elicitation but instead to point out the assumptions made for the selection of reusable aspects. In fact, this is indeed influenced by the mental model of a domain expert, determining required aspects such as *Strategy*, *Organization* or *Process* (cf. top-left of Figure 3). To be able to model Roles, Goals and `Contribution Links` in-between, prospective language concepts are known from the *i** method [21], hence being the first potential reusable aspect. In a similar way, `Process` and `Activity` concepts could be reused from UML's activity diagram and the `Organisational Unit` concept could be found in a method called Adonis-BPMS [22]. Note that the above mentioned concepts may also be available in other modelling methods as well, i.e., the selected methods could be arbitrarily exchanged. Finally, support for naming elements (i.e., 'Sales Manager', for instance) is required as well although this is rather a design aspect than a matter of conceptualization. Let's assume the availability of a *Language Conceptualization* as given by the sample scenario and the *isComposable* relation defining the composition semantics for the `Process` and `Task` concept. Remember, the latter is addressed by *Matching*. Provided that the traceability between language concepts and design elements is ensured, reusable aspects at the language design level can be obtained. Considering the highlighted *Strategy Aspect*, *Process Aspect* and *Organization Aspect*, it becomes clear that they fit the above identified requirements of the pursued language. While separating these language concerns in terms of reusable aspects is dedicated to *Modularization*, their composition for a specific problem domain is part of *Composition*. The composition strategy applied for composing these two symmetric aspects involves (i) *Concern Merge* (cf. (1)) for `Role` elements from the *Strategy* and *Organization Aspect*, thereby rectifying attribute duplications, i.e., the `name` attribute in this scenario and (ii) *Concern Override* (cf. (2)) for `Task` and `Process` elements from the *Strategy* and *Organization Aspect* by keeping the latter element. In both cases, the defined composition semantics on the conceptual level serves as a foundation for the performed aspect compositions. Assuming that *isComposable* is an equivalent relation (cf. Section 2.1) the composition of the `Role` elements become obvious. Finally, let's consider the asymmetric *Element Naming Aspect* and how it is woven into the other three considered aspects to fulfill the requirement for naming modelled elements (at the instance level). One obvious step to achieve this requirement is to inherit from the `NamedElement` design element. In this way, a *Class Pointcut* (cf. 3) has been applied to enforce the composition directive that each element of the *Strategy*, *Organization* and *Process Aspect* need to be inherited from `NamedElement`. The last aspect weaving changes the viewpoint of defining element specialization as in this case the class pointcut encapsulates the necessary statements at a central point instead of adapting each affected element.

3 Contribution Expected from Method Reuse

Three main contributions expected by ReusMe are discussed in the following.

Development of Method Reuse Process. Establishing a comprehensive method reuse library requires support particularly when existing modelling methods are going to be separated in reusable aspects and these separated aspects become composed to form new methods. In fact, modularization is not restricted to be applied on existing modelling methods, only, but instead proactively separating language concerns during method development, i.e., the construction of innovative (reusable) aspects leverage the reuse principle even better. The latter implies, however, domain experts explicate composition semantics between reusable aspects in terms of matching since a useful set of related concepts facilitates composition and its automation. In this way, the first main contribution is the development of a method reuse process although it is not claimed that this process can fully be automated. The finding of correspondences between language concepts for defining composition semantics, for instance, requires human interpretation and cognitive capabilities since a language's intrinsic meaning can not easily be expressed through an explicit conceptualization. When turning the focus on realizing concrete functionality supporting the method reuse process, available formalisms (cf. ECORE, EMOF or KM3, to mention just a few) for meta-modelling and intractable diversities (e.g., different terminology for concepts identical in meaning) that come along with them affect its applicability for a broad range of method development scenarios. Since most formalisms, however, adhere to class-based concepts (cf. [23]), adapting realized functionality for different platforms is feasible. Considering modularization [24] may serve as a source for deriving requirements while on the other hand, literature addressing meta-model composition (as further discussed in Section 4) and approaches introducing aspect-orientation into DSML (cf. [25]) pose grounding for further investigation on weaving reusable aspects.

Collection of Reusable Language Aspects. To allow utilizing a concrete method reuse library populated with various different reusable language aspects, the second main contribution is separating such aspects from existing modelling methods and their cataloguing. This investigation is initiated by considering areas such as knowledge, requirements or business process engineering but not restricted to them. The latter is of particular interest due to the diversity of available formalisms with different expressiveness but also concepts that are common to all of them. A valuable source for existing modelling methods provides the Open Model Initiative currently hosting more than 10 projects, most of them dealing with the conceptualization, design and implementation of modelling methods. Concrete projects address the area of requirements engineering[5], business process engineering[6] or knowledge management[7]. In this way, a method reuse library addressing different problem domains becomes established primarily for experiments to validate the proposed method reuse approach but also possibly useful for method engineers developing new modelling methods.

Reuse Enhanced Open Model Repository. One major prerequisite for providing useful support to the method reuse process and establishing a library populated with reusable aspects is the availability of a repository powerful enough to cope with language definition artefacts from different development phases, their traceability from early phases down to the actual implementation and aspect-oriented techniques incorporated for realizing method reuse. Potential reusable aspects become in this way anchored to the body of domain knowledge [11] a modelling

---

[5] www.openmodels.at/web/istar
[6] www.openmodels.at/web/ben
[7] www.openmodels.at/web/melca

method is (explicitly or implicitly) committing to. Providing a reuse enhanced open model repository is, hence, the third main contribution. Openness in this context is considered similar to comprehensive programming libraries usually available for contemporary general-purpose languages, thereby making such a repository the first place for sharing results during modelling method development and even more important reusable aspects. The repository reflects the shift of method artefacts from ordinary elements in the repository to reusable aspects in case the potential for reuse has been understood. This implies incorporating aspect-orientation as a concept into model repositories.

4 Related Work

The investigation of existing approaches is primarily focused on their capabilities to deal with the reuse principle in general and composition of language concerns (or modules) in particular. A selected set of representative approaches has been characterized and analyzed according to (1) the way they define *Composition Semantics*, i.e., either implicit or explicit, (2) restrictions concerning *Composable Parts*, (3) the *Reuse Granularity*, i.e., black-box or white box-reuse and (4) the ability to allow for explicit *Composition Directives*, as summarized in Figure 4.

	Composition Characteristics	Composition Semantics		Composable Parts		Reuse Granularity		Composition Directives
		implicit	explicit	restricted	any	black-box	white-box	
Approach	White et al. (2009) — Feature Model-based Refinement	+					+	
	Emerson & Sztipanovits (2006) — Template-based extension	+		+		+		−
	Di Ruscio et al. (2010) — Package-based extension			+	+	+	+	−
	Blanc et al. (2005) — Package-based composition	+			+	+		−
	Weisemöller & Schürr (2008) — Component-based composition			+	+	+		−
	Krahn et al. (2008) — Grammar-based composition			+	+	+		−
	Quintero & Valderrama (2007) — Aspect-based extension	+			+	+	+	+
	ReuseMe — Aspect-based composition		+		+	+	+	+

Fig. 4. Comparison of ReuseMe with Related Composition Approaches

Recent work incorporating ontological foundation in the area of MDE needs to be considered as well since significant results may influence the development lifecycle of modelling methods particularly when their conceptualization is requested in an explicit way. The availability of explicit language conceptualizations is obviously of considerable interest for the current work. Sharing the analysis results of a particular domain across methods with similar needs, requires carefully considering their intended meaning which may include operational semantics particularly when methods are behavioral in nature. Available literature aiming to couple ontologies and meta-modelling in general (cf. [26] a workshop series dedicated to ontologies in MDE), and proposals for capturing method concepts in terms of ontological descriptions (cf. [27]) and model-based (cf. [28]) as well as ontology-based search (cf. [29]) in particular are of relevance.

Modelling Language Reuse. In the work of [30] techniques known from software-product lines are adopted to improve the reuse in DSML development by refinement of existing DSMLs. Although this approach does not actually compose language elements (the composable parts and composition directives criteria have, thus, not been evaluated), the way semantics for potential refinements becomes defined is, however, interesting. White et al. [30] suggest feature models to define correspondences between language concepts, related to design elements. Similarly, in ReuseMe a language's conceptualization is considered as the first place for explicating composition semantics.

A template-based reuse approach to alleviate reoccurring language design problems is advocated in the work of [31]. Templates capture these design problems and allow their instantiation. In fact, instantiated templates become embedded in languages, hence extending them. The extension of Architecture Description Languages (ADLs) is discussed in [32], addressing concrete operators (e.g., inherit) that allow for extending a given base ADL. Language elements are obliged to be connected to a fixed set of meta-classes, thus restricting the scope of composable parts.

Another approach for reuse comprises the composition of existing language elements as suggested in [33] and [34]. Whereas the former approach is inspired by UML's package merge mechanism and particularly addresses the generalization of reused elements of different packages, the latter suggests components in terms of UML to provide reuse. Their actual composition is based on coupling required interfaces and provided interfaces related to concrete elements of the reused components. Another compositional approach is proposed by [35] discussing the concept of modularity in terms of textual domain-specific languages defined by a grammar-based approach, thus integrating the abstract and a textual concrete syntax into a single language design. The approaches of Weisemller & Schürr [34] and Krahn et al. [35] provide composition semantics through interfaces of language elements whereas in ReuseMe the latter is clearly separated from the language design.

Considering proposals relying on AO techniques, in [36] extension mechanisms for EMF-based meta-models are discussed. Concerning composable parts, a rather liberal approach is advocated by ReuseMe. Theoretically, any language element of a reusable aspect could be addressed during the composition, although a dedicated join point model defines possible pointcuts as known from aspect-oriented modelling which may also include to delete language elements. The consideration of reusable aspects as logically connected language design elements and the separation of their composition semantics by addressing composable parts independent of the conducted modularization allows a composition at an arbitrary granularity. Composition directives are provided by Quintero & Valderrama [36] although their approach is restricted to language extension in terms of element specialization only.

Ontologies in Language Development. In [37], a domain-specific modelling language development framework relying on class-based meta-concepts enriched by description logics (DLs) using the Web Ontology Language (OWL) is proposed. Another alternative approach to the traditional class-based development of modelling languages is [38], proposing a meta-language based on a philosophical theory although a reference implementation is missing. While both approaches expose insights into ontology-based meta-modelling, their focus is not on reuse.

5 Strategy for Evaluating Aspect-Driven Reuse

ReuseMe will be evaluated according to a three-level strategy.

Assessment of Reuse Library. To evaluate the utility of a reuse library populated with reusable aspects from various different domains both the technical as well as the human viewpoint will be considered according to the work of Mili et al. [39], supporting criteria for each viewpoint (e.g., precision and recall or difficulty of use and transparency, respectively). Regarding the human viewpoint, empirical studies based on questionnaires are planned to be conducted with partners of the plugIT[8] project. This project proposes a model-based approach for the currently imposed practice of a tight coupling between business and IT, achieving integration [40]. Members of the Open Model Initiative may also contribute to evaluate ReuseMe since high reusability is also one success factor of this initiative.

Controlled experiments with Reusable Aspects. Considering this criterion, students from our lectures will be instructed to evaluate the feasibility and applicability of the proposed method reuse process and reusable aspects from the business process modelling area. The task involves reassembling modelling methods separated into useful structural language concerns and extend assembled ones with new method artefacts by relying on a predefined baseline. The exploitation of the reuse capability assumed needs to be evaluated based on corresponding metrics [41] (e.g., ratio of reused to total size of life-cycle constructs and properties). Furthermore, these controlled experiments are a first attempt to assess the validity of ReuseMe. The adoption of ReuseMe on an industrial use case is currently being elaborated in cooperation with plugIT partners. This should indicate whether ReuseMe scale to an industrial setting. Research work that put effort in similar experiments (cf. [42]) and address structural refactoring on graph-based structures (cf. [43]) are useful sources for this criterion.

Increase of Productivity and Quality. To assess this criterion, several small development teams composed of students with similar experience are going to realize an excerpt of a modelling method specification. One half of the teams need to implement the specification from scratch, while the other half is allowed

---

[8] www.plug-it-project.eu

accessing a method reuse library consisting of potential reusable aspects. The evaluation is conducted based on empirical studies, investigating the productivity and quality of reuse in modelling method development while applying corresponding reuse metrics [41] (e.g., ratio of reused to manually implemented 'code' or error rates, respectively).

6 Current Status and Next Steps

In this work, a research roadmap for promoting reuse in modelling method development by incorporating aspect-orientation as a fundamental ingredient has been outlined. ReuseMe is a novel aspect-oriented reuse approach that puts forth a first attempt to establish a comprehensive method reuse process on top of an open model repository, thereby leveraging the reuse principle in developing new modelling methods. This research effort is still in an initial state currently addressing the elaboration of an environment that allows conducting experiments. The scope is currently on structural language concerns and their reuse in terms of reusable aspects. Analyzing the potential of such reusable aspects in existing domain-specific modelling languages and conceptual investigations on the pursued method reuse process are considered as next steps.

Acknowledgements. Many thanks to Dimitris Karagiannis, Werner Retschitzegger, Manuel Wimmer and Wieland Schwinger for their support and valuable comments, and to the anonymous reviewers for their critical reflection and suggestions.

References

1. Ter Hofstede, A.H.M., Verhoef, T.F.: Meta-CASE: Is the game worth the candle? Inf. Syst. J. 6(1), 41–68 (1996)
2. Karagiannis, D., Kühn, H.: Metamodelling Platforms. In: Bauknecht, K., Tjoa, A.M., Quirchmayr, G. (eds.) EC-Web 2002. LNCS, vol. 2455, p. 182. Springer, Heidelberg (2002)
3. Mernik, M., Heering, J., Sloane, A.M.: When and how to develop domain-specific languages. ACM Comput. Surv. 37(4), 316–344 (2005)
4. Karsai, G., Krahn, H., Pinkernell, C., Rumpe, B., Schindler, M., Völkel, S.: Design Guidelines for Domain Specific Languages. In: Proceedings of the 9th OOPSLA Workshop on Domain-Specific Modeling (DSM 2009) Helsinki School of Economics. TR no B-108 (October 2009)
5. Brinkkemper, S.: Method engineering: engineering of information systems development methods and tools. Information and Software Technology 38(4), 275–280 (1996)
6. Reddy, Y.R., Ghosh, S., France, R.B., Straw, G., Bieman, J.M., McEachen, N., Song, E., Georg, G.: Directives for Composing Aspect-Oriented Design Class Models. Transactions on Aspect-Oriented Software Development I 3880, 75–105 (2006)
7. Abazi, F., Bergmayr, A.: Knowledge-Based Process Modelling for Nuclear Inspection. In: Karagiannis, D., Jin, Z. (eds.) KSEM 2009. LNCS, vol. 5914, pp. 406–417. Springer, Heidelberg (2009)

8. Spinellis, D.: Notable design patterns for domain-specific languages. J. Syst. Softw. 56, 91–99 (2001)
9. Guizzardi, G.: On Ontology, ontologies, Conceptualizations, Modeling Languages, and (Meta)Models. In: Proceeding of the 2007 Conference on Databases and Information Systems IV, pp. 18–39. IOS Press, The Netherlands (2007)
10. Tairas, R., Mernik, M., Gray, J.: Using Ontologies in the Domain Analysis of Domain-Specific Languages. In: Chaudron, M.R. (ed.) Models in Software Engineering, pp. 332–342. Springer, Heidelberg (2009)
11. Chandrasekaran, B., Josephson, J.R., Benjamins, V.R.: What Are Ontologies, and Why Do We Need Them? IEEE Intelligent Systems 14(1), 20–26 (1999)
12. Schwab, M., Karagiannis, D., Bergmayr, A.: i* on ADOxx: A Case Study. In: Castro, J., Franch, X., Mylopoulos, J., Yu, E. (eds.) Fourth International i* Workshop (iStar 2010) at CAiSE 2010, pp. 92–97 (June 2010)
13. Bork, D., Sinz, E.J.: Design of a SOM Business Process Modelling Tool based on the ADOxx Meta-modelling Platform. In: de Lara, J., Varro, D., Margaria, T., Padberg, J., Taentzer, G. (eds.) 4th International Workshop on Graph Based Tools (GraBaTs 2010), Enschede, The Netherlands, pp. 89–101 (September, 2010)
14. Atkinson, C., Kühne, T.: Concepts for Comparing Modeling Tool Architectures. In: Briand, L.C., Williams, C. (eds.) MoDELS 2005. LNCS, vol. 3713, pp. 398–413. Springer, Heidelberg (2005)
15. France, R.B., Ray, I., Georg, G., Ghosh, S.: Aspect-oriented approach to early design modelling. IEE Proceedings - Software 151(4), 173–186 (2004)
16. Kramer, J.: Is abstraction the key to computing? Commun. ACM 50(4), 36–42 (2007)
17. Sen, S., Moha, N., Baudry, B., Jézéquel, J.M.: Meta-model Pruning. In: Schürr, A., Selic, B. (eds.) MODELS 2009. LNCS, vol. 5795, pp. 32–46. Springer, Heidelberg (2009)
18. Cottenier, T., Berg, A.V., Elrad, T.: The Motorola WEAVR: Model Weaving in a Large Industrial Context. In: Proceedings of the International Conference on AspectOriented Software Development, Industry Track (2006)
19. Jacobson, I., Ng, P.W.: Aspect-Oriented Software Development with Use Cases (Addison-Wesley Object Technology Series). Addison-Wesley Professional, Reading (2004)
20. Harrison, W., Ossher, H., Tarr, P.: Asymmetrically vs. Symmetrically Organized Paradigms for Software Composition. Research Report RC22685 (W0212-147), IBM (December 2002)
21. Mylopoulos, J., Chung, L., Yu, E.: From object-oriented to goal-oriented requirements analysis. Commun. ACM 42(1), 31–37 (1999)
22. Junginger, S., Kühn, H., Strobl, R., Karagiannis, D.: Ein Geschäftsprozessmanagement-Werkzeug der nächsten Generation - ADONIS: Konzeption und Anwendungen. Wirtschaftsinformatik 42(5), 392–401 (2000)
23. Sprinkle, J., Rumpe, B., Vangheluwe, H., Karsai, G.: Metamodelling: State of the Art, and Research Challenges. In: Model-Based Engineering of Embedded Real-Time Systems, pp. 59–78. Springer, Heidelberg (2010)
24. Henderson-Sellers, B., Ralyté, J.: Situational Method Engineering: State-of-the-Art Review. Journal of Universal Computer Science 16(3), 424–478 (2010)
25. Schauerhuber, A., Wimmer, M., Schwinger, W., Kapsammer, E., Retschitzegger, W.: Aspect-Oriented Modeling of Ubiquitous Web Applications: The aspectWebML Approach. In: ECBS 2007: Proceedings of the 14th Annual IEEE International Conference and Workshops on the Engineering of Computer-Based Systems, pp. 569–576. IEEE Computer Society, Washington, DC (2007)

26. Ghosh, S. (ed.): Second Workshop on Transforming and Weaving Ontologies in Model Driven Engineering (TWOMDE 2009), vol. 6002. Springer, Heidelberg (2010)
27. Kappel, G., Kapsammer, E., Kargl, H., Kramler, G., Reiter, T., Retschitzegger, W., Schwinger, W., Wimmer, M.: Lifting Metamodels to Ontologies: A Step to the Semantic Integration of Modeling Languages. Model Driven Engineering Languages and Systems 4199, 528–542 (2006)
28. Lucrédio, D., de M. Fortes, R.P., Whittle, J.: MOOGLE: A Model Search Engine. In: Busch, C., Ober, I., Bruel, J.-M., Uhl, A., Völter, M. (eds.) MODELS 2008. LNCS, vol. 5301, pp. 296–310. Springer, Heidelberg (2008)
29. Jasper, R., Uschold, M.: A Framework for Understanding and Classifying Ontology Applications. In: Proceedings of the IJCAI 1999 Workshop on Ontologies and Problem-Solving Methods KRR5, Stockholm, Sweden, August 2 (1999)
30. White, J., Hill, J.H., Gray, J., Tambe, S., Gokhale, A.S., Schmidt, D.C.: Improving Domain-Specific Language Reuse with Software Product Line Techniques. IEEE Softw. 26, 47–53 (2009)
31. Emerson, M., Sztipanovits, J.: Techniques for metamodel composition. In: The 6th OOPSLA Workshop on Domain-Specific Modeling, OOPSLA 2006, pp. 123–139. ACM Press, New York (2006)
32. Di Ruscio, D., Malavolta, I., Muccini, H., Pelliccione, P., Pierantonio, A.: Developing next generation ADLs through MDE techniques. In: Proceedings of the 32nd ACM/IEEE International Conference on Software Engineering. ICSE 2010, vol. 1, pp. 85–94. ACM, New York (2010)
33. Blanc, X., Ramalho, F., Robin, J.: Metamodel Reuse with MOF. Model Driven Engineering Languages and Systems 3713, 661–675 (2005)
34. Weisemöller, I., Schürr, A.: Formal Definition of MOF 2.0 Metamodel Components and Composition. In: Busch, C., Ober, I., Bruel, J.-M., Uhl, A., Völter, M. (eds.) MODELS 2008. LNCS, vol. 5301, pp. 386–400. Springer, Heidelberg (2008)
35. Krahn, H., Rumpe, B., Völkel, S.: MontiCore: Modular Development of Textual Domain Specific Languages. In: TOOLS (46), pp. 297–315 (2008)
36. Reina Quintero, A.M., Torres Valderrama, J.: Using Aspect-orientation Techniques to Improve Reuse of Metamodels. Electron. Notes Theor. Comput. Sci. 163(2), 29–43 (2007)
37. Walter, T., Silva Parreiras, F., Staab, S., Ebert, J.: Joint Language and Domain Engineering. In: Kühne, T., Selic, B., Gervais, M.-P., Terrier, F. (eds.) ECMFA 2010. LNCS, vol. 6138, Springer, Heidelberg (2010)
38. Laarman, A., Kurtev, I.: Ontological Metamodeling with Explicit Instantiation. In: van den Brand, M., Gašević, D., Gray, J. (eds.) SLE 2009. LNCS, vol. 5969, pp. 174–183. Springer, Heidelberg (2010)
39. Mili, A., Mili, R., Mittermeir, R.T.: A survey of software reuse libraries. Ann. Softw. Eng. 5, 349–414 (1998)
40. Woitsch, R., Karagiannis, D., Plexousakis, D., Hinkelmann, K.: Business and IT alignment: the IT-Socket. E & I Elektrotechnik und Informationstechnik 126, 308–321 (2009)
41. Frakes, W., Terry, C.: Software reuse: metrics and models. ACM Comput. Surv. 28(2), 415–435 (1996)
42. Whittle, J., Jayaraman, P.K., Elkhodary, A.M., Moreira, A., Araújo, J.a.: MATA: A Unified Approach for Composing UML Aspect Models Based on Graph Transformation. T. Aspect-Oriented Software Development VI 6, 191–237 (2009)
43. Mens, T., Taentzer, G., Runge, O.: Detecting Structural Refactoring Conflicts Using Critical Pair Analysis. Electronic Notes in Theoretical Computer Science 127(3), 113–128 (2005)

A Model-Based Framework for Software Performance Feedback

Catia Trubiani

Dipartimento di Informatica, University of L'Aquila
Via Vetoio n.1, 67010 Coppito, L'Aquila, Italy
catia.trubiani@univaq.it

Abstract. The problem of interpreting the results of performance analysis is quite critical in the software performance domain: mean values, variances, and probability distributions are hard to interpret for providing feedback to software architects. Support to the interpretation of such results that helps to fill the gap between numbers and architectural alternatives is still lacking.

The goal of my PhD thesis is to develop a model-based framework addressing the results interpretation and the feedback generation problems by means of performance antipatterns, that are recurring solutions to common mistakes (i.e. bad practices) in the software development. Such antipatterns can play a key role in the software performance domain, since they can be used in the search of performance problems as well as in the formulation of their solutions in terms of architectural alternatives.

Keywords: Software Architecture, Performance Evaluation, Antipatterns, Feedback Generation, Architectural Alternatives.

1 Problem

The trend in modeling and analyzing the performance of software systems is to build a cycle where models are derived form design artifacts, and results from models are evaluated in terms of design artifacts, so that the performance issues are brought to the forefront early in the design process [30]. Most of the activities connected to this cycle should be automated to make it actually applicable and able to provide timely feedbacks.

Figure 1 schematically represents the typical steps that must be executed in the software life-cycle to run a complete performance process. Rounded boxes in the figure represent operational steps whereas square boxes represent input/output data. Arrows numbered from 1 through 4 represent the typical forward path from an (annotated) software architectural model all the way through the production of performance indices of interest. While in this path quite well-founded approaches have been introduced for inducing automation in all steps (e.g. [31]), there is a clear lack of automation in the backward path that shall bring the analysis results back to the software architecture.

The *core* step of the backward path (i.e. the shaded box of Figure 1) is the results interpretation and feedback generation: the performance analysis results

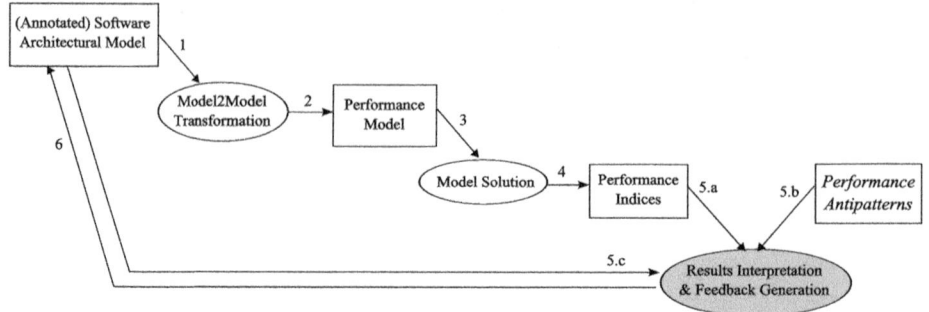

Fig. 1. Automated software performance process

have to be interpreted in order to detect, if any, performance problems, and once performance problems have been detected (with a certain accuracy) somewhere in the model, solutions have to be applied to remove those problems[1]. A performance problem is an unfulfilled requirement (e.g. the estimated response time of a service is higher than the required one), and if all the requirements are satisfied then the feedback obviously suggests no changes.

The introduction of sophisticated performance modeling notations (e.g. Queueing Networks (QNs) [21], Generalized Stochastic Petri Nets (GSPNs) [22]) and powerful tools to solve such models (e.g. WinPEPSY-QNS [5], GreatSPN [1]) makes indeed the problem of interpreting the results of performance analysis quite complex as each modeling notation is intended to give a certain representation of the software system, expressed in its own syntax, and the performance results are necessarily tailored to that modeling notation [6].

Additionally, a large gap exists between the representation of performance analysis results and the feedback expected by software architects. The former usually contains numbers (such as mean response time, throughput variance), whereas the latter should embed architectural suggestions useful to overcome performance problems (such as split a software component in two components and re-deploy one of them).

The search of performance problems in the architectural model may be quite complex and needs to be smartly driven towards the problematic areas of the model. The complexity of this step stems from several factors: (i) performance indices are basically numbers and often they have to be jointly examined: a single performance index (e.g. the utilization of a service center) is not enough to localize the critical parts of a software architecture, since a performance problem can be detected only if other indices (e.g. the throughput of a neighbor service center) are analyzed; (ii) performance indices can be estimated at different levels of granularity (e.g. the response time index can be evaluated at the level of a

---

[1] Note that this task very closely corresponds to the work of a physician: observing a sick patient (the model), studying the symptoms (some bad values of performance indices), making a diagnosis (performance problem), prescribing a treatment (performance solution).

cpu device, or at the level of a service that spans on different devices) and it is unrealistic to keep under control all indices at all levels of abstraction; (iii) architectural models can be quite complex, and the origin of performance problems emerges only looking at the architectural elements described in different views of a system (such as static structure, dynamic behaviour, etc.).

The research activity of this work is focused on the core step, and in Figure 1 the most promising elements that can drive this search have been explicitly represented, i.e. *performance antipatterns* (input labeled 5.b to the core step). The rationale of using performance antipatterns is two-fold: on the one hand, a performance antipattern identifies a bad practice in the software model that affects the performance indices negatively, thus to support the *result interpretation* operational step; on the other hand, a performance antipattern definition includes a solution description that lets the software architect devise refactoring actions, thus to support the *feedback generation* operational step.

The aim is to introduce automation in the backward path providing a feedback to the software model (label 6 of Figure 1) in the form of an architectural alternative that removes the original performance problems. Such automation provides several gains since it notifies the software architect of the interpretation of the analysis results by outlining the performance issues, and of the subsequent architectural emendations aimed at removing such issues, without the intervention of performance experts.

The main reference we consider for performance antipatterns is the work done across the years by Smith and Williams [25] that have ultimately defined fourteen modeling notation-independent antipatterns (one example is presented in Section 2). Some other works present antipatterns that occur throughout different technologies, but they are not as general as the ones defined in [25] (more references are provided in Section 3).

The benefit of using antipatterns when closing the software performance cycle is that they base on a comprehensive view of the system, thus to capture complex phenomena. An antipatterns-based approach differs from: (i) design space exploration techniques that blindly examine all architectural alternatives with a doubtful efficiency; (ii) rule-based approaches that identify problems based on a predefined set of rules with a questionable level of abstraction; (iii) metaheuristic search techniques (e.g. genetic algorithms) that search for local changes in the architectural model with uncertain optimality.

The remainder of the paper is organized as follows. Section 2 briefly provides some background on performance antipatterns by showing one example of the ones we examine. Section 3 discusses existing work in the research area. Section 4 presents the framework to automate the software performance feedback, and in Section 5 the expected contributions of the proposed approach are listed. Section 6 describes the methodologies being used in order to outline a prototype implementation. Finally, Section 7 concludes the paper by pointing out the pros and cons of using antipatterns in the software performance process.

2 Performance Antipatterns: One Example

Performance antipatterns have only been defined, up to now, in natural language [25]. From the original list of fourteen antipatterns defined by Smith and Williams two antipatterns are not considered for the following reason: the *Falling Dominoes* antipattern refers to reliability and fault tolerance issues and it is out of interest; the *Unnecessary Processing* antipattern deals with the semantics of the processing by judging the importance of the application code that it is an abstraction level not included in software architectural models. Hence, twelve is the total number of the antipatterns we examine.

Table 1 reports one example (i.e. the *Blob* antipattern [25]): the *problem* column identifies the system properties that define the antipattern and are useful for detecting it[2]; the *solution* column suggests the architectural changes useful for solving the antipattern.

Table 1. One example of Performance Antipatterns [25]

Antipattern	Problem	Solution
Blob	Occurs when a single class or component either 1) performs all of the work of an application or 2) holds all of the applications data. Either manifestation results in excessive message traffic that can degrade performance.	Refactor the design to distribute intelligence uniformly over the applications top-level classes, and to keep related data and behavior together.

Figure 2 provides a graphical representation of the Blob antipattern (see Table 1), and visualized here in UML[3]-like notation for a quick comprehension. Note that the graphical representation of the Blob antipattern provides our interpretation of the informal definition reported in Table 1. Different formalizations of antipatterns can be originated by laying on different interpretations of their textual specification [25].

The upper side of Figure 2 describes the system properties of a *(Annotated) Software Architectural Model S* with a *BLOB problem*. Such properties are grouped accordingly to the Three-View Model [29]: *(a) Static View*, a complex software resource, i.e. S_x, is connected to other software resources, e.g. S_y, through *many* usage dependencies; *(b) Dynamic View*, the software resource S_x generates *excessive* message traffic to elaborate data belonging to the software resource S_y; *(c) Deployment View*, it includes two sub-cases: *(c1) centralized*, i.e. if the communicating software resources are deployed on the same hardware resource then the latter one will show *high* utilization value, i.e. $\$utilHwRes$; *(c2) distributed*, i.e. if the communicating software resources are deployed on different hardware resources then network resource will be a critical one with a *high* utilization value, i.e. $\$utilNet$[3]. The occurrence of such properties leads to assess

---

[2] Such properties refer to software and/or hardware architectural characteristics as well as to the performance indices obtained by the analysis.

[3] The characterization of antipattern parameters related to system characteristics (e.g. *many* usage dependencies, *excessive* message traffic) or to performance results (e.g. *high*, *low* utilization) is based on thresholds values (see more details in Section 4).

A Model-Based Framework for Software Performance Feedback 23

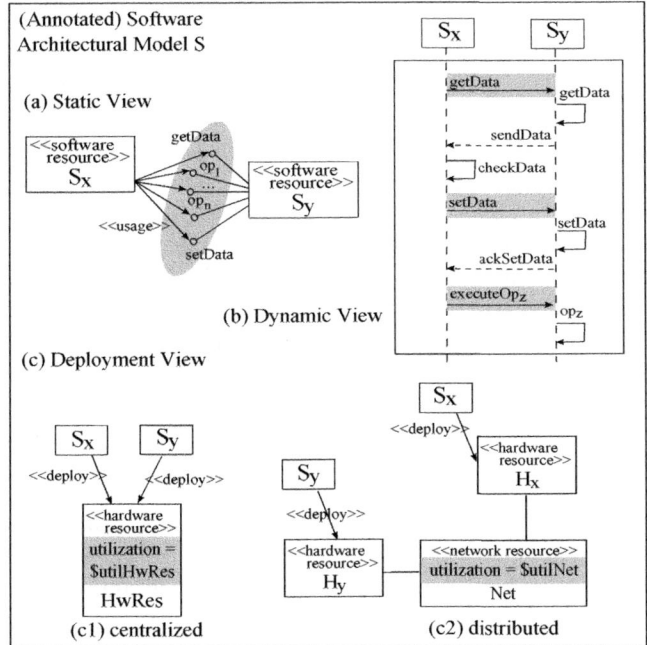

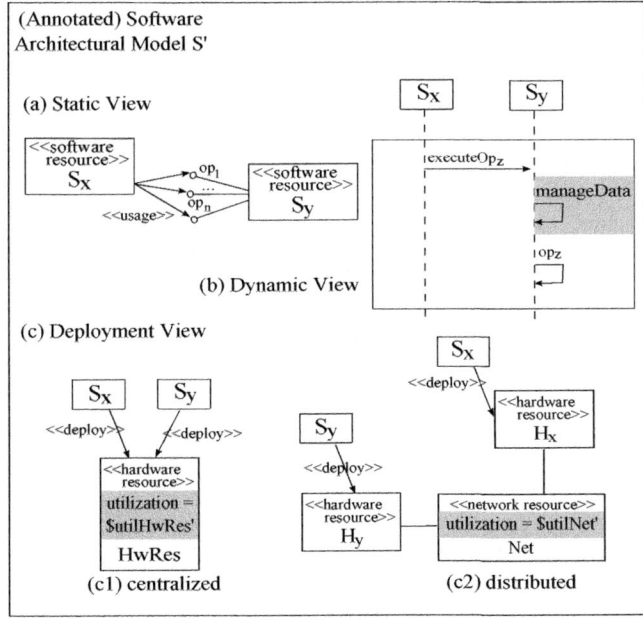

Fig. 2. A graphical representation of the *Blob* antipattern

that the software resource S_x originates an instance of the Blob antipattern in the Software Architectural Model S.

The lower side of Figure 2 contains the architectural changes that can be applied accordingly to the *BLOB solution*, thus a new software model is built (i.e. the *(Annotated)Software Architectural Model S'*). The following refactoring actions are represented: (a) the number of usage dependencies between software resources S_x and S_y must be decreased by delegating some functionalities to the resource S_y; (b) the number of messages sent by S_x must be decreased by removing the management of data belonging to S_y. As consequences of previous actions: (c1) if the communicating software resources were deployed on the same hardware resource then the latter will not be a critical resource anymore by showing a *low* utilization value, i.e. $utilHwRes'$; (c2) if the communicating software resources are deployed on different hardware resources then the network will not be a critical resource anymore by showing a *low* utilization value, i.e. $utilNet'$.

3 Related Work

The term *antipattern* appeared for the first time in [11] in contrast to the trend of focus on positive and constructive solutions. Differently from patterns, antipatterns look at the negative features of a software system and describe commonly occurring solutions to problems that generate negative consequences.

Performance Antipatternshave been previously documented and discussed in different works: technology independent performance antipatterns have been defined in [25] and they represent the main reference in this work; technology specific such as J2EE and EJB antipatterns have been specified in [17] and [26].

Few related works can be found in literature that deal with the interpretation of performance results and the generation of architectural feedback. Most of them are based on monitoring techniques [7] and therefore are conceived to only act after software deployment for tuning its performance.

An approach that aims at achieving good performance results through a deep understanding of the architectural features has been introduced in [28]. Such approach is the one that better defines the concept of antipatterns, however it is strongly based on the interactions between software architects and performance experts, therefore its level of automation is quite poor.

One of the first proposals of generation of feedback due to the software performance analysis can be found in [15], where the detection of performance flaws is demanded to the analysis of a specific performance modeling notation, i.e. Layered Queued Network (LQN) models, and informal interpretation matrices are used as support for the feedback generation.

The issue of solving performance issues through antipatterns has been addressed in [24], where a Performance Antipattern Detection (PAD) tool is presented. However, PAD only deals with Component-Based Enterprise Systems and targets Enterprise Java Bean (EJB) applications. It is based on monitoring data from running systems from which it extracts the run-time system design and detects only EJB antipatterns. Its scope is restricted to running EJB systems, therefore it is not applicable in the early development stages.

Another interesting work on the software performance diagnosis and improvements has been proposed in [32]: performance flaws are identified before the implementation, even if they are related only to bottlenecks and long paths. Performance antipatterns, compared to simple bottleneck and long paths identification, help to find more complex situations that embed software and/or hardware problems. Additionally in [32] performance issues are identified at the level of the LQN performance model, and the translation of these model properties into architectural changes might hide some possible refactoring solutions, whereas performance antipatterns give a wider degree of freedom for architectural alternatives since they embed the solutions in their definition.

By taking a wider look out of the performance domain, the management of *antipatterns* is a quite recent research topic, whereas there has already been a significant effort in the area of software design *patterns*. It is out of scope to address such wide area, but it is worth to mention some works that use model-driven instruments to deal with patterns.

In [18] a metamodeling approach to pattern specification has been introduced. In the context of the OMGs 4-layer metamodeling architecture, the authors propose a pattern specification language (i.e. Epattern, at the M3 level) used to specify patterns in any MOF-compliant modeling language at the M2 layer. In [19] a UML-based pattern specification technique has been introduced. Design patterns are defined as models in terms of UML metamodel concepts: a pattern model describes the participants of a pattern and the relations between them in a graphical notation by means of roles, i.e. the properties that a UML model element must have to match the corresponding pattern occurrence.

4 Proposed Approach

In this Section a vision of the approach is discussed: the problem of interpreting the performance results and generating architectural alternatives is addressed with a model-based framework that supports the management of antipatterns.

The main activities performed within such framework are schematically shown in Figure 3: *specifying antipatterns*, to define in a well-formed way the properties that lead the software system to reveal a bad practice as well as the changes that provide a solution; *detecting antipatterns*, to locate antipatterns in software models; *solving antipatterns*, to remove the detected performance problems with a set of refactoring actions that can be applied on the system model.

The activity of specifying antipatterns is performed by introducing a metamodel (i.e. a neutral and a coherent set of interrelated concepts) to collect the system elements that occur in the definition of antipatterns (e.g. software resource, network resource utilization, etc.), which is meant to be the basis for a machine-processable definition of antipatterns. An antipattern definition includes: (i) the specification of the problem, i.e. a set of *rules* that interrogate the system elements to look for occurrences of the corresponding antipattern; (ii) the specification of the solution, i.e. a set of *actions* that are applied on the system elements to remove the original performance issues.

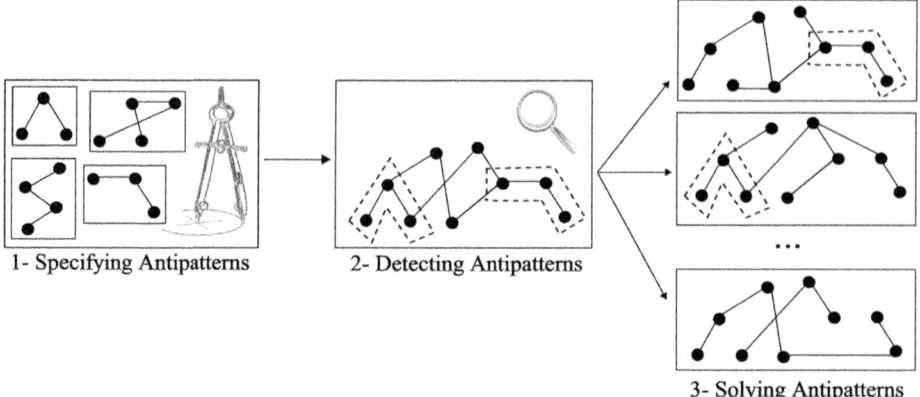

Fig. 3. The main activities of the model-based framework

The activities of detecting and solving antipatterns are performed by respectively translating the antipatterns rules and actions into concrete modeling notations. In fact, the modeling language used for the target system, i.e. the box *(annotated) software architectural model* of Figure 1, is of crucial relevance, since the antipatterns neutral concepts must be translated into the actual concrete modeling languages, if possible[4]. The framework is currently considering three notations: a system modeling language such as UML [3] and Marte profile[5] [4]; an architectural language such as Æmilia [9]; a domain specific modeling language such as Palladio Component Model (PCM) [8]. In general, the subset of target modeling languages can be enlarged as far as the concepts for representing antipatterns are available; for example, architectural description languages such as AADL [2] can be also suited to validate the approach.

As stated in Section 2, the "Blob" antipattern [25] can be detected, for example, when a software resource requires a lot of information from another one, it generates excessive message traffic that lead to over utilize the available network resource (i.e. the distributed case). Figure 4 shows an example of the *Blob problem* in the UML and Marte profile modeling language where the shaded boxes highlight the excerpts of the architecture evidencing the "Blob" instance (i.e. the *libraryController* UML component)[6]. Such antipattern can be solved by applying the *Blob solution*, e.g. by balancing in a better way the business logic among the available software resources with a consequent improvement for the utilization of the network resource (see the lower side of Figure 4).

More technical details on the main activities of the framework (i.e. specifying, detecting and solving antipatterns) are reported in the following.

---

[4] It depends on the expressiveness of the target modeling language.
[5] MARTE profile provides facilities to annotate UML models with information required to perform performance analysis.
[6] For example, a software resource can be represented as a *UML component*, the network resource utilization can be represented as the tagged value *utilization* of the MARTE stereotype *GaCommHost* applied to a *UML node*, etc.

A Model-Based Framework for Software Performance Feedback 27

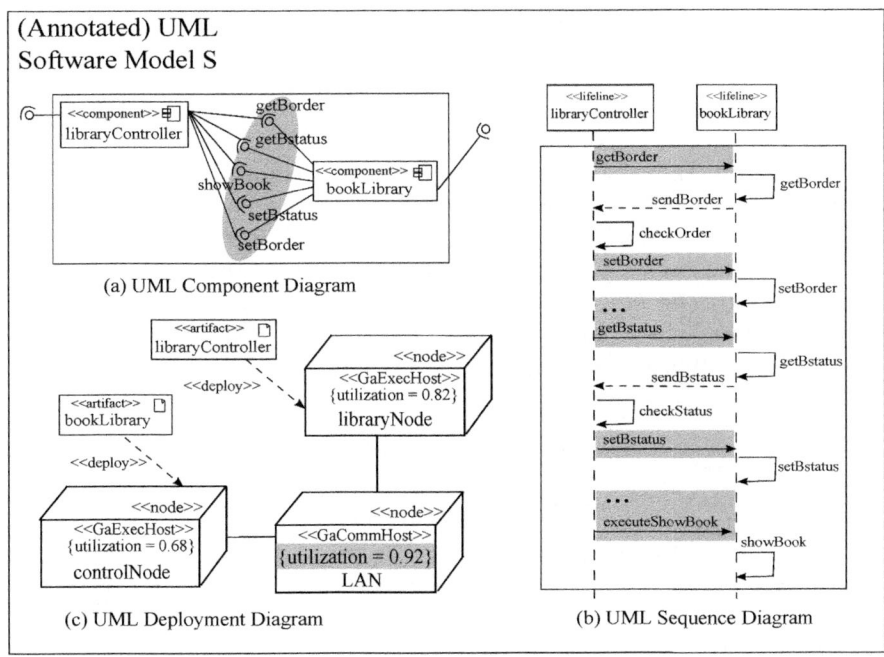

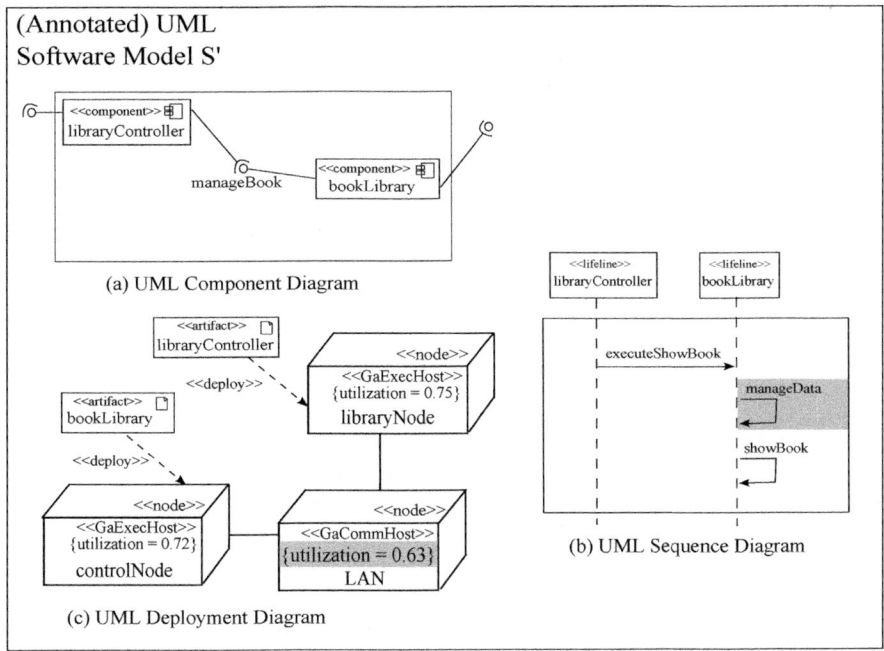

Fig. 4. An example of the "Blob" antipattern in the UML and Marte profile modeling language

4.1 Specifying Antipatterns

This section briefly presents the metamodel, named Performance Antipattern Modeling Language (PAML), collecting all the system elements identified by analyzing the antipatterns definition in literature [25].

The PAML metamodel structure is shown in Figure 5. It is constituted of two main parts as delimited by the horizontal dashed line: (i) the *Antipattern Specification* part is aimed at collecting the high-level features such as the views of the system (i.e. static, dynamic, deployment) characterizing the antipatterns' specification; (ii) the *Model Elements Specification* part is aimed at collecting the concepts that will be used to explore the software architectural models and the performance indices (see Figure 1).

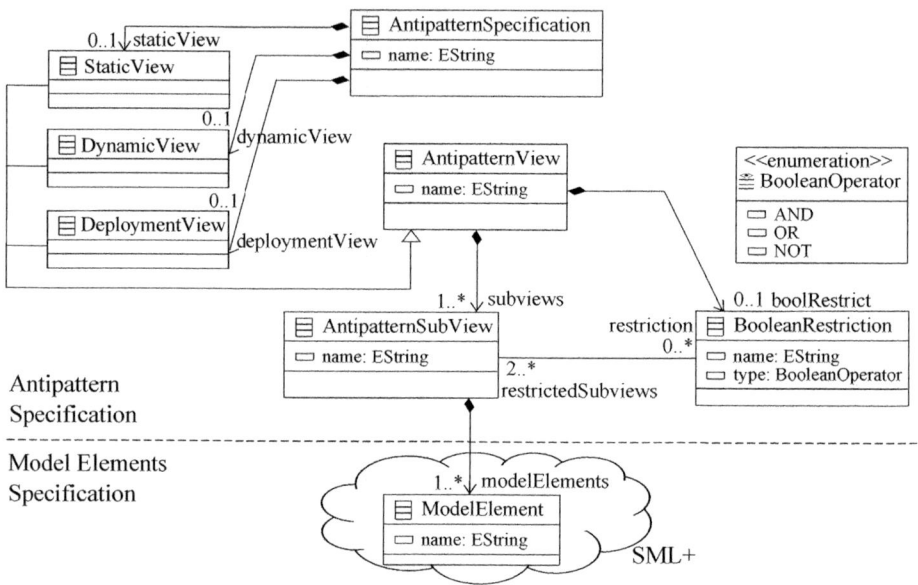

Fig. 5. The Performance Antipattern Modeling Language (PAML) structure

The specification of *model elements* to describe antipatterns is a quite complex task, because such elements can be of different type: (i) elements of a software architectural model (e.g. software resource, message, hardware resource); (ii) performance analysis outcoming indices (e.g. utilization of a network resource); (iii) structured information that can be obtained by processing the previous ones (e.g. the number of messages sent by a software resource towards another one); (iv) bounds that give guidelines for the interpretation of the system features (e.g. the upper bound for the network resource utilization).

These two latter model elements, i.e. (iii) structured information and (iv) bounds, are respectively defined by introducing supporting *functions* that elaborate a certain set of system elements, and *thresholds* that need to be compared with the observed properties of the software system. Note that threshold numerical values (e.g. the utilization of a network resource is considered high if greater than 0.8) can be assigned by software architects basing on heuristic evaluations, or they can be obtained by the monitoring of the system[7].

All the architectural model elements and the performance indices occurring in antipatterns' specifications are grouped in a metamodel called SML+ (see Figure 5). SML+ obviously shares many concepts with existing Software Modeling Languages, however, it is not meant to be another modeling language, rather it is oriented to specify the basic elements of performance antipatterns[8].

In this way an antipattern can be specified as a PAML-based model that is intended to formalize its textual description [25]. For example, following the graphical representation of the Blob antipattern (see Figure 2), the corresponding Blob model (see Figure 4) will be constituted by an `AntipatternSpecification` with three `AntipatternViews`: (a) the `StaticView`, (b) the `DynamicView`, (c) the `DeploymentView` for which two `AntipatternSubViews` are defined, i.e. (c1) the centralized one and (c2) the distributed one. A `BooleanRestriction` can be defined between these sub-views, and the *type* is set by the `BooleanOperator` equal to the *OR* value. Each subview will contain a set of `ModelElements`.

4.2 Detecting and Solving Antipatterns

Performance antipatterns are built on the basis of SML+ that contains the minimal amount of concepts essentials for their specification. The activities of detecting and solving antipatterns are performed by translating the concepts of SML+ into the corresponding elements of the concrete notations the framework considers (i.e. UML and Marte profile, Æmilia, and PCM).

Figure 6 shows how the specification of performance antipatterns can be translated into the actual modeling languages. Each antipattern will shadow on a set of model elements belonging to the modeling language *SML+* we propose. For example, the *blob* antipattern specification (see Figure 2) contains the *softwareResource* and *hardwareResource* model elements, whereas it is not related to the *resourceDemand* element (see Figure 6).

SML+ is aimed at providing the infrastructure upon which constructing the semantic relations among different modeling languages. Note that such semantic relations depend on the expressiveness of the target modeling language. For example, a *softwareResource* is respectively translated in a *UML component*, a *ARCHI_ELEM_TYPE*, and a *PCM basic component*; on the contrary, the full mapping is not possible for the *hardwareResource* whose translation is only possible with a *UML node* and a *PCM resource container*, whereas in Æmilia the concept remains uncovered.

---

[7] For example, the threshold numerical value for the upper bound of network resource utilization can be estimated as the average utilization value overall the network instances in the software system under analysis, plus the corresponding variance.

[8] For sake of space we do not detail SML+ here. However, a restricted set of model elements, such as software resource, resource demand, etc., are shown in Figure 6.

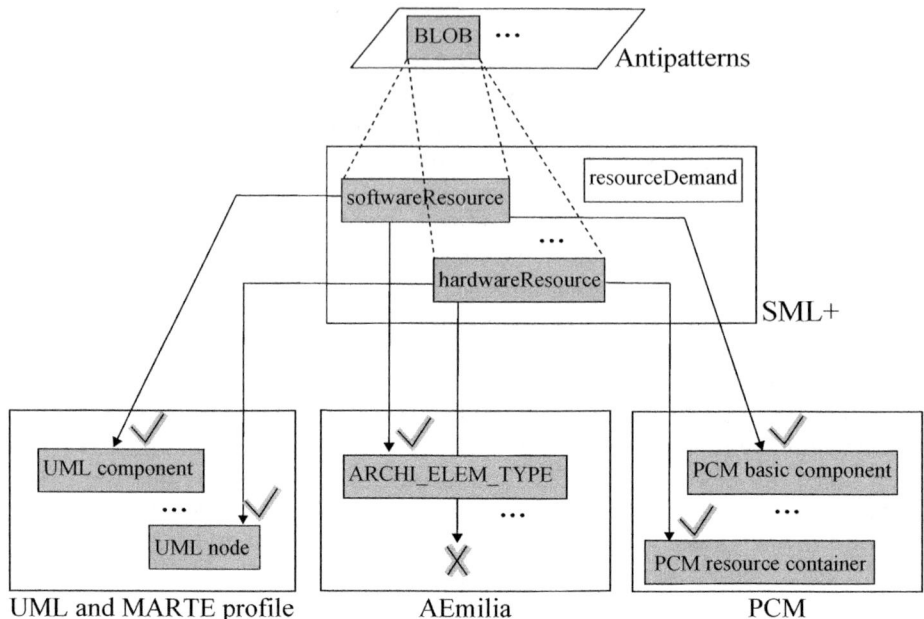

Fig. 6. Translating the specification of antipatterns into concrete modeling languages

We can conclude that in a concrete modeling language there are antipatterns that can be automatically detected and/or automatically solved (i.e. the entire set of model elements is translated) and some others that are neither detectable and solvable (i.e. no model element is translated). There is an intermediate level of antipatterns that are semi-automatically detectable by relaxing some rules, and/or semi-automatically solvable by devising some actions to be manually performed (i.e. a restricted set of model elements is translated).

5 Expected Contributions

The activity of specifying antipatterns provides several contributions: (i) the identification of the system elements of the antipatterns specification (e.g. software resource, network resource utilization, hardware resource, etc.); (ii) the formalization of the antipatterns specification as logical predicates that identify the system properties characterizing their occurrence in software architectural models (e.g. a software resource generates an excessive message traffic); (iii) the definition of a metamodel able to capture the antipatterns properties.

The benefit of introducing a metamodel approach is manifold: (i) *expressiveness*, it currently contains all the concepts needed to specify twelve performance antipatterns introduced in [25]; (ii) *usability*, it allows a user-friendly representation of all antipatterns as models capturing performance flaws; (iii) *reusability*, i.e. if new antipatterns will be found, then it can also represent the new ones, if based on the same concepts; (iv) *extensibility*, i.e. if new antipatterns are based on additional concepts the metamodel can be refined to introduce such concepts.

The subset of the antipatterns types can be enlarged as far as the concepts for representing such types are available. Technology-specific antipatterns such as EJB and J2EE antipatterns [17] [26] can be also suited to validate how the current metamodel is reusable in domain-specific fields. For example, the EJB Bloated Session Bean Antipattern [17] can be currently specified as a PAML-based model, since it describes a situation in EJB systems where a session bean has become too bulky and it is very similar to the Blob antipattern in the Smith-Williams' classification.

The activities of detecting and solving antipatterns, based on their specifications, provide the operational support to the results interpretation and feedback generation problems, thus to automate the backward path in the software performance process.

6 Current Status

The activity of *specifying antipatterns* is addressed in [14]: a structured description of the system elements that occur in the definition of antipatterns is provided, and performance antipatterns are modeled as logical predicates. Such predicates could be further refined by looking at probabilistic model checking techniques, as Grunske experimented in [20]. Additionally, in [14] the operational counterpart of the antipattern declarative definitions as logical predicates is implemented with a java rule-engine application. Such engine is able to detect performance antipatterns in an XML representation of the software system that groups the software architectural model and the performance indices data.

A Performance Antipattern Modeling Language, i.e. a metamodel specifically tailored to describe antipatterns, is introduced in [12]. It is also discussed a vision on how model-driven techniques (e.g. weaving models [10]) can be used to build a notation-independent approach that addresses the results interpretation and feedback generation steps via performance antipatterns management.

The activities of *detecting* and *solving antipatterns* are currently implemented by translating the antipattern rules and actions into two modeling languages: (i) the UML and Marte profile notation in [13]; (ii) the PCM notation in [27]. In particular, in [13] performance antipatterns are automatically detected in UML models using OCL [23] queries, whereas in [27] a restricted set of antipatterns is automatically detected and solved in PCM models through a benchmark tool.

The current work is on investigating how to specify, detect, and solve performance antipatterns in the Æmilia architectural language.

Additionally, instead of blindly moving among the antipattern solutions without eventually achieving the desired results, a technique to rank the antipatterns on the basis of their guiltiness for violated requirements is defined in [16], thus to decide how many antipatterns to solve, which ones and in what order.

7 Plan for Evaluation

The aim of this work is to provide automation in the backward path from the performance analysis to software modeling by means of antipatterns. The experimentation on the UML and Marte profile and PCM modeling languages validates the applicability of the whole approach, i.e. the support to results interpretation and feedback generation by specifying, detecting, and solving antipatterns.

As a short term future goal the approach has to be validated in order to determine the extent to which it can offer support to user activities. The validation of the approach includes two dimensions: (i) it has to be exposed to a set of target users, such as graduate students in a software engineering course, model-driven developers, more or less experienced software architects, in order to analyze its scope and usability; (ii) it has to be applied to complex case studies by involving industry partners, in order to analyze its scalability. Such experimentation is of worth interest because the final purpose would be to integrate the framework in the daily practices of the software development process.

In a longer term, some critical pending issues have to be faced in order to automate the whole process. The detection of antipatterns generates two main categories of problems: (i) the accuracy problem, i.e. false positive/negative instances might be introduced; (ii) the relationship problem, i.e. the detected instances might be related each other, e.g. one instance can be the generalization or the specialization of another instance. The solution of antipatterns generates three main categories of problems: (i) the convergence problem, i.e. the solution of one or more antipatterns might introduce new antipatterns; (ii) the requirement problem, i.e. when one or more antipatterns cannot be solved due to pre-existing (functional or non-functional) requirements; (iii) the coherency problem, i.e. when the solution of a certain number of antipatterns cannot be unambiguously applied due to incoherencies among their solutions.

Acknowledgments. I would like to thank my PhD Advisor Vittorio Cortellessa and my co-authors of the cited papers for their fundamental contribution on this topic.

References

1. GreatSPN, a GRaphical Editor and Analyzer for Timed and Stochastic Petri Nets, http://www.di.unito.it/~greatspn/index.html
2. SAE, Architecture Analysis and Design Language (AADL), June 2006, as5506/1, http://www.sae.org
3. UML 2.0 Superstructure Specification, Object Management Group, Inc. (2005), http://www.omg.org/cgi-bin/doc?formal/05-07-04
4. UML Profile for MARTE beta 2, Object Management Group, Inc. (2008), http://www.omgmarte.org/Documents/Specifications/08-06-09.pdf
5. WinPEPSY-QNS, a tool for calculating performance measures of Queueing Networks, http://www7.informatik.unierlangen.de/prbazan/pepsy

6. Balsamo, S., Di Marco, A., Inverardi, P., Simeoni, M.: Model-based Performance Prediction in Software Development: A Survey. IEEE TSE 30(5), 295–310 (2004)
7. Barber, K.S., Graser, T.J., Holt, J.: Enabling Iterative Software Architecture Derivation Using Early Non-Functional Property Evaluation. In: International Conference on Automated Software Engineering (ASE), pp. 172–182 (2002)
8. Becker, S., Koziolek, H., Reussner, R.: The Palladio Component Model for model-driven performance prediction. JUSS 82, 3–22 (2009)
9. Bernardo, M., Donatiello, L., Ciancarini, P.: Stochastic Process Algebra: From an Algebraic Formalism to an Architectural Description Language. In: Performance, pp. 236–260 (2002)
10. Bézivin, J.: On the unification power of models. Software and System Modeling 4(2), 171–188 (2005)
11. Brown, W.J., Malveau, R.C., McCormick III, H.W., Mowbray, T.J.: AntiPatterns: Refactoring Software, Architectures, and Projects in Crisis (1998)
12. Cortellessa, V., Di Marco, A., Eramo, R., Pierantonio, A., Trubiani, C.: Approaching the Model-Driven Generation of Feedback to Remove Software Performance Flaws. In: EUROMICRO-SEAA, pp. 162–169 (2009)
13. Cortellessa, V., Di Marco, A., Eramo, R., Pierantonio, A., Trubiani, C.: Digging into UML models to remove Performance Antipatterns. In: ICSE Workshop Quovadis, pp. 9–16 (2010)
14. Cortellessa, V., Di Marco, A., Trubiani, C.: Performance Antipatterns as Logical Predicates. In: IEEE International Conference on Engineering of Complex Computer Systems (ICECCS), pp. 146–156 (2010)
15. Cortellessa, V., Frittella, L.: A framework for automated generation of architectural feedback from software performance analysis. In: Wolter, K. (ed.) EPEW 2007. LNCS, vol. 4748, pp. 171–185. Springer, Heidelberg (2007)
16. Cortellessa, V., Martens, A., Reussner, R., Trubiani, C.: A process to effectively identify "Guilty" performance antipatterns. In: Rosenblum, D.S., Taentzer, G. (eds.) FASE 2010. LNCS, vol. 6013, pp. 368–382. Springer, Heidelberg (2010)
17. Dudney, B., Asbury, S., Krozak, J.K., Wittkopf, K.: J2EE Antipatterns (2003)
18. Elaasar, M., Briand, L.C., Labiche, Y.: A metamodeling approach to pattern specification. In: Wang, J., Whittle, J., Harel, D., Reggio, G. (eds.) MoDELS 2006. LNCS, vol. 4199, pp. 484–498. Springer, Heidelberg (2006)
19. France, R.B., Kim, D., Ghosh, S., Song, E.: A UML-Based Pattern Specification Technique. IEEE Trans. Software Eng. 30(3), 193–206 (2004)
20. Grunske, L.: Specification patterns for probabilistic quality properties. In: ICSE, pp. 31–40 (2008)
21. Lazowska, E., Kahorjan, J., Graham, G.S., Sevcik, K.C.: Quantitative System Performance: Computer System Analysis Using Queueing Network Models (1984)
22. Ajmone Marsan, M., Balbo, G., Conte, G., Donatelli, S., Franceschinis, G.: Modelling with Generalized Stochastic Petri Nets (1995)
23. Object Management Group (OMG). OCL 2.0 Specification, 2006. OMG Document formal/2006-05-01
24. Parsons, T., Murphy, J.: Detecting Performance Antipatterns in Component Based Enterprise Systems. Journal of Object Technology 7(3), 55–90 (2008)
25. Smith, C.U., Williams, L.G.: More new software performance antipatterns: Even more ways to shoot yourself in the foot. In: Comp. Meas. Group Conf. (2003)
26. Tate, B., Clark, M., Lee, B., Linskey, P.: Bitter EJB (2003)

27. Trubiani, C., Koziolek, A.: Detection and Solution of Software Performance Antipatterns in Palladio Architectural Models. In: Proceedings of the 2nd ACM/SPEC International Conference on Performance Engineering (ICPE), Karlsruhe, Germany, pp. 19–30. ACM, New York (2011)
28. Williams, L.G., Smith, C.U.: PASA(SM): An Architectural Approach to Fixing Software Performance Problems. In: International Computer Measurement Group Conference, pp. 307–320 (2002)
29. Woodside, C.M.: A Three-View Model for Performance Engineering of Concurrent Software. IEEE Trans. Software Eng. 21(9), 754–767 (1995)
30. Woodside, C.M., Franks, G., Petriu, D.C.: The Future of Software Performance Engineering. In: FOSE, pp. 171–187 (2007)
31. Woodside, C.M., Petriu, D.C., Petriu, D.B., Shen, H., Israr, T., Merseguer, J.: Performance by Unified Model Analysis (PUMA). In: WOSP, pp. 1–12 (2005)
32. Xu, J.: Rule-based Automatic Software Performance Diagnosis and Improvement. In: WOSP, pp. 1–12. ACM, New York (2008)

Software Modeling in Education: The 6th Educators' Symposium at MODELS 2010

Martina Seidl[1,*] and Peter J. Clarke[2]

[1] Business Informatics Group, Vienna University of Technology, Austria
Institute for Formal Models and Verification, JKU Linz, Austria
Martina.Seidl@jku.at
[2] School of Computing and Information Sciences, Florida Int'l University, USA
clarkep@cis.fiu.edu

Abstract. The Educators' Symposium (EduSymp) yields a major forum for software modeling education. Traditionally collocated with the ACM/IEEE International Conference on Model-Driven Engineering Languages and Systems (MODELS), EduSymp offers a unique opportunity for educators to present and discuss innovative pedagogical software modeling approaches. In this paper, a short retrospective on the 6th edition of EduSymp hosted in Oslo is presented. The program was a manifold of activities including interesting and thought-provoking oral presentations, an interactive breakout-session, and a panel discussion.

1 Overview

Research and academic instruction complement each other and eventually, the results of research become the foundation of the curriculum in academic disciplines. Whereas in some academic disciplines the knowledge taught to students is well established for a long time, in other disciplines, such as computer science, the knowledge mainly used is the result of recent or ongoing research. The training of computer scientists requires both established and cutting-edge knowledge, which are indispensable in preparing scientists for the challenges of the professional world.

In the field of software modeling, which continues to be an emerging research field with many highly innovative and practically relevant technological advancements, knowledge rapidly gets outdated. The challenge for teachers in the field of software modeling is to communicate well-established basic principles to the students, as well as to educate them on the scope and limitations of the novel and exciting technologies being developed. The Educators' Symposium (EduSymp), collocated with the ACM/IEEE International Conference on Model-Driven Engineering Languages and Systems (MODELS), offers a unique opportunity for educators to present and discuss innovative pedagogical software modeling approaches.

---

[*] This work has been partly funded by the Austrian Federal Ministry of Transport, Innovation, and Technology and the Austrian Research Promotion Agency under grant FIT-IT-819584.

Although many of the software modeling technologies are very mature from a conceptual point of view, the concrete implementations often provide several pitfalls to the users. Consequently, there are many questions educators are confronted with when developing software engineering curricula. A few of these questions are as follows:

- The field of software modeling continues to change rapidly. At what point in the continuum of change shall we start to teach modeling?
- Do students consider models to aid in software development or are they viewed as pretty pictures only?
- Can the benefits of modeling be realized without having proper tool support?
- Are tools imposing an extra inhibition/threshold in teaching modeling?
- Is it necessary for modeling tools to conform to standards or is it more important that they provide simplified concepts tailored for didactical purposes?
- Is it positive/negative when students are forced to use a specific tool implementation from a specific vendor? Do we teach them knowledge with an expiration date?

The 2010 EduSymp started with the thought provoking keynote "Formality in Education – Bitter Medicine or Bitter Administration?" given by Thomas Kühne[1]. The results of an online survey[2] conducted prior to the symposium offered an open forum for people interested and involved in software modeling education to discuss and exchange ideas on the questions previously listed.

The general consensus of the attendees at the 2010 EduSymp was that in software modeling education hands-on experience is extremely valuable for the students. The requirements for the modeling tools naturally vary based on the specific aims of the different courses (e.g., basic modeling, software engineering, model-driven engineering, and model engineering, among others). Overall it was thought that the available tools are mature enough, with respect to stability and documentation, that they may be successfully applied in software modeling courses. A huge point of criticism was their usability and user-friendliness which still poses a major burden to the students. In the context of these discussions many experiences and ideas were exchanged between the participants of the symposium.

This year's symposium was very well attended (between 20 and 50 participants attended the various sessions) which clearly indicates that software modeling education is an important issue within the modeling research community. We hope that the discussions initiated at the 2010 EduSymp will result in interesting and novel pedagogical ideas to support software modeling education. In addition, we expect the next edition of EduSymp will continue to increase the awareness on the importance of high quality education, and provide a forum for educators to meet, share, and discuss relevant issues in software modeling education.

---

[1] Associate Professor, School of Engineering and Computer Science, Victoria University of Wellington, New Zealand.
[2] A summary of the survey results is available at
http://edusymp.big.tuwien.ac.at/slides/survey.pdf

2 Contributions

Seven papers (three long papers and four short papers) were selected to be presented at the 2010 edition of EduSymp covering a broad spectrum in software modeling education.

Teaching Model Driven Language Handling
Terje Gjøsæter and Andreas Prinz

Many universities teach computer language handling by mainly focussing on compiler theory, although MDD (model-driven development) and meta-modelling are increasingly important in the software industry, as well as in computer science. In this article, we share some experiences from teaching a course in computer language handling where the focus is on MDD principles.

The Role of User Guidance in the Industrial Adoption of AUKOTON MDE Approach
Jari Rauhamäki, Outi Laitinen, Seppo Sierla, and Seppo Kuikka

Model-Driven Engineering (MDE) has emerged as an actively researched and established approach for next generation control application development. Technology transfer to the industry is a topical research problem. Since most professional factory process control engineers do not have computer science backgrounds, there is an urgent need for studies of the role of user guidance in the professional learning, and thus, of industrial adoption of MDE approaches. In this study professionals were invited to a hands-on assessment of the AUKOTON MDE approach for factory process control engineering. Qualitative empirical material was collected and analyzed to identify the role of user guidance in the context of other factors impacting industrial adoption. Challenges in adoption that could be solved by user guidance were identified with the theory of organizational knowledge creation (SECI) model.

Implementation of the Concept-Driven Approach in an Object-Oriented Analysis and Design Course
Ven Yu Sien

As one of the most important tasks in object-oriented analysis and design (OOAD) is the abstraction of the problem domain into specific concepts or objects, information technology (IT) students need appropriate skills of abstraction in order to identify the essential concepts and relationships within a problem domain. However students in higher education generally find difficulty performing abstractions of real-world problems within the context of OOAD.

Concept mapping is a popular tool used in education for facilitating learning, comprehension and the development of knowledge structures. We have successfully adopted concept maps as stepping-stones to assist students in constructing class and sequence diagrams. In this paper, we present a framework for teaching object-oriented (OO) modelling using concept maps. This framework comprising four teaching modules could be integrated into existing OOAD courses at the undergraduate or postgraduate level, and OOAD workshops to help software engineering educators resolve some of the difficulties they face in trying to teach OOAD. We also report results of an evaluative study on the effectiveness of integrating concept mapping techniques into an introductory OOAD course.

Teaching OCL Standard Library: First Part of an OCL 2.x Course
Joanna Chimiak-Opoka, Birgit Demuth

Our aim is to provide a complete set of materials to teach OCL. They can be used in bachelor or master programs of computer science curricula and for training in an industrial context. In this paper we present the first part of the course related to the OCL Standard Library. This part provides model independent examples to teach OCL types and their operations. It enables users to gain a basic understanding of the OCL Standard Library, which can be used as a starting point to write model constraints (OCL specifications) or model queries. Additionally, to the content of the paper, we provide a set of OCL packages, exercise proposals and lecture slides.

Role Allocation and Scheme in Software Engineering Course-Project
Ghafour Alipour

Role is a set of behavioural actions and responsibilities one takes in a specific situation. We all have many roles in our life. Differences among the role definitions reach mainly from the different emphasis of the software development method itself. Agile software development methods define roles to enhance communication and to produce a better product. In this paper, we describe a role allocation and scheme method whose data were gathered in students projects in software engineering course in the university.

New Media in Teaching UML in the Large - an Experience Report
Marion Brandsteidl, Konrad Wieland, and Christian Huemer

Huge classes with more than 800 students pose a major challenge to lecturers as well as to students, especially when a practical part is included. In order to successfully master lectures of this size, novel kinds of teaching media provide a multitude of enhanced opportunities. In this paper, we present our experiences with the application of new media in our undergraduate course Introduction to Object-Oriented Modeling (OOM). In this course, we teach approximately 800-1000 students per year the principles and techniques of UML 2.0. New media, i.e., technologies other than the traditional blackboard presentation like a document camera, web-based self assessments, or lecture recordings, are applied to support both, students and lecturers when learning and teaching, respectively. We empirically underline the acceptance of our concept with the feedback of our students concerning the newly used technologies gained through an extensive survey.

m2n: Translating Models to Natural Language Descriptions
Petra Brosch and Andrea Randak

To describe the structure of a system, the UML Class Diagram yields the means-of-choice. Therefor, the Class Diagram provides concepts like class, attribute, operation, association, generalization, aggregation, enumeration, etc. When students are introduced to this diagram, they often have to solve exercises where texts in natural language are given and they have to model the described systems. When analyzing such exercises, it becomes evident that certain kinds of phrases describing a particular concept appear again and again contextualized to the described domain.

In this paper, we present an approach which allows the automatic generation of textual specifications from a given Class Diagram based on standard phrases in natural language. Besides supporting teachers in preparing exercises, such an approach is also valuable for various e-learning scenarios.

3 Program Committee

The papers presented at EduSymp have been selected based on the novelty of the ideas, the impact of modeling during software development education, and relevance to the topics of the symposium. All papers passed through a rigorous review process, each paper received at least three detailed reviews prepared by internationally renowned experts. The list of the International Program Committee is shown below:

- Jordi Cabot, École des Mines de Nantes, France
- Fábio Costa, Universidade Federal de Goiás, Brazil
- Gregor Engels, University of Paderborn, Germany
- Robert France, Colorado State University, USA
- Martin Gogolla, University of Bremen, Germany
- Jeff Gray, University of Alabama, USA
- Øystein Haugen, SINTEF, Norway
- Gerti Kappel, Vienna University of Technology, Austria
- Ludwik Kuźniarz, Blekinge Institute of Technology, Sweden
- Timothy Lethbridge, University of Ottawa, Canada
- Werner Retschitzegger, Johannes Kepler University Linz, Austria
- Jean-Paul Rigault, University of Nice, France
- Patricia Roberts, University of Westminster, UK
- Michal Smialek, Warsaw University of Technology, Poland
- Dániel Varró, Budapest University of Technology and Economics, Hungary

Novel Communication Channels in Software Modeling Education

Marion Brandsteidl, Konrad Wieland, and Christian Huemer

Institute of Software Technology and Interactive Systems,
Vienna University of Technology, Austria
brandsteidl@ifs.tuwien.ac.at,
{wieland,huemer}@big.tuwien.ac.at

Abstract. Huge classes with more than 800 students pose a major challenge to lecturers as well as to students, especially when a practical part is included. In order to successfully master lectures of this size, novel kinds of teaching media provide a multitude of enhanced opportunities.

In this paper, we present our experiences with the application of new media in our undergraduate course Introduction to Object-Oriented Modeling (OOM). In this course, we teach approximately 800-1000 students per year the principles and techniques of UML 2.0. New media, i.e., technologies other than the traditional blackboard presentation like a document camera, web-based self assessments, or lecture recordings, are applied to support both, students and lecturers when learning and teaching, respectively. We empirically underline the acceptance of our concept with the feedback of our students concerning the newly used technologies gained through an extensive survey.

Keywords: Teaching Object-Oriented Modeling, Teaching UML, Basic Modeling Course.

1 Introduction

Since computers have become a consumer product and the internet has become a mainstream medium, many tools and techniques supporting teaching electronically as well as learning have emerged. The rich variety poses a major challenge for teachers in order to effectively apply the new possibilities.

The application of new media in education has also always been an active research field. New technologies emerge bringing new ways for teaching and learning. Today, e-learning, d-learning[1] or m-learning[2] have become indispensable in education [3]. Also other digital media affect education. In the area of modeling, Qi et al. [2] present the application of e-whiteboards, which serve perfectly for modeling in small teams. Another example is given by Zupancic et al. [8]. They have recorded the whole lectures and have streamed them together with

---
[1] Distance learning.
[2] Mobile learning.

the notes of the lecturer. Mock et al. [6] presented their experiences of using a tablet PC for teaching computer science courses.

In this paper we present our experiences with the selection of new media tools we used for our course Introduction to Object-Oriented Modeling (OOM), namely lecture recordings, a document camera, and self assessment tests. Those tools help us to teach a big number of students at the same time while still supporting the students as good as possible and offering them multiple learning channels.

At the end of summer term 2010, the students were asked to voluntarily take part in a survey covering the teaching methods of the lecture and about 180 out of 500 students took part in the survey which results in a participation rate of 36%. The results of parts of this survey are presented within this paper.

The paper is structured as follows: In the next section, we introduce our course and teaching environment. In Section 3 we present the self assessments for students in our e-learning platform. In addition, the platform also provides lecture streams, which we present in Section 4. The application of our document camera is discussed in Section 5. Before we conclude in Section 7, we present our ongoing work in Section 6.

2 Background

Our course *Introduction to Object-Oriented Modeling* (OOM) is offered twice per year and attended by 800-1000 undergraduate students who study computer science or business informatics at the Vienna University of Technology. In OOM we teach modeling basics by introducing syntax and semantics of UML 2 models[3] [4,7]. Despite the huge number of students, we try to avoid mass processing, but we establish personal mentoring instead. Besides a traditional lecture where structural as well as behavioral modeling techniques are introduced, we organize the lab as exercise courses in smaller groups where the theoretical contents of the lecture are practiced. Furthermore we provide support via online forums on the e-learning platform TUWEL[4] (a Moodle adaptation of the Vienna University of Technology). A detailed description of the course is given in [1].

The *lecture* consists of six units covering the following UML 2 diagrams: class and object diagram, sequence diagram, state diagram, activity diagram, and use case diagram. Each lecture is given with powerpoint slides accompanied by small practical modeling examples and syntax illustrations which are developed live during the lecture.

For the *practical part* the students are divided into groups of about 50 persons. Each group meets six times during the semester for a so-called "lab session" in order to discuss the solution of exercise sheets for practicing modeling. For each exercise the assistant professor chooses one student who must present and explain his/her solution.

For *further support*, we provide various e-learning exercises including multiple-choice questions and practical modeling exercises. The students can voluntarily

---
[3] http://www.uml.org/
[4] http://tuwel.tuwien.ac.at

use the e-learning exercises to test their knowledge about the syntax and the theoretical background of the diagrams as well as the interpretation of given diagrams and they can gain some modeling practice.

In our course, we use different media to teach UML supporting the different learning methods and needs of our students. The students can choose between learning the UML diagrams with the help of a book [4,7], attending the lecture, listening to the lecture at home or a combination of the three. The lab sessions are not simply used for assessing the students' knowledge, but also to answer questions and to examine each covered UML diagram from a more practical point of view — given that the students already have a basic knowledge of the syntax after the corresponding lecture as well as the preparation of the lab exercises have taken place. Three exams assess whether the students have reached the learning goals — if they understand the teaching material as well as if they are able to apply the taught concepts to small "real world problems".

To apply this teaching concept, we use traditional methods and material such as powerpoint or the blackboard as well as more recent methods such as lecture videos or e-learning. In this paper we concentrate on the more recent methods and technologies which assist us in teaching OOM.

3 Self Assessments

In OOM, the students have the possibility to practice all UML diagram types presented in the lecture with the help of our e-learning platform. In 2008, we started the first experiments on web-based self assessments for modeling [1], which we have extended providing now a higher amount of questions and more different types of questions presented in the following. In general, we distinguish between multiple choice and open questions with the overall goal that our students learn to understand both the syntax and semantics of UML by exercising on the basis of several examples on their own responsibility. Beside multiple choice questions checking the theory of object-oriented modeling, we mainly focus on multiple choice questions with practical background, where examples of UML diagrams are given and the students have to understand and interpret them. When exercising open questions where a textual description of a UML model is given, students have to develop the dedicated model from scratch.

All questions may be exercised during the whole term and may be repeated by the students as often as they like. Solving these exercises is not mandatory. Moreover, they are also a good starting point for fruitful discussions in our online forum, which is actively used by most students.

Multiple choice questions are evaluated immediately and presented to the students, where wrong answers are marked. In contrast, open questions where students have to develop a model are not checked automatically by the system. However, the students may control their exercise by fading in the correct solution.

In summer term 2010, 73% of all students used the multiple choice questions for practising and approximately 50% of all students tried them two or more times, whereas 43% of all students worked through the open examples and only

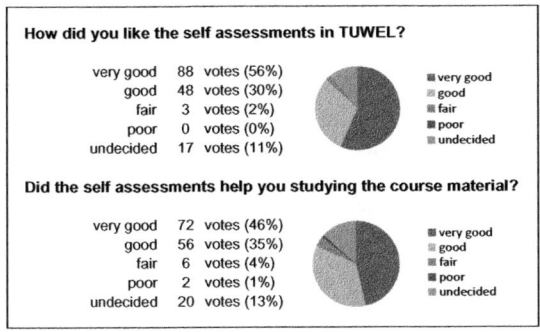

Fig. 1. Survey results concerning the self assessments

approximately 15% of all students repeated them. Of course, there is a huge increase of attempts a few days before the tests. Nearly 100% of all attempts happen during these days.

The self assessments support various types of learning (cf. [5]) in the following sense:

- *Learning by doing.* In the lecture the students get a profound theoretical background of UML and in the lab they have to work out several exercises. Our students enhance their practical modeling skills with the help of the self assessments.
- *Learning by repeating.* Another major advantage of the self assessments is that students may exercise whenever and wherever they want. If a student has some problems with a specific topic, he/she may repeat the exercises as often he/she likes to consolidate the newly acquired knowledge.
- *Fast feedback for students.* By getting feedback immediately, students may quickly find out their strengths and weaknesses in the specific topics.
- *Qualified feedback.* If the students select a wrong answer to a multiple choice question, they get qualified feedback to know why this answer is wrong.
- *Self-evaluations during the learning process.* Another advantage for our students, which we have identified, are self-evaluations during the whole term. Students may check with the help of the assessments how much progress they make in studying.

According to the survey, 86% of our students appreciate the self assessments and 64% out of them even appreciate them very much as depicted in Figure 1. Furthermore, only 5% of the students stated the self assessments as not helpful for studying the UML diagrams.

In the following, students' comments about the self assessments are summarized:

- The self assessments are a good method to learn UML.
- The slides are not enough to understand the principles and techniques of UML. The self assessments support the learning process very well.

- More exercises would be helpful.
- More qualified feedback would be supportive.

As mentioned before, only multiple choice questions can be evaluated automatically by our e-learning system and we assume that this is one of the reasons why a much higher percentage of the students do the multiple choice questions than the opening modeling examples. Therefore, in future work, we will concentrate on extending the multiple choice questions about given diagrams and on developing new e-learning exercise types where the solutions can be checked automatically. In particular, we will focus on the five exercise types described in the following:

Questions about given diagrams. In this type of exercise, a small UML diagram is presented to the student and he/she has to mark if certain statements about this diagram are true or false. The given model can either be a concrete example about a defined problem domain or an abstract diagram as shown in Exercise 1. Doing such exercises is an easy way to find out if the syntax of a given diagram is understood correctly.

Exercise 1. The given Use Case diagram was modeled strictly according to the UML 2 standard. Are the following statements true or false?

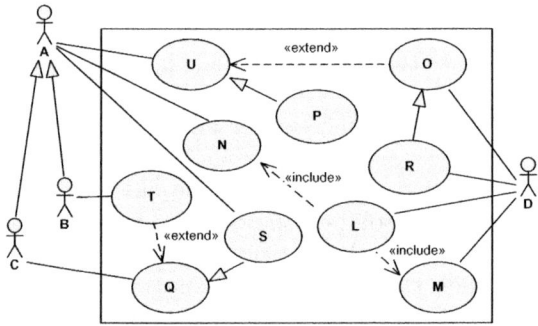

Actor B is involved in use case O.	☐ true ☐ false
Actor A can execute Q.	☐ true ☐ false
The behavior of O may be extended by the behavior of P.	☐ true ☐ false
Every time N is executed, L is also executed.	☐ true ☐ false
T can extend Q.	☐ true ☐ false

Fill in missing diagram elements. This kind of e-learning task focuses on the practice of certain concepts of a UML diagram type. The student is given an incomplete diagram and a corresponding description of the problem domain and he/she has to fill out the missing parts of the model. In Exercise 2, the student has to fill in the multiplicities of the associations between classes in a class diagram by choosing from several options. By doing this, he/she can test and/or practice the knowledge about multiplicities and the answers can still be checked automatically. Furthermore, feedback for the student is provided if a wrong multiplicity is selected. For example if the student states the multiplicity of the association between Room and House incorrect, resulting in the fact that one room is part of mutliple (*) houses. The feedback would be: "You marked the multiplicity next to the Aggregation with *, which would mean that one Room can be part of zero houses, one house or more than one houses. Due to the fact that one room is always part of exactly one house, the correct multiplicity is 1." This very detailed feedback helps the student finding out what he/she did wrong and why it is wrong. In the best case, it also gives a possible explanation why this particular mistake happened.

Exercise 2. You are given the following textual specification about a certain situation and a corresponding class diagram which has been modeled using UML 2.0. Unfortunately, all the multiplicities have been deleted. Fill in the multiplicities!
A House consists of several rooms whereas a room can be part of one house. Each house is owned by a company or by a (private) Person, companies and (private) persons can own multiple houses.

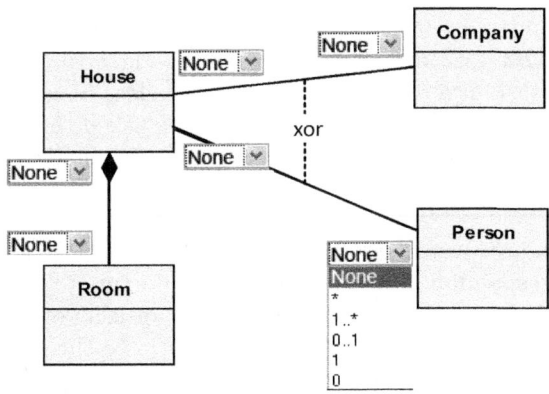

Modeling very small diagrams. In this challenge, a very short description of a domain that has to be modeled and several ways how to model that clipping are given. The student has to decide which of the given choices would be an adequate model of the given situation. If the student marks an incorrect model as correct, feedback tells him/her why this is not a convenient way to model the given problem. In Exercise 3, a model for the fact that "a person either wears one pair of boots or one pair of slippers" has to be found. Out of the five possible solutions, two model clippings fulfill the assignment specification.

Exercise 3. You are given the following textual specification about a certain situation that has to be modeled using a UML 2.0 class diagram. Look at the different answers beyond the specification and mark if the certain clipping of the UML diagram is consistent with the textual description.
A person either wears one pair of boots or one pair of slippers.

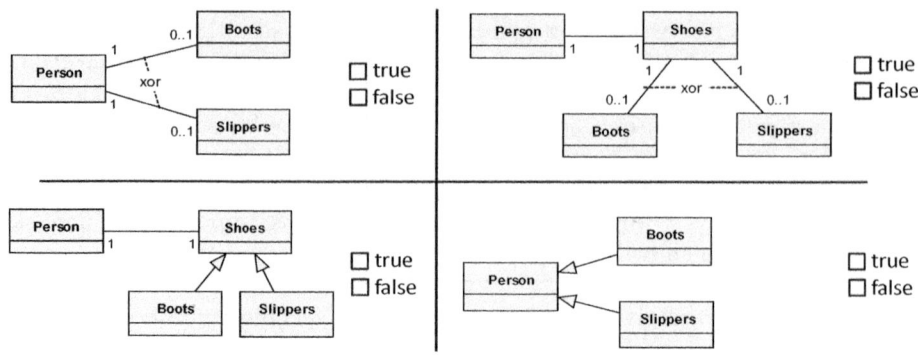

Linking between different diagram types. That exercise type offers a good possibility to show the students that the taught UML diagram types are not isolated everyone for itself, but are linked to each other and the student can find out if he/she interprets those links correctly. Two diagrams of different diagram types showing the same modeled situation are presented to the student. One of the two diagrams is considered correct, the other one contains some mistakes and the task is to find those mistakes and correct them – how to correct them depends on the concrete task. Exercise 4 shows a correct class diagram and an incorrect corresponding object diagram and the student is asked to delete as many associations and objects as necessary – but not more – to make it compliant to the class diagram.

Exercise 4. You are given the following UML 2 Class Diagram. A modeler tried to create a corresponding Object Diagram. Unfortunately, the modeler made some mistakes. Delete as many associations and objects of the Object Diagram as necessary to make the Object Diagram conform to the Class Diagram.

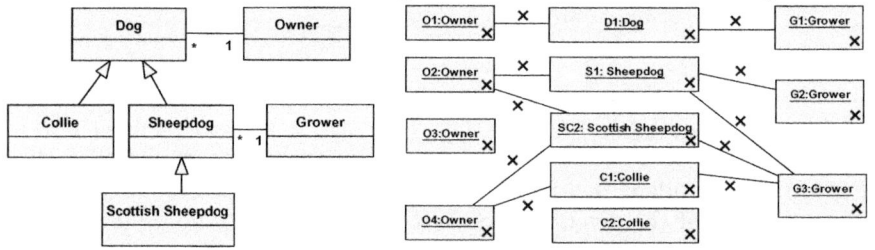

Linking code fragments to diagrams. The last variety of an e-learning task addresses the ability to link source code to a UML diagram. In the specification, a clipping of pseudo-code and a corresponding diagram, which is supposed to represent the given code correctly, are given. Once again, the diagram contains some errors and the student has to mark the errors by clicking on the diagram parts that are supposed to be wrong. With this kind of exercise, it can be checked automatically if the student found all the wrong parts, unfortunately, it is not possible to check if the student stated a diagram part as wrong for the right reason. For example in Exercise 5, the syntax of the arrow of m2() is definitely wrong. However, the system cannot determine if the student marked it as wrong for this reason.

Exercise 5. You are given the following pseudo-code. A modeler tried to visualize the communication with a UML 2 Sequence Diagram. Unfortunately, the modeler made some mistakes. Find 3 errors and mark them in the diagram by clicking on the parts that are wrong.
Assume that all used variables are already declared and initialized and that the method calls are modeled correctly.

```
class Main {
...
    Worker x = new Worker();
    if (x == 8) { y = x.m2(); }
    else { y = x.m1(); }
    for (int c = 0; c < 3; c++)
        x.m3();
}
...
}
```

4 Lecture Streams

One part of the course OOM are six lectures covering the theoretical background of the five taught UML diagrams (class and object diagram, sequence diagram, state diagram, activity diagram, and use case diagram). These lectures proceed in quite "traditional" ways, a professor or assistant professor is standing in a big lecture hall, presenting powerpoint slides and answering questions whenever they occur. The attendance of the lectures is not mandatory, nevertheless about 40% of the students visit the lectures.

In the long run, we plan to enhance all the lecture slides with spoken text thus producing lecture videos and exchanging the classical lecture with lectures that prepare the students for the lab sessions and focus more on the practical use of UML (for further information please refer to Section 6). Before actually combining our presentations with audio recordings we decided to do a test run with a less time-consuming method and, therefore, we simply recorded the actual lectures[5] to find out if the students find lecture videos useful and which features are important to them. With the kind help of the Teaching Support Center of the Vienna University of Technology we recorded the lectures and made them available through our e-learning platform TUWEL. The students had to be online and logged in to the platform to view the recordings. The videos were provided "just the way they were" with hardly any post processing at all. One file for each lecture exist, which is played directly in TUWEL, allowing the students to

---
[5] http://www.big.tuwien.ac.at/external/OOM.html

pause the recording, control the volume and jump back or forward, but without any chapter structure, subtitles or similar mechanisms helpful for navigating through a video file. Simply recording the lecture and publishing it in TUWEL did not require a lot of additional work or knowledge, but pleased the students a lot. The greatest advantages of recording lectures in general and our method of doing it are the following:

- *Low effort, big effect.* The teachers' workload does not change when recording his/her lectures. He/she simply attaches the laptop to a lecture recorder which is then attached to the LCD projector (instead of directly connecting the laptop to the LCD projector) and starts the recording.
- *Nearly time- and place-independent.* Students who are motivated to learn but cannot attend the lecture, can watch the video independently of time and place. Especially in the field of computer science a lot of students are already working part time or full time during their study, recording lectures is one way of facilitating that.
- *High learning outcome.* In the lab sessions, we also explain the theoretical background and syntax of the UML model, because after the lecture about a specific diagram type most students still did not have enough background knowledge to fully understand and discuss all the lab exercises concerning that diagram type. In summer term 2010, we increased the focus on practical issues in the labs, for the students seemed to have gained much more knowledge out of the lectures.
- *Student satisfaction.* Offering the students one more learning channel and giving them more flexibility than they are used to make them satisfied — even the ones who did not watch the videos at all seemed to feel more confident, because they "could watch them if they wanted".

When we decided to record the lectures, we were sure that the students would like it, but we did not expect that much acceptance. The students' comments on the newly used tool were not only good, they were almost enthusiastically encouraging us even more in our plans to produce lecture videos. An overview of the statements is given in the following:

- Students with previous knowledge of UML may decide only watching parts of the recordings.
- The students may choose time and place of watching the lecture by themselves, depending on when and where they can concentrate best.
- The students may take a break whenever they feel that their concentration is dropping.
- The students may watch parts they did not understand (either during the classical lecture or when watching the recording for the first time) again or they can watch the video again right before the test to refresh their memory about the specific topic.
- During the lecture, the students may concentrate on the speaker instead of taking notes, because they know that they may listen to the lecture again if they want.

According to the survey, students prefer lecture videos to traditional lectures held in a lecture hall, but even more students like a combination of both. Furthermore, for most of the students, completely disposing traditional lectures is not an option since they want the opportunity to ask questions personally and meet fellow students instead of sitting in front of their PC all the time and only communicating via Skype or similar tools. More detailed results about the survey questions concerning the lecture recordings may be found in Figure 2.

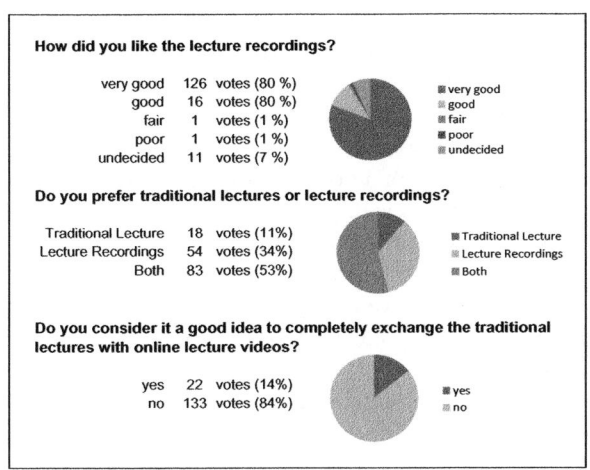

Fig. 2. Survey results concerning the lecture recordings

We also asked the students what they would like to improve about the recordings, thereby gathering valuable information for our future project. The desired features stated in the survey are as follows:

- Downloading the videos to view them offline on laptops and other mobile devices.
- Chapters or a structure of any kind to facilitate the navigation through the video.
- The option to search the video for certain words or phrases.
- A possibility to take notes comfortably while watching the video.
- Improved sound (due to some technical problems the sound of most lectures was only mono).
- The lecturer picture-in-picture with the video of the slides.
- Questions from the audience have to be repeated by the teacher to make sure they are recorded.

Most of the students' wishes can be fulfilled when enhancing the powerpoint slides with spoken text. During this summer, built-in lecture recorders are going to be installed in the first few lecture rooms of the Vienna University of Technology, eliminating the only hard factor, namely having to carry a lecture recorder with you for each lecture you wish to record. Due to the great success of the lecture recordings compared to the small extra effort, we think about using this technique in other lectures as well.

5 Document Camera

During our lectures, the lecturer often demonstrates how to model concrete scenarios with a UML diagram "on the fly" while the students are watching. Sometimes the teacher even develops small UML models together with the students. Before summer term 2010, a blackboard was used for this task, but with the ambitions to record the lectures as described in Section 4, we had to find an alternative which allows us to record these demonstrations and to easily include them in the lecture recordings.

The solution was the usage of a document camera[6] in combination with a LCD projector. A document camera is basically a camera which is fixated on a holding. Connected to a LCD projector, it is possible to place paper documents or other objects under the camera and project them onto a screen. For demonstrations the lecturer formerly would have done at the blackboard, he/she now sits down next to the camera, places a sheet of paper under it and develops the UML model on the paper.

In our teaching environment, the document camera is the best solution for our needs. We can use the LCD projectors and the screens which are already installed in every lecture room, so we just have to take the document camera with us for each lecture — hopefully there will be built-in document cameras at least in the larger lecture rooms of the Vienna University of Technology soon. The document camera has many advantages for the students as well as for the teachers, the most important advantages we have identified during our lectures are listed below:

- *People are used to paper.* Teachers as well as students are used to model on paper and they usually prefer it to writing on a blackboard, tablet PC, or overhead projector. They usually also write or draw more readable on a piece of paper, clean neat writing on other material such as overhead sheets requires much more training.
- *Document cameras are easy to use.* Most document cameras are designed with only a small set of functions, enabling easy usage. The handling is very intuitive, basically it just has to be switched on and connected to a LCD projector.
- *Document cameras also work in very large lecture rooms.* The filmed image can also be projected on large screens in big lecture halls and the document camera can even zoom in on certain parts of a document. In contrast to blackboards, the teacher may write or draw as small as he/she likes and even the students in the last row can see the drawings.

---

[6] http://www.big.tuwien.ac.at/external/OOM.html (In this video, the document camera is used, e.g. at minute 45).

- *Teacher stays turned to the students all the time.* The teacher does not have to turn around to look to the blackboard, he/she can stay focused on the students all the time.
- *Document cameras support vivid teaching.* Developing models on the fly makes lectures more interesting, the document camera is offering a simple possibility to not monotonously presenting the whole lecture with powerpoint slides but still being able to preserve the results and to provide them in TUWEL together with the lecture slides, videos etc.

Since the document camera proved its value in the lectures, we decided to use it in the lab sessions as well. In the past years, the students had to copy their solutions from their personal sheets to an overhead sheet or the blackboard before they could explain the UML model and discuss it with the teacher. Depending on the size of the model this could take very long time and the risk of a nervous student making copy-paste errors was very high. With the usage of the document camera, the student simply places his/her solution under the camera or — if developing the model together with the class and/or the one student is more appropriate for the given exercise — the student can sit down next to the camera and draw the model on paper instead of nervously scribbling on the blackboard. According to the survey, 82% of the students prefer the document camera to the blackboard or the overhead projector and they like the usage of it in the lab sessions and even more in the lectures — Figure 3 shows the results of this part of the survey. Among others, they stated the following advantages of the use of a document camera during the lab sessions:

- The students can present their own notes.
- Showing the results with the document camera instead of copying the solution to the blackboard saves time, especially with large diagrams. The teacher can use the extra time for giving more examples and explanations.
- The teacher does not have to clean the blackboard all the time.
- The students are less nervous because they can use a medium they are already used to (paper).
- The students can fully concentrate on explaining their model and answering questions instead of worrying about nice handwriting or copy-paste errors.

To sum up, the main advantage for the students seems to be the fact that they do not have to copy their solution to the blackboard before presenting it to the teacher, which seems to reduce their nervousness and the risk of making errors.

With the use of the document camera in the lectures, the fact that the whole lecture content can easily be preserved and that the lecture is more varied are the most important advantages from the students' point of view. Concretely, they stated the following advantages:

- Students who cannot attend the lecture for whatever reason get all lecture material instead of only the powerpoint slides.
- The students can also see details from behind rows.

- Demonstrations help the students understanding the teaching matter.
- The teacher does not talk to a blackboard while giving "live" examples.

During the summer term 2010, we used the document camera in our lecture for the first time and both, the students as well as the instructors, first had to get used to the different technology. Most of the problems the students mentioned are linked to this lack of experience in the use of the document camera. The students specified the following drawbacks concerning the use in the lab sessions, some of them also apply to the lectures:

- The light in the lecture room is too bright to see the projection.
- Pencil-drawn models and models on squared paper are very difficult to see.
- Errors cannot be corrected as easily as with the use of a blackboard.
- There sometimes is a time interval between the students' actions on the paper and the display on the screen.
- In contrast to models on a blackboard, the paper sheets often "disappear" too quick, giving the students not enough time to take a detailed look at the model and take notes.
- The teachers should be trained in using the camera.

After this term's test run, keeping those things in mind, most of the mentioned downsides can be overcome and the document camera can also be of great use in our lab sessions. In future, we will tell the students to properly prepare their solutions like modeling each diagram on a separate white sheet of paper and ask each teacher to train a little bit with the camera before using it in the course like watching their speed and the lighting conditions.

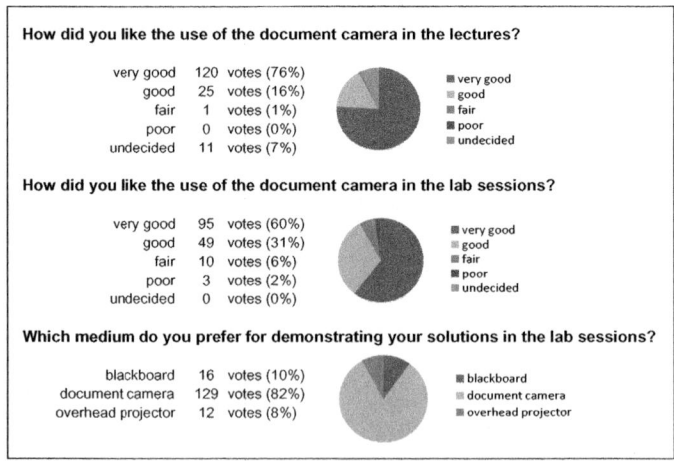

Fig. 3. Survey results concerning the document camera

6 Ongoing Work

In the near future, we will start to enhance our lecture slides with voice recordings. First an appropriate tool for combining slides and audio has to be found. The software has to allow the combination of each slide (separately) with spoken text and be able to exchange single slides and their audio later on. Then, we will prepare text for each of the slides and apply some minor changes to the slides themselves to prepare them for operation in a video. Finally, we ourselves will record the text passages and combine them with the powerpoint presentation, generating one video for each of the five taught UML diagrams. It is planned that the videos will provide a search function not only to search for text in the slides but also to search for parts of the spoken text as well as a navigation bar and a chapter structure to easily navigate within the video. Furthermore, possibilities to watch the videos online and to download them will be offered. Video versions to watch it on a laptop or other mobile device such as a mobile phone will be provided.

We plan to have the first lectures combined with audio ready for use in the winter term of 2010. In our survey, we also asked the students if they would still need a traditional lecture given that lectures enhanced with spoken text are available. Most students stated that they would still want an additional traditional lecture — it should be noted that the quantity of students that want traditional lectures is significantly higher than the quantity of students that actually visited the traditional lectures. The following reasons for still additionally offering traditional lectures were named:

- They want to ask questions personally.
- The teacher listens and responds to the students, adapting the lecture to the student's needs and interests.
- Personal contact to teachers and fellow students is important.
- A fixed timetable is good for those who need to be forced a little bit.
- In a lecture room a higher level of concentration is possible than at home with lots of distractions.

We agree that personal contact and the possibility to ask questions are essential for each university course, thus we will not completely eliminate the lectures but exchange them with tutorials, preparing the students for the lab sessions and the test by modeling and discussing a lot of examples "live" together with the students. This offers the students an additional possibility to gain more practical knowledge about UML diagrams.

We consider this approach very valuable, not at last because OOM is taught each semester and we would not be forced to explain the theoretical basics in traditional lectures each semester any more. The lecture videos sort of teach the students the theoretical background whereas we can concentrate on the practical aspects, questions and discussions.

7 Conclusion

In this paper, we have presented our experiences in our undergraduate course *Object-Oriented Modeling*. Due to the huge number of participants we apply alternative media like a document camera instead of the traditional blackboard on the one hand to support the learning process of our students and on the other hand to reduce time and effort for teaching. Furthermore, to improve the quality of our course we have introduced web-based self assessments, which are used by our students to exercise UML modeling. Additionally, we recorded the lecture allowing the students to listen to it at any time. Especially when learning modeling, practical exercising (e.g., by self assessments) is of significant importance for students. Furthermore, developing small UML diagrams live in the lecture together with the students is more effective than just presenting powerpoint slides. However, since the lecturers' knowledge is based on personal experiences (e.g., in modeling Use Case Diagrams), traditional face-to-face lectures are indispensable.

To evaluate our newly designed course, we have done an extensive survey, where we got responses of 180 students and beneficial feedback. In summary, our e-learning support providing self assessments and lecture streams, as well as the application of our document camera are considered very useful for studying. However, for our students it is of huge importance, despite the time of Web 2.0, to have personal contact to the teachers and to have, beside lecture streams, face-to-face lectures.

References

1. Brandsteidl, M., Seidl, M., Wimmer, M., Huemer, C., Kappel, G.: Teaching Models @ BIG: How to Give 1000 Students an Understanding of the UML. In: Promoting Software Modeling Through Active Education, Educators' Symposium Models 2008, pp. 64–68. Warsaw University of Technology (2008)
2. Chen, Q., Grundy, J., Hosking, J.: An E-whiteboard Application to Support Early Design-stage Sketching of UML Diagrams. In: HCC 2003: Proceedings of the 2003 IEEE Symposium on Human Centric Computing Languages and Environments, pp. 219–226. IEEE Computer Society Press, Washington, DC (2003)
3. Garrison, R.D., Anderson, T.: E-Learning in the 21st Century: A Framework for Research and Practice. Routledge/Falmer, London (2003)
4. Hitz, M., Kappel, G., Kapsammer, E., Retschitzegger, W.: UML@Work, Objektorientierte Modellierung mit UML 2. dpunkt.verlag, Heidelberg (2005)
5. Kolb, D.: Learning Styles Inventory. The Power of the 2x2 Matrix: Using 2x2 Thinking to Solve Business Problems and Make Better Decisions, 352 (2004)
6. Mock, K.: Teaching with tablet pc's. J. Comput. Small Coll. 20(2), 17–27 (2004)
7. Rupp, C., Queins, S., Zengler, B.: UML Glasklar. Praxiswissen für die UML-Modellierung. Hanser Fachbuch (2007)
8. Zupancic, B., Horz, H.: Lecture recording and its use in a traditional university course. In: ITiCSE 2002: Proceedings of the 7th Conference on Innovation and Technology in Computer Science Education, pp. 24–28. ACM, New York (2002)

Implementation of the Concept-Driven Approach in an Object-Oriented Analysis and Design Course

Ven Yu Sien

HELP University College, Kuala Lumpur, Malaysia
sienvy@help.edu.my

Abstract. One of the most important tasks in object-oriented analysis and design (OOAD) is the abstraction of the problem domain into specific concepts or objects. Information technology (IT) students need appropriate skills of abstraction in order to identify the essential concepts and relationships within a problem domain. However students in higher education generally find difficulty performing abstractions of real-world problems within the context of OOAD. In this paper, we present a framework comprising four teaching modules for teaching object-oriented (OO) modelling using concept maps. We also report results of an evaluative study on the effectiveness of integrating concept mapping techniques into an introductory OOAD course by classifying the UML diagrams produced by the participants in design categories.

Keywords: abstraction, UML models, concept map, class diagram, sequence diagram.

1 Introduction

Abstraction skills are especially important for solving complicated problems as they enable the problem solver to think in terms of conceptual ideas rather than their details [1]. Abstraction skills are also necessary for the construction of the various models, designs, and implementations that are required for a software system. As models are a simplification of reality that help us to understand and analyse large and complex systems, students must therefore possess the necessary abstraction skills to produce them [2]. However, being able to understand what details are important to the problem is a difficult skill that requires a great deal of practice. Kramer [2] believes that the reason why '*some software engineers and computer scientists are able to produce clear, elegant designs and programs, while others cannot, is attributable to their abstraction skills*'.

In this paper we present a set of guidelines for teaching OO modelling using concept mapping techniques to assist students with their abstraction skills within the context of OOAD. We also report results of an evaluative study on the effectiveness of integrating this approach in an introductory OOAD course by comparing the results of participants who were exposed to concept mapping techniques with participants who were not exposed to concept mapping techniques.

2 Background Review

A model of an OO system is an abstract representation of the system. It represents the problem domain and emphasises some characteristics of the real-world. Modelling a system, however, requires the representation of different perspectives or views of the system and therefore there are different types of diagrams for modelling each of these views.

Frosch-Wilke [3] found in his teaching experience that his students:

- may have an *'extensive knowledge of diagram notations but the majority of them are not able to put this (theoretical) knowledge into an application context'*; and
- may be successful in drawing some OO models separately but do not understand the relationship and interdependencies between these different models.

Cianchetta [4] considers teaching the fundamental concept of identifying objects from the problem domain to be one of the most difficult tasks that he encountered when training OO developers. He found that even though object-oriented analysis (OOA) and object-oriented design (OOD) can be easily defined as *'the modeling of a specific problem domain and a pragmatic solution for that domain'*, the essential problem is *'defining how one should go about modeling a problem domain and its practical, efficient, and cost-effective solution'*.

Bolloju and Leung [5] conducted a study to identify errors produced by novice systems analysts in use case diagrams, use case descriptions, and class and sequence diagrams. The errors that they found in class diagrams were:

- operations that had not been included in classes;
- misassigned operations;
- incorrect multiplicities;
- misassigned attributes; and
- incorrect usage of generalisation-specialisation hierarchies.

Some of the faults they found in sequence diagrams were:

- missing messages;
- missing message parameters;
- missing objects; and
- incorrect delegation of responsibilities.

Concept mapping is a technique for representing the structure of information visually. It was developed by Joseph Novak [6] in 1972 at Cornell University and is commonly used for visualising relationships between concepts. Concept maps are two-dimensional diagrams that represent the structure of knowledge within a particular domain as nodes (or concepts) and connecting links. A concept is *'an idea or notion that we apply to the things, or objects, in our awareness'* [7]. Concepts are related to each other by a link, and each link has a word or word-phrase describing the relationship between the concepts. In this paper we use concept maps as a graphical representation of fundamental concepts and their relationships within a problem domain. Instead of a class diagram, the concept map is the initial domain model to be derived from a set of functional requirements or textual use cases.

3 Proposed Concept-Driven Approach

In order to resolve some of the issues discussed in Section 2, we presented a concept-driven approach to introduce concept mapping as a tool to help students with OO modelling [8, 9]. There are many inherent problems associated with modelling the problem domain with class and sequence diagrams – these are discussed in Section 2. We do not claim that it is easy to model the problem domain by using concept maps. We do however consider that concept maps have the following advantages over class diagrams:

- It is easier to distinguish between classes and attributes in concept maps by using specifically defined labelled links e.g., 'has'.
- It is easier to identify generalisation-specialisation hierarchies in concept maps by using specifically defined labelled links e.g., 'is-a'.
- Relationships between concepts that do not fall in the 'is-a' or 'has' categories are defined by an appropriate transitive verb from the case study.
- Substantial guidelines to produce concept maps have been developed. These are defined in [8, 9].
- It is relatively easy to teach concept maps. There are only two types of notations used in a concept map – nodes and links [10].

An evaluation study [8] was conducted to determine the effectiveness of adopting concept maps as the first and essential model to be derived from a set of functional requirements. The data from this study was analyzed and there is sufficient statistical evidence to support the claim that the participants do produce more comprehensive class diagrams after being exposed to concept mapping techniques.

3.1 Static and Dynamic Concept Maps

Within the context of OO modelling, we used concept maps as an initial abstraction of the problem domain. A static concept map is a type of static structure diagram that describes the structure of a system by illustrating the system's concepts and the relationships between these concepts. The concepts defined in the static concept map model classes (and attributes) in the analysis class diagram. For example, a static concept map (see Fig. 1) is constructed by identifying concepts and their relationships from an expanded use case (Table 1). We adapted some processes from [11] for constructing static concept maps. These processes involve the identification of candidate concepts and their relationships from expanded use cases. We included some construction constraints by defining only three types of relationships that concepts can have with each other i.e., attribute, generalisation-specialisation and association. If the type of relationship between two concepts does not fall into the first two relationship categories, then it is considered to be an association.

The static concept map is built incrementally from the use cases – it is subsequently transformed to a UML class diagram using the rules described in [8]. These rules were constructed by examining the linking words between two concepts to determine whether:

- a concept should be converted to a class *or* an attribute; and
- a link should be converted to an association *or* generalisation-specialisation hierarchy.

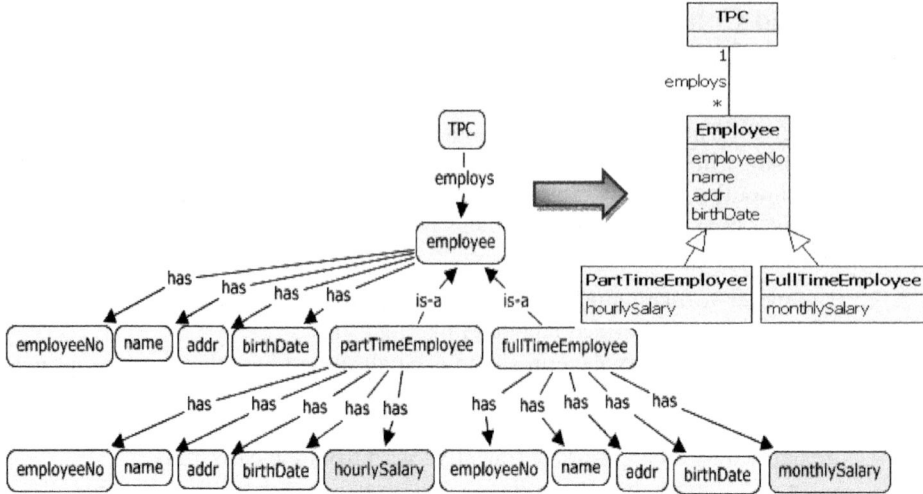

Fig. 1. Static concept map converted to a class diagram

Table 1. Expanded use case

Use Case 1	Add New Employee	
Goal in Context	An employee is correctly entered into the system.	
Primary Actor	HR Manager	
Main Course Description	Step	Action
	1	The HR Manager enters the employee's name, address and birth date.
	2	A unique employee number is allocated by the system.
Alt. Course Description	Step	Branching Action
	1a	The HR Manager enters the full-time employee's name, address, birth date and monthly salary.
	1b	The HR Manager enters the part-time employee's name, address, birth date and hourly rate.

A dynamic concept map provides a dynamic view of the system behaviour by showing the key responsibilities that need to be fulfilled by specific concepts in order to fulfil a particular scenario of a use case. The concepts defined in the dynamic concept map model *objects* in the sequence diagram. For each use case, its key responsibilities are identified and added to the static concept map so as to produce a dynamic concept map. A dynamic concept map is constructed and subsequently transformed to a UML sequence diagram using the rules described in [9].

Fig. 2 illustrates an example of how a dynamic concept map for creating a part-time employee concept is transformed to a sequence diagram.

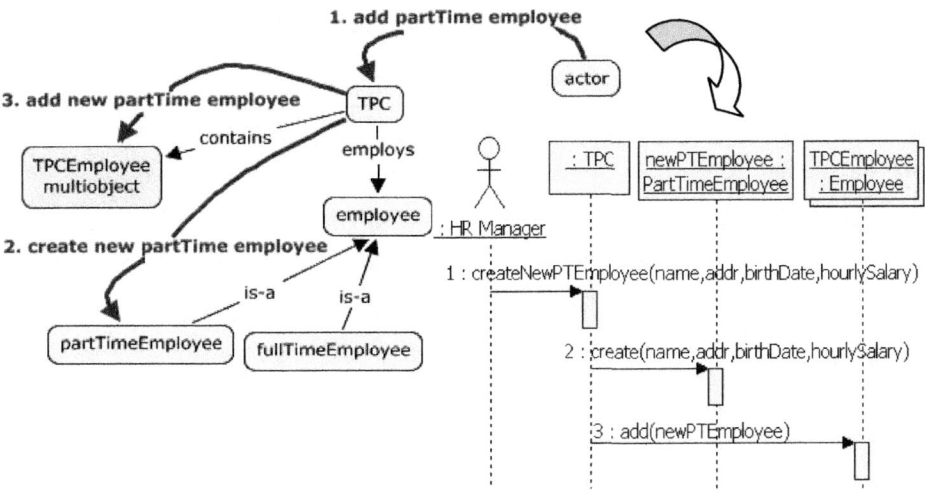

Fig. 2. Dynamic concept map converted to a sequence diagram

The class and sequence diagrams are selected for our study because they represent the essential static and behavioural aspects of a problem domain. The class diagram is fundamental to the OO modelling process and provides a static description of system components and structures in terms of classes and their relationships. The sequence diagram is selected because it is identified as the *'major UML diagram that captures the detailed behaviour of objects in the system'* [12] and it is one of the most widely used dynamic diagrams in UML [13].

One of the main motivations for developing this concept-driven approach is to assist students produce more appropriate class and sequence diagrams. Our concept mapping techniques are developed based on some of the design errors that are reported in Section 2:

- The processes for deriving appropriate concepts from use cases should help novices avoid producing inappropriate classes, missing controller classes, and missing attributes.
- Labelled links between concepts should help prevent misassigned attributes and inappropriate relationships.
- As the dynamic concept map is based on the static concept map, there should be fewer inconsistent objects, missing objects, and missing controller objects defined in the sequence diagrams.
- The processes involved in identifying responsibilities and the assignment of these responsibilities to candidate concepts should help novices understand how objects can interact with each other via messages to fulfil the responsibilities of a particular scenario of a use case.

It must be emphasised that the concepts defined in the static concept map are transformed to classes (and attributes) in the analysis class diagram, whilst the concepts defined in the dynamic concept map are transformed to objects in the sequence diagram.

3.2 Integrating the Concept-Driven Approach into an Existing OOAD Course

Teaching OOAD is not easy. Educational institutions have developed/adopted various approaches [14, 15] to help resolve the problems discussed in Section 2. Our framework consists of the following four modules with three guided practice sessions in each module.

Module 1: Static Concept Map (estimated duration: 1 hour 30 minutes). This module covers real-world problems conceptualised as abstractions; introduction to concept maps; guidelines for producing concept maps to represent a problem domain within the context of OOAD [8]; exercises to produce a static concept map representing the problem domain from a case study. The students are provided with a case study containing three expanded use cases that describe the functional requirements of the system, and are expected to work on them during the following practice sessions:

- First practice session: the students are provided with a partially completed concept map and a list of concepts derived from the first use case (UC1).The students have to update the concept map using the supplied concepts and linking words.
- Second practice session: the students are provided with an incomplete list of concepts derived from the second use case (UC2). The students have to update the concept map produced from UC1. They are allowed to add their own concepts.
- Third practice session: the students are asked to individually produce a concept map from the third use case (UC3).

Module 2: Static Concept Map → Analysis Class Diagram (estimated duration: 1 hour 15 minutes). This module covers transformation rules for converting a static concept map to an analysis class diagram [8]; exercises to produce a class diagram – students continue with the case study that they worked on in Module 1.

- First practice session: the students are provided with a static concept map for UC1. They are shown how to generate a class diagram from this concept map using the rules supplied.
- Second practice session: the students are provided with a static concept map for UC1 and UC2. The students are expected to generate a class diagram from this concept map using the rules supplied.
- Third practice session: the students are provided with a static concept map for UC1, UC2 and UC3. The students are expected to generate a class diagram from this concept map using the rules supplied.

Module 3: Dynamic Concept Map (estimated duration: 2 hours). This module covers multi-objects/containers in a concept map; naming convention for messages; identification of responsibilities from the use case; assignment/delegation of responsibilities to appropriate concepts using basic design patterns; guidelines for producing dynamic concept maps [9]; exercises to produce dynamic concept maps – students continue with the case study that they worked on in Module 1. They will be provided with a static concept map and a class diagram representing the problem domain.

- First practice session: the students are provided with a static concept map for UC1. The students are shown how to identify responsibilities from the use case and how to translate them to messages in the concept map.
- Second practice session: the students are provided with a static concept map and responsibilities for UC2. They are expected to translate the responsibilities to messages in the concept maps.
- Third practice session: the students are provided with a static concept map for UC3. The students are expected to identify appropriate responsibilities from the use case and to translate them into messages in the concept map.

Module 4: Dynamic Concept Map → Sequence Diagram (estimated duration: 1 hour 45 minutes). This module covers transformation rules for converting a dynamic concept map to a sequence diagram using the rules defined in [9]; exercises to produce sequence diagrams – students continue with the case study that they worked on in Module 1.

- First practice session: the students are provided with a dynamic concept map for UC1. The students are shown how to generate a sequence diagram from this concept map using the rules supplied.
- Second practice session: the students are provided with a dynamic concept map for UC2. The students are expected to generate a sequence diagram from the dynamic concept map using the rules supplied.
- Third practice session: the students are provided with a dynamic concept map for UC3. They are expected to generate a sequence diagram from this concept map using the rules supplied.

These modules can be used as a stand-alone workshop or integrated into existing OOAD courses or workshops. The times allocated to the modules are based on our experience conducting concept mapping workshops. There are many constraints to consider e.g., the time that the facilitator can afford for these topics in his/her syllabus, the speed with which the students can complete the guided sessions, the amount of help that the students require, etc.

In a typical introductory OOAD course, many OO concepts and definitions are presented first (e.g., objects, classes, inheritance, encapsulation, polymorphism, UML notation) followed by the application of these notations in the various types of UML analysis models. Once these topics have been covered, the facilitator can integrate Module 1 into the curriculum. It should be noted that the students do not need to know how to produce an analysis class diagram from the expanded use cases at this stage – the students only need to reach a basic understanding of the UML notations that are used in the class diagram. Module 2 can commence immediately after Module 1. The facilitator can then continue with the remaining syllabus in the analysis phase. Modules 3 and 4 can only be introduced when the topics on sequence diagrams have been covered. Once all the concept mapping techniques have been covered, the facilitator can continue teaching the remaining OOAD syllabus.

We incorporated these modules in the workshops reported in [8, 9] to evaluate the effectiveness of using concept maps to produce class and sequence diagrams. Since the evaluation results provided strong evidence that the concept-driven approach can be used successfully, we implemented the modules in an introductory OOAD course in the February 2009 semester at HELP University College, Malaysia.

3 Evaluation Study

A study was conducted to evaluate the pedagogical effectiveness of adopting concept maps as a stepping stone to assist novices in developing class and sequence diagrams. The research question for this study is:

Are there any improvements in the class and sequence diagrams produced by students as a consequence of using our concept mapping techniques?

We use the Goal/Question/Metric (GQM) template (see Table 2) to help us define the goal of this study.

Table 2. Goal according to GQM

Analyse	the integration of concept mapping techniques in an OOAD course
For the purpose of	minimising the types of errors in class and sequence diagrams, and evaluating whether the concept mapping techniques improve the appropriateness of class and sequence diagrams produced by OOAD students
With respect to	the students' OO modelling skills
From the point of view of	software engineering educators
In the context of	teaching students how to develop UML class and sequence diagrams during the analysis and design phases of a software development project

Therefore, in order to investigate the effectiveness of integrating the concept mapping techniques in an introductory OOAD course, we compared the results of two studies. The participants in Study 1 were not exposed to concept mapping techniques while the participants in Study 2 were taught concept mapping techniques as part of their OOAD course. Consequently, we expect the students in Study 2 to individually produce more concise models in terms of complexity and completeness – suggesting that concept maps have helped in the overall understanding of abstraction. While we are aware that we are comparing results from two different sets of students, we can nonetheless use the outcome as a basis for considering the implications of incorporating concept mapping techniques in an OOAD course. Study 1 consisted of fifty-one Year 2 IT undergraduate students and Study 2 consisted of twenty-one Year 2 IT undergraduate students. All the participants were volunteers and were not paid to take part in the study. Information captured on the background of the participants and their experience with OOAD is summarised in Table 3. The OO experience reported for these participants is based on the experience they gained from their university courses that include OO concepts.

Table 3. Background information on participants

	Study 1 (N=51)	Study 2 (N=21)
Average age (years)	22	22
Age range (years)	20-27	19-28
Gender		
• male	61%	90%
• female	39%	10%
OO experience		
• < 1 year	35%	48%
• 1- 2 years	49%	52%
• 3-5 years	16%	0%
• > 5 years	0%	0%

The participants from both studies were asked to work on a case study containing four expanded use cases that describe the functional requirements of the system. The solution for the case study consists of nine appropriate classes, two generalisation-specialisation hierarchies and eight associations. The participants in Study 1 were given a case study to work on after they had completed their OOAD course at HELP University College, Malaysia. In the subsequent semester Modules 1, 2, 3 and 4 were integrated into the OOAD course. After completing Module 4, the participants in Study 2 were given the same case study to work on. The participants in Study 1 were given 1 hour to work on the case study as they were required to produce a class and sequence diagram. The participants in Study 2, however were given 1 hour 30 minutes to work on the case study as they were required to produce a static concept map, a class diagram, a dynamic concept map and a sequence diagram.

4 Results

In order to evaluate the effectiveness of the concept-driven approach, an analysis of the UML diagrams produced by participants from Studies 1 and 2 are provided as follows.

Expected classes. Study 2 shows a significant improvement in the identification of expected classes – see Table 4.

Table 4. Analysis of class diagrams with expected classes

	Classes[1]							
	1	2	3	4	5	6	7	8
Study 1 (N=51)	2%	2%	8%	14%	10%	22%	35%	8%
Study 2 (N=21)	0%	0%	0%	0%	5%	14%	33%	48%

---

[1] The totals do not add up to 100% due to rounding errors.

Inappropriate Class Names. In Study 1, 26% of class diagrams have one or more class names that do not represent a real-world concept. All the classes produced in Study 2 represent appropriate real-world concepts.

Attributes. There is a significant improvement in assigning attributes to appropriate classes in Study 2 – see Table 5. A higher percentage of missing attributes for Study 2 is caused by the larger number of appropriate classes defined in the class diagrams (the percentage of misassigned and missing attributes is calculated based on the appropriate classes that have been defined in the class diagrams).

Table 5. Analysis of class diagrams with one or more inappropriate attributes identified

	Misassigned Attributes	**One or More Missing Attributes**
Study 1 (N=51)	86%	20%
Study 2 (N=21)	38%	24%

Associations. In Study 2, 76% of associations were defined inappropriately in the class diagrams produced. Study 2 has a higher percentage of associations that have been defined inappropriately and missing associations because this percentage is calculated with respect to the number of appropriate classes defined in the participants' class diagrams – see Table 6.

Table 6. Class diagrams with one or more inappropriate associations

	One or More Associations Defined Inappropriately	**One or More Missing Associations**
Study 1 (N=51)	65%	49%
Study 2 (N=21)	76%	76%

Generalisation-Specialisation Hierarchies. The results in Table 7 show a significant improvement in the identification of generalisation-specialisation hierarchies in Study 2. The totals do not add up to 100% for both studies because:
- 6% of participants in Study 1 produced some appropriate and some inappropriate generalisation-specialisation hierarchies in their class diagrams.
- 5% of participants in Study 2 produced some appropriate and some inappropriate generalisation-specialisation hierarchies in their class diagrams. The remaining 1% is due to rounding errors.

Table 7. Analysis of class diagrams with generalisation-specialisation

	Inappropriate Use of Inheritance Hierarchy	**Appropriate Use of Inheritance Hierarchy**	**Inheritance Hierarchies not Defined**
Study 1 (N=51)	12%	45%	49%
Study 2 (N=21)	10%	86%	10%

Objects. The sequence diagrams produced in Study 2 were greatly improved – see Table 8. Only 47% of the sequence diagrams in Study 1 included an appropriate controller object (representing the façade controller). All the sequence diagrams in Study 2 however included an appropriate controller object. 70% of the students in Study 1 were able to produce at least one appropriate object, and some of the objects defined in the sequence diagrams did not relate to corresponding classes identified in the class diagram. These examples provide evidence that some students from Study 1 do not understand that they should use the objects that have been identified from the problem domain (defined in the class diagram) in their sequence diagram. In Study 2, however all the objects defined in the sequence diagrams relate to corresponding classes in the class diagrams.

Table 8. Sequence diagrams with objects identification

	Controller Object Included	One or More Objects Correctly Identified	One or More Missing Objects	One or More Multi-Objects Correctly Included & Accessed
Study 1 (N=51)	47%	70%	100%	20%
Study 2 (N=21)	100%	100%	43%	71%

Messages. The correct identification of parameters and delegation of responsibilities improved significantly in Study 2.

Table 9. Analysis of messages defined in sequence diagrams

	Correct Identification of 1 or 2 Parameters Defined in Messages	Evidence of Some Delegation of Responsibilities
Study 1 (N=51)	27%	40%
Study 2 (N=21)	77%	88%

We classified the class and sequence diagrams produced by our participants according to the design categories proposed by Eckerdal et al. [16]. The design categories, in order of appropriateness are: Complete, Partial, First Step, Skumtomte[2], Restatement and Nothing. The descriptions of the categories for class diagrams have been modified to make them more appropriate for our study e.g.,

- Complete: diagrams contain all of the expected classes, attributes and associations. Generalisation-specialisation hierarchies and whole-part associations are appropriately applied.
- Partial: diagrams are a good representation of the problem domain with most of the expected classes, attributes and associations defined.
- First Step: diagrams are a good representation of a partial overview of the problem domain with an appropriate number of expected classes.

---

[2] Skumtomte is a Swedish word referring to a pink-and-white marshmallow, shaped like a Santa Claus. It looks as if it contains some matter but in reality it does not contain much substance.

- Skumtomte: incomplete diagrams with missing classes, misassigned or irrelevant attributes, and missing or inappropriately defined associations.
- Restatement: level of detail provided is insufficient. There are significant errors and misunderstandings.
- Nothing: diagrams do not contain any logical content.

The descriptions of the categories for sequence diagrams have been modified to make them more appropriate for our study e.g.,

- Complete: diagrams contain appropriate sequence of messages passed to the relevant objects to fulfil the responsibilities of the use case.
- Partial: diagrams include an appropriate number of correct objects fulfilling some responsibilities of the use case.
- First Step: evidence of some understanding of the required delegation of responsibilities among the objects.
- Skumtomte: diagrams are incomplete but contain at least 1 appropriate interaction between 2 appropriately defined objects. The majority of messages are inappropriate.
- Restatement: diagrams are incomplete but contain at least 2 appropriate objects. All the messages are inappropriate.
- Nothing: diagrams contain significant errors and misunderstandings.

This method allows us to adopt a holistic approach for evaluating the appropriateness of the UML diagram. We are, however, aware that this may not be a reliable assessment as it does not explicitly assess the appropriateness of individual components of the diagram.

In Table 10, the names of the design categories have been abbreviated: Complete=CP, Partial=PT, First Step=FS, Skumtomte=SK, Restatement=RS and Nothing=NT. A higher percentage of class and sequence diagrams produced in Study 2 are found to be in better design categories than the diagrams produced in Study 1 – see Table 10. There are 36% of class diagrams produced in Study 1 that belong in the Restatement and Nothing categories – participants in Study 2 did not produce any class diagrams belonging in these two categories. There are no sequence diagrams produced in Study 1 that belong in the Complete category, compared to 35% of sequence diagrams produced in Study 2 belonging in the Complete category.

Table 10. Analysis of diagrams produced by participants

Group	Diagram	CP	PT	FS	SK	RS	NT
Study 1	Class	2%	10%	21%	31%	23%	13%
Study 2	Class	57%	14%	14%	14%	0	0
Study 1	Sequence	0%	3%	3%	10%	17%	67%
Study 2	Sequence	35%	6%	12%	6%	24%	18%

Some of the most common faults found in the models produced in Study 1 were similar to the types discussed in Section 2. We find in Study 2 that the number of faults has significantly decreased especially in the following areas:

- identification of expected classes representing the key concepts in the problem domain;
- assignment of attributes to appropriate classes;
- identification of appropriate generalisation-specialisation hierarchies.
- identification of appropriate objects participating in the scenario of the use case;
- identification of objects in the sequence diagram that correspond to classes defined in the class diagram; and
- delegation/assignment of responsibilities to objects.

5 Threats to Validity

This section discusses some threats to validity that may affect this study.

Internal Validity. Internal validity refers to the extent to which we can correctly state that the introduction of concept mapping techniques caused the participants to produce more appropriate class and sequence diagrams. One of the threats to internal validity consists of the expectations of a particular result by the researcher. In this context, the researcher was responsible for marking the class and sequence diagrams produced by the two groups of participants, and she is fully aware that the scores for the diagrams may bias the hypotheses. To this end, the marking scheme was strictly adhered to. However, in order to eliminate this threat, we should consider using independent assessors to mark the pre-test and post-test diagrams. We have not 'employed' the services of independent assessors due to logistical problems e.g., lack of funding and time constraints. Note: the case study, marking scheme and a sample of the marked diagrams were moderated by independent assessors.

There may be other factors that contributed to the quality of class and sequence diagrams produced by the participants of Study 2 e.g.,

- the students from Study 2 may be more intelligent than the students from Study 1;
- as the students from Study 2 are currently enrolled in the OOAD course, their knowledge of OOAD concepts and experience in OO modelling is still fresh in their minds;
- the students in Study 2 have been given a good foundation on OOAD concepts;
- sufficient emphasis has been placed on the necessary topics that are being evaluated.

Construct Validity. Construct validity refers to whether the study was actually evaluating what it was trying to evaluate. Study subjects are likely to be anxious about being evaluated and this apprehension may influence the results. We did not detect any evaluation apprehension as the students were assured that the results of the exercises would not contribute towards their overall course scores

External Validity. The main threat to external validity is generalising our results as our sample may not be representative of all IT undergraduate students.

6 Conclusion

We have presented an approach that introduces a concept-driven approach to help novices in OOAD understand and master the technique of abstraction in order that they can improve their OO modelling skills. We have also provided a set of teaching modules that can be easily integrated into existing introductory OOAD courses or can be used independently in workshops. There are several clear benefits to adopting these modules:

- Students are explicitly taught how to identify concepts to represent the problem domain, how to distinguish classes from attributes and how to identify appropriate relationships for the concepts.
- Students are taught how to produce sequence diagrams that use objects derived from the classes defined in the class diagrams.
- The modules include graduated exercises for students to practise with.

Results of two studies were compared to investigate the effectiveness of integrating the concept mapping techniques in an introductory OOAD course. The participants in Study 1 were not exposed to concept mapping techniques while the participants in Study 2 were taught concept mapping techniques as part of their OOAD course. It is evident from the results reported that the quality of class and sequence diagrams improved in Study 2. We find that concept maps are particularly effective at helping students identify appropriate classes and associations in class diagrams; and appropriate objects and feasible sequence of messages in sequence diagrams. Hence, we can state that concept maps can play an important and effective role in helping novices produce more appropriate class and sequence diagrams.

References

1. Kramer, J., Hazzan, O.J.: The Role of Abstraction in Software Engineering. In: 28th International Conference on Software Engineering, pp. 1017–1018. ACM, New York (2006)
2. Kramer, J.: Is Abstraction the Key to Computing? Communications of the ACM (2007)
3. Frosch-Wilke, D.: Using UML in Software Requirements Analysis - Experiences from Paractical Student Project Work. In: Informing Science & Information Technology Education Joint Conference, Pori, Finland (2003)
4. Cianchetta, T.: Teaching Object-Oriented Analysis and Design by "Cruisin' the Classifieds for Business Objects". In: 1995 Conference of the Centre for Advanced Studies on Collaborative Research. IBM Press, Toronto (1995)
5. Bolloju, N., Leung, F.: Assisting Novice Analysts in Developing Quality Conceptual Models with UML. Communications of the ACM 49, 108–112 (2006)
6. Novak, J.D., Cañas, A.J.: The Origins of the Concept Mapping Tool and the Continuing Evolution of the Tool. Information Visualization 5, 175–184 (2006)
7. Martin, J., Odell, J.: Object-Oriented Methods: A Foundation. Prentice-Hall International Inc., Englewood Cliffs (1995)
8. Sien, V.Y., Carrington, D.: A Concepts-First Approach to Object-Oriented Modelling. In: 3rd IASTED International Conference on Advances in Computer Science and Technology, Phuket, Thailand (2007)

9. Sien, V.Y., Carrington, D.: Using Concept Maps to Produce Sequence Diagrams. In: IASTED International Conference on Software Engineering, Innsbruck, Austria (2008)
10. Novak, J.D., Cañas, A.J.: The Theory Underlying Concept Maps and How to Construct and Use Them. Technical Report IHMC CmapTools (2008)
11. Naidu S, Blanchard P.: Concept Mapping, http://www.infodiv.unimelb.edu.au/telars/flds/documents/conceptmappingwbook.pdf#search=%22concept%20mapping%20naidu%22
12. George, J.F., Batra, D., Valacich, J.S., Hoffer, J.A.: Object-Oriented Systems Analysis and Design. Pearson Higher Education, London (2007)
13. Dobing, B., Parsons, J.: How UML is Used. Communications of the ACM 49, 109–113 (2006)
14. Box, R., Whitelaw, M.: Experiences when Migrating from Structured Analysis to Object-Oriented Modelling. In: The Australasian Conference on Computing Education. ACM International Conference Proceeding Series, pp. 12–19 (2000)
15. Beheshti, R., Dado, E.: Simplified UML Techniques for System Development in an Educational Setting. In: 6th International Conference on Information Technology Based Higher Education and Training, pp. S2C/1– S2C/6 (2005)
16. Eckerdal, A., McCartney, R., Moström, J.E., Ratcliffe, M., Zander, C.: Can Graduating Students Design Software Systems? In: 37th SIGCSE Technical Symposium on Computer Science Education, Houston, Texas (2006)

Model Based Architecting and Construction of Embedded Systems (ACES-MB 2010)

Stefan Van Baelen[1], Iulian Ober[2], Huascar Espinoza[3],
Thomas Weigert[4], Ileana Ober[5], and Sébastien Gérard[6]

[1] K.U. Leuven - DistriNet, Belgium
Stefan.VanBaelen@cs.kuleuven.be
[2] University of Toulouse - IRIT, France
Iulian.Ober@irit.fr
[3] Tecnalia, Spain
Huascar.Espinoza@tecnalia.com
[4] Missouri University of Science and Technology, USA
weigert@mst.edu
[5] University of Toulouse - IRIT, France
Ileana.Ober@irit.fr
[6] CEA - LIST, France
Sebastien.Gerard@cea.fr

Abstract. The third ACES-MB workshop brought together researchers and practitioners interested in model-based software engineering for real-time embedded systems, with a particular focus on the use of models for architecture description and domain-specific design, and for capturing non-functional constraints. Twelve presenters proposed contributions on metaheuristic search techniques for UML, modelling languages and mappings, model based verification and validation, software synthesis, and embedded systems product lines. In addition, a lively group discussion tackled these issues in further detail. This report presents an overview of the presentations and fruitful discussions that took place during the ACES-MB 2010 workshop.

1 Introduction

The development of embedded systems with real-time and other critical constraints raises distinctive problems. In particular, development teams have to make very specific architectural choices and handle key non-functional constraints related to, for example, real-time deadlines and to platform parameters like energy consumption or memory footprint. The last few years have seen an increased interest in using model-based engineering (MBE) techniques to capture dedicated architectural and non-functional information in precise (and even formal) domain-specific models in a layered construction of systems.

MBE techniques are interesting and promising because they allow to capture dedicated architectural and non-functional information in precise (and even formal) domain-specific models, and they support a layered construction of systems, in which the (platform independent) functional aspects are kept separate from architectural and non-functional (platform specific) aspects, where the final system is obtained by combining these aspects later using model transformations.

The Third Workshop on *Model Based Architecting and Construction of Embedded Systems* (ACES-MB 2010) brought together researchers and practitioners interested in all aspects of model-based software engineering for real-time embedded systems. The participants discussed this subject at different levels, from requirements specifications, model specification languages and analysis techniques, embedded systems product lines, model synthesis, to model based verification and validation.

2 Workshop Contributions

The keynote [2] was given by Prof. Lionel C. Briand from the University of Oslo and the Simula Research Laboratory, Norway, who discussed the use of metaheuristic search for the analysis and verification of UML models.

There is a growing research activity around the use of metaheuristic search techniques (e.g., genetic algorithms) in software engineering, for example to support test case generation, often referred to as search-based software engineering (SBSE). Several years of research have focused on using metaheuristic search to support the analysis and verification of UML models and its extensions such as MARTE and OCL. Examples include the analysis of real-time deadlines (schedulability analysis), concurrency problems, and constraint solving, for example for supporting model-based test case generation. Results suggest that applying metaheuristic approaches to these problems lead to practical and scalable solutions that rely solely on UML and extensions, and does not require translations into other languages and formalisms.

6 full papers and 5 short papers had been accepted for the workshop, see [1]. A synopsis of each presentation is given below. Extended versions of articles [5] and [6] are included in this workshop reader.

[3] presents a MARTE to AADL mapping that is valuable for MARTE users in order to enable the use AADL analysis tools on MARTE models. For example, CAT, the Consumption Analysis Toolbox, allows for system-level power and energy consumption estimation for AADL models.

[4] addresses the problem that real-time embedded software today is commonly built using programming abstractions with little or no temporal semantics. The paper discusses the use of an extension to the Ptolemy II framework as a coordination language for the design of distributed real-time embedded systems. Specifically, the paper shows how to use modal models in the context of the PTIDES extension of Ptolemy II.

[5] uses UML Interaction Overview Diagrams as the basis for a user-friendly, intuitive, modelling notation that is well-suited for the design of complex, heterogeneous, embedded systems developed by domain experts with little background on modelling software based systems. To allow designers to precisely analyse models written with this notation, a part of it is provided with a formal

semantics based on temporal logic, upon which a fully automated, tool supported verification technique is built.

[6] argues that system development and integration with a sufficient maturity at entry into service is a competitive challenge in the aerospace sector, and can only be achieved using efficient model-based techniques for system design as well as for system testing. Building on the general idea of model-based systems engineering, an integrated virtual verification environment for modelling systems, requirements, and test cases is proposed, so that system designs can be simulated and verified against the requirements in the early stages of system development. The paper exemplifies its application in a ModelicaML modelling environment.

[7] addresses the early validation of automobile electronic systems by providing a transformation of EAST-ADL models to SystemC at different layers of abstraction. This allows specific analysis with hardware-software co-simulation iteratively in the development process. The proposed approach is realized in a tool chain and demonstrated by an automotive use case, showing the potential of an early validation of system and software designs based on architecture models.

[8] argues that modelling tools should become development environments and support a methodologically guided development in which milestones are indicated and warnings are generated to inform the user about issues that are to be solved to reach these milestones. The paper indicates model maturity levels that correspond to an underlying development method and shows in the model maturity view which elements or parts of the model do not yet reach a certain level and why.

[9] proposes to abstract away from architectural platforms and their induced architectural styles to more abstract representation of applications. Architecture-independent application models, developed using modern model-based development techniques, can be mapped to application architectures in a variety of architectural styles. Architectural mappings therefore play an important role in synthesis of software implementations from abstract application models.

[10] proposes to integrate multiple partially overlapping models from different tools, since each tool and associated modelling language have different strengths and weaknesses. It is crucial that relevant dependencies between models and related timing properties are explicitly captured, allowing the analysis of the impact of changes on the timing properties and timing requirements. The paper proposes to use the concept of megamodels as a solution for the support of those dependencies relevant for timing properties, so that no violation may remain undetected.

[11] presents a model of an evolutionary product line process based on architecture transformations. The model attempts to give an accurate description of how real architects actually work. Key elements of the approach are how the transformations interact with consistency constraints and with feasibility in terms of resource limitations.

[12] proposes an approach for the identification of features supported by class models annotated with stereotypes. The models are automatically reverse engineered by a tool called Rejasp/Dmasp where attributes and methods are

stereotyped if they have some relation with candidate features. The approach consists of four guidelines and focuses on identifying features in embedded systems for ground vehicles.

[13] states that much meaning can be given to a model using a domain specific language (DSL), and the code generation rate can be increased. Model-based product line development is possible using code generation to realize variability. The paper presents a case study where a high rate of code generation was achieved by using two DSLs, the characteristics of which supplement each other. Structure is described by a highly general DSL and behaviour by a specialised DSL. Various kinds of products have been developed from a product line efficiently by using code generation from DSLs to realize variability.

3 Summary of the Workshop Discussions

The workshop was divided into 3 sessions: modelling languages and mappings, verification and validation, and a position statement session. After each session, a group discussion was held on issues raised during the session presentations. The following integrates and summarizes the conclusions of the discussions.

Mappings between modelling languages

An important issue for mappings between modelling formalisms concerns the level of detail that can be expressed in each formalism and the ability to transform information from one modelling formalism into another. One viewpoint is to consider a mapping between modelling formalisms as a dedicated transformation for a specific purpose, e.g., model analysis in the case of the MARTE to AADL mapping. This means that a mapping can abstract away certain details from the source model that are useless for the transformation purpose. In addition, specific information can be refined or added to the target model by enlarging the target model or by using an in-between Platform-Specific Model (PSM) profile on top of the source model, e.g., an AADL profile for MARTE. OCL constraints can added to the PSM profile in order to validate the correctness of the added information. In order to bridge the semantic gap between the two modelling levels, abstraction patterns can be introduced, e.g., by creating user-defined extensions for AADL.

Constructing architectural models

The construction of architectural models raises a number of issues, such as dealing with a multitude of inter-model dependencies and coping with model changes and the ripple effects they can cause. In addition, a product line approach can be beneficial but even further complicates the architectural modelling phase, since one should focus on an architecture for the whole product line instead of for a single product. When generative techniques are used, there was a common agreement on never touching the generated models or code. If changes seem necessary, either the source model or the generator itself should be changed.

Using a megamodel approach
Although the use of megamodels was recognised as a need in order to support different modelling formalisms, it was not clear if one should stay in the same technological space or not. It can be difficult to arrive at a combined megamodel. Therefore, it is sometimes better to use transformations or filters to combine different models rather than try to squeeze them into a single megamodel.

Acknowledgements

This workshop was supported by the IST-004527 ARTIST2 Network of Excellence on Embedded Systems Design (http://www.artist-embedded.org), the research project EUREKA-ITEA EVOLVE (http://www.evolve-itea.org), the research project EUREKA-ITEA VERDE (http://www.itea-verde.org), the research project EUREKA-ITEA OPEES (http://www.opees.org), and the research project ICT FP7-INTERESTED (http://www.interested-ip.eu).

References

1. Van Baelen, S., Ober, I., Espinoza, H., Weigert, T., Ober, I., Gérard, S. (eds.): Third International Workshop on Model Based Architecting and Construction of Embedded Systems. CEUR Workshop Proceedings Vol.644, CEUR, Aachen, Germany (2010)
2. Briand, L.C.: Using metaheuristic search for the analysis and verification of UML models. In: [1], p. 9
3. Turki, S., Senn, E., Blouin, D.: Mapping the MARTE UML profile to AADL. In: [1], pp. 11–20
4. Eidson, J.C., Lee, E.A., Matic, S., Seshia, S.A., Zou, J.: A time-centric model for cyber-physical applications. In: [1], pp. 21–35
5. Baresi, L., Morzenti, A., Motta, A., Rossi, M.: From interaction overview diagrams to temporal logic. In: [1], pp. 37–51
6. Schamai, W., Helle, P., Fritzson, P., Paredis, C.J.J.: Virtual verification of system designs against system requirements. In: [1], pp. 53–67
7. Weiss, G., Zeller, M., Eilers, D., Knorr, R.: Approach for iterative validation of automotive embedded systems. In: [1], pp. 65–83
8. Grosse-Rhode, M.: Model maturity levels for embedded systems development, or working with warnings. In: [1], pp. 85–99
9. Bagheri, H., Sullivan, K.: Towards a systematic approach for software synthesis. In: [1], pp. 101–105 (2010)
10. Neumann, S., Seibel, A.: Toward mega models for maintaining timing properties of automotive systems. In: [1], pp. 107–111
11. Axelsson, J.: A transformation-based model of evolutionary architecting for embedded system product lines. In: [1], pp. 113–117
12. Durelli, R.S., Conrado, D.B.F., Ramos, R.A., Pastor, O.L., de Camargo, V.V., Penteado, R.A.D.: Identifying features for ground vehicles software product lines by means of annotated models. In: [1], pp. 119–123
13. Tokumoto, S.: Product line development using multiple domain specific languages in embedded systems. In: [1], pp. 125–129

Virtual Verification of System Designs against System Requirements

Wladimir Schamai[1], Philipp Helle[2], Peter Fritzson[3], and Christiaan J.J. Paredis[4]

[1] EADS Innovation Works, Germany
wladimir.schamai@eads.net
[2] EADS Innovation Works, UK
philipp.helle@airbus.com
[3] Department of Computer and Information Science, Linköping University, Sweden
petfr@ida.liu.se
[4] Georgia Institute of Technology, Atlanta, USA
chris.paredis@me.gatech.edu

Abstract. System development and integration with a sufficient maturity at entry into service is a competitive challenge in the aerospace sector. With the ever-increasing complexity of products, this can only be achieved using efficient model-based techniques for system design as well as for system testing. However, natural language requirements engineering is an established technique that cannot be completely replaced for a number of reasons. This is a fact that has to be considered by any new approach. Building on the general idea of model-based systems engineering, we aim at building an integrated virtual verification environment for modeling systems, requirements, and test cases, so that system designs can be simulated and verified against the requirements in the early stages of system development. This paper provides a description of the virtual verification of system designs against system requirements methodology and exemplifies its application in a ModelicaML modeling environment.

Keywords: Requirements, Verification, ModelicaML, Modelica, MBSE, Model-based testing.

1 Introduction

The ever-increasing complexity of products has had a strong impact on time to market, cost and quality. Products are becoming increasingly complex due to rapid technological innovations, especially with the increase in electronics and software even inside traditionally mechanical products. This is especially true for complex, high value-added systems such as aircraft and automobile that are characterized by a heterogeneous combination of mechanical and electronic components. System development and integration with sufficient maturity at entry into service is a competitive challenge in the aerospace sector. Major achievements can be realized through efficient system specification and testing processes. Limitations of traditional approaches relying on textual descriptions are progressively addressed by the development of model-based systems engineering[1] (MBSE) approaches. Building on this general idea of MBSE, we aim at building a virtual verification environment for modeling systems, requirements and test cases, so that a system design can be simulated and verified against the requirements in the early system development stages.

1.1 Scope

For our methodology we assume that the requirements from the customer have been elicited[2] as requirement statements according to common standards in terms of quality, e.g. according to Hull et al.[4] stating that the individual requirements should be unique, atomic, feasible, clear, precise, verifiable, legal, and abstract, and the overall set of requirements should be complete, non-redundant, consistent, modular, structured, satisfied and qualified. The methods to achieve this have been well defined and can be considered to be established. Furthermore, the overall MBSE approach to system design, that is the development of a system design model from textual requirements, is not within the scope of this paper[3].

Paper structure: First we establish and describe the idea of virtual verification of system designs against system requirements (Section 2). Then we present background information on ModelicaML and the running example (Section 3) before we will explain the methodology in detail with the help of said running example (Section 4). Tool support and automation will be discussed in section 5. Finally, we close with a summary of the current status and propose a number of ideas for future research (Sections 6 and 7).

2 Virtual Verification of System Designs against System Requirements

This chapter provides the motivation behind our work, a general description thereof and the benefits of using the virtual verification of system design against system requirements (vVDR) approach. Furthermore, related work is discussed.

2.1 Objectives

A number of studies have demonstrated that the cost of fixing problems increases as the lifecycle of the system under development progresses, e.g. Davis[7].

---

[1] The International Council on Systems Engineering (INCOSE) defines MBSE as follows: "Model-based systems engineering (MBSE) is the formalized application of modelling to support system requirements, design, analysis, verification and validation activities beginning in the conceptual design phase and continuing throughout development and later life cycle phases"[1].
[2] A description of the various requirement elicitation, i.e. capturing, techniques can be found in [2] and [3].
[3] The interested reader can find a detailed overview of existing solutions for that in [5] and [6].

Thus, the business case for detecting defects early in the life cycle is a strong one. Testing thus needs to be applied as early as possible in the lifecycle to keep the relative cost of repair for fixing a discovered problem to a minimum. This means that testing should be integrated into the system design phase so that the system design can be verified against the requirements early on. To enable an automatic verification of a design model against a given set of requirements, the requirements have to be understood and processed by a computer. MBSE typically relies on building models that substitute or complement the textual requirements. Links between the model elements and the textual requirements are usually kept at the requirements' granularity level, meaning that one or more model elements are linked to one requirement. This granularity is good enough for basic traceability and coverage analysis but fails when an interpretation of a requirement's content by a computer is necessary. There is research concerning the automatic translation of natural language requirements into behavioral models to support the automation of system and acceptance testing (see e.g. [8]) but it is not widely adopted in industrial practice[9]. Formal mathematical methods may be used to express requirements, but their application requires high expertise and, hence, they are not very common in industrial practice. A recent survey came to the conclusion that "in spite of their successes, verification technology and formal methods have not seen widespread adoption as a routine part of systems development practice, except, arguably, in the development of critical systems in certain domains."[10]. The bottom line is that natural language is still the most common approach to express requirements in practice[9]. We want to provide a solution to the question of how to formalize requirements so that they can be processed and evaluated during system simulations in order to detect errors or inconsistencies in a way that is easy to understand and to apply.

2.2 vVDR Concept

Figure 1 depicts the relationship of the various engineering artifacts in the frame of vVDR.

A subset of a given set of textual requirements is selected and formalized into so-called requirement violation monitors by identifying measurable properties addressed in the requirement statement. A requirement violation monitor is basically an executable model for monitoring if the constraints expressed by the

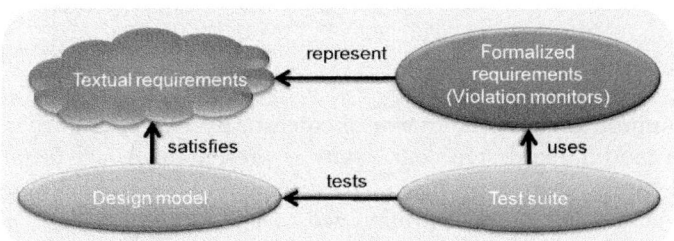

Fig. 1. Engineering data relations overview

requirement statement are adhered to. To test a given design model, the requirement violation monitors are linked to the design model using explicit assignment statements. Furthermore, a test suite consisting of a test context and a number of test cases has to be built manually. The test suite uses the formalized requirements as test oracles for the test cases, i.e., if a requirement is violated during a test, the test case is deemed failed. The separation of requirement and system design modeling provides a degree of independence that ensures a high fidelity in the testing results. The test cases, requirement violation monitors and the design model can be instantiated and run automatically. Visual graphs (e.g. plots) allow the monitoring of the requirement violation monitors during run-time to see if the design model fails to implement a requirement.

2.3 Benefits

Our approach contributes to three main steps in the system development lifecycle: requirements analysis, system design and system testing. Experience shows that the main benefit of modeling in general is a contribution to the identification of ambiguities and incompleteness in the input material. Even though we assume that the textual requirements that are provided as an input to the process adhere to a high quality standard, vVDR enables the requirements analyst to further improve the quality by modeling the requirements in a formal representation as this forces a detailed analysis of the requirements. The main contribution of vVDR is to the quality of the system design. The automatic verification of a design model based on the formalized requirements allows the detection of errors in the system design. The separation of requirements modeling and design modeling allow a reuse of the requirements for the verification of several alternative system designs. Furthermore, even for one design model the same requirements violation monitors can be instantiated several times. As described in [11], the benefits of using a model-based testing approach during the system design phase facilitates error tracing and impact assessment in the later integration and testing stages by providing a seamless traceability from the initial requirements to test cases and test results. Furthermore, it allows reusing the artifacts from the engineering stage at the testing stage of the development cycle which results in a significant decrease in overall testing effort. By integrating the requirements model in a test bench the test models can also be reused for hardware-in-the-loop test setups.

2.4 Related Work

In [12] an approach to the incremental consistency checking of dynamically definable and modifiable design constraints is presented. Apart from focusing on design constraints instead of design requirements which can be argued as being a marginal issue, the main difference to vVDR is that the constraints are expressed using the design model variables whereas our approach is based on a separation of the requirements and the design model. Only for a specific test context are they connected using explicit assignment statements. Additionally, the monitoring of model changes and the evaluation of the defined constraints is done by a separate "Model Analyzer Tool" whereas our approach relies on out-of-the-box modeling capabilities. The Behavior Modeling Language (BML) or more specifically the Requirement Behavior Tree technique that is a vital part of the BML is another method for formalizing requirements into a form that can be processed by computers[13][14]. But whereas vVDR relies on a separation between the set of independent requirements that are used to verify a design model and the building of a design model by the system designer, the BML methodology merges the behavior trees that each represent single requirements into an overall design behavior tree (DBT). In other words, the transition from the requirements space to the solution space is based on the formalized requirements.

3 Background

This chapter provides background information on the graphical modeling notation ModelicaML [15] and its underlying language Modelica [16] which was used to implement our approach, and introduces the running example that will be used to illustrate the vVDR methodology in Section 4.

3.1 Technical Background

Modelica is an object-oriented equation-based modeling language primarily aimed at physical systems. The model behavior is based on ordinary and differential algebraic equation (OAE and DAE) systems combined with difference equations/discrete events, so-called hybrid DAEs. Such models are ideally suited for representing physical behavior and the exchange of energy, signals, or other continuous-time or discrete-time interactions between system components.

The Unified Modeling Language (UML) is a standardized general-purpose modeling language in the field of software engineering and the Systems Modeling Language (SysML) is an adaptation of the UML aimed at systems engineering applications. Both are open standards, managed and created by the Object Management Group (OMG), a consortium focused on modeling and model-based standards.

The Modelica Graphical Modeling Language is a UML profile, a language extension, for Modelica. The main purpose of ModelicaML is to enable an efficient and effective way to create, visualize and maintain combined UML and Modelica models. ModelicaML is defined as a graphical notation that facilitates different views (e.g., composition, inheritance, behavior) on system models. It is based on a subset of UML and reuses some concepts from SysML. ModelicaML is designed to generate Modelica code from graphical models. Since the ModelicaML profile is an extension of the UML meta-model it can be used as an extension for both UML and SysML[4].

---

[4] SysML itself is also a UML Profile. All ModelicaML stereotypes that extend UML meta-classes are also applicable to the corresponding SysML elements.

3.2 Running Example: Automated Train Protection System

In this section we introduce an example, which will be used in the remainder of this paper to demonstrate the vVDR approach. It is based on the example from[13]. Most railway systems have some form of train protection system that uses track-side signals to indicate potentially dangerous situations to the driver. Accidents still occur despite a train protection system when a driver fails to notice or respond correctly to a signal. To reduce the risk of these accidents, Automated Train Protection (ATP) systems are used that automate the train's response to the track-side signals. The ATP system in our example design model has three track-side signals: proceed, caution and danger. When the ATP system receives a caution signal, it monitors the driver's behavior to ensure the train's speed is being reduced. If the driver fails to decrease the train's speed after a caution signal or the ATP system receives a danger signal then the train's brakes are applied. The textual requirements for the ATP can be found in Appendix A.

4 Methodology Description

The following subsections contain a description of the method steps and illustrate the methodology using our running example.

4.1 Role: Requirements Analyst

Generally speaking, a requirements analyst acts as the liaison between the business professionals and the customer on the one hand and the system design team on the other hand. The requirements analyst is responsible for ensuring the correctness and completeness of the input requirements that are handed down from a business analyst. The objective is to create a set of requirements, which ensure that the product fulfils its original intent. The analyst needs analytical skills to critically evaluate the information gathered from multiple sources, reconcile conflicts and distinguish solution ideas from requirements[17]. In our scope, the requirements analyst is responsible for translating the textual requirements into a set of requirement violation monitors. This task includes selecting suitable requirements, creating the requirements in a formal model, identifying measurable properties and defining the requirements violation monitors.

4.2 Role: System Designer

A system designer develops the system design based on the system requirements received from the requirements analyst. An engineer in this role creates the static architecture and defines the dynamic behavior of the system. The system designer needs technical and creative skills in his work[18]. As the building of the system model is not in the scope of this paper, the system designer only has a supporting role here. He/she supports the requirements analyst in selecting the requirements for formalization and the tester in linking the formalized requirements' properties to the system design model.

4.3 Role: System Tester

[4] states that "in its broadest sense, testing is any activity that allows defects in the system to be detected or prevented, where a defect is a departure from requirements". The system tester therefore has to confirm that a particular system design meets the system requirements. The system tester builds a test model that defines the test context for a given system. He creates test cases, links requirements to design models, executes test cases, and reports test results.

4.4 Method Step: Select Requirements to Be Verified

From the set of agreed input requirements the requirements analyst selects requirements that are to be verified by means of simulation. The selection criteria depend on the requirement types as well as on the system design models that are planned to be created. Generally speaking, the requirements analyst needs to decide if the vVDR approach is suitable to test a given requirement. This step requires a close collaboration between the requirements analyst and the system designer. The output of this activity is a selected subset of the input requirements. This activity contributes to the system design modeling by clarifying the level of detail that is required of the model for an automatic evaluation of the selected requirements. For example, the requirements 001, 001-2 and 002 would not be selected because appropriate models will be missing or simulation is not best suited[5] for their verification. In contrast, the requirements 003-009 are good candidates for the verification using simulations. The selected subset of requirements will then be transferred into the modeling tool and used in the subsequent steps.

4.5 Method Step: Formalize Textual Requirements

The second step is to formalize each requirement in order to enable its automatic evaluation during simulations. Note, that in an ideal world, i.e. in a company where the vVDR method is used throughout the development process, the requirements were already formalised at a higher engineering level by the person that formulated the requirements and allocated them to our system under development in the first place.

Consider requirement 006-1: "If at any time the controller calculates a "caution" signal, it shall, within 0.5 seconds, enable the alarm in the driver cabin." Based on this statement we can:

- Identify measurable properties included in the requirement statement, i.e., the reception of a caution signal, the activation of the alarm and the time frame constant,
- Formalize properties as shown in Fig. 2 and define a requirement violation monitor as illustrated in Fig. 3.

---

[5] For example, design inspection could be sufficient.

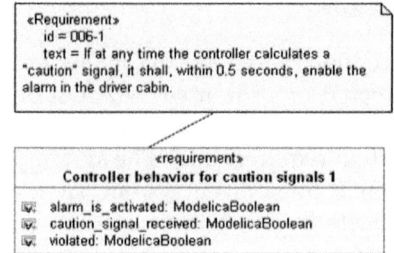

Fig. 2. Formalized requirement properties in ModelicaML

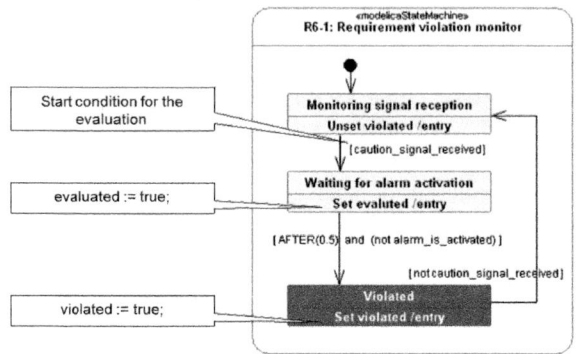

Fig. 3. Requirement violation monitor example

In order to determine if a requirement is fulfilled the following assumption is made: A requirement is implemented in and met by a design model as long as its requirement violation monitor is evaluated but not violated. Now the violation relations can be defined. This example uses a state machine[6] (as shown in Fig. 3) to specify when the requirement is violated. In general, it is recommended to create the following attributes for each requirement:

- evaluated: Indicates if the requirement was evaluated at least once,
- violated: Indicates if this requirement was violated at least once.

The evaluated attribute is necessary, because, while a violation during a simulation provides sufficient indication that a requirement is not met, a non-violation is not enough to ensure the satisfaction of a requirement. For example, if the value of "caution_signal_received" is never true during a particular test case simulation this can mean that either this requirement is not addressed by the design (i.e., the caution signals are not received by the controller at all), or that this requirement is not verified by this test case because the test case does not provide appropriate stimuli for the design model.

---

[6] A ModelicaML state machine is one possible means to express the violation of a requirement. It is also possible to use other formalisms, equations or statements for it.

This method step supports the requirements analyst in improving the quality of the selected requirements by identifying ambiguities or incompleteness issues. Any issues that are identified in this step have to be resolved with the stakeholders and all affected textual requirements have to be updated accordingly.

4.6 Method Step: Select or Create Design Model to Be Verified against Requirements

The actual system design is not in the scope of this paper. The system designer builds a design model for each design alternative that he comes up with[7]. Since the requirements are kept separate from the design alternatives, the same requirements can be reused to verify several designs, and the same requirement violation monitors can be reused in multiple test cases.

4.7 Method Step: Create Test Models, Instantiate Models, Link Requirement Properties to Design Model Properties

After the formalization of the requirements and the selection of one design model for verification, the system tester starts creating test models, defining test cases and linking requirement properties to values inside the design model. The recommended procedure is as follows:

- Define a test model that will contain test cases, a design model, the requirements and their requirement violation monitors.
- Define test cases for evaluating requirements. One test case can be used for evaluating one or more requirements.
- Create additional models if necessary, for example, models that simulate the environment, stimulate the system or monitor specific values.
- Bind the requirements to the design model by setting the properties of a requirement to values inside the design model using explicit assignments.

Particularly the last step will require the involvement of the system designer in order to ensure that the requirement properties are linked properly, i.e. to the correct properties values inside the design model. For example, the assignment for the requirement property *caution_signal_received* is as follows:

```
caution_signal_received =
design_model.train1.pc1.tcs.controller.tracks_signals_status == 1
```

This means that the requirement property *caution_signal_received* will become true when the controller property *tracks_signals_status* is equal to one[8].

---

[7] For ease of use, the design will normally be modelled in the same notation and the same tool as the requirements. However, it can be imagined to build interfaces to executable models that were built using different modelling notations in different tools and then subsequently use vVDR to test these models.

[8] "1" denotes a caution signal in the design model.

Another example is the assignment of the requirement property alarm_is_activated. Here the system tester will have to decide which design property it should be linked to. It could be accessed from the ATP controller or from the HMI system, that is between the controller and the driver, or from the driver HMI port directly. The answer will probably be: It should be accessed from the driver HMI port because failures in HMI system may also affect the evaluation result. Furthermore, it is recommended to create the following attributes and statements[9] for each test model:

- `test_passed := evaluated and not violated;`
  Indicates if the test is passed or failed.
- `evaluated := if req1.evaluated and ... and reqN.evaluated then true ...;`
  Indicates if the test case has evaluated all requirements.
- `violated := when {req1.violated,... ,reqN.violated} then true ...;`
  Indicates if any of requirements was violated.

These definitions enable an automated test case results evaluation by using the requirement violation monitors of the involved requirements as a test oracle for the test case. Figure 4 presents an example of a test case that drives the simulation.

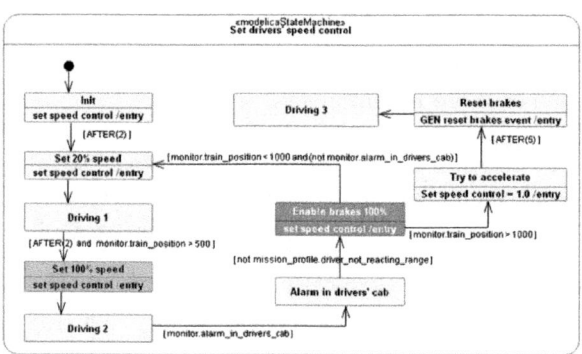

Fig. 4. Test case example

4.8 Method Step: Test and Observe Requirement Violations

After having created the test models, the system tester can run simulations and observe the results. Hereby, the system tester will be interested in knowing if test cases have passed or failed. A test case is deemed to have failed when not all requirements were evaluated or some requirements were violated during the execution of the test case.

---

[9] These statements are written in Modelica.

4.9 Method Step: Report and Analyze Test Results

After the execution of all test cases, the system tester creates a simulation report. This information is the basis for discussions among the involved parties and may lead to an iterative repetition of the system design and testing process described here. Furthermore, it allows the precise reproduction of test results at a later state. Additionally, these reports can be reused as a reference for later product verification activities, i.e., the physical system testing at a test bench.

5 Tool Support and Automation

Past experience shows that the acceptance of new methods by systems engineers highly correlates with the ease of application of said new method. The field of formal methods, although it is proven that its application can reduce errors drastically, is just one example were a good method was not adapted widely in the daily work of the engineers mainly due to its steep learning curve. To ease the adaptation of vVDR by systems engineers, a number of assistant tools has been developed that is constantly growing. These tools that are integrated into the vVDR development environment aim at simpliyfing complex and/or repetitive tasks within the vVDR method by automation.

For the linking of requirement properties to design properties a wizard for preparing the binding statements has been developed as shown by Fig. 5. The wizard collects all requirements that have been instantiated within a selected simulation model and prepares a Modelica modification in that simulation model with assignment statements that have the input variables of the requirements on the left hand side of the equation and "TBD" on the right hand side of the equation. Therefore, the tester who prepares the simulation now only has to go through these statements and can replace the "TBD" on the right hand side with a pointer to the appropriate variable in the design model. Without this helper, the tester would need to look manually through each instantiated requirement and the manually write the complete assignment statement for all the requirement's input variables.

A second improvement in the vVDR development environment aims at simplifying the same task for the system tester. As shown in Fig. 6 a dedicated view supports the task of binding requirements properties to design model properties and the task of discovering the right stimuli for the design model in a test case. This view filters the model instance tree for inputs and outputs. Inputs are potential stimuli. Outputs are potential observation points. This view limits the potential possibilities that can be placed on the right hand side of the properties binding assignment and gives the system tester an easy tool for identifying the right ones.

Another helper was built for automatically writing the overall test evaluation code (see 4.7) were the evaluation and violation of the individual requirements is combined to provide an overall test verdict. The helper is able to create the code and update it after a model change.

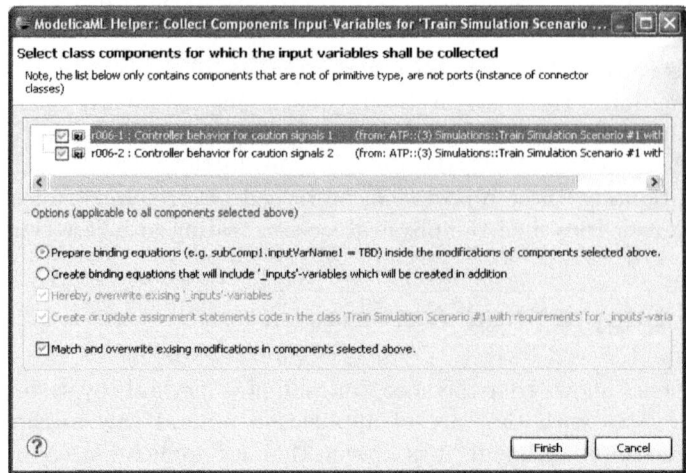

Fig. 5. Wizard for variables binding support

6 Current Status and Future Directions

The methodology presented in this paper has been successfully applied in several case studies. However, the case studies included only a small number of requirements. In the future, a real-sized case study is planned, i.e., one that contains more than a hundred requirements to be verified using the vVDR method to determine the applicability and scalability of this approach.

The traceability between requirements and design artefacts is a critical issue in the daily engineering work, particularly with regards to change impact analysis. vVDR already support this but we aim at improving its capabilities. We see the need to improve the level of granularity at which requirements and model elements are linked with each other to support change impact analysis more efficiently. For example, parts of a requirement statement, i.e.,. single words, can be linked to the model elements that they are referring to. Moreover, an effective visualization and dependencies exploration is necessary.

A model-based development approach enables an effective and efficient reporting on and monitoring of the requirements implementation. For example, a bidirectional traceability between requirement and design allows the determination of the system development status and supports project risk management and planning. Template-based reporting engines support automatic generation of various kinds of reports on demand.

While the test cases for our running example can be easily derived directly from the input requirements, manual test case generation becomes an increasingly tedious task for real-life specifications with hundreds of requirements. Model-based testing provides methods for automated test case generation some of which already work on UML models[19] and look promising to be adapted to vVDR.

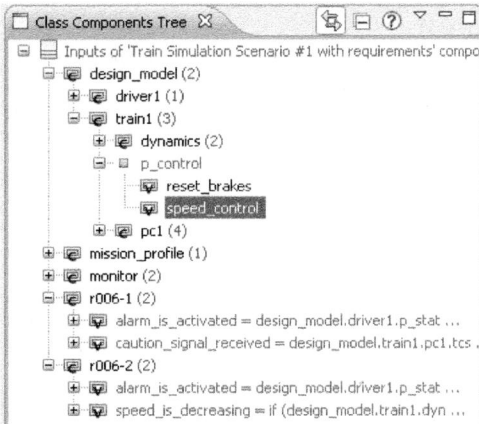

Fig. 6. View to support input and output variables connection

Requirements traceability, a higher test automation through adaptation of model-based testing techniques as well as reporting topics are subject to our future work.

7 Conclusion

This paper presents a method for the virtual verification of system designs against system requirements by means of simulation. It provides a detailed description of all method steps and illustrates them using an example case study that was implemented using ModelicaML. It points out that this method strongly depends on the design models that are planned to be created and that not all type of requirements can be evaluated using this method. In the vVDR approach, formalized requirements, system design and test cases are defined in separate models and can be reused and combined into test setups in an efficient manner. In doing so, a continuous evaluation of requirements along the system design evolution can be done starting in the early system design stages. This approach enables an early detection of errors or inconsistencies in system design, as well as of inconsistent, not feasible or conflicting requirements. Moreover, the created artifacts can be reused for later product verification (i.e., physical testing) activities.

References

1. Haskins, C. (ed.): Systems Engineering Handbook: A guide for system life cycle processes and activities. In: INCOSE (2006)
2. Gause, D., Weinberg, G.: Exploring requirements: quality before design. Dorset House Pub., New York (1989)

3. Loucopoulos, P., Karakostas, V.: System requirements engineering. McGraw-Hill, Inc., New York (1995)
4. Hull, E., Jackson, K., Dick, J.: Requirements engineering. Springer, Heidelberg (2005)
5. Estefan, J.: Survey of model-based systems engineering (MBSE) methodologies. Incose MBSE Focus Group 25 (2007)
6. Helle, P., Mitschke, A., Strobel, C., Schamai, W., Rivière, A., Vincent, L.: Improving Systems Specifications - A Method Proposal. In: Proceedings of CSER 2008 Conference, Los Angeles, CA, April 4-5 (2010)
7. Davis, A.: Software requirements: objects, functions, and states. Prentice-Hall, Inc., Upper Saddle River (1993)
8. Santiago Jr., V.A.d.: Natural language requirements: automating model-based testing and analysis of defects. Instituto Nacional de Pesquisas Espaciais, São José dos Campos (2010)
9. Mich, L., Franch, M., Novi Inverardi, P.: Market research for requirements analysis using linguistic tools. Requirements Engineering 9(2), 151 (2004)
10. Woodcock, J., Larsen, P., Bicarregui, J., Fitzgerald, J.: Formal methods: Practice and experience. ACM Computing Surveys (CSUR) 41(4), 1–36 (2009)
11. Helle, P., Schamai, W.: Specification model-based testing in the avionic domain - Current status and future directions. In: Proceedings of the Sixth Workshop on Model-Based Testing 2010, Paphos, Cyprus (2010)
12. Groher, I., Reder, A., Egyed, A.: Incremental Consistency Checking of Dynamic Constraints. In: Fundamental Approaches to Software Engineering, pp. 203–217 (2010)
13. Myers, T., Fritzson, P., Dromey, R.: Seamlessly Integrating Software & Hardware Modelling for Large-Scale Systems. In: 2nd International Workshop on Equation-Based Object-Oriented Languages and Tools, Paphos, Cyprus (2008)
14. Powell, D.: Requirements evaluation using behavior trees-findings from industry. In: Australian Software Engineering Conference, ASWEC 2007 (2007)
15. Schamai, W., Fritzson, P., Paredis, C., Pop, A.: Towards Unified System Modeling and Simulation with ModelicaML: Modeling of Executable Behavior Using Graphical Notations. In: Proc. of the 7th International Modelica Conference, Como, Italy (2009)
16. Fritzson, P.: Principles of object-oriented modeling and simulation with Modelica 2.1. Wiley-IEEE Press (2004)
17. Sheard, S.: Twelve systems engineering roles. In: Proceedings of INCOSE (1996)
18. Morrell, J., Mawhinney, C., Morris, G., Haga, W., Smolkina, A.: The systems analyst: a post mortem?. In: Proceedings of the Fourth International Conference of the Academy of Business and Administrative Sciences, Quebec City, Canada (2001)
19. Prasanna, M., Sivanandam, S., Venkatesan, R., Sundarrajan, R.: A survey on automatic test case generation. Academic Open Internet Journal 15 (2005)

A ATP Requirements

ID	Requirement Text (based on [13])
001	The ATP system shall be located on board the train.
001-2	The ATP system shall consist of a central controller and five boundary subsystems that manage the sensors, speedometer, brakes, alarm and a reset mechanism.
002	The sensors shall be attached to the side of the train and read information from approaching track-side signals, i.e. they detect what the signal is signaling to the train driver.
002-2	Within the driver cabin, the train control display system shall display the last track-side signal values calculated by the controller.
003	Three sensors shall generate values in the range of 0 to 3, where 0, 1 and 2 denote the danger, caution, and proceed track-side signals respectively. Each sensor shall generate the value 3 if a track-side signal that is out of the range 0..2 is detected.
004	The controller shall calculate the majority of the three sensor readings. If no majority exists then the value shall be set to "undefined" (i.e. 3).
005	If the calculated majority is "proceed" (i.e. 0) then the controller shall not take any action with respect to the activation of the braking system.
006-1	If at any time the controller calculates a "caution" signal, it shall, within 0.5 seconds, enable the alarm in the driver cabin.
006-2	If the alarm in the driver cabin has been activated due to a "caution" signal and the train speed is not decreasing by at least $0.5 m/s^2$ within two seconds of the activation, then the controller shall within 0.5 seconds activate the automatic braking.
007-1	If at any time the controller calculates a "danger" signal it shall within 0.5 seconds activate the braking system and enable the alarm in the driver cabin.
007-2	If the alarm in the driver cabin has been activated due to a "caution" signal, it shall be deactivated by the controller within 0.5 seconds if a "proceed" signal is calculated and the automatic braking has not been activated yet.
008	If at any time the automatic braking has been activated, the controller shall ignore all further sensor input until the system has been reset.
009	If the controller receives a reset command from the driver, then it shall within 1 second, deactivate the train brakes and disable the alarm within the driver cabin.

From Interaction Overview Diagrams to Temporal Logic[*]

Luciano Baresi, Angelo Morzenti, Alfredo Motta, and Matteo Rossi

Politecnico di Milano
Dipartimento di Elettronica e Informazione, Deep-SE Group
Via Golgi 42 – 20133 Milano, Italy
{baresi,morzenti,motta,rossi}@elet.polimi.it

Abstract. In this paper, we use UML Interaction Overview Diagrams as the basis for a user-friendly, intuitive, modeling notation that is well-suited for the design of complex, heterogeneous, embedded systems developed by domain experts with little background on modeling software-based systems. To allow designers to precisely analyze models written with this notation, we provide (part of) it with a formal semantics based on temporal logic, upon which a fully automated, tool supported, verification technique is built. The modeling and verification technique is presented and discussed through the aid of an example system.

Keywords: Metric temporal logic, bounded model checking, Unified Modeling Language.

1 Introduction

Complex embedded systems such as those found in the Aerospace and Defense domains are typically built of several, heterogeneous, components that are often designed by teams of engineers with different backgrounds (e.g., telecommunication, control systems, software engineering, etc.). Careful modeling starting from the early stages of system development can greatly help increase the quality of the designed system when it is accompanied and followed by verification and code generation activities. Modeling-verification-code generation are three pillars in the model driven development of complex embedded systems; they are most effective when (i) modeling is based on user-friendly, intuitive, yet precise notations that can be used with ease by experts of domains other than computer science; (ii) rigorous, possibly formal, verification can be carried out on the aforementioned models, though in a way that is hidden from the system developer as much as possible; (iii) executable code can be seamlessly produced from verified models, to generate implementations that are correct by construction.

---

[*] This research was supported by the European Community's Seventh Framework Program (FP7/2007-2013) under grant agreement n. 248864 (MADES), and by the Programme IDEAS-ERC, Project 227977-SMScom.

This work, which is part of a larger research effort carried out in the MADES European project[1] [1], focuses on aspects (i) and (ii) mentioned above. In particular, it is the first step towards a complete proposal for modeling and validating embedded systems. The plan is to exploit both "conventional" UML diagrams [15] and a subset of the MARTE (Modeling and Analysis of Real-Time and Embedded systems) UML profile [14]. We want to use Class Diagrams to define the key components of the system, State Diagrams to model their internal behaviors, and Sequence and Interaction Overview Diagrams to model the interactions and cooperations among the different elements. These diagrams will be augmented with clocks and resources taken from MARTE. The result is a multi-faceted model of the system, automatically translated into temporal logic to verify it. Temporal Logic helps glue the different views, create a single, consistent representation of the system, discover inconsistencies among the different aspects, and formally verify some global properties.

This paper starts from Interaction Overview Diagrams (IODs) since they are often neglected, but they provide an interesting means to integrate Sequence Diagrams (SDs) and define coherent and complex evolutions of the system of interest. IODs are ascribed a formal semantics, based on temporal logic, upon which a fully automated, tool supported, verification technique is built.

The choice of IODs as the starting point for a modeling notation that is accessible to experts of different domains, especially those other than software engineering, is borne from the observation that, in the industrial practice, SDs are often the preferred notation of system engineers to describe components' behaviors [3]. However, SDs taken in isolation are not enough to provide a complete picture of the interactions among the various components of a complex system; hence, system designers must be given mechanisms to combine different SDs into richer descriptions, which is precisely what IODs offer.

In this article we provide a preliminary formal semantics of IODs based on metric temporal logic. While this semantics is not yet complete, as it does not cover all possible mechanisms through which SDs can be combined into IODs, it is nonetheless a significant first step in this direction. The provided semantics has been implemented into the Zot bounded satisfiability/model checker [16][2], and has been used to prove some properties of an example system.

This paper is structured as follows. Section 2 briefly presents IODs; Section 3 gives an overview of the metric temporal logic used to define the formal semantics of IODs, and of the Zot tool supporting it; Section 4 introduces the formal semantics of IODs through an example system, and discusses how it has been used to prove properties of the latter; Section 5 discusses some relevant related works; finally, Section 6 draws some conclusions and outlines future works.

2 Interaction Overview Diagrams

Most UML behavioral diagrams have undergone a significant revision from version 1.x to version 2.x. To model interactions, UML2 offers four kinds of

---
[1] http://www.mades-project.org
[2] Zot is available at http://home.dei.polimi.it/pradella/Zot

diagrams: communication diagrams, sequence diagrams, timing diagrams and interaction overview diagrams. In this work we focus on Sequence Diagrams (SDs) and Interaction Overview Diagrams (IODs).

SDs have been considerably revised and extended in UML2 to improve their expressiveness and their structure. IODs are new in UML2. They allow a designer to provide a high-level view of the possible interactions in a system. IODs constitute a high-level structuring mechanism that is used to compose scenarios through mechanisms such as sequence, iteration, concurrency or choice. IODs are a special and restricted kind of UML Activity Diagrams (ADs) where nodes are interactions or interaction uses, and edges indicate the flow or order in which these interactions occur. Semantically, however, IODs are more complex compared to ADs and they may have different interpretations. In the following the fundamental operators of IODs are presented. Figure 2 shows an example of IOD for the application analyzed in Section 4, which will be used throughout this section to provide graphical examples of IOD constructs. IODs include also other operators whose study is left to future works.

IODs include the **initial node**, **final node** and **flows final node** operators, which have exactly the same meaning of the corresponding operators found in ADs. For example, The IOD of Figure 2 has an initial node at the top, but no final or flow final nodes.

A **control flow** is a directed connection (flow) between two SDs (e.g., between diagrams *delegateSMS* and *downloadSMS* in Figure 2). As soon as the SD at the source of the flow is finished, it presents a token to the SD at the end of the flow.

A **fork node** is a control node that has a single incoming flow and two or more outgoing flows. Incoming tokens are offered to all outgoing flows (edges). The outgoing flows can be guarded, which gives them a mechanism to accept or reject a token. In the IOD of Figure 2, there is one fork node at the top of the diagram (between the initial node and SDs *waitingCall* and *checkingSMS*) modeling two concurrent execution of the system. The dual operator is the join node, which synchronizes a number of incoming flows into a single outgoing flow. Each (and every) incoming control flow must present a control token to the join node before the node can offer a single token to the outgoing flow.

A **decision node** is a control node that has one incoming flow and two or more outgoing flows. In the IOD of Figure 2 there are four decision operators (e.g., the one between SDs *waitingCall* and *delegateCall*) with their corresponding Boolean conditions. Conversely, a **merge node** is a type of control node that has two or more incoming flows and a single outgoing flow.

3 TRIO and Zot

TRIO [7] is a general-purpose formal specification language suitable for describing complex real-time systems, including distributed ones. TRIO is a first-order linear temporal logic that supports a metric on time. TRIO formulae are built out of the usual first-order connectives, operators, and quantifiers, as well as a single basic modal operator, called Dist, that relates the *current time*, which is left implicit in the formula, to another time instant: given a formula F and

Table 1. TRIO derived temporal operators

OPERATOR	DEFINITION
$\text{Past}(F, t)$	$t \geq 0 \wedge \text{Dist}(F, -t)$
$\text{Futr}(F, t)$	$t \geq 0 \wedge \text{Dist}(F, t)$
$\text{Alw}(F)$	$\forall d : \text{Dist}(F, d)$
$\text{AlwP}(F)$	$\forall d > 0 : \text{Past}(F, d)$
$\text{AlwF}(F)$	$\forall d > 0 : \text{Futr}(F, d)$
$\text{SomF}(F)$	$\exists d > 0 : \text{Futr}(F, d)$
$\text{SomP}(F)$	$\exists d > 0 : \text{Past}(F, d)$
$\text{Lasted}(F, t)$	$\forall d \in (0, t] : \text{Past}(F, d)$
$\text{Lasts}(F, t)$	$\forall d \in (0, t] : \text{Futr}(F, d)$
$\text{WithinP}(F, t)$	$\exists d \in (0, t] : \text{Past}(F, d)$
$\text{WithinF}(F, t)$	$\exists d \in (0, t] : \text{Futr}(F, d)$
$\text{Since}(F, G)$	$\exists d > 0 : \text{Lasted}(F, d) \wedge \text{Past}(G, d)$
$\text{Until}(F, G)$	$\exists d > 0 : \text{Lasts}(F, d) \wedge \text{Futr}(G, d)$

a term t indicating a time distance (either positive or negative), the formula $\text{Dist}(F, t)$ specifies that F holds at a time instant whose distance is exactly t time units from the current one. While TRIO can exploit both discrete and dense sets as time domains, in this paper we assume the nonnegative integers $\mathbb{N}$ as discrete time domain. For convenience in the writing of specification formulae, TRIO defines a number of *derived* temporal operators from the basic Dist, through propositional composition and first-order logic quantification. Table 1 defines some of the most significant ones, including those used in this paper.

The TRIO specification of a system includes a set of basic *items*, such as predicates, representing the elementary modeled phenomena. The system behavior over time is formally specified by a set of TRIO formulae, which state how the items are constrained and how they vary in time, in a purely descriptive (or declarative) fashion.

The goal of the verification phase is to ensure that the system S satisfies some desired property R, that is, that $S \models R$. In the TRIO approach S and R are both expressed as logic formulae Σ and ρ, respectively; then, showing that $S \models R$ amounts to proving that $\Sigma \Rightarrow \rho$ is valid.

TRIO is supported by a variety of verification techniques implemented in prototype tools. In this paper we refer to Zot [16], a bounded model checker which supports verification of discrete-time TRIO models. Zot encodes satisfiability (and validity) problems for discrete-time TRIO formulae as propositional satisfiability (SAT) problems, which are then checked with off-the-shelf SAT solvers. More recently, we developed a more efficient encoding that exploits the features of Satisfiability Modulo Theories (SMT) solvers [2]. Through Zot one can verify whether stated properties hold for the system being analyzed (or parts thereof) or not; if a property does not hold, Zot produces a counterexample.

4 Formal Semantics of Interaction Overview Diagrams

This section introduces the formal semantics of IODs defined in terms of the TRIO temporal logic. The semantics is presented by way of an example system, whose behavior modeled through a IOD is described in Section 4.1. Then, Section 4.2 discusses the TRIO formalization of different constructs of IODs, and illustrates how this is used to create a formal model for the example system. Section 4.3 briefly discusses some properties that were checked for the modeled system by feeding its TRIO representation to the Zot verification tool. Finally, Section 4.4 provides a measure of the complexity of the translation of IODs into metric temporal logic.

4.1 Example Telephone System

The example system used throughout this section is a telephone system composed of three units, a *TransmissionUnit*, a *ConnectionUnit* and a *Server*, depicted in the class diagram of Figure 1. The *ConnectionUnit* is in charge of checking for the arrival of new SMSs on the *Server* (operation *checkSMS* of class *Server*) and to handle new calls coming from the *Server* (operation *IncomingCall* of class *ConnectionUnit*). The *TransmissionUnit* is used by the *ConnectionUnit* to download the SMSs (operation *downloadSMS*) and to handle the call's data (operation *beginCall*). The *TransmissionUnit* receives the data concerning SMSs and calls from the *Server* (operations *receiveSMSToken* and *receiveCallData*).

The behavior of the telephone system is modeled by the IOD of Figure 2. The fork operator specifies that the two main paths executed by the system are in parallel; for example the *checkingSMS* and *receiveCall* sequence diagrams run in parallel. Branch conditions are used in order to distinguish between different possible executions; for example after checking for a new SMS on the *Server* the system will continue with downloading the SMSs if one is present, otherwise it will loop back to the same diagram. It can be assumed that the *Server* allocates a dedicated thread to each connected telephone; this is why the sequence diagrams of Figure 2 report the interaction between only one *ConnectionUnit*, one *TransmissionUnit* and one *Server*.

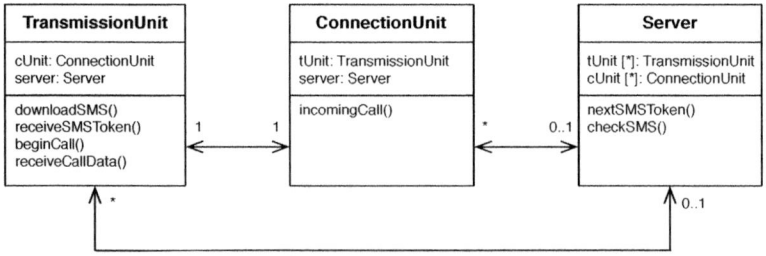

Fig. 1. Class diagram for the telephone system

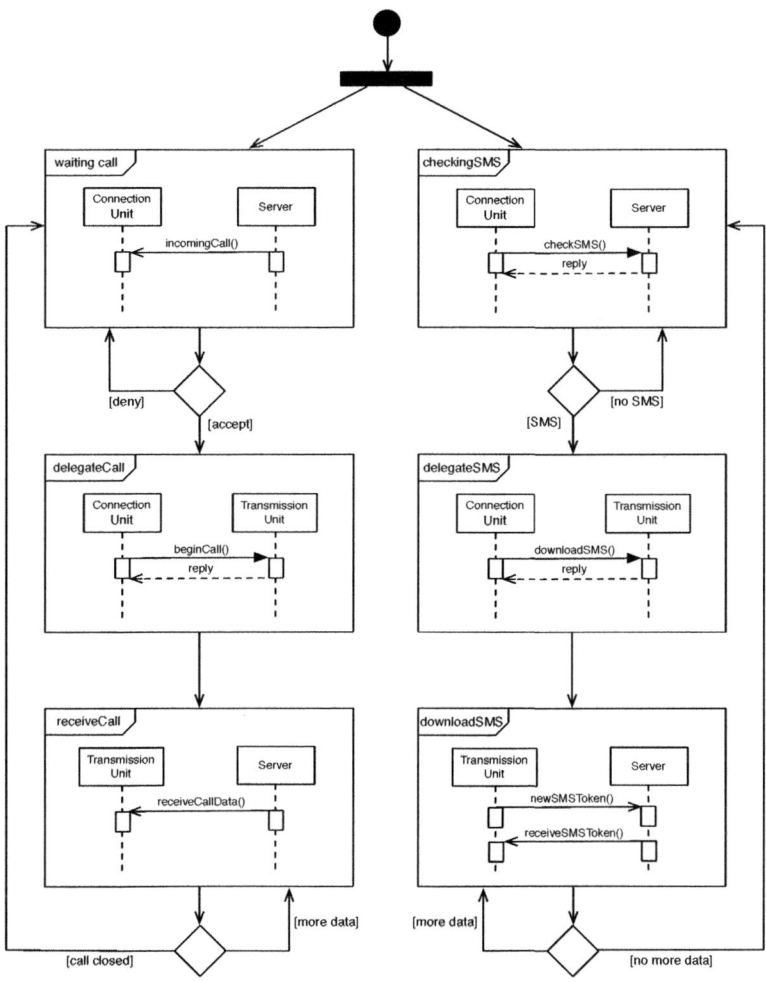

Fig. 2. Interaction Overview diagram for the telephone system

4.2 TRIO Formalization

The formalization presented here was derived from the diagram of Figure 2 by hand. The availability of a tool, which we are building, will allow us to analyze more complex models and assess the actual scalability of the proposed technique. The formalization is organized into sets of formulae, each of them corresponding to one of the SDs appearing in the IOD. Every set can be further decomposed into three subsets modeling different aspects of the SDs:

- **diagram-related formulae**, which concern the beginning and the end of the execution of each SD, and the transition between a SD and the next one(s);

- **message-related formulae**, which concern the ordering of the events within a single SD;
- **component-related formulae**, which describe constraints on the execution of operations within single components.

These subsets are presented in the rest of this section.

Diagram-related Formulae. In this presentation of the semantics of IODs we assume, for the sake of simplicity, that, within each SD of an IOD, messages are totally ordered, hence we can clearly identify a begin message and an ending message. This assumption is not restrictive because, given any IOD that does not satisfy it, we can use the fork/join operators to obtain an equivalent IOD that satisfies the assumption, simply by splitting diagrams where messages may occur in parallel, into diagrams where messages are totally ordered. Then, for each SD D_x, it is possible to identify two messages, m_s and m_e, which correspond to the start and the end of the diagram. For each SD D_x, we introduce predicates D_xSTART and D_xEND that are true, respectively, at the beginning and at the end of the diagram. We also introduce, for each message m appearing in diagram D_x, a predicate m that holds in all instants in which the message occurs in the system (this entails that components synchronize on messages: send and receive of a message occur at the same time). Then, the correspondence between D_xSTART (resp. D_xEND) and the starting (resp. ending) message m_s (resp. m_e) is formalized by formulae (1-2)[3]. In addition, we introduce a predicate D_x that holds in all instants in which diagram D_x is executing; hence, predicate D_x holds between D_xSTART and D_xEND, as stated by formula (3).

$$D_xSTART \Leftrightarrow m_s \qquad (1)$$
$$D_xEND \Leftrightarrow m_e \qquad (2)$$
$$D_x \Leftrightarrow D_xSTART \vee \text{Since}(\neg D_xEND, D_xSTART) \qquad (3)$$

For example, the instances of formulae (1-3) for diagram *delegateSMS* correspond to formulae (4-6).

$$delegateSMSSTART \Leftrightarrow downloadSMS \qquad (4)$$
$$delegateSMSEND \Leftrightarrow reply3 \qquad (5)$$
$$delegateSMS \Leftrightarrow delegateSMSSTART \vee \qquad (6)$$
$$\text{Since}(\neg delegateSMSEND, delegateSMSSTART)$$

Notice that if the IOD contains k different occurrences of the same message m, k different predicates $m_0...m_k$ are introduced. For this reason in formula (5) *reply3* appears instead of *reply*.

---

[3] Note that TRIO formulae are implicitly temporally closed with the Alw operator; hence, $D_xSTART \Leftrightarrow m_s$ is actually an abbreviation for $\text{Alw}(D_xSTART \Leftrightarrow m_s)$.

A diagram D_x is followed by a diagram D_y for either of two reasons: (1) D_x is directly connected to D_y, in this case the end of D_x is a sufficient condition to start D_y; (2) D_x is connected to D_y through some *decision* operator, in this case a sufficient condition for D_y to start is given by the end of D_x, provided (i.e. conjoined with the requirement that) the condition associated with the decision operator is true. If a diagram D_x is preceded by p sequence diagrams, we introduce p predicates $D_x ACTC_i$ ($i \in \{1...p\}$), where $D_x ACTC_i$ holds if the i-th sufficient condition to start diagram D_x holds. We also introduce predicate $D_x ACT$, which holds if any of the p necessary conditions holds, as defined by formula (7). After the necessary condition to start a diagram is met, the diagram will start at some point in the future, as stated by formula (8). Finally, after a diagram starts, it cannot start again until the necessary condition to start it is met anew, as defined by formula (9).

$$D_x ACT \Leftrightarrow D_x ACTC_0 \vee ... \vee D_x ACTC_m \qquad (7)$$
$$D_x ACT \Rightarrow \mathrm{SomF}(D_x START) \qquad (8)$$
$$D_x START \Rightarrow \neg \mathrm{SomF}(D_x START) \vee \mathrm{Until}(\neg D_x START, D_x ACT) \qquad (9)$$

In the case of SD *downloadSMS* of Figure 2, the instances of formulae (7-9) are given by (12-14). In addition, formulae (10-11) define the necessary conditions to start diagram *downloadSMS*: either diagram *delegateSMS* ends, or diagram *downloadSMS* ends and condition *moredata* holds. Currently, we can only deal with atomic Boolean conditions. The representation of more complex data, and conditions upon them, is already in our research agenda.

$$downloadSMSACTC_1 \Leftrightarrow delegateSMSEND \qquad (10)$$
$$downloadSMSACTC_2 \Leftrightarrow downloadSMSEND \wedge moredata \qquad (11)$$
$$downloadSMSACT \Leftrightarrow \begin{pmatrix} downloadSMSACTC_1 \\ \vee\ downloadSMSACTC_2 \end{pmatrix} \qquad (12)$$

$$downloadSMSACT \Rightarrow \mathrm{SomF}(downloadSMSSTART) \qquad (13)$$
$$downloadSMSSTART \Rightarrow$$
$$\neg \mathrm{SomF}(downloadSMSSTART) \vee$$
$$\mathrm{Until}(\neg downloadSMSSTART, downloadSMSACT) \qquad (14)$$

Message-related Formulae. Suppose that, in a SD, a message m_i is followed by another message m_j. Then the occurrence of m_i entails that m_j will also occur in the future; conversely, the occurrence of m_j entails that m_i must have occurred in the past. This is formalized by formulae (15-16). In addition, after an instance of m_j, there can be a new instance of the same message only after a new occurrence of m_i; this is stated by formula (17), which defines that, after m_j, there will not be a new occurrence of m_j until there is an occurrence of m_i.

$$m_i \Rightarrow \text{SomF}(m_j) \land \neg m_j \tag{15}$$
$$m_j \Rightarrow \text{SomP}(m_i) \land \neg m_i \tag{16}$$
$$m_j \Rightarrow \neg\text{SomF}(m_j) \lor \text{Until}(\neg m_j, m_i) \tag{17}$$

If, for example, formulae (15-17) are instantiated for SD *checkingSMS* of Figure 2, one obtains formulae (18-20).

$$checkSMS \Rightarrow \text{SomF}(reply1) \land \neg reply1 \tag{18}$$
$$reply1 \Rightarrow \text{SomP}(checkSMS) \land \neg checkSMS \tag{19}$$
$$checkSMS \Rightarrow \neg\text{SomF}(checkSMS) \lor \text{Until}(\neg checkSMS, reply1) \tag{20}$$

Component-related Formulae. This set of formulae describes the conditions under which the entities of the system are busy, hence cannot perform further operations until they become free again. For example, in the telephone system of Figure 2, when the execution is inside the *checkingSMS* diagram, the *ConnectionUnit* cannot perform any other operations during the time interval between the invocation of operation *ckechSMS* and its corresponding *reply* message, since the invocation is synchronous (as highlighted by the full arrow).

In general, a synchronous invocation between objects A and B that starts with message m_i and ends with message m_j blocks both components from the moment of the invocation until its end; this is formalized by formulae (21-22), in which h and k are indexes identifying the occurrences of invocations (either received of issued) related to objects A and B in the IOD. In case of an asynchronous message m between A and B (such as, for example, *incomingCall* in SD *waitingCall*, as denoted by the wire-like arrow), the semantics is the one defined by formulae (23-24), which state that the objects are blocked only in the instant in which the message occurs.

$$m_i \lor \text{Since}(\neg m_j, m_i) \Leftrightarrow ABLOCKED_h \tag{21}$$
$$m_i \lor \text{Since}(\neg m_j, m_i) \Leftrightarrow BBLOCKED_k \tag{22}$$
$$m \Leftrightarrow ABLOCKED_h \tag{23}$$
$$m \Leftrightarrow BBLOCKED_k \tag{24}$$

Finally, if n is the number of occurrences of invocations involving object A in the IOD, formula (25) states that all executions involving A are mutually exclusive.

$$\forall 1 \leq i, j \leq n (i \neq j \land ABLOCKED_i \Rightarrow \neg ABLOCKED_j) \tag{25}$$

The following formulae are instances of (21-25) for object *ConnectionUnit*, which is involved in four separate invocations in the IOD of Figure 2:

$ConnectionUnitBLOCKED1 \Leftrightarrow checkSMS \vee$
$\qquad \text{Since}(\neg reply1, checkSMS)$
$ConnectionUnitBLOCKED2 \Leftrightarrow incomingCall$
$ConnectionUnitBLOCKED3 \Leftrightarrow downloadSMS \vee$
$\qquad \text{Since}(\neg reply2, donwloadSMS)$
$ConnectionUnitBLOCKED4 \Leftrightarrow beginCall \vee$
$\qquad \text{Since}(\neg reply3, beginCall)$
$\forall 1 \leq i, j \leq 4 (i \neq j \wedge ConnectionUnitBLOCKED_i \Rightarrow$
$\qquad \neg ConnectionUnitBLOCKED_j)$

4.3 Properties

Using the formalization presented above, we can check whether the modeled system satisfies some user-defined properties or not, by feeding it as input to the Zot verification tool.[4]

We start by asking whether it is true that, if no SMS is received in the future, then nothing will ever be downloaded. This property is formalized by the following formula:

$$\neg \text{SomF}(SMS) \Rightarrow \neg \text{SomF}(downloadSMS) \qquad (26)$$

After feeding it the system and the property to be verified, the Zot tool determines that the latter *does not* hold for the telephone system of Figure 2. In fact, between the check for a new SMS and its download there can be an arbitrary delay; hence, the situation in which the last SMS has been received, but it has not yet been downloaded, violates the property. Zot returns this counterexample in around 8.5 seconds.[5]

The following variation of the property above, instead, holds for the system:

$$\neg(\text{SomP}(SMS) \vee SMS) \Rightarrow \neg \text{WithinF}(downloadSMS, 3) \qquad (27)$$

Formula (27) states that, if no SMS has yet been received, for the next 3 instants there will not be an SMS download. Zot takes about 7 seconds to determine that formula (27) holds.

The following formula states that after a *nextSMSToken* request from *TransmissionUnit* to *Server*, no data concerning an incoming call can be received by the *TransmissionUnit* until a new SMS is received.

$$nextSMSToken \Rightarrow \text{Until}(\neg receiveCallData, receiveSMSToken) \qquad (28)$$

---

[4] The complete Zot model can be downloaded from
  http://home.dei.polimi.it/rossi/telephone.lisp
[5] All tests have been performed with a time bound of 50 time units (see [16] for the role of time bounds in Bounded Model/Satisfiabliity Checking), using the Common Lisp compiler SBCL 1.0.29.11 on a 2.80GHz Core2 Duo laptop with Linux and 4 GB RAM. The verification engine used was the SMT-based Zot plugin introduced in [2], with Microsoft Z3 2.8 (http://research.microsoft.com/en-us/um/redmond/projects/z3/) as the SMT solver.

Zot verifies that property (28) does not hold in around 8 seconds. As witnessed by the counterexample produced by Zot, the reason why (28) does not hold is that the *downloadSMS* diagram and the *receiveCall* diagram can run in parallel, and after sending a *nextSMSToken* message the *TransmissionUnit* and the *Server* are free to exchange a *receiveCallData* message.

4.4 Complexity

In this section we estimate the complexity of the translation from the IOD of the system into a set of temporal logic formulas. The purpose of this analysis is to provide an *a priori* estimation of the feasibility of the approach, i.e., to ensure that the approach is scalable and effectively implementable by means of an automatic software tool. It is to be noted that the estimation of the number of predicates and formulas produced by the translation procedure does not allow us to draw conclusions about the complexity of the algorithms for model verification (e.g., through simulation or property proof), because this depends on several features of the verification engine that will be employed by the verification tool (which could be, for instance, a SAT-based or SMT-based solver). Such an analysis is therefore left for future work.

We measure the complexity of the translation in terms of the number of predicates and the size of the TRIO formulas that are produced, and we consider, as parameters of such evaluation, the number n_d of SDs in the IOD and the number n_o of objects composing the system. The worst case occurs when every SD is connected to all the others (including itself) in an IOD, and thus every SD has n_d incoming flows. Moreover, still in a worst case scenario, every object in every SD sends one synchronous message to all the other objects in the system. According to these hypotheses, an estimation of the number of predicates and of the order of magnitude of the number of logic formulae generated by the translation can be carried out as follows.

For every SD the translation generates $3n_d$ predicates (D_x, D_xSTART, D_xEND) and $3n_d$ formulae according to axioms (1–3). Further, since every SD has n_d incoming flows the translation generates $n_d(n_d+1)$ predicates (D_xACTC_0, ..., $D_xACTC_{n_d}$, D_xACT) and $n_d(n_d + 3)$ formulae (7–9).

If we assume that every object in every SD sends one synchronous message to every other object in the same SD, we have $2n_dn_o(n_o - 1)$ messages. Every message instance has its own predicate and this results in $2n_dn_o(n_o-1)$ generated predicates. Moreover we have $5 \cdot 2n_dn_o(n_o - 1)$ generated formulae, according to axioms (15–17,21,22).

Finally, since every object is blocked while sending or receiving a message, in every SD the number of operation executions for a single object is $2(n_o - 1)$ (the object sends $n_o - 1$ messages and receives $n_o - 1$ messages). This generates $n_dn_o2(n_o - 1)$ predicates overall. The mutual exclusion of these predicates is stated in axiom (25); because every object has $n_d2(n_o-1)$ operation executions, we have $n_d2(n_o - 1)(n_d2(n_o - 1) - 1)$ instances of axiom (25) for each object, and $n_on_d2(n_o - 1)(n_d2(n_o - 1) - 1)$ formulae overall.

If n_{dec} is the number of decision operators in the IOD, the overall number of predicates is:
$$3n_d + n_d(n_d + 1) + 4n_d n_o(n_o - 1) + n_{dec}$$
which is in the order of $O(n_d^2 + n_d n_o^2)$, since the number n_{dec} of decision operators can be safely assumed to be $O(n_d)$; also, the overall number of formulae is:
$$3n_d + n_d(n_d + 3) + 5 \cdot 2n_d n_o(n_o - 1) + n_o n_d 2(n_o - 1)(n_d 2(n_o - 1) - 1)$$
which is in the order of $O(n_d^2 * n_o^3)$.

Note, however, that real-world models do not follow this kind of worst-case topology. For a more realistic analysis, we can assume that each diagram is connected to a constant number of diagrams (n_d^c, number of diagrams connected, which also entails that the number of decision operators is a constant n_{dec}^c), and that each object sends a constant number of messages (e.g., m synchronous messages) to the other objects. In this case, the number of predicates becomes:
$$3n_d + n_d(n_d^c + 1) + 4n_d n_o m + n_{dec}^c$$
which is in the order of $O(n_d n_o)$, and the number of formulae becomes:
$$3n_d + n_d(n_d^c + 3) + 5 \cdot 2n_d n_o m + n_o n_d 2m(n_d 2m - 1)$$
which is in the order of $O(n_d^2 n_o)$.

Looking at the number of formulae, the term that weighs the most is the last one, which originates from the fact that every execution occurrence cannot be true at the same time instant as another execution occurrence. This can only happen if the execution occurrences are inside diagrams that can be executed in parallel (because of fork operators). If we assume, like in our example, that the system only has p parallel paths, then the generated number of formulae becomes: $3n_d + n_d(n_d^c + 3) + 5 \cdot 2n_d n_o m + n_o n_d 2m(\frac{n_d}{p} 2m - 1)$, but its complexity remains in the order of $O(n_d^2 n_o)$. Also, the number of predicates is not affected.

If the system is implemented in a modular fashion, we can also assume that each object does not appear in every SD, but that each diagram comprises a maximum number n_o^d of objects. This means that an object is used in $\frac{n_d n_o^d}{n_o}$ diagrams, and it has $2m \frac{n_d n_o^d}{n_o}$ execution occurrences. These hypotheses transform the number of generated predicates into:
$$3n_d + n_d(n_d^c + 1) + 4n_d n_o^d m + n_{dec}^c$$
which is in the order of $O(n_d)$ and the number of generated formulae into:
$$3n_d + n_d(n_d^c + 3) + 5 \cdot 2n_d n_o^d m + n_o(2m \frac{n_d n_o^d}{n_o})((2m \frac{n_d n_o^d}{n_o}) - 1)$$
with a further reduction to the order of $O(\frac{n_d^2}{n_o})$.

The above complexity figures agree with the intuition that the verification can be carried out more efficiently if the model of the system under analysis is adequately modularized.

Finally, note that the current formal model has not yet been optimized to minimize the number of generated formulae: improvements can surely be obtained, at least as far as the constant factors in the above complexity measures are concerned.

5 Related Work

The research community has devoted a significant effort to studying ways to give a formal semantics to scenario-based specifications such as UML sequence diagrams, UML interaction diagrams, and Message Sequence Charts (MSCs).

Many works focus on the separate formalization of sequence diagrams and activity diagrams. Störrle analyzes the semantics of these diagrams and proposes an approach to their formalization [18]. More recently, Staines formalizes UML2 activity diagrams using Petri nets and proposes a technique to achieve this transformation [17]. Also, Lam formalizes the execution of activity diagrams using the $\pi - Calculus$, thus providing them with a sound theoretical foundation [13]. Finally, Eshuis focuses on activity diagrams, and defines a technique to translate them into finite state machines that can be automatically verified [9][8].

Other works investigate UML2 interaction diagrams. Cengarle and Knapp in [6] provide an operational semantics to UML 2 interactions, and in [5] they address the lack of UML interactions to explicitly describe variability and propose extensions equipped with a denotational semantics. Knapp and Wuttke translate UML2 interactions into automata and then verify that the proposed design meets the requirements stated in the scenarios by using model checking [12].

When multiple scenarios come into play, like in IODs, there is the problem of finding a common semantics. Uchitel and Kramer in [19] propose an MSC-based language with a semantics defined in terms of labeled transition systems and parallel composition, which is translated into Finite Sequential Processes that can be model-checked and animated. Harel and Kugler in [10] use Live Sequence Charts (LCSs) to model multiple scenarios, and to analyze satisfiability and synthesis issues.

To the best of our knowledge very little attention has been paid to IODs. Kloul and Küster-Filipe [11] show how to model mobility using IODs and propose a formal semantics to the latter by translating them into the stochastic process algebra PEPA nets. Tebibel uses hierarchical colored Petri nets to define a formal semantics for IODs [4]. Our work is quite different, because it uses metric temporal logic to define the semantics of IODs; as briefly discussed in Sections 1 and 6, this opens many possibilities as far as the range of properties that can be expressed and analyzed for the system is concerned.

6 Conclusions and Future Works

In this paper we presented the first steps towards a technique to precisely model and analyze complex, heterogeneous, embedded systems using an intuitive UML-based notation. To this end, we started by focusing our attention on Interaction

Overview Diagrams, which allow users to describe rich behaviors by combining together simple Sequence Diagrams. To allow designers to rigorously analyze modeled systems, the basic constructs of IODs have been given a formal semantics based on metric temporal logic, which has been used to prove some properties of an example system.

The work presented in this paper is part of a longer-term research, and it will be extended in several ways.

First, the metric features of TRIO will be used to extend the formalization of SDs and IODs to real-time features that will be introduced in the modeling language by providing support for the MARTE UML profile.

Furthermore, we will provide semantics to constructs of IODs that are not yet covered. This semantics will be used to create tools to automatically translate IODs into the input language of the Zot tool, and to show designers the feedback from the verification tool (e.g., counterexamples) in a user-friendly way. In particular, we will define mechanisms to render graphically the counterexamples provided by Zot as SDs. These tools will allow domain experts who have little or no background in formal verification techniques to take advantage of these techniques in the analysis of complex systems.

References

1. Bagnato, A., Sadovykh, A., Paige, R.F., Kolovos, D.S., Baresi, L., Morzenti, A., Rossi, M.: MADES: Embedded systems engineering approach in the avionics domain. In: Proceedings of the First Workshop on Hands-on Platforms and Tools for Model-Based Engineering of Embedded Systems, HoPES (2010)
2. Bersani, M.M., Frigeri, A., Pradella, M., Rossi, M., Morzenti, A., San Pietro, P.: Bounded reachability for temporal logic over constraint systems. In: Proc. of the Int. Symp. on Temporal Representation and Reasoning (TIME), pp. 43–50 (2010)
3. Blohm, G., Bagnato, A.: D1.1 requirements specification. Technical report, MADES Consortium, Draft (2010)
4. Bouabana-Tebibel, T.: Semantics of the interaction overview diagram. In: Proc. of the IEEE Int. Conf. on Information Reuse Integration (IRI), pp. 278–283 (2009)
5. Cengarle, M.V., Graubmann, P., Wagner, S.: Semantics of UML 2.0 interactions with variabilities. Elec. Notes in Theor. Comp. Sci. 160, 141–155 (2006)
6. Cengarle, M.V., Knapp, A.: Operational semantics of UML 2.0 interactions. Technical Report TUM-I0505, Technische Universität Mnchen (2005)
7. Ciapessoni, E., Coen-Porisini, A., Crivelli, E., Mandrioli, D., Mirandola, P., Morzenti, A.: From formal models to formally-based methods: an industrial experience. ACM TOSEM 8(1), 79–113 (1999)
8. Eshuis, R.: Symbolic model checking of UML activity diagrams. ACM Trans. Softw. Eng. Methodol. 15(1), 1–38 (2006)
9. Eshuis, R., Wieringa, R.: Tool support for verifying UML activity diagrams. IEEE Trans. Software Eng. 30(7), 437–447 (2004)
10. Harel, D., Kugler, H.: Synthesizing state-based object systems from LSC specifications. In: Yu, S., Păun, A. (eds.) CIAA 2000. LNCS, vol. 2088, pp. 1–33. Springer, Heidelberg (2001)
11. Kloul, L., Küster-Filipe, J.: From intraction overview diagrams to PEPA nets. In: Proc. of the Work. on Process Algebra and Stochastically Timed Activities (2005)

12. Knapp, A., Wuttke, J.: Model checking of UML 2.0 interactions. In: Models in Software Engineering. LNCS, vol. 4634, pp. 42–51 (2007)
13. Lam, V.S.W.: On π-calculus semantics as a formal basis for uml activity diagrams. International Journal of Software Engineering and Knowledge Engineering (2008)
14. Object Management Group. UML Profile for Modeling and Analysis of Real-Time Embedded Systems. Technical report, OMG (2009) formal/2009-11-02
15. Object Management Group. OMG Unified Modeling Language (OMG UML), Superstructure. Technical report, OMG (2010) formal/2010-05-05.
16. Pradella, M., Morzenti, A., San Pietro, P.: The symmetry of the past and of the future: bi-infinite time in the verification of temporal properties. In: Proceedings of ESEC/SIGSOFT FSE, pp. 312–320 (2007)
17. Staines, T.S.: Intuitive mapping of UML 2 activity diagrams into fundamental modeling concept petri net diagrams and colored petri nets. In: Proc. of the IEEE Int. Conf. on the Engineering of Computer-Based Systems, pp. 191–200 (2008)
18. Störrle, H., Hausmann, J.H.: Towards a formal semantics of UML 2.0 activities. In: Software Engineering. Lect. Notes in Inf., vol. 64, pp. 117–128 (2005)
19. Uchitel, S., Kramer, J.: A workbench for synthesising behaviour models from scenarios. In: Proc. of the Int. Conf. on Software Engineering, pp. 188–197 (2001)

Report of the 15th International Workshop on Aspect-Oriented Modeling

Jeff Gray[1], Dominik Stein[2], Jörg Kienzle[3], and Walter Cazzola[4]

[1] Department of Computer and Information Sciences, University of Alabama, Tuscaloosa, AL, USA
[2] Institute for Computer Science and Business Information Systems, University of Duisburg-Essen, Essen, Germany
[3] School of Computer Science, McGill University, Montreal, QC, Canada
[4] Department of Informatics and Communication, University of Milano, Italy
gray@cs.ua.edu, dominik.stein@icb.uni-due.de, Joerg.Kienzle@mcgill.ca, cazzola@dico.unimi.it

Abstract. This report summarizes the outcome of the 15th Workshop on Aspect-Oriented Modeling (AOM) held in conjunction with the 13th International Conference on Model Driven Engineering Languages and Systems – MoDELS 2010 – in Oslo, Norway, on the 4th of October 2010. The workshop brought together researchers and practitioners from two communities: aspect-oriented software development (AOSD) and software model engineering. This report gives an overview of the accepted and presented submissions, and summarizes the questions addressed in the discussion.

1 Introduction

This report summarizes the outcome of the 15th edition of the successful Aspect-Oriented Modeling Workshop series. An overview of what happened at previous editions of the workshop can be found at http://dawis2.icb.uni-due.de/aom/. The workshop took place at the Oslo Congress Center in Oslo, Norway on Monday, October 4th 2010, as part of the 13th International Conference on Model Driven Engineering Languages and Systems – MoDELS 2010.

Participation to the workshop was open to anyone attending the conference, and as a result there were approximately 25 participants. A total of 9 position papers were submitted and reviewed by the program committee, 7 of which were presented at the workshop.

The rest of this report is structured as follows: Section 2 gives an overview of the presentations of the accepted papers that took place in the morning sessions. Section 3 gives an overview of the questions that were voiced in the second afternoon session. Section 4 concludes the report.

2 Overview of Presentations

Marko Boscovic from Athabasca University in Canada presented the paper "Aspect-Oriented Feature Models" [1]. In his presentation he argued that feature models for real-world systems tend to grow very large in size, citing as an example the feature model of the Linux Kernel which contains over 6000 features. Since feature models are trees, repetition of features or even entire subtrees of features is not uncommon. In consequence he suggests to apply aspect-oriented modularization techniques to reuse subtrees of features at several places within a model and also to share subtrees of features among different feature models. The proposed Aspect Feature Models (AFM) make it possible to define features of crosscutting concerns separately, and then to define a Pointcut Feature Model (PFM) to express patterns and composition rules that define how the AFM is to be composed with a base feature model. Tagging of model elements in the PFM allows a developer to specify which features of the base are to be matched, which features are to be added to the base, which features are to be removed from the base, and, as an interesting novelty, which features are to be removed from the AFM. This last technique makes it possible to define generic AFMs that can be applied in the context of different software product lines, even if not all features from the AFM are to be used in the base model.

Leonardo Tizzei from the University of Campinas in Brazil presented "An Aspect-oriented View to Support Feature-oriented Reengineering" [2]. He pointed out that feature selection impacts the product line architecture, which impacts the design, and that hence early identification of concerns is important. He showed how to add aspect-oriented feature views to the feature-oriented reengineering process, an approach that provides guidelines for developers to build software product lines from legacy applications. In Tizzei's approach, an aspect-oriented feature view comprises crosscutting features (represented by a diamond in the feature diagram) and standard non-crosscutting features, as well as "crosscuts" and "preceded-by" relationships among them. The resulting feature view is therefore an acyclic graph, as opposed to standard feature diagrams which are usually trees. Tizzei also showed how to extend the feature-oriented reengineering process with aspect-oriented feature analysis, defining guidelines on how to produce an aspect-oriented feature view.

Mauricio Alférez from the Universidade Nova de Lisboa in Portugal presented the paper "Towards Consistency between Features and SPL Use Cases" [3]. He argued that in the context of software product line (SPL) engineering consistency checking, i.e. the description and verification of semantic relationships among system views and models, between feature models in the domain space and their realizations in the solution space is crucial. In his presentation he proposed an aspect-oriented, requirements-specific composition language that allows developers to describe consistency constraints between a feature model for a SPL and a set of use cases of the SPL. The work goes beyond checking for syntactic conformness of the feature model and use case model to their meta models. With the approach it is possible to verify the consistency of domain constraints (e.g., *requires* and *excludes* relationships in feature models) with the relationships among elements in a use case model (e.g. *includes*, *generalization* and *containment* between use cases) according to the established mapping between the models.

Everton Tavares from the Pontifical Catholic University of Rio de Janeiro in Brazil presented an empirical study in his paper entitled "Analyzing the Effects of Aspect Properties on Model Composition Effort: A Replicated Study" [4] that compared the effects of aspect-oriented modeling to non-aspect-oriented modeling when developers need to perform model composition. The study, which was the second of this kind performed by the authors, aimed in particular at analyzing if obliviousness has an effect on the number of model composition conflicts. The experiment was performed on component models and aspect-oriented component models of subsequent releases of the Health Watcher system. The composition conflict rates were gathered manually and quantified by a set of conflict metrics. The results confirmed the results from a previous study, which showed that the advanced modularization of aspect-oriented models was beneficial in localizing model conflicts. The experiment also confirmed that a higher degree of obliviousness between the base model and the aspect model led to a significant decrease of conflicts, whereas aspects with higher degree of quantification were the cause of higher conflict rates.

Aram Hovsepyan from the Catholic University of Leuven in Belgium presented the design of an empirical study in his paper entitled "An Experimental Design for Evaluating the Maintainability of Aspect-Oriented Models Enhanced with Domain-Specific Constructs" [5], which aimed at investigating if there is a benefit to keeping concerns that have been identified at the modeling level also separate at the implementation level, or, in other words, if weaving should be done at the model level or if is it better to map models to apsect-oriented code and rely on a code weaver to produce the executable model. To answer this question, Aram proposes three empirical studies: 1) a quantitative one, which uses static analysis of the final systems obtained using both approaches to collect size metrics, coupling and cohesion, and scattering and tangling metrics; 2) a quantitative user study, in which the time developers need to complete a set of maintenance tasks (2 functional with impact on non-functional aspects, and 2 non-functional tasks with impact on functionality) using either of the two approaches as well as the number of errors made is gathered and evaluated; 3) an open interview and task specific questionnaire with positive and negative questions.

Max Kramer from McGill University in Canada talked about the challenge of "Mapping Aspect-Oriented Models to Aspect-Oriented Code" [6]. By showing how to map a concrete aspect modeled using the Reusable Aspect Models modeling approach to the aspect-oriented programming language AspectJ, Max highlighted the general issues that need to be addressed when defining such a mapping: mapping structure and behaviour of a single aspect, mapping the instantiation of structure and behaviour within a target model, mapping conflict resolution between aspect models, and mapping aspect dependencies and variabilities, if any. The solutions he presented make use of AspectJ's annotation and reflection mechanisms and support sophisticated aspect-oriented modeling constructs such as recursive advice and generic aspects with type parameters. Other mapping rules ensure for example that all intended information from the modeling level is conveyed to the code by automatically reusing Java libraries and by generating default implementations for common design patterns. In addition to these solution strategies, Max presented a first evaluation of this model to code mapping using an extended case study for transactions. More than 84% of the final AspectJ code for the transaction system and more than 96% of the code for its extension were obtained using the presented mapping.

Dominik Stein from the University of Duisburg-Essen in Germany presented the paper "Facilitating the Exploration of Join Point Selection In Aspect-Oriented Models [7]". He outlined a scenario in which developers frequently look at the woven results of an aspect-oriented weaver in order to understand how a join point selection is effectuated, and he detailed the problems that they are facing when they need to gather all relevant model chunks (or code chunks) from the woven result, and to infer their interdependencies. As a solution, he presents a mapping which translates the specification of a join point selection (expressed as a "JPDD") into a description of the selection process (expressed in terms of states and state transitions). He argues that by means of such (state-based) description of the selection *process*, developers are freed from reconstructing that selection process from the woven results. Instead, they are pointed to the (and only the) relevant steps of join point selection right away as well as to their interdependencies. In consequence, developers are expected to understand easier why certain join points are (are not) selected. The description of the selection process may be still complex, but it is not tangled with the base model. Stein sees possible application domains for this mapping in the development of new aspect weavers or in the debugging of applications.

3 Question Addressed in the Discussion Session

The following research questions have been gathered by the audience and have been addressed during the discussion session in the afternoon:

- How do we map requirements to features? What kind of process can be used?
- Should we preserve feature modularity at the code level?
- What is the relation between features and model fragments?
- Is the information in a feature model sufficient to compose the model fragments?
- What are advantages and disadvantages of different ways to resolve conflicts among aspects in feature models (LTL, Alloy, SAT solvers...)?
- How can we assess aspect-oriented feature models quantitatively and qualitatively?
- Is there any metric suite to evaluate AOM at early phases?
- Is aspect-oriented programming vs. aspect-oriented modeling similar to feature-oriented programming vs. feature-oriented modeling?
- How much modeling should we do with MDD in general and with AOM in particular (simpler structure vs. complex behaviour vs. full specification)?
- How do the aspects/concerns that are identified on different levels relate to each other (e.g. requirements → feature model → design → code)?

- What are some large and open experimental platforms that can be used for assessment?
- What kind of validation can be done? Syntactic? Semantic?
- Can we define a model for aspect interferences?

4 Concluding Remarks

The organizers for this edition of the workshop were Walter Cazzola, Jeff Gray, Jörg Kienzle, and Dominik Stein. An expert program committee provided assistance in reviewing the submitted papers. The members of the program committee were Aswin van den Berg, Phil Greenwood, Stefan Hanenberg, Philippe Lahire, Ana Moreira, Alfonso Pierantonio, Ella Roubtsova, Pablo Sánchez, Bedir Tekinerdogan, and Julie Vachon. Last but not least, we'd like to thank all submitters and participants of the workshop who contributed with their papers and positions.

References

1. Boskovic, M., Mussbacher, G., Bagheri, E., Amyot, D., Gasevic, D., Hatala, M.: Aspect-oriented Feature Models. In: Proceedings of the 15th International Workshop on Aspect-Oriented Modeling (October 2010)
2. Tizzei, L., Lee, J., Rubira, C.M.: An Aspect-oriented View to Support Feature-oriented Reengineering. In: Proceedings of the 15th International Workshop on Aspect-Oriented Modeling (October 2010)
3. Alferez, M., Lopez-Herrejon, R.E., Moreira, A., Amaral, V., Egyed, A.: Towards Consistency between Features and SPL Use Cases. In: Proceedings of the 15th International Workshop on Aspect-Oriented Modeling (October 2010)
4. Guimaraes, E., Garcia, A., Ferias, K.: Analyzing the Effects of Aspect Properties on Model Composition Effort: A Replicated Study. In: Proceedings of the 15th International Workshop on Aspect-Oriented Modeling (October 2010)
5. Hovsepyan, A., Baelen, S., Scandariato, R., Joosen, W.: An Experimental Design for Evaluating the Maintainability of Aspect-Oriented Models Enhanced with Domain-Specific Constructs. In: Proceedings of the 15th International Workshop on Aspect-Oriented Modeling (October 2010)
6. Kramer, M.E., Kienzle, J.: Mapping Aspect-Oriented Models to Aspect-Oriented Code. In: Proceedings of the 15th International Workshop on Aspect-Oriented Modeling (October 2010)
7. Stein, D., Sanchez, P., Hahnenberg, S., Fuentes, L., Unland, R.: Facilitating the Exploration of Join Point Selection In Aspect-Oriented Models. In: Proceedings of the 15th International Workshop on Aspect-Oriented Modeling (October 2010)

Aspect-Oriented Feature Models

Marko Bošković[1,3], Gunter Mussbacher[2], Ebrahim Bagheri[1,4], Daniel Amyot[2], Dragan Gašević[1,3], and Marek Hatala[3]

[1] SCIS, Athabasca University
{marko.boskovic,ebagheri,dgasevic}@athabascau.ca
[2] SITE, University of Ottawa
{gunterm,damyot}@site.uottawa.ca
[3] SIAT, Simon Fraser University Surrey
mhatala@sfu.ca
[4] National Research Council Canada

Abstract. Software Product Lines (SPLs) have emerged as a prominent approach for software reuse. SPLs are sets of software systems called families that are usually developed as a whole and share many common features. Feature models are most typically used as a means for capturing commonality and managing variability of the family. A particular product from the family is configured by selecting the desired features of that product. Typically, feature models are considered monolithic entities that do not support modularization well. As industrial feature models tend to be large, their modularization has become an important research topic lately. However, existing modularization approaches do not support modularization of crosscutting concerns. In this paper, we introduce Aspect-oriented Feature Models (AoFM) and argue that using aspect-oriented techniques improves the manageability and reduces the maintainability effort of feature models. Particularly, we advocate an asymmetric approach that allows for the modularization of basic and crosscutting concerns in feature models.

Keywords: Software Product Lines, Feature Models, Aspect-oriented Modeling.

1 Introduction

The increase in the number of software systems containing extensive sets of common requirements has led to widespread interest in Software Product Line Engineering (SPLE) [26]. Software Product Line Engineering is a methodological framework for engineering Software Product Lines (SPLs), or *software families*. SPLs are sets of software systems with an extensive number of common functional and non-functional properties. SPLs are developed as a whole and share many assets, herewith increasing reusability.

An SPL generally consists of three kinds of artifacts, representing the problem space, the solution space, and the mappings between problem and solution spaces [10]. Artifacts in the solution space represent design and implementation of all members of the family. The problem space, on the other hand, is comprised of all the features for the family members. Typically, the problem space is captured with feature models. A *feature model*, first introduced by Kang [17], is represented with a feature diagram, a tree-like structure whose root represents the whole SPL and whose descendant nodes represent potential features of its members. A particular product of the family is defined by selecting the desired features from the feature model. Based on such feature selection and with the help of defined mappings, artifacts of the solution space are composed to form the desired product. The process of selecting desired features is called *configuration* and the set of selected features a *feature model configuration* [11].

Contemporary feature models often tend to grow very large in size and different groups of experts are usually dedicated to different parts of feature model development [14]. These parts must be assembled into one large feature model. Treating such large feature models as monolithic entities makes them very hard to develop, manage, understand, and evolve. Typically, every change performed on a feature model must be verified by experts with different expertise [23], which is time consuming and costly.

To address this problem, recent work by Mannion et al. [23], Hubaux et al. [14], and others introduce approaches for the modularization of feature models. However, separation of concerns can still be improved as these approaches lack support for the modularization of *crosscutting concerns* such as security and other non-functional properties. In this paper, we leverage principles of Aspect-oriented Modeling (AOM) [9] to address this issue. In dealing with similar problems, AOM has been applied in several requirement formalisms like use cases [15], problem frames [22], URN [25], and UML models [28]. By applying these principles, we therefore aim at enabling better understandability, maintainability, and scalability of feature models.

This paper presents Aspect-oriented Feature Models (AoFM), which introduce the notion of concerns in feature models. Particularly, we distinguish between non-crosscutting concerns called *base concerns* and crosscuting concerns called *aspects*. AoFM describes feature models for these two types of concerns as well as the specification of their *composition rules* with the aim to reduce the impact of changes in one concern's feature model on other concerns' feature models.

The reminder of the paper is as follows. Section 2 describes the basics of feature models. Our extension of basic feature modeling, i.e., AoFM, is introduced in Section 3. A validation of our approach by application to a trial case is given in Section 4. Section 5 highlights potential and promising enhancements to AoFM that require further investigation. Section 6 summarizes identified contemporary related work. Finally, Section 7 concludes the paper and discusses future work.

2 Feature Models

Feature models are widely accepted means of capturing commonality and managing variability within SPLs. They are modeled as feature diagrams, i.e., tree-like structures consisting of nodes that represent features of a modeled SPL and their

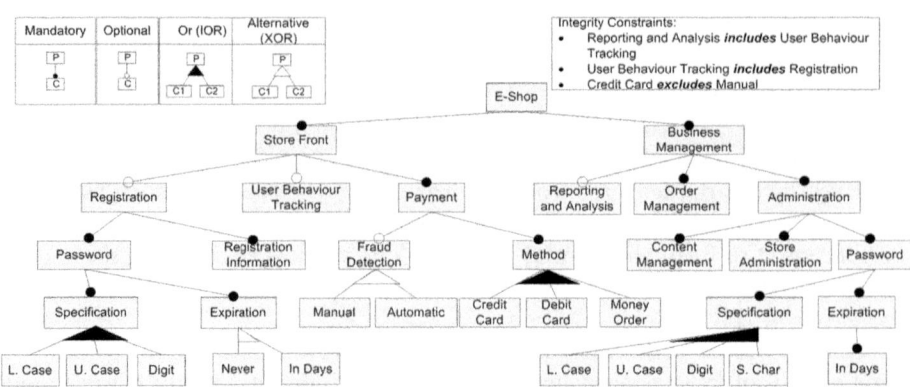

Fig. 1. An E-shop Feature Model

interrelationships. Figure 1 shows an example of a feature diagram of an E-shop SPL, inspired by Lau [21].

Typically, a feature diagram consists of features, specified as nodes, and of interfeature relationships. The latter are either *mandatory* and *optional* parent-child feature relationships or *alternative feature groups* and *or feature groups*, graphically presented in Figure 1. *Mandatory* parent-child relationships specify that, if a parent feature is included in a certain feature model configuration, its mandatory child features also have to be included (e.g., the relationships between the E-shop and Store Front features and the E-shop and Business management features specifying that every E-shop consists of the interface that the customer uses for accessing the E-shop and one concerned with back office operations, respectively). An *optional* parent-child relationship specifies that when a parent feature is selected in a configuration, its optional child features may but do not have to be included (e.g., the relationship between the Store Front and User Behaviour Tracking features). *Alternative feature groups* consist of features from which exactly one must be selected (XOR) (e.g., the group consisting of the Manual and Automatic features - fraud detection in an E-shop application can be either manual or automatic, but not both). An *or feature group* specifies a group of features from which at least one must be selected (IOR) (e.g., the group consisting of the Credit Card, Debit Card, and Money Order features - to enable customers to pay for selected items, at least one payment method must be selected).

Finally, feature models also contain feature relationships that cannot be captured with a tree structure. Such relationships are called cross-tree constraints, or integrity constraints [6]. Most often, these constraints are includes and excludes constraints. An *includes* constraint specifies a relationship between two features that ensures that one feature is selected when the other is. In the feature model in Figure 1, includes constraints exist between the Reporting and Analysis and User Behaviour Tracking features and between the User Behaviour Tracking and Registration features. The *excludes* integrity constraint specifies a relationship between two features that ensures that one feature is not selected when another one is. Such a constraint exists between the Credit Card and the Manual features.

Even in such a small example as in Figure 1, it can be recognized that not all features are of interest to the same stakeholders. While features for password policies are the major concern for security experts, they are not of high relevance to higher management. Furthermore, the developers of user interface functionality are not interested in back office operations and vice versa. Moreover, different parts of a family might require different security policies. Namely, the password policy for back office administration of an E-shop application is usually stricter compared to the user interface's and might require the inclusion of special characters and an expiration after a certain amount of days. For this reason, a subtree for password policy specification of back office administration contains the additional (S. Char) and (In Days) features. Finally, the addition of new security policies would result in revisions to sub-models related to security policy in the store front and back office sub-parts. Considering the size of contemporary feature models, separation of different concerns is an important task for achieving better understandability, maintainability, and scalability of models. To provide separation of concerns in feature models, we introduce AoFM in the next section.

3 Aspect-Oriented Feature Models

Aspect-oriented Modeling (AOM) applies concepts originating from Aspect-oriented Programming (AOP) [18] to requirements and design models. AOM emerged as one of the most prominent approaches for software modularization. Particularly, AOM facilitates modularization of aspects, i.e., concerns which cannot be encapsulated properly with other contemporary modularization techniques. Aspects are concerns that often repeat with small variations in other concerns. Examples of aspects are performance and security, each being implemented by different mechanisms such as load-balancing/caching and authentication/encryption, respectively. In AoFM, we distinguish between non-crosscutting concerns, or base concerns, and crosscutting concerns, or aspects. Note that this distinction, however, does not preclude aspects from being applied to other aspects.

3.1 Base Concerns in AoFM

Base concerns in feature models are specific *viewpoints* of a feature model [27]. Viewpoints are different perspectives on the same feature model. A viewpoint contains those parts of a feature diagram that are of interest to the users associated with the viewpoint. In the E-shop case study in Figure 1, we have identified three concerns as illustrated in Figure 2.

The E-shop System Concern is a high level business concern representing the major functionalities of the E-shop SPL. This base concern contains the root feature E-Shop and its two child features Store Front and Business Management. The User Interface Concern is a concern of particular interest to developers of user requirements and interactions. It contains the parts of the feature model representing Registration, User Behaviour Tracking, and Payment functionalities.

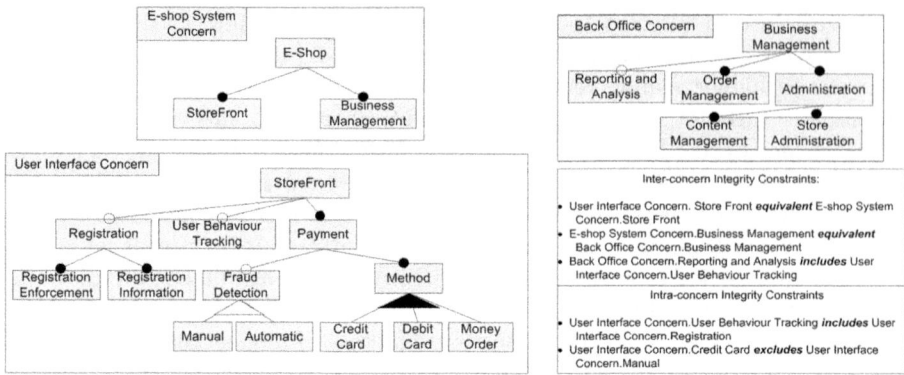

Fig. 2. Base Concerns in the E-shop Feature Model

In addition to the features in Figure 1, the User Interface Concern contains the Registration Enforcement feature which represents actions that mandate user registration such as buying products. Finally, the Back Office Concern contains all functionality related to the operation of an E-shop application.

Concerns in AoFM have the same tree-like structure and relationships as the basic feature models introduced in Section 2. However, the modularization of feature models into base concerns introduces two kinds of integrity constraints, namely intra- and inter-concern integrity constraints. *Intra-concern* integrity constraints exist between features of one concern. They are essentially the same as the integrity constraints of the basic feature models, i.e., includes and excludes constraints. In the example in Figure 2, there is an includes constraint between the User Behaviour Tracking and Registration features of the User Interface Concern and an excludes constraint between the Credit Card and Manual features of the User Interface Concern.

Inter-concern integrity constraints are specified between features in different concerns. The set of possible inter-concern constraints also contains includes and excludes constraints. To provide a way of representing the same feature in different concerns, we introduce the *equivalent* inter-concern integrity constraint. Such constraints enable the separation of base concerns that are not highly crosscutting but still should be encapsulated into their own modules based on the viewpoint principle mentioned earlier. Hence, inter-concern integrity constraints constitute the composition rules for base concerns. For example, an equivalent constraint exists between the Store Front feature of the E-shop System Concern and the Store Front feature of the User Interface Concern, allowing these two concerns to be sufficiently separated. Using equivalent constraints, the feature diagrams of base concerns can be re-composed, if desired, into the original, much larger, and more monolithic feature diagram.

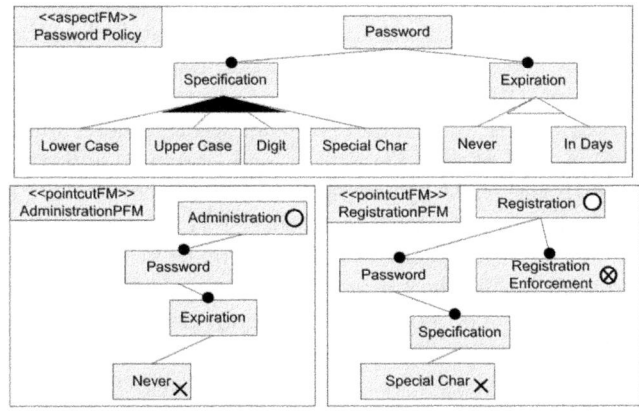

Fig. 3. Excerpt of Security Aspect Feature Model for E-shop SPL

3.2 Aspects in AoFM

To facilitate modeling of aspects in feature models, AoFM must support the specification of feature models for crosscutting concerns and their composition with base concerns. This composition requires the specification of:

- Patterns defining where the aspect is to be applied,
- Composition rules specifying how the aspect is to be applied at the locations identified by the patterns, and
- A join point model, i.e., the set of all locations that an aspect is allowed to change and hence may be matched by the patterns.

Therefore, we introduce the concepts of a) join point model for feature models, b) aspects, c) aspect feature models, d) pointcut feature models, e) patterns, and f) composition rules.

The *join point model* for feature models contains the feature nodes and integrity constraints of a feature diagram, allowing any feature node or integrity constraint to be changed by an aspect. *Aspects* are purely organizational units consisting of aspect feature models and pointcut feature models. An example of an aspect is the Security aspect of the E-shop case study, a portion of which is presented in Figure 3. It contains one aspect feature model and two pointcut feature models.

Aspect Feature Models (AFMs) are feature models of crosscutting concerns. Structurally, they do not differ from feature models of base concerns. In Figure 3, the Password Policy is the crosscutting concern of password policies, a sub-concern of the Security aspect. The Password Policy aspect defines the feature model for all possible password policies configurations.

Pointcut Feature Models (PFMs) express patterns as well as composition rules. Structurally, they are again not different from feature models of base concerns except that they may be tagged with two kinds of markers. Patterns and composition rules together must enable all changes an aspect in AoFM may possibly want to impose on a base concern, i.e., the adding and removal of feature diagram elements. To achieve this, the *pattern* to be matched in the base concern is first identified by the ◯ tag in the PFM. Second, any element from an AFM that is also used on a PFM is, by default, added to the matched base concern. The element from the AFM is added together with its descendant features and their relationships. In addition, we can also add features and relationships that are not specified in the AFM by simply specifying them in the PFM.

Third, any element tagged with × in the PFM is removed from the feature model. The × tag may be applied to an element from the AFM or an element already tagged with ◯. In the former case, this tag indicates that the element from the AFM is not to be added to the composed model. The same applies to the descendant features of the element from the AFM and their integrity constraints. In the latter case, the tag may be visualized as ⊗ and indicates that the matched element from the base concern is to be removed. Again, this applies to its descendant features and their relationships.

Beside features, integrity constraints can also be part of the matching pattern. Therefore, we apply the same operators on integrity constraints. Namely, if an integrity constraint needs to be matched it will be marked with the ◯ marker in the PFM. If it needs to be removed from the aspect, it will be marked with the × operator. Finally, if it needs to be matched in the base concern and removed, the operator ⊗ is used.

Therefore, the *composition rule* consists of a) the set of links in the PFM that connect elements tagged with ◯ and elements from the AFM, b) any remove operations indicated by the × tag, and c) any new integrity constraints between features of the target feature model and features of the aspect.

It is necessary to allow the specification of elements from the AFM that are not to be added to the matched base concern, because aspects in AoFM should be very generic and applicable to multiple SPLs from very different domains, i.e., an aspect is applied multiple times not to just one SPL but multiple times to multiple SPLs. Therefore, it is very likely that not all features of the aspect are applicable to all domains. Consequently, the × marker is necessary to indicate such features. Note that a PFM is invalid if the links among features from an AFM are not the same as the links defined in the AFM.

For example, two PFMs are defined in Figure 3. AdministrationPFM specifies adding a password policy to the Administration operations, while RegistrationPFM adds a password policy to the Registration feature in the base feature model. For AdministrationPFM, the pattern to be matched is the Administration feature as indicated by the ◯ tag. The composition rule for AdministrationPFM states that the complete Password feature sub-tree from the AFM except for the Never feature is to be attached to the Administration feature with a mandatory parent-child relationship. The Never feature and its relationship to the Expiration feature are excluded because of the × tag.

For RegistrationPFM, the pattern to be matched is the Registration and Registration Enforcement features connected with a mandatory parent-child relationship. The composition rule for RegistrationPFM states that the complete

Password feature sub-tree from the AFM except for the Special Char feature is to be attached to the Registration feature with a mandatory parent-child relationship. In addition, the Registration Enforcement feature and its relationship to the Registration feature must be removed from the base concern, as indicated by the ⊗ tag.

Finally, if there is a need for integrity constraints between features of target feature models and aspects, they are specified as part of the PFM.

4 Validation

To validate the proposed approach to feature modeling, we apply it to a trial case [24]. As a crosscutting concern, we use fault tolerance, and particularly the AspectOptima [19] framework, a framework consisting of aspects for implementing various transaction concurrency control and recovery mechanisms. We apply it to the Online Auction System, a case study introduced by Kienzle et al. [20] and whose feature model is presented in Figure 4.

The Online Auction System is a family of web-based systems that allows for selling and buying items by means of different types of auctions, like English, Dutch, and 1st Price. A particular member of the family may support any combination of these auction types. A User Interface of the system supports Starting Auction, Browsing Auction, Participating and Bidding in an auction, Closing an open auction, and browsing through the History of a user. Prior to performing these operations, a user has to carry out Registration and Login activities. Delivery of goods may be the responsibility of the seller, and quality of the delivery is in this case computed by buyers' Voting. Alternatively, a system may provide a special Escrow service that blocks the money of the buyer until the goods are received and the buyer is satisfied.

In an Online Auction System member, crashes of any of the client computers must not corrupt the state of the auction system. Therefore, there is a need for adding fault tolerance in the form of transactions to the system. As previously mentioned, we use the AspectOptima framework for this purpose and add transaction configuration options to the Registration and English Auction features. An AspectOptima feature model aspect is presented in Figure 5.

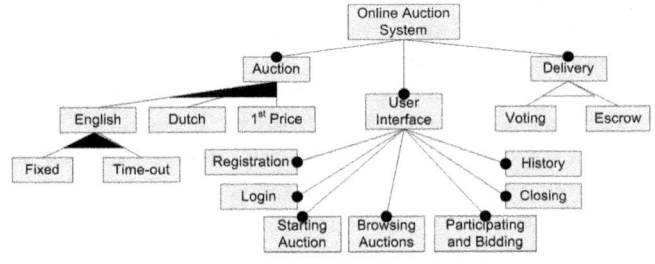

Fig. 4. An Online Auction System Feature Model

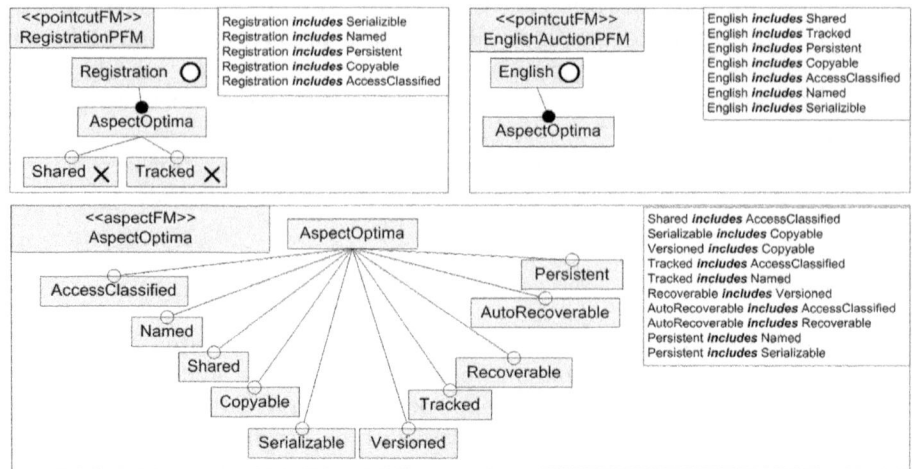

Fig. 5. An AspectOptima Framework Aspect-oriented Feature Model

The AFM of the AspectOptima framework is modeled as a set of optional features, because in different methodologies, like PLUS [13], aspects are considered as means for implementing optional features. The AspectOptima framework consists of ten reusable aspects: 1) AccessClassified for classifying methods of a transactional object into read, write, and update operations, 2) Named for associating a unique name with the object that is created, 3) Shared for ensuring mutual exclusion of shared object modifications within one transaction, 4) Copyable for enabling copying of object states, 5) Serializable for moving an object's state to another location in the system, 6) Versioned for encapsulating multiple versions of the same object, 7) Tracked for generic monitoring of transactional objects, 8) Recoverable for providing the ability to undo state changes in case of an aborted transaction, 9) AutoRecoverable for region-based recovery, and 10) Persistent for writing the state of an object to a stable storage. Additionally, interdependencies between these aspects are specified as integrity constraints.

In an Online Auction System, such as the one previously presented, user information is of central importance to the auction process. For this reason, a system must ensure that a crash in a communication with a user during the entry of the information will not allow for participation in an auction with incomplete user information. Therefore, the entry of user information must be one transaction. Due to the fact that user information can be entered only by the user himself, this transaction is single threaded. To facilitate the configuration of this transaction, AspectOptima features are added to the Registration feature with the RegistrationPFM PFM. Features Shared and Tracked, are used for multithreaded transactions and therefore undesirable for this case. By adding the *includes* integrity constraints to the RegistrationPFM, the selection of Serializable, Named, Persistent, Copyable, and AccessClassified is mandatory, and ensures that fault tolerance is added to the system. However, the selection of Recoverable,

AutoRecoverable, and Versioned is left optional to allow for different recovery and concurrency controls, such as optimistic and pessimistic concurrency control.

Even more important than registration is the fault tolerance of auctions. The system must ensure that when the auction is successful, the money is withdrawn from the buyer, and sent to the seller. Furthermore, if the auction is unsuccessful, the state must be returned to the state before the auction. Therefore, an auction must also be considered as one transaction. Due to the fact that in one auction several users may participate, an auction should be a multithreaded transaction. To enable the specification of fault tolerance for English auctions, as in [20], we add the AspectOptima aspect to the English feature by the means of the EnglishAuctionPFM PFM. Furthermore, to ensure that the fault tolerance mechanism treats auctions as multithreaded transactions, the selection of Shared, Tracked, Persistent, Copyable, AccessClassified, Named and Serializible is mandated, similarly to RegistrationPFM, by the means of *includes* integrity constraints.

5 Potential Enhancements

AoFM introduces a new way of modularizing very large feature models that exist in real world applications. However, the work presented in this paper is still in its initial phase, and several enhancements may be introduced to even further support modularization and reduce the maintainability effort.

One potential enhancement is adding a *substitution* composition rule. The *substitution* rule allows for features to be substituted while all relationships of the substituted and of the substituting feature are retained. The potential benefits of such an operator can be seen when using aspects for feature model evolution [8]. Namely, new relationships may be added by aspects, while retaining the old ones.

An enhancement to the specification of aspects is the additional specification of ordering of compositions in cases where several aspects are added to the same feature. An example of a problem that might appear when applying several aspect to the same part of the feature model is that a feature may be deleted in one of the aspects, and matched for the purpose of adding some new features in another aspect. Similarly to the case presented by Jayaraman et al. [16], the pattern matching mechanism will not work. Therefore, there is a need for specifying an appropriate ordering, which will enable the application of all selected aspects.

One more possible enhancement is the support for regular expressions in the specification of the names of features and integrity constraints. Regular expressions could be as simple as a wildcard (*) combined with a partial name (e.g., *Case would match Upper Case and Lower Case in our example). This kind of specification may reduce the number of PFMs in a feature model aspect and increase the matching power of the pattern. For a more complex example, consider the Password Policy aspect. If the same password policy were to be applied to both the Administration and Registration and no elements of the base concerns needed to be removed, only one PFM would be sufficient and the feature tagged with ○ could be named (Admin|Reg)istration. This example also demonstrates the modularization power of this approach. Namely, the number of PFMs and repetition of features from base concerns in PFMs depend only on the differences between subsets of AFMs that are added to different join points. However, whether support for full regular expressions is beneficial requires further investigation.

Wildcards could also be allowed on relationships in the feature model to be able to match *mandatory* and *optional* parent-child feature relationships at the same time as well as *alternative feature groups* and *or feature groups* at the same time.

To enhance manageability and maintainability even more, semantic-based pattern matching specifications could also be considered. One semantic-based pattern matching example could be the specification of general parent-child relationships in the pattern of the aspect. When specifying such a general parent-child relationship, it is possible to match any child feature of a feature, and hence, it is possible to apply an aspect to all of its child features. This may not be constrained to just the immediate child features of a feature, but also the child features of each child feature, possibly up to a specified depth. Finally, AoFM may also be extended to enable the specification of an ancestor/descendant feature relationship. If the relationship between two features is specified as ancestor/descendant in a pattern, a match of the pattern is successful if a hierarchical trace through the feature model from one feature to the other feature exists. Benefits of such relationships are twofold. First, the size of PFMs can be significantly reduced. Second, AoFM models become more robust to changes and modifications in base concerns, hence mitigating the fragile pointcut problem.

6 Related Work

Due to the large size of feature models, the need for modularization has been recognized by several researchers.

Czarnecki et al. [11] introduce a reference concept in feature models as the principal means for modularization. A reference points to one feature of a feature model that defines a subtree, which will be copied to the reference location. Compared to this approach, AoFM allows for variability and flexibility in the composition rules of concerns, herewith better encapsulating crosscutting concerns.

Mannion et al. [23] propose a viewpoint-based approach for the development of feature models that facilitates the development of large feature models by merging several smaller ones. Smaller feature models represent viewpoints from the perspective of different stakeholders. This approach allows for the modularization of feature models similar to base concerns in AoFM, but fails at capturing crosscutting concerns, which is the main benefit of AoFM.

Hubaux et al. [14] also introduce an approach for multiview feature models. According to Hubaux et al., a large feature model is supported by multiple views, or concerns, which are used for configuration performed by different stakeholders. Compared to this approach, AoFM additionally supports the specification of crosscutting concerns.

Acher et al. [1] present a textual, domain-specific language for managing and evolving feature models[1]. This language includes operators for feature composition (e.g., for inserting and merging models), comparison and analysis (e.g., to determine the validity of the resulting model). Compared to AoFM, their approach does not support crosscutting concerns well as their feature composition targets a single feature in a model where another can be, for instance, inserted. Their feature merging is name-based but is limited to only one operator at a time (e.g., union or difference), whereas AoFM supports a mixture of operators simultaneously.

Dhungana et al. [12] observe that problem and solution space models may both have crosscutting concerns. For this reason, they introduce model fragments, i.e., models of reusable assets and their variability points, as separate modules. In their approach, crosscutting concerns in the problem space are merged with base concerns by means of placeholders. If there is a need for different variants of a crosscutting concern, the concern needs to be copied and adapted for each placeholder. AoFM allows for better modularization as base models are unaware of crosscutting concerns and different variants of crosscutting concerns can be specified in PFMs.

At this time, AOM techniques are used mostly for solution space models instead of feature models. Zschaler et al. [30] present VML*, which addresses variability management across several modeling notations such as feature models, use cases, activity diagrams, and UML 2.0 architectural models. While AOM techniques are used to ease the engineering of new family members from a given feature model, feature models themselves are not structured in an aspect-oriented way. An example related to SPL is the DiVA Project[2], which intends to manage dynamic variability in adaptive systems with the help of AOM techniques. Again, variability models in the problem space are not structured in an aspect-oriented way but solution space artifacts are. AoFM, on the other hand, structures feature models based on aspect-oriented principles.

Jayaraman et al. [16] also introduce an approach where aspect-oriented models are considered only in the solution space. To specify aspect-oriented solution space models, they apply the MATA technique [28]. In their approach, kernel features, i.e., features that exist in all models, are specified as base concerns. Optional features and features that do not appear in all models are hence specified as aspects. As a method for detecting inconsistencies, they apply Critical Pair Analysis. A recent research proposal by Barreiros and Moreira [4] attempts to extend this approach by applying this analysis not only to feature interactions but also to the verification of traceability relationships between different solution space models. Our work is complementing this work as we introduce aspect-oriented modularization in problem space models.

Also recently, Zhang [29] introduced a notion of aspect-oriented feature modeling. According to Zhang's method, feature models should be extended with aspectual features representing system concerns. Aspectual features are used for

---

[1] See also the FAMILIAR Web page at http://nyx.unice.fr/projects/familiar/
[2] http://www.ict-diva.eu

adapting the base feature model according to selected system concerns. AoFM is somewhat different as AFMs capture commonalities and manage variabilities of a crosscutting concern, and rules for their integration into major concerns are provided. Furthermore, a crosscutting concern is not necessarily a system concern in AoFM, but may be a part of a subsystem.

7 Conclusions and Future Work

In this paper we have introduced the notion of Aspect-oriented Feature Models (AoFM). We argue that AoFM further enhances the modularization of feature models by enabling encapsulation of crosscutting concerns. The approach has been validated by adding a fault tolerance crosscutting concern to a family of web based software systems. For validation, the AspectOptima framework has been used as a fault tolerance framework and an Online Auction System as a trial case. The validation has shown benefits of the proposed approach by demonstrating reuse of feature models of the fault tolerance framework. However, full integration of AoFM in the process of SPLE is still in its early stage. Particularly, there is a need for extending composition rules, providing tool support, and automatically analyzing SPLs consisting of problem space models in AoFM and their aspect-oriented implementations for the solution space.

For tool support, we intend to extend *FeaturePlugin* [2], an Eclipse plug-in for feature model development. To avoid overwhelming users of the tool with new concepts, we plan to perform a lightweight extension to the existing notation used by the FeaturePlugin. The extensions will facilitate only the annotation of existing elements of the *FeaturePlugin* notation with concepts needed for AoFM.

Due to the large size of feature models, there is a need for automated analysis of feature model designs [5]. A comprehensive set of analysis operations can be found in [6]. To provide analysis operations and explanations for different stakeholders, and to reduce the time required for the analysis, we plan to use Distributed Description Logics (DDL) [7]. DDL is a formalism for modularized conceptual modeling and reasoning. In our previous work [3], we have applied DDL for the verification of inconsistencies in modular feature model specifications and irregular FM configurations. Our initial results show a significant reduction of reasoning time, because only needed information from other modules is imported when reasoning about a particular module. To evaluate the claimed benefits of using DDL, we intend to analyze the time needed for the verification of feature models specified by AoFM and their DDL representation, and compare it to the equivalent, monolithic feature model represented in basic description logic.

Typically, in an SPL, problem space models in AoFM are connected to the solution space implementation of the family. During design time, there is a need for ensuring that interdependencies of crosscutting concerns in the problem space are not contradictory to mappings and crosscutting concerns in the solution space, i.e., we need to ensure that every valid configuration produces a valid product. We also intend to use DDL for this kind of verification.

Acknowledgments. This research was in part supported by Alberta Innovates – Technology Futures through the New Faculty Award program, the Discovery Grants program of the Natural Sciences and Engineering Research Council of Canada, and the Ontario Graduate Scholarship Program.

References

1. Acher, M., Collet, P., Lahire, P., France, R.: Composing feature models. In: van den Brand, M., Gašević, D., Gray, J. (eds.) SLE 2009. LNCS, vol. 5969, pp. 62–81. Springer, Heidelberg (2010)
2. Antkiewicz, M., Czarnecki, K.: Featureplugin: feature modeling plug-in for eclipse. In: Eclipse 2004: Proceedings of the 2004 OOPSLA WS on Eclipse technology eXchange, pp. 67–72. ACM, New York (2004)
3. Bagheri, E., Gasevic, D., Ensan, F.: Modular Feature Models: Representation and Configuration. Technical report, Athabasca University (2009)
4. Barreiros, J., Moreira, A.: Managing features and aspect interactions in software product lines. In: Int. Conf. on Software Engineering Advances, pp. 506–511 (2009)
5. Batory, D., Benavides, D., Ruiz-Cortés, A.: Automated Analysis of Feature Models: Challenges Ahead. Communications of ACM 49(12), 45–47 (2006)
6. Benavides, D., Segura, S., Ruiz-Cortés, A.: Automated analysis of feature models 20 years later: A lit. review. Inf. Systems 35(6), 615–636 (2010)
7. Borgida, A., Serafini, L.: Distributed description logics: Assimilating information from peer sources. Journal of Data Semantics 1, 153–184 (2003)
8. Cazzola, W., Chiba, S., Saake, G.: Aspects and software evolution. In: Rashid, A., Liu, Y. (eds.) Transactions on Aspect-Oriented Software Development IV. LNCS, vol. 4640, pp. 114–116. Springer, Heidelberg (2007)
9. Chitchyan, R., Rashid, A., Sawyer, P., Garcia, A., Alarcon, M.P., Bakker, J., Tekinerdogan, B., Clarke, S., Jackson, A.: Survey of analysis and design approaches. Technical report, AOSD-EUROPE, Del. 11 (2005)
10. Czarnecki, K., Eisenecker, U.W.: Components and generative programming. SIGSOFT Software Engineering Notes 24(6), 2–19 (1999) (invited paper)
11. Czarnecki, K., Helsen, S., Eisenecker, U.W.: Staged configuration through specialization and multilevel configuration of feature models. Software Process: Improvement and Practice 10(2), 143–169 (2005)
12. Dhungana, D., Grünbacher, P., Rabiser, R., Neumayer, T.: Structuring the Modeling Space and Supporting Evolution in Software Product Line Engineering. Journal of Systems and Software 83(7), 1108–1122 (2010)
13. Gomaa, H.: Designing Software Product Lines with UML: From Use Cases to Pattern-Based Software Architectures. Addison Wesley Longman Publishing Co., Inc., Redwood City, CA (2004)
14. Hubaux, A., Heymans, P., Schobbens, P.-Y., Deridder, D.: Towards multi-view feature-based configuration. In: Wieringa, R., Persson, A. (eds.) REFSQ 2010. LNCS, vol. 6182, pp. 106–112. Springer, Heidelberg (2010)
15. Jacobson, I., Ng, P.-W.: Aspect-Oriented Software Development with Use Cases. Addison-Wesley, Reading (2004)
16. Jayaraman, P., Whittle, J., Elkhodary, A., Gomaa, H.: Model composition in product lines and feature interaction detection using critical pair analysis. In: Engels, G., Opdyke, B., Schmidt, D.C., Weil, F. (eds.) MODELS 2007. LNCS, vol. 4735, pp. 151–165. Springer, Heidelberg (2007)

17. Kang, K.C., Cohen, S.G., Hess, J.A., Novak, W.E., Peterson, A.S.: Feature-oriented domain analysis (foda) feasibility study. Technical report, Carnegie-Mellon University SEI (November 1990)
18. Kiczales, G., Lamping, J., Mendhekar, A., Maeda, C., Lopes, C.V., Loingtier, J.-M., Irwin, J.: Aspect-oriented programming. In: ECOOP, pp. 220–242 (1997)
19. Kienzle, J., Duala-Ekoko, E., Gélineau, S.: AspectOptima: A Case Study on Aspect Dependencies and Interactions. In: Transactions on Aspect-Oriented Software Development, pp. 187–234. Springer, Berlin (2009)
20. Kienzle, J., Strohmeier, A., Romanovsky, A.: Auction system design using open multithreaded transactions. In: Proc. of the 7th IEEE Int. Workshop on Object-Oriented Real-Time Dependable Systems (WORDS 2002), pp. 95–104. IEEE Computer Society Press, Washington, DC (2002)
21. Lau, S.Q.: Domain analysis of e-commerce systems using feature-based model templates. Master's thesis, University of Waterloo, Waterloo (2006)
22. Lencastre, M., Araujo, J., Moreira, A., Castro, J.: Analyzing crosscutting in the problem frames approach. In: IWAAPF 2006: Proc. of the 2006 Int. Workshop on Advances and Applications of Problem Frames, pp. 59–64. ACM, New York (2006)
23. Mannion, M., Savolainen, J., Asikainen, T.: Viewpoint-oriented variability modeling. Int. Computer Software and Applications Conf. 1, 67–72 (2009)
24. Marcos, E.: Software Engineering Research versus Software Development. SIGSOFT Software Engineering Notes 30, 1–7 (2005)
25. Mussbacher, G., Amyot, D.: Extending the user requirements notation with aspect-oriented concepts. In: Reed, R., Bilgic, A., Gotzhein, R. (eds.) SDL 2009. LNCS, vol. 5719, pp. 115–132. Springer, Heidelberg (2009)
26. Pohl, K., Böckle, G., van der Linden, F.J.: Software Product Line Engineering: Foundations, Principles and Techniques. Springer, Heidelberg (2005)
27. Sommerville, I., Sawyer, P.: Viewpoints: principles, problems and a practical approach to requirements engineering. Annals of Softw. Eng. 3, 101–130 (1997)
28. Whittle, J., Jayaraman, P.K., Elkhodary, A.M., Moreira, A., Araújo, J.: MATA: A Unified Approach for Composing UML Aspect Models Based on Graph Transformation. Transactions on Aspect-oriented Software Development 6, 191–237 (2009)
29. Zhang, G.: Aspect-oriented feature modelling for software product line web: http://ecs.victoria.ac.nz/twiki/pub/Events/ACDC2010/Zhang.pdf
30. Zschaler, S., Sánchez, P., Santos, J., Alférez, M., Rashid, A., Fuentes, L., Moreira, A., Araújo, J., Kulesza, U.: VML* – A Family of Languages for Variability Management in Software Product Lines. In: van den Brand, M., Gašević, D., Gray, J. (eds.) SLE 2009. LNCS, vol. 5969, pp. 334–353. Springer, Heidelberg (2010)

Mapping Aspect-Oriented Models to Aspect-Oriented Code

Max E. Kramer[1] and Jörg Kienzle[2]

[1] Karlsruhe Institute of Technology, Karlsruhe, Germany
max.kramer@student.kit.edu
[2] McGill University, Montréal, Canada
joerg.kienzle@mcgill.ca

Abstract. When aspect-oriented modeling techniques are used in the context of Model-Driven Engineering, a possible way of obtaining an executable from an aspect-oriented model is to map it to code written in an aspect-oriented programming language. This paper outlines the most important challenges that arise when defining such a mapping: mapping structure and behavior of a single aspect, mapping instantiation of structure and behavior in target models, mapping conflict resolution between aspects, and mapping aspect dependencies and variability. To explain these mapping issues, our paper presents details on how to map REUSABLE ASPECT MODELS (RAM) to ASPECTJ source code. The ideas are illustrated by presenting example models and corresponding mapped code from the AspectOPTIMA case study.

1 Introduction

Aspect-Oriented Software Development (AOSD) aims at providing systematic means for the identification, separation, representation, and composition of crosscutting concerns. Aspect-Oriented Modeling (AOM) applies aspect technology in the context of Model-Driven Engineering (MDE), and therefore focuses on modularizing and composing crosscutting concerns during the design of a software system. The resulting models can be used to describe or analyze system properties, and eventually be executed.

Although there is a growing community of researchers that build virtual machines that can interpret and execute software models at runtime [3], code generation is for performance and portability reasons still by far the most popular way of turning models into running software.

There are two ways to obtain code from an aspect-oriented design model:
1) One can use a model weaver to generate a non-aspect-oriented model, and then use standard code generation technology to generate code for a non-aspect-oriented programming language, or 2) One can map the aspect-oriented model directly to aspect-oriented code and rely on the weaver of the aspect-oriented target language to deal with crosscutting concerns.

Weaving at the model level has the obvious advantage of allowing the developer to exploit existing code generation technology and to target any platform.

It also gives the developer the possibility to verify that the different aspects were composed correctly by analyzing the woven model. Most aspect-oriented modeling techniques have focused on model weaving in the past.

Mapping aspect-oriented models to an AOP language, however, has also several advantages. It has been shown that the resulting code is in general smaller, more modular and hence easier to understand. In some cases this is beneficial during the maintenance phase of software development [8].

This paper presents a step-by-step transformation that maps models specified using the REUSABLE ASPECT MODELS (RAM) approach to ASPECTJ source code. The goal of this exercise is to illustrate the challenges that have to be faced when a aspect-oriented model consisting of several interdependent aspects is mapped to AOP code. The presented mapping preserves the modularity of the model within the generated code in order to maintain traceability of concerns and to ease maintenance. The generated code-level aspects are individually reusable – just like their model counterparts – and they contain all information that was modeled in order to minimize the necessity of manual implementation efforts.

The paper outline is as follows: Section 2 presents the background on RAM and ASPECTJ ; Section 3 describes the mapping of a single aspect model; Section 4 and Section 5 show how to generate code that allows one aspect to reuse structure and behavior provided by another aspect; Section 6 demonstrates how conflict resolution models can be mapped to code equivalents; Section 7 shows how our mapping supports aspect variability; Section 8 summarizes the solution strategies that we developed; Section 9 discusses related work, and the last section draws some final conclusions.

2 Background

2.1 Reusable Aspect Models

RAM [12, 13] is an aspect-oriented multi-view modeling approach that 1) integrates existing class diagram, sequence diagram, and state diagram AOM techniques into one coherent approach; 2) packages aspect models for easy and flexible reuse; 3) supports the creation of complex aspect dependency chains; 4) performs consistency checks at the model level to verify correct aspect composition and reuse; 5) defines a detailed model weaving algorithm that resolves dependencies to generate independent aspect models and the final application model.

How our mapped ASPECTJ code for RAM achieves 1), 2) and 3) is outlined in the rest of the paper. The interested reader is referred to [12] and [11] for additional details and explanations on 4) and 5).

2.2 AspectJ

ASPECTJ [10] is an aspect-oriented extension of the JAVA [6] programming language. Crosscutting structure and behavior is encapsulated in a class-like construct called an *aspect* that may contain constructs of four new concepts: *join points*, *pointcuts*, *advice*, and *inter-type declarations*.

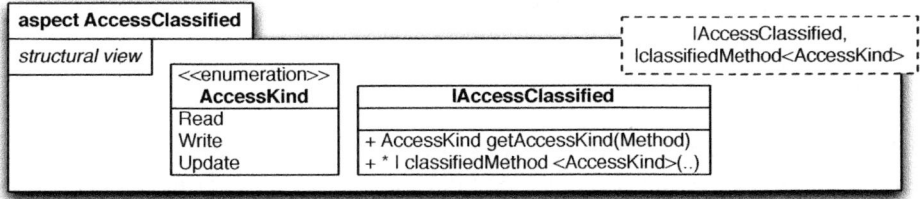

Fig. 1. The aspect *AccessClassified* from the AspectOPTIMA case study

Join points are well-defined points in the execution of a program. These include method and constructor calls, their executions, field access operations, object and class initializations, and others. A *pointcut* is a construct used to designate a set of join points of interest. It can expose to the programmer the context of a matched join point, such as the current executing object (with expressions like `this(ObjectIdentifier)`), the target object of a call or execution (`target(ObjectIdentifier)`) and the arguments of a method call (`args(..)`).

An *advice* defines the actions to be taken at the join point(s) captured by a pointcut. A `before` advice runs just before the captured join point; an `after` advice runs immediately after the captured join point; an `around` advice surrounds the captured join point and has the ability to augment, bypass or allow its execution. Finally, *inter-type declarations* allow an aspect to define methods and fields for other classes and interfaces.

3 Mapping a Single Aspect Model

In RAM, the structure and behavior of an aspect is encapsulated inside a UML package that contains three different types of diagrams. The structural view compartment of a RAM aspect is a UML class diagram that contains all the classes pertaining to the design of the aspect together with their attributes, operations and associations. The set of public operations defined in the structural view of an aspect model define the aspect's interface [1].

Figure 1 shows a simple RAM aspect model of ASPECTOPTIMA, an aspect-oriented framework that realizes run-time support for transactions. The aspect makes it possible to associate an access kind (i.e., read, write, or update) with every operation of a class. To achieve this, the aspect model defines a class |AccessClassified that contains a method parameter |classifiedMethod. The "|" that was prepended to the names marks the class and its method as mandatory instantiation parameters, which means that they have to be bound to a complete class and its method(s) when the aspect is used. In RAM, every class that is not a parameter and that contains a constructor is complete. Incomplete classes can be completed by binding complete classes to them. Incomplete elements are exposed in the top right corner of the RAM aspect package similar to UML's template parameters.

To keep the mapping from models to code as simple as possible, we map each RAM aspect model to a JAVA package. Each class in the structural view is then analyzed to determine if it is a *complete class*, an *incomplete class*, or if it can be implemented by reusing the JAVA library.

Reusing the Java Library. In order to allow modelers to reuse existing JAVA library classes we maintain a list of supported classes and interfaces and associate every interface on that list to a default implementation class. If a complete class in the aspect model bears the name of a class or interface of the library list and the signatures of the modeled operations match the signatures of the methods defined on the class or interface, then the JAVA library is automatically reused. In cases where modeled classes define template parameters, their types and number must also match that of the JAVA library class.

As an example of JAVA library reuse, imagine a modeled class named Map with template parameters Context and |AccessClassified, and operations put(Context,|AccessClassified) and remove(|AccessClassified). Such a class would be recognized as an instance of the library interface java.util.Map, and the modeled parameters Context and |AccessClassified would be mapped to the template parameters K and V. Every call to a constructor of Map would be mapped to a call to a constructor of the class java.util.HashMap as we defined this class as the default implementation of the interface java.util.Map.

Mapping of Classes. If a *complete class* (i.e. a class that contains a constructor) in the aspect model is not recognized as an instance of an existing JAVA class, a JAVA implementation is generated from scratch. The straightforward idea of mapping the complete class to a standard JAVA class is unfortunately not a good solution, because it is possible that the modeled class is later bound to another class when the aspect is used (see Section 4). Therefore we create a new public JAVA interface and an ASPECTJ aspect for every complete class of the model. In this aspect we introduce fields and methods into the interface using ASPECTJ's inter-type declaration mechanism. This allows us to implement the merging of modeled classes with JAVA classes that implement multiple interfaces that have been augmented as described in Section 4. In order to instantiate complete classes we create empty JAVA classes that implement the created interfaces.

An *incomplete class* (i.e. a class that contains no constructor and is exposed as a parameter or bound to a parameter) is mapped in the same way as a complete class, except that no empty implementation class is generated, since incomplete classes cannot be instantiated.

Since one of the goals of our mapping is to reduce manual implementation refinements to a minimum, we also map modeled attributes and associations to JAVA fields and methods that we introduce into the generated interfaces. Declared operations that follow common signature patterns like getters, setters, incrementors etc. are completely generated using default implementations.

Mapping of Instantiation Parameters. If an incomplete class is exposed as a mandatory instantiation parameter of the aspect model, we create a custom

```
@Target({ElementType.TYPE})
@Retention(RetentionPolicy.RUNTIME)
public @interface AccessClassifiedClass {
  // empty
}
```

Fig. 2. Custom JAVA annotation for the parameter class |AccessClassified

JAVA annotation for it so that binding the parameter can be done by annotating existing classes. Figure 2 presents such a custom annotation for the mandatory instantiation parameter |AccessClassified of the aspect presented in Figure 1.

Likewise, for each operation that is exposed as a mandatory instantiation parameter, a JAVA annotation is created. Sometimes, parameters themselves are parameterized, such as the operation |classifiedMethod<AccessKind> of the aspect *AccessClassified* that we presented in Figure 1. The AccessKind parameter associates a concrete type of access with the operation. In case of such a parameterization, we add corresponding methods for each parameter to the generated annotation. Figure 3 presents the annotation for the |classifiedMethod operation that contains the method AccessKind value as a parameter.

4 Enabling Reuse of Structure

In RAM, an aspect model is applied within a target model using instantiation directives that map (at least) all mandatory instantiation parameters to target model elements. A target model can either be a base model that uses the functionality of the aspect model or it can be another aspect model that extends or modifies the functionality of the reused aspect model.

Traceable is an aspect of the AspectOPTIMA case study that reuses the structure and behavior of the *AccessClassified* aspect in order to provide the infrastructure that is necessary to create traces of calls to access classified operations. The structural view of the aspect *Traceable* is shown in Figure 4.

Mapping Instantiation Directives. RAM's instantiation directives are used to map mandatory instantiation parameters to target model elements. For example, the directive in Figure 4 specifies that the |AccessClassified class should be merged with |Traceable, and that the method parameter |classifiedMethod corresponds to the |traceableMethod parameter. This means that every class that is bound to the parameter |Traceable is also an |AccessClassified class and if an operation of it is bound to the |traceableMethod parameter this operations is also a |classifiedMethod.

```
@Target({ElementType.METHOD})
@Retention(RetentionPolicy.RUNTIME)
public @interface ClassifiedMethod {
  AccessKind value();
}
```

Fig. 3. Mapped code for the method parameter |classifiedMethod<AccessKind>

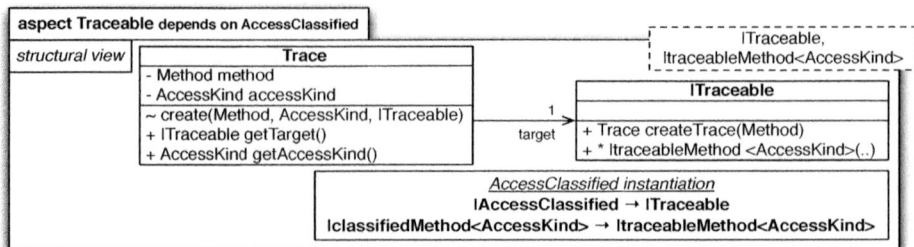

Fig. 4. The *Traceable* aspect that reuses the aspect *AccessClassified*

In our mapping, instantiation directives are implemented by type hierarchy modifications and annotation inheritance. The JAVA interface of the instantiating class extends the interface of the instantiated class and corresponding parameter annotations of the instantiated class are added to the instantiating class. As a result, the directive |AccessClassified → |Traceable is mapped to an *extends* inheritance relation between the JAVA interfaces of |AccessClassified and |Traceable (see Figure 5, line 1). At the same time, if the target model element is also a mandatory instantiation parameter like it is the case for |Traceable, we also make sure that the corresponding JAVA annotations are inherited. In our example, this results in a statement that tells the ASPECTJ compiler to automatically add the annotation @AccessClassifiedClass to each class that has been annotated using @TraceableClass (Figure 5, line 2).

If a parameterized method parameter is instantiated using another parameter, we use a similar mechanism to inherit the annotation while preserving parameter values: for every possible parameter value we create an ASPECTJ statement that passes the annotation together with the parameter value on to the target annotation of the instantiated method (Figure 5, line 3-5).

```
1 public interface Traceable extends AccessClassified {
  ...
  }
2 aspect TraceableAspect {
   declare @type :
     @TraceableClass * : @AccessClassifiedClass;
3  declare @method :
     (@TraceableMethod(AccessKind.READ) * *.*(..)) :
       @ClassifiedMethod(AccessKind.READ);
4  declare @method :
     (@TraceableMethod(AccessKind.WRITE) * *.*(..)) :
       @ClassifiedMethod(AccessKind.WRITE);
5  declare @method :
     (@TraceableMethod(AccessKind.UPDATE) * *.*(..)) :
       @ClassifiedMethod(AccessKind.UPDATE);
  }
```

Fig. 5. Implementing instantiation directives through annotation inheritance

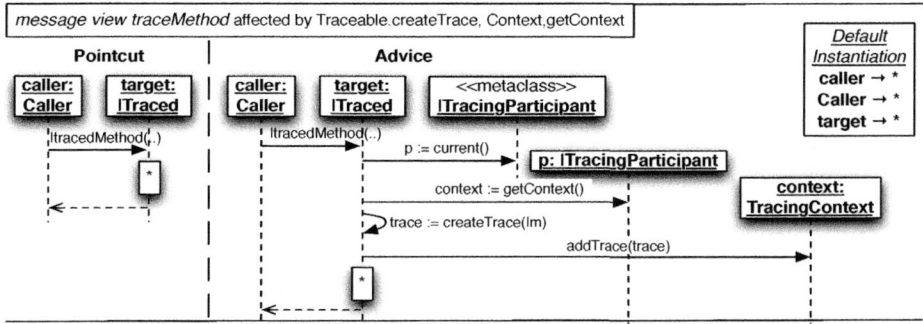

Fig. 6. The message view *traceMethod* from the *Tracing* aspect showing the advisory of the mandatory instantiation parameter |tracedMethod

5 Enabling Reuse of Behavior

In RAM, an aspect model specifies the behavior of operations defined in the interface of the aspect using message views. A message view is a UML sequence diagram that supports advice and describes how instances of the classes of the aspect collaborate to achieve the desired functionality.

For space reasons we cannot present the mapping for message views in detail. We assume that the reader is familiar with the mapping of sequence diagrams to code in general, and concentrate our discussion on the most challenging circumstances in which message views can be used in RAM.

A message view either defines the behavior of a method that was newly declared, or it advises an existing concrete method, or it advises a method parameter. The resulting ASPECTJ advice and their pointcuts are slightly different for concrete methods and parameters, but since the generation of a pointcut for a single specific method is straightforward it is not discussed in this paper.

Advising Method Parameters. In the AspectOPTIMA case study, the aspect *Tracing* reuses the infrastructure that is provided by *Traceable* in order to trace every call to an operation. To achieve this, *Tracing* contains a message view *traceMethod* that advises the mandatory instantiation parameter |tracedMethod as shown in Figure 6. The pointcut models an arbitrary call to a method that is bound to the parameter. The involved `caller` and `target` objects are named in order to be able to refer to them in the advice model, but we specify with a default instantiation that the `caller` can be arbitrary and that the name of the `target` is not fixed. As we cannot know in advance which methods are going to be bound to the parameter |tracedMethod, we represent the original behavior of an advised method with a box that contains a star as wildcard parameter. In the advice we can use this box in order to specify that the newly defined behavior should occur before the original method behavior.

The mapped code for the message view *traceMethod* is an ASPECTJ `before` advice that is presented in Figure 7. It makes use of the annotation that was

```
@AdviceName( "traceMethod" )
before(Traced target):
1 execution(@TracedMethod * *.*(..))
2 && target(target) {
    TracingParticipant p = TracingParticipant.current();
    TracingContext context = (TracingContext) p.getContext();
3   Method tracedMethod =
      ((MethodSignature) thisJoinPointStaticPart.getSignature()).
       getMethod();
4   Trace trace = target.createTrace(tracedMethod);
    context.addTrace(trace);
}
```

Fig. 7. Mapped code for *traceMethod*

created for the mandatory instantiation parameter |tracedMethod in order to restrict the advice to executions of bound methods (Figure 7, line 1) and binds the target object to a variable (Figure 7, line 2). As such message views may contain logic that needs to know exactly which method is currently advised, we support this by retrieving the corresponding *java.lang.reflect.Method* object from ASPECTJ 's join point information (Figure 7, line 3). In our example this information is used as an argument for a method call during the creation of a trace (Figure 7, line 4).

Instead of proceeding with the unmodified behavior of an advised method, a message view can also contain a new call to the advised method. The result is a new invocation of the method, which can trigger the re-execution of aspects that are linked to the advised method, including the current aspect. To implement such calls we obtain the currently advised method from the join point information object of the advice and invoke it using JAVA's REFLECTION API. An example for such a new call that leads to a recursive application of an advice is found in the message view *addChildrensResults* that we present in Figure 9.

Mapping Behavior Involving Generic Types. Whenever a method parameter makes use of a generic type we cannot use our mapping with annotations, as ASPECTJ does not support pointcuts with type parameters. For this reason we resort to abstract aspects that can be parameterized with a type. We wrap the advice that corresponds to a message view with type parameters in an abstract aspect and define an abstract pointcut that is used in the advice. Instead of binding parameters to such message views with annotations, we need to define concrete aspects that extend the abstract aspect, provide values for the type parameters and instantiate the abstract pointcut in order to specify which method(s) should be bound. This means that the code of models with generic types, in contrast to all other code that can be obtained with our mapping, cannot be used in legacy systems where adding ASPECTJ code is not an option.

An example use of this technique can be shown with the *Nested* aspect of the AspectOPTIMA case study, which makes it possible for transaction contexts to be nested inside each other. *Nested* defines a behavioral template with a generic type in a message view *addChildrensResults* as shown in Figure 8. In the model the unmodified behavior of the advised method is executed, and then an iteration

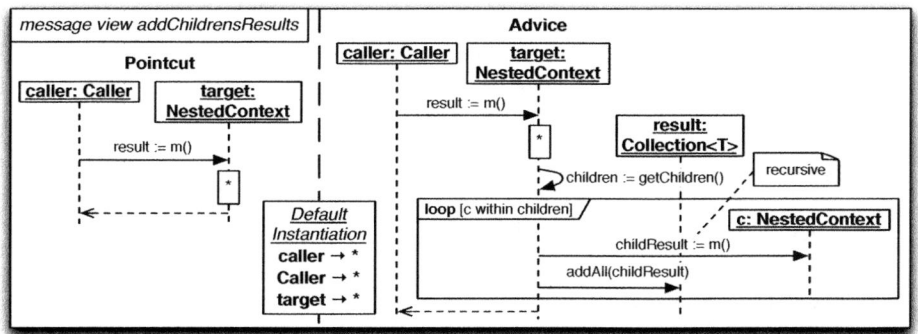

Fig. 8. The template message view *addChildrensResults* showing a non-recursive proceed in form of a wildcard box and a recursive call for the method parameter m

over all children contexts is performed and the parameter method is recursively applied to every child context. The result of each recursive invocation is added to the overall result which is returned after the iteration is completed.

In the code that corresponds to the message view *addChildrensResults* (Figure 9) the type parameter T is created and it is specified that this type parameter extends the JAVA library class java.util.Collection (line 1), so that it becomes unnecessary to include this information in every instantiation of our abstract pointcut (line 2). It is sufficient to use T as return type of our around advice (line 3) and wherever it is used for variables. The currently executing method is retrieved from ASPECTJ's join point information (line 4) in order to invoke it recursively on the children objects (line 5). The invoke method can throw exceptions if it is used improperly so it has to be wrapped in a try-catch block (line 6) even if our code is generated in a way that ensures that no reflection exceptions are ever thrown. However, the bound method itself may throw arbitrary exceptions that JAVA's REFLECTION API wraps in InvocationTargetExceptions. These exceptions need to be re-thrown (line 7)[1]. An example use of the template *addChildrensResults* and the corresponding code is given in the context of a conflict resolution aspect in Section 6 in Figure 10 and Figure 11.

6   Mapping Conflict Resolutions

In order to automatically detect and resolve conflicts between reused aspects RAM support the definition of conflict resolution aspects. These aspects have all features of ordinary aspects, but they cannot be instantiated. Instead, they are automatically applied if their *interference criteria* are met. To support that,

---

[1] Since the advised methods do not need to declare to throw the checked InvocationTargetException, we must wrap all exceptions in ASPECTJ's predefined SoftException similarly to the result of ASPECTJ's declare soft expression.

```
public abstract aspect AddChildrensResultsAspect
1 <T extends java.util.Collection<?>> {
2   public abstract pointcut m(NestedContext target);
    @AdviceName( "addChildrensResults" )
3   T around(NestedContext target) : m(target) {
      T result = null;
      try {
        result = proceed(target);
        Set<NestedContext> children = target.getChildren();
        for (NestedContext c : children) {
4         Method m = ((MethodSignature) thisJoinPointStaticPart.
            getSignature()).getMethod();
5         T childResult = (T) m.invoke(c, (Object[]) null);
          result.addAll(childResult);
        }
6     } catch (Exception e) {
        if (e instanceof InvocationTargetException)
7         throw new SoftException(e);
        e.printStackTrace(); // swallow reflection exceptions
      }
      return result;
    }
}
```

Fig. 9. Mapped code for the template *addChildrensResults* involving a generic type parameter

our mapping has to generate code for conflict resolution aspects that is only executed when the corresponding criteria hold.

If a conflict resolution aspect contains a criterion of the type `ClassA = ClassB` and a message view that advises a method parameter, we need to make sure that the behavior of the method is only changed if both classes are merged. We achieve this by inserting an additional class parameter to the annotation of the advised method. This class parameter defaults to the class that contains the method parameter. In a conflict resolution aspect the parameter can be used to specify the class of which the executing object needs to be an instance of in order for the advice to apply. In our code we retrieve the corresponding annotation with a `@annotation` pointcut and bind it to a variable. After we obtained the parameter value `targetClass` from the annotation variable, we frame the complete advice in the block of an if-statement that defines `targetClass.isInstance(target)` as condition. The effect is that the advice is only applied when the `target` object is an instance of the class that was provided by the annotation.

In the AspectOPTIMA case study there is a conflict between the aspects *Nested* and *Tracing*: traces gathered in a child context should also be made available

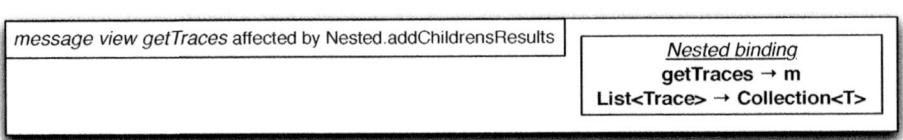

Fig. 10. The message view *getTraces* binding the template *addChildrensResults*

```
aspect GetTracesAddChildrensResultsAspect
 extends AddChildrensResultsAspect<List<Trace>> {
    public pointcut m(NestedContext target) :
      execution(List<Trace> TracingContext.getTraces())
      && target(target);
}
```

Fig. 11. Code for *getTraces* extending the abstract aspect for *addChildrensResults*

to the parent context. To achieve the desired effect, a RAM conflict resolution aspect applies the behavior of the message view addChildrensResults that we discussed in the previous section (Figure 8) to the method getTraces (Figure 10). The results is that all traces of children contexts are added to the traces of a context before the result is returned.

To achieve the same effect in ASPECTJ, our mapping produces a concrete aspect that extends the abstract aspect (Figure 9) as shown in Figure 11. The conflict criteria TracingContext = NestedContext is also visible in the generated code: in the pointcut definition we intercept executions of the getTraces method of a TracingContext, but the declared target type of the call is NestedContext.

7 Mapping Variability

The RAM approach can be used effectively in the context of product line development thanks to its support for optional and alternative aspect dependencies. The dependencies between aspect models are captured using feature diagrams. Figure 12 shows an extract of the feature diagram of the AspectOPTIMA case study, which defines 35 aspects that can be combined in different ways to implement run-time support for transactions. To generate a specific product, it suffices to choose which optional or alternative features are to be included in the product as conflicts are automatically resolved.

To support variability, each individual RAM aspect model must specify the structure and behavior needed for each variant. Figure 12 specifies, for example, that the *Recovering* aspect either depends on the *Checkpointing* aspect or on the *Deferring* aspect. In the aspect model of *Recovering*, instantiation directives and message views are tagged with a variant name (e.g. Checkpointing variant) if they are relevant to a particular variant only.

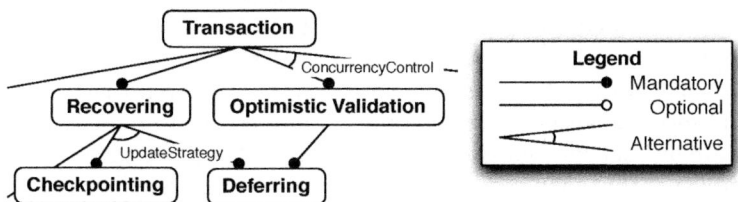

Fig. 12. Feature diagram extract demonstrating variability support

If we map an aspect model with support for variability to code, we need to implement every possible variation. In case of an alternative variant we create a JAVA enumeration that lists all possibilities. The enumeration is named according to the feature diagram and it is used in involved annotations to specify the chosen alternative. Optional dependencies are represented by boolean variables.

We then determine for every class whether it contains variation specific structure or behavior as a result of varying instantiation directives or variant-specific message views. If a class is not variation independent, we create a variant-specific interface that extends the original interface of that class and has the name of the aspect that causes the variation appended to its name. Additionally, we parameterize the class's annotation to account for the variation.

As variations are preserved in reusing aspects we need to apply the same technique to classes that are merged with varying classes in reusing aspects. This means that for every class we need to account for every possible configuration that results in a different structure or behavior for this class. An example where such indirect variation effects occur is the *Transaction* aspect as it inherits the alternative *UpdateStrategy* from the reused *Recovering* aspect (Figure 12).

All code that results from the variation independent part of the structural view and from message views that do not list a special variant is introduced into the variation independent interfaces. These general interfaces extend all interfaces that correspond to bound or instantiated classes of directives that are valid for all variations. The remaining variation specific structure and behavior is introduced into the variant-specific interfaces for those variants. This strategy of keeping as much code as possible in the general interfaces helps to avoid code duplication and keeps the size and complexity of the resulting implementation as small as the model permits it. To ensure that a user or modeler can never choose both options of an alternative we declare weaver errors whenever an involved class is marked with annotations that correspond to both alternatives.

8 Solution Strategies

After our detailed description of some of the mapping rules we summarize the problems that we encountered together with the solution strategies that we applied to them. We hope that these general implementation strategies can help other researchers that map aspect-oriented models to aspect-oriented code to solve similar problems.

We help to minimize the design efforts for the modeler by providing an unobtrusive and automatic possibility to reuse the JAVA library if class names and method signatures are matched. The work load for the modeler is further decreased by automatic default implementations for common design patterns like getters and setters. Both strategies make it unnecessary to model already existing structure or behavior but do not impose target language specific constraints.

The problems that may arise from the merging of modeled classes as a result of instantiation or binding are indirectly avoided as we decided to use interfaces as introduction containers for fields and methods. This gives us the possibility to make classes implement multiple interfaces whenever a merge of the corresponding classes is modeled and bypasses JAVA's prohibition of multiple inheritance.

We achieve bindable parameters by generating custom JAVA annotations. Parameter instantiation is implemented with type hierarchy modifications and annotation inheritance. The advisory of parameters is possible thanks to ASPECTJ's parameter-based pointcuts and thanks to its REFLECTION API that gives access to additional context information. This information is also used for recursive method invocations that make it possible to re-apply advice.

Due to ASPECTJ's incapability to directly support dynamic advice that involves type parameters we create parameterized abstract aspects with abstract pointcuts. When such a generic advice is used the corresponding abstract pointcuts are instantiated in concrete aspects that extend the abstract aspect.

Aspects that have to apply if and only if some conditions are met are implemented through additional restrictions in pointcuts or additional check clauses. These checks use information that was obtained from parameterized annotations.

Variation-specific structure and behavior is achieved by creating variation-specific interfaces that serve as introduction containers. These variations are preserved in reusing aspects by propagating annotation parameters and specific interfaces to reusing aspects. Variation independent information is kept separate.

In order to maintain the modeled order of advice, the precedence that is implicitly defined by the order of reuse is made explicit in corresponding statements that declare a precedence of reusing aspects over reused aspects.

9 Related Work

In 2004 Clarke and Walker present a detailed mapping from THEME/UML to ASPECTJ [5], [4]. THEME/UML [2] is an asymmetric AOM approach that has some points in common with RAM, and thus leads to a similar mapping. Analogous to our mapping, pattern classes are implemented with interfaces and non-template operations become methods that are introduced in these interfaces. If a template operation has no supplementary behavior it is mapped to abstract methods in contrast to our mapping. Template operations with additional behavior are mapped to abstract pointcuts. That means that template methods without supplementary behavior need to be bound by implementing the corresponding abstract method with a delegating call. This is more verbose than marking existing methods with annotations but it makes it possible to adapt to incompatible signatures. The disadvantage of this solution, however, is that concrete pointcuts have to be defined for bound methods. This makes it difficult to use the code that is obtained from the THEME/UML mapping in projects were ASPECTJ constructs in the code base have to be avoided. For our mapping this is not true as our generated annotations are pure JAVA that can be ignored during compilation whenever the aspectual information is not wanted.

The main difference, however, is that RAM and our mapping support more complex constructs like generic or recursive advice and aspect variations than the THEME/UML approach and the corresponding mapping. This higher expressiveness has also to be taken into account when the size and readability of the resulting code for both mappings is compared. Furthermore, the code for THEME/UML is less flexible when seen from a user perspective. This is mainly due to the fact that when the THEME/UML mapping was defined, ASPECTJ did not support annotations and JAVA did not include GENERICS yet.

Apart from an article by Jackson et al. [9] that describes the adaption of the THEME/UML mapping to the requirements of CAESARJ we are not aware of any furhter work that discusses a detailed mapping from constructs of an aspect-oriented modeling language to aspectual code. Much work (e.g. [7], [14]) mentions the generation of AOP code without providing any details on which modeling artifacts correspond to which code elements and how common problems are solved.

10 Conclusions

When using aspect-oriented modeling in the context of Model-Driven Engineering, one possible way of obtaining an executable from the models is to map them to aspect-oriented code. As opposed to weaving at the model level and then generating object-oriented code, traceability of concerns is made easier if aspects at the model level are mapped to code-level aspects. This in turn can benefit software evolution and maintenance.

This paper presents solutions to the most important challenges that a modeler has to face when mapping aspect-oriented models to an aspect-oriented programming language: mapping structure and behavior of a single aspect, mapping instantiation of structure and behavior in target models, mapping conflict resolution between aspects, and mapping aspect dependencies and variability. To illustrate the mapping issues, the paper presents details on how to map REUSABLE ASPECT MODELS to ASPECTJ source code. Finally, general solution strategies that can be used to solve similar problems when attempting to map other aspect-oriented modeling techniques to aspect-oriented code are outlined.

We implemented the AspectOPTIMA case study and an extension to it that supports Open Multithreaded Transactions (OMTTs)[2]. 84% of the base code and 96% of the code of the extension could be obtained by a rigorous application of the mapping presented in this paper. This gives us hope that a future code generator for RAM will lead to very elaborate implementations with little need for manual refinement.

We believe that this mapping in a combination with a meta-model for RAM and a textual representation of it may be a first step on our way to automatic transformations of aspect models to aspect-oriented code.

References

[1] Al Abed, W., Kienzle, J.: Aspect-Oriented Modeling and Information Hiding. In: 14th Aspect-Oriented Modeling Workshop, Denver, CO, USA, pp. 1–6 (October 4, 2009)

---

[2] The complete model and implementation for the AspectOPTIMA case study and its OMTT extension are available at www.cs.mcgill.ca/~joerg/SEL/RAM.html

[2] Baniassad, E., Clarke, S.: Theme: An approach for aspect-oriented analysis and design. In: ICSE 2004, pp. 158–167. IEEE Computer Society, Washington, DC (2004)
[3] Bencomo, N., Blair, G., France, R.: Proceedings of the International Workshops on models@run.time, 2006-2010.
[4] Clarke, S., Baniassad, E.: Aspect-Oriented Analysis and Design. Addison-Wesley Professional, Reading (2005)
[5] Clarke, S., Walker, R.J.: Towards a standard design language for aosd. In: AOSD 2002, pp. 113–119. ACM, New York (2002)
[6] Gosling, J., Joy, B., Steele, G.L.: The Java Language Specification. The Java Series. Addison Wesley, Reading (1996)
[7] Groher, I., Schulze, S.: Generating aspect code from uml models. In: Workshop on Aspect-Oriented Modeling with UML @ AOSD (2003)
[8] Hovsepyan, A., Scandariato, R., Van Baelen, S., Berbers, Y., Joosen, W.: From aspect-oriented models to aspect-oriented code?: the maintenance perspective. In: AOSD 2010, pp. 85–96. ACM, New York (2010)
[9] Jackson, A., Casey, N., Clarke, S.: Mapping design to implementation. AOSD-Europe-TCD-D111, www.aosd-europe.net
[10] Kiczales, G., Hilsdale, E., Hugunin, J., Kersen, M., Palm, J., Griswold, W.G.: An Overview of AspectJ. In: Lee, S.H. (ed.) ECOOP 2001. LNCS, vol. 2072, pp. 327–357. Springer, Heidelberg (2001)
[11] Kienzle, J., Al Abed, W., Fleurey, F., Jézéquel, J.-M., Klein, J.: Aspect-Oriented Design with Reusable Aspect Models. Transactions on Aspect-Oriented Software Development 7, 279–327 (2010)
[12] Kienzle, J., Al Abed, W., Klein, J.: Aspect-Oriented Multi-View Modeling. In: AOSD 2009, pp. 87–98. ACM Press, New York (2009)
[13] Klein, J., Kienzle, J.: Reusable Aspect Models. In: 11th Aspect-Oriented Modeling Workshop, Nashville, TN, USA (September 30, 2007)
[14] Kulesza, U., Garcia, A., Lucena, C.: Generating aspect-oriented agent architectures. In: Workshop on Early Aspects: Aspect-Oriented Requirements Engineering and Architecture Design (2004)

Equation-Based Object-Oriented Modeling Languages and Tools
Report on the Workshop EOOLT 2010 at MODELS 2010
Oslo, Norway, October 3, 2010

Peter Fritzson[1], Edward A. Lee[2], François E. Cellier[3], and David Broman[1]

[1] Linköping University, Sweden
peter.fritzson@liu.se, david.broman@liu.se
[2] UC Berkeley, CA, USA
eal@eecs.berkeley.edu
[3] ETH Zurich, Switzerland
fcellier@inf.ethz.ch

Abstract. EOOLT 2010 was the third edition of the EOOLT workshop series. The workshop is intended to bring together researchers and practitioners from different equation-based object-oriented (EOO) modeling language communities. This year's workshop also expands the scope to include the whole design space of languages for cyber-physical systems, where physical dynamics are mixed with networks and software. The workshop gathered 31 participants to present and discuss thirteen different papers grouped into the four areas of real-time oriented modeling languages and tools, modeling language design, simulation and model compilation, and modeling and simulation tools.

1 Introduction

During the last decade, integrated model-based design of complex cyber-physical systems (which mix physical dynamics with software and networks) has gained significant attention. Hybrid modeling languages based on equations, supporting both continuous-time and event-based aspects (e.g. Modelica, SysML, VHDL-AMS, and Simulink/ Simscape) enable high-level reuse and integrated modeling capabilities of both the physically surrounding system and software for embedded systems. Using such equation-based object-oriented (EOO) modeling languages, it has become possible to model complex systems covering multiple application domains at a high level of abstraction through reusable model components.

The interest in EOO languages and tools is rapidly growing in the industry because of their increasing importance in modeling, simulation, and specification of complex systems. There exist several different EOO language communities today that grew out of different application areas (multi-body system dynamics, electronic circuit simulation, chemical process engineering). The members of these disparate communities rarely talk to each other in spite of the similarities of their modeling and simulation needs.

The EOOLT workshop series aims at bringing these different communities together to discuss their common needs and goals as well as the algorithms and tools that best support them.

It was a good response to the call-for-papers. Eleven papers were accepted for full presentations and two papers for short presentations in the workshop program out of eighteen submissions. All papers were subject to rather detailed reviews by the program committee, on the average four reviews per paper. The workshop program started with a welcome and introduction to the area of equation-based object-oriented languages, followed by paper presentations. Discussion sessions were held after presentations of each set of related papers. There were 31 participants in the workshop, more than doubled compared to EOOLT 2008 which was held in conjunction with ECOOP 2008.

After the event of the workshop, a nomination request for the best paper of the workshop was sent out to all PC members, authors, and workshop participants. Authors were not allowed to nominate themselves. Seven different papers were nominated, where the paper "Modal Models in Ptolemy" by Edward A. Lee and Stavros Tripakis received a clear majority of the nominations. This paper was selected as the best paper of EOOLT 2010, and the abstract is published in a post proceedings of the MODELS conference.

The venue for EOOLT 2010 was Oslo, Norway, in conjunction with the MODELS 2010 conference.

2 Program Chairs/Organizers and Program Committee

Peter Fritzson, Chair	Linköping University, Linköping, Sweden
Edward A. Lee, Co-Chair	U.C. Berkeley, USA
François E. Cellier, Co-Chair	ETH, Zurich, Switzerland
David Broman, Co-Chair	Linköping University, Linköping, Sweden
Bernhard Bachmann	Univ. of Applied Sciences, Bielefeld, Germany
Bert van Beek	Eindhoven Univ. of Technology, Netherlands
Felix Breitenecker	Technical University of Vienna, Vienna, Austria
Jan Broenink	University of Twente, Netherlands
Peter Bunus	Linköping University, Linköping, Sweden
Francesco Casella	Politecnico di Milano, Italy
Hilding Elmqvist	Dassault Systèmes, Lund, Sweden
Olaf Enge-Rosenblatt	Fraunhofer Inst. for Integrated Circuits, Dresden
Petter Krus	Linköping University, Linköping, Sweden
Sven-Erik Mattsson	Dassault Systèmes, Lund, Sweden
Jacob Mauss	QTronic GmbH, Berlin, Germany
Pieter Mosterman	MathWorks, Inc., Natick, MA, USA
Toby Myers	Griffith University, Brisbane, Australia
Henrik Nilsson	University of Nottingham, Nottingham, UK
Dionisio de Niz Villasensor	Carnegie Mellon University, Pittsburgh, USA
Hans Olsson	Dassault Systèmes, Lund, Sweden
Martin Otter	DLR Oberpfaffenhofen, Germany
Chris Paredis	Georgia Institute of Technology, Atlanta, USA
Peter Pepper	TU Berlin, Berlin, Germany
Adrian Pop	Linköping University, Linköping, Sweden
Nicolas Rouquette	NASA Jet Propulsion Laboratory, USA

Peter Schwarz   Fraunhofer Inst. for Integrated Circuits, Dresden
Christian Sonntag   TU Dortmund, Dortmund, Germany
Martin Törngren   KTH, Stockholm, Sweden
Alfonso Urquía   National Univ. for Distance Education, Madrid
Hans Vangheluwe   McGill University, Montreal, Canada
Dirk Zimmer   DLR Oberpfaffenhofen, Germany
Johan Åkesson   Lund University, Lund, Sweden

3 Publication

All papers are published electronically by Linköping University Electronic Press [1] and available in the electronic proceedings at http://www.ep.liu.se/ecp/047/.

All presentations (together with the papers) are also available at the EOOLT 2010 web site: http://www.eoolt.org/2010/.

4 Sessions

The workshop sessions are briefly described below. Each session starts with paper presentations, followed by a discussion related to the topic of that particular session. Some discussion also took place during the paper presentations.

4.1 Real-Time Oriented Modeling Languages and Tools

Session chair: David Broman

In this session, research work was presented related to graphical modeling languages, real-time applications, and profiling. Three papers were presented and discussed.

In "Execution of UML State Machines Using Modelica," Wladimir Schamai, Uwe Pohlmann, Peter Fritzson, Christiaan J.J. Paredis, Philipp Helle, and Carsten Strobel present the ModelicaML language and how it can be used for modeling UML state machines. Wladimir presented a translational approach for code generation of Modelica code as well as a priority schema for handling the problem of conflicting transitions in UML diagrams.

In "Modal Models in Ptolemy," Edward A. Lee and Stavros Tripakis discuss the concepts and semantics of modal models and how time is handled in refined submodels in finite state machines (FSMs). Examples were given in the Ptolemy II environment. One conclusion is that refined modes should have a local notation of time that does not advance while a mode is inactive. Hence, the gap between local time and global time is monotonically increasing.

In "Profiling of Modelica Real-Time Models," Christian Schulze, Michaela Huhn, and Martin Schüler present an approach and implementation for profiling of Modelica models used in real-time applications. It was concluded using a case study that profiling can help identifying the workload for parts of a model. It was also pointed out that it is important to separate the process of saving result data to a hard disk drive into a non real-time application.

In the following discussion session, questions and comments from the audience concerned all three paper presentations. The main questions and comments for the first presentation related to Stategraph, static checking, and possibility of round-trip engineering. For the second presentation, questions concerned the similarity to Simulink and semantics for stream processing in Ptolemy. It was pointed out that the semantics are not built into the system, but are defined by different directors. The discussions concerning the last presentation focused on different challenges of implementation of a profiling system, in particular regarding the possibility of tracing back to the original Modelica model.

4.2 Modeling Language Design

Session chair: Edward A. Lee

The second session focused on design and implementation aspects of Modelica.

"Towards Improved Class Parameterization and Class Generation in Modelica," Dirk Zimmer introduces the idea that class parameterization and class generation should be separate concepts in Modelica. The goal is to partially redesign Modelica, to unify concepts, and to simplify the language.

In "Notes on the Separate Compilation of Modelica," Christoph Höger, Florian Lorenzen, and Peter Pepper discuss different problems and implications of introducing separate compilation of Modelica models, e.g., runtime instantiation, introducing coercion functions, and handling of dynamic binding. It is noted that the Modelica language is very complex and that special cases of the semantics need to be reduced.

In "Import of Distributed Parameter Models into Lumped Parameter Model Libraries for Linearly Deformable Solid Bodies," Tobias Zaiczek and Olaf Enge-Rosenblatt show how distributed parameter models can be included in libraries of lumped parameter models. Discretization, connector definitions, and model order reduction are analyzed with regards to flexible bodies modeling and simulation.

In the following discussion session, the discussion related to the first talk concerned types, models as first class, and different aspects of concrete syntax. The discussion about the second talk focused on when elaboration/flattening and symbolic manipulation should take place. Should it be at compile-time, link-time, or at run-time? Finally for the last talk, questions were raised about related work, i.e., performance comparison with simulation tools such as Dymola and comparison to other PDE Modelica efforts.

4.3 Simulation and Model Compilation

Session chair: François E. Cellier

In this session, three research papers were presented related to synchronous event handling together with a numerical solver, distributed simulation using TLM techniques, and profiling.

In "Synchronous Events in the OpenModelica Compiler with a Petri Net Library Application," Willi Braun, Bernhard Bachmann, and Sabrina Proß describe improved techniques for synchronous event handling using the DASSL solver in OpenModelica, with applications in a Petri Net library.

In "Towards Efficient Distributed Simulation in Modelica using Transmission Line Modeling," Martin Sjölund, Robert Braun, Peter Fritzson, and Petter Krus describe the TLM model partitioning technique, how this can be integrated in Modelica to enable efficient simulation, and results from a prototype implementation.

In "Compilation of Modelica Array Computations into Single Assignment C for Efficient Execution on CUDA-enabled GPUs," Kristian Stavåker, Daniel Rolls, Jing Guo, Peter Fritzson, and Sven-Bodo Scholz describe methods to compile repetitive equations and array equations to SAC code running on GPUs, with measurements.

Discussions touched issues like convergence of event iteration, synchronous event handling (1st talk), fixed or flexible time steps, interpolation (2nd talk), and large arrays, need for combination of task and data parallelism, size of equation systems that can be handled, and handling models with algebraic loops (3rd talk).

4.4 Modeling and Simulation Tools

Session chair: Peter Fritzson

This session presented research related to tool functionality such as XML representation of systems of equations, computer algebra operations on models, a comparison between DASSL and QSS numeric solvers, and model debugging through model reduction. Two long papers followed by two short were presented and discussed.

In "An XML Representation of DAE Systems Obtained from Continuous-time Modelica Models," Roberto Parrotto, Johan Åkesson, and Francesco Casella describe an XML format for model equations and its usage for model export to other tools.

In "Towards a Computer Algebra System with Automatic Differentiation for Use with Object-Oriented Modelling," Joel Anderson, Boris Houska, and Moritz Diehl describe a special-purpose small C++ based tool for automatic differentiation.

In "Discretising Time or States? A Comparative Study between DASSL and QSS," Xenofon Floros, François E. Cellier, and Ernesto Kofman describe a new simulation run-time system for OpenModelica based on quantized state systems (QSS) simulation and compares this approach to the standard DASSL solver.

In "Model Verification and Debugging of EOO Models Aided by Model Reduction Techniques," Anton Sodja and Borut Zupančič give an overview of model reduction techniques and argue that such techniques are useful for debugging and verification.

The following discussion covered e.g., the difference between FMI and the XML, advantages / issues with QSS, the current status of model reduction techniques, etc.

References

[1] Fritzson, P., Lee, E., Cellier, F., Broman, D. (eds.): Proceed-ings of the 3rd International Workshop on Equation-Based Object-Oriented Mod-eling Languages and Tools, Oslo, Norway. LIU Electronic Press (October 2010) ISSN 1650-3740

Model-Driven Interoperability: MDI 2010

Jean Bézivin[1], Richard M. Soley[2], and Antonio Vallecillo[3]

[1] INRIA and Ecole de Mines de Nantes, France
[2] Object Management Group, USA
[3] Atenea Research Group, Universidad de Málaga, Spain
`jbezivin@gmail.com`, `soley@omg.org`, `av@lcc.uma.es`

Abstract. This paper provides a summary of the First International Workshop on Model Driven Interoperability (MDI 2010), held on October 5, 2010, in conjunction with the MODELS 2010 conference in Oslo, Norway.

1 Introduction

The MDI 2010 workshop was held on October 5, 2010, in conjunction with the MODELS 2010 conference in Oslo, Norway. This was the first edition of this workshop, which is devoted to discuss the potential role of models as key enablers for all kinds of systems and data interoperability.

The MDI workshop was created with the goal to provide a venue where researchers and practitioners concerned with all aspects of models and systems interoperability could meet, disseminate and exchange ideas and problems, identify some of the key issues related to model-driven interoperability, and explore together possible solutions and the challenges ahead.

This paper contains a summary of the MDI 2010 workshop. It is an extended version of [1], which provided an editorial introduction to the full MDI 2010 workshop Proceedings [2].

2 Model-Driven Interoperability

Interoperability can be defined as the ability of separate entities, systems or artifacts (organizations, programs, tools, etc.) to work together. Although there has always been the need to achieve interoperability between heterogeneous systems and notations [3], the difficulties involved in overcoming their differences, the lack of consensus on the common standards to use and the shortage of proper mechanisms and tools, have severely hampered this task.

Model-Driven Engineering (MDE) is an emergent discipline that advocates the use of (software) models as primary artifacts of the software engineering process. In addition to the initial goals of being useful to capture user requirements and architectural concerns, and to generate code from them, models are proving to be effective for many other engineering tasks. New model-driven engineering approaches, such as model-driven modernization, models-at-runtime, model-based testing, etc. are constantly emerging.

Model interoperability is much more complex than simply defining a local serialization format, e.g., XMI. This would just resolve the syntactic (or "plumbing") issues between models and modeling tools. However, interoperability should also involve further aspects, including behavioral specifications of models (which in turn describe the behavioral aspects of the systems being modeled), and other "semantic" issues [4] such as agreements on names, context-sensitive information, agreements on concepts (ontologies), integration conflict analysis (including for example automatic data model matching), semantic reasoning, etc. Furthermore, interoperability not only means being able to exchange information and to use the information that has been exchanged [5], but also to exchange services and functions to operate effectively together. All these interoperability issues and needs become clear in any complex system, as it has recently happened in the HL/7 and DICOM healthcare projects, for instance.

Models and MDE techniques (especially metamodeling and model transformations) can play a fundamental role for fully accomplishing these tasks. Thus, models can become cornerstone elements for enabling and achieving interoperability between all kinds of systems and artifacts, including data sets (under the presence of different data schemata, and possibly at different levels of abstraction), services (despite their differences in data representation, access protocols and underlying technological platforms), event systems (with different complex types and origins), languages (that use different notations and may have different semantics), tools (with different data formats and semantic representations), technological platforms (with different notations, tools and semantics), etc. It should also be emphasized that the success of MDE has created accidental complexity, for example by generating a number of overlapping metamodels (UML, SySML, BPML, etc.) and this situation reveals itself in a number of contexts as an additional metamodel interoperability problem.

3 The MDI 2010 Workshop

The organizers decided to set up a workshop with the goal of gathering rearchers and practitioners working on topics related to interoperability, coming from different communities and with different backgrounds. The idea was to exchange experiences and proposals, and to foster potential cross-fertilization of ideas among participants.

An excellent Program Committee was assembled to help with the review process, which included very well-known and respected experts in the topics of the workshop: Patrick Albert, Uwe Assmann, Colin Atkinson, Jorn Bettin, Jean Pierre Bourey, Tony Clark, Robert Claris, Gregor Engels, Jean Marie Favre, Robert France, Dragan Gasevic, Sbastien Grard, Martin Gogolla, Jeff Gray, Esther Guerra, Tihamer Levendovszky, Richard Paige, Alfonso Pierantonio, Bernhard Rumpe, Jim Steel, Hans Vangheluwe, Andrew Watson, Jon Whittle and Manuel Wimmer.

In response to the call for papers, a total of 19 submissions were received. Submitted papers were formally peer-reviewed by three referees, and 12 papers were finally accepted for presentation at the workshop and publication at the Proceedings, that have been published in the ACM Digital Library [2].

We counted on some external reviewers that helped PC members to review the papers: Fabian Buettner, Lars Hamann, Mirco Kuhlmann, Ivano Malavolta, Antonio Navarro Perez, Ingo Weisemoeller, Christian Wende and Claas Wilke.

4 Workshop Papers

The following 12 papers were presented in the workshop:

- "Model Driven Interoperability in practice: preliminary evidences and issues from an industrial project" by Youness Lemrabet, David Clin, Michel Bigand, Jean-Pierre Bourey and Nordine Benkeltoum. [6]
- "Semantic Interoperability of Clinical Data Exchange" by Idoia Berges, Jess Bermudez, Alfredo Goi and Arantza Illarramendi. [7]
- "A Process Model Discovery Approach for Enabling Model Interoperability in Signal Engineering" by Wikan Danar Sunindyo and Thomas Moser. [8]
- "Efficient Analysis and Execution of Correct and Complete Model Transformations Based on Triple Graph Grammars" by Frank Hermann, Hartmut Ehrig, Ulrike Golas and Fernando Orejas. [9]
- ⊛ "Towards an Expressivity Benchmark for Mappings based on a Systematic Classification of Heterogeneities" by Manuel Wimmer, Gerti Kappel, Angelika Kusel, Werner Retschitzegger, Johannes Schoenboeck and Wieland Schwinger. [10]
- ⊛ "Specifying Overlaps of Heterogeneous Models for Global Consistency Checking" by Zinovy Diskin, Yingfei Xiong and Krzysztof Czarnecki. [11]
- "Anticipating Unanticipated Tool Interoperability using Role Models" by Mirko Seifert, Christian Wende and Uwe Aßmann. [12]
- "Behavioural Interoperability to Support Model-Driven Systems Integration" by Alek Radjenovic and Richard Paige. [13]
- "Aligning Business and IT Models in Service-Oriented Architectures using BPMN and SoaML" by Brian Elvesæter, Dima Panfilenko, Sven Jacobi and Christian Hahn. [14]
- "Domain-specific Templates for Refinement Transformations" by Lucia Kapova, Thomas Goldschmidt, Jens Happe and Ralf Reussner. [15]
- "Advanced Modelling Made Simple with the Gmodel Metalanguage" by Jorn Bettin and Tony Clark. [16]
- "Model-driven Rule-based Mediation in XML Data" by Yongxin Liao, Dumitru Roman and Arne.J. Berre. [17]

These papers contribute in different aspects to the area of model driven interoperability, from its foundations to the potential benefits it may bring to the emerging field of MDE. The slides of these presentations are available from the workshop Web site http://mdi2010.lcc.uma.es. Two of the papers (these marked with a circled asterisk ⊛ in the list above) were invited to submit an extended version for this LNCS volume, and are included in this volume, after this workshop summary.

5 Workshop Discussions

The workshop was organized in four sessions. The first three were dedicated to the presentation of the selected papers. The last session was dedicated to discussions among the participants about the open issues and topics identified during the paper presentations. The detailed agenda of the workshop is in http://mdi2010.lcc.uma.es/Agenda.html.

The first session started with a welcome to the participants and a keynote opening talk by Jean Bézivin, who described the key concepts related to Model-Driven Interoperability, identified the essential aspects involved in this topic and presented some of the efforts currently in progress within the software community. The talk served as an introduction to the workshop and also helped setting a context for the rest of the presentations and discussions. The slides of the talk are available from http://mdi2010.lcc.uma.es/slides/MDI2010-JBezivinPresentation.ppsx.

The remainder of the first session and the next two were devoted to paper presentations and short questions and answers.

A final session was dedicated to discuss some of the issues that came up during the paper presentations. More than 30 people participated in the discussions, that covered different topics including syntactical vs. semantic interoperability, why it the problem of interoperability so hard, what kinds of mechanisms are required to deal with some of the issues that were identified during the workshop, etc.

Finally, it was agreed that a mail list was set up in order to distribute information related to the topics of the workshop. Such a list is already in use: mdi@lcc.uma.es. Subscription can be done on-line via http://sol10.lcc.uma.es/mailman/listinfo/mdi.

Acknowledgements

We would like to thank the MODELS 2010 organization for giving us the opportunity to organize this Workshop, especially to the Workshop Chairs, Juergen Dingel and Arnor Solberg. Many thanks to all those that submitted papers, and particularly to the contributing authors. Our gratitude also goes to the paper reviewers and the members of the MDI 2010 Program Committee, for their timely and accurate reviews and for their help in choosing and improving the selected papers. Thanks to the ACM Digital Library for producing and publishing the MDI Worskhop Proceedings, and specially to Craig Rodkin for his excellent support. Finally, we would like to acknowledge the research projects TIN2008-03107 and P07-TIC-03184 that have helped supporting this workshop.

References

1. Bézivin, J., Soley, R.M., Vallecillo, A.: Editorial to the proceedings of the first international workshop on model-driven interoperability. In: Proceedings of the First International Workshop on Model-Driven Interoperability, MDI 2010, pp. 1–2. ACM, Oslo (2010)
2. Bézivin, J., Soley, R.M., Vallecillo, A. (eds.): MDI 2010: Proceedings of the First International Workshop on Model-Driven Interoperability, Oslo, Norway. ACM, New York (2010); ISBN: 978-1-4503-0292-0, http://portal.acm.org/citation.cfm?id=1866272&picked=prox&CFID=11191541%7&CFTOKEN=16058625
3. Wegner, P.: Interoperability. ACM Computing Surveys 28(1), 285–287 (1996)
4. Heiler, S.: Semantic interoperability. ACM Computing Surveys 27(2), 271–272 (1995)
5. Institute of Electrical and Electronics Engineers: IEEE Standard Computer Dictionary: A Compilation of IEEE Standard Computer Glossaries (1990)

6. Lemrabet, Y., Bigand, M., Clin, D., Benkeltoum, N., Bourey, J.P.: Model driven interoperability in practice: preliminary evidences and issues from an industrial project. In: Proceedings of the First International Workshop on Model-Driven Interoperability, MDI 2010, Oslo, Norway, pp. 3–9. ACM, New York (2010)
7. Berges, I., Bermudez, J., Goñi, A., Illarramendi, A.: Semantic interoperability of clinical data. In: Proceedings of the First International Workshop on Model-Driven Interoperability, MDI 2010, Oslo, Norway, pp. 10–14. ACM, New York (2010)
8. Sunindyo, W.D., Moser, T., Winkler, D., Biffl, S.: A process model discovery approach for enabling model interoperability in signal engineering. In: Proceedings of the First International Workshop on Model-Driven Interoperability, MDI 2010, Oslo, Norway, pp. 15–21. ACM, New York (2010)
9. Hermann, F., Ehrig, H., Golas, U., Orejas, F.: Efficient analysis and execution of correct and complete model transformations based on triple graph grammars. In: Proceedings of the First International Workshop on Model-Driven Interoperability, MDI 2010, Oslo, Norway, pp. 22–31. ACM, New York (2010)
10. Wimmer, M., Kappel, G., Kusel, A., Retschitzegger, W., Schoenboeck, J., Schwinger, W.: Towards an expressivity benchmark for mappings based on a systematic classification of heterogeneities. In: Proceedings of the First International Workshop on Model-Driven Interoperability, MDI 2010, Oslo, Norway, pp. 32–41. ACM, New York (2010)
11. Diskin, Z., Xiong, Y., Czarnecki, K.: Specifying overlaps of heterogeneous models for global consistency checking. In: Proceedings of the First International Workshop on Model-Driven Interoperability, MDI 2010, Oslo, Norway, pp. 42–51. ACM, New York (2010)
12. Seifert, M., Wende, C., Aßmann, U.: Anticipating unanticipated tool interoperability using role models. In: Proceedings of the First International Workshop on Model-Driven Interoperability, MDI 2010, Oslo, Norway, pp. 52–60. ACM, New York (2010)
13. Radjenovic, A., Paige, R.F.: Behavioural interoperability to support model-driven systems integration. In: Proceedings of the First International Workshop on Model-Driven Interoperability, MDI 2010, Oslo, Norway, pp. 98–107. ACM, New York (2010)
14. Elvesæter, B., Panfilenko, D., Jacobi, S., Hahn, C.: Aligning business and IT models in service-oriented architectures using BPMN and SoaML. In: Proceedings of the First International Workshop on Model-Driven Interoperability, MDI 2010, Oslo, Norway, pp. 61–68. ACM, New York (2010)
15. Kapova, L., Goldschmidt, T., Happe, J., Reussner, R.H.: Domain-specific templates for refinement transformations. In: Proceedings of the First International Workshop on Model-Driven Interoperability, MDI 2010, Oslo, Norway, pp. 69–78. ACM, New York (2010)
16. Bettin, J., Clark, T.: Advanced modelling made simple with the Gmodel metalanguage. In: Proceedings of the First International Workshop on Model-Driven Interoperability, MDI 2010, Oslo, Norway, pp. 79–88. ACM, New York (2010)
17. Liao, Y., Roman, D., Berre, A.J.: Model-driven rule-based mediation in xml data exchange. In: Proceedings of the First International Workshop on Model-Driven Interoperability, MDI 2010, Oslo, Norway, pp. 89–97. ACM, New York (2010)

From the Heterogeneity Jungle to Systematic Benchmarking*

M. Wimmer[1], G. Kappel[1], A. Kusel[2], W. Retschitzegger[2],
J. Schoenboeck[1], and W. Schwinger[2]

[1] Vienna University of Technology, Austria
lastname@big.tuwien.ac.at
[2] Johannes Kepler University Linz, Austria
firstname.lastname@jku.at

Abstract. One of the key challenges in the development of model transformations is the resolution of recurring semantic and syntactic heterogeneities. Thus, we provide a systematic classification of heterogeneities building upon a feature model that makes the interconnections between them explicit. On the basis of this classification, a set of benchmark examples was derived and used to evaluate current approaches to the specification of model transformations. We found, that approaches on the conceptual level lack expressivity whereas execution level approaches lack support for reuse. Moreover, only few of the approaches evaluated provide key features such as an automatic trace model or the ability to reuse specifications by inheritance.

Keywords: Syntactic and Semantic Heterogeneities, Mapping Benchmark.

1 Introduction

With the rise of model-driven engineering (MDE), models and associated transformations for migrating, merging, or evolving models have become the main artifacts of the software engineering process [3]. One of the key challenges in this respect is the resolution of recurring heterogeneities between the corresponding metamodels (MMs) to preserve semantics, (i) at the conceptual level by means

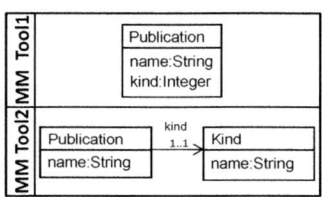

Fig. 1. Heterogenous MMs

of mapping tools that provide reusable components as, for instance proposed in [7] and [21], and (ii) at the execution level by means of dedicated transformation languages [5]. Heterogeneities result from the fact that semantically similar metamodeling concepts (M2) can be defined by different meta-metamodeling concepts (M3), which leads to differently structured metamodels. As a simple example, Fig. 1 shows two MMs of fictitious, domain-specific tools that administrate publications. Whereas Tool1 models the type of a publication by the

---

* This work has been funded by the Austrian Science Fund under grant P21374-N13.

attribute `Publication.kind` (e.g., conference or journal), `Tool2` represents the same semantics by using the class `Publication`, which refers to a class `Kind`, to determine the kind of publication.

Up to now, it has been unclear which kinds of heterogeneity must be resolved in model-to-model transformations. Therefore, this paper proposes a systematic classification of heterogeneities between object-oriented MMs by adapting and extending existing classifications in data and ontology engineering. The design rationale was to identify a complete set of potential points of variation between two Ecore-based MMs. This provided the basis for establishing a benchmark that allows evaluation of existing approaches with respect to their ability to resolve heterogeneities. To show the applicability of this benchmark, existing mapping tools and transformation languages from different domains were evaluated by using selected example scenarios defined for our benchmark, each posing certain challenges to the benchmarked approaches. Further example scenarios of our benchmark can be found in [22] and on our project web page[1].

The remainder of this paper is structured as follows. Section 2 presents the identified points of variation of meta-metamodels and gives a first overview of our classification. The exemplary benchmark scenarios together with their challenges and how existing approaches deal with them are discussed in Section 3. Lessons learned are summarized in Section 4. Finally, related work is referred to in Section 5, and Section 6 reports on future work.

2 Systematic Classification of Heterogeneities

According to a substantial body of literature [2,4,9,12,13,14,15,18,20], heterogeneities can be divided into two main classes: (i) *syntactic heterogeneities*, i.e., differences with respect to *how* something is represented by a MM and (ii) *semantic heterogeneities*, i.e., differences with respect to *what* is represented by a MM.

Syntactic Heterogeneities. Syntactic heterogeneities result from the fact that semantically similar concepts can be defined by different metamodeling concepts, which leads to differently structured metamodels. To obtain a systematic classification of different kinds of syntactic heterogeneity,

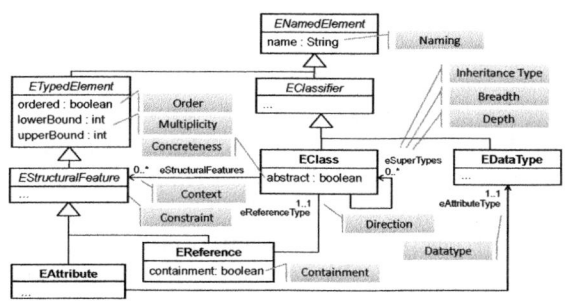

Fig. 2. Variation Points in Ecore-based MMs

we investigated potential points of variation between two Ecore[2]-based metamodels. Fig. 2 depicts the relevant part of the Ecore meta-metamodel potentially causing syntactic heterogeneities, and omits all the Ecore concepts which

---

[1] www.modeltransformation.net
[2] http://www.eclipse.org/modeling/emf/

Table 1. Common Core Concepts in Different Domains

Common Core Concepts	Ecore	XML Schema	OWL
Class	EClass	<xs:complexType>	<owl:Class>
Attribute	EAttribute	<xs:attribute>	<owl:DatatypeProperty>
Reference	EReference	<xs:key>, <xs:keyRef>	<owl:ObjectProperty>
Inheritance	eSuperTypes	<xs:extension base>	<rdfs:subClassOf>

are used merely for Java code generation in the EMF framework. It must be emphasized at this point that the core concepts of Ecore resemble the fundamental ingredients of semantic data models [11], which are also prevalent in other domains such as data and ontology engineering (as depicted in Table 1). Hence, the following findings apply to a broader field.

Based on this design rationale, we introduce a classification of heterogeneities (cf. Fig. 3). It is expressed by means of the feature model formalism [6], which allows us to identify clearly the interconnections between the different kinds of heterogeneity. We distinguish two types of *syntactic heterogeneity*: simple *naming differences* (i.e., differences in the values of the name attribute of ENamedElement: cf. Fig. 2) and more challenging *structural differences*. Although names play an important role when deriving the semantics of a concept, the semantics cannot be inferred automatically, which leads to the synonym and homonym problem. With respect to structural differences, two main cases can be distinguished: *core concept differences* and *inheritance differences*. The former occur due to different usage of classes, attributes, and references (represented by C, A, and R in Fig. 3) and can be further divided into heterogeneities between (a) the same and (b) different metamodeling concepts. Two main differences may emerge in case (a) – either the concepts exhibit different attribute/reference settings (cf. Fig 2) or a different number of concepts has been used in the MMs to express the same semantic concept (cf. *Source-Target-Concept Cardinality* in Fig. 3). An example of the first case would be that one of two EClasses used is defined as abstract, which leads to a *concreteness heterogeneity*. An example of the second case is that in the left hand side (LHS) MM, two EAttributes, firstName and lastName, are used whereas in the right hand side (RHS) MM, this information is contained in just one EAttribute: name. Concerning case (b), heterogeneities are derived by systematically combining the identified core concepts. For instance, an EAttribute in the LHS MM is represented by an EClass in the RHS MM (cf. example in Fig. 1). Finally, heterogeneities may not only be caused by the concepts of classes, attributes, and references but also by the concept of inheritance. In this respect, we distinguish between heterogeneities that may occur although both MMs use inheritance (cf. *"same metamodeling concept inheritance"* in Fig. 3) and heterogeneities that occur if only one MM makes use of inheritance (cf. *"different metamodeling concept inheritance"* in Fig. 3).

Semantic Heterogeneities. Two main cases of semantic heterogeneity can be distinguished: (i) differences in the *number of valid instances* and (ii) differences in the *interpretation of the instance values* [12]. In case (i), all the set-theoretic relationships may occur as modeled by the corresponding subfeatures. In case (ii), a variety of modifications of the values may be necessary

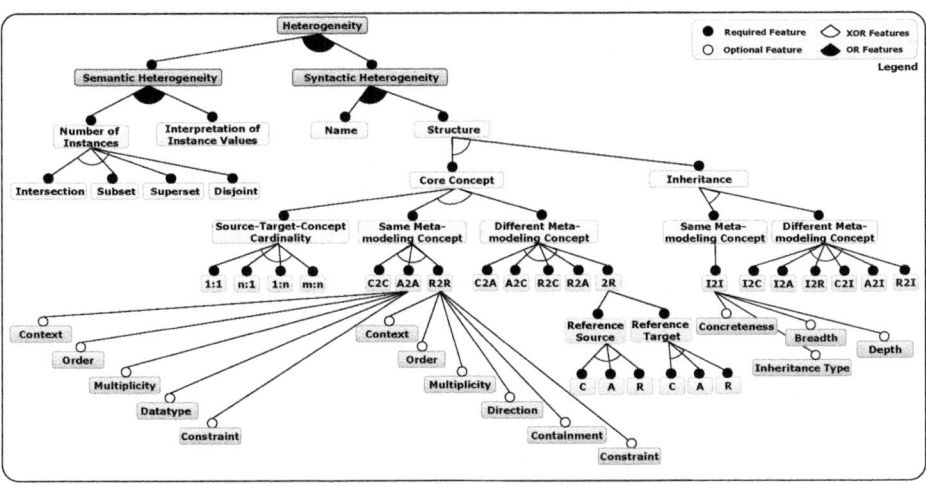

Fig. 3. Heterogeneity Feature Model

to translate LHS MM values into RHS MM values such that the values conform to the *interpretation* of the RHS MM. Thus, semantic heterogeneities cannot be derived from the syntax (since in both cases the MMs can be represented syntactically in the same way) but only by incorporating *interpretation*, i.e., by assigning meaning to each piece of data [10]. For further details about the classification the reader is referred to [22].

3 Benchmark Examples Applied

The proposed classification was then used to derive appropriate benchmark examples. Since the classification makes the interconnections between heterogeneities explicit, a systematic set of benchmark examples, i.e., a set that fully covers the feature model, can be built. Each benchmark example is characterized by a description, source and target metamodels and corresponding models. To aid comprehension, examples using ontological concepts were preferred over those using linguistic concepts. Below, we present three of the proposed examples that we used to evaluate the ability of mapping tools and transformation languages to resolve certain heterogeneities. Each example is a representative of a main branch in the feature model: (i) core concepts with same metamodeling concept heterogeneities, (ii) core concept with different metamodeling concept heterogeneities and (iii) inheritance heterogeneities.

Evaluated Approaches. The benchmark examples were applied to a carefully selected bundle of approaches: at the conceptual level, three mapping tools from different domains and, at the execution level, two dedicated model transformation languages. Among the mapping tools were *AMW* [7] from the area of model engineering, the commercial tool *MapForce*[3] from data engineering, and

---

[3] http://www.altova.com/de/mapforce.html

$MAFRA^4$ from ontology engineering. *AMW* allows the definition of so-called weaving links between Ecore-based MMs to form a mapping definition which can be transformed into executable *ATL* code. In contrast, *MapForce* allows mapping definitions between diverse schema languages, for instance, relational or XML schemas. For executing the specified mapping definitions, several target languages such as Java and XSLT are supported. Finally, *MAFRA* supports for mappings between RDF- and OWL-based ontologies and XML schemas which are directly executed within the tool. Among the transformation languages evaluated were ATL^5, a representative of hybrid rule-based transformation languages, and AGG^6, a declarative graph-based transformation language. The results of the comparison are summarized in Table 2 and described in detail below.

3.1 Benchmark Example 1

The first benchmark example belongs to the category of core concept heterogeneities between the same MM concepts (cf. Fig. 3), and poses four main challenges, as detailed below (cf. Fig. 4). Since the overall goal of all our transformations is to minimize *information loss* and to produce only *valid instances*, instance P2 remained in the RHS although it does not reference any journal publication in the LHS model. Interestingly, the RHS MM in this example is more restrictive than the LHS MM, since the EAttribute Prof.bornIn always requires a value, and since each instance of Prof requires at least one link to a journal publication. Since these restrictions do not exist in the LHS MM, instances of it may break them. Therefore, some resolution strategy is needed – either by auto-generating values or by incorporating user-interaction in order to produce valid instances of the RHS MM.

Challenge 1: A2A, Multiplicity Difference, Datatype Difference. In our example, this challenge arises between the EAttributes Professor.dateOfBirth and Prof.bornIn. The main challenge is to extract the year of birth as an integer value from the LHS date structure. In the absence of a date either (i) a null-value (with semantics *exists but not known*, leading to an invalid target model), or (ii) a (user- or auto-generated) value requiring a corresponding *function* is produced. All evaluated approaches were able to meet this challenge, although the specification effort varied. For example, in *MapForce* dedicated components such as substitute-missing (cf. Fig. 5 (a)) are available, whereas in the other tools the function must be defined from scratch.

Challenge 2: Semantic Heterogeneity, A2A. The *second challenge* exhibits a *semantic heterogeneity* between the EAttributes Professor.salary and Prof.salary, since Professor.salary is encoded in dollars, whereas Prof.salary is encoded in euros, i.e., there is a difference in the interpretation of the values. A conversion of values from dollars to euros must thus be realized in a *function*. This imposes requirements similar to those in the first challenge, and

---

[4] http://mafra-toolkit.sourceforge.net
[5] http://www.eclipse.org/atl
[6] http://user.cs.tu-berlin.de/~gragra/agg

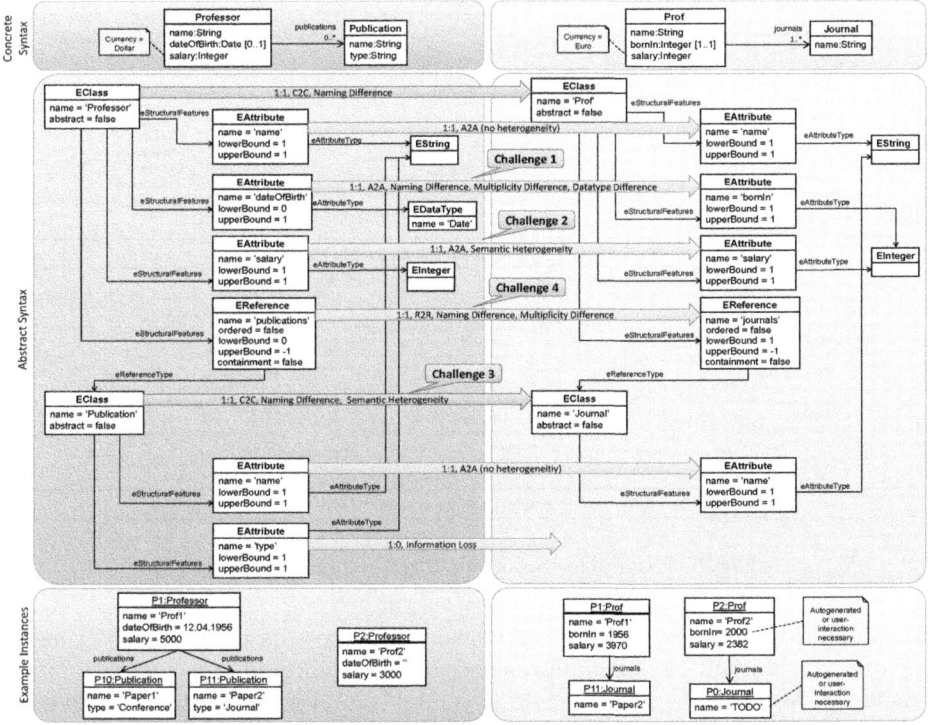

Fig. 4. Benchmark Example 1 – Heterogeneities between same MM concepts

the evaluation therefore results in similar findings. The exemplary solution of this challenge in *MapForce* is shown in Fig. 5 (a).

Challenge 3: Semantic Heterogeneity, C2C. The *third challenge* again includes a *semantic heterogeneity* – but this time a difference in the number of valid instances, since only journal instances should be transformed. Resolving the heterogeneity requires a corresponding *condition*, that identifies instances that remain valid in the context of the RHS `EClass`. All approaches were able to achieve this. The exemplary solution of this challenge in *AMW* is shown in Fig. 5 (b).

Challenge 4: R2R, Multiplicity Difference. Finally, the *fourth challenge* consists of a multiplicity difference between the `EReferences Professor.publications` and `Prof.journals`. Since challenge 3 requires transformation only of journal instances, the first sub-challenge here is to identify links that do not refer to journal instances. Ideally, this should be achieved automatically by a built-in trace model that keeps track of which source elements have been used to create certain target elements. Moreover, since the goal is to generate only valid target instances, the second sub-challenge is to generate journals and link them correctly (instead of generating null values with semantics *does not exist* when a professor does not have any). All approaches were able to resolve the heterogeneity of the first sub-challenge. However, the effort needed differed, since

156   M. Wimmer et al.

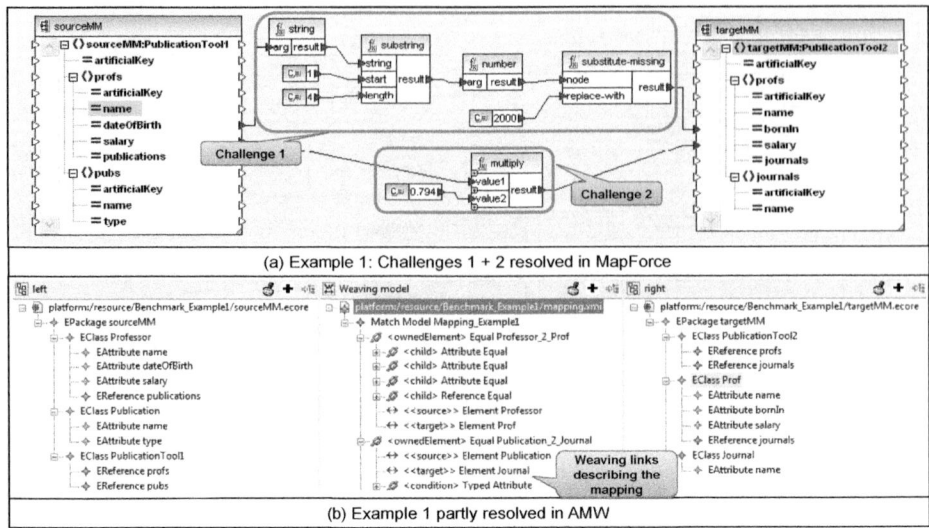

Fig. 5. Exemplary Solutions for Benchmark Example 1

the condition required for filtering journal instances (as in challenge 3) had to be duplicated in all mapping approaches due to insufficient trace model support. As for the second sub-challenge, *AMW* and *MAFRA* were not able to link newly generated objects due to insufficient trace model support. Although *MapForce* does not support a trace model, it resolved this example, since only one journal object with a fixed key value had to be generated, and this can be referred to by the foreign key. Both, *ATL* and *AGG* were able to resolve this heterogeneity using their trace models. *ATL* provides a built-in trace model which can be queried (`resolveTemp` mechanism), whereas in *AGG* the trace model must be maintained manually.

In summary, the fourth challenge appeared to be the most problematic one in this example for the approaches evaluated.

3.2 Benchmark Example 2

The second benchmark example belongs to the category of core concept heterogeneities when using different metamodeling concepts (cf. Fig. 3) and poses two main challenges. The example instances reveal that the intention is to create a Kind object only for distinct values of the attribute Publication.kind. Therefore, the RHS model contains only a single Kind object named Journal (cf. K1 in Fig. 6), which is referenced by the Publication objects P1 and P2.

Challenge 1: A2C. The first challenge in this benchmark example is the generation of Kind objects for distinct values of the kind attribute. A trace model is required to keep track of whether an object has already been created for a value. Since no explicit trace model is available in *AMW* and *MAFRA*, they were not able to resolve this heterogeneity. Although *MapForce* also does

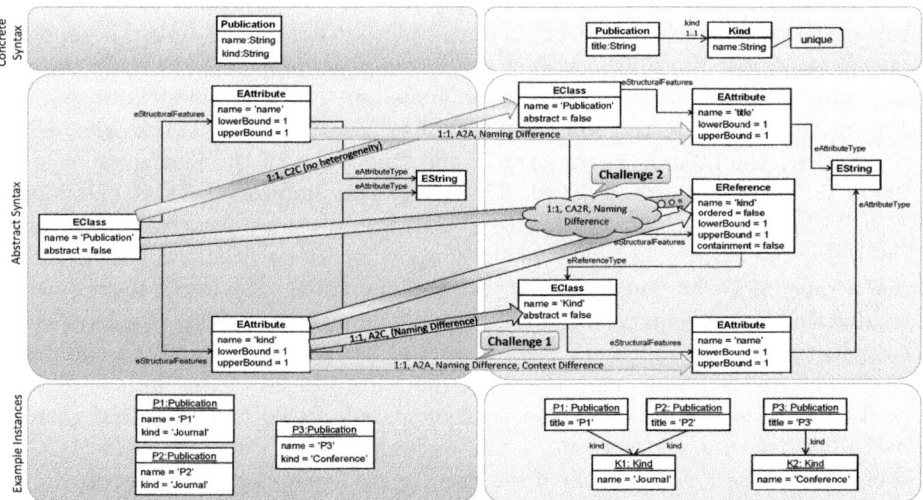

Fig. 6. Benchmark Example 2 – Different Metamodeling Concept Heterogeneities

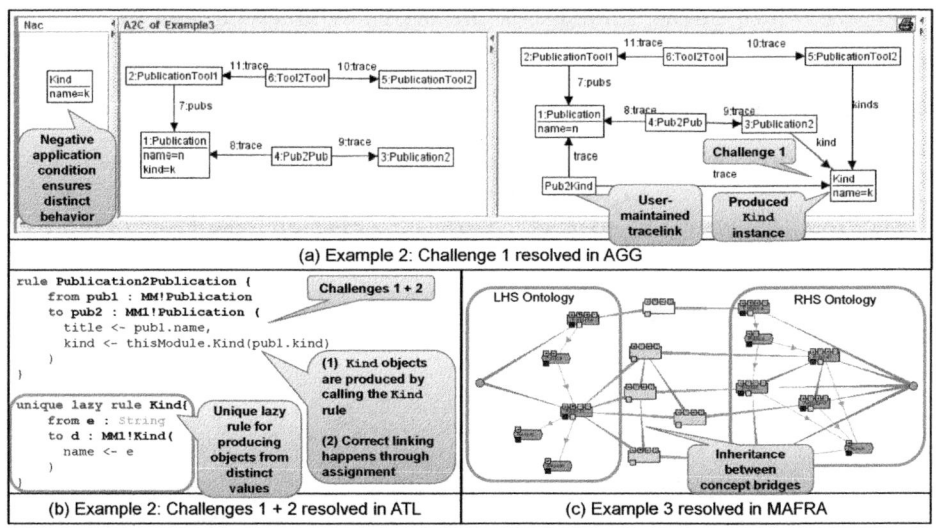

Fig. 7. Exemplary Solutions for Benchmark Examples 2 and 3

not provide explicit trace information, it offers a dedicated `distinct-values` component, which produces target elements for distinct input values only. In *ATL* a so-called *unique lazy rule* can be applied (cf. Fig. 7 (b)). Using the built-in trace model, this type of rule always generates and returns the same target object. *AGG* offers no dedicated support: the heterogeneity must be resolved by using user-defined graph transformation rules and a negative application condition that prevents multiple creation of `Kind` objects (cf. Fig. 7 (a)).

158   M. Wimmer et al.

Challenge 2: CA2R. In addition to creating objects based on distinct LHS values, the second challenge in this example is to correctly link the generated target elements. Establishing such links requires information about the relationships between the concepts to be linked in the LHS model. In the LHS MM of this example, the source of the EReference Publication.kind is represented by the EClass Publication and the target of the EReference by the EAttribute Publication.kind. Therefore, this heterogeneity is classified as *C(lass)A(ttribute)2R(eference)*. To obtain the information needed to establish the links, the approaches must again support queries to the trace model. Since *AMW* and *MAFRA* could not cope with challenge 1, they were also not able to resolve this heterogeneity. *MapForce* was also unable to resolve this kind of heterogeneity, since the internal trace model of the distinct-values component cannot be queried. Although the trace model produced by the *unique lazy rule* in *ATL* also cannot be queried, the elements produced can be linked correctly by calling the *unique lazy rule* in the assignment (cf. Fig. 7 (b)). In *AGG* the user-maintained trace model can be used to resolve this heterogeneity.

In summary, the mapping tools evaluated provide only limited support for resolution of the various metamodeling concept heterogeneities. Detailed knowledge of the transformation languages is required when using them to resolve heterogeneities, which further emphasizes the need for direct support by dedicated components.

3.3 Benchmark Example 3

The third benchmark example belongs to the category of inheritance heterogeneities with different metamodeling concepts (cf. Fig. 3) and poses one challenge. As the example instances show (cf. Fig. 8), the type of an LHS

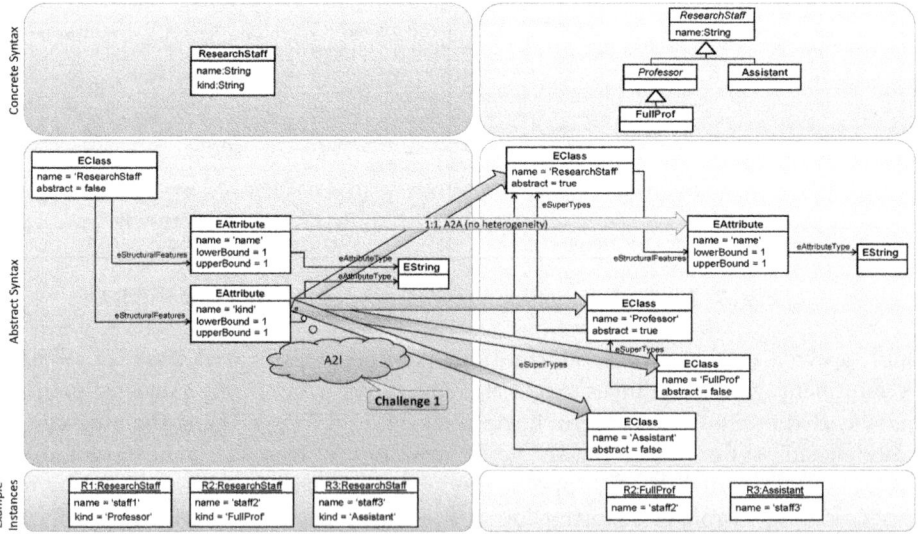

Fig. 8. Benchmark Example 3 – Different Metamodeling Concept Heterogeneities

ResearchStaff object is identified by the value of its EAttribute Research-Staff.kind, whereas the RHS MM provides an explicit type hierarchy. Thus, the problem may arise, that the EAttribute of the LHS MM contains values that do not correspond to any (concrete) EClass in the RHS MM. This is the case in the example with the instance R1, since the corresponding EClass Professor in the RHS MM is abstract and can thus not be instantiated, which causes information loss.

Challenge 1: A2I. To resolve this heterogeneity, objects must be filtered by using a certain attribute value and should provide means to deal with inheritance in order to reduce the specification overhead. With the exception of *MapForce*, which cannot display correctly XML schemas that make use of type derivation, all mapping tools were able to resolve this heterogeneity, although no dedicated components are available. In contrast to *AMW*, *MAFRA* allows for inheritance between mappings and thus reduces specification overhead (cf. Fig. 7 (c)). Of the transformation languages evaluated, only *ATL* supports inheritance between rules, whereas *AGG* does not.

In summary, although the resolution of this heterogeneity can be achieved in all approaches except in *MapForce*, no approach provides dedicated support. The approaches that enable resolution can be further divided into those supporting inheritance (*ATL*, *MAFRA*), which allow reuse in specifications, and those not supporting inheritance (*AMW*, *AGG*), which require duplication of parts of the specification.

Table 2. Comparison of Approaches

Challenges		Model Engineering			Data Engineering	Ontology Engineering
		AMW	ATL	AGG	MapForce	MAFRA
Example 1						
1	A2A, Multiplicity and Datatype Difference	User-defined extension ~	Conditional assignment with function ~	User-defined Java-function ~	Function library ✓ (value translations and substitute-missing component for default-value generation)	Property bridge with a user-defined service ~
2	A2A, Semantic Heterogeneity	User-defined extension ~	User-defined Function ~	User-defined Java-function ~	Function library ✓ available for diverse value translations	Property bridge with a user-defined service ~
3	C2C, Semantic Heterogeneity	Equivalence component with condition ✓	Condition ~	Condition ~	Condition ~	Concept bridge with condition ✓
4	R2R, Multiplicity Difference	No reference to newly generated objects possible ✗	Query of the trace model ~	User-maintained tracelinks ~	Has to be simulated by the generation of foreign-key-values according to a query ~	No reference to newly generated objects possible ✗
Example 2						
1	A2C	No distinct semantics supported ✗	Unique lazy rule ~	User-maintained tracelinks ~	Distinct-values component ✓	No distinct semantics supported ✗
2	CA2R	No tracemodel available ✗	Query of the trace model ~	User-maintained tracelinks ~	No tracemodel available ✗	No tracemodel available ✗
Example 3						
1	A2I	No inheritance support - simulation by code duplication ~	Inheriting rules ~	No inheritance support - simulation by code duplication ~	No support for inheritance ✗	Inheriting concept bridges ~

✓ supported ~ resolvable (no dedicated support) ✗ non-resolvable

4 Lessons Learned

In this section, we present the lessons learned from applying our examples.

Absence of Trace Model Limits Applicability. Current mapping tools in the area of data engineering typically rely on the specification of simple correspondences between source and target elements, which may be refined by conditions or functions. However, these correspondences do not offer trace information, which would support the definition of dependent mappings. For instance, a value mapping always occurs in the context of a certain object mapping and is thus dependent on the element mapping. This deficiency leads to less expressive mapping specifications, as also discussed in [16]. The developers of mapping tools in the area of ontology engineering and model engineering recognized this need and thus implemented dependent mappings. However, simple dependencies between mappings, for instance, composition of mappings, are still insufficient, which leads to the problems, for example, in an A2C heterogeneity, in which explicit queries to the trace model are needed. Transformation languages can be divided into approaches providing automatic trace information, as in *ATL*, and approaches requiring manual generation of trace information, as in *AGG*. *ATL* provides trace information only for the declarative parts (`matched rules`) and not for the imperative parts of the language. Finally, a user-specified trace model leaves the entire tedious and error-prone process of setting up the trace information correctly to the transformation designer.

Transformation Languages Lack Reuse Facilities. Transformation languages such as *ATL* and *AGG* provide the expressivity to overcome the heterogeneities identified in our examples. Nevertheless, they lack adequate reuse facilities, which forces the transformation designer to respecify the resolution of recurring heterogeneities over and over. Especially in complex scenarios (e.g., when generating new target elements, as in the first example, or when dealing with unequal concept heterogeneities, as in the second example), the transformation designer must handle low-level intricacies of the transformation language. In order to avoid this tedious and error-prone task, transformation languages should provide idioms that resolve these structural heterogeneities, for instance, predefined, parameterizable rules in *ATL* or in *AGG*. A fact that hinders the provision of such predefined components is that transformation rules are based on the specific types defined in the corresponding metamodels. Thus, a notion of generic transformations which resembles the concept of templates in C++ or generics in Java is required.

Lack of Inheritance Support Encourages Code Duplication. Inheritance, which is heavily used in metamodels, supports the reuse of attribute and reference definitions. Thus, when a mapping is specified between subclasses, then it should be able to reuse attribute and reference mappings of mappings between superclasses; i.e., inheritance between mappings should be supported. The same holds true for transformation languages. Otherwise, duplicated mapping definitions or transformation rules induce both, a bigger specification overhead and maintenance problems in the future, as is the case in *AGG*.

Mapping Tools Struggle with Function/Condition Definitions. Mapping tools have the main advantage of providing predefined components for the resolution of heterogeneities, but the definition of functions and conditions poses a major problem. Each mapping tool provides a specific basic set of components. For instance, *MapForce* provides a library of low-level functions such as string conversion functions. However, such a library is naturally never complete, which leads to limitations in expressivity. Thus, incorporating an expressive language with which the transformation designer is familiar could resolve this problem.

Mapping Tools Lack Adequate Extension Mechanisms. Since mapping tools struggle with resolving certain kinds of heterogeneity, an adequate extension mechanism that allows addition of user-defined components should be offered. *MapForce* supports user-defined components but only on the basis of predefined ones. Although this enhances the scalability of the approach by composing several low-level components, expressivity is not increased. In contrast, both *AMW* and *MAFRA* allow increasing expressivity by user-defined components but require heavyweight programmatic extensions. In *AMW*, both, the metamodel describing the set of predefined components and the transformation generating *ATL* code from a mapping specification must be extended. *MAFRA* supports new components, but they must be coded manually in so-called user-defined services.

Mapping Tools Lack Comprehensive Validation Support. A major advantage of describing model transformations at a conceptual level by means of mapping tools is that comprehensive validations can be done at design time. To verify that the components are configured correctly, *structural validations* examine the required input and output parameters and *metamodel-based validations* check the interpretation of the mapped metamodels. For instance, a reference is only mapped correctly if both its source and target class have also been mapped. *MapForce* and *MAFRA* support only structural validations. *AMW* does not support validation at all, which results in potentially erroneous *ATL* code.

5 Related Work

Two threads of related work are considered: First, we compare our feature-based classification to existing classifications. Second, we relate the mapping benchmark to existing mapping benchmarks. We start with examining the most closely related area, model engineering, and then proceed to the more widely related areas of data engineering and ontology engineering.

5.1 Heterogeneity Classifications

Model Engineering. Although model transformations, and thus the resolution of heterogeneities between MMs, play a vital role in MDE, to the best of our knowledge no dedicated survey exists that examines potential heterogeneities.

Data Engineering. In the area of data engineering, in contrast, extensive literature exists, over decades, highlighting various aspects of heterogeneities in the context of database schemata. Batini et al. [2] presented a first classification of semantic and structural heterogeneities that arise when two different schemas are integrated. Kim et al. [13] introduced a systematic classification of possible variations in an SQL statement, detailing *Table-Table* and *Attribute-Attribute* heterogeneities (e.g., with respect to cardinalities). The classification of Kashyap et al. [12] provides a broad overview of potential heterogeneities in a data integration scenario with semantic heterogeneities and conflicts that occurr between the same modeling concepts. Blaha et al. [4] described patterns that resolve syntactic heterogeneities, both between the same and different MM concepts. Finally, the classification of Härder [9] and Legler [15] presented a systematic approach to attribute mappings by combining attribute correspondences with potential cardinalities.

Ontology Engineering. In ontology engineering, both pattern collections and classifications exist. A pattern collection by Scharffe et al. in [17] presented correspondence patterns for ontology alignments, but on a rather coarse-grained level. For instance, their conditional patterns dealing with attribute differences and transformation patterns deal only vaguely with different metamodeling concept heterogeneities. Visser et al. [20] and Klein [14] provided classifications in the form of comprehensive lists of semantic heterogeneities but neglected syntactic heterogeneities.

In summary, although there are several classifications available, none focuses explicitly on the domain of MDE. Since the benchmarks in the area of data engineering base on the relational data model, they do not include potential heterogeneities stemming from the explicit concepts of references and inheritance in object-oriented metamodels. Although in ontology engineering references and inheritance are explicit concepts, their interest is to resolve semantic heterogeneities rather than syntactic heterogeneities. Finally, current classifications fail to explicate how types of heterogeneity relate to each other. We formalized these relationships in a feature model.

5.2 Mapping Benchmarks

Model Engineering. To the best of our knowledge, no benchmark for mapping systems in the area of MDE exists. However, a benchmark for evaluating the execution performance of graph transformations [19] has been proposed.

Data Engineering. In the area of data engineering Alexe et. al. [1] proposed a first benchmark for mapping systems that focuses on resolving syntactic and semantic heterogeneities in information integration. Although the benchmark provides a first set of mapping scenarios, it remains unclear how the scenarios were obtained and whether they provide full coverage in terms of expressivity. Even though XQuery expressions are given to define the semantics, some of the XQuery functions assume the availability of custom functions which are not provided. Since RHS models are also not given, it is hard to know the actual outcome of the transformation. A further benchmark called THALIA was presented by Hammer et. al [8], which provides researchers with a collection of twelve benchmark queries expressed in XQuery. They focus on the resolution of syntactic and semantic heterogeneities in an information integration scenario. For each query a so-called *reference schema* (i.e., global schema) and a *challenge schema* (i.e., the schema to be integrated) are provided together with corresponding instances. Although the authors claim to provide a systematic classification of semantic and syntactic heterogeneities resulting in the queries, the rational behind the systematic is not explained further.

Ontology Engineering. In ontology engineering, no dedicated mapping benchmark exists. However, there have been efforts to evaluate matching tools, i.e., tools for automatically discovering alignments between ontologies, which resulted in an ontology *matching benchmark*[7]. Although the goal of the evaluation is different, the examples could also be of interest for a dedicated mapping benchmark.

In summary, although both benchmarks from the area of data engineering provide useful scenarios in the context of XML, they do not provide a systematic classification that results in a systematic set of benchmark examples for evaluating the expressivity of a mapping tool.

6 Conclusion and Future Work

In this paper we have introduced a systematic classification of heterogeneities between Ecore-based MMs. This classification can also be applied to other domains, that use the same core concepts on which this classification is based, i.e., classes, attributes, references and inheritance. Furthermore, three of the proposed benchmark examples were used to evaluate mapping tools from diverse engineering domains and to compare solutions realized with the transformation languages *ATL* and *AGG*. Further work includes the completion of the benchmark examples to fully cover the classification and the evaluation of further approaches.

References

1. Alexe, B., Tan, W.-C., Velegrakis, Y.: STBenchmark: Towards a Benchmark for Mapping Systems. VLDB Endow 1(1), 230–244 (2008)
2. Batini, C., Lenzerini, M., Navathe, S.B.: A Comparative Analysis of Methodologies for Database Schema Integration. ACM Comp. Surv. 18(4), 323–364 (1986)
3. Bézivin, J.: On the Unification Power of Models. Journal on SoSyM 4(2), 31 (2005)
4. Blaha, M., Premerlani, W.: A catalog of object model transformations. In: Proc. of the 3rd Working Conf. on Reverse Engineering (WCRE 1996), pp. 87–96 (1996)
5. Czarnecki, K., Helsen, S.: Feature-based Survey of Model Transformation Approaches. IBM Systems Journal 45(3), 621–645 (2006)
6. Czarnecki, K., Helsen, S., Eisenecker, U.: Staged Configuration Using Feature Models. In: Proc. of Third Software Product Line Conf., pp. 266–283 (2004)
7. Del Fabro, M., Bézivin, J., Valduriez, P.: Model-driven Tool Interoperability: an Application in Bug Tracking 1. In: Proc. of the 5th Int. Conf. on Ontologies, DataBases, and Applications of Semantics (ODBASE 2006), pp. 863–881 (2006)

---

[7] http://oaei.ontologymatching.org/2010/

8. Hammer, J., Stonebraker, M., Topsakal, O.: THALIA: Test harness for the assessment of legacy information integration approaches. In: Proc. of the Int. Conf. on Data Engineering (ICDE 2005), pp. 485–486 (2005)
9. Härder, T., Sauter, G., Thomas, J.: The intrinsic problems of structural heterogeneity and an approach to their solution. The VLDB Journal 8(1), 25–43 (1999)
10. Harel, D., Rumpe, B.: Meaningful modeling: What's the semantics of "semantics"? IEEE Computer 37, 64–72 (2004)
11. Hull, R., King, R.: Semantic Database Modeling: Survey, Applications, and Research Issues. ACM Comp. Surv. 19(3), 201–260 (1987)
12. Kashyap, V., Sheth, A.: Semantic and schematic similarities between database objects: A context-based approach. The VLDB Journal 5(4), 276–304 (1996)
13. Kim, W., Seo, J.: Classifying Schematic and Data Heterogeneity in Multidatabase Systems. Computer 24(12), 12–18 (1991)
14. Klein, M.: Combining and relating ontologies: an analysis of problems and solutions. In: Proc. of Workshop on Ontologies and Information Sharing (IJCAI 2001), pp. 53–62 (2001)
15. Legler, F., Naumann, F.: A Classification of Schema Mappings and Analysis of Mapping Tools. In: Proc. of the GI-Fachtagung für Datenbanksysteme in Business, Technologie und Web (BTW 2007), pp. 449–464 (2007)
16. Raffio, A., Braga, D., Ceri, S., Papotti, P., Hernández, M.A.: Clip: a visual language for explicit schema mappings. In: Proc. of the 24th Int. Conf. on Data Engineering (ICDE 2008), pp. 30–39 (2008)
17. Scharffe, F., Fensel, D.: Correspondence Patterns for Ontology Alignment. In: Gangemi, A., Euzenat, J. (eds.) EKAW 2008. LNCS (LNAI), vol. 5268, pp. 83–92. Springer, Heidelberg (2008)
18. Sheth, A.P., Larson, J.A.: Federated Database Systems for Managing Distributed, Heterogeneous, and Autonomous Databases. ACM Comput. Surv. 22(3), 183–236 (1990)
19. Varro, G., Schürr, A., Varro, D.: Benchmarking for graph transformation. In: Proc. of the 2005 IEEE Symposium on Visual Languages and Human-Centric Computing (VLHCC 2005), pp. 79–88 (2005)
20. Visser, P.R.S., Jones, D.M., Bench-Capon, T.J.M., Shave, M.J.R.: An analysis of ontological mismatches: Heterogeneity versus interoperability. In: Proc. of AAAI 1997 Spring Symposium on Ontological Engineering, pp. 164–172 (1997)
21. Wimmer, M., Kappel, G., Kusel, A., Retschitzegger, W., Schoenboeck, J., Schwinger, W.: Surviving the Heterogeneity Jungle with Composite Mapping Operators. In: Tratt, L., Gogolla, M. (eds.) ICMT 2010. LNCS, vol. 6142, pp. 260–275. Springer, Heidelberg (2010)
22. Wimmer, M., Kappel, G., Kusel, A., Retschitzegger, W., Schönböck, J., Schwinger, W.: Towards an Expressivity Benchmark for Mappings based on a Systematic Classification of Heterogeneities. In: Proc. of the First Int. Workshop on Model-Driven Interoperability (MDI 2010) @ MoDELS 2010, pp. 32–41 (2010)

Specifying Overlaps of Heterogeneous Models for Global Consistency Checking

Zinovy Diskin, Yingfei Xiong, and Krzysztof Czarnecki

Generative Software Development Lab.,
University of Waterloo, Canada
{zdiskin,y6xiong,kczarnec}@gsd.uwaterloo.ca

Abstract. Software development often involves a set of models defined in different metamodels, each model capturing a specific view of the system. We call this set a *multimodel*, and its elements *partial* or *local* models. Since partial models overlap, they may be consistent or inconsistent wrt. a set of *global* constraints.

We present a framework for specifying overlaps between partial models and defining their global consistency. An advantage of the framework is that heterogeneous consistency checking is reduced to the homogeneous case yet merging partial metamodels into one global metamodel is not needed. We illustrate the framework with examples and sketch its formal semantics based on category theory.

1 Introduction

Software development often involves a set of heterogeneous models, such as use cases, process models, UML design models, and code. These models are defined by different metamodels, and are often built by different teams, but collectively represent a single system. Due to possible overlaps between models, individually consistent models may be *globally* inconsistent if taken together. Many existing approaches focus on checking consistency of a single model or a pair of models [1]. However, individual consistency or pairwise consistency do not guarantee global consistency. For example, Fig. 1 shows three UML class diagrams $D_{1,2,3}$, where the classes

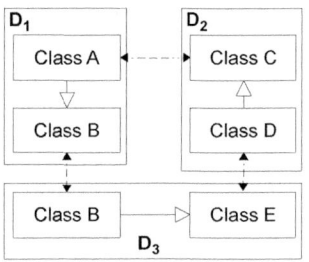

Fig. 1. Three globally inconsistent models

connected by a dashed line are considered to be the same class (even though named differently). Each of the three diagrams is consistent, and each pair of them is consistent, but taken together the three diagrams are inconsistent: there is a cycle in the inheritance chain.

The example shows two phases in checking global consistency. First, we need to specify the models' overlap. For models like code and UML class diagrams extracted from code, we may know their overlap by matching the elements by name. But for models in the conceptual stage, we cannot deduce their overlap automatically. For example, an entity "Person" created by a business analyst and a table "Employee" existing in a legacy database may refer to the same concept despite their different names. Moreover, there are cases when elements in different models are related but their relationship cannot be specified by direct linking and we need something more intelligent. For example, Fig. 2 shows two models that present basically the same information but structure it differently. Whatever means are used for specifying the overlap, in the second phase we need to check the global consistency of the system (= models + overlap).

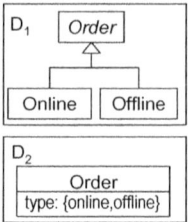

Fig. 2. Indirect correspondence

Sabezadeh et al.[2] proposed to check global consistency of homogeneous models by their merging. The models' overlap is specified by a *correspondence diagram*: a set of auxiliary models and mappings "in-between" the local model, which declare some elements in different local models as being actually the same. Then all local models are merged into one model modulo the correspondence, i.e., elements declared to be the same in the correspondence diagram become one element. Finally, consistency of the merged model is checked against the constraints declared in the metamodel. Thus, verifying global consistency amounts to checking consistency of a single model. However, the approach was developed for the case of homogeneous models only, and indirect overlaps (like shown in Fig. 2) were not considered.

The goal of the paper is to adopt the *consistency-checking-by-merging (CCM) idea* for the heterogeneous situation. A straightforward solution could be, first, to merge all involved metamodels so that all local models become instances of the same global metamodel; then we can merge these instances and check the result wrt. the constraints in the global metamodel. Though theoretically possible, in practice this approach leads to dealing with huge models and metamodels resulting from the merge, which is cumbersome and not effective. We present another approach in which merging metamodels is significantly reduced to an unavoidable minimum, and merging models is reduced to only merging their relevant parts. Briefly, we find common views between metamodels, project related models to spaces of instances (*overlaps*) determined by those views, and then apply the CCM approach to each of the homogeneous sets of projections.

Realization of the approach requires several challenging issues to be solved: type-safe model matching, specification of indirect overlap between metamodels, inter-metamodel constraints, and constraints over the entire schema of metamodels and their overlaps. We will discuss these issues in more detail in Section 2.2 after we briefly outline the basics of CCM-approach in Section 2.1. Section 3 describes our main techniques with simple examples. In Section 4 we abstract the examples and sketch a much more general framework. Section 5 presents a brief survey of approaches to heterogeneous multimodeling, and highlights the advantages of our framework. Section 6 concludes.

The present paper is an extended version of our MDI'2010 Workshop paper [3]. It presents a new issue of consistency between correspondence spans, and a

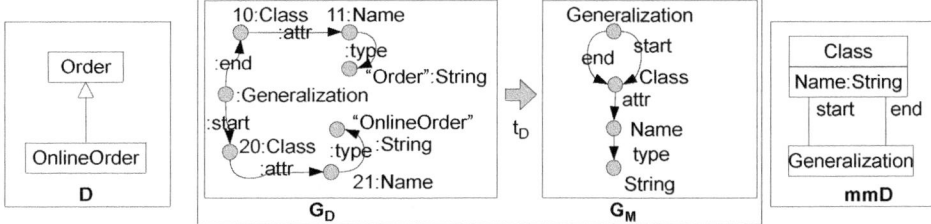

Fig. 3. Graph representation of a UML class diagram

new survey of approaches to heterogeneous multimodeling. Description of our formal framework is omitted due to space limits but Section 4 presents a rough sketch of the ideas.

2 From Homo- to Heterogeneous Multimodeling

2.1 Background: Homogeneous Overlap and Consistency

We briefly review the basics of the CCM-approach, and also show how to manage conflicts between values.

Software models are typed graphs. We follow the approach to metamodeling developed by the graph transformation community, and treat models as typed graphs. A metamodel is a pair $M = (G_M, C_M)$ with G_M a graph and C_M a set of constraints. A model (M's instance) is a graph *typed* over M, i.e., a pair $D = (G_D, t_D)$ with G_D a graph (typically much bigger than G_M) and $t_D \colon G_D \to G_M$ a graph mapping (which preserves the incidence relationship between arrows and nodes) such that all constraints in set C_M are satisfied.

For example, Fig. 3 shows how to represent a UML class diagram D as a typed graph $t_D \colon G_D \to G_M$ with G_M being the graph representing a simple metamodel mmD for class diagrams. Classes, attributes, primitive values and generalization relations are represented as nodes; their relationships are captured by arrows. The value of mapping t_D at element $e \in G_D$ is given after colon, e.g., expression "10:Class" means $t_D(10)$=Class for node 10; identifiers of arrows are omitted but their types are kept.

Any UML class diagram can be represented by a typed graph as above but not the converse. To ensure that a typed graph is a correct diagram, constraints must be declared and added to the metamodel. Examples of constraints are (C1) a class has only one name; (C2) a class has only one parent class; (C3) classes with stereotype 'singleton' are instantiated with at most one object.

Matching models via spans. Suppose two business analysts have independently built two UML diagrams, D_1 and D_2 in Figure 4. To check their global consistency, we first need to specify overlap between the diagrams. Suppose we know that class 'OnlineOrder' in diagram D_1 and class 'Order' in D_2 refer to the same class of objects, and their 'price' attributes refer to the same attribute.

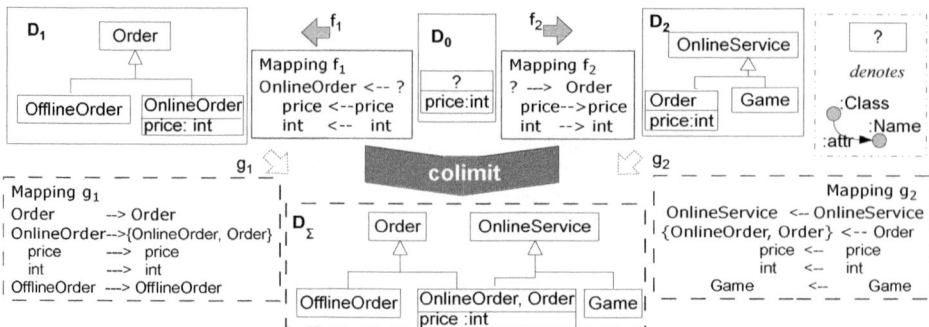

Fig. 4. Homogeneous Model Matching. Frames of models provided by the user are solid, those computed automatically are dashed; user-defined mappings are shaded, computed mappings are blank.

We could write the following two informal equations: (E1) OnlineOrder@D_1 = Order@D_2; (E2) price@D_1 = price@D_2.

These equations conform to the type system of class diagrams: we match a class to a class and an attribute to an attribute. Hence, we can represent the set of equations by a class diagram D_0 shown in the middle of Fig. 4 equipped with two functions $f_i\colon D_0 \to D_i$, $i = 1, 2$, mapping "equations" to their left and right terms resp. Formally, f_1 and f_2 are graph mappings which map nodes to nodes and arrows to arrows so that their incidence is preserved. The question mark indicates that the name of the class is unknown and the corresponding Name-slot is empty (see the fragment in the top-right corner of the figure). Thus, equation (E1) encodes two formal equations (for classes and Name-slots) and (E2) gives three (equating, in addition, two string values).

We call a pair of mappings with a common source a *(binary) span*. The source (model D_0) is called the *head* of the span, mappings f_1, f_2 are *legs* and their targets (models D_1, D_2) are *feet* (these names are borrowed from category theory). Thus, an overlap of two homogeneous models is specified by a *correspondence span* over the same metamodel; for n models we need an n-ary span with n legs and feet. Note that the span pattern allows us to record inconsistencies and keep them for future resolution according to the *living with inconsistencies* paradigm [4]. A precise formalization and details can be found in [5, Section 3].

Merging and conflicts. After specifying the overlap by a correspondence span, we merge two models into one and check whether it satisfies all constraints declared in the metamodel.

The merge procedure consists of two parts. We first disjointly merge the graphs underlying the models, and then glue together elements declared to be the same by the span. The result is shown as diagram D_Σ in Fig. 4, in which the merged graph has five rather than six class nodes because of gluing. Class named {OnlineOrder,Order} has one Name-slot because the two local slots were glued, but this slot holds two names since they are not (and cannot be) equated in the head. Besides graph D_Σ, merging also produces two graph mappings $g_i\colon D_i \to D_\Sigma$ that show how the local models are embedded into the merge.

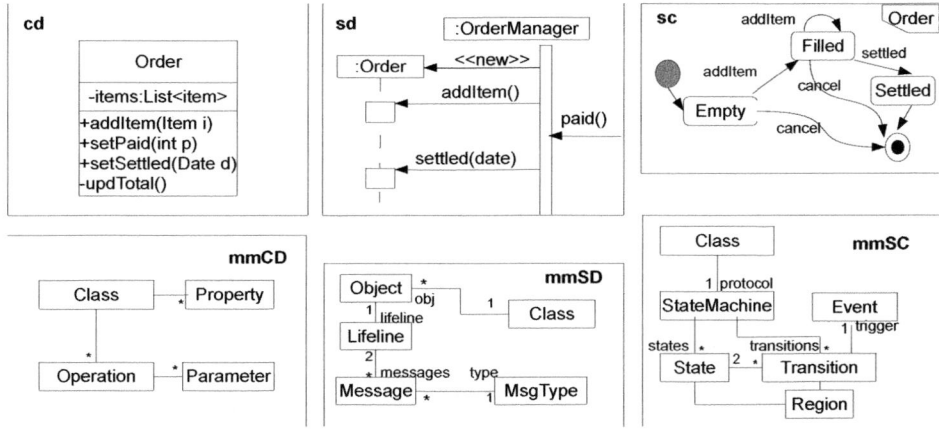

Fig. 5. Motivating example: mmXX is the metamodel of model xx

The merge procedure is fully automatic and can be precisely formalized in terms of the *colimit* operation developed in category theory. A detailed explanation and examples of how colimit works can be found in [6] or [5]. It follows from general properties of colimit that the merged graph G_{D_Σ} is correctly typed over graph G_M (with M denoting the metamodel of class diagrams).

To make reading figures like Fig. 4 easier, we adopt the following notation. Frames of models provided by the user, and those computed automatically, are solid and dashed resp; user-defined mappings are shaded whereas computed mappings are blank.

After the merged graph is built, we can check whether it satisfies all constraints declared in the metamodel (say, with a checking tool). In our example, we find that constraints (C1) and (C2) specified above are violated.

2.2 The Problems

Existing CCM-approaches [2] handle the homogeneous case well, but software models are often heterogeneous. For example, Fig. 5 presents three UML models of the same system developed independently by three teams: a class diagram cd, a sequence diagram sd, and a statechart sc (with their simplified metamodels). Since the models are developed independently, we need to specify their overlap and check the global consistency. However, the heterogeneity of the models gives rise to several new problems.

A) Type-safety is important for overlap specification. In the homogeneous situation, we allow only elements of the same type to be matched to ensure type safety. However, in heterogeneous cases different models are declared in different metamodels, and hence their elements have disjoint types. We need a new method to ensure type-safety in overlap specifications.

B) Indirect overlap often occurs in heterogeneous multimodeling. For example, in class diagrams operations are linked to their owning classes. Such linking also exists but is implicit in sequence diagrams (through consecutive linking

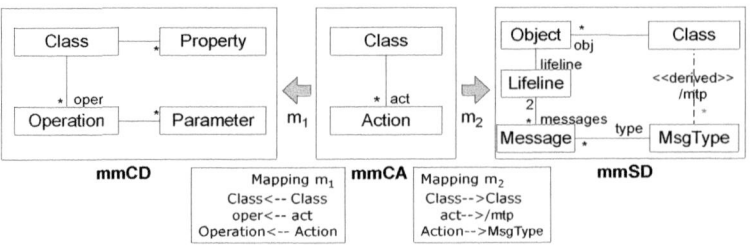

Fig. 6. Matching basic and derived meta-elements

Classes, Objects, Lifelines, Messages, and MsgTypes). Hence, we cannot use direct matching to describe overlap between sets of Class-Operation links in class diagrams and Class-MsgType links in sequence diagrams.

C) Inter-metamodel constraints appear in heterogeneous multimodeling. For example, we may require that the interaction described by the sequence diagram should conform to the state machine described by the state chart. Such constraints regulate *interaction* of partial models, and hence are not captured by metamodels of any of them. Such constraints are inherently global and should be explicitly specified.

D) Metamodel inter-relations are crucial for heterogeneous multimodeling. "The metamodel" of a heterogeneous multimodel is a system of metamodels *together* with their relationships rather than a discrete set of isolated metamodels. We need a language for specifying systems of interacting metamodels.

3 Heterogeneous Overlap and Consistency by Examples

In this section we incrementally introduce our approach. We will consider very simple examples addressing the four challenges.

3.1 Type-Safety and Indirect Overlap

To ensure type-safety in heterogeneous case, we first need to know which types are safe to be matched. We get this information by asking the user to specify the overlap between metamodels first. For example, suppose in Fig. 5 we know that class Order together with methods addItem, setSettled in cd refer to the same elements as class Order together with message types addItem, settled in sd. To match these elements, we first match their metamodels, mmCD and mmSD, as shown in Fig. 6. Since metamodels are graphs, we can match them as homogeneous models. We state that metaclasses Class@mmCD and Class@mmSD refer to the same concepts, and Operation@mmCD and MsgType@mmSD are also "the same".

However, as we described in the previous section, there is also an indirect overlap between the metamodels: operations and message types are both related to classes, but operations are directly related by an association while message types are indirectly related via four associations. To declare this indirect overlap,

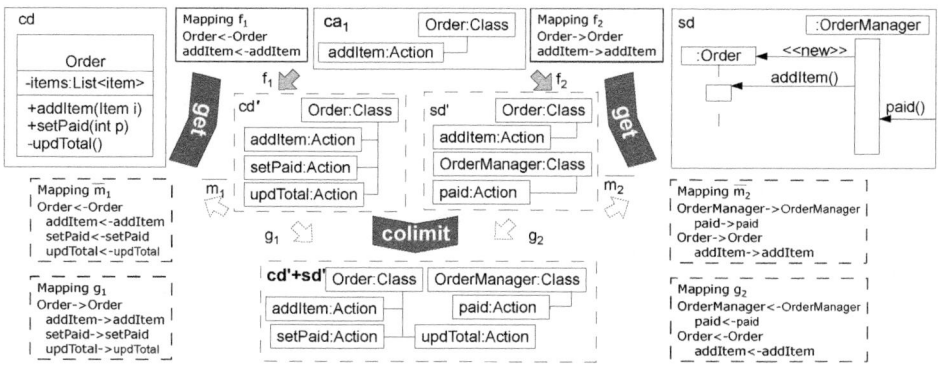

Fig. 7. Matching basic and derived elements (see Fig. 6 for view definitions)

we augment metamodel mmSD with a new element mtp (read "messageType") and specify how it is derived (e.g., in OCL):
context Class
inv: self.mtp=self.objects.lifeline.messages.type.

Now we declare the sameness of associations oper@mmCD and mtp@mmSD by placing association act into the head of the span as shown in Fig. 6, and defining $m_1(\text{act}) = \text{oper}$, $m_2(\text{act}) = /\text{mtp}$. The indirect overlap in Fig. 2 can be specified in a similar way. We first augment diagram D_2 with two derived subclasses of class Order (defined by the respective two queries), and then declare their sameness with the corresponding classes in diagram D_1.

After we have the overlap of metamodels, we can match models type-safely. Consider again the span we declared. We may consider the head of the span mmCA as a view on both models, and the two legs m_1 and m_2 as view definitions. Then the view definitions can be executed on models. For example, view definition m_1 : mmCA → mmCD can be executed for any instance of mmCD (i.e., for any class diagram) by extracting its mmCA-portion and its respective retyping. A concrete view execution is shown in Fig. 7, where class diagram cd shown in left upper corner is translated into diagram cd′ typed over metamodel mmCA. We write cd′ = get^{m_1}(cd) with get^{m_1} denoting the operation of view execution (*getView*) determined by view definition m_1 (in figures we omit the superscript). We will also say that model cd is *projected* into the *overlap space* mmCA, and call model cd′ the mmCA-*projection* of cd. Note also that *getView* not only produces cd′ but also the traceability mappings $\overline{m_1}$: cd′ → cd.

Similarly, sequence diagram sd in the top right corner of Fig. 7 is translated into diagram sd′ = get^{m_2}(sd) also typed over mmCA, along with its traceability mapping $\overline{m_2}$. (This translation involves execution of the OCL-query specified above). Since both views are instances of the same metamodel, we can type-safely build a span (ca_1, f_1, f_2) to match them and check consistency. This span and the corresponding merge (colimit) are shown in the middle part of Fig. 7, and the two models are consistent with respect to the constraints in mmCA.

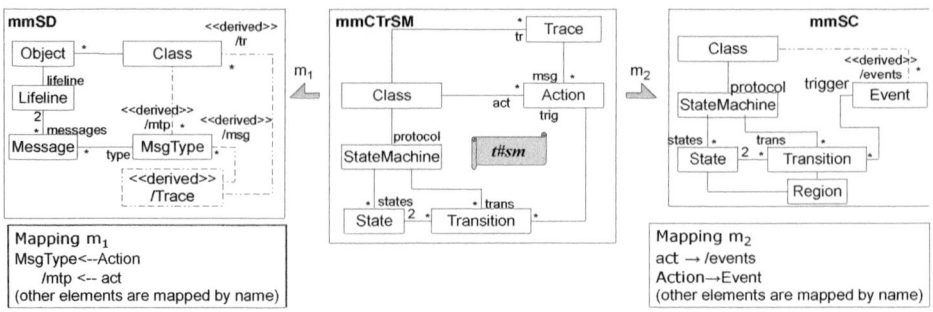

Fig. 8. Specifying inter-metamodel constraints

3.2 Inter-metamodel Constraints

So far we only checked the constraints declared in the head of the correspondence span (mmCA in our examples). These constraints are common for both feet metamodels (mmCD and mmSD). However, there may be important constraints residing in neither of the feet metamodels. For example, traces of actions exhibited by a sequence diagram must conform to the state machine specified by the corresponding statechart. We will denote this constraint by $t\sharp sm$ meaning "Traces are to conform to the StateMachine". Since constraint $t\sharp sm$ involves elements of both metamodels, mmSD and mmSC, it cannot be declared in either of them. Hence, a new metamodel in which $t\sharp sm$ could be specified has to be built. Below we first show how to build such a metamodel; then we show how to project partial models sd and sc to the space of this metamodel instances, in which projections can be matched, merged and checked against $t\sharp sm$.

To declare $t\sharp sm$, we need a metamodel encompassing metaclasses for Classes, Traces (sequences of actions), StateMachines, and related notions: States, Transitions, Events as specified by metamodel mmCTrSM in the middle of Fig. 8. The upper half of this metamodel is "taken" from the sequence diagram metamodel mmSD as specified by mapping m_1 in Fig. 8. Note that m_1 maps class Trace@mmCTrSM to derived class /Trace@mmSD, whose instances are sequences of actions described by the sequence diagram and hence can be computed by a suitable query. The lower half of mmCTrSM is taken from the statechart metamodel mmSC as specified by mapping m_2 in Fig. 8 (and we again use derived elements). Having built metamodel mmCTrSM, we declare in it the constraint $t\sharp sm$ with its intended semantics. We call the configuration $(m_1, \text{mmCTrSM}, m_2)$ a *partial* span because mappings m_1 and m_2 are partially defined (on the upper and lower halves of mmCTrSM resp.). In Fig. 8 and other figures below, a semi-arrow head indicates partiality of the mapping.

The next step is to project models sd and sc to the metamodel mmCTrSM. We cannot directly execute view definitions m_1, m_2 because they are partial, but we can execute them in three steps.

Step 0. We explicitly specify the domains mmCTr and mmCSM of mappings m_j on which they become totally defined mappings $m!_j$ ($j = 1, 2$; see Fig. 9); inclusion mappings i_j embed the domains into the head of the span.

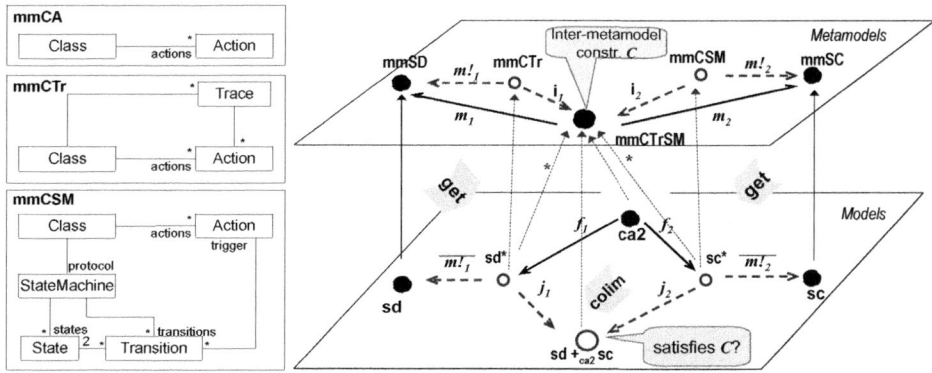

Fig. 9. Verifying inter-metamodel constraints

Step 1. Total view definitions $m!_j$ are executed for models sd and sc and produce views sd* and sc* over metamodels mmCTr and mmCSM resp.

Step 2. As the two latter metamodels are included into mmCTrSM, we may consider their instances as "partial" instances of mmCTrSM. Formally, we compose typing mappings of models sd*, sc* with inclusion mappings i_1, i_2 and get new typing mappings into mmCTrSM (marked by ∗ in Fig. 9).

The three steps are performed automatically and may be hidden from the user, for whom operations get^{m_1} and get^{m_2} appear as if mappings m_j were ordinary total view definitions.

Now we have two models sd* and sc* over the same metamodel mmCTrSM. To finish consistency checking, the user must match the models and build a correspondence span, say, $(f_1, \text{ca2}, f_2)$. The head is denoted by ca2 because it is an instance of metamodel mmCA built in Section 4.2 (it can be formally proved). After that, models are automatically merged modulo the span and checks the result against the constraints in mmCTrSM, including the inter-metamodel constraint $t \sharp sm$. The right half of Fig. 9 specifies the entire procedure: data provided by the user are shown with bullet nodes and solid arrows (and are black), data automatically computed are shown with blank nodes and dashed arrows (and are blue). Note that span $(f_1, \text{ca2}, f_2)$ is a part of the multimodel.

3.3 Metamodel Inter-relations

We consider our full example with three models, cd, sd and sc.

First we build a ternary span $(\text{mmCA}, m_1, m_2, m_3)$ specifying "the sameness" of the concepts of operation, message and transition in the respective metamodels as shown in Fig. 10(a); superscript '+' near a target metamodel indicates that it is augmented with derived elements defined by queries. Ternary span mmCA is a straightforward extension of binary span mmCA built in Section 3.1 with a new leg towards mmSC. Then we turn to models. We project the three models to head mmCA (see Fig. 10(b)), match projections ca', sd', sc' with a ternary correspondence span ca3, merge projections modulo ca3, and finally check the merge against the constraints declared in mmCA.

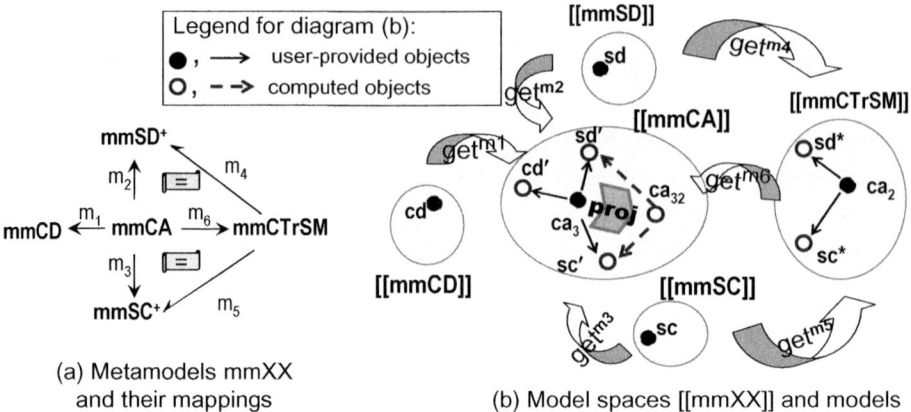

Fig. 10. Consistency checking of the example in Fig. 5

In a similar way we check consistency of models sd and sc wrt. the inter-model constraint $t\sharp sm$ declared in mmCTrSM as explained above (span ca_2 describes correspondences between projections sc^* and sd^*). However, now a new aspect of global consistency checking appears: we need to check that model correspondence spans ca_3 and ca_2 are consistent between themselves.

An important property of the metamodel schema in Fig. 10(a) is commutativity of the two triangle diagrams (denoted by "=" labels):

$(=)_m$ $\quad m_6; m_4 = m_2$ and $m_6; m_5 = m_3$.

Because view execution and retyping are compatible with metamodel mapping composition, we have commutativity for view execution mappings as well:

$(=)_{\text{get}}$ $\quad \text{get}^{m_4}; \text{get}^{m_6} = \text{get}^{m_2}$ and $\text{get}^{m_5}; \text{get}^{m_6} = \text{get}^{m_3}$.

Hence, the mmCA-views of xx*-models must be equal to the respective xx'-models. Now we can check the consistency between spans. We first derive a binary projection ca_{32} of the ternary span ca_3, which relates sd' and sc'. Then we check whether the mmCA-view of the span ca_2 is equal to ca_{32}.

The simple example above shows how local model interaction is governed by the multimodel schema specifying metamodels' inter-relationships. The example also demonstrates that N-ary multimodeling may exhibit sufficiently complex metamodels schemas bearing their own constraints like commutativity.

4 Making Multimodeling Precise: A General Framework

A key message of the paper is that a multimodel is not just a set of models. A multimodel is a set of *base* models *and* a structure of auxiliary models and model mappings specifying *correspondences* between base models. For instance, the multimodel of our example in the previous section consists of three models (cd,sd,sc) *and* two inter-model spans (ca_3, ca_2) shown in Fig. 10(b). Respectively, the metamodel of a multimodel is a graph consisting of base metamodels *and* a system of spans specifying their overlap like shown in Fig. 10(a); we call it the *metamodel schema*.

In a nutshell, a heterogeneous multimodel is a pair $(\mathcal{A},\mathcal{C})$ with $\mathcal{A} = \{A_1{:}M_1..$ $..A_k{:}M_k\}$ a family of base models A_i over their metamodels M_i, and $\mathcal{C} = \{C_1{:}O_1..$ $..C_l{:}O_l\}$ a system of model correspondence spans C_j over a system of (heads of) spans O_j specifying metamodel overlap. In other words, the correspondence part of a multimodel is a network of auxiliary models and model mappings in-between models A_i, which resides over the respective network of auxiliary metamodels and mappings in-between metamodels M_i. The two-level structure of the overlap specification is essential: models may overlap only via paths declared in the metamodel schema.

Our formal framework [7] provides a detailed description of the sketch above. The three basic ingredients are (a) metamodels and their mappings, (b) models and their mappings, and (c) a mechanism of model translation from one metamodel to another. A (minimal in a sense) mathematical framework integrating these constructs turns out close to the *institution* theory [8] — a framework for model translation developed in mathematical logic and model theory. In more detail, the concept of *abstract multimodeling framework* described in [7] is a variant of the so called *liberal institutions*, which have two translation mechanisms corresponding to our view computation and retyping. The framework is fairly abstract: no details are given on what conformance of a model to a metamodel is, or how the view mechanism is realized. Nevertheless, the notions of heterogeneous multimodel and its consistency can be well defined and give rise to the corresponding algorithm for global consistency checking.

To bridge the gap between the abstract framework and practical applications, the notion of a *concrete multimodeling framework* is also defined in [7]. For a concrete framework, conformance of models to metamodels is realized via typing mappings (and retyping plainly amounts to mapping composition), and the view mechanism is realized via an algebra of query operations. A wide class of multimodeling systems appearing in practice are instances of concrete frameworks. Any concrete framework gives rise to an abstract framework, and thus the general algorithm of global consistency checking can be applied.

5 Related Work and Discussion

Approaches to heterogeneous multimodeling can be roughly divided into *global* and *local*. For the global approaches, heterogeneity is managed by relating all local models to one global model, and checking consistency wrt. this global model. In contrast, there is no global model in local approaches (including ours). Another crucial dimension of multimodeling is how correspondences between local models and their inter-relationships are specified. Below the space of existing approaches is discussed in more detail.

Global approaches. We distinguish two main types.

1) Monitoring satisfiability of consistency rules. This is the most direct global approach to consistency checking. All local models are considered as partial instances of some all-embracing global model given a priori, e.g., *System model* in [9] or the entire UML model (if UML modeling is treated as suggested by OMG). Inter-model consistency is given by *rules* specified in a special language "understanding" all local models. For this goal, local models are translated into an expressive common formalism, e.g., FOL in the well-known *Viewpoints* framework [10], XMI in *xlinkit* [11], description logic in [12], and again FOL in Egyed's framework [13]. Configuration of model overlap (which may be very intricate as our examples show) is thus flattened and hidden in arrays of formulas. As a result, the approaches mainly handle cases with simple overlap structures, e.g., binary overlaps with elements matched by names.

2) Consistency checking via merging. Close relations between consistency and model merging are noticed in [14] for behavioral, and in [2] for structural modeling. The global model is not given a priori but is computed by merging all local models modulo their correspondences; the latter must be explicitly specified. Much work in this direction is done in databases in the context of *view integration*, where they work mainly with enhanced ER-diagrams [15] or similar but more expressive formalisms [16]. A serious limitation of this work is that only the homogeneous case is considered because so far it was unclear how to merge heterogeneous models.

To manage heterogeneity, local models can be translated into an a priori given common expressive formalism (e.g., *generalized sketches* [17] or graph transformation systems [18]), where they are merged. A more intelligent approach is to *build* a minimal common formalism by merging together all local metamodels. Different versions of this idea have been elaborated in the area of model composition [19]; a survey can be found in [20]. Of course, composition of local metamodels requires correspondences between them to be explicitly specified. Usually only binary cases are considered, but [17,18,2] address also the general N-ary case by using the colimit operation.

Local approaches. Although the idea of local consistency checking seems intuitive, we are not aware of its practical realization. A partial reason for this may be that an abstract general formulation of the framework is not easy (compare our concrete examples in Section 4 and their abstract description in [7]). The problem is currently being investigated by the Algebraic Specification community within the institution framework [8]. Models are translated into theories in suitable institutions, and relationships between the latter are specified by spans (or cospans) of institution comorphisms (resp., morphisms) [21]. The community is experimenting with different types of structures specifying institution overlaps, and a recent paper [22] uses mixed pairs (comorphism, morphism) to relate two institutions. It is not clear how this mixed setting can be extended to the multi-ary situation.

A fundamental distinction between these and our frameworks is that they do not consider derived elements in correspondence specifications. It makes the theory much simpler but much less expressive (and inapplicable to practically interesting situations we considered in the paper). Another fundamental distinction is that they consider local models consistent if their projections to the overlap are equal (or one is a subset of the other), but matches between projections are not considered. In contrast, in our framework model matches are an integral part of the multimodel. Other distinctions are (a) they consider only binary correspondences, (b) do not work with inter-metamodel constraints, and (c) treat consistency semantically (the set of instances is not empty) rather than syntactically (as in our framework). However, if the institution satisfies the corresponding completeness theorem, syntactic and semantic consistencies coincide. Also, we do not translate metamodels into theories: for us metamodels *are* theories, and model translation is given by the view execution mechanism.

Correspondences via spans. For local and global-2 approaches, explicit specification of inter-model correspondences is a central issue, and different types of notation and techniques were developed [23]. A distinctive feature of our approach is that the set of correspondences is reified as a special model endowed with projection mappings — a span. This is a standard categorical idea, which was repeatedly employed in homogeneous multimodeling frameworks based on category theory, eg, [24,17,18,6,25]. Independently, the same idea of reifying correspondences by a model was discovered in work on model management in databases [26,16].

The most difficult issue is *indirect correspondences*, when sets of elements in different models are related but their relationships cannot be specified by equating the elements (e.g., Fig. 2). Such correspondences are usually specified by *correspondence rules* [23] or *expressions* [26] attached to nodes reifying correspondences. When such annotated spans are composed, it is not clear how to compose the rules — the importance and difficulty of this problem was stressed in [26]. In our approach, the problem is solved with specifying indirect correspondences by equations involving derived elements, then composition amounts to term substitution (see [5,27] for examples and details). Moreover, the use of derived elements allows us to specify structural conflicts between models uniformly by equations; e.g., all structural conflicts considered in [16] can be managed in this way [28].

6 Conclusion

The paper describes a general approach to global consistency checking of heterogeneous multimodels. It is based on finding common views between metamodels of the models involved, projecting all models to these views, merging projections and checking the result against the constraints specified in the view. The approach gives rise to a novel framework for heterogeneous multimodeling, in which a network of interrelated metamodels — the metamodel schema — plays the central role.

The framework has a number of advantages. First, heterogeneous consistency checking is reduced to homogeneous with a minimal amount of metamodel merging; the latter is unavoidable if we want to treat inter-metamodel constraints yet we work as locally as possible. Second, the framework is applicable to a wide class of models and metamodels satisfying not too restrictive conditions. Third is the adaptability of the framework to the *living with inconsistencies* paradigm [4]: conflicts between models can be recorded in the heads of the correspondence spans and resolved later. Forth, heterogeneous multimodeling becomes directly related to the institution theory and hence to a source of important mathematical results about interrelation of logical theories and their models.

However, the approach still needs practical, and in part also theoretical, validation. On the practical side, the main question is how effectively a multimodeling tool based on the framework could be implemented. On the theoretical side, the cornerstone of the approach is a default assumption that our "as local as possible" consistency checking is equivalent to consistency checking via building a global metamodel (global-2 approaches). There are strong formal arguments justifying this assumption but an accurate proof is still to be completed.

Another important theoretical line of future work is to develop a useful classification of heterogeneous multimodels. We may classify multimodels by the type of their metamodel schema: whether it is a plain collection of spans, or there are spans over spans over spans, or perhaps even more complex configurations. Types of mappings in the metamodel schema are also essential: whether they are plain projections or complex views involving non-trivial queries. Complexity of queries involved in the metamodel schema of a multimodel is its important property, and many useful results can be found in the database literature. Defining multimodeling in abstract mathematical terms [7] would allow useful interaction of the two fields.

Acknowledgement. We are grateful to the organizers of the MDI'10 Workshop for encouragement and the invitation to prepare this paper. Thanks to Antonio Vallecillo for pointing out several important related papers. Special thanks to Michał Antkiewicz for valuable discussions of multimodeling.

Financial support was provided by the Ontario Research Fund.

References

1. Egyed, A.: Instant consistency checking for the UML. In: ICSE, pp. 381–390 (2006)
2. Sabetzadeh, M., Nejati, S., Liaskos, S., Easterbrook, S., Chechik, M.: Consistency checking of conceptual models via model merging. In: RE, pp. 221–230 (2007)
3. Diskin, Z., Xiong, Y., Czarnecki, K.: Specifying overlaps of heterogeneous models for global consistency checking. In: First Int. Workshop on Model-Driven Interoperability, MDI 2010, pp. 42–51. ACM Press, New York (2010)
4. Balzer, R.: Tolerating inconsistency. In: ICSE, pp. 158–165 (1991)
5. Diskin, Z.: Model synchronization: mappings, tile algebra, and categories. In: Fernandes, J.M., Lämmel, R., Visser, J., Saraiva, J. (eds.) Generative and Transformational Techniques in Software Engineering III. LNCS, vol. 6491, Springer, Heidelberg (2011)
6. Sabetzadeh, M., Easterbrook, S.: View merging in the presence of incompleteness and inconsistency. Requir. Eng. 11(3), 174–193 (2006)
7. Diskin, Z.: Towards a formal semantics for consisternCy of heterogeneous multimodels. Technical Report 2010-07, The University of Waterloo (2011), http://gsd.uwaterloo.ca/node/330
8. Mossakowski, T., Tarlecki, A.: Heterogeneous logical environments for distributed specifications. In: Corradini, A., Montanari, U. (eds.) WADT 2008. LNCS, vol. 5486, pp. 266–289. Springer, Heidelberg (2009)

9. Broy, M., Cengarle, M., Rumpe, B.: Semantics of UML — towards a system model for UML: The structural data model. Technical Report TUM-IO612, Techniche Universität München (2006)
10. Nuseibeh, B., Kramer, J., Finkelstein, A.: Viewpoints: meaningful relationships are difficult? In: ICSE, pp. 676–683 (2003)
11. Nentwich, C., Emmerich, W., Finkelstein, A.: Consistency management with repair actions. In: ICSE, pp. 455–464 (2003)
12. Van Der Straeten, R., Mens, T., Simmonds, J., Jonckers, V.: Using description logic to maintain consistency between UML models. In: Stevens, P., Whittle, J., Booch, G. (eds.) UML 2003. LNCS, vol. 2863, pp. 326–340. Springer, Heidelberg (2003)
13. Egyed, A.: Fixing inconsistencies in UML design models. In: ICSE, pp. 292–301 (2007)
14. Easterbrook, S.M., Chechik, M.: A framework for multi-valued reasoning over inconsistent viewpoints. In: ICSE, pp. 411–420 (2001)
15. Spaccapietra, S., Parent, C.: View integration: A step forward in solving structural conflicts. IEEE Trans. Knowl. Data Eng. 6(2), 258–274 (1994)
16. Bernstein, P., Pottinger, R.: Merging models based on given correspondences. In: VLDB (2003)
17. Cadish, B., Diskin, Z.: Heterogenious view integration via sketches and equations. In: ISMIS, pp. 603–612 (1996)
18. Engels, G., Heckel, R., Taentzer, G., Ehrig, H.: A combined reference model- and view-based approach to system specification. Int. Journal of Software and Knowledge Engeneering 7, 457–477 (1997)
19. Bézivin, J., Bouzitouna, S., Del Fabro, M.D., Gervais, M.-P., Jouault, F., Kolovos, D.S., Kurtev, I., Paige, R.F.: A canonical scheme for model composition. In: Rensink, A., Warmer, J. (eds.) ECMDA-FA 2006. LNCS, vol. 4066, pp. 346–360. Springer, Heidelberg (2006)
20. Vallecillo, A.: On the combination of domain specific modeling languages. In: Kühne, T., Selic, B., Gervais, M.-P., Terrier, F. (eds.) ECMFA 2010. LNCS, vol. 6138, pp. 305–320. Springer, Heidelberg (2010)
21. Wirsing, M., Knapp, A.: View consistency in software development. In: Wirsing, M., Knapp, A., Balsamo, S. (eds.) RISSEF 2002. LNCS, vol. 2941, pp. 341–357. Springer, Heidelberg (2004)
22. Boronat, A., Knapp, A., Meseguer, J., Wirsing, M.: What is a multi-modeling language? In: Corradini, A., Montanari, U. (eds.) WADT 2008. LNCS, vol. 5486, pp. 71–87. Springer, Heidelberg (2009)
23. Romero, J., Jaen, J., Vallecillo, A.: Realizing correspondences in multi-viewpoint specifications. In: EDOC, pp. 163–172. IEEE Computer Society, Los Alamitos (2009)
24. Fiadeiro, J.L., Maibaum, T.S.E.: Interconnecting formalisms: Supporting modularity, reuse and incrementality. In: SIGSOFT FSE, pp. 72–80 (1995)
25. Liang, H., Diskin, Z., Dingel, J., Posse, E.: A general approach for scenario integration. In: Busch, C., Ober, I., Bruel, J.-M., Uhl, A., Völter, M. (eds.) MODELS 2008. LNCS, vol. 5301, pp. 204–218. Springer, Heidelberg (2008)
26. Bernstein, P.: Applying model management to classical metadata problems. In: Proc. CIDR 2003, pp. 209–220 (2003)
27. Diskin, Z.: Mathematics of generic specifications for model management. In: Rivero, Doorn, Ferraggine (eds.): Encyclopedia of Database Technologies and Applications, pp. 351–366. Idea Group, USA (2005)
28. Diskin, Z., Easterbrook, S., Miller, R.: Integrating schema integration frameworks, algebraically. Technical Report CSRG-583, University of Toronto (2008), http://ftp.cs.toronto.edu/pub/reports/csrg/583/TR-583-schemaIntegr.pdf

Models and Evolution - ME2010

Dirk Deridder[1], Alfonso Pierantonio[2], Bernhard Schätz[3], and Dalila Tamzalit[4]

[1] Vrije Universiteit Brussel, Belgium
dirk.deridder@vub.ac.be
[2] University of L'Aquila, Italy
alfonso@di.univaq.it
[3] fortiss GmbH, Germany
schaetz@fortiss.org
[4] University of Nantes, France
dalila.tamzalit@univ-nantes.fr

1 Introduction

In general, software artifacts and applications are subject to many kinds of changes, which range from technical changes due to rapidly evolving technology platforms, to modifications in the applications themselves due to the natural evolution of the businesses supported by those software applications. These modifications include changes at all levels, from requirements through architecture and design, to source code, documentation and test suites. They typically affect various kinds of models including data models, behavioral models, domain models, source code models or goal models. Coping with and managing the changes that accompany the evolution of software assets is therefore an essential aspect of Software Engineering as a discipline.

In this context, models can play an important role. They can help and guide software evolution and can enforce and reduce critical risks and important resources (e.g., costs, personnel, time) involved in software evolution, by employing high-level abstractions. Models can thus help to direct evolution. Model-Driven Engineering (MDE) is an approach to software design and development in which models are the primary artifacts, and play a key role. The major objective of MDE is to increase productivity and reduce time-to-market by raising the level of abstraction and using concepts closer to the problem domain at hand, rather than those offered by programming languages. Models represent domain-specific concepts and conform to metamodels. A core task of MDE is the manipulation and transformation of models. Manipulating and transforming models can be very useful to manage software evolution. The objective is to enforce and reduce critical risks and important costs involved in software evolution, by employing high-level abstractions and by considering several facets.

Similar to traditional software engineering approaches, MDE is also susceptible to evolution. The MDE context poses unique challenges which require the conception and development of novel techniques, dedicated approaches, and advanced tool support. In fact, there is an increasing need for more research investigating disciplined techniques and engineering tools to support a wide range of model evolution activities, including model-driven software evolution, model differencing, model comparison, model refactoring, model inconsistency management, model versioning and merging, and (co-)evolution of models.

The different dimensions of evolution in the MDE context make the problem intrinsically difficult. This is because modifications can reflect coherent adaptations of correlated artifacts at several layers of the metamodeling architecture and at several levels of abstractions. For example, some well-formed rules can be invalidated when a metamodel evolves. The same happens with the associated model transformations. Furthermore, model adaptations should be propagated to artifacts interconnected by means of model transformations. Finally, evolution of model transformations should be reflected in both source and target models. In addition, the exploitation of differences is an appropriate solution for version management, because in general the complete system model is far larger than the modifications that occur from one version to another.

Furthermore, there is a substantial difference between the modeling of evolution and the evolution of models. There are plenty of works on the former topic, while the focus of this workshop is on the evolution of models, hence its name: "Models and Evolution" (ME). ME 2010 was the result of merging two successful series of international yearly workshops that were in existence since 2007 (for the MoDSE workshop), and 2008 (for the MCCM workshop).

2 Workshop Contributions

In addition to the content-wise objectives described above, one of the main goals of the workshop series is to provide an open discussion space where the MDE and software evolution communities can meet on a yearly basis. As usual we also encouraged young researchers to participate and submit their work to get into contact with this growing community.

The full-day workshop included four thematic sessions which we used to group the presentations and focus the discussions:

Semantics

- **A Manifesto for Semantic Model Differencing,**
  by Shahar Maoz, Jan Ringert and Bernhard Rumpe
- **Towards Semantics-Preserving Model Migration,**
  by Markus Herrmannsdoerfer and Maximilian Koegel
- **Documenting Stepwise Model Refinement using Executable Design Decisions,**
  by Matthias Biehl

Model merging

- **Representation and Visualization of Merge Conflicts with UML Profiles,**
  by Petra Brosch, Philip Langer, Martina Seidl, Konrad Wieland, Manuel Wimmer, Horst Kargl and Gerti Kappel

- **Decoupling Operation-Based Merging from Model Change Recording,**
  by *Stephen Barrett, Patrice Chalin and Greg Butler*
- **Merging Model Refactorings - An Empirical Study,**
  by *Maximilian Koegel, Markus Herrmannsdoerfer, Otto von Wesendonk and Jonas Helming*
- **The Case for Batch Merge of Models Issues and Challenges,**
  by *Lars Bendix, Maximilian Koegel and Antonio Martini*

Model Inconsistencies, Model Differences

- **Automated Planning for Resolving Model Inconsistencies: A Scalability Study,**
  by *Jorge Pinna Puissant, Ragnhild Van Der Straeten and Tom Mens*
- **RCVDiff - a stand-alone tool for representation, calculation and visualization of model differences ,**
  by *Zvezdan Protic, Mark van den Brand and Tom Verhoeff*

Meta models and transformations

- **Semi-Automated Correction of Model-to-Text Transformations,**
  by *Gábor Guta, András Pataricza, Wolfgang Schreiner and Dániel Varró*
- **Transformation Migration After Metamodel Evolution,**
  by *David Méndez, Anne Etien, Alexis Muller and Rubby Casallas*
- **Towards Metamodel Evolution of EMF Models with Henshin,**
  by *Stefan Jurack and Florian Mantz*
- **Comparing Model-Metamodel and Transformation-Metamodel Co-evolution,**
  by *Louis Rose, Anne Etien, David Méndez, Dimitrios Kolovos, Richard Paige and Fiona Polack*

As a tradition in the workshop series we always organise a plenary debate. The basis for these debates comes from the questions and challenges provided by the authors, program chairs, and participants. Below we briefly summarize the ones that were used to guide and fuel this year's discussion(s):

- Why don't we focus more on proactive support for model evolution (possibly facilitated and backed up by a MDE process), instead of fixing problems after they occur?
- How to deal with the semantic aspect of model evolution?
- How to preserve model semantics when evolving models, meta-models, transformations, ...?
- When to use semantic model differencing instead of syntactic model differencing?
- How to manage model-metamodel co-evolution and transformation-metamodel co-evolution? And what about the link between both?
- Isn't it time to move towards a unification of model evolution approaches (terminology, frameworks, ...)? And how would this impact/advance our research (and collaborations)?

- There is still a lot of work to be done in resolving the problems detected when evolving models. Knowing the problem is one thing, resolving it another?
- Wouldn't a benchmarking methodology/tool be benificial for comparing our different approaches?
- Which types of models do we want to consider in ME research (e.g. physical models, process models, domain specific models, design models, hardware models, ...)?
- What are the limitations of evolution approaches with respect to the kinds of models they can address and is it possible to make these more generic?
- How to make models and transformations more resilient to changes in the meta-models? Is there a way to encapsulate changes (e.g. in a first class artifact) and apply them to all impacted artifacts?
- How to deal with ME when confronted with a heterogeneous set of meta-models?
- What about large scale models and evolution?

3 Summary and Outlook

The Models and Evolution workshop series is maturing, and every year we witness an increase of interest by the MoDELS community. This is clearly evidenced by the steady growing number of participants that we are happy to welcome each year (over 50). The quality of the submissions we received was exceptionally high, which is why we have set up a theme issue on Models and Evolution in the Springer *Software and Systems Modelling* journal (www.sosym.org). Given the fact that the Models and Evolution research community is a very lively one, we are looking forward to learn about the results in future editions of the ME workshops. Full versions of the presented contributions are available online at www.modse.fr.

Acknowledgements

We thank our programme committee members for their help in the paper selection process: Hubert Dubois, Jeff Gray, Tom Mens, Pierre-Yves Schobbens, Stefan Wagner, Arnaud Albinet, Benoit Baudry, Mireille Blay-Fornarino, Jean-Michel Bruel, Jordi Cabot, Rubby Casallas, Antonio Cicchetti, Davide Di Ruscio, Anne Etien, Jean-Marie Favre, Mehdi Jazayri, Gerti Kappel, Udo Kelter, Olivier Le Goaer, Richard Paige, Antonio Vallecillo, Ragnhild Van Der Straeten, Hans Vangheluwe, Dennis Wagelaar.

Conflicts as First-Class Entities: A UML Profile for Model Versioning[*]

Petra Brosch[1], Horst Kargl[3], Philip Langer[2], Martina Seidl[1],
Konrad Wieland[1], Manuel Wimmer[1], and Gerti Kappel[1]

[1] Business Informatics Group, Vienna University of Technology, Austria
`lastname@big.tuwien.ac.at`
[2] Department of Telecooperation, Johannes Kepler University Linz, Austria
`firstname.lastname@jku.at`
[3] SparxSystems, Austria
`firstname.lastname@sparxsystems.at`

Abstract. The urgent demand for optimistic version control support for software models induced active research within the modeling community. Recently, several approaches have been proposed addressing the task of detecting conflicts when merging two concurrently changed versions of a model. In this context, the holistic representation and supportive visualization of detected merge conflicts pose a challenge.

In this paper, we present a modeling language independent *conflict model* comprising all necessary information to profoundly represent merge conflicts. From this conflict model, we leverage the dynamic extension power of UML profiles by introducing a dedicated *conflict profile* to visually assist modelers in resolving merge conflicts of UML models. As a result, modelers may resolve conflicts in the concrete graphical syntax conducting their familiar UML editors without tool extensions.

Keywords: model versioning, conflict visualization, UML profile.

1 Introduction

Like traditional program code, software models are not resistant to change, but evolve over time by steadily undergoing extensions, corrections, and updates. Especially in the context of model-driven engineering (MDE) models are not used for mere documentation purposes only. Instead, models are leveraged as first-class development artifacts. Hence, models are subject to continuous evolution requiring adequate techniques to manage the development process in general and to support the collaborative creation and modifications in particular [8,17].

The application of version control systems (VCS) is one important way to improve cooperation in software development [6]. Following the optimistic versioning paradigm, every modeler works independently from other team members

---

[*] This work has been partly funded by the Austrian Federal Ministry of Transport, Innovation, and Technology and the Austrian Research Promotion Agency under grant FIT-IT-819584 and by the fFORTE WIT Program of the Vienna University of Technology and the Austrian Federal Ministry of Science and Research.

on her personal local copy. When merging the isolated updates into one common version, conflicts might be raised due to divergences in the different replicas triggering the conflict resolution process necessary to obtain a consolidated and reconciled merged version of the modified artifacts [13].

To provide collaborative modeling support, text-based versioning systems successfully applied for the versioning of code such as Subversion[1] and CVS[2] have been reused. It has been quickly realized that XMI serializations are not the appropriate representation for detecting and resolving conflicts between concurrently edited model versions, because modelers are familiar with the concrete graphical syntax but not with computer internal representations. Thus, some dedicated approaches have been proposed for visualizing differences of UML models. They construct a dedicated view using the concrete syntax, which combines and highlights changes of both models using coloring techniques [12,15]. Hence, the modeler remains in her familiar modeling environment. However, these approaches require the implementation of special editor extensions.

In this paper we pursue this idea by proposing an approach for representing and visualizing merge conflicts for UML models based on UML profiles. As a conceptual basis, we first present a holistic and language independent model for representing conflicts. From this model, we derive a dedicated conflict diagram view with additional annotations for marking changes and conflicts between UML models. These annotations are defined by a UML profile, which allows on the one hand, to display annotated models in arbitrary UML editors without requiring any tool extensions. On the other hand, it yields a specification for tool vendors to integrate mechanisms for user friendly conflict resolution and filtering support. This additional information is valuable for the final merge process.

Starting with a brief motivating example in Section 2, we continue with discussing how to represent conflicts emerging from two concurrently modified versions of one model in Section 3. In Section 4, we present a visualization of conflicts using UML profiles. Finally, in Section 5 we conclude and give an outlook on future work.

2 Motivating Example

Harry and Sally check out the UML Class Diagram V0 depicted in Fig. 1 from a central repository and concurrently perform several modifications.

Sally renames the class Element (C1) to Shape and sets this class abstract. Next, she performs the refactoring pullUpField by removing the common attribute area from all subclasses Square (C2), Circle (C3), and Line (C4) and adding it to the common superclass Element (C1). Furthermore, she adds two new attributes to the class Circle (C3), namely perimeter and radius. Finally, the class Square (C2) is set as superclass of Rectangle (C6). The result of Sally's work is depicted as V0' in Fig. 1, which she commits to the repository.

---

[1] http://subversion.tigris.org
[2] http://cvs.nongnu.org

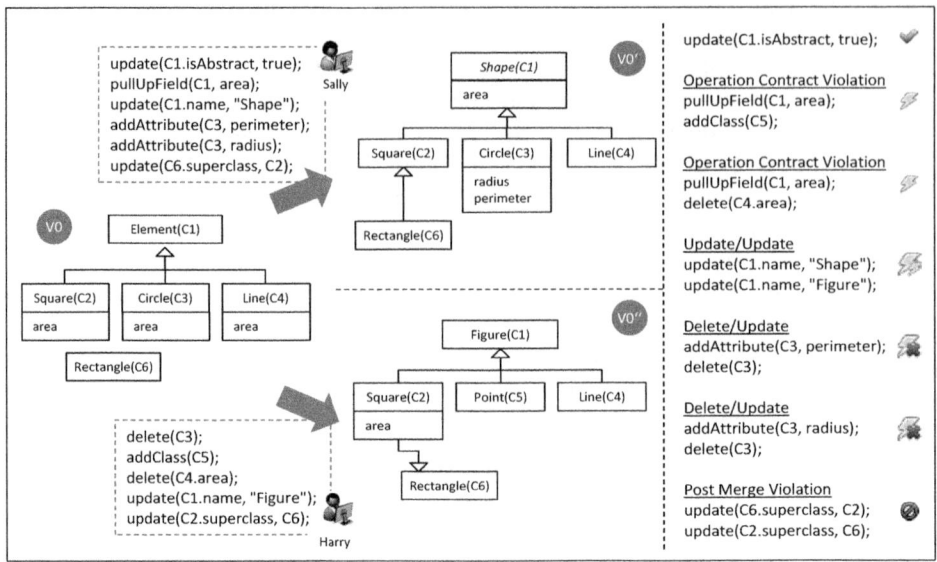

Fig. 1. An example scenario

In parallel, Harry removes the class Circle (C3) as well as the attribute area from the class Line (C4). Next, he introduces a new class Point (C5) which is set as subclass of Element (C1). In addition, he renames Element (C1) to Figure. Finally, Harry sets the class Rectangle (C6) as superclass of the class Square (C2).

When Harry tries to check in his modifications, several conflicts are reported (cf. right part of Fig. 1). Only the operation update(C1.isAbstract, true) may be merged unproblematically (depending on the unit of versioning). The refactoring pullUpField(C1, area) is conflicting with both, the introduction of the class Point (C5) and the deletion of the attribute area of the class Line (C4). Neither the new class Point (C5), nor the updated class Line (C4) provide the required attribute, which results in a contract violation of the refactoring operation. Since both, Harry and Sally, have renamed the class Element (C1), an *update/update* conflict is reported. Furthermore, two *delete/update* conflicts have occurred, because Harry deleted the class Circle (C3) in which Sally added the attributes perimeter and radius. Finally, the violation "Inheritance Cycle" is reported between the classes Square (C2) and Rectangle (C6) which is raised by a constraint in the metamodel.

3 A Holistic Conflict Model

In this section, we present a conceptual representation of changes and conflicts between two independent modifications of a common base model. An outright representation is mandatory for modeling environments to construct a supportive visualization of all occurred conflicts.

3.1 Prerequisites

Before elaborating on the representation of conflicts, we shortly discuss preceding steps which are mandatory to finally explicate conflicts. These steps are *(i)* capturing the changes performed between two versions of a model, and subsequently, *(ii)* identifying conflicting pairs of changes.

(i) Capturing changes. A prerequisite for detecting conflicts is to capture the actual changes that have been concurrently performed by two modelers on the same original model. Generally, there are two different techniques to accomplish this task [6]: *State-based* approaches compare different states, i.e., versions of a model to derive the differences between these states. In contrast, *change-based* approaches capture changes by observing and recording the modifications while the user performs them.

Recently, it has been widely recognized that the additional knowledge on applied composite operations like refactorings is highly beneficial for versioning. Respecting refactorings enables a faster and better understanding of the modeler's original intention and enables a smarter conflict detection and resolution [1,7]. Some change-based approaches allow to directly capture applied refactorings at execution time (e.g., [9]). However, such approaches strongly depend on the modeling environment and only predefined refactorings for a specific modeling language may be detectable. Manually performed refactorings remain unrevealed. To overcome these shortcomings, refactoring occurrences may also be retrospectively detected using state-based approaches as realized in the model versioning system AMOR [1]. Nevertheless, state-based refactoring detection may accomplish a lower precision compared to change-based refactoring detection.

(ii) Detecting conflicts. Having captured all performed changes, conflicts may be detected. In this paper, we consider three kinds of conflicts which are indepth discussed in [2]. The simplest kind of conflict arises if two opposite changes modify the same feature of a model element in a contradicting way resulting in *update/update* and *delete/update* conflicts. Regarding refactorings, another kind of conflict may occur, if the execution of a refactoring is not possible anymore after incorporating the opposite modeler's changes. Such conflicts are referred to as *operation contract violation* since opposite changes violate the preconditions of a refactoring. Finally, so called *post merge violations* may also arise if the merged model violates metamodel constraints.

The first kind of conflict is supported by several approaches like [1,4,10,14,16]). Additionally, refactorings are regarded in the approaches presented in [10], [16], and [1], however, only the approach introduced in [1] has explicitly specified preconditions of refactorings and, thus, also supports more complex *operation contract violations*. Violations of the metamodel are usually revealed by reusing existing validation frameworks as done by [1] and [10].

3.2 A Model for Conflicts

The essence of a conflict are the involved model elements, the performed changes as well as the violated constraints. These constraints are either preconditions of a

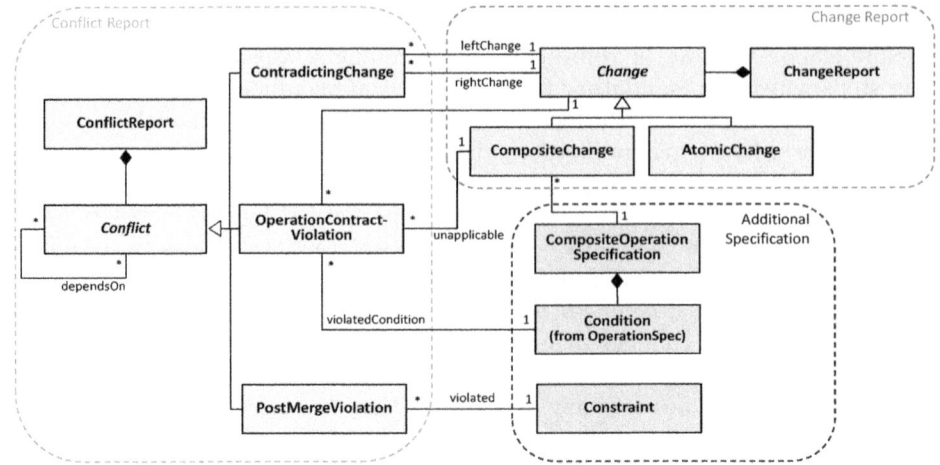

Fig. 2. Conflict Model

change or conformance rules defined in the metamodel of a modeling language. Hence, in our conflict model depicted in Fig. 2, we assemble two sources of information for obtaining a *conflict report*, namely the *change report*, comprising all applied changes, and *additional language specifications* formulating language specific operations like refactorings and conformance rules. With this conflict model we may profoundly express the three different kinds of conflicts.

- *ContradictingChange.* A conflict caused by contradicting changes always references two changes which interfere each other. These changes may either be atomic or composite changes. For example, in Fig. 1 the two concurrent updates of C1's name are contradicting changes as well as the introduction of an attribute into a class which is concurrently deleted.
- *OperationContractViolation.* A conflict due to the violation of an operation contract always involves at least one composite change like a refactoring. This change cannot be performed because another change violates a precondition. Composite changes may be specified with a tool like the Operation Recorder as proposed in [3]. We distinguish between two cases: a composite change is either not applicable because a model element violating the change's precondition has been added (e.g., class C5 in Fig. 1) or an existing model element necessary for the execution has been changed or deleted (e.g., an attribute of class C4 in Fig. 1).
- *PostMergeViolation.* Furthermore, conflicts may arise if the merged model violates metamodel constraints. For example in Fig. 1, a naively merged version would contain a cyclic inheritance relationship between the classes C2 and C6.

The idea of representing conflicts in terms of a model is not new. Cicchetti et al. [5] recently proposed a metamodel to describe conflict patterns used to

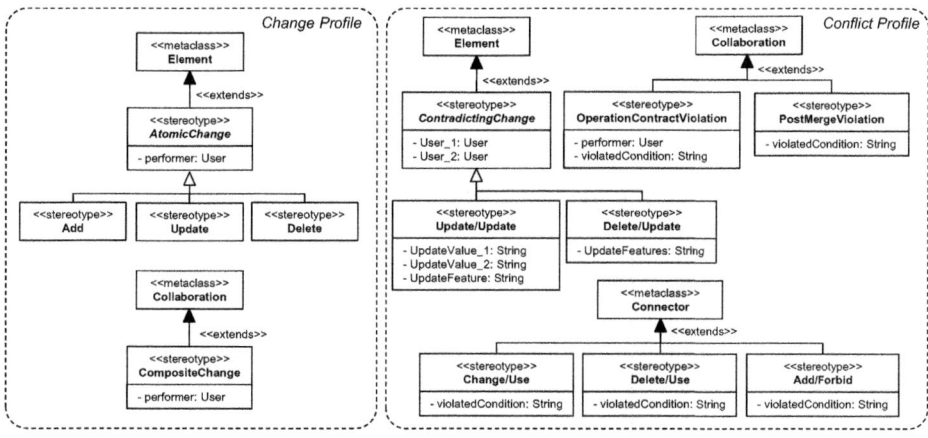

Fig. 3. Change Profile and Conflict Profile

match against a change report for detecting conflicts. In contrast to Cicchetti et al., our approach is designed for the automatic calculation of conflicts by using additional language information like composite change specifications and metamodel constraints. The detection of contradicting changes does not require any additional information. Thus, we are able to derive conflict descriptions automatically.

4 Representing and Visualizing Conflicts in UML Models

In the previous section, we have introduced a model for representing conflicts. However, when it comes to showing the conflicts to the user, appropriate visualization techniques are a must. Thus, in this section we leverage the dynamic extension power of UML profiles by introducing a dedicated *change profile* and *conflict profile* (cf. Fig. 4). Both profiles are used to visualize the evolution of a model and occurred conflicts. The design rationale for choosing UML profiles is based on the following requirements:

- *User-friendly visualization*: Merge conflicts as well as the information on performed changes shall be presented in the concrete syntax of UML.
- *Integrated view*: All information shall be visualized within a single diagram to provide a complete overview of conflicts.
- *UML-conform models*: The models incorporating the conflict information shall be compliant with the UML metamodel.
- *No editor modifications*: The visualization of conflicts in UML models shall be possible without modifying the graphical editors of UML tools.
- *Model-based representation*: If models are exchanged between UML tools, the conflict information shall not be lost. Thus, conflicts should be explicitly represented as model elements. Then, conflicts may be resolved later.

UML profiles typically comprise *stereotypes*, *tagged values*, and additional *constraints* stating how profiled UML models may be built. Stereotypes are used to introduce additional modeling concepts to extend standard UML metaclasses. Once a stereotype is specified for a metaclass, the stereotype may be applied to instances of the extended metaclass to provide further semantics. With tagged values, additional properties may be defined for stereotypes. These tagged values may then be set on the modeling level for applied stereotypes. Furthermore, syntactic sugar in terms of icons for defined stereotypes may be configured to improve the visualization of profiled UML models. The major benefit of UML profiles is that profiled models are still compliant to UML and, thus, are naturally handled by current UML tools.

In the remainder of this section, we first present the *Change Profile* and the *Conflict Profile*. Second, we elaborate on the algorithm for computing the *Conflict Diagram View*, i.e., the merged model including change information as well as conflicts in terms of stereotypes and tagged values. Finally, we discuss possible *interaction techniques* with this conflict diagram view from a user perspective.

4.1 A UML Profile for Conflicts

As depicted in Fig. 2, the conflict model assembles the change report comprising all atomic and composite changes as well as the conflict report which subsumes all detected conflicts. A conflict links to the actual conflicting changes in the change report. This separation is also considered in the UML profile by providing a dedicated profile for visualizing changes and a dedicated profile for visualizing conflicts (cf. Fig. 4). Both profiles are derived from the previously presented conflict model. Please note that the UML profile comprises additional information, e.g., subtypes and properties, which is implicitly stated in the conflict model.

Change Profile. The change profile provides stereotypes for each kind of change. The stereotypes for atomic changes, like adds, updates, and deletions may be applied to all concrete UML concepts. Thus, the stereotype ≪AtomicChange≫ extends the root metaclass Element of the UML metamodel. In contrast to atomic changes, composite changes involve several model elements. Therefore, we decided to explicitly introduce a UML Collaboration annotated with a ≪CompositeChange≫ stereotype for each composite change. The collaboration links via UML Connectors to the involved model elements to which appropriate ≪Add≫, ≪Delete≫, and ≪Update≫ stereotypes are applied. Finally, for each change the responsible user is saved as meta information.

Conflict Profile. For each of the aforementioned conflict kinds, the conflict profile provides a stereotype with appropriate tagged values. For contradicting changes, the profile provides an ≪Update/Update≫ and ≪Delete/Update≫ stereotype. Both may be applied to any UML element. In contrast to contradicting changes, violations may involve several model elements. Hence, similar as for composite changes, for each violation a UML Collaboration annotated with the respective stereotype ≪OperationContractViolation≫ or ≪PostMergeViolation≫ is introduced. A collaboration refers to elements involved in the violation using UML Connectors. In case of *operation contract violations*, to add more semantics to these connectors, they are annotated with respective stereotypes (inspired from graph transformation theory [11]) for marking how the contract is violated by the model element (cf. lower right hand side of Fig. 4).

4.2 Generating the Conflict Diagram View

Resolving conflicts by manually exploring the base model as well as changed models in combination with the change report and a list of conflicts seems to be too cumbersome and error-prone in practice. Thus, we generate a dedicated *Conflict Diagram View* showing the merged model comprising all relevant changes and detected conflicts at a single glance (cf. Fig. 4 for the running example). This view is obtained as follows:

1. All non-conflicting atomic updates and additions are applied to the common base model. Deletions are skipped, to allow annotating deleted elements with the respective stereotype (e.g., area in class Line in Fig. 4). Also composite changes are left out in this step since they are handled in Step 4.
2. To each changed element, the corresponding change type is annotated by applying the respective stereotype of the change profile (e.g., Point in Fig. 4).
3. Contradicting changes are annotated by applying ≪Delete/Update≫ and ≪Update/Update≫ stereotypes to the involved elements (e.g., Element in Fig. 4). Updated features and its changed values are stored in tagged values.
4. The applied composite changes are considered by checking their preconditions with the merged model. If the preconditions are still valid, they are re-executed on the merged model. If the preconditions are invalid, an *operation contract violation* is at hand. Since such conflicts involve several model elements, we add a UML Collaboration for each of these conflicts. The added collaboration references *(i)* model elements to which the composite change has been originally applied (e.g., gray lines from Pull Up Field in Fig. 4), *(ii)* the elements which are no longer fulfilling the precondition, i.e., all classes must have the field to be pulled up, due to changes by another user (e.g., red line annotated with ≪Delete/Use≫ in Fig. 4), and *(iii)* elements added by another user which violate the change's preconditions (e.g., red line annotated with ≪Add/Forbid≫ in Fig. 4).
5. Finally, all *post merge violations* are marked adding collaborations referring to the involved model elements (e.g., Inheritance Cycle in Fig. 4).

4.3 Interaction with the Conflict Diagram View

The *Conflict Diagram View* provides several benefits concerning the resolution of the conflicts. First of all, necessary information to resolve the occurred conflicts is provided at a single glance. Furthermore, different diagram filters based on the stereotypes may be used. With the help of these filters, specific kinds of stereotypes, i.e., conflicts, may be hidden enabling the user to focus on a specific conflict scenario. For example, a conflict resolution process can be supported such as firstly representing contradicting changes, subsequently, operation

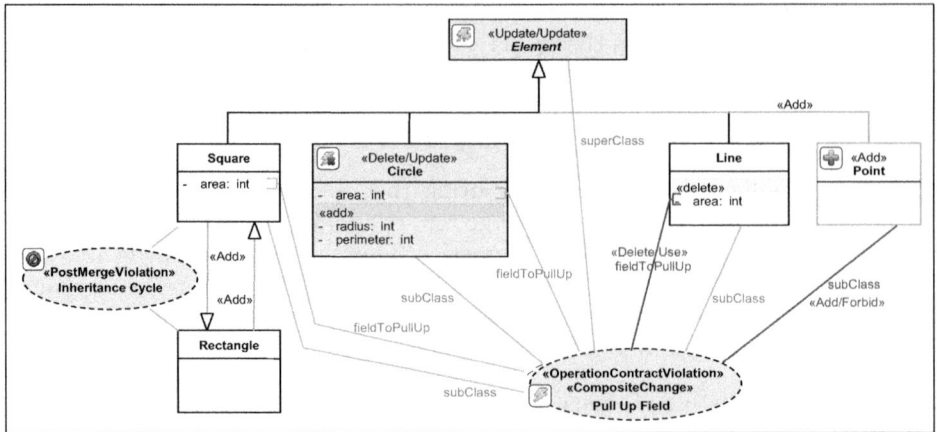

Fig. 4. Conflict Diagram View for the Running Example

contract violations, and finally, post merge conflicts. Based on the stereotypes, additional mechanisms for visualizing conflicts are supported by state-of-the-art UML modeling tools. As depicted in Fig. 4, specialized colors are used for stereotyped elements. Moreover, for each stereotype, possible resolution methods may be provided and, in addition, after resolving a conflict the selected resolution is stored for preserving the history of the resolution process. Finally, conflicts may be temporarily tolerated and kept in the model to be handed over to another user as issue report.

5   Conclusions and Future Work

In this paper, we proposed a holistic conflict model for optimistic model versioning. By using information of the modeling language such as metamodel constraints and specifications of refactorings, we are able to automatically detect conflicts which go beyond trivial update/update and delete/update conflicts. For representing and visualizing conflict reports in UML modeling tools, we proposed a UML conflict profile. By this, we achieved a tool independent representation and visualization without any additional implementation effort for editor extensions. We realized this approach within Enterprise Architect[3] which provides powerful visualization and filtering techniques based on UML profiles. The conflict profile and example models are available on our project homepage[4].

In future work, we will perform user studies in order to explore the usability of conflict profiled models. With this, we want to empirically measure how our visualization approach influences the conflict resolution process. Furthermore, we will increase the usage of smart filtering techniques to improve the support of huge and intensely modified models. We also plan to apply our approach to other Ecore-based modeling languages.

---

[3] http://www.sparxsystems.eu
[4] http://www.modelversioning.org/conflict-profile

References

1. Brosch, P., Kappel, G., Langer, P., Seidl, M., Wieland, K., Wimmer, M., Kargl, H.: Adaptable Model Versioning in Action. In: Modellierung 2010, pp. 221–236 (2010)
2. Brosch, P., Langer, P., Seidl, M., Wieland, K., Wimmer, M.: Colex: A Web-based Collaborative Conflict Lexicon. In: Proc. of the 1st Int. Workshop on Model Comparison in Practice @ TOOLS 2010, pp. 42–49. ACM, New York (2010)
3. Brosch, P., Langer, P., Seidl, M., Wieland, K., Wimmer, M., Kappel, G., Retschitzegger, W., Schwinger, W.: An Example Is Worth a Thousand Words: Composite Operation Modeling By-Example. In: Schürr, A., Selic, B. (eds.) MODELS 2009. LNCS, vol. 5795, pp. 271–285. Springer, Heidelberg (2009)
4. Brun, C., Pierantonio, A.: Model Differences in the Eclipse Modeling Framework. UPGRADE, The Europ. Journal for the Informatics Professional (2008)
5. Cicchetti, A., Di Ruscio, D., Pierantonio, A.: Managing Model Conflicts in Distributed Development. In: Busch, C., Ober, I., Bruel, J.-M., Uhl, A., Völter, M. (eds.) MODELS 2008. LNCS, vol. 5301, pp. 311–325. Springer, Heidelberg (2008)
6. Conradi, R., Westfechtel, B.: Version Models for Software Configuration Management. ACM Computing Surveys 30(2), 232–282 (1998)
7. Dig, D., Manzoor, K., Johnson, R.E., Nguyen, T.N.: Effective Software Merging in the Presence of Object-Oriented Refactorings. IEEE Transactions on Software Engineering 34(3), 321–335 (2008)
8. France, R., Rumpe, B.: Model-driven Development of Complex Software: A Research Roadmap. In: Future of Software Engineering, pp. 37–54. IEEE, Los Alamitos (2007)
9. Herrmannsdoerfer, M., Kögel, M.: Towards a Generic Operation Recorder for Model Evolution. In: Proc. of the 1st Int. Workshop on Model Comparison in Practice @ TOOLS 2010, pp. 76–81. ACM, New York (2010)
10. Kögel, M., Herrmannsdoerfer, M., von Wesendonk, O., Helming, J.: Operation-based Conflict Detection. In: Proc. of the 1st Int. Workshop on Model Comparison in Practice @ TOOLS 2010, pp. 21–30. ACM, New York (2010)
11. Lambers, L., Ehrig, H., Orejas, F.: Conflict Detection for Graph Transformation with Negative Application Conditions. In: Corradini, A., Ehrig, H., Montanari, U., Ribeiro, L., Rozenberg, G. (eds.) ICGT 2006. LNCS, vol. 4178, pp. 61–76. Springer, Heidelberg (2006)
12. Mehra, A., Grundy, J., Hosking, J.: A Generic Approach to Supporting Diagram Differencing and Merging for Collaborative Design. In: Proc. of the 20th Int. Conference on Automated Software Engineering, pp. 204–213. ACM, New York (2005)
13. Mens, T.: A State-of-the-Art Survey on Software Merging. IEEE Transactions on Software Engineering 28(5), 449–462 (2002)
14. Murta, L., Corrêa, C., Prudêncio, J.G., Werner, C.: Towards Odyssey-VCS 2: Improvements over a UML-based Version Control System. In: Proc. of the 2nd Int. Workshop on Comparison and Versioning of Software Models @ ICSE 2008(2008)
15. Ohst, D., Welle, M., Kelter, U.: Differences between Versions of UML Diagrams. In: Proc. of the 9th Europ. Software Engineering Conf., pp. 227–236. ACM, New York (2003)
16. Schneider, C., Zündorf, A., Niere, J.: CoObRA—A Small Step for Development Tools to Collaborative Environments. In: Proc. of the Workshop on Directions in Software Engineering Environments @ ICSE 2004 (2004)
17. Van Der Straeten, R., Mens, T., Van Baelen, S.: Challenges in Model-Driven Software Engineering. In: Chaudron, M.R.V. (ed.) MODELS 2008. LNCS, vol. 5421, pp. 35–47. Springer, Heidelberg (2009)

A Manifesto for Semantic Model Differencing

Shahar Maoz*, Jan Oliver Ringert**, and Bernhard Rumpe

Software Engineering
RWTH Aachen University, Germany
http://www.se-rwth.de/

Abstract. Models are heavily used in software engineering and together with their systems they evolve over time. Thus, managing their changes is an important challenge for system maintainability. Existing approaches to model differencing concentrate on heuristics matching between model elements and on finding and presenting differences at a concrete or abstract syntactic level. While showing some success, these approaches are inherently limited to comparing syntactic structures.

This paper is a manifesto for research on **semantic model differencing**. We present our vision to develop **semantic diff operators** for model comparisons: operators whose input consists of two models and whose output is a set of **diff witnesses**, instances of one model that are not instances of the other. In particular, if the models are syntactically different but there are no diff witnesses, the models are semantically equivalent. We demonstrate our vision using two concrete diff operators, for class diagrams and for activity diagrams. We motivate the use of semantic diff operators, briefly discuss the algorithms to compute them, list related challenges, and show their application and potential use as new fundamental building blocks for change management in model-driven engineering.

1 Introduction

Effective change management, a major challenge in software engineering in general and in model-driven engineering in particular, has attracted much research efforts in recent years (see, e.g., [5,7,12,13,15]). Due to iterative development methodologies, changing requirements, and bug fixes, models continuously evolve during the design, development, and maintenance phases of a system's lifecycle. Managing their changes using formal methods to follow their different versions over time is thus an important task. Fundamental building blocks for this task are *diff operators* one can use for model comparisons.

Existing approaches to model differencing concentrate on matching between model elements using different heuristics related to their names and structure and on finding and presenting differences at a concrete or abstract syntactic level. While

---

* S. Maoz acknowledges support from a postdoctoral Minerva Fellowship, funded by the German Federal Ministry for Education and Research.
** J.O. Ringert is supported by the DFG GK/1298 AlgoSyn.

showing some success, these approaches are also limited. Models that are syntactically very similar may induce very different semantics (in the sense of 'meaning' [9]), and vice versa, models that semantically describe the same system may have rather different syntactic representations. Thus, a list of syntactic differences, although accurate, correct, and complete, may not be able to reveal the real implications these differences have on the correctness and potential use of the models involved. In other words, such a list, although easy to follow, understand, and manipulate (e.g., for merging), may not be able to expose and represent the semantic differences between two versions of a model, in terms of the bugs that were fixed or the features (or new bugs...) that were added.

This paper is a manifesto for research on **semantic model differencing**. We present our vision to develop **semantic diff operators** for model comparisons: operators whose input consists of two models and whose output is a set of **diff witnesses**, instances of the first model that are not instances of the second. Such diff witnesses serve as concrete proofs for the real change between one version and another and its effect on the meaning of the models involved.

We demonstrate our ideas using two examples of concrete semantic diff operators, for class diagrams (CDs) and for activity diagrams (ADs), called *cddiff* and *addiff*, respectively. Given two CDs, *cddiff* outputs a set of diff witnesses, each of which is an object model that is an instance of the first CD and not an instance of the second. Given two ADs, *addiff* outputs a set of diff witnesses, each of which is a finite action trace that is possible in the first AD and is not possible in the second. Each operator considers the specific semantics of the relevant modeling languages, e.g., in terms of multiplicities, inheritance, etc. for CDs, and decision nodes, fork nodes, etc. for ADs.

In addition to finding concrete diff witnesses (if any exist), our operators can be used to compare two models and decide whether one model semantics includes the other model semantics (the latter is a refinement of the former), whether they are semantically equivalent, or whether they are semantically incomparable (each allows instances that are not allowed by the other). When applied to the version history of a certain model, such an analysis provides a semantic insight into the model's evolution, which is not available in existing syntactic approaches.

We have already implemented prototype versions of *cddiff* and *addiff*: all examples shown in this paper were computed by our prototype implementations. Section 4 gives a brief overview of the algorithms and tools we have used.

It is important not to confuse diffing with merging. Merging is a very important problem, dealing with reconciling the differences between two models that have evolved independently from a single source model, by different developers, and now need to be merged back into a single model (see, e.g., [2,7,12]). Diffing, however, is the problem of identifying the differences between two versions, for example, an old version and a new one, in order to better understand the course of a model evolution during some step of its development. Thus, diff witnesses are not conflicts that need to be reconciled. Rather, they are proofs of features that were added or bugs that have been fixed from one version to another along the history of the development process.

Finally, our vision of semantic diffing does not come to replace existing syntactic diffing approaches. Rather, it is aimed at augmenting and complementing existing approaches with capabilities that were not available before. As semantic differencing is so different from existing syntactic differencing approaches, it brings about new research challenges. We overview these challenges in Section 5.

The next section presents motivating examples, demonstrating the unique features of our vision. Section 3 presents a formal definition of a generic semantic diff operator and its specializations for CDs and ADs. Section 4 briefly describes the algorithms used to compute the two operators and their prototypes implementations, and Section 5 discusses new challenges emerging from our vision. Related work is discussed in Section 6 and Section 7 concludes.

2 Examples

We start off with a number of motivating examples, demonstrating the unique features of our vision.

Example 1. Consider $cd1.v1$ of Fig. 1, describing a first version of a model for (part of) a company structure with employees, managers, and tasks. A design review with a domain expert has revealed two bugs in this model: first, employees should not be assigned more than two tasks, and second, managers are also employees, and they can handle tasks too.

Following this design review, the engineers created a new version $cd1.v2$, shown in the same figure. The two versions share the same set of named elements but they are not identical. Syntactically, the engineers added an inheritance relation between Manager and Employee, and set the multiplicity on the association between Employee and Task to 0..2. What are the semantic consequences of these differences?

Using the operator $cddiff$ we can answer this question. $cddiff(cd1.v1, cd1.v2)$ outputs om_2, shown in Fig. 1, as a diff witness that is in the semantics of $cd1.v1$ and not in the semantics of $cd1.v2$; thus, it demonstrates that the bug of having more than two tasks per employee was fixed. In addition, $cddiff(cd1.v2, cd1.v1)$ outputs om_1, shown in Fig. 1, as a diff witness that is in the semantics of $cd1.v2$ and not in the semantics of $cd1.v1$. Thus, the engineers should perhaps check with the domain expert whether the model should indeed allow managers to manage themselves.

Example 2. $cd5.v1$ of Fig. 2 is another class diagram from this model of company structure. In the process of model quality improvement, an engineer has suggested to refactor it by introducing an abstract class Person, replacing the association between Employee and Address by an association between Person and Address, and redefining Employee to be a subclass of Person. The resulting suggested CD is $cd5.v2$.

Using $cddiff$ we are able to prove that despite the syntactic differences, the semantics of the new version is equivalent to the semantics of the old version, formally written $cddiff(cd5.v1, cd5.v2) = cddiff(cd5.v2, cd5.v1) = \emptyset$. The refactoring is indeed correct and the new suggested version can be committed.

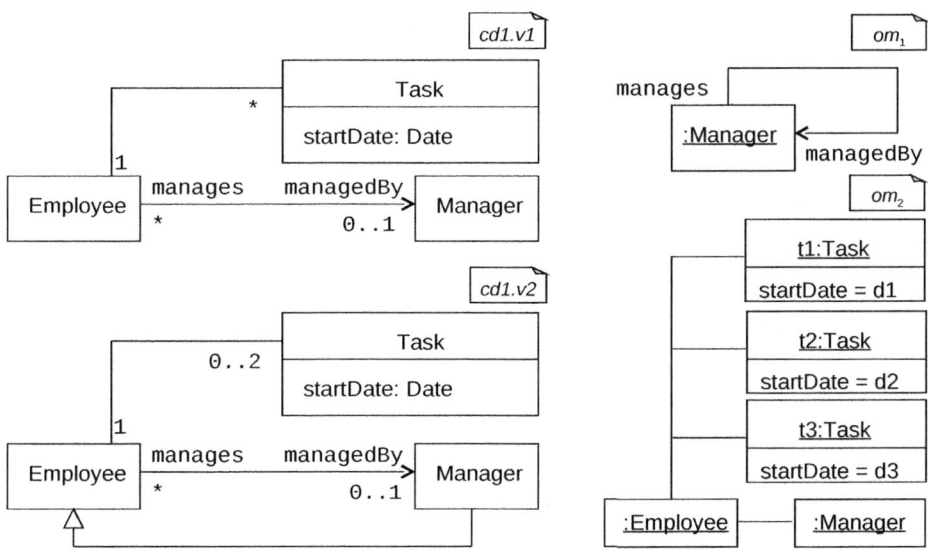

Fig. 1. *cd1.v1* and its revised version *cd1.v2*, with example object models representing the semantic differences between them

Example 3. AD *ad.v1* of Fig. 3 describes the company's workflow when hiring a new employee. Roughly, first the employee is registered. Then, if she is an internal employee, she gets a welcome package, she is assigned to a project and added to the company's computer system (in two parallel activities), she is interviewed and gets a manager report, and finally her payments are authorized. Otherwise, if the new employee is external, she is only assigned to a project before her payments are authorized.

After some time, the company deployed a new security system and every employee had to receive a key card. A revised workflow was created, as shown in *ad.v2* of Fig. 3.

Later, a problem was found: sometimes employees are assigned to a project but cannot enter the building since they do not have a key card yet. This bug was fixed in the next version, *ad.v3*, shown in Fig. 4. Finally, the company has decided that external employees should report to managers too. Thus, the merge between the two branches for internal and external new employees has moved

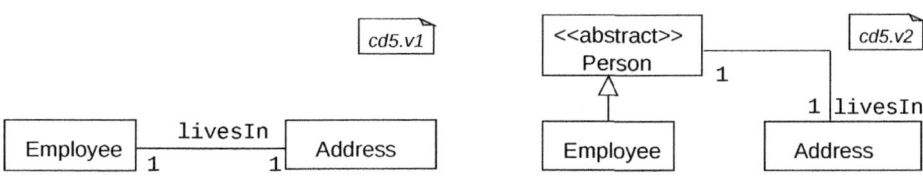

Fig. 2. Two example class diagrams of equivalent semantics

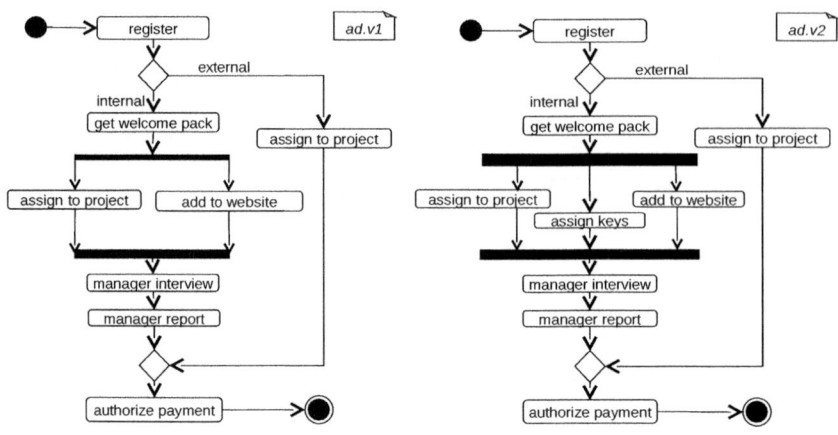

Fig. 3. Version 1 and version 2 of the hire employee workflow

'up', in between the interview and the report nodes. The resulting 4th version of the workflow, *ad.v4*, is shown in Fig. 4.

Comparing *ad.v1* and *ad.v2* using *addiff* reveals that they are incomparable: some executions of *ad.v1* are no longer possible in *ad.v2*, and some executions of *ad.v2* were not possible in *ad.v1*. Moreover, it reveals that handling of internal employees has changed, but handling of external ones remained the same between the two versions.

Comparing *ad.v2* and *ad.v3* reveals that the latter is a refinement of the former: *ad.v3* has removed some traces of *ad.v2* and did not add new traces. In particular, *addiff*(*ad.v2*, *ad.v3*) shows that the trace where a person is assigned to a project before she gets a security card was possible in *ad.v2* and is no longer possible in *ad.v3*, i.e., it demonstrates that the bug was fixed.

Finally, comparing *ad.v3* and *ad.v4* using *addiff* reveals that although hiring of external employees has changed between the two versions, hiring of internal employees did not: *addiff*(*ad.v3*, *ad.v4*) contains a single trace, where the employee is external, not internal. That is despite the syntactic change of moving the merge node from after to before the report node, which is part of the handling of internal employees.

3 Formal Definitions

Consider a modeling language $ML = \langle Syn, Sem, sem \rangle$ where Syn is the set of all syntactically correct (i.e., well-formed) expressions (models) according to some syntax definition, Sem is a semantic domain, and $sem : Syn \rightarrow \mathcal{P}(Sem)$ is a function mapping each expression $e \in Syn$ to a set of elements from Sem (see [9]).

The semantic diff operator $diff : Syn \times Syn \rightarrow \mathcal{P}(Sem)$ maps two syntactically correct expressions e_1 and e_2 to the (possibly infinite) set of all $s \in Sem$ that are in the semantics of e_1 and not in the semantics of e_2. Formally:

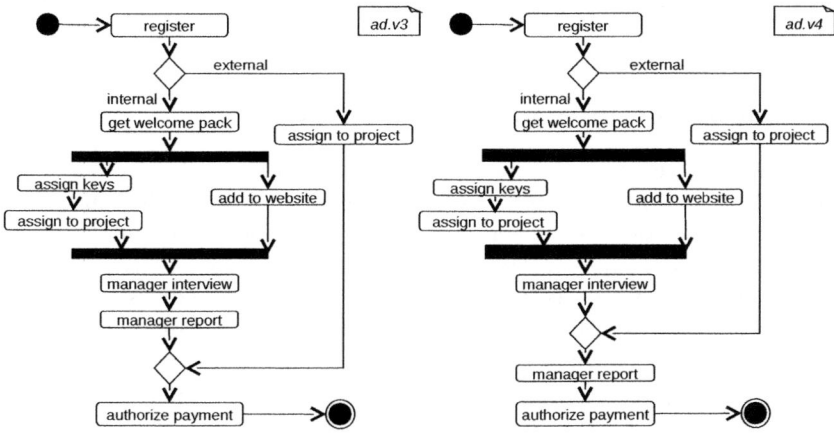

Fig. 4. Version 3 and version 4 of the hire employee workflow

Definition 1. $\mathit{diff}(e_1, e_2) = \{s \in \mathit{Sem} | s \in \mathit{sem}(e_1) \land s \notin \mathit{sem}(e_2)\}$.

Note that *diff* is not symmetric, $\mathit{diff}(e_1, e_1) = \emptyset$, and $\mathit{diff}(e_1, e_2) \cap \mathit{diff}(e_2, e_1) = \emptyset$. The elements in $\mathit{diff}(e_1, e_2)$ are called *diff witnesses*. We define specializations of *diff* for CDs and ADs.

Our semantics of CDs is based on [8] and is given in terms of sets of objects and relationships between these objects. More formally, the semantics is defined using three parts: a precise definition of the syntactic domain, i.e., the syntax of the modeling language CD and its context conditions (we use MontiCore [11,14] for this); a semantic domain - for us, a subset of the System Model (see [3,4]) OM, consisting of all finite object models; and a mapping $\mathit{sem} : CD \to \mathcal{P}(OM)$, which relates each syntactically well-formed CD to a set of constructs in the semantic domain OM. For a thorough and formal account of the semantics see [4].

To make the operator *cddiff* computable and finite, we bound the number of objects in the witnesses we are looking for. Thus, we define a family of bounded operators. Formally:

Definition 2 (cddiff). $\forall k \geq 0, \mathit{cddiff}_k(cd_1, cd_2) = \{om | om \in \mathit{sem}(cd_1) \land om \notin \mathit{sem}(cd_2) \land |om| \leq k\}$, where $|om|$ is the maximal number of instances per class in om.

We use UML2 Activity Diagrams for the syntax of our ADs. In addition to action nodes, pseudo nodes (fork, decision, etc.), the language includes input and local variables (over finite domains), transition guards, and assignments. Roughly, the semantics of an AD is made of a set of finite action traces from an initial to a final node, considering interleaving execution of fork branches, the guards on decision nodes etc. (a formal and complete semantics of ADs is outside the scope of this paper).

In diffing ADs, we are looking only for shortest witnesses: diff traces that have another diff trace as prefix are not considered interesting. Formally:

Definition 3 (addiff). $addiff(ad_1, ad_2) = \{tr | tr \in sem(ad_1) \land tr \notin sem(ad_2) \land \nexists tr' : tr' \in sem(ad_1) \land tr' \notin sem(ad_2) \land tr' \sqsubseteq tr\}$.

4 Implementations and Applications

To evaluate our vision and demonstrate its feasibility, we have defined and implemented prototype versions of *cddiff* and *addiff*. Indeed, all examples shown in the previous section have been computed by our prototype implementations.

We compute a variant of *cddiff* using a transformation to Alloy [10]. Given two CDs, cd_1 and cd_2, we construct a single Alloy model consisting of the joint set of class signatures from the two CDs and a set of predicates that describe the relations between them in each of the CDs. We do not compute all instances of each CD and compare the two sets of instances; rather, we define a diff predicate, which specifies that all the cd_1 predicates hold and that at least one of the cd_2 predicates does not hold. We then use the Alloy Analyzer to compute instances of this diff predicate: these instances represent object models of the first CD that are not object models of the second CD. The transformation to Alloy considers the semantics of CDs, including multiplicities, inheritance, singleton and abstract classes etc.

Our implementation of *cddiff* can be used to compute diff witnesses, if any, or to show that no diff witnesses exist (up to a user-defined bound on the number of objects of each class in the model).

We compute a variant of *addiff* by modeling ADs as finite state machines, and defining a transformation to SMV [17]. Given two ADs, ad_1 and ad_2, we construct two SMV modules whose possible execution traces are exactly the set of possible traces of each of the ADs. We then use BDD-based algorithms, implemented using JTLV APIs [16], to find whether there are traces of ad_1 that are impossible in ad_2. The transformation to SMV and the algorithms used consider the semantics of ADs, including input variables, guarded branching in decision nodes, parallel interleaving execution following fork nodes, etc.

Our implementation of *addiff* can be used to compute diff witnesses, each of which is a finite trace which is a sequence of actions possible in one AD and not possible in the other (a trace includes the values of its input variables). If no such traces are found, we know that all traces of the first are also possible in the second, i.e., that the first is a refinement of the second. If, in addition, no such traces are found when reversing first and second, we know that the two ADs have equal semantics: their syntactic differences, if any, have no effect on their meaning.

We have integrated our implementations into Eclipse plug-ins. The plug-ins allow an engineer to compare two models from a project or two versions of a model from the history of a version repository. The engineer can then browse the diff witnesses that were found, if any.

Moreover, we have used *addiff* and *cddiff* to implement a COMPARE command, used to compare two selected models and output one of four answers: $\equiv$ if the two models are semantically equivalent, < or >, if the second (first) is a semantic refinement of the first (second), and <> if the two are incomparable, that is, if each of them allows instances (i.e., object models, traces) not possible in the other (in the case of *cddiff* the results of COMPARE are limited by the user-defined bound). COMPARE can be integrated with existing SVN history view, to provide a high-level semantic differencing summary of a model's evolution.

The details of the above transformations and algorithms for *cddiff* and *addiff*, and their related Eclipse plug-ins, are omitted from this workshop paper. We hope to present them in detail in follow-up publications.

5 Challenges

Semantic differencing is rather different from syntactic differencing approaches, so it raises a number of new research challenges.

5.1 Computation

Computing diff witnesses may not be algorithmically easy and sometimes even impossible. When computable, its complexity depends on the specific modeling language semantics at hand. For example, computing *cddiff* requires the use of a constraint solver (such as Alloy); to make it tractable, it must be bounded (see Section 3). Computing *addiff* requires a traversal of the state space induced by the ADs at hand. Depending on the use of fork nodes, input variables, and guards, this state space may be exponential in the size of the ADs themselves.

In general, depending on the available syntactic concepts and the semantics of the relevant modeling language, computing diff witnesses may be undecidable. In some cases, the set of computed witnesses may be sound but incomplete: all computed witnesses are indeed correct, but there may be infinitely many others that are harder to find. Thus, for each modeling language, a language specific diff operator needs to be defined and a new algorithm needs to be developed for its computation. Abstraction/refinement methodologies, partial-order reductions, and other approaches may be required in order to improve the efficiency of the computations and allow them to scale.

5.2 Presentation

To be useful, diff witnesses must be presented textually or visually to the engineer. Just like for computation, the presentation of diff witnesses is language specific; it depends on the specific modeling language of the models involved and its semantics. For example, for *cddiff*, differencing object models may be visually presented using generated object diagrams; for *addiff*, differencing traces may be visually presented on the ADs themselves, e.g., by coloring and numbering the nodes that participate in the diff trace on both diagrams, from the initial node up until the point where the two diagrams differ. Alternatively, one may use a collaboration diagram like notation, possibly with the aid of animation.

Moreover, as there may be (possibly infinitely) many diff witnesses, it is necessary to define sorting and filtering mechanisms, to select the 'most interesting' witnesses for presentation and efficiently iterate over them at the user's request.

5.3 Integration with Syntactic Differencing

Many works have suggested various syntactic approaches to model differencing (see Section 6). It may be useful to combine syntactic differencing with semantic differencing, for example:

- Extend the applicability of semantic diffing in comparing models whose elements have been renamed or moved in the course of evolution, by applying a syntactic matching before running a semantic diffing: this would result in a mapping plus a set of diff witnesses.
- Use information extracted from syntactic diffing as a means to localize and thus improve the performance of semantic diffing computations.

6 Related Work

The challenge of model change management and versioning has attracted much research efforts in recent years. In particular, many works have investigated various kinds of model comparisons. We review some of these briefly below.

[1] describes the difference between two models as a sequence of elementary transformations, such as element creation and deletion and link insertion and removal; when applied to the first model, the sequence of transformations yields the second. A somewhat similar approach is presented in [12] in the context of process models, focusing on identifying dependencies and conflicts between change operations. [7] presents the use of a model merging language to reconcile model differences. Comparison is done by identifying new/old MOF IDs and checking related attributes and references recursively. Results include a set of additions and deletions, highlighted in a Diff/Merge browser. [15] compares UML documents by traversing their abstract-syntax trees, detecting additions, deletions, and shifts of sub-trees.

As the above shows, some works go beyond the concrete textual or visual representation and have defined the comparison at the abstract-syntax level, detecting additions, removals, and shifts operations on model elements. However, to the best of our knowledge, no previous work considers model comparisons at the level of the semantic domain, as suggested in our vision.

Some works, e.g., [6,18], use similarity-based matching before actual differencing. As our vision focuses on semantics, it assumes a matching is given. Semantic diffing can be applied after the application of matching algorithms.

7 Conclusion

In this paper we described our vision on semantic diff operators for model comparison, as new fundamental building blocks for change management in model-driven engineering. We motivated our vision with examples, and gave a brief overview of the formal background and the algorithms used in our prototype implementations. Finally, we listed new research challenges that emerge from our vision, related to the computation and presentation of semantic model differences.

Acknowledgments. We thank Assaf Marron and the anonymous reviewers for their comments on a draft of this paper.

References

1. Alanen, M., Porres, I.: Difference and Union of Models. In: Stevens, P., Whittle, J., Booch, G. (eds.) UML 2003. LNCS, vol. 2863, pp. 2–17. Springer, Heidelberg (2003)
2. Altmanninger, K.: Models in Conflict – Towards a Semantically Enhanced Version Control System for Models. In: Giese, H. (ed.) MODELS 2008. LNCS, vol. 5002, pp. 293–304. Springer, Heidelberg (2008)
3. Broy, M., Cengarle, M.V., Grönniger, H., Rumpe, B.: Definition of the System Model. In: Lano, K. (ed.) UML 2 Semantics and Applications. Wiley, Chichester (2009)
4. Cengarle, M.V., Grönniger, H., Rumpe, B.: System Model Semantics of Class Diagrams. Informatik-Bericht 2008-05, Technische Universität Braunschweig (2008)
5. Ebert, J., Kelter, U., Systä, T.: Workshop on comparison and versioning of software models (CVSM 2009). In: ICSE Companion, pp. 457–458 (2009)
6. EMF Compare, http://www.eclipse.org/modeling/emft/?project=compare
7. Engel, K.-D., Paige, R.F., Kolovos, D.S.: Using a Model Merging Language for Reconciling Model Versions. In: Rensink, A., Warmer, J. (eds.) ECMDA-FA 2006. LNCS, vol. 4066, pp. 143–157. Springer, Heidelberg (2006)
8. Evans, A., France, R.B., Peng, S.-L.: The UML as a Formal Modeling Notation. In: Bézivin, J., Muller, P.-A. (eds.) UML 1998. LNCS, vol. 1618, pp. 336–348. Springer, Heidelberg (1999)
9. Harel, D., Rumpe, B.: Meaningful Modeling: What's the Semantics of "Semantics"?. IEEE Computer 37(10), 64–72 (2004)
10. Jackson, D.: Software Abstractions: Logic, Language, and Analysis. MIT Press, Cambridge (2006)
11. Krahn, H., Rumpe, B., Völkel, S.: MontiCore: a framework for compositional development of domain specific languages. Int. J. on Software Tools for Technology Transfer (STTT) 12(5), 353–372 (2010)
12. Küster, J.M., Gerth, C., Engels, G.: Dependent and Conflicting Change Operations of Process Models. In: Paige, R.F., Hartman, A., Rensink, A. (eds.) ECMDA-FA 2009. LNCS, vol. 5562, pp. 158–173. Springer, Heidelberg (2009)
13. Mens, T., Demeyer, S. (eds.): Software Evolution. Springer, Heidelberg (2008)
14. MontiCore project, http://www.monticore.org/
15. Ohst, D., Welle, M., Kelter, U.: Differences between versions of UML diagrams. In: Proc. ESEC / SIGSOFT FSE, pp. 227–236. ACM, New York (2003)
16. Pnueli, A., Sa'ar, Y., Zuck, L.: JTLV: A framework for developing verification algorithms. In: Touili, T., Cook, B., Jackson, P. (eds.) CAV 2010. LNCS, vol. 6174, pp. 171–174. Springer, Heidelberg (2010)
17. SMV model checker, http://www.cs.cmu.edu/~modelcheck/smv.html
18. Xing, Z., Stroulia, E.: Differencing logical UML models. Autom. Softw. Eng. 14(2), 215–259 (2007)

Summary of the 5th International Workshop on Models@run.time

Nelly Bencomo[1], Gordon Blair[1], Franck Fleurey[2], and Cédric Jeanneret[3]

[1] Computing Department, Lancaster University, UK
[2] SINTEF, Oslo, Norway
[3] Department of Informatics, University of Zurich, Switzerland
nelly@acm.org, gordon@comp.lancs.ac.uk,
Franck.Fleurey@sintef.no, jeanneret@ifi.uzh.ch

Abstract. The 5th edition of the workshop Models@run.time was held at the 13th International Conference MODELS. The workshop took place in the exciting city of Oslo, Norway, on the 5th of October 2010. The workshop was organised by Nelly Bencomo, Gordon Blair, Franck Fleurey, and Cédric Jeanneret. It was attended by at least 33 people from more than 11 countries. In this summary we present a synopsis of the presentations and discussions that took place during the workshop.

Keywords: runtime adaptation, MDE, reflection, run-time abstractions.

1 Introduction

The Models@run.time workshop series provides a forum for exchange of ideas on the use of run-time models. The workshop series targets researchers from different communities, including model-driven software engineering, software architectures, computational reflection, adaptive systems, autonomic and self-healing systems, and requirements engineering. This edition of the workshop successfully brought together researchers from different communities and, at least, thirty three (33) people from eleven (11) countries attended the workshop.

In response to the call for papers, fifteen (15) papers were submitted, of which four (4) papers and six (6) posters were accepted. Every submitted paper was reviewed by at least 3 program committee members. The papers presented during the workshop are published in a workshop proceeding [1]. Two papers were selected as the best papers. Extended and improved versions of these two papers are published in this post workshop proceedings with other selected papers from all the workshops at MODELS 2010.

2 Workshop Format and Session Summaries

The workshop activities were structured into presentations, posters, and discussion sessions. In the opening presentation, Nelly Bencomo and Franck Fleurey set the context of the workshop by summarizing the major results from past workshop editions and outlining the path to follow during the workshop. The opening presentation was followed by the papers and posters sessions.

In the paper sessions four (4) papers were presented. Authors presented their papers in a twenty-minute-time slot, and five minutes were allowed for questions and discussion. *Robert France and Arnor Solberg* chaired these presentations. In the poster session, six (6) authors also presented their work to the workshop attendees.

Ppaper and poster presentations were done during the morning to allow enough time for discussion during the second part of the day. In the afternoon, the workshop participants formed three groups. Each group took care of discussing specific relevant topics. At the end of the workshop, each group selected a delegate who presented the conclusions and research questions raised by the group. More details about the discussion session can be found in Section 3. The four (4) paper presentations and the six (6) posters were divided into the following two sessions:

Session 1: Fundamental Concepts

- *Meta-Modeling Runtime Models*, by Grzegorz Lehmann, Marco Blumendorf, Frank Trollman and Sahin Albayrak.
- *Toward Megamodels at Runtime*, by Thomas Vogel, Andreas Seibel and Holger Giese.

Session 2: Evaluation and Experimentation

- *Applying MDE Tools at Runtime: Experiments upon Runtime Models*, by Hui Song, Gang Huang, Franck Chauvel and Yanchun Sun.
- *Run-Time Evolution through Explicit Meta-Objects*, by Jorge Ressia, Lukas Renggli, Tudor Girba and Oscar Nierstrasz.

Session 3: Applications

The following posters were displayed, presented and discussed with the workshop attendees.

- *A Model-Driven Approach to Graphical User Interface Runtime Adaptation*, by Javier Criado, Cristina Vicente-Chicote, Nicolás Padilla and Luis Iribarne
- *Monitoring Model Specifications in Program Code Patterns,* by Moritz Balz, Michael Striewe and Michael Goedicke
- *Separating Local and Global Aspects of Runtime Model Reconfiguration,* by Frank Trollmann, Grzegorz Lehmann and Sahin Albayrak.
- *Using Models at Runtime For Monitoring and Adaptation of Networked Physical Devices: Example of a Flexible Manufacturing System,* by Mathieu Vallee, Munir Merdan and Thomas Moser.
- *Monitoring Executions on Reconfigurable Hardware at Model Level,* by Tobias Schwalb, Graf Philipp and Klaus D. Müller-Glaser.
- *.Knowledge-based Runtime Failure Detection for Industrial Automation Systems,* by Martin Melik-Merkumians, Thomas Moser, Alexander Schatten, Alois Zoitl and Stefan Biffl.

3 Discussions

During the afternoon, three discussions groups were established. Each group was asked to discuss *a* set of topics based on the questions raised during the presentations and the research interests of the attendees. The following are the main topics discussed during the afternoon:

Topic of discussion group 1:
- *Classification and applications of models@run.time*

Topics of discussion group 2:
- *Abstraction gap*
- *Causal connection.*
- *Temporal Gap.*

Topic of discussion group 3:
- *Difference between design time and run-time models*

After spending two hours debating the presentations and shared research interests, each group presented a summary of their discussions and conclusions.

Thomas Moser was the representative of the breakout discussion group with the topic "*classification and applications of models@run.time*". The discussions of the group started based on the figure "Categories of run-time models" from the paper by Thomas Vogel et al. (Fig 1, page 15 in [1]). Thomas Vogel et al. identified the following types of models: implementation models, configuration and architectural models, configuration space and variability models, context and resource models, as well as rules, strategies, constraints, requirements and goals. Based on this figure, the group defined reasoning (analysis) and decision as the two major purposes of models@run.time. Examples for reasoning could be faults and defects detection and model checking; examples for decisions could be changes to running systems such as runtime adaptation or the generation of reports about behaviour.

Using these two major purposes for models@run.time, the group developed a table-based structure showing which types of models are used and for which purposes, i.e., for which type of reasoning and for which type of decision. The columns of the table can also be considered as the dimensions of models@run.time: namely type of model, type of reasoning and type of decision. Thomas commented that a fourth dimension could also be considered if context is included.

Mathieu Vallee was the representative of the group with the topic "*causal connection and abstraction gap*". The causal connection, i.e., how a running system is reflected in a runtime model (and conversely), has been discussed in previous editions of the workshop. However, this year participants focused on the difficulties that arise when the abstraction gap between a runtime model and the modelled system expands. Typically, as systems become more complex (larger, and distributed), it looks relevant the use of models that are more abstract and therefore easier to understand. However, and at the same time, this makes the causal connection more difficult to establish and to maintain. A lengthy discussion took place to clarify the problems, and is summarized as follows:

- In state-of-the-art solutions using runtime models, the abstraction gap is kept small, so that the relation between the system and the models is relatively easy to establish. A typical example is the use of a runtime architectural model together with a component-based infrastructure, in which concepts in the model (e.g., component) directly represent elements in the system.
- In some works, the abstraction gap becomes broader due to the adoption of higher level models. For instance, research on requirements at runtime raises questions on how to establish a causal link between a model of requirements and components in an underlying system.
- In other works, the abstraction gap may become broader due to the manipulation of the system at a finer level of granularity. For instance, using meta-objects at runtime enables the manipulation of a system at a fine granularity, but it was not clear to the group how it can be linked to an architectural model.

Similar issues arise regarding the *"temporal gap"*, which appears when the model and the system cannot be synchronized anymore or at least temporarily, i.e., the system still evolves while building the runtime model. In some pure software systems (i.e. no hardware is taken into account), it is possible to keep the model and the system always synchronized (e.g. by freezing execution while building the model). In systems involving physical components, as well as in more complex software systems, continuously maintaining the synchronization may not be possible. Mathieu emphasized that we need to take into account that a runtime model may not always accurately reflect the current system state, and that we need to design methods for estimating the temporal gap, as well as compensating it (e.g. through prediction of future states). From the discussions in the group, it appears that addressing these issues is a rather long-term objective. Nevertheless, the group believe that difficulties arise more due to the purpose of a runtime model than from its level of abstraction. As a consequence, the group recommended the following steps:

1. Elaboration of a classification of runtime models, according to their purpose.
2. Elaboration of concrete examples involving several models/levels of abstraction.
3. Study of the relationship between different runtime models in a given system.
4. Study of general solutions for managing models with different levels of abstraction. The last presentation was given by *Betty Cheng* who was the representative of the group that discussed *"differences between design time and run-time models"*. The discussions of this topic focused on the identification of requirements for run-time models. Betty reported that the group discussed about the contents of a run-time model (in contrast to a design model). According to Betty and colleagues, run-time model comprises:
    - Environmental conditions depicted by design info (e.g., plant model) and run-time info (e.g., plant model with values). Run-time info would be more abstract.
    - System conditions depicted by design info (traditional models like class, state, etc.) and run-time info (e.g., current task, service, attributes, processing node). Run-time info would also contain traceability information to design-time info.

The group also discussed about the purposes of run-time models and specifically focused on the case of self-adaptive systems. The following were the purposes identified:
- Monitoring the state of the system and the environment
- Decision-making: to process data to adapt; validation and simulation are also included
- Adaptation (mode change; reconfiguration). The changes can affect the structure and behaviour of the system.

The group presented the following recommendations:
- Move towards multiple run-time models, rather than using a monolithic run-time model
- Take into account the purpose for run-time models. The kinds of run-time models strongly depend on what we want to do with the system (e.g. performance analysis; fault tolerance, diagnosis; adaptive; safety)
- Identify possible purposes of run-time models and find additional ones (change existing model types, and consider to develop new ones)

Final Remarks: It is interesting to note that discussions of the different groups converged to similar outcomes and recommendations; as for example the need of a classification for run-time models and identification of the purposes and relationships between the models. A general wrap-up discussion was held at the very end of the afternoon. The workshop was closed with a friendly "thank you" from the organizers to all participants for a fruitful workshop. After the workshop, the organizers used the feedback from attendees and PC members to select the best 2 papers. After careful discussion, the best papers were selected and are presented in this book.

Acknowledgments. No workshop is successful by the efforts of only a few people. *We would also like to thank the members of the program committee who acted as anonymous reviewers and provided valuable feedback to the authors: Uwe Assman, Franck Chauvel, Betty Cheng, Peter J. Clark, Fabio Costa, Jeff Gray, Holger Giese, Oystein Haugen, Jozef Hooman, Gang Huang, Paola Inverardi, Jean-Marc Jezequel, Rui Silva Moreira, Flavio Oquendo, Arnor Solberg, Mario Trapp, and Thaís Vasconcelos Batista.* We thank Mathieu Vallee and Thomas Moser in the elaboration of Section 3 of this summary. Last but not least, we thank the authors for their interesting submissions and for helping us making this workshop possible.

References

[1] Bencomo, N., Blair, G.S., Fleury, F., Jeanneret, C. (eds.): Proceedings of the 5th Workshop on Models@run.time, held at the ACM/IEEE 13th International Conference on Model Driven Engineering Languages and Systems (MODELS 2010). CEUR Workshop Proceedigns. CEUR, vol. 641 (2010)

Meta-modeling Runtime Models

Grzegorz Lehmann, Marco Blumendorf, Frank Trollmann, and Sahin Albayrak

DAI-Labor, Technische Universität Berlin, Ernst-Reuter-Platz 7, 10587 Berlin, Germany
{Grzegorz.Lehmann,Marco.Blumendorf,Frank.Trollmann,
Sahin.Albayrak}@dai-labor.de

Abstract. Runtime models enable the implementation of highly adaptive applications but also require a rethinking in the way we approach models. Metamodels of runtime models have to be supplemented with additional runtime concepts that have an impact on the way how runtime models are built and reflected in the underlying runtime architectures. The goal of this work is the generalization of concepts found in different approaches utilizing runtime models and the provision of a basis for their meta-modeling. After analyzing recent work dealing with runtime models, we present a meta-modeling process for runtime models. Based on a meta-metamodel it guides the creation of meta-models combining design time and runtime concepts.

Keywords: Meta-modeling, Models@Runtime, runtime models, meta-metamodel.

1 Introduction

(Self-)Adaptive applications are required to adapt dynamically at runtime, often to situations unforeseeable at design time. Application code generated from design time models fails to provide the required flexibility, as the design rationale held in the models is not available at runtime. To address this issue the use of runtime models (or models@run.time) has been proposed. Runtime models enable the reasoning about the decisions of developers when they are no longer available. Additionally, they provide appropriate abstractions from code-level details of the applications at runtime.

Although the idea of utilizing models at runtime is not new, there is still a lack of common understanding and suitable methodologies for the definition of runtime models. Moving the models from design time to runtime raises questions about the connection of the models to the runtime architecture, about synchronization and valid modifications of the models at runtime and the identification of model parts specified at design time and those determined at runtime.

The goal of this work is to generalize common concepts found in different approaches utilizing runtime models and to provide a basis for their meta-modeling. The approach brings:

- A common understanding of runtime models and their concepts
- Means for comparing and discussing different runtime models
- A basis for achieving interoperability of models@run.time approaches
- A basis for the definition of a meta-modeling process for runtime models

The next section presents exemplary works dealing with runtime models (2.1) and discusses their common properties (2.2). In Section 3 our approach to meta-modeling runtime models is described. Section 4 discusses the EMF-based implementation of an example application utilizing runtime models. Section 5 concludes the paper.

2 Related Work

Model-driven engineering is a promising approach for the development of complex systems and applications. Since its emergence, model-based development aims at expressing different aspects of an application on different levels of abstraction within different models. Utilizing formal models takes the design process to a computer-processable level, on which design decisions become understandable for automatic systems. The principles of model-driven architecture [9] have been successfully applied in different domains, e.g. the user interface engineering domain, where application code is generated from models.

Modern applications are required to adapt dynamically to context of use situations unforeseeable at design time. This requirement extends the scope of model utilization from design time to runtime.

2.1 Utilizing Models at Runtime

Models are utilized at runtime in different domains and for different purposes. This section analyzes exemplary approaches from several fields, including model-based simulation and validation, adaptive and self-managing systems, executable and reconfigurable models. Depending on the application domain the models fulfill different roles, but some similarities can be identified.

[12] describes the Cumbia platform for executable runtime models, aiming at the provisioning of reusable monitoring and control tools. Integrating the execution logic and semantics behind the evolution of the model over time as part of the model leads to self-contained executable models. Cumbia's models are based on the idea of open objects, consisting of an *entity*, a state machine describing the entity's lifecycle and a set of actions triggered by the transitions of the state machine. Cumbia identifies four types of runtime model information:

- Structure of models - the static information about the application
- State of the elements in the models
- Historical information - the trace of model elements' state during the execution
- Derived information - information not directly included in the model but derived from it, e.g. by means of calculations

A slightly different approach to application monitoring is presented in [1]. The authors show how state machine logic can be embedded in object-oriented code. A runtime environment extracts the annotated state chart information at runtime and executes it. This way the runtime environment provides control of the application, enables the logging of its workflow and the debugging of events. In the implementation, Java code is connected to the state charts by means of special classes, interfaces and annotations. Rather than being created and manipulated at design time, the state machine model is extracted from code at runtime.

Another approach for model-based (rapid) development of software is discussed in [7]. The authors propose a layered debugging architecture for their model-based applications. In an example the authors extend the UML state diagram metamodel with elements holding dynamic runtime information. The metamodel is thus split into a static and a dynamic part. However the categorization of design and runtime information is not further generalized.

The usage of models at runtime is also common in approaches dealing with model-based design and adaptation of large, (self-) adaptive systems, like [14], [5] and [6]. The configuration of the systems and the possible adaptations are held in models at runtime. Adaptations are performed on the running system by transforming the models of the system.

In the ALIVE approach [14] executable code is generated from application models by means of transformations. If an adaptation is necessary at runtime, the models are modified and the executable code is regenerated. A monitoring mechanism assures that the application is paused for the time of adaptation and restarted when the new executable code is loaded.

In [5] an adaptation model holds information about possible variants of the system, constraints expressing valid configurations of the system and rules defining when adaptations should be performed. A context model represents the environment of the application and is the basis for the adaptation rules. Sensors deployed in the environment and in the system assure that the information in the models is up-to-date.

In the Rainbow framework [6] the architecture monitors and adapts the system through abstract models. The system layer consists of probes and effectors. The former observe and measure system states. The latter carry out the adaptations performed on the model level in the system. On the architecture layer, adaptation operators and strategies are provided. A set of operators determines the reconfiguration actions that can be performed on the system. Strategies describe how operators need to be applied to achieve certain system properties.

The idea of utilizing models at runtime drives the design of executable models and languages. Kermeta, presented in [11], extends the Essential Meta Object Facility (EMOF) with action semantics. The composition of an existing meta language with an action metamodel results in an executable meta-language, enabling the definition of domain specific languages with precisely defined operational semantics. The Kermeta metamodel enhances the EMOF metamodel with typical action expressions (e.g. Conditional, Assignment, Loop).

[10] presents Kermeta at RunTime (K@RT), a framework for adaptive software systems reconfigurable at runtime. K@RT supervises component-based systems by maintaining a reference model at runtime. The model provides a high-level view of the system. Modifications performed on the model are propagated into the underlying running system by automatically generated reconfiguration scripts. The authors propose a generic and extensible Metamodel for Runtime Models that represents component-based systems at runtime and aims at abstracting a running system. Composed of three packages (type, instance and implementation) and compatible with the Service Component Architecture (SCA), the metamodel enables the description of component-based software structures.

[8] proposes FAME as a polyglot library capable of maintaining the connection of models and code at runtime. FAME enables the adaptation of software at runtime

through modifications of the models and even the meta-models by means of a set of basic operations (Get, Set, Create, Delete). FAME is capable of maintaining the causal connection to several programming languages, e.g. Smalltalk, Ruby or Java.

After presenting different approaches to utilize models at runtime in this section, the next section discusses common properties of the different approaches are and definitions that can be used to generalize runtime models.

2.2 Generalizing Runtime Models

Although many approaches utilize models at runtime, we are not aware of an approach that explicitly deals with the creation of metamodels of runtime models. Most works in the area of runtime models focus on defining special adaptation (e.g. as transformations executable at runtime) or system models (e.g. component networks), rather than looking at the common characteristics of runtime models.

An analysis of model executability has been performed in [3], resulting in a classification of elements in executable models, which comes close to a definition of a meta-metamodel. The authors differentiate three parts of dynamic models:

- Definition part – is the static part of a model, defined at design time
- Situation part – includes all elements describing the dynamic state of a model during its execution
- Execution part – specifying the transitions of the model from one state to another, in other words its execution logic

The proposed classification has been a good starting point for our work, but, because of its focus on executable models, it does not fully apply to runtime models. For example, not every runtime model must have a definition part defined at design time. There are runtime models generated completely at runtime. Thus a different or modified basis is needed for classifying runtime models.

In our view, the key for classifying and generalizing elements of runtime models lies in their causal connection. In [2] a model@run.time is defined as a *causally connected self-representation of the associated system that emphasizes the structure, behavior, or goals of the system from a problem space perspective*. A runtime model provides up-to-date information about the system under study (SUS) and enables to perform adaptations of the system by means of model modifications.

In [13] and [4] the classification of descriptive and specification (also called prescriptive) models is discussed. According to [13] a model is descriptive if *all statements made in the model are true for the SUS*. On the other side a specification model prescribes how the system should be: *a specific SUS is considered valid relative to this specification if no statement in the model is false for the SUS*. Favre [4] proposes to distinguish whether the model or the system *has the truth*. In case of runtime models, both the system and the runtime model have (parts of) the truth. Due to their causal connection, runtime models describe systems with their states and, at the same time, specify how the systems should behave.

The importance of the causal connection can be observed in the approaches presented in section 2.1. Most of them possess means for connecting the runtime models with the system under study, although the description/specification ratios strongly differ. In works focusing on model executability, e.g. [11], the models have an either strong or sole prescriptive role. In self-adaptive systems, like [5] and [6], the utilized runtime models mostly have both, descriptive and specification, parts. On the other end, when runtime models are used to debug or monitor applications (e.g. [1]), the descriptive character dominates.

Another common property of runtime models is their ability to evolve over time. Modifications of models can be performed in different ways, e.g. by means of transformations, predefined operations or by special tools. Depending on whether the prescriptive or descriptive part of the model is modified, the changes have different consequences. Modifications of the prescriptive elements (e.g. performed by an adaptation engine) lead to changes in the system. Modifications of the descriptive parts of runtime models are mostly triggered by the system (e.g. probes in [6]) - whenever the system changes, its representation in the model must also change.

The identified typical properties of runtime models lead to requirements posed on their metamodels. Metamodels of runtime models must provide modeling constructs enabling the definition of:

- prescriptive part of the model specifying how the system should be
- descriptive part of the model specifying how the system is, i.e. the state of the SUS at runtime (similar to the situation part defined in [3])
- valid model modifications of the descriptive parts, executable at runtime
- valid model modifications of the prescriptive parts, executable at runtime
- causal connection in the form of an information flow between the model and its SUS

The following sections present a meta-modeling process addressing the above requirements.

3 Meta-modeling Runtime Models

This part presents a process guiding the meta-modeling of runtime models (Sections 3.1-3.4). Section 3.5 describes the meta-metamodel underlying this process.

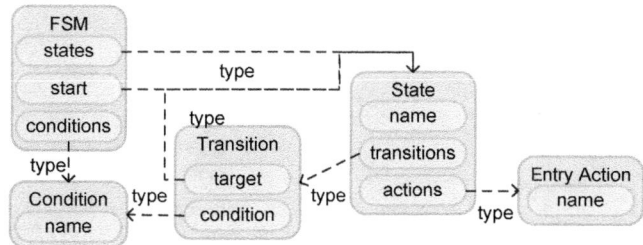

Fig. 1. Metamodel of finite state machines consisting of *States* with *Entry Actions* and *Transitions* bound to *Conditions*

For illustration purposes, the process is applied to a simplified finite state machine (FSM) metamodel, depicted in Fig. 1. The metamodel defines a finite state machine element *FSM* consisting of *states*, of which one *State* is the *start* state. *States* are connected with each other via *Transitions*. The *FSM* provides *conditions* bound to transitions. Additionally each *State* can be associated with entry actions (*EntryAction* elements) executed upon the activation of the state.

The presented metamodel describes typical design-time models, with no runtime concepts included. It can be used to statically describe state machines but provides limited utility at runtime. However, in our example scenario we wish to use the FSM models both at design- and runtime. At design-time we wish to specify the behavior of software components in form of FSMs. At runtime we want to execute, monitor and inspect the state of the application through runtime FSM models.

In the following the metamodel is extended with runtime concepts so it enables the definition of FSM runtime models. The meta-modeling process consists of four steps; each of the following subsections is dedicated to one of the subsequent steps.

3.1 Identify the Prescriptive and Descriptive Parts

To use the FSM models at runtime we must first identify elements of the models, which describe the runtime state of the system under study. At runtime, *Conditions* of a FSM become fulfilled and lead to the execution of the associated *Transitions*, which then activate *target* states. The example metamodel is therefore extended by adding an *active* attribute to the *State* and an *isFulfilled* attribute to the *Condition*. These descriptive attributes, marked orange in Fig. 2, hold the state of a FSM at runtime.

The distinction between the prescriptive and descriptive elements is necessary to clearly separate parts of a model altered in order to change the behavior of the system from the parts storing the runtime state of the system. In the example FSM metamodel, a state and the conditions of its transitions belong to the specification part, but whether a state has been activated or a condition fulfilled belongs to the descriptive part and is determined at runtime.

The differentiation between prescriptive and descriptive elements is not based on their type or class, but depends on the relationship of the element to other elements. Model elements of a specific type may in some cases be descriptive elements and in other cases prescriptive elements. It only counts whether the element is aggregated in a prescriptive- or descriptive field.

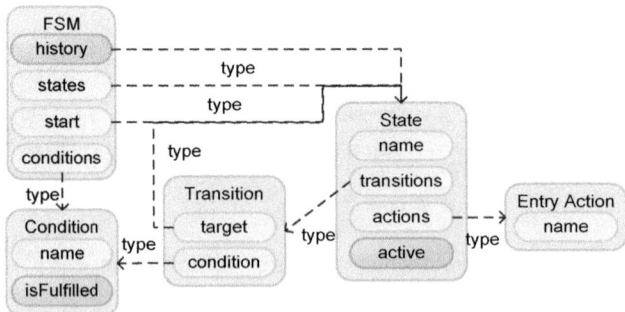

Fig. 2. Finite state machine metamodel with the orange marked descriptive elements *history*, *isFulfilled* and *active*, holding the state of the FSM at runtime

In case of the example runtime FSM models, the state and transition hierarchy is defined by the model developer at design time. The states composing the FSM are thus prescriptive elements (e.g. elements held in *FSM.states*, *FSM.start* or *Transition.target*). However, an FSM may also store a *history* list of states activated in the past. The history is a result of runtime execution of the model and thus belongs to its descriptive part. This way, model elements of type *State* are either prescriptive or descriptive depending on their relationship to other model elements. As shown in Fig. 2, *States* are descriptive elements, if they are part of *FSM.history*, or prescriptive elements, if they belong to the design-time state network specification (*FSM.states*). The latter are defined by the developer, the former are determined at runtime.

3.2 Modifications of Descriptive Elements

In the previous section the example metamodel has been enhanced with descriptive elements that enable to describe the state of a FSM model at runtime. In the next step of the meta-modeling process, available operations that can be performed on the descriptive part of the model are identified. The example FSM metamodel is thus enhanced with operations, which describe the transitions of FSM models from one state to another (i.e. the FSM execution logic). We refer to these operations as *DescriptionModificationElements*.

Fig. 3 pictures the FSM metamodel with *DescriptionModificationElements* altering the state of FSMs at runtime. The *State* type has been enhanced with the *DescriptionModificationElements activate* and *deactivate*, which *alter* the *active* attribute of *States*. Activation of a *State* leads to the execution of its entry actions, so the *activate* operation *uses* the *execute* operation of *EntryAction*. States become activated and deactivated by executed transitions. Transitions are triggered by the fulfillment of the associated conditions.

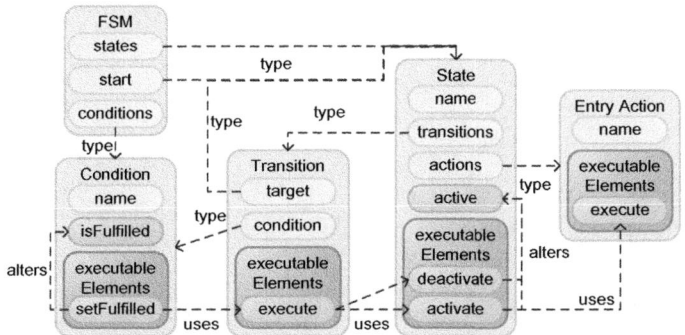

Fig. 3. Finite state machine metamodel with *DescriptionModificationElements setFulfilled, execute, activate* and *deactivate*

The *DescriptionModificationElements* represent procedures or actions altering the elements of conforming runtime models. Through them a metamodel provides the ability to insert new information about the system into the models in a well-defined manner, even at runtime. For example, the *DescriptionModificationElement setFulfilled* makes it possible to inform an FSM model about a condition fulfilled in the system under study.

At this point of the process the FSM metamodel enables the definition of runtime models with state information and execution logic as alteration of this information (*DescriptionModificationElements*). The next step deals with the identification of *SpecificationModificationElements* that enable the modification of the prescriptive part of the conforming FSM models. We refer to the modifications of prescriptive elements as adaptations, because they change the behavior of the system under study.

3.3 Modifications of Prescriptive Elements

One of the main purposes of runtime model utilization is the adaptation of the modeled application to varying context situations by means of model modifications. However, arbitrary reconfiguration of application models soon leads to inconsistencies and can destroy the integrity of the adapted models.

The definition of possible model adaptations is an integral part of the meta-modeling process. It is the task of the meta-modeler to define possible modifications of the conforming models and their impact on the models. Only in this way can the correctness of the adaptations and the consistency of the adapted models at runtime be assumed.

The meta-modeling of model adaptations can again be exemplified using the FSM metamodel. A feasible adaptation of a FSM-based application is the adding of special states or entry actions. Such adaptations are necessary if e.g. the context of the application changes and parts of the state network must be replaced with alternatives.

To enable the adding and removing of states in a finite state machine at runtime, the example metamodel is extended with *SpecificationModificationElements addState* and respectively *delState*. Fig. 4 shows the FSM metamodel with the new elements. Both *alter* the *states* of the adapted *FSM*. To retain the readability of the figure, we did not draw the *SpecificationModificationElements addTransition* and *delTransition* needed for reconfiguration of the transition network.

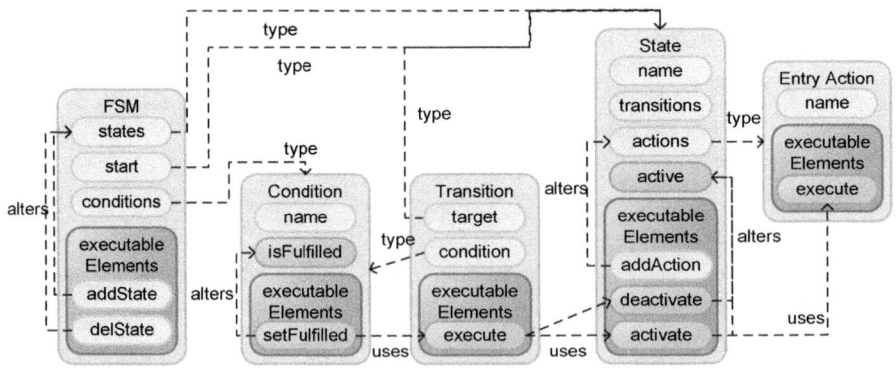

Fig. 4. FSM metamodel with *SpecificationModificationElements addState*, *delState*, *addAction*

The difference between the *Description-* and *SpecificationModificationElements* is essential. While the former only change the model, so it reflects the state of the SUS at runtime (e.g. *activate* or *deactivate* in the example FSM metamodel), the latter have the power to modify the structure and behavior of the SUS (e.g. *FSM.addState* or *FSM.delState*). The *SpecificationModificationElements* have thus a much stronger impact on the models and their adaptation capabilities.

After identifying the runtime elements of a runtime model and defining the valid modification of both its descriptive and prescriptive parts, the meta-modeler has to deal with one final runtime concept. The next section describes the last step of the meta-modeling process, which is the identification of the causal connection between the runtime model and its system under study.

3.4 Identify the Causal Connection

The connection between a runtime model and its system under study is referred to as the *causal connection*. The concept expresses the interrelation or causal loop between the model that represents a system and a system that must act according to the model. During the meta-modeling process the causal connections between the conforming runtime models and their systems under study must be identified.

Meta-modeling the causal connection comprises the definition of both directions of communication between the runtime models and their SUS. The influence of the model on the system and the synchronization of the model, based on the occurrences in the system, must be specified. It is thus essential to identify, how descriptive and prescriptive elements of the models communicate with the SUS.

The approaches described in Section 2.1 present different ways of handling the causal connection. In Rainbow [6] the *effectors* are responsible of adapting the system to the current structure of the model. *Probes*, or *sensors* in [5], assure the information flow in the opposite direction – from the system and its environment into the model. We generalize such elements by the term of *proxy* elements.

A proxy element fulfills the role of an interface between the runtime model and its system under study. The proxy type enables the explicit definition of proxies

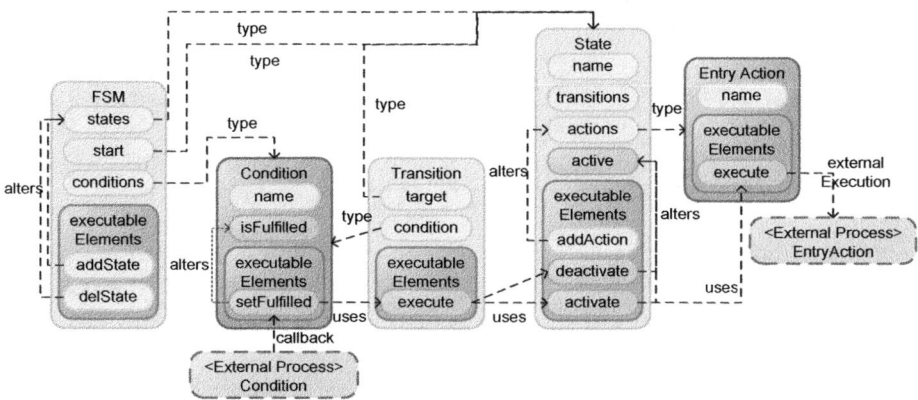

Fig. 5. FSM metamodel with *Condition* and *EntryAction* proxies handling the causal connection

within metamodels and a classification of model elements connected to entities outside of the model.

The information flow between the proxy elements and the outside world can be bidirectional. On the one side proxies synchronize the descriptive elements of the model with the state of the SUS, and on the other side they adapt the system according to the prescriptive part of the model. To achieve the first the proxies expose *callback DescriptionModificationElements* to external SUS processes. For the model to SUS synchronization, the proxies forward *externalExecution* calls to the SUS.

In the example FSM metamodel two proxy types have been identified: *Condition* and *EntryAction*. An FSM model must become aware of condition fulfillment occurring in the SUS. Therefore, as shown in Fig. 5, the *Condition* proxies expose the *setFulfilled* operation to external condition processes. This way, whenever a condition is fulfilled, external components inform the FSM model using the *setFulfilled* element. The *EntryAction* proxies do not expose any operations to the external processes, but trigger action execution in external processes outside of the model.

The identification of proxy elements enables an explicit and clear definition of the boundaries of runtime models. The communication between the model and the system via *Description-* and *SpecificationModificationElements* ensures that the synchronization occurs in a metamodel conformant way and does not interfere with the execution logic of the model. In the FSM example, the *Condition* proxies ensure that the FSM model reflects the state of the SUS at runtime. The *EntryAction* proxies enable the model to influence the SUS upon state changes.

We have presented a meta-modeling process, which identifies and makes explicit the runtime concepts necessary for the utilization of models at runtime. The next section sums up the ideas behind this process in form of a meta-metamodel.

3.5 Meta-metamodel

Defining metamodels of runtime models requires a meta-modeling language that provides means for the expression of the described runtime concepts within the metamodels. Meta-modeling languages are defined in form of special metamodels, so called meta-metamodels. We thus present a meta-metamodel, which provides necessary constructs for formalizing metamodels of runtime models.

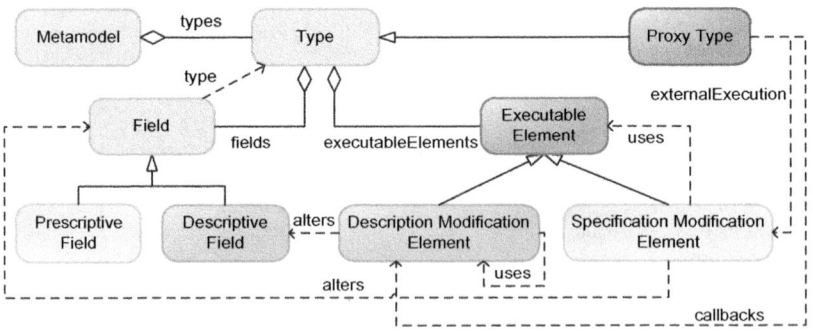

Fig. 6. Meta-metamodel of runtime models

The meta-metamodel, shown in Fig. 6, prescribes that each conforming metamodel defines *Types* composed of *Fields* and *ExecutableElements*. *Fields* represent relationships between types (often referred to as attributes, associations, references, etc.) and are classified as either *Prescriptive-* or *DescriptiveFields*. Intuitively, model elements held in prescriptive fields are prescriptive elements and those held in descriptive fields are descriptive elements. The differentiation of fields enables the identification of descriptive and prescriptive parts of conforming models during the meta-modeling process.

The *ExecutableElements* represent operations enabling the modification of model elements. Depending on whether the modifications influence the descriptive or the prescriptive part of the model, *ExecutableElements* are refined as either *DescriptionModificationElements* (DME) or *SpecificationModificationElements* (SME). As explained in previous sections, the DMEs encapsulate the state synchronization of the models conforming to the metamodel, whereas the SMEs represent possible model and system adaptations.

The descriptive elements of the model are held in the *DescriptiveFields*. Therefore each DME defines, which *DescriptiveFields* it modifies, using the *alters* association. Associating a DME with other DMEs by means of the *uses* association the meta-modeler expresses that the execution of the DME is composed of or includes the execution of the associated DMEs (as the *State.activate* DME using *EntryAction.execute* in case of the FSM metamodel example).

Performing an adaptation of the model may not only influence its prescriptive part, but will often impact its state as well. For this reason the SMEs can define *alters* and *uses* associations to both types of *Fields* and *ExecutionElements*.

Finally, the special *Proxy* type enables the formalization of the causal connection of runtime models. It classifies model elements connecting the model with its SUS. At runtime a proxy element mediates with an external element through a clearly defined communication interface. The interface is specified in form of *ExecutableElements*, either called during the model adaptation to influence the SUS (*externalExecution*) or available to the proxies to push information about the SUS into the model (*callbacks*).

4 Implementation

In this section we first discuss an example application created on the basis of runtime models. Then we present a context metamodel created according to the meta-modeling process introduced in this paper.

Our implementation is based on the Eclipse Modeling Framework (EMF). To assure compatibility of our models with EMF we define our metamodels as plain EMF metamodels enhanced with special annotations (e.g. annotating that an attribute expressed in Ecore is a *DescriptiveField*). The use of annotations makes the metamodels readable and usable for EMF tools (which ignore our custom annotations) and at the same time enables to extract the additional information about the runtime concepts of the conforming models.

Because EMF does not provide meta-metamodeling capabilities, the meta-metamodel is also defined as an Ecore metamodel. Transformations between the annotated Ecore metamodels and the meta-metamodel notation provide the necessary "meta-step". This enables to define metamodels of runtime models with full advantages of EMF tools while using the meta-metamodel constructs and semantics.

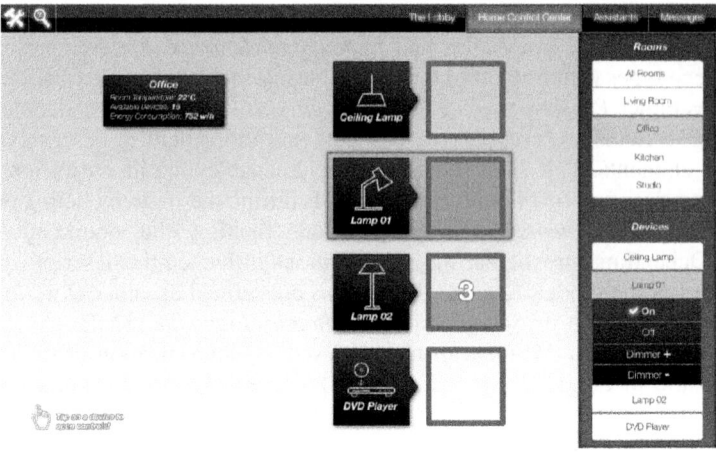

Fig. 7. Home Control Center application visualizing appliances available in the *Office* room. The HCC uses finite state machine networks for device configuration and control.

4.1 Example Application

The Home Control Center (HCC) application communicates with networked appliances in a smart home environment e.g. networked light controls, multimedia devices, kitchen appliances like ovens or fridges. Through a user interface the HCC presents an overview of the connected home appliances (their status, power consumption, etc.) and enables the user to control them.

The HCC is based on a FSM model, which guides its workflow at runtime. The model describes the state of the application and prescribes its transitions during the interaction with the user. The FSM model is connected to user interface (UI) components through proxies. By communicating with the UI components at runtime, the proxies assure that, on the one side, state changes in the FSM model are reflected in the user interface and, on the other side, the model reacts to user interaction. Device proxies are responsible for the communication between HCC's FSM model and the devices. *Condition* proxies trigger transitions based on the state of the devices; *EntryAction* proxies send control requests from the model to the devices.

The user interface mask shown in Fig. 7 presents a list of appliances in one of the rooms. The user can select a device and turn it on or off. Depending on the device, the user has some additional control possibilities (e.g. setting the light dimming level or playing a movie in case of a DVD player).

The set of control functionalities and protocols for home appliances strongly varies from one device type or manufacturer to another. For example, turning on a lamp or an oven are two completely different processes, requiring different backend calls and user interactions. However, an extensibility requirement posed on the HCC demands that the application is capable of *learning* the control processes of new devices, not known at design time. If, for example, a manufacturer produces a new series of ovens, with new features and functions, the HCC must be able to cope with that. To address this requirement, the appliance control functionality of the HCC has been based on an adaptable FSM runtime model. Each device connected to the HCC provides its own FSM, describing the interaction with the user and the control process. The FSM is integrated in the state network of the HCC at runtime by means of *SpecificationModificationElements* of the FSM metamodel. This way, previously unknown types of devices can be integrated into the HCC at runtime.

A part of HCC's finite state machine responsible for controlling an oven is shown in Fig. 8 (the figure presents an excerpt, the models implemented in the HCC are significantly larger). The presented model conforms to the FSM metamodel introduced in the previous sections. The FSM starts with a configuration of the oven's heating curve (*Heating curve configuration* state). While entering this state the HCC executes the *Ask user for heating curve* entry action. The action activates appropriate user interface components, which are presented to the user. Depending on the user's response one of the *Conditions* associated with the following transitions is fulfilled. If the user decides to configure a pre-heating process (*User selected pre-heating* condition), the interaction branches into the configuration of a time delay for the pre-heating process. Selecting any other program (*User selected a heating curve*) leads directly to the *Temperature configuration*. After specifying the temperature (*User specified temperature* condition) the oven is programmed in the *Oven programming* state by means of the *Set oven temperature* entry action.

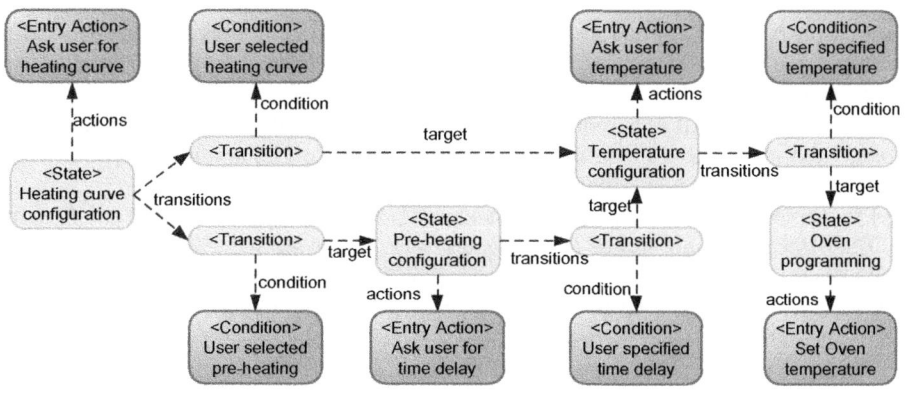

Fig. 8. FSM model describing the HCC interaction and control process of an oven. The device FSMs are connected to the FSM of the HCC at runtime.

Besides the communication with the device, the HCC uses the explicit state information held in the runtime FSM models to provide help functionality to the user. The information about the active / inactive states and fulfilled / unfulfilled conditions, stored in the descriptive part of the FSM models, is used to inform the user about the current state of the application and the devices. At any point of time the HCC can inform the user about the currently active state and the possible transitions based on conditions that need to be fulfilled.

The explicitly modeled causal connection, wrapped in the proxy elements, enables the information exchange between the model and the system under study. In HCC's FSM models the *Condition* and *EntryAction* proxies handle the communication between the application, the users and the devices.

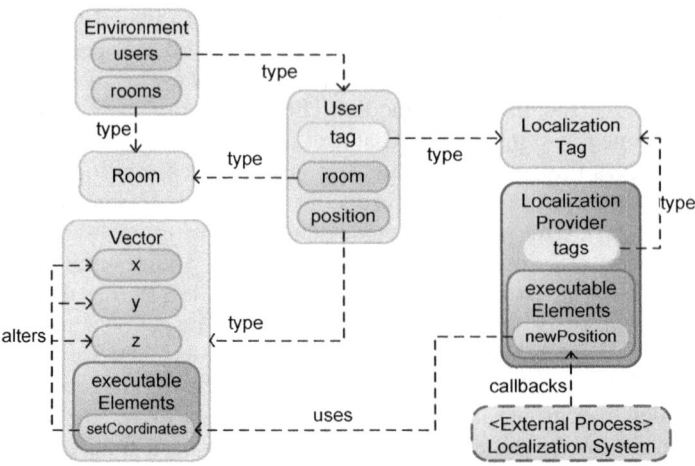

Fig. 9. Excerpt from a metamodel of runtime context models, used for observing and reasoning about an environment at runtime

4.2 Context Metamodel

To demonstrate the applicability of our approach to metamodels other than the FSM example, we present a context metamodel. It enables the modeling of the context seen as a combination of the environment, the users and the available platforms. This information is crucial for ubiquitous applications that have to adapt to changing situations. Runtime context models provide means for reasoning about the dynamic situation of the application and the user.

Fig. 9 pictures an excerpt from a metamodel of runtime context models. It defines an *Environment* composed of *Rooms* and *Users*. *Users* are located in rooms and have a 3D position in the environment expressed as *Vector*. Each user is associated with a *LocalizationTag* (e.g. a RFID tag). The context metamodel furthermore specifies the necessary *DescriptionModificationElements*, e.g. the *setCoordinates* element that allows updating the coordinates at runtime.

Building a context model that reflects the state of the environment at runtime requires the connection of the model with the real world context sensors and actors available in the environment. According to the proxy concept, the context metamodel describes a *LocalizationProvider* proxy, which represents a localization system in the environment. As visualized in Fig. 9, the *LocalizationProvider* defines the *newPosition* callback element for updating position information of entities based on their localization tag and the data gathered from the localization sensors. Whenever a tag position change is detected in the environment, the *newPosition* callback element is triggered by the *LocalizationSystem* to update the position.

5 Conclusions and Outlook

On the basis of our experiences with runtime models, we have presented a meta-modeling process that identifies core runtime concepts reoccurring in runtime models. The process and the constructs of the meta-metamodel are sufficient to distinguish the descriptive and prescriptive (specification) parts of runtime models as well as to identify operations for their modification *(ExecutableElements)*. Furthermore the causal connection of the runtime model and its system under study can be described using the *Proxy* type. This way the meta-metamodel covers all aspects of meta-modeling runtime models identified in section 2.2. The example FSM and context metamodels, as well as the HCC application, demonstrate the usefulness of the presented approach while designing, building and executing runtime models.

In the future we will explore the possibilities of using the meta-metamodel to achieve interoperability between different runtime model approaches (across technological spaces). We are working on additional metamodel transformations that will enable us to transform metamodels from technological spaces other than Ecore into the format of the meta-metamodel. We are also working on a reconfiguration metamodel, defined on the basis of the meta-metamodel. Combined with the transformations it will enable us to reconfigure and adapt runtime models from different technological spaces in one reconfiguration model.

References

[1] Balz, M., Striewe, M., Goedicke, M.: Embedding State Machine Models in Object-Oriented Source Code. In: 3rd Int. Workshop on Models@run.time (2008)
[2] Blair, G., Bencomo, N., France, R.B.: Models@run.time. Computer 42(10) (2009)
[3] Breton, E., Bézivin, J.: Towards an understanding of model executability. In: Proc. of the International Conference on Formal Ontology in Information Systems (2001)
[4] Favre, J.: Foundations of Model (Driven) (Reverse) Engineering – Episode I: Story of The Fidus Papyrus and the Solarus. In: Post-Proc. of Dagstuhl Seminar on Model Driven Reverse Engineering (2004)
[5] Fleurey, F., Dehlen, V., Bencomo, N., Morin, B., Jézéquel, J.-M.: Modeling and validating dynamic adaptation. In: 3rd Int. Workshop on Models@run.time (2008)
[6] Cheng, S.-W., Huang, A.-C., Schmerl, B., Steenkiste, P., Garlan, D.: Cheng. Rainbow: Architecture-based self-adaptation with reusable infrastructure. Computer 37(10) (2004)
[7] Graf, P., Müller-Glaser, K.D.: Gaining insight into executable models during runtime: Architecture and mappings. IEEE Distributed Systems Online 8(3) (2007)
[8] Kuhn, A., Verwaest, T.: Fame, a polyglot library for metamodeling at runtime. In: 3rd Int. Workshop on Models@run.time (2008)
[9] Miller, J., Mukerji, J.: Model Driven Architecture (MDA). Object Management Group, omg document ormsc/2001-07-01 edition (2001)
[10] Morin, B., Barais, O., Jézéquel, J.-M.: K@rt: An aspect-oriented and model-oriented framework for dynamic software product lines. In: 3rd Int. Workshop on Models@run.time (2008)
[11] Muller, P.A., Fleurey, F., Jézéquel, J.M.: Weaving executability into object-oriented meta-languages. In: Proc. of the 8th International Conference on Model Driven Engineering Languages and Systems (2005)
[12] Sanchez, M., Barrero, I., Villalobos, J., Deridder, D.: An execution platform for extensible runtime models. In: 3rd Int. Workshop on Models@run.time (2008)
[13] Seidewitz, E.: What models mean. IEEE Software 20(5) (2003)
[14] Staikopoulos, A., Saudrais, S., Clarke, S., Padget, J., Cliffe, O., De Vos, M.: Mutual dynamic adaptation of models and service enactment in alive*. In: 3rd Int. Workshop on Models@run.time (2008)

The Role of Models and Megamodels at Runtime

Thomas Vogel, Andreas Seibel, and Holger Giese

Hasso Plattner Institute at the University of Potsdam
Prof.-Dr.-Helmert-Str. 2-3, 14482 Potsdam, Germany
thomas.vogel@hpi.uni-potsdam.de

Abstract. In model-driven software development a multitude of interrelated models are used to systematically realize a software system. This results in a complex development process since the models and the relations between the models have to be managed. Similar problems appear when following a model-driven approach for managing software systems at runtime. A multitude of interrelated runtime models are employed simultaneously, and thus they have to be maintained at runtime. While for the development case *megamodels* have emerged to address the problem of managing models and relations, the problem is rather neglected for the case of runtime models by applying ad-hoc solutions.

Therefore, we propose to utilize megamodel concepts for the case of multiple runtime models. Based on the current state of research, we present a categorization of runtime models and conceivable relations between them. The categorization describes the role of interrelated models at runtime and demonstrates that several approaches already employ multiple runtime models and relations. Then, we show how megamodel concepts help in organizing and utilizing runtime models and relations in a model-driven manner while supporting a high level of automation. Finally, the role of interrelated models and megamodels at runtime is discussed for self-adaptive software systems and exemplified by a case study.

1 Introduction

According to France and Rumpe, there are two broad classes of models in *Model-Driven Engineering* (MDE): *development models* and *runtime models* [10]. Development models are employed during the model-driven development of software. Starting from abstract models describing the requirements of a software, these models are systematically transformed and refined to architectural, design, implementation, and deployment models until the source code level is reached.

In contrast, a runtime model provides a view on a running software system that is used for monitoring, analyzing or adapting the system through a causal connection between the model and the system [6,10]. Most approaches, like [11,14], employ *one* causally connected runtime model that reflects a running system. While it is commonly accepted that developing complex software systems using *one* development model is not practicable, we argue that the whole complexity of a running software system cannot be covered by one runtime model defined by one metamodel. This is also recognized by Blair et al. who state "that in practice, it is likely that multiple [runtime] models will coexist and that different styles of models may be required to capture different system concerns" [6, p.25].

At the *2009 Workshop on Models@run.time* we presented an approach for simultaneously using multiple runtime models at different levels of abstraction for monitoring and analyzing a running software system [17]. While abstracting from the running system, each runtime model provides a different view on the system since each model is defined by a different metamodel that focuses on a specific concern, like architectural constraints or performance. At the workshop, our approach raised questions and led to a discussion about simultaneously coping with these models since concerns that potentially interfere with each other are separated in different models. For example, any adaptation being triggered due to the performance of a running system, which is reflected by one runtime model, might violate architectural constraints being reflected in a different model. Thus, there exists relations, like trade-offs or overlaps, between different concerns or models, which have to be considered and managed at runtime.

A similar issue appears during the model-driven development of software. A multitude of development models and relations between those models have to be managed, especially to maintain traceability information and consistency among the models. An example is the *Model-Driven Architecture* (MDA) approach that considers, among others, transformations of platform-independent to platform-specific models. Thus, different development models are related with each other, and if changes are made to any model, the related models have to be updated by synchronizing these changes or repeating the transformation. In this context, *megamodels* have emerged as one means to cope with the problem of managing a multitude of development models and relations. The term megamodel originates from ideas on modeling MDA and MDE, which basically consider *a megamodel as a model that contains models and relations between those models or between elements of those models* (cf. [2,4,5,9]).

In contrast, the problem of managing multiple models and relations is neglected for the runtime case and to the best of our knowledge there is no approach that explicitly considers this problem beyond ad-hoc and code-based solutions. In this paper, which is a revision of [18], we present a categorization of runtime models derived from the current state of research, and conceivable relations between models of the same or different categories. The presented categories and relations demonstrate the role of models at runtime and that multiple interrelated models are already or likely to be used simultaneously at runtime. Based on that, we propose to apply existing concepts of megamodels for managing runtime models and relations. Such an approach provides a high level of automation for organizing and utilizing multiple runtime models and their relations, which supports the domain of runtime system management, for example, by automated impact analyses across related models. Moreover, we especially discuss the conceptual role of interrelated models and megamodels for self-adaptive systems.

The rest of the paper is structured as follows. Section 2 presents the categorization of runtime models, conceivable relations between models, and the application of megamodel concepts at runtime. The role of interrelated models and megamodels for self-adaptive systems is discussed in Section 3 and exemplified by a case study in Section 4. Finally, the paper concludes with Section 5.

2 Models, Relations and Megamodels at Runtime

In this section, we present categories of runtime models and conceivable relations between models of the same or different categories. The categorization is derived from literature, primarily the *Models@run.time* workshops [1] and our own work [12,15,16,17]. However, we do not claim that the categories are complete or that each category has to exist in every approach. Nevertheless, they indicate the role of models at runtime and demonstrate that different kinds of interrelated runtime models are already or likely to be employed simultaneously.

2.1 Categories of Runtime Models

Both of the already mentioned approaches [11,14] employ one runtime model that is causally connected to a running system. In contrast, our approach [15,16,17] provides multiple runtime models simultaneously, each of which is causally connected to the system and specified by a distinct metamodel. Nevertheless, the other approaches also maintain additional model artifacts at runtime, which are not causally connected to a system, but which are used to manage the system.

In the case of *Rainbow* [11], such artifacts are invariants that are checked on a causally connected architectural model, and adaptation strategies that are applied if the invariants are violated. Morin et al. [14] even have in addition to a causally connected architectural model, a feature model describing the system's variability, a context model describing the system's environment, and a so called reasoning model specifying which feature should be activated or deactivated on the architectural model depending on the context model.

Thus, even if only one causally connected runtime model is used for managing a running system, several other models that do not need to be causally connected are employed at runtime. For the following categories[1] as depicted in Figure 1, we consider any conceivable runtime models regardless whether they are causally connected to a running system or not. The models are categorized in a rather abstract manner according to their purposes and contents. As shown in Figure 1, runtime models (*M1*) of all categories are usually instances of metamodels (*M2*) that are defined by meta-metamodels (*M3*), which leverages typical MDE techniques, like model transformation or validation, to the runtime.

Implementation Models are similar to models used in the field of reflection to represent and modify a running system through a causal connection. Such models are based on the solution space of a system as they are coupled to the system's implementation and computation model [6]. Therefore, these models are platform-specific and at a rather low level of abstraction. As modeling languages, class or object diagrams are often employed to provide structural views, and sequence diagrams or automatons for behavioral views.

---

[1] A detailed description of the categories and supporting literature can be found in [18].

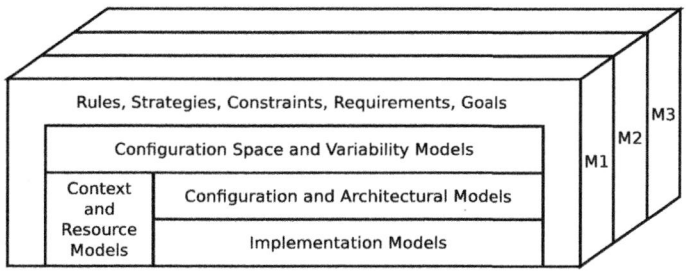

Fig. 1. Categories of Runtime Models

Configuration and Architectural Models are usually also causally connected to a running system and they reflect the current configuration of the system. Since software architectures are considered to be at an appropriate abstraction level for analysis or adaptation, these models provide architectural views similar to component diagrams [11,14,15,17]. These diagrams are often enhanced with non-functional properties to directly support analysis or to transform them to specific analysis models, like queueing networks to reason about the performance. At a higher level of abstraction, process or workflow models are also feasible to describe a running system from a business-oriented view. Moreover, model types of the *Implementation Models* category are also conceivable in this category, but at a higher level of abstraction. For example, a sequence diagram would consider the interactions between component instances instead of the interactions between objects.

In general, models of this category and *Implementation Models* are often both causally connected to a system. However, *Configuration and Architectural Models* are at a higher level of abstraction, less complex and often platform-independent, while *Implementation Models* are at a lower level of abstraction, more complex and platform-specific. Thus, *Configuration and Architectural Models* are rather related to problem spaces, and *Implementation Models* to solution spaces. This is similar to the view of Blair et al. [6] on runtime models and reflection models.

Context and Resource Models describe the operational environment of a running system. This comprises the context, which is "any information that can be used to characterise the situation of an entity", while "an entity is a person, place, or object that is considered relevant to the interaction between a user and an application" [8, p.5] or in general to the operation of the application. To represent a context, semi-structured tags and attributes, key value pairs, object-oriented or logic-based models, or even feature models can be used. Moreover, the operational environment consists of resources a running system requires and actually uses for operation. These are logical resources, like any form of data, or physical resources, like the hardware the system is running on.

Configuration Space and Variability Models specify potential variants of a system, while *Configuration and Architectural Models* reflect the currently running variant of the system. Therefore, models of this category describe a system at the type level to span the system's configuration space and variability.

Using these models, adaptation points in a running system and possible adaptation alternatives can be identified. Examples for models in this category are aspect and feature models [14], or component type diagrams [12,15].

Rules, Strategies, Constraints, Requirements and Goals may refer to any model from the other categories and, therefore, their levels of abstraction are similar to the levels of the referred models. Models in this category define, among others, when and how a running system should be adapted by following one of two general approaches. First, rules or strategies usually in some form of event-condition-action rules describe when and under which conditions, a system is adapted by performing reconfiguration actions. The second approach is based on goals a running system should achieve, and guided by utility functions, adaptation aims at optimizing the system with respect to these goals.

Moreover, constraints on models of the other categories regarding functional and non-functional properties are used for runtime validation and verification. Constraints can be expressed, among others, in the *Object Constraint Language* (OCL)or formally in some form of *Linear Temporal Logic* (LTL). Though constraints can be seen as requirements that are checked at runtime, recently the idea of *requirements reflection* has emerged, which explicitly considers requirements as adaptive runtime entities [3]. Thus, requirements models, like goal models, become runtime models above the abstraction level of architectures.

The presented model categories show that different aspects have to be considered for managing a system at runtime. These aspects are at least the running system at different levels of abstraction, the system's environment, the system's variability, and the validation, verification and adaptation. Rather than covering all these aspects in a monolithic runtime model being highly complex, multiple and different kinds of models are possible, and even employed simultaneously for that. Which categories and especially which kind of and how many models are employed is specific to each approach. This depends, among others, on the purposes of an approach and on the domain of the system. Nevertheless, separating aspects in different models requires to consider relations among these models.

2.2 Relations between Runtime Models or Model Elements

In the following, we use the presented model categories to outline exemplars of relations between runtime models or between elements of different runtime models. Note that a relation between elements of two different models also constitutes a more abstract relation between these two models. These exemplars motivate the need for managing relations together with the models at runtime.

As already mentioned, models of the category *Rules, Strategies, Constraints, Requirements and Goals* may refer to models of the other categories. For example, goal modeling approaches refine a top-level goal to subgoals recursively until each subgoal can be satisfied by an agent being a human or a component (cf. [3]). Having a goal model at runtime, it is of interest which component of a running system actually satisfies or fails in satisfying a certain goal. Therefore, goals being reflected in a goal model refer to corresponding components of *Configuration and Architectural Models*, which also relates the goal and architectural model with each other. Moreover, goal satisfaction can be influenced by the current context of a system, such that goals and elements of a context model are related with each other. As an example, consider an e-mail client application that has the subgoal of actually sending a message to a mail server for distribution. This subgoal is fulfilled by a client component that establishes a connection to the server and transmits the message. Thus, this subgoal and component are related with each other. Moreover, satisfying this subgoal is influenced by the availability of a network connection to the server, which is part of the context. This constitutes a relation between the goal model and the context or resource model.

Configuration and Architectural Models can also be related to *Configuration Space and Variability Models* by means of effects the selection of a variant as defined by a variability model has on the current system configuration or architecture. For example, activating or deactivating features in a feature model specifying the system's variability requires the adaptation of the currently active architecture by adding or removing corresponding components. Thus, components and their supported features are related with each other. Regarding the same dimension of abstraction, *Implementation Models* can be seen as refinements of *Configuration and Architectural Models* as they describe how a configuration or architecture is actually realized using concrete technologies. Thus, refinement relations are conceivable between models of these two categories.

Another relation can reflect the deployment or resource utilization of a system by means of relating *Architectural Model* elements and *Resource Model* elements, or in other words, which components of a running systems are deployed on which nodes and are consuming which resources. *Context and Resource Models* can also refer to *Configuration Space and Variability Models* since the configuration space and variability of a system can be influenced by the current context or resource conditions. For example, a certain variant is disabled due to limited resources.

Besides relations between models of different categories, there may also exist relations between models of the same category. In [17], several *Architectural Models* are employed reflecting the same system, but providing different views on it. However, these views are overlapping, which can be considered as a relation. Furthermore, each model focuses on a certain concern, like performance or architectural constraints, and any adaptation optimizing one concern might interfere with another concern. As an example, due to a decline in the system performance, an additional component of a certain type should be deployed to balance the load, which however violates the architectural constraint restricting the number of deployed components of the specific type. Thus, overlaps, trade-offs or conflicts between concerns respectively between the models are conceivable.

The presented exemplars show that runtime models are usually not isolated and independent from each other, but they rather compose a network of models. Therefore, besides the runtime models also the relations between those models have to be managed at runtime. The concrete relations emerging in an approach depend, among others, on the purposes of the approach, the domain of the system and on the models that are employed.

2.3 Megamodels at Runtime

As it turned out, different kinds of models and relations between them emerge when managing a system at runtime. In such scenarios, it is important that these relations are modeled and maintained at runtime because this makes the relations *explicit* and, therefore, amenable for analysis or other runtime activities. For example, an impact analysis is leveraged when knowing which models are related with each other. Then, the impact of any model change to related models can be analyzed by following transitively the relations and propagating the change. Moreover, relations can be classified, for example in critical and non-critical ones, and for certain costly analyses only the critical relations may be considered.

Nevertheless, relations to other models are usually not covered by all models because they were not foreseen when designing the corresponding modeling languages. Thus, a language for explicitly specifying all kinds of relations between various models and between elements of different models is required. Rather than applying ad-hoc and code-based solutions to relate models with each other, megamodels provide a language that supports the modeling of arbitrary models and relations between those models or between elements of those models. Therefore, the management of models and relations itself is done in a model-driven manner enabling the use of existing MDE techniques for it.

In general, megamodels for the model-driven software development serve organizational and utilization purposes that should also be leveraged at runtime. Organizational purposes are primarily about managing the complexity of a multitude of models. Therefore, like some kind of a model registry [5], megamodels help in organizing a huge set of different models together with their relations by storing and categorizing them. Likewise, megamodels can serve as a means to explicitly organize and maintain runtime models and their relations in the domain of runtime system management since several models and relations can be employed simultaneously at runtime (cf. Sections 2.1 and 2.2).

Utilization purposes of megamodels are primarily about navigation and automation by actually using the relations that are made explicit due to the organizational purposes. Utilizing relations, megamodels can be the basis for navigating through various models. Thus, starting from a model, all related models can be reached in a model-driven manner instead of using mechanisms at a lower level of abstraction like programming interfaces. Having the conceivable runtime models and relations in mind (cf. Sections 2.1 and 2.2), navigating between runtime models is essential for a comprehensive system management approach. Thus, explicit relations can be utilized by typical operations to *read* or *write* models, or to *apply* a model on another model. Navigating between models can be considered as reading models, while writing can be a model update by propagating model changes along relations. Finally, models, like transformation or generation rules, can be applied on models resulting in models. This leads to the aspect of automation aiming to increase efficiency. Relations between models are treated as executable units that take models as input and produce models as output. Thus, a megamodel can be considered as an executable process for runtime activities, like automatically analyzing the impact of changes. Therefore, relations can be

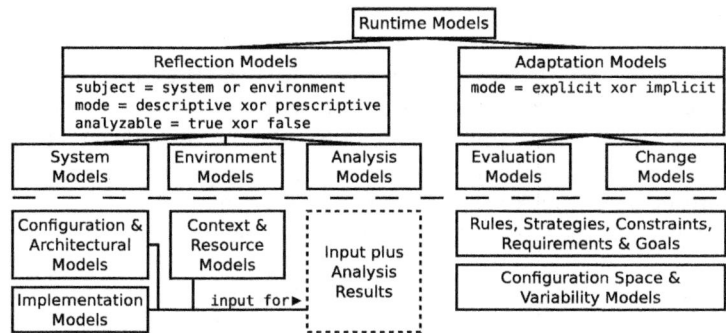

Fig. 2. Categories of Runtime Models for Self-Adaptive Software Systems

used to synchronize model changes to related models and these synchronized models are then analyzed to investigate the impact of the initial changes.

Finally, automation considers the efficient maintenance of models and relations by means of their validity and consistency, because models and relations are often both dynamic and they change over time.

3 Self-adaptive Software Systems

While in the previous section the model categories are derived from literature and broken down according to the purposes and primarily the contents of the models, now we will approach a different categorization by taking a conceptual view on self-adaptive software systems. Based on the typical feedback loop of a self-adaptive system, we investigate the role of runtime models and especially how they are used throughout the loop. This results in a different model categorization that focuses on the usage of models and that will be compared to the previously presented categorization in order to foster the comprehension of conceivable models and their roles at runtime for self-adaptive systems.

3.1 Runtime Models for Self-adaptive Software Systems

Before investigating the usage of models in self-adaptive software systems, we describe the categories of these models as depicted on top of Figure 2. *Runtime Models* are divided into two top categories, *Reflection* and *Adaptation Models*, based on the way they are used at runtime.

Reflection Models reflect the system or the system's environment either in a descriptive or prescriptive manner as indicated by the attributes subject and mode, respectively. Descriptive models describe the as-is situation of the running system or environment, while prescriptive models prescribe the to-be situation, primarily the designated target state of the system. Though it is not possible to prescribe the environment, to-be environment models are conceivable for reflecting predictions of the future environment. Reflection models can be analyzable to support reasoning about the system or environment. Thus, using basic and incomplete attribute assignments, *System Models* (subject = system), *Environment Models* (subject = environment), and *Analysis Models* (analyzable = true) are considered as typical reflection models, while other models are conceivable regarding the possible combinations of the reflection models' attributes. In general, reflection models are primarily *read* and *written* to describe, prescribe or analyze the system and environment.

Adaptation Models on the other hand are primarily *applied* on reflection models as they define how reflection models are evaluated or changed. Thus, *Evaluation Models* specify the reasoning and analyses that are performed on descriptive or prescriptive reflection models, while *Change Models* specify how prescriptive reflection models can be obtained. This can be done either in an explicit or implicit mode. Explicit models enumerate patterns that can be directly compared to reflection models for evaluation or that precisely define fragments of possible prescriptive reflection models. In contrast, implicit models, like rules, define operations that are applied on reflection models, which returns either evaluation results or changed and potentially new reflection models.

This model categorization can be mapped to the categorization previously presented in Section 2, which is outlined in Figure 2. *System Models* directly correspond to *Configuration & Architectural Models* and *Implementation Models*, while *Environment Models* are equivalent to *Context & Resource Models*. In contrast, *Analysis Models* are only implicitly represented in the previous categorization by mentioning that analysis can be performed on *Configuration & Architectural Models* or on models derived from them. However, this view neglected the important role of the environment for the analysis. Thus, besides models reflecting the system, also environment models have to be considered when creating analysis models. Thus, *Configuration & Architectural*, *Implementation*, and *Context & Resource Models* serve as the input for analysis models that also contain the analysis results. Technically, these input models or parts of them can be copied or transformed into the analysis models, or the analysis models can reference the relevant parts of the original input models. A main difference between both categorizations is that the previous categorization does not distinguish between descriptive and prescriptive reflection models.

Finally, *Adaptation Models* can be mapped to *Rules, Strategies, Constraints, Requirements & Goals* and to *Configuration Space & Variability Models*. The previous categorization does not clearly distinguish whether the corresponding models are exclusively used for reasoning (*Evaluation Models*) or for specifying and executing changes (*Change Models*). From a conceptual view, applying *Evaluation Models* does not modify *Reflection Models* as they are only read for reasoning purposes, while the application of *Change Models* modify or create new *Reflection Models*, primarily prescriptive *System Models*. However, from a technical view, *Evaluation* and *Change Models* can be quite similar as both can be specified, for example, in some form of rules.

Moreover, *Configuration Space & Variability Models* can be especially mapped to *explicit Adaptation Models* as they, for example, explicitly describe potential variants for prescriptive system models. On the other hand, *Rules* or *Strategies* can be mapped to *implicit Adaptation Models* as the prescriptive *System Models* are obtained by sequentially applying the rules or strategies on a descriptive *System Model*. Thus, *explicit Adaptation Models* in the form of *Configuration Space & Variability Models* are not necessarily required as the adaptation might also be specified by *implicit Adaptation Models* in the form of rules or strategies.

3.2 Model Operations and Relations for Self-adaptive Systems

Using the *Reflection* and *Adaptation Models* and their specializations as described in Section 3.1, and having both categorizations in mind, we outline how a self-adaptive system uses runtime models throughout the feedback loop.

The concept of feedback loops is an inherent part of each self-adaptive system since the loop controls the self-adaptation [7]. A generic loop is proposed in [13] and whose building blocks can be identified in Figure 3. The *Managed System* operates in an *Environment* and contains the business logic offered to users or other systems. It provides *Sensor* and *Effector* interfaces to enable its management by autonomic managers implementing the feedback loop. Using sensors, the manager *monitors* and *analyzes* the system and environment to decide whether the system fulfills the given goals or not. If not, adaptation is required and thus, changes are *planned* and *executed* to the system through effectors. A manager itself also provides sensors and effectors to support the hierarchical composition of managers. Additionally, the original loop [13] considers a generic notion of *Knowledge* that is used and shared by the loop activities. In contrast to the activities, the knowledge remains rather abstract as it is not clearly substantiated. Therefore, we elaborated the role of models for the knowledge by investigating from a conceptual view what types of models are shared and how they are used by the activities. This has lead to the extended loop as shown in Figure 3.

Since the loop activities use models to perform their tasks and to communicate with each other, each loop activity can be conceptually considered as a complex and high level model operation taking models as input and producing models as output. Thus, the activities can be seen as relations between the input and output models (cf. Section 2.3). However, from a technical view the models need not to be completely copied from one activity to another as the same model instances can also be shared among activities or only single model changes, the deltas, can be exchanged between the activities. In the following we discuss *one* reasonable and conceptual scenario for the loop behavior, while considering the loop activities as complex model operations that consist of the basic operations of reading, writing, and applying models. The semantics of these basic operations are substantiated through the application domain of self-adaptive systems. Moreover, the basic operations are the foundation for advanced MDE techniques, like model transformation, synchronization, or merge, being relevant for engineering self-adaptive systems employing runtime models.

The monitor *writes descriptive System* and *Environment Models* to continuously provide up-to-date views on the running system and environment, respectively. In general, writing a model includes the *reading* of the model, such

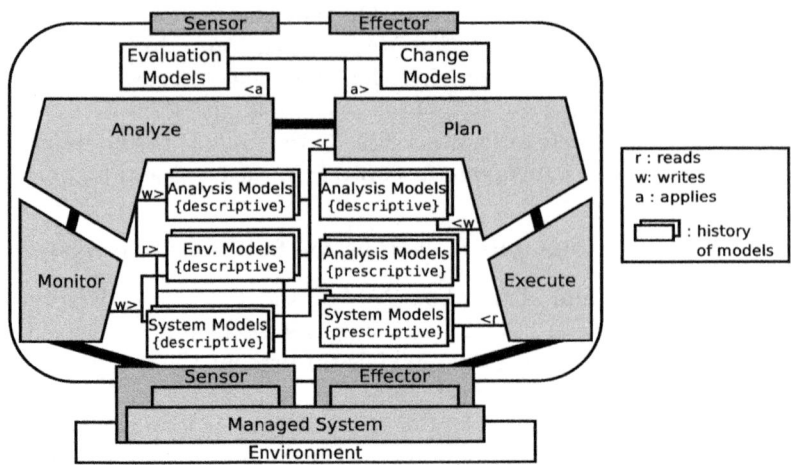

Fig. 3. Runtime Models and their Usage along the Feedback Loop

that the models do not have to be created every time from scratch but they can also be maintained and updated at runtime. Likewise, a history of models can be maintained to keep track on their evolution over time, like the past states of the system or environment. Moreover, the monitor may filter, merge, abstract, etc. the monitored data to provide several system and environment models simultaneously, that differ, for example, in their abstraction levels.

The descriptive system and environment models are *read* by the analyze step to transform, synchronize or generally *write* them to *descriptive Analysis Models* for reasoning, like a queueing network model for performance analysis. Moreover, *prescriptive System Models* are *read* since they serve as reference models for descriptive system models to analyze whether the current system converges to the designated target state. The analysis itself is defined by *Evaluation Models* that describe implicitly or explicitly the goals of the system in an operationalized form (cf. Section 3.1). Thus, the fulfillment of goals can be analyzed by *applying* evaluation models on system, environment, or analysis models. Based on the analysis results, usually annotated to analysis models, a decision about the need of adaptation is made. If adaptation is required, the planner comes into play.

The planner *reads* the descriptive analysis, system and environment models to devise a plan on how the system should be adapted such that the system fulfills its goals. This planning process is guided by *Change Models* that are *applied* on the descriptive system and environment models to obtain and *write prescriptive System Models* reflecting suitable target configurations. Likewise to evaluation models, change models specify implicitly or explicitly how prescriptive system models can be obtained (cf. Section 3.1). Since the planner has to select one among many possible target configurations, analysis is performed to determine the best or at least the most appropriate target configuration with respect to the current system and environment state. Therefore, the planner *reads* and *writes descriptive* and *prescriptive Analysis Models* by *applying Evaluation Models* to reason about the current and the possible future situations. The planning result is a predictive system model describing the final target system configuration.

Finally, this *predictive* and the current *descriptive System Models* are *read* by the execute step, and compared with each other to derive the set of reconfiguration actions. These actions move the managed system from the current to the target configuration. Therefore, they are executed on the system through effectors, while considering the latest *descriptive System* and *Environment Models* to find a point in time when the running system can be safely reconfigured.

As already mentioned, an autonomic manager providing sensors and effectors can be managed by another manager, which leads to a hierarchical composition of managers. A higher level manager comes into play when the lower level manager cannot cope with the adaptation of the system, like the planner is not able to find any target configuration fulfilling the goals. Therefore, the higher level manager can perform more sophisticated planning, even at the level of goals, and provide new *Evaluation* and *Change Models* specifying new adaptation mechanisms to the lower level manager. Thus, the higher level manager senses all required models from the lower level one, but it only effects the evaluation and change models and thus, the adaptation mechanisms of the lower level manager. Other triggers for adapting the evaluation and change models of a manager are the emergence of new application or adaptation goals for this manager.

3.3 Megamodels at Runtime for Self-adaptive Systems

From the previous sections it can be concluded that different kinds of models are used in different ways throughout the feedback loop of self-adaptive systems. The models are not only used by the loop activities, but they are also shared between the different activities and even between different loops. The relations between models that are described in Section 2.2 also hold for the case of self-adaptive systems. Moreover, each loop activity can be considered as a complex model operation taking models as input and producing models as output, which similar to the view of megamodels on relations as executable units (cf. Section 2.3). Thus, the whole feedback loop can be interpreted as an executable process that can be modeled and enacted with a megamodel. By modeling, the comprehension of the feedback loop will be leveraged, and by enacting, the level of automation for executing a loop will be increased through model-driven techniques.

4 Case Study: Self-adaptive Software Systems

In this section, we outline a case study in the field of self-adaptive software that exemplifies the role and benefits of models and megamodels at runtime. The case study is based on our previous work that employs several runtime models simultaneously for monitoring [17] and adapting [15] a system as outlined in Figure 4. Using stereotypes, the models are mapped to the categories presented in Section 3.1 while neglecting the distinction between descriptive and prescriptive models due to space constraints. The *Managed System* is reflected by an *Implementation Model* and both are causally connected to realize the

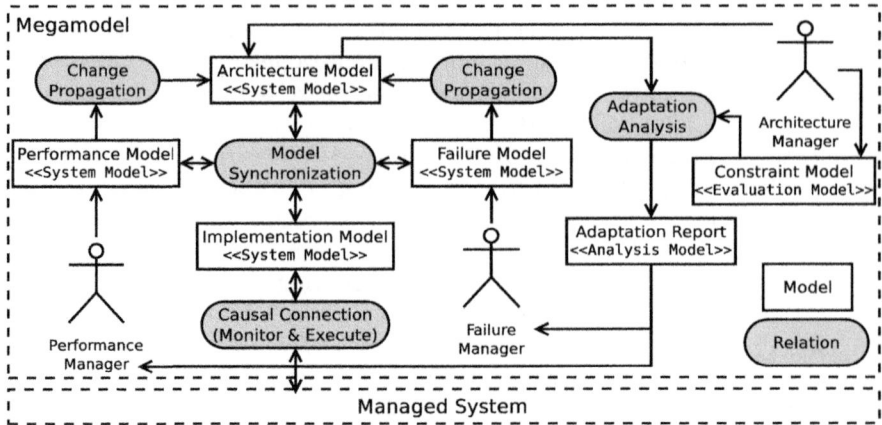

Fig. 4. A Megamodel Example for a Self-Adaptive Software System

monitoring and the execution of changes. However, the implementation model is platform-specific, complex, at a low level of abstraction, and related to the system's solution space. Therefore, abstract runtime models are derived from the implementation model using incremental and bidirectional *Model Synchronization* techniques. These abstract models can be causally connected to the system via the implementation model, and they are similar to *Configuration and Architectural Models* (cf. Section 2.1). Each of these abstract models focuses on a specific concern of interest, which leverages models related to problem spaces. An *Architecture Model*, a *Performance Model*, and a *Failure Model* are derived focusing on architectural constraints, performance, and failures of the system, respectively. Thus, specific self-management capabilities are supported by distinct models, like self-healing by the failure model or self-optimization by the performance model. Consequently, specialized autonomic managers, like a *Performance Manager* working on the performance model, can be employed. The managers' tasks are the analysis of the system and primarily the planning of adaptations with respect to the specific concerns.

However, adaptations planned by a certain manager due to a specific concern might interfere with other concerns covered by other managers. For example, adaptations based on the performance model, like deploying an additional component to balance the load, might violate architectural constraints covered by the *Architecture Model*, like the affected component can only be deployed once.

Since each concern is covered by a different model, megamodels can be used to describe relations, like interferences or trade-offs, between the different models or concerns. This makes these relations explicit such that they can be utilized for modeling coordination mechanisms between different managers to balance multiple concerns. Besides describing these mechanisms, they can also be enacted at runtime as outlined by the following scenario. Before any adaptation planned by the performance or failure manager who change the performance or failure model, respectively, is executed on the system by triggering the *Model Synchronization*, the changes are automatically propagated to the architecture model (cf. *Change Propagation* relations in Figure 4). Then, the architecture manager applies the *Constraint Model* on the updated architecture model to analyze the planned adaptations (*Adaptation Analysis*) by writing an *Adaptation Report*. This report is sent to the manager proposing the adaptation and it instructs either the execution of the planned adaptation on the system or the rollback of the corresponding model changes depending on the analysis results.

The presented case study exemplified a potential use case and benefits of megamodel concepts for self-adaptive systems in organizing and utilizing multiple runtime models and relations, especially regarding the execution of a loop.

5 Conclusion and Future Work

In this paper we have shown that the issue of complexity in model-driven software development, caused by the amount of development models and their relations, is also a problem in the domain of runtime system management and self-adaptive systems. Since for the latter domain this problem is rather neglected by applying ad-hoc solutions, we proposed to use megamodel concepts at runtime. Therefore, we presented a categorization of runtime models and potential relations between the models, which outlined the role of models at runtime. Moreover, it demonstrated that advanced approaches already or likely use multiple models and relations simultaneously. Based on that, we showed that megamodels are an appropriate formalism to manage multiple runtime models and their relations. We especially discussed the role of interrelated models and megamodels at runtime for the case of self-adaptive systems, which was also exemplified by a case study.

The discussions at the *2010 Models@run.time* workshop basically concluded that multiple runtime models are required to provide views at different levels of abstraction, for different time scales regarding the feasible performance of activities working on runtime models, and for various purposes, like monitoring, analysis, decision-making, or adaptation. These discussions further motivate our work on investigating multiple runtime models and their relations.

As future work, we plan to elaborate our categorization to incorporate other preliminary classifications comparing development and runtime models [10], and describing dimensions of runtime models, like structural/behavioral or procedural/declarative models [6]. This includes possible categorizations of model relations, which requires a more profound understanding of the different kinds of runtime models and their usage. Finally, we will investigate the application of megamodel concepts in our approach [15,16,17], which will potentially uncover yet unknown specifics of megamodel concepts for the case of runtime models.

References

1. Models@run.time Workshops, www.comp.lancs.ac.uk/~bencomo/MRT (2006-2009)
2. Barbero, M., Fabro, M.D.D., Bézivin, J.: Traceability and Provenance Issues in Global Model Management. In: Proc. of 3rd ECMDA Traceability Workshop (ECMDA-TW), pp. 47–55 (2007)

3. Bencomo, N., Whittle, J., Sawyer, P., Finkelstein, A., Letier, E.: Requirements reflection: requirements as runtime entities. In: Proc. of the 32nd ACM/IEEE Intl. Conference on Software Engineering (ICSE), pp. 199–202. ACM, New York (2010)
4. Bézivin, J., Gérard, S., Muller, P.A., Rioux, L.: MDA components: Challenges and Opportunities. In: Proc. of the 1st Intl. Workshop on Metamodelling for MDA, pp. 23–41 (2003)
5. Bézivin, J., Jouault, F., Valduriez, P.: On the Need for Megamodels. In: Proc. of the OOPSLA/GPCE Workshop on Best Practices for Model-Driven Software Development (2004)
6. Blair, G., Bencomo, N., France, R.B.: Models@run.time: Guest Editors' Introduction. Computer 42(10), 22–27 (2009)
7. Brun, Y., Serugendo, G.D.M., Gacek, C., Giese, H., Kienle, H.M., Litoiu, M., Müller, H.A., Pezzè, M., Shaw, M.: Engineering Self-Adaptive Systems through Feedback Loops. In: Cheng, B.H.C., de Lemos, R., Giese, H., Inverardi, P., Magee, J. (eds.) Software Engineering for Self-Adaptive Systems. LNCS, vol. 5525, pp. 48–70. Springer, Heidelberg (2009)
8. Dey, A.K.: Understanding and Using Context. Personal Ubiquitous Comput. 5(1), 4–7 (2001)
9. Favre, J.M.: Foundations of Model (Driven) (Reverse) Engineering: Models – Episode I: Stories of The Fidus Papyrus and of The Solarus. In: Language Engineering for Model-Driven Software Development. No. 04101 in Dagstuhl Seminar Proceedings, IBFI, Schloss Dagstuhl (2005)
10. France, R., Rumpe, B.: Model-driven Development of Complex Software: A Research Roadmap. In: Proc. of the ICSE Workshop on Future of Software Engineering (FOSE), pp. 37–54. IEEE, Los Alamitos (2007)
11. Garlan, D., Cheng, S.W., Huang, A.C., Schmerl, B., Steenkiste, P.: Rainbow: Architecture-Based Self-Adaptation with Reusable Infrastructure. Computer 37(10), 46–54 (2004)
12. Giese, H., Seibel, A., Vogel, T.: A Model-Driven Configuration Management System for Advanced IT Service Management. In: Proc. of the 4th Intl. Workshop on Models@run.time. CEUR-WS.org, vol. 509, pp. 61–70 (2009)
13. Kephart, J.O., Chess, D.: The Vision of Autonomic Computing. IEEE Computer 36(1), 41–50 (2003)
14. Morin, B., Barais, O., Jézéquel, J.M., Fleurey, F., Solberg, A.: Models@Run.time to Support Dynamic Adaptation. Computer 42(10), 44–51 (2009)
15. Vogel, T., Giese, H.: Adaptation and Abstract Runtime Models. In: Proc. of the 5th ICSE Workshop on Software Engineering for Adaptive and Self-Managing Systems (SEAMS), pp. 39–48. ACM, New York (2010)
16. Vogel, T., Neumann, S., Hildebrandt, S., Giese, H., Becker, B.: Model-Driven Architectural Monitoring and Adaptation for Autonomic Systems. In: Proc. of the 6th Intl. Conference on Autonomic Computing and Communications (ICAC), pp. 67–68. ACM, New York (2009)
17. Vogel, T., Neumann, S., Hildebrandt, S., Giese, H., Becker, B.: Incremental model synchronization for efficient run-time monitoring. In: Ghosh, S. (ed.) MODELS 2009. LNCS, vol. 6002, pp. 124–139. Springer, Heidelberg (2010)
18. Vogel, T., Seibel, A., Giese, H.: Toward Megamodels at Runtime. In: Proc. of the 5th Intl. Workshop on Models@run.time. CEUR-WS.org, vol. 641, pp. 13–24 (2010)

MoDeVVa 2010 Workshop Summary

Levi Lúcio[1], Elisangela Vieira[2], and Stephan Weißleder[3]

[1] University of Luxembourg, Luxembourg
levi.lucio@uni.lu
[2] Alcatel-Lucent, France
elisangela.vieira@alcatel-lucent.com
[3] Fraunhofer FIRST, Germany
stephan.weissleder@first.fraunhofer.de

1 Modeling, Verification, and Validation

The MoDeVVa workshop series is focused on Model-Driven Engineering, Verification, and Validation.

Models are purposeful abstractions. They are used to support the focus on the important aspects and to make complex systems easy to understand. Beyond their use as documentation, models can also be used for automatic transformation or code generation. For this, a formal foundation of models with fixed semantics is necessary. One typical application is the automatic generation of large parts of system source code. The automation can result in a decrease of system engineering costs. Thus, the usage of models, model transformations, and code generation is becoming more and more important for industrial applications. As one of the most important representatives for the application of models, Model-Driven Engineering (MDE) is a development methodology that is based on models, meta models, and model transformations. There is already a lot of tool support for models, (domain-specific) modeling languages, model transformations, and code generation. The constant pace at which scientific and industrial development of MDE-related techniques moves forward shows that MDE is quickly changing and that new approaches and corresponding issues arise frequently. Most important, there is a crucial need for verification and validation (V&V) techniques in the context of MDE. Likewise, V&V is very important in many domains (e.g., automotive or avionics) and the use of MDE techniques in the context of V&V is an interesting topic. One prominent representative of this approach is model-based testing (MBT).

2 Objectives of the Workshop

The objective of the workshop on model-driven engineering, verification, and validation (MoDeVVa) in 2010 was to offer a forum for researchers and practitioners who are working on V&V and MDE. The main goals of the workshop were to identify the mutual impact of MDE and V&V: How can MDE improve V&V and how can V&V leverage the techniques around MDE? Thus, we asked for submissions that target the following areas:

- V&V techniques for MDE activities, e.g. V&V for model-to-model or model-to-text transformations;
- V&V at the level of the models: techniques for validating a model or generating test cases from models, including simulation, model-checking, model-based testing, etc.;
- V&V at the level of meta models: techniques for validating meta-models (languages) or for using meta-models to validate other artifacts;
- The application of MDE to validation, testing and verification;
- Impact analysis of (meta) model changes on validation, i.e. the result of a change in a (meta-)model on the previous results of validation;
- V&V techniques supporting refinement, abstraction and structuring;
- Difficulties and gains of applying V&V to MDE and vice versa;
- Case studies and experience reports;
- Tools and automation.

This year we especially encouraged the submission of papers on the most discussed topic in MoDeVVa 2009: the combination of model transformations and model-based testing.

3 Submissions and Acceptance in 2010

In 2010, there were 14 submissions to MoDeVVa from 8 countries. In the review process, we chose 9 papers on mainly three topics: *transformation verification*, *modeling* and *model-based testing*. The transformation verification session was the largest one, with topics such as the application of mutation analysis to transformation verification or the formal validation of an implementation of a transformation language. Given that transformations are taking on a fundamental role in MDE, their verification seems to be also assuming an important role in the community's research.

4 Discussions during the Workshop

One of the major topics was the applicability of MBT in safety-relevant domains: "Would you fly an airplane that had been tested ONLY by model-based testing?"

The use of a development based on models is a common practice in several domains of application. The applicability of model-based strategies in the validation phase, such as model-based testing, is less common in daily practice of large companies. The main question is: if MBT offers interesting advantages, why is it not widely applied? What are the thresholds to overcome?

This question has caught some attention of the academic community and also of the industrial one. In MoDeVVA 2010, the participation of Antti Huima as keynote speaker created an interesting opportunity for discussion. Some of the identified challenges that need to be overcome are:

- *The need for mature tools*
  One inconvenience of applying MBT in industry is that mature tools able to automatically generate test code are in general a costly investment. Worst, the return on investment is not immediately observed when the users are not familiar with models. On the other hand, in general academic centers develop their own prototype tools, languages, and small case studies. If this context allows valuable time to investigate new alternatives on modeling, algorithms, and strategies for test case generation and selection, it does necessarily promote of applying such approaches in industrial cases.

  One alternative to tackle this issue is the collaboration of both worlds by introducing MBT in industry using prototype tools. This scenario seems interesting: industrial reduces the risks on investments and academics have real case studies to analyze. In practice, however, this is not easy to implement. It requires both knowledge of tools proposed by research groups and identifying interested groups from the industry.

- *Does validation require formal verification?*
  Some points that seem natural steps for academics may seem expensive for industrials. For instance, the idea that models used for MBT purposes should be verified. This brings questions such as: what is the definition of verification? How far should we go in this phase? Why are MBT tools and model verification tools are seldom integrated?

  Those familiar with model verification know by experience that it is not possible to do test generation using a model that has not been verified. A minimum of verification is required, e.g., to detect deadlocks, live locks, or dead transitions.

  The practice in the industry shows that, except for organizations dealing with critical and safety properties, industrials do not use or even mention verification in formal terms (for instance, model checking). In general, it is expected that the test generation tool will verify some basic properties before launching any test generation. However, in general, only in tools that come from the academic world these checks seem to be explicit.

- *Modeling for test generation*
  MBT requires time for modeling. This phase can be long, according to the modeling level of the testers and the knowledge about the feature/system/use case to be modeled. One reason for this difficulty comes from the university years: engineers are prepared for modeling for the development phase but not for validation purposes.

  Another problem is the number of modeling languages proposed to describe a system. How to distinguish a model that describes the system under test from the model that is going be used for test generation? A possible response to this question is that we can restrict ourselves to particular modeling languages for which MBT can be done automatically and for which coverage metrics have been studied and are available.

- *Meta models, models, or code?*
  Many approaches, languages, tools, and methodologies for V&V and MDE have been proposed, but the trend seems to be on "keeping on proposing" rather than evaluating. A possible answer to this question would be to apply in larger scale at the industrial level or let the questions from industry permeate into research in a more "open" fashion, i.e. to rethink the research questions in terms of what is demanded from industry. This may also mean that a step up from current research is needed in order to find "meta" tools that will allow this research to take place.

- *Model transformations*
  Model transformations are becoming part of MBT. Transformations can be used in order to add information relevant for testing to models used by the development team. Development and validation phases may start from a common model, however, according to the features under test, it may be required to abstract some information or go further in detailing other information.

  And the problem may go even further. When we want the generation of test cases able to be automatically executed, it requires including information for code generation in the modeling phase. The model may become very complex and discourage beginners in this practice.

  An alternative, especially for those starting on MBT, is going step by step. First, modeling without taking into consideration the test execution phase. Second, when automation of test case execution is required, the model is transformed to include additional information for code generation.

  There again, tools developed in academia can be helpful. These tools are developed having other primary goals than the test execution phase. For instance, they are developed for the analysis of new algorithms for generating scenarios or for test case reduction. In addition, academics are interested in having case studies coming from different industrial domains. Depending on the industrial partner a distinct programming language may be used during test execution. The result is thus not automatically executed, but it can be if a test harness is associated to it.

  Another usage of model transformation is for coping automatically with model changes during the whole test phase.

- *Test case reduction*
  Model transformation has also been used to deal with test case reduction, test case selection, and even to avoid state explosion problem.

  The slicing technique, for instance, is a way to avoid the state explosion problem. From an initial model, several sub-models are sliced that will contain only the essential information for the test generation. Each slice or sub-model is generated according to the test objectives. Ideally, this slice is automatically done such that all sub-models put together recreate the global model. In addition we guarantee that all parts of the initial global model are in at least one sub-model.

Concerning the selection or reduction of automatically generated test cases, this is a problem that is very present in the industry even for manual test generation. Which test cases should be prioritized? How to select the most important ones? Another way to see this problem in MBT is: how to automatically identify a given requirement in a model? A possibility is that in the modeling phase the tester would be able to identify important transitions or states by tagging or labeling. The criteria for test generation from such labeling could be: cover all scenarios where a certain requirement is involved. The results may still require a phase of test case reduction, but using such a technique could provide an idea about how many tests are required to cover a specific requirement from a given model. Nowadays, few tools are able to provide these features.

Acknowledgments

We would like to thank all the authors for their contributions and high quality presentations. A big thank you also to the Program Committee for their help and advice while selecting the best contributions: Vasco Amaral, Paul Ammann, Benoit Baudry, Fabrice Bouquet, Ruth Breu, Gregor Engels, John Derrick, Alain Faivre, Mark Harman, Antti Huima, Eliane Martins, Mercedes Merayo, Roman Nagy, Alexander Pretschner, Holger Schlingloff, Dehla Sokenou, and Yves Le Traon.

Finally, we would like to especially thank Antti Huima for having helped us kicking off MoDeVVa with his keynote speech. His enthusiasm for MBT and his many application and research questions on the topic have added value to this year's edition of MoDeVVa.

Efficient Test Suite Reduction by Merging Pairs of Suitable Test Cases

Harald Cichos[1] and Thomas S. Heinze[2]

[1] Real-time Systems Lab, TU Darmstadt, Darmstadt, Germany
[2] Institute of Computer Science, Friedrich Schiller University of Jena, Jena, Germany

Abstract. During the development and maintenance of software, the size of a test suite often increases to such an extent that the costs allocated for its execution are exceeded. In this case, the test suite needs to be reduced. A number of approaches address the problem of test suite reduction. Most of them consider the removal or merging of test cases. However, less attention has been paid to the identification of test cases that are suitable for merging.

In this paper, we present a novel approach to fill this gap. Using this approach allows for the identification of test case pairs that, when merged, have a high potential for test suite reduction. We show that two test suites reduced by our approach are considerably smaller in size than those, whose merged test cases were selected randomly. Additionally, we examine the effect of composite test goals on the reduction ratio.

1 Introduction

Over the last few years, the complexity of software has significantly increased, which in turn led to a dramatic increase in test cases [14]. Since resources are typically limited within the testing process, only a restricted number of test cases (*test suite*) can be executed. In model-based testing, a coverage criterion [12] is often used to select a finite and manageable number of test cases. A coverage criterion primarily measures how well a test suite covers the model, but it can also be used as a function that returns *test goals* for the model [13]. Thereby, a test goal is satisfied iff the corresponding parts of the model are covered by at least one test case. Thus, when all test goals in a test suite are satisfied, the test suite fulfills the chosen coverage criterion. As the number of test goals is influenced by the used coverage criterion, it can vary for the same model. Furthermore, a large number of test goals is usually accompanied by a large number of test cases.

In the testing process, an important figure is the *size of a test suite*. This figure correlates with the number and the total length of test cases contained in the test suite. When the size of a test suite becomes too large, resources assigned to the creation and execution of the test suite can be easily exceeded. In such a situation, the reduction of the test suite should be taken into account. So far, many approaches [4,5,6,9,10,14] consider the problem of *test suite reduction*.

The goal of test suite reduction is to identify a minimal set of test cases that are required to satisfy the given test goals. In [6] the problem of test suite reduction is defined as follows:

Given: A test suite T, a set of test goals $\{g_1, g_2,..., g_n\}$ that must be satisfied to provide the desired test coverage of the model, and subsets $\{T_1, T_2,..., T_n\}$ of T, one associated with each of the g_i's such that any one of the test cases t_j belonging to T_i covers g_i.

Problem: Find a *minimal cardinality* subset of T that fulfills all g_i's exercised by the original test suite T.

In case a test suite has already been reduced to such a degree that removing another test case is impossible without decreasing the number of satisfied test goals, any further reduction can only be achieved by merging test cases. Two test cases are *merged* by the time these are substituted by one newly generated test case that satisfies the same test goals. Merging a test case pair always leads to a reduction in the number of test cases. In contrast, the reduction of the test suite's total length depends on the chosen test case pair and therefore, merging a randomly selected pair of test cases may not cause the test suite to be reduced in its total length at all.

For this reason, we introduce a new approach which allows us to identify those test case pairs that, when merged, are substituted more often by a shorter test case, compared to randomly selected test case pairs. Our approach is based on the finding that the substituting test case often integrates the functionality of both initial test cases. In addition, if both initial test cases partly fulfill the same functionality, the substituting test case often integrates this shared functionality only once instead of twice. Thus, a high reduction is to be expected if the test case pair has a high functional similarity. To evaluate our approach, we reduce two test suites, TS_t and TS_{tp}, that were derived from the same model but satisfy different test goals. In test suite TS_t, each test goal corresponds to exactly one transition of the model. In contrast, the test goals of test suite TS_{tp} are each mapped to one transition-pair. Since all test goals of test suite TS_t are satisfied by at least one test case, the *all-transitions coverage* [12, page 117] is fulfilled. The same applies to test suite TS_{tp} that fulfills the *all-transition-pairs coverage* [12, page 118]. In this extended version of our previous work [2], we also examine the effect of composite test goals on the achieved reduction ratio. A *composite test goal* can be formed by combining test goals. Furthermore, we discuss reasons why our approach is only effectively applicable for systematically generated test cases.

The remainder of the paper is organized as follows: In Section 2, we discuss related work. Thereafter, we derive test suite TS_t in Section 3. In Section 4, we introduce our approach and thereafter use it for reducing test suite TS_t. Section 5 and 6 present results and discuss the effect of composite test goals on the reduction ratio. Finally, Section 7 concludes the paper.

2 Related Work

A detailed and comprehensive survey about approaches to the test suite reduction problem is given in [14]. The test suite reduction problem is usually classified as an NP-hard optimization problem [8]. Consequently, often heuristics have to be applied to achieve an almost minimal size of a test suite. The test suite reduction problem only allows for the removal of a test case from a test suite if the number of the satisfied test goals remains the same. This requirement is fulfilled by redundant test cases only.

Definition 1. *A test case t is redundant in a test suite if the number of satisfied test goals with and without t stays the same.*

Unfortunately, many case studies [10] show that test suite reduction can lead to a big loss in total fault detection effectiveness of a test suite. The total fault detection effectiveness is based on the number of satisfied test goals and, additionally, on the paths that are taken to satisfy the test goals. The latter is reasoned by the fact that such a path can identify faults also en passant and, therefore, a path can contribute to the total fault detection effectiveness, too. As a result, different approaches [4,5] attempt to keep the total fault detection effectiveness constant.

Test suite reduction techniques can be divided into pre- and post-processing techniques. The pre-processing should prevent the generation of test cases that only contribute little to the total fault detection effectiveness of a test suite but cause high costs. Therefore, test goals are used to be prioritized before test case generation so that resources are used first for more useful test cases [9].

If a test suite already exists, it only can be reduced in a post-processing phase. Today it is a common technique that a test case can be removed from a test suite if the complete sequence of the test case is already subsumed as prefix in a longer test case [1]. Thus, in this method the total fault detection effectiveness of the test suite remains constant despite the reduction. Even if a test suite no longer contains subsumed test cases there may still exist some test cases that have an identical prefix sequence. That means, their sequence is the same from the beginning up to a certain point. These identical prefix sequences also represent a kind of redundancy related to the total fault detection effectiveness, which can be removed by merging test cases. Therefore, the method in [4] either expands a test case for the test goals of another test case with an identical prefix sequence or substitutes both test cases by a newly generated one that satisfies all test goals. If there are several test cases with an identical prefix sequence it remains unclear which of them should be substituted or be extended in order to satisfy the test goals by a rather short test case. For this purpose a heuristics is presented in [3]. However, the biggest drawback of using the heuristics compared to our approach is that, if anything at all, test goals and not sequences of already generated test cases are taken into account as an information resource. Our presented approach is the first that uses the existing test cases as an information resource to identify particular pairs of test cases that are especially suited for merging [14].

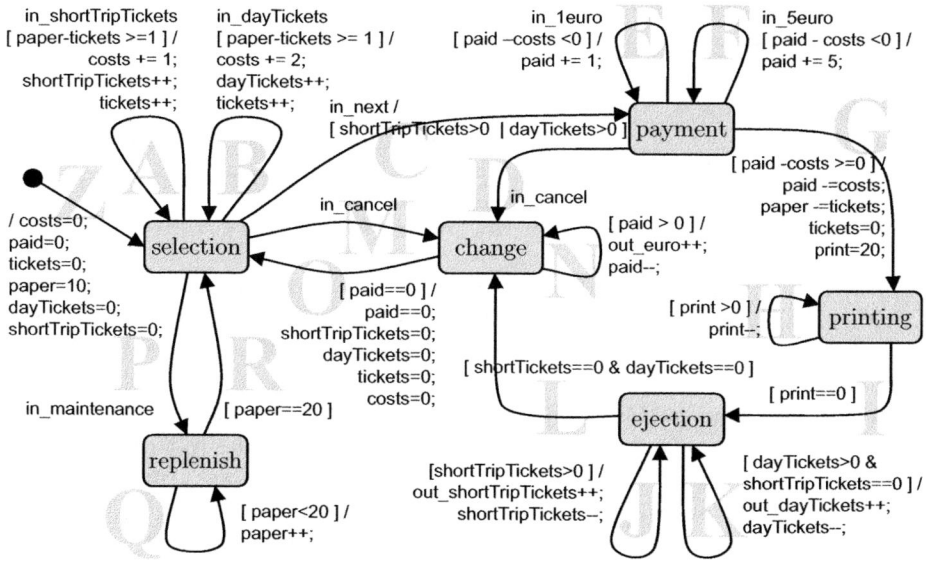

Fig. 1. Test model of a ticket machine

3 Generation and Representation of Test Cases

To prepare the presentation of our approach, we next introduce a test suite TS_t which is derived from a test model of a ticket machine. The ticket machine is our system under test (SUT) and it dispenses tickets at tram stops for public transport. The associated test model is a UML state machine (see Figure 1) that formally describes the behavior of the SUT. Due to the fact that the SUT is a reactive system and, therefore, never terminates there exists an infinite number of test cases. In order to limit the effort spent on testing the SUT, the all-transitions coverage criterion [12, page 117] is chosen as test selection criterion for test suite TS_t. Based on the all-transitions coverage criterion, test goals are derived for the test model such that each test goal covers a certain transition of the model. The UML state machine in Figure 1 contains 19 transitions, hence 19 test goals exist.

Having defined the test goals, the test cases can be automatically generated based on the test model by using a test case generator. For our purpose, the model-based testing framework Azmun [7], instantiated with the model checker NuSMV, was chosen as test case generator. Using this generator allows us to generate the shortest test cases for structural test goals like states, transitions, and transition-pairs. Using the test case generator, for each of the 19 test goals a single test case is generated.

Several of the generated test cases are redundant (see Definition 1). Consequently, redundant test cases can be removed from the test suite without changing the number of satisfied test goals. Afterwards, each test case in test suite TS_t

Table 1. Test suite TS_t without redundant test cases

#	created for test goals	transition path	length
101	Z, A, J	ZACEGHHHHHHHHHHHHHHHHHHHHHH I J	27
102	F,G,H,I,K,L	ZBCFGHHHHHHHHHHHHHHHHHHHHHH I K L	28
103	B,C,D,E,N	ZBCEDN	6
104	M, O	ZMO	3
105	P, Q, R	ZPQQQQQQQQQQR	13

satisfies exclusively at least one test goal that no other test case in the test suite satisfies. In the end, the number of 19 test cases is decreased to five test cases (see Table 1). The such reduced test suite TS_t does not contain any redundant test case.

A test case generated by the test generator is a finite sequence of input values and expected output values. The input values represent the test data while the expected output values represent the test oracle during the test execution. In case of our test model in Figure 1, the inputs are incoming signals and the outputs are outgoing signals. Furthermore, in Figure 1, each transition is labeled with an alphabetic character. Thus, each test case can be uniquely transformed from a signal sequence into a transition path.

Definition 2. *A transition path tp of length n is a sequence of n consecutive transitions in a state machine.*

An example for both notations of a test case is given next:

Signal sequence: *in_dayTickets, in_next, in_cancel, in_dayTickets, in_cancel*
Transition path: *Z, B, C, D, O, B, M, O*

While transforming a signal sequence into a transition path, particular test inputs are neglected, such that only those transitions remain that are actually used in the test case.

The advantage of representing a test case in terms of a transition path is that any section of the path can be mapped to a unique part of the test model's structure. Consequently, if multiple transition paths include the same sections, it can be assumed that these sections are responsible for traversing the same transitions in the same order. In contrast, identical sections of signal sequences can map to different parts of the test model, because an incoming signal can affect different transitions. For example, the signal *in_cancel* in our test model can be related to two different transitions, i.e. D and M (see Figure 1). Due to the fact that our approach exploits this mapping to identify suitable test case pairs, in the following, test cases are represented as transition paths only.

4 Similarity-Based Test Suite Reduction

To motivate our approach, we assume the following situation: Due to limited testing resources, it is not possible to handle all test cases in a test suite, in order that the number of n test cases has to be decreased by one. In case the test suite contains only non-redundant test cases, the required reduction is only achievable by merging test cases since, otherwise, the number of satisfied test goals is also decreased. Furthermore, we assume that all test goals are not mutually exclusive and, thus, each possible pair of test cases can be merged.

Obviously, a reduction in the number of test cases can be achieved by merging an arbitrary pair of test cases. A reduction in the total length of the test suite is also of interest, in order to save even more testing resources. Therefore, however, a test case pair first has to be identified, that, when merged, leads to a high reduction in length.

In a first try, a brute-force approach may be used to find the pair of test cases that leads to the highest absolute reduction in length. For this purpose, for each possible pair combination of test cases in the test suite a substituting test case is generated. The pair whose merging achieves the highest reduction is finally chosen and substituted by the respective new test case. As the generation of a test case consumes resources, the brute-force approach is impracticable in the real-world due to its complexity of $O(n^2)$. The problem with the brute-force approach is that a new test case is generated for all possible pair combinations although only one test case is used for substitution and all other generated test cases are discarded.

It would be an advantage to avoid the expensive generation of those test cases that are finally discarded. For this purpose, a method for estimating the potential of test case pairs for test suite reduction is needed. In the following, we present our new approach that effectively and efficiently identifies test case pairs that, when merged, allow for a high absolute reduction in the total length of the comprising test suite.

4.1 Identification of Similarity

Our approach is based on the following finding: The new test case that results from merging a test case pair often integrates sections of the test case pair's transition paths to satisfy the test goals. In addition, if the test cases of the test case pair share identical path sections, the sections often only appear once in the new test case, instead of twice as before. Thus, a high reduction is to be expected if the transition paths of the test case pair have a large number of identical transitions. For example, in Figure 2, the transition paths of test cases 101 and 102 have 24 identical transitions in the same order, i.e. Z, C, G, H, and I. The newly generated test case 201 integrates these transitions, but only once

#	transition path	length
101	Z - AC - EG [H×20] I J - -	27
102	Z B - CF - G [H×20] I - KL	28
matches: + + + +...+ +		

merging

#	transition path	length
201	Z B A C F G [H×20] I J K L	30

similarity: ~87%   reduction: ~45%

Fig. 2. Two aligned transition paths

instead of twice. However, because the identical path sections can be distributed differently in the transition paths of the test case pair, their identification is rather complex. In this paper, the problem of identifying the highest number of identical transitions is solved by applying the Smith-Waterman-Algorithm [11], well-known from bioinformatics. The Smith-Waterman-Algorithm efficiently determines the highest number of identical transitions for two transition paths by using a local sequence alignment. The algorithm generates the alignment by inserting gaps (depicted as "-" in Figure 2) into the aligned sequences such that an optimal number of identical transitions is shifted to matching positions. Thereby, the algorithm maintains the order of transitions within each transition path. For example, in Figure 2, the transition paths of test cases 101 and 102 are aligned to each other.

The *similarity* of a test case pair can be calculated as follows: The number of identical transitions in the two aligned transition paths of test cases t_i and t_j is set in relation to the total length of both transition paths (see Formula 1, where $match(t_i, t_j)$ denotes the number of identical transitions in the alignment). For example, test cases 101 and 102 have a similarity value of approx. 87%. Note that the calculated similarity value for a test case pair depends on the used test model. Using a different, but semantically equivalent model might result in different values.

$$similarity(t_i, t_j) = \frac{match(t_i, t_j) \cdot 2}{t_i.length + t_j.length}. \qquad (1)$$

4.2 Algorithm

In the following the functionality of our approach is described in detail by means of the test suite TS_t that was derived from our test model (see Figure 1). The consecutive numbering "#" in the following text refers to the corresponding line number in the pseudo-algorithm presented in Figure 3.

At the beginning, for each pair of test cases contained in the test suite the similarity is calculated by applying the sequence alignment (1.-5.). Referring to test suite TS_t, 10 pairs (see Table 2 col. "test case pair") can be generated by combining the original five test cases (see Table 1). For example, the calculated similarity for pair 101×102 would be approx. 87% (see Table 2 col. "similarity").

After that, each test case pair and its calculated similarity is added to the list *listCombinations* (5.). Finally, the pairs contained in the list *listCombinations* are sorted in descending order according to their similarity (6.). In test suite TS_t, the test case pairs would be arranged as follows: 101×102, 103×104, ...

Subsequently, the test case pairs are successively taken from top (highest similarity first) of list *listCombinations* (8.) until function *exitCondition*() becomes true (7.). The function can be substituted by different exit conditions (e.g. "Only generate n test cases" or "The similarity of test case pairs should not be below $n\%$"). Afterwards, the test generator creates (if feasible) a new test case t_{new} (10.) for each selected test case pair in order to satisfy their combined test goals (9.). For example, we assume that, due to the exit condition, only

```
input      testsuite : set of test cases
output     testsuite : reduced set of test cases

0.    listCombinations, listCandidates = null;
1.    for each t_i and t_j in testsuite
2.        if ( i > j ) then
3.            pair = pair( t_i, t_j )
4.            pair.similarity = calcSimilarity( align( pair ) )
5.            listCombinatons.add( pair )
          endif
      endfor
6.    listCombinations.sort()   //...pairs with highest similarity on top

7.    while ( ! exitCondition() ) do   //...e.g. pair.similarity < 70%
8.        pair = listCombinations.getNextFromTop()
9.        t_new.testgoals = mergeTestGoals( pair )
10.       t_new.transitionpath = TestGen.generate( t_new.testgoals )
11.       if t_new.transitionpath exists then
12.           listCandidates.add( t_new, reduction( t_new, pair ) )
          endif
      endwhile

13.   testsuite.substitute( listCandidates.identifyMaxReductionSet() )
14.   return testsuite
```

Fig. 3. Algorithm used in our approach

five new test cases are allowed to be generated for test suite TS_t. Then, the test goals of the following five test case pairs, which have the highest similarity in list $listCombinations$, are combined: 101×102, 103×104, 101×103, 102×103, and 104×105. The combined test goals (A, J and Z, F, G, H, I, K, L) of test case pair 101×102 are satisfied, for example, by the new test case 201.

For each newly created test case t_{new} the achieved reduction is calculated. Subsequently, the reduction value and the newly generated test case t_{new} are added to the list $listCandidates$ (11.-12.). Referring to test suite TS_t, the five newly generated test cases 201, 208, 202, 205, and 210 are in this list.

After that, a set of newly created test cases is selected from list $listCandidates$ so that the highest absolute reduction in total length is achieved. While doing so, no test case pair in this set is allowed to contain test cases that are also used for another test case pair in the set. For example, such a set consists of test cases 201 and 202 for test suite TS_t. In this case, this selection is inappropriate, since test case 101 is substituted by both test cases. On the other hand, a set which consists of test cases 201 and 208 is appropriate. Furthermore, this set also achieves the highest absolute reduction in total length for test suite TS_t.

Finally, for each test case in the set, the corresponding test case pair is substituted in the test suite (13.). This means that after substitution test suite TS_t contains three test cases, i.e. 201, 208, and 105.

Table 2. All test case combinations for test suite TS_t

test case pair	simil.*	#	created for test goals	transition path	length	reduction rel.*	reduction abs.
101 × 102	87%	→ 201	Z,A,J,F,G,H,I,K,L	Z BACFG [H×20] I J K L	30	45%	25
101 × 103	18%	→ 202	Z,A,J,B,C,D,E,N	Z BCEDNO ACEG [H×20] I J	33	0%	0
101 × 104	7%	→ 203	Z, A, J, M, O	ZMOACEG [H×20] I J	29	3%	1
101 × 105	5%	→ 204	Z, A, J, P, Q, R	ZAP [Q×10] RCEG [H×20] I J	39	3%	1
102 × 103	18%	→ 205	F,G,H,I,K,L,B,C,D,E,N	Z ACDOBCEFG [H×20] I K L N	34	0%	0
102 × 104	6%	→ 206	F,G,H,I,K,L,M,O	ZMOBCFG [H×20] I K L	30	3%	1
102 × 105	5%	→ 207	F,G,H,I,K,L,P,Q,R	Z BP [Q×10] RCFG [H×20] I K L	40	2%	1
103 × 104	22%	→ 208	B,C,D,E,N,M,O	ZMOBCEDN	8	11%	1
103 × 105	11%	→ 209	B,C,D,E,N,P,Q,R	Z BP [Q×10] RCEDN	18	5%	1
104 × 105	13%	→ 210	M, O, P, Q, R	Z P [Q×10] RMO	15	6%	1

* = rounded

5 Evaluation of the Achieved Reduction Results

So far we presented how to derive and how to apply our approach on test suite TS_t. Test suite TS_t contains five test cases that can be combined to 10 pairs. These 10 pairs are shown on the left side in Table 2 with their corresponding similarity. For each test case pair the corresponding test case, that would be generated when the pair would be merged, is shown on the right side. The resultant relative and absolute reduction value, also shown on the right side, refers to the difference between the length of a newly generated test case and the total length of the corresponding test case pair.

In the following, we will further evaluate our approach by comparing the reduction results achieved for test suite TS_t with those achieved for test suite TS_{tp}, which have already been partly presented in [2]. The test goals for test suite TS_{tp} are derived by applying the all-transition-pairs coverage criterion [12, page 118] to the test model presented in Section 3. As a result, each test goal corresponds to exactly one of the 62 transition pairs of the model. However, only 55 of these test goals can be satisfied by a test case. For each of the remaining seven goals, no test case can be generated that satisfies the respective test goal. Subsequently, redundant test cases are removed such that, in the end, 26 test cases are contained in the test suite TS_{tp}. These 26 test cases can be combined to 325 pairs.

5.1 Similarity in Relation to Achieved Relative Reduction

In Figure 4, the calculated similarity for all 10 test case pairs of test suite TS_t and all 325 test case pairs of test suite TS_{tp} is set in relation to the achieved relative reduction by merging them. With the assistance of trend lines it can be seen that for test case pairs of TS_t and TS_{tp} most of the time the following is valid: The higher the similarity of a test case pair, the higher is the reduction achieved by substitution.

It is further in evidence that merging test case pairs can also result in growth of test case length. But this happens more often for test case pairs with low similarity. This is clearly to be seen in Figure 4(b), where many test case pairs

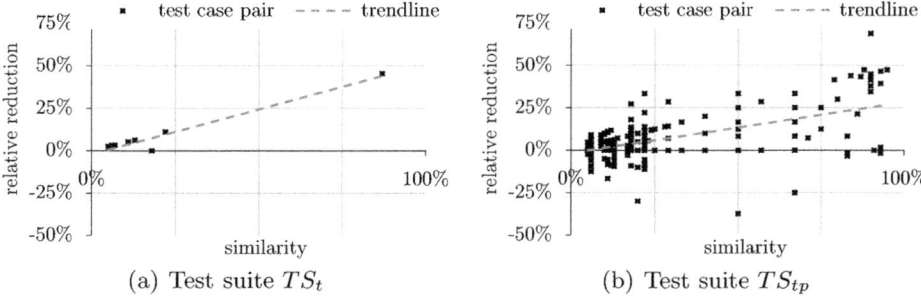

Fig. 4. The similarity of test case pairs compared with the achieved relative reduction

with a low similarity value of around 10% are substituted by a test case whose length exceeds the total length of the test case pair.

5.2 Comparison of Differently Reduced Test Suites

Next, we reduce test suites TS_t and TS_{tp} in various ways and compare the achieved results. We therefore use, in addition to our approach, three other techniques to select particular pairs of test cases for merging:

- **Best:** Only pairs are selected that in combination achieve the highest absolute reduction in total length (using the brute-force approach).
- **Worst:** Only pairs are selected that in combination achieve the lowest reduction in total length.
- **Random:** The pairs are selected randomly.

The objective was to substitute two test case pairs in test suite TS_t and 10 test case pairs in test suite TS_{tp} by newly generated test cases. In other words, the number of contained test cases in test suite TS_t should be decreased from five to three (40%) and in test suite TS_{tp} from 26 to 16 (approx. 38%).

In Figure 5 the total length of five differently reduced test suites is depicted in comparison to the original test suites TS_t and TS_{tp}. For test suites TS_t^{Rnd} and TS_{tp}^{Rnd}, which are reduced by merging randomly selected pairs, the total length of contained test cases stays nearly the same compared to the original test suites TS_t and TS_{tp}. For the test suite TS_{tp}^{Worst} the total length of contained test cases has increased significantly. Test suites TS_t^{Best} and TS_{tp}^{Best}, which are reduced by using the brute-force approach, achieved the highest reduction in total length. However, 10 new test cases have to be generated for test suite TS_t^{Best} and, in the end, 9 of these are discarded. For test suite TS_{tp}^{Best}, 325 test cases have to be generated and, in the end, 315 are discarded. Our approach is able to achieve similar good results (refer to test suites TS_t^{Appr} and TS_{tp}^{Appr}) though consuming less resources. In particular, for test suite TS_t, only two new test cases are generated, and only 10 for test suite TS_{tp}, respectively.

These results confirm that our approach is very effective in identifying test case pairs that lead to a high reduction in the total length of a test suite. Due to its

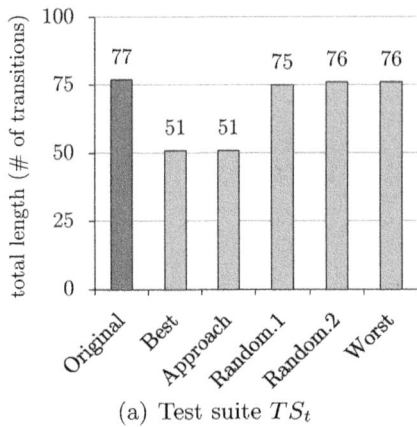
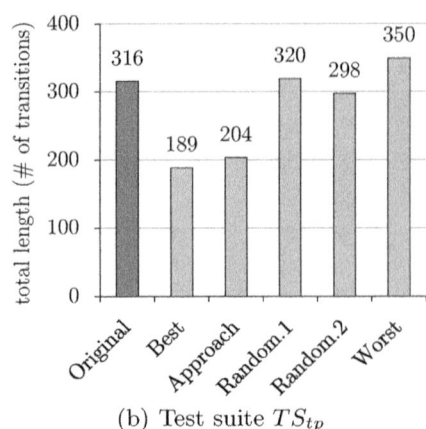

(a) Test suite TS_t (b) Test suite TS_{tp}

Fig. 5. Total length of 5 differently reduced test suites in relation to the original one

high efficiency, our approach should be preferred over the brute-force approach or the random selection of test case pairs. Our approach should also be effectively applicable in more complex scenarios related to industrial case studies with test goals that are derived by other coverage criteria (e.g. MC/DC).

It is important to note that our approach is not limited to model-based techniques; it can also be applied to code-based techniques. In this case, branches of the control flow of a program would be used instead of transitions.

6   Effect of Composite Test Goals on the Reduction Ratio

Topics like *Scalability*, *Reachability of Combined Test Goals*, and *Total Fault Detection Effectiveness* have already been discussed in [2]. In the following, we additionally examine the effect of composite test goals on the reduction ratio achieved by our approach.

In this paper, we have derived test goals by applying a coverage criterion, used as our *test selection criterion* [12, page 107], on the test model. For example, for test suite TS_t the all-transitions coverage criterion is used and the resulting test goals are, therefore, transitions. From now on, test goals that were derived in such a way are called *atomic test goals*. An atomic test goal is satisfied only, if there exists a valid sequence of inputs for the test model, that leads to states where the test goal is fulfilled. Executing this sequence on the model, typically, more than one transition is traversed. As the transitions have conditions that have to be fulfilled for traversing them, a test goal can also be defined in terms of such conditions guarding the reachability of the test goal. For example, let transition C in our test model (see Figure 1) be an atomic test goal. To satisfy this test goal, the corresponding transition-condition "$[shortTripTickets > 0$ or $dayTickets > 0]$" has to be fulfilled. Furthermore, in order to reach transition C, test cases definitely have to traverse transition A or B. Therefore, the conditions of transitions A, B, and C can be used in combination to define the corresponding test goal.

A *composite test goal* is composed of atomic test goals and/or other composite test goals. To satisfy a composite test goal, all of its associated test goals have to be satisfied by one and the same test case. For example, a composite test goal can be formed by merging test case pairs, as done for our approach. In this case, the single, newly generated test case must satisfy the composite test goal that consists of all test goals of the substituted test case pair. Thereby, the conditions of the combined atomic test goals are taken over.

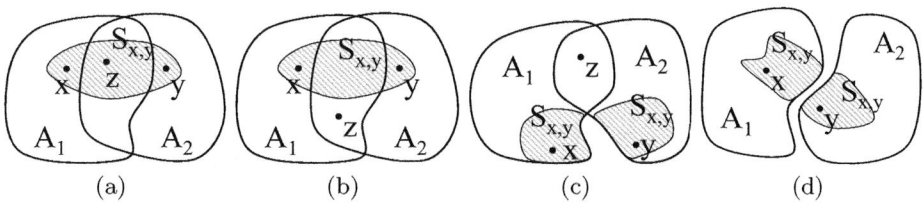

Fig. 6. Merging a test case pair is influenced by the composite test goal

We identified different cases (see Figure 6) how a composite test goal can influence the generation of a new test case z that is used as substitute for a pair of test cases, i.e. x and y. In Figure 6, A_i is the set of all test cases that satisfy test goal i. Test case x satisfies test goal 1 ($x \in A_1$). Test case y satisfies test goal 2 ($y \in A_2$). Test case z is generated by merging test case pair $x \times y$ ($z \in (A_1 \cap A_2)$). Consequently, test case z satisfies the composite test goal that is formed by combining test goals 1 and 2. $S_{x,y}$ is the set of all test cases that have a high similarity with respect to test case x and test case y. Consequently, the test case pair $x \times y$ has a high similarity ($x, y \in S_{x,y}$). The similarity for a test case pair is high, if the similarity value (calculated by using Formula 1) is $\geq 85\%$.

Our reduction approach exploits the case represented in Figure 6(a). In this case test case z has a high similarity with respect to test cases x and y. That means, a large number of transitions in the transition path of the test case z are identical and are traversed in the same order as in test cases x and y. As a result, the identical transitions in the newly generated test case z were integrated only once, instead of twice, which caused a reduction in the length of the test suite. For example, in Table 3 the similarity for all pair combinations of test cases x, y, and z of test suite TS_t is presented. As can be seen, test case z achieved a high reduction in length if it exhibits a high similarity with respect to test cases x and y. The situation in Figure 6(a) typically arises if the composite test goal for test case z is formed by test goals that depend on each other as little as possible. Otherwise, situations as depicted in Figure 6(c) or 6(d) can occur.

In case test goals of a composite test goal influence each other, the following often happens: A new test case z is generated that satisfies the composite test goal, which itself is formed by combining test goals of other test cases x and y.

Table 3. All similarity values for test cases x, y, and z of test suite TS_t

# of test case			similarity for ...			relative reduction
x	y	z	x and y	x and z	y and z	(merging x and y)
101	102	201	87%	91%	97%	45%
101	103	202	18%	87%	31%	0%
101	104	203	7%	93%	19%	3%
101	105	204	5%	76%	50%	3%
102	103	205	18%	87%	15%	0%
102	104	206	6%	93%	18%	3%
102	105	207	5%	76%	49%	2%
103	104	208	22%	71%	55%	11%
103	105	209	11%	33%	84%	5%
104	105	210	13%	22%	93%	6%

However, the new test case z exhibits a rather low similarity with respect to test cases x and y, since the interdependence of test goals for test cases x and y prevents the generation of a more similar test case. This situation is depicted in Figure 6(c) and frequently occurs if a high number of test goals are combined into a composite test goal.

Due to the low similarity of test case z with respect to test cases x and y, a reduction based on the principle "integrate once instead of twice" is not effectively applicable. Therefore, our approach is not useful in such a situation, though substituting test cases x and y by the new test case z may still imply a reduction in length: Test case z can exhibit shortcuts and detours, and can therefore be shorter or longer with respect to the total length of test cases x and y. However, shortcuts and detours are on average equally distributed such that the change in length is typically rather marginal.

The number of test goals, which have to be satisfied by one single test case z, correlates with the probability for the mutual exclusion of fulfillment conditions for these test goals. In consequence, a new test case z cannot always be derived for a composite test goal (see Figure 6(d)). Nevertheless, such a situation is prevented in test suites TS_t, due to reachability of the start state for every other state. As a result, all test goals of test suite TS_t can theoretically be satisfied by one single test case. However, this comprehensive test case is of huge length. In comparison, in test suite TS_{tp} several test goals are mutually exclusive, e.g. the transition pairs ZA and ZB.

As mentioned above, our approach is only effectually applicable, if the case depicted in Figure 6(a) occurs. For this case to happen, test cases x, y, and z shall be generated systematically, e.g. by using a model checker, and not randomly, as we assume that the generation of a test case z with a high similarity with respect to x and y is more frequent if test cases are systematically derived. This can be justified by the fact that even the repeated random generation of a test case for one and the same test goal results in different test cases. Due to random generation, a newly generated test case z does not exhibit a high similarity with respect to test cases x and y (see Figure 6(b)). Therefore, a reduction based on the principle "integrate once instead of twice" is not effective.

In summary, the following conclusions can be drawn: The more test goals are combined into one composite test goal, the larger is the probability that there exists no single test case z satisfying the composite test goal (see Figure 6(d)). However, if such a test case z still exists, this test case is often dissimilar to the test case pair $x \times y$ (see Figure 6(c)). Due to the dissimilarity no high reduction can be on average achieved by merging the test case pair $x \times y$.

As a consequence, the number of test goals, which have to be satisfied by the new test case z, is also of interest when selecting test cases x and y for merging. Furthermore, our approach performs better for test suites that are derived from large test models, containing a high number of transitions and weak transition conditions, since these positively affect the size of sets A and S shown in Figure 6.

In our discussion, we have only considered common test models. Of course, specific models can be used that fail in meeting the above-listed requirements for our approach.

7 Conclusion and Future Work

Test suite reduction has been a major focus of interest in software testing. As a result, a number of methods were proposed to reduce the size of a test suite by merging contained test cases [4,5]. Nevertheless, this paper (an extended version of [2]) is the first that proposes and develops a technique to identify pairs of test cases that are especially suited for merging [14]. We therefore introduced a new approach that efficiently identifies test case pairs that, when merged, are often capable of largely reducing the size of the test suite. Our approach determines those test case pairs based on their similarity. For this purpose, test cases are depicted as transition paths and can then be compared by analyzing their overall lengths and the number of identical path sections. The identical path sections can be efficiently identified by applying a local sequence alignment algorithm. Our new approach is evaluated using two different test suites which were automatically derived from the same test model. It could be shown that the reductions achieved by our approach were very close to the optimum, while random reduction, used for comparison, only achieved average results. Additionally, we discussed the effect of composite test goals on the reduction ratio that can be achieved by applying our approach. Based on the promising results, which we were able to achieve, we will further evaluate and validate our approach by using larger test suites provided by our industrial partners.

References

1. Black, P.E., Ranville, S.: Winnowing Tests: Getting Quality Coverage from a Model Checker without Quantity. In: Proc. of the 20th Conf. in Digital Avionics Systems, vol. 2, 9B6/1–9B6/4 (2001)
2. Cichos, H., Heinze, T.: Efficient Reduction of Model-based Generated Test Suites through Test Case Pair Prioritization. In: MoDeVVa 2010: Workshop for Model-Driven Engineering, Verification and Validation (2010)

3. Fraser, G., Wotawa, F.: Creating Test-Cases Incrementally with Model-Checkers. GI Jahrestagung (2). LNI 110, 381–386 (2007)
4. Fraser, G., Wotawa, F.: Redundancy Based Test-Suite Reduction. In: Dwyer, M.B., Lopes, A. (eds.) FASE 2007. LNCS, vol. 4422, pp. 291–305. Springer, Heidelberg (2007)
5. Hamon, G., Moura, L., Rushby, J.: Generating Efficient Test Sets with a Model Checker. In: Proc. of the Software Eng. and Formal Methods, pp. 261–270. IEEE, Los Alamitos (2004)
6. Harrold, M.J., Gupta, R., Soffa, M.L.: A Methodology for Controlling the Size of a Test Suite. ACM Trans. Software Eng. Methodol. 2(3), 270–285 (1993)
7. Haschemi, S.: Azmun - The Model-Based Testing Framework, http://www.azmun.de (last checked: 2010-12-28)
8. Hong, H.S., Cha, S.D., Lee, I., Sokolsky, O., Ural, H.: Data Flow Testing as Model Checking. In: ICSE 2003: Proc. of the 25th Int. Conf. on Software Eng., pp. 232–242. IEEE, Los Alamitos (2003)
9. Korel, B., Koutsogiannakis, G., Tahat, L.H.: Model-Based Test Prioritization Heuristic Methods and their Evaluation. In: Proc. of the 3rd Int. Workshop on Advances in Model-Based Testing, A-MOST 2007, pp. 34–43. ACM, New York (2007)
10. Rothermel, G., Harrold, M.J., von Ronne, J., Hong, C.: Empirical Studies of Test-Suite Reduction. Journal of Software Testing, Verification, and Reliability 12, 219–249 (2002)
11. Smith, T.F., Waterman, M.S.: Identification of Common Molecular Subsequences. Journal of Molecular Biology 147(1), 195–197 (1981)
12. Utting, M., Legeard, B.: Practical Model-Based Testing: A Tools Approach. Morgan Kaufmann Publishers Inc., San Francisco (2006)
13. Weißleder, S.: Simulated Satisfaction of Coverage Criteria on UML State Machines. In: ICST 2010: Proc. of the 2010 Int. Conf. on Software Testing Verification and Validation, pp. 117–126. IEEE, Los Alamitos (2010)
14. Yoo, S., Harman, M.: Regression Testing Minimization, Selection and Prioritization: A Survey. In: Software Testing, Verification and Reliability (2008)

Traceability for Mutation Analysis in Model Transformation

Vincent Aranega[1], Jean-Marie Mottu[2], Anne Etien[1],
and Jean-Luc Dekeyser[1]

[1] LIFL - UMR CNRS 8022, INRIA, University of Lille 1
Lille, France
`firstname.lastname@lifl.fr`
[2] LINA - UMR CNRS 6241, University of Nantes
Nantes, France
`jean-marie.mottu@univ-nantes.fr`

Abstract. Model transformation can't be directly tested using program techniques. Those have to be adapted to model characteristics. In this paper we focus on one test technique: mutation analysis. This technique aims to qualify a test data set by analyzing the execution results of intentionally faulty program versions. If the degree of qualification is not satisfactory, the test data set has to be improved. In the context of model, this step is currently relatively fastidious and manually performed.

We propose an approach based on traceability mechanisms in order to ease the test model set improvement in the mutation analysis process. We illustrate with a benchmark the quick automatic identification of the input model to change. A new model is then created in order to raise the quality of the test data set.

1 Introduction

When a program written in C has not the expected behavior or is erroneous, the programmers look for the faults in their program. Indeed, they trust in the compiler. The C compilers have been largely tested for two major reasons. First, a fault in a compiler may spread over lot of programs since a compiler is used many times to justify the efforts relative to its development. Secondly, compilers have to be trustworthy. Indeed, when the execution of a C program leads to an unexpected behavior, the faults have to be looked for in the program and not in the compiler. Similarly, model transformations that form the skeleton of model based system development, and so enable to generate code from high level model specifications, have to be largely tested and trustworthy.

Model transformations may be considered programs and tested as such. However, the data structures they manipulate (models conform to metamodels) implies specific operations that do not occur in traditional programs such as navigating the metamodels or filtering model elements in collections. Thus, classical but also specific faults may appear in model transformations. For instance, the programmer may have navigated a wrong association between two classes, thus manipulating incorrect class instances of the expected type. The emergence of the object paradigm has implied an evolution in the verification techniques [13]. Similarly, verification techniques have to be adapted to model transformation specificity to make profit from the model paradigm. New issues relative to the generation, the selection and the qualification of input model data are met.

There exist several test techniques. In this paper, we only focus on mutation analysis. This technique relies on the following assumption: if a given test data set can reveal the fault in voluntarily faulty programs, then this set is able to detect involuntary faults. Mutation analysis [6] aims to qualify a test data set for detecting faults in a program under test. For this purpose, faulty versions of this program (called *mutants*) are systematically created by injecting one single fault by version. The efficiency of a given test data set to reveal the faults in these faulty programs is then evaluated. If the proportion of detected faulty programs [20] is considered too low, new data tests have to be introduced [16].

Only the test data improvement step of the mutation analysis process dedicated to model transformation is apprehended in this paper. Indeed, in [12], the authors argue, with a survey of the development of mutation testing, that few works deals with that test set improvement step. The creation of new test models relies on a deep analysis of the existing test models and the execution of the unrevealed faulty transformations. Currently, this work is manually performed and fastidious; the tester deals with a large amount of information. Thus, in this paper, we propose an approach to fully automate the information collection. This automation relies on traceability mechanisms enhanced with mutation analysis characteristics. An algorithm is proposed to effectively collect the required and sufficient information. Then, the collected information is used to create new test models. Our enhanced traceability mechanisms helps to reduce the testers intervention to particular steps where their expertises are essential.

This paper is composed as follows. Section 2 presents mutation analysis to qualify test data set in model transformation testing. Section 3 describes our metamodels, foundations of our approach to improve test data set. Section 4 validates our approach with the *class2table* transformation. Section 5 introduces works related to the qualification and the improvement of the test data set. Section 6 draws some conclusions and introduces future work.

2 Mutation Analysis to Qualify Test Data Set

Assuring that a program is undoubtedly fault free is a difficult task requiring a lot of time and expertise. However, qualifying a test data set (*i.e.* estimate its pertinence and its effectiveness) is easier. If this estimation is considered too low, the test set must be improved. In the following subsections, we briefly describe the mutation analysis process [6], one way to qualify a given test data set. We then explain why that software testing method has to be adapted to the model paradigm.

2.1 Mutation Analysis Process

The mutation analysis process may be divided into four activities as sketched in Figure 1. The preliminary step (*i.e.* activity (a)) corresponds to the definition of an initial test set, that the tester wants to qualified and the creation of variants $(P_1, P_2, \ldots, P_k)$ (called mutants) of the program P under test by injecting one atomic change. In practice, each change corresponds to the application of a single mutation operator on P. Then, P and all the mutants are successively executed with each test data of the set that has to be qualified (*i.e.* activity (b)).

If the behavior of P with one of the test data differs from anyway from the behavior of at least one of the P_i with the same test data, these mutants are said to be *killed*. The faults introduced in those P_i were indeed highlighted by the test data. In the other case, if P returns the same results as some P_j, they are said to be *live* mutants. The activity (c) computes the ratio of killed mutants also called the mutation score. If this ratio is considered too low, this means that the test data set is not sensitive enough to highlight the faults injected in the program. In that latter case, the test data set has to be improved (activity (d)) until it kills each mutant or it only leaves live mutants that are equivalent to P [6]; *i.e.* no test data can distinguish P and these live mutants (*e.g.* the fault is inserted in dead code).

The mutation analysis process is stopped when the test data set is qualified *i.e.* when the mutation score reached 100 % or when it rose above a threshold beforehand fixed.

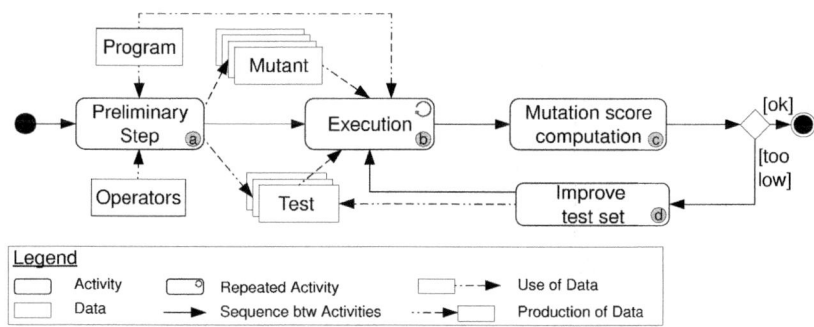

Fig. 1. Mutation analysis process

2.2 A Largely Manual Process

Part of the mutation analysis process is automatic but work remains for the tester. The mutant creation can be automated. However, usually the operators are specific to the language used in the program to test. For each new language the mutation operators have to be defined and implemented. The execution of P and its associated mutants with the test data is obviously automated as well as the comparison of the outputs. The analysis of a live mutant is manual up to now. Indeed, on the one hand, the automatic identification of equivalent mutants is an undecidable problem [6,17]. On the other hand, the test data set improvement can be difficult. The improvement of the test data set is manually performed. Indeed, the unrevealed injected fault should be analyzed both statically and dynamically in order to create a new test data that will kill the considered mutant.

The purpose of this paper is to help in the automation of the test data set improvement in case where test data are models and program is a model transformation. But let us explore in the next subsection the specificity of model transformation testing.

2.3 Adaptation to Model Transformation

Model transformations can be considered programs and therefore techniques previously explained can be used. However, the complexity and the specificity induced by the data structures (*i.e.* models conform to their metamodels) manipulated by the transformations imply modifications in the mutation analysis process described in the subsection 2.1.

Each step of the mutation analysis process has to be adapted to model transformations. [18] deals with the generation of test models. In [14], dedicated mutation operators have been designed independently from any transformation language. They are based on three abstract operations linked to the basic treatments of a model transformation: the navigation of the models through the relations between the classes, the filtering of object collections, and the creation and the modification of the model elements. The execution of the transformation under test T and its mutants $T_1, T_2, \ldots, T_k$ differs from the execution of a program but remains common. The comparison of the output model produced by T and those produced by the T_i can be performed using adequate tools such as EMFCompare [1]. If a difference is raised by EMFCompare, the mutant is considered *killed*, otherwise new test models are built to kill the (non equivalent) live mutants.

The remainder of this paper focuses on the improvement of the test set (activity (d)) in the mutation analysis process dedicated to model transformation. Our proposition relies on the following hypothesis: Building new test models from scratch can be complex whereas creating a new test model could benefit from the existing models. Thus we have developed an approach that creates new test model by adaptation of other existing and pertinent ones.

3 Traceability, a Means to Automatically Collect Information

Considering that creating a new test model from another one is easier than from scratch, the issue of the test set improvement raises three questions:

- Among all the existing couples (test model, mutant), which ones are relevant to be studied?

- What should the output model look like if the mutant was killed? *i.e.* what could be the difference we want to make appear in the output model?
- How to modify the (input) test model to produce the expected output model and thus kill the mutant?

To help the tester to answer these questions, we provide a method based on a traceability mechanism.

3.1 Traceability for Model Transformation

According to the IEEE Glossary, *Traceability allows one to establish degrees of relationship between products of a development process, especially products bound by a predecessor-successor or master-subordinate relationship* [11]. Regarding MDE and more specifically model transformations, the trace links elements of different models by specifying which ones are useful to generate others.

Our traceability approach [9,2] relies, among others, on the local trace metamodel presented in Figure 2.

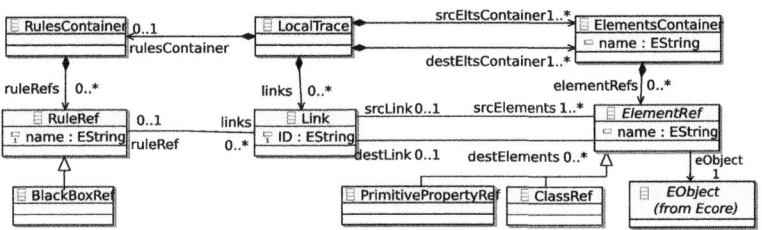

Fig. 2. Local Trace Metamodel

The local trace metamodel is built around two main concepts: *Link* and *ElementRef* expressing that one or more source elements are possibly bound to target elements. Furthermore, for each link, the transformation rule producing it is traced using the *RuleRef* concept. Finally, for implementation facilities, an *ElementRef* has a reference to the real object in the source or target model. As our environment is based on the Eclipse platform, models are implemented with EMF, the reference named *EObject* is an import of the *ECore* metamodel. The local trace metamodel and local trace models are independent of any transformation language. However, the generation of the local trace model strongly depends on the used transformation language.

For each *Link* instance, the involved elements of the input or output models are clearly identified thanks to the *ClassRef* directly referring the *EObject*. A continuity between the traceability and the transformation worlds is ensured. Furthermore, the transformation rule that has created a link is associated to it via the *ruleRef* reference. Each time a rule is called a unique new *Link* is created. Thus, from a rule, the *localTraceModel* enables the tester to identify, for each call (*i.e.* for each associated link), two sets of elements: those of the input model and those of the output model created by the rule. In the case of a faulty rule, these sets respectively correspond to the elements to modify and the elements that may be different if the mutant is killed.

3.2 Mutation Matrix Metamodel

Mutation analysis results and traces information are combined to automate a part of the test data set improvement process. Mutation analysis results are usually gathered in a matrix. Each cell indicates if an input model has killed a given mutant or not. A mutant is alive if none of its corresponding cells indicate a killing. From information contained in all the cells concerning a mutant, it can be deduced if it is alive or not.

Links between mutants, test models and their traces are managed using a dedicated matrix at a model level. The advantages are multiple. A cell corresponds to an abstraction of the execution of a mutant T_i for the test model D_k. By associating its trace to each cell, the matrix model becomes a pivot model. In this way a continuity is ensured between the traces, the test models and the information gathered in the mutation matrix. The navigation is eased between the different worlds. Moreover, the mutation matrix benefits from tools dedicated to models. Thus, the mutation matrix model is automatically produced from the results of the comparisons between the model produced by the original transformation and the one generated by T_i.

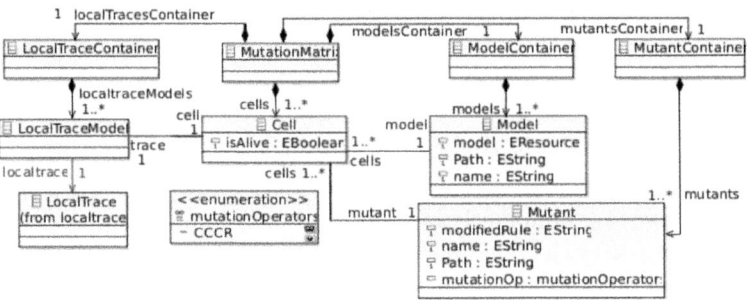

Fig. 3. Mutation Matrix Metamodel

The mutation matrix metamodel, presented in Figure 3, is organized around three main concepts. *Mutant* refers to mutants created from the original transformation. The mutants have one rule (*modifiedRule* attribute) modified thanks to one mutation operator (*mutationOp* attribute). *Model* refers to input test data. *Cell* corresponds to an abstraction of the couple (mutant T_i, test model D_k). Its value (*false* or *true*) of the property *isAlive* specifies the state (killed or live respectively) of the *Mutant* T_i regarding to the specific *Model* D_k. The *LocalTraceModel* corresponding to the execution of T_i with D_k is thus associated to the *Cell*.

The matrix model is generated during the mutation analysis process. It is the doundation of the test model improvement process presented in the next subsection.

3.3 Data Improvement Process Assisted by Traces

This section aims to clarify and expose the data improvement process enhanced with our traceability mechanism. An overview of our proposition is shown before detailing the different steps of this process.

Overview. The data improvement process (activity (d) in Figure 1) is composed of three activities as shown in Figure 4: (1) the selection of a live mutant, (2) the identification of a relevant test model and (3) the creation of a new test model by adaptation of the existing test model previously identified. These three activities rely on either the mutation matrix, the trace model or both. Indeed, in the mutation matrix, each cell corresponds to a couple (mutant, test model). The results of the execution of the considered mutant with the model in question are gathered in a trace model. We developed some algorithms to scan the mutation matrix and the trace model in order to gather adequate information. In this paper we focus on the second activity and give some exploratory ideas on the third one.

Step 1: Selection of a Live Mutant. A mutant is alive if no test model has killed it. Live mutants can thus be easily and automatically identified by exploring the matrix cells. Each cell relative to a mutant is scanned. If for all of them the property *isAlive* is set to *true*, the mutant is considered alive.

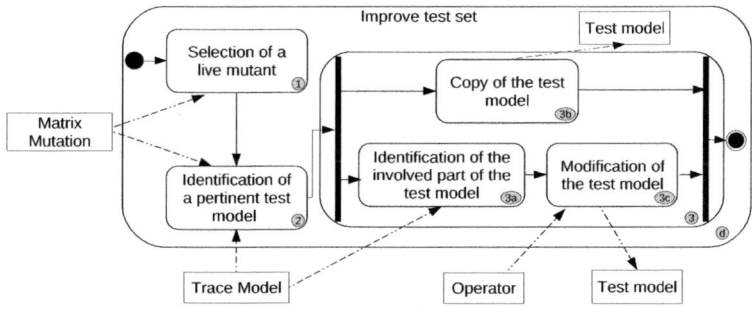

Fig. 4. Test Model Improvement Process

Step 2: Identification of a Relevant test model. Identifying a good candidate, among the test models, to kill a given live mutant is more difficult. Our approach relies on the principle that test models for which the faulty rule of the mutant has been called are better candidates. Indeed, the conditions to apply this rule were satisfied. Our traceability mechanism helps us to identify these models and for each of them to highlight the elements impacted by the faulty rule. The algorithm 1 implements this part of the improvement process (*i.e.* corresponding to step 2 and gathering information to perform step 3).

The first five lines correspond to the initialization of the different variables. The *trace* variable stores the trace associated to the execution of the mutant

Algorithm 1. Information Recovering for a Live Mutant

```
 1: trace ← null
 2: rule ← null
 3: modifiedRule ← mutant.modifiedRule
 4: modelsHandled ← ∅
 5: eltsHandledSrc ← ∅
 6: eltsHandledDest ← ∅
 7: for each mutant.cells do
 8:     trace ← cell.trace
 9:     rule ← trace.findRule(modifiedRule)
10:     if rule ≠ null then
11:         modelsHandled + = cell.model
12:         tempEltsSrc ← ∅
13:         tempEltsDest ← ∅
14:         for each rule.links do
15:             tempEltsSrc + = link.srcElements
16:             tempEltsDest + = link.destElements
17:         end for
18:         eltsHandledSrc + = tempEltsSrc
19:         eltsHandledDest + = tempEltsDest
20:     end if
21: end for
```

T_i for a given test model D_k. *rule* refers to a RuleRef in the trace model. *modifiedRule* is a String initialized with the name of the modified rule associated to T_i. The *modelsHandled* variable is a model list containing the test models for which the execution of the mutant requires the modified rule. The *eltsHandledSrc* and *eltsHandledDest* variables are similar to the previous one. They contain lists of input (respectively output) elements (one list by test model) that are involved in the application of the faulty rule.

The algorithm then scans each cell relative to the studied mutant. The trace corresponding to the execution of T_i on one input model D_k is stored (line 8). The trace model is navigated to check if the modified rule has been called during the corresponding transformation. This search is performed through the *findRule* method (not detailed in the algorithm). This method explores the *RulesContainer* of the *LocalTraceModel* associated to the cell until it finds the *RuleRef* instance whose name corresponds to the one of the faulty rule (*i.e.* the assigned value of the modifiedRule property of the *Mutant*). This method returns a *RuleRef* instance or null if the rule doesn't appear in the trace. The result is stored in the *rule* variable (line 9). If the content of the *rule* variable is *null*, the analysis stops here for this cell and goes on with the next one. On the other hand, the model D_k is stored in the *modelHandled* (line 10). For each link associated to the *rule*, the list of the input model elements (*srcElements*) is stored in the *eltsHandledSrc* variable using the temporary variable *tempEltsSrc*. The management of the output model elements is performed from the same way. (line 12 to 17).

For a given live mutant T_i, this algorithm provides: (1) some test models (*modelsHandled*) (2) their elements (*eltsHandled*) involved in the application of the faulty rule and (3) the elements of the output models created by this rule. If the content of the *modelHandled* variable is empty, the faulty rule has never been called, whatever the test model. A new model has to be created, possibly from scratch, containing elements satisfying the application of the faulty rule. On the other hand, if the *modelHandled* variable is not empty, the faulty rule has been called at least once. However, since the mutant is alive, this rule has never produced a result different from the one generated by the original transformation T. A new test model is created by adapting the considered test model.

Step 3: Creation of a New Test Model. During this step, a new test model is produced using the information gathered in the previous one. The step is composed of three sub-steps. The most important ones are the $3(a)$ and $3(c)$ (figure 4), that modify a test model previously identified as relevant. As these sub-steps deliberately modify a chosen test model among the existing ones, the sub-step $3(b)$ copies the considered test model in order to conserve it unchanged in the produced new test model set.

The modification of the test model requires both the previously identified elements and the applied operator. Indeed, based on a static analysis, the tester must understand why the mutant remains alive whereas the mutated rule has been called on the identified elements. He then must consequently modify the model. These two activities are currently manually performed. However, we observe that for each mutation operator, the number of situations letting the mutant alive is low. We have initiated to list, for each operator, all these situations and identify some related modifications to perform on the model to kill the mutant. For each mutant, the list of the situations must be exhaustive, but for each of these situations, only one modification enabling the tester to kill the mutant is enough. We foresee to develop a tool that, given an operator and the identified relevant model, will automatically detect one of these situations and perform the modification on this model.

The *RSMA* mutation operator [14] is taken for the following example. It adds a useless navigation to an existing navigation sequence while respecting the metamodel involved in the transformation. Thus, for example, the original transformation navigates the sequence *self.a.b* and the mutant navigates *self.a.b.c*. In only three cases, the mutant may remain alive: (1) the original and the mutated navigation sequence finally point to the same instance; (2) the original and the mutated navigation sequence finally point to *null*; (3) the property values pointed by the original and the mutated navigation sequence are the same. The way to modify the test model differs in each of these three cases. The first case occurs when the added navigation is the same that the last one in the original sequence. Such a situation is possible if the added navigation corresponds to a reflexive reference in the metamodel. The mutated navigation is thus *self.a.b.b* (for the original navigation sequence *self.a.b*). The mutant can be killed if the original and the mutated navigation point to two different instances of the same metaclass. A new instance (with different properties) of this metaclass must thus be added in the test model and references consequently updated. The second case occurs if one intermediate navigation is not set. In our example, if the a reference points to *null*, neither the original navigation sequence $self.a.b$ nor the mutated one $self.a.b.c$ can be fully performed, the object retrieved in both sequences is *null*. The test model can be modified in order to fill in the empty references. The third case occurs when the class recovered by the sequence $self.a.b$ and the class recovered by the sequence $self.a.b.c$ both own a property with the same label (*e.g.* the property *name*). The mutant remains alive if, in the test model, these properties are set to the same value for the two recovered instances (of possibly two different metaclasses). To solve this problem, the testers can modify one of the properties changing its value.

By extending such a work on all the operators identified in [14], the creation of a new test model can be even more automated. However, the algorithm underlying this automation will rely on the used transformation language. In order to capitalize this work whatever the used transformation language it seems inevitable to use generic definition of mutation operators. In [19] the authors propose MuDeL, a language enabling the description of mutant operators independently from the used language. Thus a given generic operator can be reused with several languages. However, the MuDeL operators are dedicated to traditional programs and not to model transformations. A generic representation of the mutation operators defined in [14], would largely benefit to the independence of our approach to any transformation language.

4 Example

This section aims to validate our approach on a case study; the classical UML to Relation Data Base Management Systems (RDBMS) transformation (*class2-rdbms*). For the example, we used a simple version of the UML class diagram (simpleCD) and a simple version of the *class2rdbms* transformation. The transformation specification we adopt is the one proposed at the MTIP workshop [5]. We have implemented this transformation with Kermeta [15]. The transformation counts around 113 lines of code in 11 operations. The choice of the Kermeta language results in the work initiated in [14]. Using the same transformation and mutant enables us to compare and evaluate the approach proposed in this paper.

4.1 Application of Our Approach

For the experimentation, 200 mutants have been manually created (105 for the *navigation* category, 75 for the *filtering* category and 20 for the *creation* category). Initially, 16 test models have been defined. The mutants are executed. The mutation matrix is filled based on the model comparison. Then, the mutation matrix is automatically explored in order to identify the alive and the killed mutants. The remainder of the algorithm is applied for an alive mutant. The first alive mutant identified is the *navigation/Class2RDBMS_19.kmt*. Listing 1.1

```
1  operation createColumnsForAssociation( ...,
2  asso : Association, prefix : String) is
3  do
4  ...
5  var fk : FKey init FKey.new
6  //fk.prefix := prefix + asso.name // orig
7  fk.prefix := prefix + asso.dest.name // mutant
8  ...
9  end
```

Listing 1.1. Mutate *createColumnsForAssociation* rule excerpt

Table 1. Test Model Elements Handled by the Modified Rule

Test Model	Src. Elements (eltsHandledSrc)	Dest. Elements (eltsHandledSrc)
ClassModel02.simpleuml	c:Association	c:FKey
ClassModel03.simpleuml	b:Association	b:FKey
ClassModel04.simpleuml	Customer:Association	Customer:FKey
ClassModel05.simpleuml	blah:Association	blah:FKey
ClassModel06.simpleuml	c:Association	c:FKey
ClassModel07.simpleuml	c:Association b:Association	c:FKey b:FKey
ClassModel08.simpleuml	a:Association b:Association	a:FKey b:FKey

represents an excerpt of this mutant. The original piece of code is marked by the *orig* flag and the modified one by the *mutant* flag. Initially, the transformation fills in the *prefix* attribute of the *FKey* class by concatenating a variable with the *name* attribute of the *Association*. The mutant concatenates the same variable with the *name* of the *dest* attribute belonging to the *Association*. A navigation has been introduced in an existing sequence using the *RSMA* mutation operator (Relation Sequence Modification with Addition) [14].

Thanks to the mutation matrix, the mutated rule is recovered from the *modifiedRule* property of the *Mutant* Class. For the studied mutant, the rule *createColumnsForAssociation* is immediately identified.

The algorithm 1 identified 7 test models that have triggered the mutated rule (the *createColumnsForAssociation* rule). The algorithm also provides the elements of the identified models (the *eltsHandledSrc* set) involved by the application of this rule. Moreover, the elements created in the output model from the elements that reach the mutated rule are, also, highlighted and gathered in the *eltsHandledDest* set. Table 1 gathers the results. For example, the *classModel04.simpleuml* model triggers the mutated rule that only handles the *Customer:Association* element and produces the *Customer:FKey* element in the destination model.

A quick static analysis of the mutated rule indicates that the *prefix* is formed using the *name* of the *dest* instead of the *name* of the *Association* directly. Based on these information and on the algorithm results, the remainder of the improvement test set process is manually performed. The *prefix* property of the *FKey* is set to *Customer*. The same occurs for the model produced by the original transformation. Thus, in order to kill the mutant, the model created by the mutated transformation must provide a different value for the *prefix* property. As no difference are raised, the tester can infer that in the 7 identified models, the *name* of the *Association* is the same as the *name* of the element pointed by *dest*. Easily, a new test model is created by modification of an existing one (for example: *ClassModel04.simpleuml*). This model is copied, then the *name* of the *Association* is changed from *Customer* to *CustomerAssoc*.

In order to check the efficiency of the new test, the mutation analysis process is performed once again. This time, 17 models are taken in account. The studied mutant is henceforth killed and this same added model also killed 2 other mutants that probably modified a rule using in the same way as the studied mutant. Once the mutation analysis is played again with the new test model set, the process goes on with another live mutant.

The modifications to perform on the test model to create a new one are not so easy than the one of the above example. However, this example illustrates the relevance and the usefulness of the information gathered thanks to our algorithm in order to raise the quality of a test model set.

4.2 Quantitative Study

This section aims to show that our approach enables the tester to save a considerable amount of time and that the execution time remains largely acceptable whereas 3200 executions are performed and so many results analyzed. For this purpose, we perform different benchmarks corresponding to 8, 9 and 16 test models, respectively.

Identification of the live mutants. The number of mutants remains 200 in the three benchmarks. The only variable parameter is the number of input model and thus the number of cells to explore for each mutant. The live mutant identification only uses the mutation matrix that is loaded once. The loading time is closely bound to the mutation matrix size. The loading time was short and approximated 1 second. The mutation matrix contains around 3200 cells + 3200 traces, corresponding to a loading time of $5107ms$. Then, once the mutation matrix is loaded, the operations performed in order to identify the live mutants are only navigations. Fortunately, this kind of operations are quite instantaneous, and the observed execution time are lower than 1 second for each benchmark (for the bag of 16 test models, the algorithm identified 24 live mutants in $461ms$).

Execution of the algorithm 1 for one live mutant. This part aims to measure the execution time of the algorithm that identifies the useful tests models. Three benchmarks with respectively 8, 9 and 16 test models are performed[1]. The algorithm identifies three elements: potential useful models, input elements and output elements impacted by the application of the faulty rule. In the three

---

[1] On a DELL Precision 490/Gentoo-2.6.34.

Table 2. Identified models for each test models set

Test set size	Number of identified models	Execution time
8	7	308ms
9	7	308ms
16	7	311ms

cases, the algorithm identifies the 7 models in 308ms for the set of 8 and 9 test models and 311ms for the set of 16 test models (Table 2). The fact that the execution time is slightly different in the latter case corresponds to the scan of the traces relative to the seven more test models (the mutation matrix is considered already loaded). Of course, these measures depend on the test model and the trace sizes, but they are largely inferior to the time spend to manually collect the information. Going in details with these results also shows that the 7 more test data added to the set are not useful for this mutant and require a more complex modification in order to reach the mutated rule and kill the mutant. Nevertheless, their presence in the test model set is relevant because they allow to kill other mutants.

Our approach has to be tested with hundreds test models and the execution time measured. However, the quantitative analysis is promising concerning the scalability of our algorithm.

Comparison with other models. Our approach has also been used with model transformations written in QVTO [3], in the context of the Gaspard 2 framework. This framework aims to generate, from a UML model enhanced with the profile dedicated to real time and embedded systems, programs in various languages depending on the purpose (simulation, execution, verification ...). The order of magnitude were approximately the same. The loading time of the matrix was smaller (around 1 second) because of the matrix size (only 1120 cells + 1120 traces). However, the execution times of the algorithm were higher because the models contained much more number of classes and referenced a UML profile.

Comparison with the manual process. The test set improvement is a hard and complex task for the testers. They have to perform static analysis to identify why a mutant has not been killed. However, they may do this analysis with test model, without leading to any relevant results. Indeed, some existing models have to be heavily modified before killing a mutant. Manually identifying an adequate test model from which it will be easy to create a new one killing the mutant may be very long. For the *class2table* transformation, the manual information collection can take from few minutes for some easy cases to few hours for the most complex ones. Using our algorithm allows the testers to recover the same piece of information in less than a minute.

5 Related Work

There are different ways to obtain a qualified test data set. Since model transformation testing has only been briefly studied, few works consider test models qualification and improvement.

Fleurey et al. [7] propose to qualify a set of test models regarding its coverage of the input domain. The input domain is defined with metamodels and constraints. The qualification is static and only based on the input domain whereas the mutation analysis relies on a dynamic analysis of the transformation. In case of very localized transformations, the approach developed by Fleurey et al. produces more models than necessary.

However, in [8], they also propose an adaptation of bacteriologic algorithm to model transformation testing. The bacteriologic algorithm [4] is designed to automatically improve the quality of a test data set. It measures the mutation score of each data to (1) reject useless test data, (2) keep the best test data, (3) "combine" the latter to create new test data. Their adaptation consists in creating new test models by covering part of the input domain still not covered. The authors use the bacteriologic algorithm to select models whereas we propose the mutation analysis associated to trace mechanisms.

In [10], authors study how to use traceability in test driven development (TDD). TDD involves writing the tests prior to the development of the system. Here, traceability can be used to help the creation of new tests considering how the system covers the requirements. The trace links the requirement and the code, and helps the developer to choose the next features which should be tested, then coded. In that approach they do not consider the fault revealing power of the test data set, but the coverage of the requirements to assist the creation of test data.

6 Conclusion

As any other program, it is important to test model transformations. For this purpose, test data set has to be qualified. Mutation analysis is an existing approach that has already been approved and adapted to model transformations. In this paper, we focus on the test model set improvement step and propose a traceability mechanism in order to ease the tester job. This mechanism completely adopts the model paradigm and relies on a local trace metamodel and a matrix metamodel.

Our approach helps the tester to drastically reduces the field of the required analysis to create a new model. We have shown on the *RSMA* operator that the number of situations where a mutated rule is executed for a test model while letting the mutant alive is low. The modifications to performed in those cases are well identified. We are currently working on a generic representation of the mutation operators in order to go towards one step further in the automation the mutation analysis process and to remain independent from the used transformation language.

References

1. EMFcompare, www.eclipse.org/emft/projects/compare
2. Aranega, V., Mottu, J.-M., Etien, A., Dekeyser, J.-L.: Traceability mechanism for error localization in model transformation. In: ICSOFT, Bulgaria (July 2009)
3. Aranega, V., Mottu, J.-M., Etien, A., Dekeyser, J.-L.: Using traceability to enhance mutation analysis dedicated to model transformation. In: Workshop MoDeVVa 2010 Associated with Models2010 Conference, Oslo, Norway (October 2010)
4. Baudry, B., Fleurey, F., Jézéquel, J.-M., Le Traon, Y.: From genetic to bacteriological algorithms for mutation-based testing. STVR Journal 15(2), 73–96 (2005)
5. Bézivin, J., Rumpe, B., Schürr, A., Tratt, L.: Model transformations in practice workshop. In: Bruel, J.-M. (ed.) MoDELS 2005. LNCS, vol. 3844, Springer, Heidelberg (2006)
6. DeMillo, R., Lipton, R., Sayward, F.: Hints on test data selection: Help for the practicing programmer. Computer 11(4), 34–41 (1978)
7. Fleurey, F., Baudry, B., Muller, P.-A., Le Traon, Y.: Towards dependable model transformations: Qualifying input test data. SoSyM Journal (2007)
8. Fleurey, F., Steel, J., Baudry, B.: Validation in model-driven engineering: testing model transformations. In: Proceedings of MoDeVVa, pp. 29–40 (November 2004)
9. Glitia, F., Etien, A., Dumoulin, C.: Traceability for an MDE Approach of Embedded System Conception. In: ECMDA Traceability Workshop, Germany (2008)
10. Hayes, J.H., Dekhtyar, A., Janzen, D.S.: Towards traceable test-driven development. In: TEFSE Workshop, USA, pp. 26–30. IEEE Computer Society, Los Alamitos (2009)
11. IEEE. IEEE standard computer dictionary : a compilation of IEEE standard computer glossaries. IEEE Computer Society Press, New York (1991)
12. Jia, Y., Harman, M.: An analysis and survey of the development of mutation testing. IEEE Transactions of Software Engineering (2010) (to appear)
13. Ma, Y.-S., Offutt, J., Kwon, Y.R.: Mujava: an automated class mutation system. Softw. Test. Verif. Reliab. 15(2), 97–133 (2005)
14. Mottu, J.-M., Baudry, B., Le Traon, Y.: Mutation analysis testing for model transformations. In: ECMDA 2006, Spain (July 2006)
15. Muller, P.-A., Fleurey, F., Jézéquel, J.-M.: Weaving Executability into Object-Oriented Meta-languages. In: Briand, L.C., Williams, C. (eds.) MoDELS 2005. LNCS, vol. 3713, pp. 264–278. Springer, Heidelberg (2005)
16. Murmane, T., Reed, K., Assoc, T., Carlton, V.: On the effectiveness of mutation analysis as a black box testing technique. In: Software Engineering Conference, pp. 12–20 (2001)
17. Offutt, A.J., Pan, J.: Detecting equivalent mutants and the feasible path problem. Software Testing, Verification and Reliability 7(3), 165–192 (1997)
18. Sen, S., Baudry, B., Mottu, J.-M.: On combining multi-formalism knowledge to select models for model transformation testing. In: ICST, Norway (April 2008)
19. Sim ao, A., Maldonado, J.C., da Silva Bigonha, R.: A transformational language for mutant description. Comput. Lang. Syst. Struct. 35(3), 322–339 (2009)
20. Voas, J.M., Miller, K.W.: The revealing power of a test case. Softw. Test., Verif. Reliab. 2(1), 25–42 (1992)

Summary of the Workshop on Multi-Paradigm Modelling: Concepts and Tools

Hans Vangheluwe[1,2], Vasco Amaral[3], Cécile Hardebolle[4], and László Lengyel[5]

[1] University of Antwerp, Antwerp, Belgium
hv@cs.mcgill.ca
[2] McGill University, Montréal, Québec, Canada
Hans.Vangheluwe@ua.ac.be
[3] Universidade Nova de Lisboa, Lisbon, Portugal
vasco.amaral@di.fct.unl.pt
[4] Supélec, Cedex, France
cecile.hardebolle@supelec.fr
[5] Budapest University of Technology and Economics, Budapest, Hungary
Lengyel.Laszlo@aut.bme.hu

Abstract. Multi-Paradigm Modelling (MPM) is a research field focused on solving the challenge of combining, coupling, and integrating rigorous models of some reality, at different levels of abstraction and views, using adequate modelling formalisms and semantic domains, with the goal to simulate (for optimization) or realize systems that may be physical, software or a combination of both. The key challenges are finding adequate Model Abstractions, Multi-formalism modelling, Model Transformation and the application of MPM techniques and tools to Complex Systems.

MPM theories/methods/technologies have been successfully applied in the field of software architectures, control system design, model integrated computing, and tool interoperability.

The fourth Workshop on Multi-Paradigm Modelling: Concepts and Tools (MPM) was held this year (2010) in Oslo. It is usually organized as a satellite event of MoDELS aimed to further the state-of-the-art as well as to define future directions of this emerging research area by bringing together world experts in the field for an intense one-day workshop.

In this paper we summarize the results of this year's event.

1 Introduction

Fred Brooks, in his seminal paper on Essence and Accidents of Software Engineering [1] makes a distinction between accidental complexity (caused by the approach chosen to solve a problem) and essential complexity (inherent to the problem and unavoidable). In his work, he analyses the issue of ever increasing complexity during software development.

A cause of this problem is the continuous increase of the complexity due to the growing needs in the specific problem domain, complexity of the tools in the solution domain and increasing complexity associated with Non-Functional Requirements.

This complexity is typically tackled by raising the level of abstraction in modelling, reducing the accidental complexity. It involves explicitly modelling every aspect of the system, including relationships between models at different levels of abstraction and in some cases to compose models in different formalisms. Multi-formalism modelling emerges as absolutely necessary to specify the different perspectives of the system. These techniques have been successfully applied and reported in the MPM workshop in the domain of software architectures, control system design, model integrated computing, and tool interoperability. Embedded systems, by nature heterogeneous, is a typical example of a field where we can find many implementation technologies where multi-paradigm modelling plays a relevant role.

In what concerns to minimizing the effects of the previously mentioned essential complexity, changes in the Software Development paradigm like to introduce Rapid Prototyping, Verification of the rigorous models that use a set of well understood semantics and Simulation are seen as a relevant support to incremental validation of the requirements.

The International Workshop on Multi-Paradigm Modelling: Concepts and Tools (MPM) is a series of annual events that have been a satellite event of the International Conference on Model-Driven Engineering Languages and Systems (MoDELS). The roots of MPM can be traced back to the 1993 – 1997 ESPRIT Basic Research Working Group 8467 "simulation for the future: new concepts, tools and applications" (Simulation in Europe – SiE) where the need for MPM was identified by a consortium of modelling and simulation researchers and industry practitioners. In 2000, Mosterman and Vangheluwe introduced the term Computer Automated Multi-Paradigm Modelling (CAMPaM) in two tracks at the IEEE CACSD conference. A series of workshops, journal special issues, keynote lectures, conference tracks, and thesis on the topic have followed since. The MoDELS MPM workshop was first held in 2006 in Genova, Italy, then in 2007 in Nashville, USA, and 2009 in Denver, USA and the current one held in Oslo, Norway, on the 3rd of October 2010. The workshop has experienced a steady growth in participation, attracting 30 participants in the 2009 edition, as it is a vibrant forum for research and industry experts to join together and discuss fundamental concepts and tools for Multi-Paradigm Modelling.

In the rest of this paper we summarize the results of this workshop's discussions and contributions.

2 Current Trends in Multi-Paradigm Modelling

An introductory talk was given by Hans Vangheluwe to define MPM and to frame the discussions of the workshop. This talk explained what makes MPM different from MoDELS. Firstly, MPM's pure goal is to tackle complexity by modelling everything explicitly, at the most appropriate level(s) of abstraction using the most appropriate formalism(s). Secondly, software/information and hardware/physical systems are treated equally (as apparent in software intensive systems). This should lead to a *unified* discipline with supporting tools. On the one hand, hardware/physical and software/information components are coupled and on the other hand, software is deployed onto physical platforms.

As explained before, Multi-Paradigm Modelling combines, transforms and relates formalisms, generates maximally constrained domain- and problem-specific formalisms, methods, and (visual) tools, and verifies consistency between multiple views.

This year's workshop had 18 submissions. The review process counted 3 to 5 reviewers per paper. Eight contributions were accepted as full papers with a presentation time of 20 minutes and five were considered short papers with 15 minutes presentations. From the reviews, both the high quality of the contributions and the progress made during the last year in MPM research were apparent.

The papers presented at the workshop approached a wide range of topics within MPM's concerns. The issue of Multi Paradigm Modelling was presented from different perspectives highlighting new challenges and re-enforcing the need to invest in this research area. As we will summarize below, the approached issues followed the trend of last year's workshop.

Megamodelling - The topic of Megamodels (or macromodels) first introduced by Favre and Bézivin is surveyed in the paper by Hebig, Seibel ang Giese[2]. The paper then proposes a core definition of Megamodels.

Transformations - One of the two highlights of this workshop is the paper, voted by the attendants as one of the two best, by Asztalos, Syriani, Wimmer and Kessentini [3] on the issue of transformation rule composition. The authors discuss the possibility of generating a single transformation derived from a chain of transformations in the context of PIM and PSM models when model evolution occurs. An example application presented is the transformation of UML models into EJB 2.0 and then to EJB 3.0. There was also a short paper presentation [4] that highlights the limitations of the traceability mechanism of QVT through different scenarios.

Model Debugging - The paper by T. Levendovsky [5] presents a novel way to develop model transformations in an interactive fashion, where the modeller is able to select the model elements for the transformation, pause the transformation engine at run-time, analyse its results, and even change the matched patterns for the further transformation steps. This interactive technique can be very useful for domain-specific modellers during refactoring operations and application of design patterns to their models. In this paper, the authors demonstrate their tool by means of the application of rules for unflattening Statecharts.

Verification and Optimization - The paper by Kerzhner and Paredis [6] (selected as one of the workshop's two best papers) presents a discussion on how to verify and optimize design alternatives with respect to system Engineering design requirements through automated generation of analyses from formal models expressed in OMG SysUML on the system engineering models. The approach is demonstrated on the design of a hydraulic subsystem. A paper by Herold [7] presents an approach for checking architectural compliance of different kinds of artifacts created in the development of component-based systems. For that purpose, the authors use first order logic in their approach. A case study on Checking

Architectural Layers for the purpose of quality assurance is presented. There was a short paper presentation by Astalos et. al. [8] outlining a possible approach for verifying automatically declarative descriptions of Graph Rewriting-based Model Transformations. In another short paper, Straeten [9], presented a strategy for specifying semantics of a Domain Specific Model through properties expressed already in the used DSL.

Multi-Formalism Composition/Integration - A short paper by Braatz and Brandt [10] discusses a possible technique for integrating heterogenous DSMLs by means of rule-based transformations. A example of a visual DSML for IT and a DSML for firewall configurations are presented as case studies.

Model Evolution - Motivated by the problem of both Model and Metamodel evolution and the need of migrating instance models Meyers, Wimmer, Cichetti and Sprinkle [11] discuss a new technique to guide the user in solving migration issues in a step-wise manner by means of in-place transformations.

Practical Case Studies - The paper by Zellag and Vangheluwe [12] presents a domain-specific language for the purpose of modelling and simulation of multi-tier systems. By using graph transformations the instance models in the referred DSL are translated into Queuing Petri Nets(QPNs) models which can be analysed and simulated by the SimQPN tool simulator. Within the focus of another specific domain a paper by Neema et. al. [13] presents a work in progress on the definition of an architecture that supports the multitude of modelling languages to address the issue of specifying both physical and computational aspects, and their relations, of Cyber Physical Systems (CPS).

3 Conclusion

Confirming the tendency of previous editions, the workshop has experienced a steady growth. More than 40 people have participated in this one day long workshop that had an intensive programme. Reflecting the nature of MPM, the audience was composed of researchers from diverse fields of research ranging from theoretical Computer Science to domain-experts (cybernetics, mechanical engineering, embedded systems, ...). This led to productive cross-disciplinary discussions.

The workshop was deemed very successful by the participants, and we plan to continue organizing future workshops. This workshop would not been possible without the help of many people besides the authors. We wish to acknowledge our Programme Committee composed of ourselves and: Antonio Vallecillo (Universidad de Málaga), Bruno Barroca (Universidade Nova de Lisboa), Bernhard Westfechtel (University of Bayreuth), Chris Paredis (Georgia Tech), Christophe Jacquet (Supélec), Didier Buchs (University of Geneva), Dirk Deridder (Free University of Brussels), Esther Guerra (Universidad Carlos III de Madrid), Eugene Syriani (McGill University), Franck Fleurey (SINTEF), Frédéric Boulanger (Supélec), Gabriela Nicolescu (Polytechnique Montréal), Gergely Mezei (Budapest University of Technology and Economics), Hessam Sarjoughian (Arizona State University), Holger Giese (Hasso-Plattner-Institut), Jeff Gray (University of Alabama), Jeroen Voeten (Eindhoven University of Technology), Jonathan Sprinkle (University of Arizona), José Luis Risco-Martín (Universidad Complutense de Madrid), Juan de Lara (Universidad Autonoma de Madrid), Laurent Safa (Silver Egg Technology), Levi Lúcio (University of Luxembourg), Luís Pedro (D'Auriol Assets), Mamadou K. Traoré (FR Sciences et Technologies), Manuel Wimmer (Vienna University of Technology), Mark Minas (University of the Federal Armed Forces), Martin Törngren (KTH Royal Institute of Technology), Matteo Risoldi (University of Geneva), Mirko Conrad (The MathWorks), Peter Bunus (Linkoping University), Pieter van Gorp (Eindhoven University of Technology), Reiko Heckel (University of Leicester), Stefan Van Baelen (K.U. Leuven), Steve Hostettler (University of Geneva), Thomas Feng (Oracle), and Thomas Kühne (Victoria University of Wellington).

References

1. Brooks, F.P.: No silver bullet: Essence and accidents of software engineering. Computer 20(4), 10–19 (1987)
2. Hebig, R., Seibel, A., Giese, H.: On the unification of megamodels. In: MPM Proceedings, ECEASST (2011)
3. Asztalos, M., Syriani, E., Wimmer, M., Kessentini, M.: Towards transformation rule composition. In: MPM Proceedings, ECEASST (2011)
4. Aranega, V., Etien, A., Dekeyser, J.L.: Using an alternative trace for QVT. In: MPM Proceedings, ECEASST (2011)
5. Mészáros, T., Levendovszky, T., Mezei, G.: Active model patterns with interactive model transformation. In: MPM Proceedings, ECEASST (2011)
6. Kerzhner, A., Paredis, C.: Model-based system verification: A formal framework for relating analyses, requirements, and tests. In: MPM Proceedings, ECEASST (2011)
7. Herold, S.: Compliance between architecture and design models of component-based systems. In: MPM Proceedings, ECEASST (2011)
8. Asztalos, M., Ekler, P., Lengyel, L., Levendovszky, T., Mezei, G., Mészáros, T.: Automated verification by declarative description of graph rewriting-based model transformations. In: MPM Proceedings, ECEASST (2011)
9. Van Der Straeten, R.: Towards a methodology for semantics specification of domain-specific models through properties. In: MPM Proceedings, ECEASST (2011)
10. Braatz, B., Brandt, C.: Rule-based integration of domain-specific modelling languages. In: MPM Proceedings, ECEASST (2011)
11. Meyers, B., Wimmer, M., Cicchetti, A., Sprinkle, J.: A generic in-place transformation-based approach to structured model co-evolution. In: MPM Proceedings, ECEASST 2011
12. Zellag, K., Vangheluwe, H.: Modelling- and simulation-based design of multi-tier systems. In: MPM Proceedings, ECEASST 2011
13. Neema, S., Bapty, T., Karsai, G., Sztipanovits, J., Corman, D., Herm, T., Stuart, D.: A multi-modeling language suite for cyber physical systems. In: MPM Proceedings, ECEASST 2011
14. Kühne, T.: A visual notation for declarative behaviour specification. In: MPM Proceedings, ECEASST 2011

Model-Based System Verification: A Formal Framework for Relating Analyses, Requirements, and Tests

Aleksandr A. Kerzhner and Christiaan J.J. Paredis

G.W. Woodruff School of Mechanical Engineering,
Georgia Institute of Technology, Atlanta, GA, USA
alek.kerzhner@gatech.edu, chris.paredis@me.gatech.edu

Abstract. As modern systems become increasingly complex, there is a growing need to support the systems engineering process with a variety of formal models, such that the team of experts involved in the process can express and share knowledge precisely, succinctly and unambiguously. However, creating such formal models can be expensive and time-consuming, making a broad exploration of different system architectures cost-prohibitive. In this paper, we investigate an approach for reducing such costs and hence enabling broader architecture space exploration-through the use of model transformations. Specifically, a method is presented for verifying design alternatives with respect to design requirements through automated generation of analyses from formal models of the systems engineering problem. Formal models are used to express the structure of design alternatives, the system requirements, and experiments to verify the requirements as well as the relationships between the models. These formal models are all represented in a common modeling language, the Object Management Group's Systems Modeling Language (OMG SysML^{TM}). To then translate descriptive models of system alternatives into a set of corresponding analysis models, a model transformation approach is used to combine knowledge from the experiment models with knowledge from reusable model libraries. This set of analysis models is subsequently transformed into executable simulations, which are used to guide the search for suitable system alternatives. To facilitate performing this search using commercially available optimization tools, the analyses are represented using the General Algebraic Modeling System (GAMS). The approach is demonstrated on the design of a hydraulic subsystem for a log splitter.

Keywords: systems engineering, SysML, model integration, model to model transformation, requirements modeling.

1 Introduction

Engineered systems are becoming increasingly complex to design because of greater consumer expectations, highly integrated products encompassing various engineering domains, and geographically distributed stakeholders. To manage this complexity, systems engineering can be applied; systems engineering is an interdisciplinary approach to creating and verifying an integrated set of system solutions to satisfy customer needs. The systems engineering process generally consists of problem definition, analysis, and interpretation [1]. Formulating the problem usually involves several common tasks, including defining the system objectives, deriving requirements for the system, and generating candidate solutions. Several iterations of these core tasks may be needed to derive a suitable final system. In an effort to precisely and unambiguously express the knowledge present in a systems engineering problem, systems engineers have begun to adopt the Model-Based Systems Engineering (MBSE) approach [2]. Within MBSE, engineers represent all aspects of the problem using formal models; such models generally include system alternatives, requirements, experiments to verify the requirements and also models relating these different aspects. There are many MBSE approaches that prescribe a work flow for modeling and solving the problem [3].

A key challenge during any MBSE process is evaluating objectives and verifying that requirements are met by a particular alternative. To accomplish this in current approaches, designers manually create the necessary analyses by incorporating thier knowledge of various domains. For complex problems, manually creating such analysis models requires significant time and effort and introduces many opportunities for error. An additional complication in many MBSE approaches is that the domain-specific knowledge used to generate these analyses is captured in diverse and incompatible tools and representation syntaxes.

This paper proposes a method for automatically generating analysis models for systems engineering problem models. In this method, the entire problem is represented in a common language, the Systems Modeling Language (SysML^{TM}) from the Object Management Group (OMG) [4]. SysML is based on the Unified Modeling Language (UML) and is chosen because it allows the representation of the very distinct elements needed to model a systems engineering problem in a single language partially overcoming the challenge of using diverse tools and representations. Because SysML is used as a common language, it also allows for the expression of relationships between different facets of the problem. Meta-data is also associated with both models and relationships to efficiently describe their role within the systems engineering problem and facilitate reuse. Using models and problem-independent model libraries captured in SysML, model transformations are utilized to automatically generate corresponding analysis models. The model libraries facilitate model reuse and can be used to express common structural components and their relationships to the appropriate analysis models. Model transformations are also used to transform the problem-specific analysis models into executable simulations which are used to evaluate an alternatives performance and verify related requirements.

Other work has identified a need for efficient architecture and have proposed computational tools for synthesizing alternatives [5,6,7]. To analyze these alternatives, usually these works generate one type of analysis model which focuses either on geometric considerations or simple functionality. This paper supports this work by presenting an approach for generating a more varied and comprehensive set of analyses to evaluate a potential solution.

The remainder of the paper is presented as follows. In Section 2, the general approach to formally modeling meta-data and relationships within SysML is presented. This general approach is applied to the modeling of a hydraulic log splitter problem in Section 3. The problem definition is then used in conjunction with model transformations to automatically produce an executable simulation in Section 4.

2 Approach: Model Management in SysML

MBSE prescribes formal modeling throughout the systems engineering process which results in a large number of models representing a complex problem. Managing the location and purpose of all these models is difficult, even if these models are contained in a common repository. To allow the models to be easily searched and identified, it is important to capture which facet of the problem each model expresses and how they relate to each other. To faciliate this, our approach relies on expressing relevant models, metadata, and relations in a common model which is represeted in SysML. The role of a particular model is characterized by associating related *aspects*. This alone is insufficient because it only facilitates expressing relationships between models; a generic, consistent, and computer interpretable approach for expressing the relationships is also needed.

SysML is chosen because it is a visual language with standardized constructs designed to represent an entire systems engineering problem [8]. The basic unit of SysML is a *Block*, which can be used to describe the system, its components, or other constructs of interest. SysML is also flexible enough to express the additional knowledge such as aspects and relationships. Because models of both the meta-data and relationships are captured within SysML, the entire representation is in a common formalism.

The approach for characterizing the models is based on Multi-Aspect Component Models (MAsCoMs) [9] where *aspects* are used to characterize analysis models by describing what the model represents, the representation syntax, and how it can be composed with other models. Unlike MAsCoMs, *aspects* are used here to characterize any model expressing the systems engineering problem, not just analysis models. We will refer to any models characterized by aspects as engineering models. The concept of aspects is similar to those in aspect-oriented programming [10] in that they characterize models based on their function. Models can have any number of associated aspects to describe their function. Unlike aspect-oriented modeling [11], these aspects are meant to characterize the models for composition and search purposes instead of describing crosscutting features.

To formally define engineering models and other relatd constructs, a profile is used to extend the SysML language[4]. A profile is a Unified Modeling Language (UML) concept that is used as a light-weight extension mechanism for adding new constructs to UML or SysML [12]. The engineering model concept is captured using a stereotype as is illustrated in Figure 1. The *EngineeringModel* stereotype has an *aspect* property which allows any *EngineeringModel* to

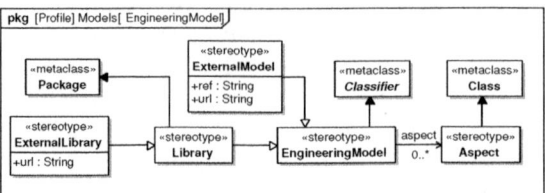

Fig. 1. Profile for defining engineering models in SysML

be unambiguously classified with aspects. The *EngineeringModel* also extends from the Classifier meta-class forcing any engineering model to allow for generalization/specialization relationships. To enable reuse, the possible aspects are captured in a model library where they are organized in a hierarchical fashion and stereotyped with the *Aspect* stereotype. This profile represents the meta-model for engineering models and aspects.

Along with capturing models of interest, relationships between them are also captured within SysML. By design, SysML provides many of the relationships necessary for modeling systems engineering problems. When existing relationships are not suitable, the UML *AssociationClass* construct is used to define a new relationship. Usages of these types can then represent a particular instance of that type of relationship. Again, a profile is used to enumerate the different relationships used in this approach, illustrated in Figure 2. For example, *CompositionRelationship*s describe how models can be composed together into more complex models.

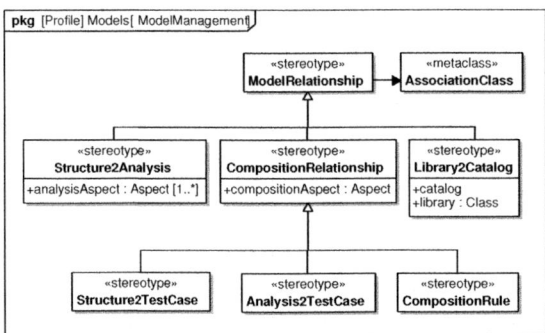

Fig. 2. Model Management Profile defining some possible model relationships

An *AssociationClass* between two models is shown in Figure 3. This illustrates the *ModelRelationship* A2B between *EngineeringModels* A and B. This relationship expresses that usages of A and B can be related by usages of *ModelRelationship* A2B. In addition, one can express how the parameters and ports of these models are linked when such a model relationship exists.

The other relationships will be discussed in more detail in the following sections. Now that the general framework for capturing models of interest and

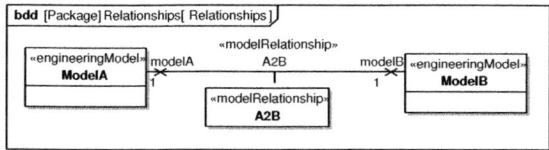

Fig. 3. Example Relationship between Model A and B in SysML

relationssships between them in SysML has been presented, the next section will cover how a systems engineering problem is expressed using this model management framework.

3 Defining the Systems Engineering Problem

This section describes how the framework presented in the previous section can be used to model a systems engineering problem. The design of a hydraulic subsystem for a horizontal acting hydraulic log splitter is used as an illustrative example in the subsequent sections. A log splitter is a simple hydraulic system which is used to divide cylindrical pieces of wood longitudinally. This example is chosen because the system is defined as a composition of well-defined, modular components. Although the system itself is simple, the design of the system is interesting because the system must satisfy several competing requirements; the hydraulic circuit should be cost effective, light weight, and capable of actuating the wedge with both high force and high velocity. The definition of this problem consists of three major parts:

- Requirements the system should be designed to meet.
- Experiments that can be performed on the system to verify that requirements are met.
- System topologies under consideration.

This section explores how each of these is captured within SysML. We will begin with the modeling of the system requirements. One advantage of SysML is the existing constructs for modeling requirements and common relationships. These existing relationships can be used to capture how requirements are decomposed, verified, and satisfied.

The requirements on the system begin with abstract specifications that qualitatively describe how the system should behave. These requirements are then decomposed into more focused specifications on the system. To simplify the verification process, in this approach the requirements are further decomposed to an abstraction level where they can be quantitatively verified through experiments; that is until a particular property of the system can be bounded. Currently, this is accomplished deterministically by constraining a variable with an equality or inequality condition.

The next step is to model the experiments or test cases needed to verify that a system satisfies the specified requirements. Experiments or test cases will be referred to as tests for the rest of this paper. To formally model tests within SysML, some additional constructs are needed to formally define a quantitatively-verifiable requirement (or testable requirement), a test, and the relationship. A profile is again used to define these constructs, as shown in Figure 4. Two stereotypes are added, the *Testable* stereotype for requirements and the *Test* stereotype for experiments. The *Testable* stereotype derives from the standard SysML Requirement with additional properties for capturing precisely which system variable is being bounded by the requirement.

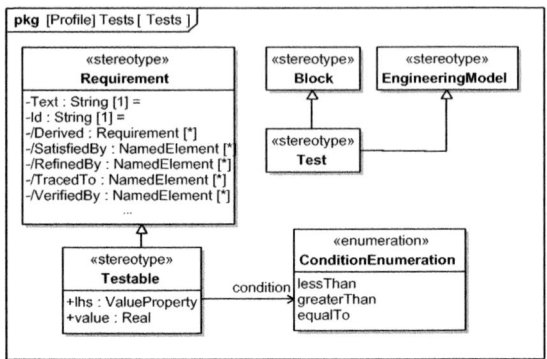

Fig. 4. Profile for defining tests and testable requirements in SysML

The use of these stereotypes along with existing SysML constructs to model requirements, derived requirements, and tests for a small portion of the log splitter's requirements is illustrated in Figure 5. In this example, a high-level requirement is decomposed into a testable requirement which can be verified by the defined test. Existing SysML relationships are used to describe that the testable requirement is derived from a high-level requirement and that the test should verify the testable requirement.

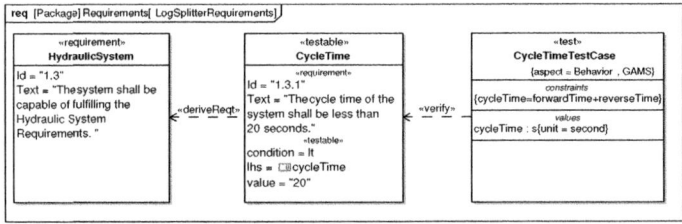

Fig. 5. Requirements Breakdown for the Log Splitter's cycle time

One important characteristic of the test definition is that it is defined independently of any particular design alternative. To separate the test definition from the structural definition, the test is defined using only a system boundary that captures the interface to the environment that all design alternatives should realize. The test specifies the state of the environment through inputs to the system as well as the parameters of the system that are to be measured. The state of the environment is described both by connecting the system boundary inputs to appropriate models and constraining the appropriate variables. Since the design alternative extends from the system's boundary, it has the same interfaces. Therefore, any constraints placed on the system boundary can be transferred to the test for a particular design alternative.

Once the modeling of the requirements and tests are complete, models of possible system topologies are needed. In this example, the system topology under consideration is that of a very simple hydraulic circuit. In this design, the wedge of the log splitter is pushed by a hydraulic piston which provides the force necessary to split the wood. An engine powers a constant displacement pump that, when engaged, causes fluid to flow through the system pushing the cylinder. The system topology as modeled in SysML is shown in Figure 6. This model is a specialization of the system boundary. It realizes the rod interface which splits the wood and the control interface that receives input from the user of the log splitter.

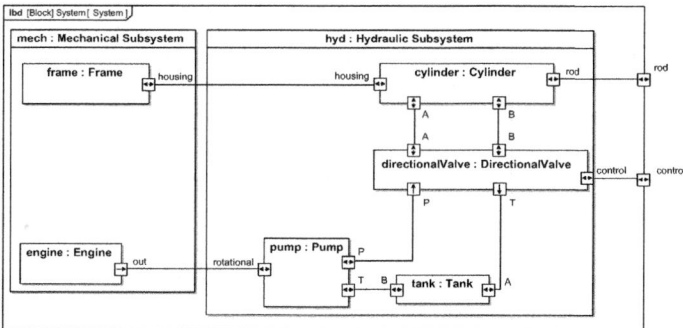

Fig. 6. A SysML model describing the Log splitter architecture. An engine provides power to the hydraulic subsystem which is used to actuate a splitting wedge.

Since the log splitter is comprised of common modular components, the modeling effort is reduced by storing these components in a model library and reusing them. The library model for the cylinder is shown in Figure 7. Within this library model, common properties and ports of the cylinder are defined, such as the stroke length or bore diameter. This cylinder model can be specialized by more specific types of cylinders or, as is the case here, specific vendor-provided products which have certain values for each attribute. A combination of vendor-provided components can represent a particular system embodiment.

Now that the systems engineering problem has been defined, the next step is to solve that problem and find a system that fulfills the requirements.

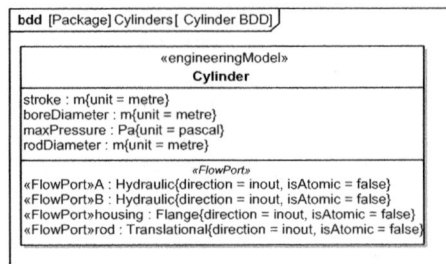

Fig. 7. A Cylinder model from the model library

4 Modeling and Composition of Analyses

Once the problem has been defined, it needs to be solved by creating appropriate simulation models from the set of tests. To execute a particular set of tests, one may need a variety of analysis models. These analysis models then can be simulated to ensure that a design alternative is capable of satisfying the requirements. This section addresses how a number of these analyses can be created for a particular design alternative, and then how they are converted into executable simulations. This focus in this section will be specifically on analyses modeled totally within the SysML language.

Analyses completely specified in SysML are modeled as *Blocks* containing only ports, constraints, and properties in a port-based modeling approach [13]. These *Blocks* can be further stereotyped to classify an analysis and provide a storage mechanism for any additional metadata needed with by the analysis. The modeled analyses are at a component-level, they model some properties of components that can be used in a particular system alternative instead of system alternatives themselves. To specify the equations or code that describes the model, constraints are used. The constraint's specification is independent of any particular syntax or semantics. This makes the constraints very flexible but also difficult to interpret. Because the equations used in this paper are purely algebraic, they are modeled using General Algebraic Modeling System (GAMS) syntax [14] to allow the problem to be solved using a number of commercial solvers that accompany GAMS. This provides a concrete syntax to use when specifying the constraints. SysML value properties are used to model any variables or constants that appear in the equations. These value properties can have types which represent the units of the variables or constants. In GAMS, variables do not have units and instead only have primitive types. In this case, it is assumed that the variables are represented using the international standard of units (SI).

UML ports are used to describe the interfaces of analyses; these interfaces often abstract interfaces of the real components being modeled. The interfaces are any inputs or outputs to the analysis model. Labeling these ports as either input or output is unnecessary in this case because this causality is automatically determined by a GAMS solver after the analyses are composed. This increases the

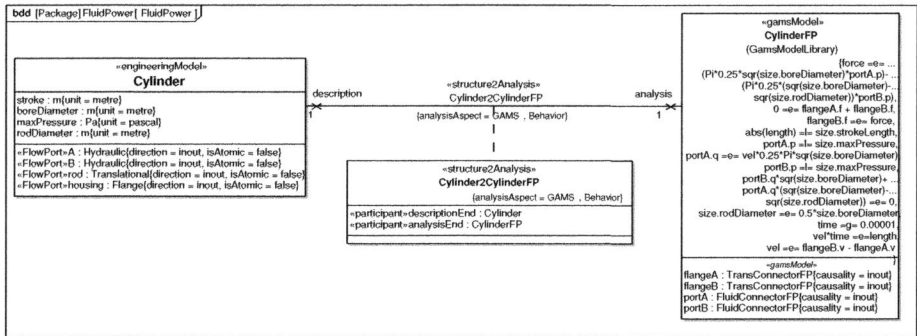

Fig. 8. Relationship between Cylinder and Behavior model

opportunity for reusing these component-level models because there are more valid combinations in which they can be connected together. To represent the connections between the analysis models, the ports are connected together using UML connectors. Stereotypes are used in cases where these connectors do not represent simple equalities but instead more complex behavior. One such example is energy flows between the ports which need to use Kirchoff's laws to sum the appropriate components of the flow.

Once component-level analyses models are constructed within SysML, model transformations can be used to automatically compose them into system-level analyses and then transform them into executable simulations. Because a SysML model can be thought of as a labeled and directed graph, graph-based model transformations are used in this approach. This transformation is broken up into two components: the first from the problem definition into a set of system-level analysis models and the second from the set of analysis models into executable simulations. Once the analysis models are created in SysML, another transformation is used to create an executable simulation in a format compatible with a paradigm-specific modeling tool.

The input to the transformation is a single model that encompasses the problem definition and any applicable model libraries. The transformation begins by locating the elements stereotyped with the *Test* stereotype; for each of these elements a corresponding system-level analysis model is necessary. For each test, a system-level analysis model is created and any variables or constraints owned by the test are copied into the analysis model. Then, the transformation finds each system that is a specialization of the system boundary owned by the test. For all components owned by each system, the transformation selects an appropriate component-level analysis model and adds it to the system-level analysis. The appropriate component-level analysis is selected by matching the aspects associated with the test to an analysis model with the appropriate aspects and correspondence relationship. One example correspondence relationship with aspects is shown in Figure 8. This particular correspondence relationship relates the cylinder component with a model described the cylinder's behavior. The

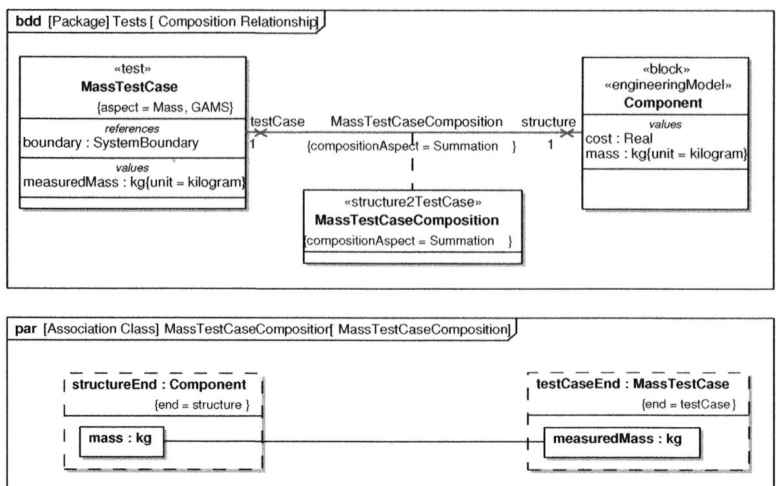

Fig. 9. Composition relationship for Mass test used to add up the mass of each component into measuredMass

relationship is stereotyped with the *Structure2Analysis* stereotype and associated with the GAMS and Behavior aspects. Properties from the cylinder, such as the stroke, are related to particular properties of the analysis. The use of similar templates for other types of analyses, mainly Finite Element Analysis (FEA) was shown by Bajaj et al. [15].

Once all the component-level analysis models are instantiated, they need to be correctly connected to other component-level models as well as the inputs and outputs of the system-level analysis model. The first step is to instantiate new connections in the system-level analysis model for any connections between the interfaces of two corresponding components. This connections are instansiated by using information contained in the *Structure2Analysis* stereotyped AssociationClasses to provide a correspondence between the structural and analytical models. Based on these AssociationClasses, the corresponding ports of the stuctural and analytical models can be matched. If two ports in the structral model have a connection, then that same connection is created in the analytical model by following the correspondence from both of these ports to the appropriate analytical ports. Using the *Structure2Test* stereotyped AssociationClasses as templates, interfaces of the component-level analysis models are connected to the inputs and outputs of the system-level model. This includes any attributes which must be added together into a single variable (i.e. mass or cost) as well as the interfaces which should be connected. As an example, the composition relationship that component masses are added into a single mass attribute is illustrated in Figure 9. The relationship is associated with the summation aspect and owns a connector between the *mass* and *measuredMass* attributes which represents that the mass from each component should be added together into a single measuredMass attribute.

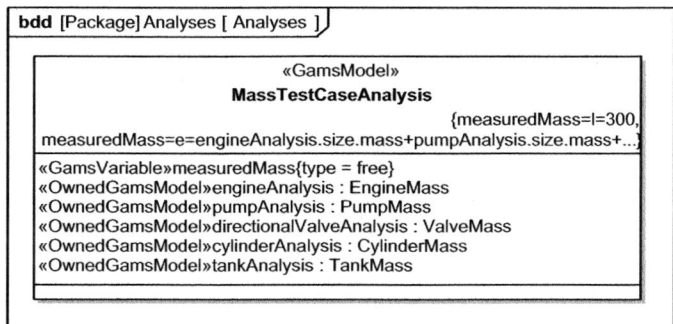

Fig. 10. Analysis generated from the test for the alternatives mass

Once all the analysis models are fully specified, a sizing model is created to explicitly connect corresponding variables describing a system's sizing across analysis models. This sizing model insures that when multiple analysis models are solved simultaneously in a solution tool the sizing parameters are consistent among the analysis models. Also, connectors are added between any created analysis model construct and the original problem definition. This allows any result of the transformation to be verified by tracing these connectors and insuring that each aspect of the problem definition has been appropriate transformed. Although the current implementation for the transformation is a completely batch process which transformations the entire model, future work will focus on incremental updates to make the entire process more efficient. These connectors can also be analyzed when the structural model changes to facilitate incremental changes to the analytical model. The result of the first phase of the transformation is system-level analysis models generated from each test such as the one illustrated in Figure 10. This analysis includes constraints generated from a composition relationship (the component masses are added into a single attribute) and from a testable requirement (the mass should be less than 300 kg).

The transformation between test and analysis models is defined with the Fujaba story-diagram [16] semantic using the MOFLON meta-case tool [17]. As is the case with many other graph-based model transformation approaches, the transformations are defined using a metamodel. To simplify the specification of this transformation, a custom SysML metamodel is used as both the source and target. This metamodel was constructed based on the standard UML infrastructure metamodel and SysML profile provided by OMG. The stereotypes in the SysML profile are converted into meta-classes so they are on the same meta-level as the UML metamodel concepts. A JMI implementation of this metamodel is created by using MOFLON's code generator [18]. This implementation is completely tool independent but requires authored models in to be transformed into it.

After the analyses are created within SysML, they need to be transformed into executable simulations. In theory, the generated simulations should test every possible design alternative using appropriate analyses to verify whether it meets the requirements. Since testing every possible combination would be computationally

Scenario	Component Sizing (Selection Id from Catalog)				Selected Variable Values				CPU Execution Time (s)
	Cylinder Id	Pump Id	Engine Id	Valve Id	Forward Force (N)	Total Mass (kg)	Total Cost ($)	Total Time (s)	
Maximize Force (N)	HMW-5032	SKP1NN_012	DP340E	NT-2020	139,833	94.9	993.5	20	2.82
Minimize Total Time (s)	HMW-3010	SKP1NN_012	DP390E	NT_Prince-2036	50,000	51.87	843.97	4.896	3.54
Minimize Total Cost ($)	HMW-4010	SKP1NN_012	DP240	NT-2020	53,698	51.3	657.4	9.69	2.45
Minimize Total Mass (kg)	PMC-5414	SNP2NN_4_0	DP160V	MSCDirect-01825629	52,013	32.25	708.6	9.15	78.13

Fig. 11. Results from the GAMS optimization

explosive, an optimization approach is used instead. The analyses are combined into a single non-linear mixed integer programming (MINLP) problem as demonstrated by Shah et al. [19]. This MINLP problem is represented using GAMS and solved using the Branch-And-Reduce Optimization Navigator (BARON) [20] to find several candidate alternatives that meet the requirements. A graph-based code generator specified using MOFLON is used to create the executable simulation code in GAMS syntax. Some solutions are shown in Figure 11. The solutions are composed of vendor products from the model library configured into the simple topology in Figure 6. Each solution meets the requirements and also maximizes a given objective function. The most likely cause of the long simulation time when finding the solution that maximizes mass is that the solver was not able to quickly eliminate a large number of the possible solutions as clearly inferior.

Although not considered in this paper, future work will investigate how external models can be integrated into this framework. Referencing external models may allow designers to tap into large existing domain-specific analysis model libraries. When an analysis model is located outside of the SysML environment, the *ExternalModel* stereotype defined in Figure 1 can be used to reference it using a black box approach. A black box model only exposes the parameters and ports of a model but leaves rest of the specification in the native language. Unfortunately, referencing external models adds additional complexity when implementing a transformation because their contents may need to be parsed in order to set parameters or instantiate connections.

In the current implementation, both the transformation from the problem definition to analysis models and the transformation from anlaysis models to executable simulation code are wrapped into ModelCenter [21]. ModelCenter is an integrated environment designed to execute multiple analyses as well as run trade studies optimizations. ModelCenter is used to control the execution order of the transformations and also to run the simulation using the prescribed simulation code. Incorporating the transformations within ModelCenter should allow future work to more easily execute resulting simulation code in a larger number of tools. Also, this provides a framework which can be expanded by including future transformations. Another benefit is that the values in the problem definition can be adjusted and multiple analyses can be run using built-in design exploration tools.

5 Discussion and Closure

As mentioned, the overall goal of MBSE is to explicitly model all aspects of the systems engineering process. This should include both the actual elements (systems structure, analyses, tests, and requirements) and the relationships between them. The overall goal is to improve traceability and reduce tedious effort by the designer during the design process. The framework presented here addresses only a small portion of this goal by formally capturing the structure, requirements, and tests and transforming this captured knowledge into executable simulations.

One limitation of the current framework is that the test execution order is implicitly handled by a domain-specific solution tool. This approach would be insufficient if the analyses needed to be executed in different modeling tools or if they modeled the problem at different levels of fidelity. How to formally model this execution process within SysML is left for future work.

We view the work presented here as an initial step towards a more complete tool set where a problem definition is transformed and analyzed to automatically search for good design alternatives. From the problem definition, design alternatives could be automatically generated using captured knowledge [22], and then each alternative could be analyzed using models at varying levels of fidelity. The entire description of the problem could be maintained in a SysML model, executable simulations could be generated from this model [19,23]. The ModelCenter implementation provides a platform for which these future transformations can be integrated and future work will focus on integrating each of these tasks within this framework.

Acknowledgments. This work has been funded by Deere & Company along with the ERC for Compact and Efficient Fluid Power, supported by the National Science Foundation under Grant No. EEC-0540834. The authors would like to thank Roger Burkhart, Sanford Friedenthal, Leon McGinnis, and Russell Peak for the discussions that helped crystallize the ideas presented in this paper. The authors would also like to thank No Magic Inc. for providing access to its MagicDraw UML/SysML tool and Andy Schürr for access to the MOFLON tool.

References

1. Sage, A., Armstrong, J.: Introduction to systems engineering. Wiley, Chichester (2000)
2. Fisher, J.: Model-Based Systems Engineering: A New Paradigm. INCOSE INSIGHT 1, 3–16 (1998)
3. Estefan, J.A.: Survey of model-based systems engineering (mbse) methodologies. Technical report, California Institute of Technology (2007)
4. OMG.: Systems Modeling Language v 1.1 (2008)

5. Alber, R., Rudolph, S.: On a grammar-based design language that supports automated design generation and creativity. In: Fifth Workshop on Knowledge Intensive CAD, vol. 19, Springer, Heidelberg (2004)
6. Bolognini, F., Seshia, A.A., Shea, A.K.: A computational design synthesis method for MEMS using COMSOL. In: COMSOL Users Conference (2007)
7. Starling, A.C., Street, T., Shea, K.: A parallel grammar for simulation-driven mechanical design synthesis. In: ASME IDETC, vol. 2, pp. 24–28 (2005)
8. Friedenthal, S., Moore, A., Steiner, R.: A Practical Guide to SysML: The Systems Modeling Language. Morgan Kaufmann, San Francisco (2008)
9. Jobe, J.M.: Multi-Aspect Component Models: Enabling the Reuse of Engineering Analysis Models in SysML. Masters, Georgia Institute of Technology (2008)
10. Irwin, J., Kickzales, G., Lamping, J., Mendhekar, A., Maeda, C., Lopes, C., Loingtier, J.: Aspect-oriented programming. In: Proceedings of ECOOP, pp. 220–242. IEEE, Finland (1997)
11. Chavez, C., Lucena, C.: A metamodel for aspect-oriented modeling. In: Workshop on Aspect-Oriented Modeling with the UML at AOSD 2002, Citeseer (2002)
12. ISO/IEC: Unified Modeling Language Specification (2005)
13. Paredis, C., Diaz-Calderon, A., Sinha, R., Khosla, P.: Composable models for simulation-based design. Engineering with Computers 17(2), 112–128 (2001)
14. Brook, A., Kendrick, D., Meeraus, A.: Gams, a user's guide. ACM SIGNUM Newsletter 23(3-4), 11 (1988)
15. Bajaj, M., Peak, R.S., Paredis, C.J.J.: Knowledge composition for efficient analysis problem formulation part 2: Approach and analysis meta-model. In: ASME IDETC & CIE (2007)
16. Fischer, T., Niere, J., Torunski, L., Zündorf, A.: Story Diagrams: A New Graph Rewrite Language Based on the Unified Modeling Language and Java. In: 6th International Workshop Theory and Application of Graph Transformations, November 16-20, 1998, vol. 1764, pp. 157–167. Springer, Heidelberg (2000)
17. Amelunxen, C., Königs, A., Rötschke, T., Schürr, A.: MOFLON: A standard-compliant metamodeling framework with graph transformations. In: Model Driven Architecture–Foundations and Applications, pp. 361–375. Springer, Heidelberg (2006)
18. Dirckze, R.: Java metadata interface (jmi) specification version 1.0. Unisys Corporation and Sun Microsystems 2002 (2002)
19. Shah, A.: Combining mathematical programming and sysml for component sizing as applied to hydraulic systems. Masters, Georgia Institute of Technology (2010)
20. Sahinidis, N.: BARON: A general purpose global optimization software package. Journal of Global Optimization 8(2), 201–205 (1996)
21. Malone, B., Papay, M.: ModelCenter: An Integration Environment for Simulation Based Design. In: Simulation Interoperability Workshop, Orlando, FL (1999)
22. Kerzhner, A.A., Paredis, C.J.J.: Using Domain Specific Languages to Capture Design Synthesis Knowledge for Model-Based Systems Engineering. In: ASME IDETC & CIE (2009)
23. Johnson, T., Paredis, C., Burkhart, R.: Integrating Models and Simulations of Continuous Dynamics into SysML. In: 6th International Modelica Conference, Modelica Association (2008)

Simplifying Model Transformation Chains by Rule Composition

Mark Asztalos[1], Eugene Syriani[2], Manuel Wimmer[3], and Marouane Kessentini[4]

[1] Budapest University of Technology and Economics, Budapest, Hungary
`asztalos@aut.bme.hu`
[2] McGill University, Montréal, Québec, Canada
`esyria@cs.mcgill.ca`
[3] Vienna University of Technology, Vienna, Austria
`wimmer@big.tuwien.ac.at`
[4] DIRO, Université de Montréal, Montréal, Québec, Canada
`kessentm@iro.umontreal.ca`

Abstract. Many model transformation problems require different intermediate transformation steps, e.g., when platform-specific models (PSM) are generated from platform-independent models (PIM). This requires the presence of several intermediate meta-models between those of the PIM and the PSM. Thus, for achieving the final PSM, a chain of transformation is needed. The solution proposed in this paper is to investigate whether it is possible to generate a single transformation from a chain of transformations, solely involving the initial PIM and final PSM meta-models. The presented work focuses on the composition of algebraic graph transformations at the rule level. Moreover, we discuss about the translation of transformations implemented in dedicated model-to-model transformation languages to algebraic graph transformation specifications. We apply the automatic procedure for composing rules in the context of the evolution of Enterprise Java Beans (EJB), transforming UML models into EJB 2.0 and then to EJB 3.0 models. The composable transformations are specified in the Atlas Transformation Language.

1 Introduction

Nowadays, software platforms evolve very rapidly. This is also true for modelling languages, which have to reflect the evolution of the underlying platforms. The evolution of a modelling language requires one to adapt its meta-model as well as any model transformation involving it. The task of adapting the transformations to the new version of the language is very tedious and error prone, especially when this is done manually. Let us take the example scenario of generating platform-specific models (PSMs) from platform-independent models (PIMs). Due to the continuous evolution of the platform, while several versions of the platform-specific meta-model have to be employed, transformations between these meta-model versions are necessary for migrating the PSMs at version

n to PSMs at version $n + 1$. These transformations can be also reused within a model transformation chain for transforming a PIM over several intermediate meta-models into a PSM for the latest platform version. Over time, such transformation chains naturally become larger and larger, which has a negative impact on maintainability and execution performance.

The goal of this paper is to reduce the manual effort of shortening transformation chains by eliminating intermediate transformation steps. The presented work proposes to compose a chain of transformations into one transformation that does not involve any intermediary meta-model. In particular, this is done by computing the transitive transformation of two given transformations. Our approach relies on the notion of graph transformations. To support dedicated model-to-model (M2M) transformation languages, which are commonly employed for generating PSMs from PIMs, we present how such languages are mapped to graph transformations by using the Atlas Transformation Language (ATL) [6] as an example.

In Section 2, we first define the composition of transformations in general. Section 3 reduces the problem to the composition of rules by (1) elaborating on the criteria for composing graph transformation rules and (2) presenting an automatic procedure to compose such rules into one. Section 4 elaborates on how M2M transformation languages can be mapped to graph transformations. In Section 5, we illustrate the composition approach in the context of the evolution of the Enterprise Java Beans (EJB) language, transforming UML models into EJB 2.0 models and then to EJB 3.0 models. Section 6 is dedicated to the related work and we conclude in Section 7.

2 Transformation Composition

In this section, we define a composition operator to precisely specify the meaning of a transformation composition. This operation is applied in the context of a chain of model transformations as defined below.

Definition 1 (Transformation chain). *Let* $\mathbf{T_n} = \langle T_1, T_2, \ldots, T_n \rangle_{n \in \mathbb{N}}$ *be an ordered sequence of transformations where each* T_i *defines a mapping from a meta-model* $\mathfrak{M}_i$ *to a different meta-model* $\mathfrak{M}_{i+1}$. *We denote such a transformation chain as* $\mathfrak{M}_1 \stackrel{T_1}{\to} \mathfrak{M}_2 \stackrel{T_2}{\to} \mathfrak{M}_3 \stackrel{T_3}{\to} \ldots \stackrel{T_n}{\to} \mathfrak{M}_{n+1}$. *Note that we enforce that all the meta-models involved in the chain* $\mathbf{T_n}$ *be different from one another, i.e., each transformation must be* exogenous *[8].*

We call $\mathfrak{M}_i$ the domain of T_i and $\mathfrak{M}_{i+1}$ its co-domain. The transformation is applied on a model m_i conforming to its meta-model $\mathfrak{M}_i$ and results in a new model $m_{i+1} = T_i(m_i)$ whose meta-model is $\mathfrak{M}_{i+1}$. Note that transformations, transformation rules, as well as the pre- and post-condition patterns of the rules are also considered as models conforming to their respective meta-models [7].

The presented approach assumes that each transformation in the chain is specified using algebraic graph transformation rules. The models involved are represented as graph objects in the category of typed attributed graphs as defined in [4]. In the remainder of the paper, a model m and its *element graph*

G will be used interchangeably. The typed attributed graph G consists of a set of nodes $V(G)$ and edges $E(G)$, where each node conforms to a specific node type in a type graph (representing $\mathfrak{M}$, the meta-model of m) and can hold attribute values. We however require that graph edges be partitioned in two sets $E(G) = E_m(G) \cup \Lambda(G)$, distinguishing *trace edges* $\Lambda(G)$ from the edges $E_m(G)$ conforming to those defined in the type graph. A trace edge represents a traceability link connecting any two nodes regardless of their type. While a transformation is applied, traceability links are created such that any newly created element must have at least a traceability link[1].

Definition 2 (Transformation composition). *Let T_1 and T_2 be two consecutive transformations in a transformation chain such that $\mathfrak{M}_1 \xrightarrow{T_1} \mathfrak{M}_2 \xrightarrow{T_2} \mathfrak{M}_3$. We denote $T' = T_2 \bullet T_1$ the composed transformation of T_1 with T_2, following the composition operator $\bullet$ which satisfies the sequence, elimination, and transitivity criteria as defined below.*

We describe the application criteria of the composition operator given an arbitrary input model m_1 for T_1, $m_2 = T_1(m_1)$, and $m_3 = T_2(m_2)$, where m_1, m_2, and m_3 conform to $\mathfrak{M}_1, \mathfrak{M}_2$, and $\mathfrak{M}_3$ respectively. We denote $m' = T_2 \bullet T_1(m_1)$ be the resulting model after the composition. In the case where traceability links are created explicitly in the rules, $\hat{m}$ represents the graph model isomorphic to m without any trace edge.

Sequence. There shall exist three injective graph morphisms $(seq_i)_{i=(1,2,3)}$ that must be defined as: $seq_1 : m_1 \to m'$, $seq_2 : \hat{m}_3 - \hat{m}_2 - \hat{m}_1 \to m'$, and $seq_3 : \hat{m}' \to m_3$. seq_1 ensures that the input model is preserved. seq_2 ensures that all the elements from $\mathfrak{M}_3$ produced by T_2 are present in m'. seq_3 ensures that m' contains no other elements than those found in m_3.

Elimination. There should not be any morphism $elem : m_2 - \hat{m}_1 \to m'$. That is, m' shall not contain any occurrence of an element from $\mathfrak{M}_2$. Moreover, no traceability links involving elements from $\mathfrak{M}_2$ shall be present.

Transitivity. We denote by λ_{ij} a traceability link (trace edge) between an element from m_i and an element from m_j. The following predicate must hold: $\exists \lambda_{12} \in \Lambda(m_3) \wedge \exists \lambda_{23} \in \Lambda(m_3) \Rightarrow \exists \lambda_{13} \in \Lambda(m')$. This ensures the transitive closure of traceability links, *i.e.*, for any instance element of $\mathfrak{M}_2$ in m_3, if it is connected through trace edges to both an instance element of $\mathfrak{M}_1$ *and* an instance element of $\mathfrak{M}_3$, then m' must have a trace edge between the latter two instance elements.

The sequence criterion ensures soundness and completeness of the composition operator. The elimination criterion ensures that the resulting transformation is independent from any intermediate meta-model. Finally, the transitivity criterion ensures that traceability links correctly map the source and target model elements of the composed transformation T'. The transformation composition definition is generalized to an arbitrary number of transformations as follows:

---

[1] Traceability links can be created implicitly such as in [6]. Otherwise, their creation must be explicitly specified in the rules.

Definition 3 (Transformation chain composition). *Given the chain* $\mathbf{T_n} = \langle T_1, T_2, \ldots, T_n \rangle_{n \in \mathbb{N}}$, *the composed transformation of* $\mathbf{T_n}$ *is a transformation* $T' = T_n \bullet (T_{n-1} \bullet \ldots (T_3 \bullet (T_2 \bullet T_1)) \ldots) \equiv T_n \bullet T_{n-1} \bullet \ldots \bullet T_3 \bullet T_2 \bullet T_1$.

3 Rule Composition

The task of composing two arbitrary transformations is a very complex problem. That is because the choice of which rule from one transformation to compose with a rule from the other transformation often depends on the domain of application. For the scope of this paper, we concentrate on applying the composition operation on two graph transformation rules. In this section, we provide a procedure for composing two individual rules into a single one such that the sequence, elimination, and transitivity criteria are satisfied.

3.1 Criteria for Rule Composability

In the following, we assume that rewriting rules or productions are defined as presented in [4]. This means that a rule $p = (L \leftarrow K \rightarrow R)$ consists of three objects in the category of typed attributed graphs: the left hand side (L), the interface K, and the right hand side (R) objects respectively. In this paper, we assume that each transformation transforms an instance of one metamodel into an instance of another, therefore, the objects L, K, and R may contain elements from both the source and the target metamodel of the current transformation.

To apply the composition operator on two individual rules, we assume that each of the transformations involved consists of a single rule for sake of completeness: $T_1 = \{r_1\}$ and $T_2 = \{r_2\}$. The procedure assumes that the rules r_1 and r_2 are monotonically increasing, *i.e.*, they can only create new elements and/or modify attribute values. Moreover, all traceability links created during the application of T_1 and T_2 shall be preserved. The output of the composition procedure is a new transformation $T_3 = T_2 \bullet T_1 = \{r_2\} \bullet \{r_1\} = \{r_3\}$ consisting of a single rule. The following proposition specifies the necessary condition for the composition procedure to satisfy Definition 2.

Proposition 1 (Composability condition). *Two rules $r_1 = L_1 \leftarrow K_1 \rightarrow R_1$ and $r_2 = L_2 \leftarrow K_2 \rightarrow R_2$ satisfy the composability condition if there exists a partial morphism $n : L_2 \rightarrow R_1$ such that: (i) the domain of n is a subgraph of L_2, which consists of all the elements that is from $\mathfrak{M}_2$, (ii) the co-domain of n is a subgraph of R_1 consisting of elements only from $\mathfrak{M}_2$, (iii) the mapping from the domain to the co-domain of n is a total injective morphism.*

The formal definition of the traditional composition of two sequential rewriting rules is described in [4], this composition is called the *E*-concurrent production. The definition states that given two rules p_1 and p_2, they can be composed into a new rule $p = (L, K, R)$. Informally, the p is composed along a new graph object E, which is produced by jointly surjective morphisms from R_1—the right-hand side (RHS) of p_1—and L_2—the left-hand side (LHS) of p_2. The application of the new rule is equal with the sequential application of the two original rules.

However, there are often more than one possible composition of the rules, because of the non-determinism of the matches.

To satisfy the elimination and transitivity criteria of Definition 2, the subprocedure in Algorithm 1 is required. Given a model m, the procedure performs two runs over the trace edges in m. In the first run (lines 1 to 7), it first looks for a trace edge λ_{12} linking an element conforming to $\mathfrak{M}_1$, say e_1, to an element conforming to $\mathfrak{M}_2$, say e_2 and another trace edge λ_{23} linking e_2 to an element conforming to $\mathfrak{M}_3$, say e_3. It then creates the transitive trace edge λ_{13}, removes the two other traceability edges as well as e_2. In the second run, the elimination procedure looks for all remaining trace links involving $\mathfrak{M}_1$ and $\mathfrak{M}_2$ elements and removes them from m. Note that there cannot be any trace edge in the form λ_{23} remaining after the first run, since any element from $\mathfrak{M}_2$ must be linked to an element from $\mathfrak{M}_1$ by construction. Therefore after the elimination procedure terminates, the only remaining trace edges in m link elements from $\mathfrak{M}_1$ to elements from $\mathfrak{M}_3$.

Algorithm 1. eliminate(m)

1: **for all** $\lambda_{12}, \lambda_{23} \in \Lambda(m)$ **do**
2:    **if** $trg(\lambda_{12}) = src(\lambda_{23})$ **then**
3:       create λ_{13} such that $src(\lambda_{13}) = src(\lambda_{12})$ and $trg(\lambda_{13}) = trg(\lambda_{23})$
4:       $\Lambda(m) \leftarrow \Lambda(m) \cup \{\lambda_{13}\} - \{\lambda_{12}, \lambda_{23}\}$
5:       $V(m) \leftarrow V(m) - \{trg(\lambda_{12})\}$
6:    **end if**
7: **end for**
8: **for all** $\lambda_{12} \in \Lambda(m)$ **do**
9:    $\Lambda(m) \leftarrow \Lambda(m) - \{\lambda_{12}\}$
10:    $V(m) \leftarrow V(m) - \{trg(\lambda_{12})\}$
11: **end for**

3.2 Composition Procedure

Let $r_1 = L_1 \leftarrow K_1 \rightarrow R_1$ and $r_2 = L_2 \leftarrow K_2 \rightarrow R_2$ be two rules that satisfy the *composability condition* of Proposition 1. We want to produce the composite rule r_3 such that $\{r_3\} = \{r_2\} \bullet \{r_1\}$ as defined in Section 2.

Algorithm 2 produces the set of all possible compositions of r_1 and r_2, based on the E-based composition where $E = R_1$. r_2 is extended with a negative application condition (NAC) corresponding to its RHS, which results in r'_2. This ensures that r_2 is only applied once on every match found in E. It is worth noting that there can be different R_3's even if r'_2 is applied exhaustively on E, if the order of application affects the result.

Before analyzing the algorithm, we demonstrate its operation on the composition of two simple rules R_1 and R_2 presented in Figure 1. Let R'_2 be rule R_2 extended by the NAC which consists of the RHS of R_2. By Algorithm 2, the E graph is RHS of R_1. If we modify R_1 by applying R'_2 once on its RHS, we get rule R. However, we apply R'_2 exhaustively, therefore, RHS of R is modified again, which results in rule R'. Note that there are no other possible matches,

Algorithm 2. compose(r_1, r_2)

1: $K_3 \leftarrow R_1$
2: $L_3 \leftarrow$ eliminate(L_1)
3: $R \leftarrow \phi$
4: $r'_2 \leftarrow r_2$ extended with R_2 as a NAC, if not present
5: **repeat**
6:     $R_3 \leftarrow$ apply r'_2 exhaustively on E
7:     eliminate(R_3)
8:     $R \leftarrow R \cup \{(L_3, K_3, R_3)\}$
9: **until** all application sequences of r'_2 have been exhausted on E
10: **return** R

because of the NAC in R'_2. The next step is the application of the elimination algorithm, which performs the transitive closure on the trace edges. RHS of R' is eliminated, which results in rule R''.

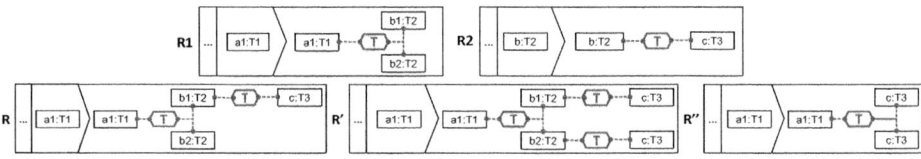

Fig. 1. Example for rule composition

The lemmas below validate the composition procedure. Lemma 1 ensures that the procedure will output all possible composed rules r_3 and Lemma 2 ensures its correctness.

Lemma 1. *If r_1 and r_2 satisfy the composability condition, then compose(r_1, r_2) outputs all compositions of r_1 and r_2 such that the exhaustive application of compose(r_1, r_2) is equivalent to the composition of r_1 and r_2 using the composition operator of Definition 2.*

Proof. Assume that there is a possible E-based composition $r = L \leftarrow K \rightarrow R$ such that the E-graph $E \neq R_1$. This implies that $\exists e \in E : e \notin R_1$ where e can be any type of element in the graph. E is produced by jointly surjective morphisms from R_1 and L_2; thus $e \in L_2$. Moreover, e is an element conforming to $\mathfrak{M}_2$ as it is the domain of r_2. However $e \notin R_1$, which implies that $e \in L$, according to the definition of the E-concurrent production. But L cannot contain elements from $\mathfrak{M}_2$ because if it did, the input model would contain elements conforming to $\mathfrak{M}_2$, which is a contradiction.

Lemma 2. *The result of the composition procedure $\{r_3\} = \{r_2\} \bullet \{r_1\}$ satisfies Definition 2.*

Proof. Assume that a model m_1 is processed by the transformations T_1 and T_2 through a possible traditional E-based composition r'_3 of the rules r_1 and r_2.

Let r_3 be a rule computed by applying the elimination procedure on the LHS, RHS, and interface graph of r_3'. Let $T_3 = \{r_3\}$, $m_2 = T_1(m_1)$, $m_3 = T_2(m_2)$, and $m' = T_3(m_1)$. We shall now prove that T_3 satisfies the sequence, elimination, and transitivity criteria.

- *Sequence Criterion:* $\exists seq_1 : m_1 \to m'$, because $L_3 = K_3$ and hence the input model m_1 is not modified. $\exists seq_2 : \hat{m}_3 - \hat{m}_2 - \hat{m}_1 \to m'$ as no elements from r_3' have been deleted during the elimination that was performed to produce r_3. Moreover, $\exists seq_3 : \hat{m'} \to m_3$ since R_3 contains elements conforming to $\mathfrak{M}_3$ because of the exhaustive application of r_2'.
- *Elimination Criterion:* m' does not contain any element from $\mathfrak{M}_2$ since applying the elimination procedure on r_3' ensures that all elements from the intermediate meta-model are removed from it.
- The *Transitivity Criterion* is also satisfied because the elimination procedure generates all the traceability links required by the condition.

When NACs come into play in r_1 or r_2, we distinguish the following case: (i) If there is a NAC in r_1 and it corresponds to R_1, then we extend each composite rule r_3 with a NAC corresponding to R_3. (ii) If there is a NAC in r_2 and it corresponds to R_2, then it is taken into account when applying r_2 to E. (iii) Any other NAC is not considered in the presented procedure.

4 From ATL to Graph Transformations

M2M transformations are typically defined with dedicated M2M languages. Especially, ATL has been successfully applied and represents the de-facto standard transformation language in Eclipse. Before presenting a case study of composing ATL transformations by applying the presented composition approach, we briefly introduce ATL and how it is mapped to graph transformations.

4.1 ATL By-Example

As running example for the rest of this paper, a transformation between UML and EJB is used. Simplified versions of the meta-models and of the transformation T_1 are depicted in Fig. 2 and List. 1, respectively. T_1 transforms Packages into EJBArchives and Classes into either SessionBeans or EntityBeans, depending on the isPersistent attribute, as well as into Interfaces. Furthermore for each Bean, an Entry in the DeploymentDescriptor is generated.

ATL transformations are defined as Modules (cf. line 1 in List. 1) comprising MatchedRules (cf. rule keyword). A MatchedRule is automatically executed by the transformation engine in case its InPattern (cf. from keyword) matches. This requires that for each InPatternElement a suitable element in the input model is found and that an optional filter condition (cf. e.g., line 14) is fulfilled. If a complete match for the InPattern is found, the OutPattern (cf. to keyword) is executed which results in creating an object in the output model for each OutPatternElement. Properties of the created objects are set as described by the Bindings of the OutPatternElements (cf. assignment operator

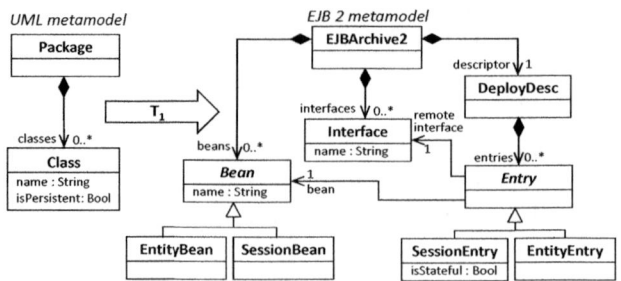

Fig. 2. Meta-models of the transformation T_1

<-). Bindings range from simple value assignments (cf. line 16) over setting links between created objects (cf. line 17) to complex assignments which need to query objects created by other rules by using resolveTemp (cf. line 7). For instance, resolveTemp is used to query EntityBeans created in rule R2 for setting the reference beans in rule R1. The input parameter for resolveTemp is a source element for which the generated output elements are retrieved via the implicitly created trace model. If several objects are generated for one input element, the variable name is used for retrieving the desired output elements.

Listing 1. T_1 defined in ATL

```
 1:  module T1;
 2:  create OUT : EJB2 from IN : UML;
 3:
 4:  rule R1 {
 5:    from p : UML!Package
 6:    to a : EJB2!EJBArchive(
 7:      beans <- p.classes -> collect(c|thisModule.resolveTemp(c, 'b')),
 8:      interfaces <- p.classes -> collect(c|thisModule.resolveTemp(c, 'i')) ),
 9:    dd : EJB2!DeploymentDescriptor(
10:      entries <- p.classes -> collect(c|thisModule.resolveTemp(c, 'e')) )
11:  }
12:
13:  rule R2 {
14:    from c : UML!Class (c.isPersistent = 'true')
15:    to b : EJB2!EntityBean(
16:      name <- c.name,
17:      entry <- e ),
18:    i : EJB2!Interfaces(
19:      name <- c.name ),
20:    e : EJB2!EntityEntry(
21:      bean <- b,
22:      remoteInterface <- i )
23:  }
24:
25:  rule R3 --analogous to R2, but different filter (c.isPersistent='false')
```

4.2 Mapping ATL to Graph Transformation

After briefly introducing the main concepts of ATL, we proceed with describing how we map ATL to graph transformations. In particular, we employ EMF Tiger as reference language for graph transformations. To adhere to the behaviour of ATL, the resulting graph transformation rules have to ensure the following properties which also comply to the criteria for rule composition:

- *Matchable Elements*: ATL is designed as a M2M transformation language meaning that the target model is completely rebuilt from the source model. Thus, the only elements that can be matched by a rule are elements of the source model and elements of the target model already created by previous rule applications. The latter are only accessible via trace links.
- *Creation and Deletion of Elements*: In ATL the source model is considered as read-only, thus elements of this model may not be altered. Furthermore, elements of the target model are created by executing the transformation, but once created, they can no longer be deleted by the transformation.
- *Trace Model*: For each rule execution, a trace element is generated linking all matched source elements to all generated target elements. Other transformation rules can build on this trace information, *e.g.*, for adding links to already created target elements.
- *Unique Matching*: Each transformation rule can only match once for a given set of elements. Thus, to ensure this behaviour in the graph transformation rules, each rule comprises a NAC corresponding to the RHS of the rule.

Fig. 3 shows the generated graph transformation for the ATL transformation depicted in List. 1. We now elaborate on how the rules are generated.

Rule R1. The LHS is generated from the InPattern, whereas each InPatternElement is transformed into an Object. For this rule, only one Object of type Package is generated. The same is done for generating the first part of the RHS from the OutPattern. In addition, the Objects in the LHS should not be deleted when executing the rule, thus

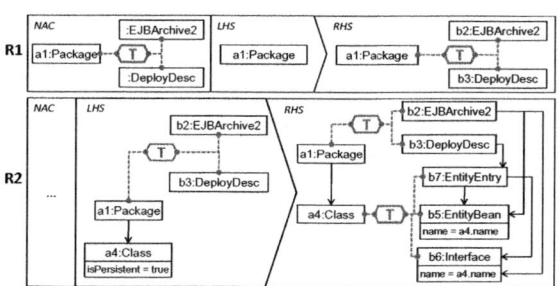

Fig. 3. Graph transformation for T_1

they have to be duplicated and assigned to the RHS. Furthermore, a TraceLink has to be explicitly declared in the RHS which links the input elements with the output elements. The transformation of the resolveTemp Bindings has to be postponed, because the referred elements are created by the rules R1 and R2. Finally, the NAC is set equal to the RHS of the rule for ensuring the unique matching constraint.

Rule R2. The generation of the LHS, RHS, and NAC is analogous to the R1. Please note that due to space limitations, the NACs are no longer shown. In addition, the property isPersistent of Class has to be set to the Constant 'true' according to the filter condition of the MatchedRule. The Bindings for setting the names of EntityBeans and Interfaces have to be translated into Variables which are assigned in the LHS and queried in the RHS. The elements created by this rule are referenced by R1 using resolveTemp, e.g., consider the binding for the beans reference. This means that in the resulting graph transformation, the links from the EJBArchive2 has to be set to the produced EntityBeans. This is ensured by merging the RHS of R1 (the *referring* rule) into the LHS and RHS of R2 (the *producer* rule). By this, R2 contains elements of the referring rule R1 for setting additional links to already produced elements of R1.

Rule R3. Analogues to R2 (cf. Fig. 5-T_1 for the resulting rule specification). Table 1 summarizes the mappings between ATL and EMF Tiger concepts.

Table 1. Mapping from ATL to EMF Tiger

ATL Concept	EMF Tiger Concept
Module	Transformation
MatchedRule	Rule
InPattern	LHS, RHS, Mapping(LHS,RHS), NAC
InPatternElement	Object
Filter	Setting Properties of Objects
OutPattern	RHS, NAC
OutPatternElement	Object
Binding:	
- VarExp	Link
- [String|Bool|Int]Exp	Constant
- NavigationOrAttributeExp	Variable, LHS Property, RHS Property
- ResolveTemp	Merging the RHS of Referring Rule into Producer Rule
Implicit Trace Model	Explicit Trace Link, NAC (same as RHS)

5 Application

We now apply the composition approach presented in Section 3 in the following scenario. A company has developed the transformation T_1 explained in the previous section for transforming UML class diagrams to EJB 2.0. However, after some time, the company decided to use EJB 3.0 due to several simplifications of the new version of the standard. In particular, the DeploymentDescriptor concept is no longer used in EJB 3.0, because no additional XML configuration files for Beans are required. Instead, a light-weight approach for configuring Beans directly in the Java code through Annotations is supported by EJB 3.0. Thus, they developed a transformation T_2 for migrating existing EJB 2.0 models to EJB 3.0 models (cf. Fig. 5). However, to support the generation of new EJB 3.0 models from UML class diagrams, they would have to implement a dedicated transformation T_3, if applying the transformation chain $\langle T_1, T_2 \rangle$ is undesired. Reasons for this may be related to performance issues for ensuring rapid generation of EJB 3.0 models. Also, direct traceability between UML models and EJB 3.0 models is desired since EJB 2.0 instances would become obsolete.

5.1 Composing the Transformations

We now apply the composition procedure to our example by composing the rules of T_1 with those of T_2. Since the composition procedure is applied on individual rules, we have implemented a program in Java that first detects which combinations of rules from T_1 can be composed with rules from T_2, based on Proposition 1. The iteration over the rules of T_2 follows the order shown in the

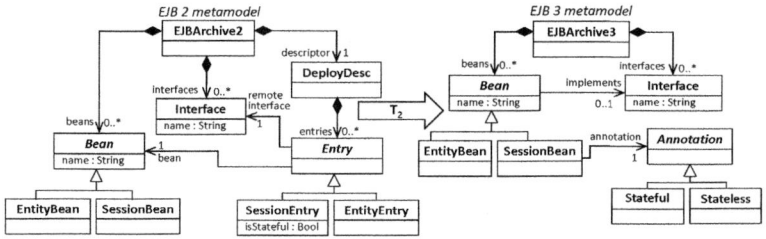

Fig. 4. Evolution of the EJB metamodel

upper left of Fig. 5. However, this may lead to several possible valid combinations of rules. The user then selects the most appropriate combination according to his knowledge of UML class diagrams and EJB. Then, the composition procedure is applied on these two rules. The result, *i.e.*, the transformation T_3, is shown at the bottom of Fig. 5.

***Composing* $T_2 : R_1$.** $T_2 : R_1$ is composable with $T_1 : R_1$, $T_1 : R_2$, and with $T_1 : R_3$ according to the composability condition. However, due to the fact that $T_1 : R_2$ and $T_1 : R_3$ both contain a subgraph of the LHS of $T_2 : R_1$ in both their LHS and RHS, $T_1 : R_1$ seems to be more appropriate for composition. The reason is that $T_1 : R_1$ actually generates the input elements for $T_2 : R_1$ in contrast to the other two rules which only check for the existence of these elements. The composite rule $T_3 : R_1$ is constructed by composing $T_1 : R_1$ and $T_2 : R_1$ as follows. The LHS of $T_3 : R_1$ remains the same as the one for $T_1 : R_1$. Then to create the RHS of $T_3 : R_1$, the composition procedure connects an EJBArchive3 element to the Package element of $T_1 : R_1$ via a trace edge. Then the elimination procedure removes both the EJBArchive2 and DeployDesc elements from the result. Finally a trace edge connecting the Package element to the EJBArchive3 is created. $T_3 : R_1$ also comprises a NAC corresponding to its RHS since $T_1 : R_1$ did have a NAC corresponding to its own RHS. For computing this NAC, we are currently not using a composition procedure. Instead we just copy the elements of the RHS into the NAC to ensure the aforementioned unique rule matching.

***Composing* $T_2 : R_2$.** $T_2 : R_2$ is only composable with $T_1 : R_2$ as it is the only rule of T_1 that has a RHS matchable by the LHS of $T_2 : R_2$. The two rules are thus composed in the same way as described in the previous case. In addition, we now have to compose not only the graph patterns but also the attribute value computations. For example, consider the assignment name = c4.name in element d6:EntityBean of the RHS of $T_2 : R_2$. It cannot be copied as is since the assignment refers to an element of the EJB 2.0 meta-model. In this example, we only have simple value assignments without using more complex functions. For setting the attribute values in the composed transformation rule, we have to find out for each attribute value assignment in T_2, how the value is actually computed in T_1. In our example, we can easily find out that the name attribute of the element c4 in $T_2 : R_2$ is actually calculated by using the name attribute value of the element a4. Thus, only this assignment has to be used in the composed

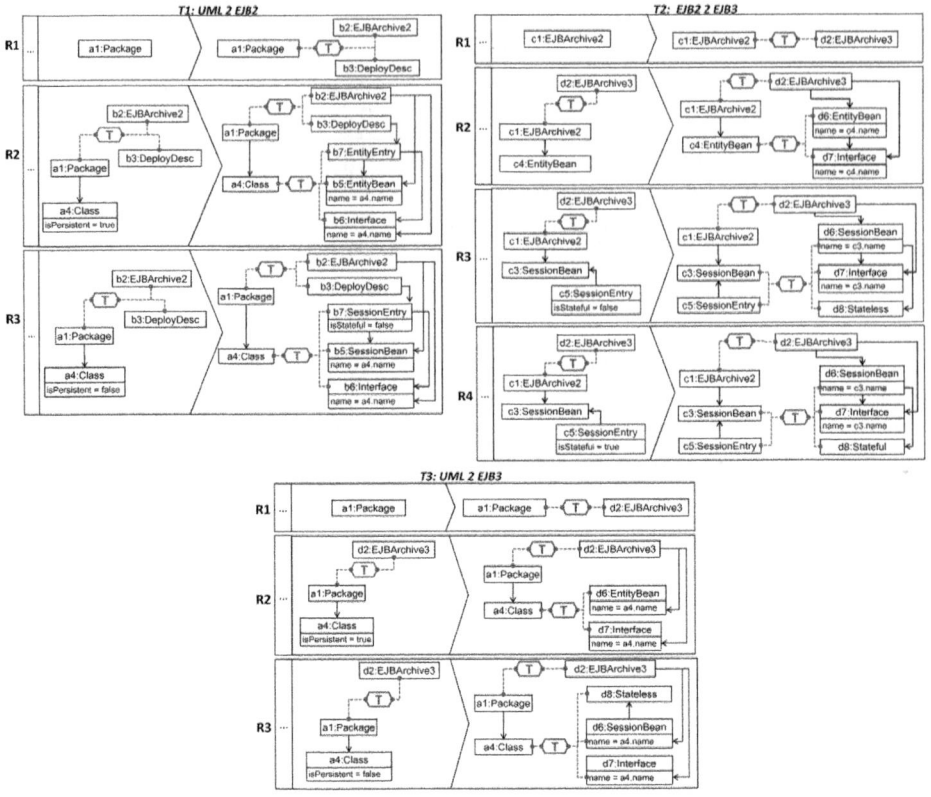

Fig. 5. Transformations of the case study

transformation rule. Finally, the elimination procedure applied on the LHS of $T_3 : R_2$ not only deletes the DeployDesc element from the RHS of $T_3 : R_2$ (as in the previous case), but also from the LHS of $T_3 : R_2$.

Composing $\mathbf{T_2 : R_3}$. $T_2 : R_3$ is only composable with $T_1 : R_3$. In this case, in addition to composing the nodes and edges of the pattern, we also consider the attribute value condition isStateful = false of the LHS of $T_2 : R_3$. However, the rest of the composition is analogous to the previous case.

Composing $\mathbf{T_2 : R_4}$. $T_2 : R_4$ is not composable with any rule of T_1.

5.2 Implementation

The presented composition procedure allows to compose T_1 and T_2 nearly automatically. The transformation T_3 can be entirely produced with the help of some heuristics to further filter out meaningful composition possibilities (*e.g.,* reasoning about if a rule generates the elements or uses them only as context, as discussed in the first composition). Furthermore, some specific extensions such as attribute value assignments as well as constraints are necessary in the future to allow for a higher automation degree. The user chooses two transformations to compose. If they are composable, the procedure outputs the composite rule. In the case where there are more than one possibility, the user can interactively select the most appropriate composition. The implementation relies on a higher-order transformation implemented in Java. The first step is the generation of templates out of the LHS of the rules from T_2. These templates are then matched against the RHS of the rules from T_1. This match model is the basis for further composition computations. In a second step, the rules of T_1 are rewritten according to the presented composition procedure. In addition, we have implemented the mentioned heuristic for filtering the composition possibilities and support simple attribute value assignments. After the composition computation has finished, the resulting transformation is serialized as T_3 expressed again as an EMF Tiger transformation.

6 Related Work

In this section, we outline how others have investigated in transformation composition: in graph transformation theory, in model-driven engineering, and more widely in the field of data engineering.

Composition of Algebraic Graph Transformations. As mentioned in Section 3.2, a formal definition for the composition of two graph transformation rules was already proposed in [4], by creating the so-called E-concurrent rule. However, the authors do not explicitly precise how this rule is constructed. In the current paper, we propose a systematic algorithm to (1) detect if two rules are composable and (2) explicitly give the steps on how to construct the E-concurrent rule. Also, the scope of the definitions and algorithms of this paper are directly applicable in model-driven frameworks.

Composition of Model Transformations. In the latest years, the sequential composition of model transformations has been an active research field. Several approaches for modelling transformation chains [10,13,5,12] have been proposed. Most of them are based on UML Activity Diagrams which orchestrate several transformations to achieve a larger goal. However, none of these approaches tries to compute new transformations out of existing transformations as done in this paper.

In [11], the authors present an approach for composing rules within one transformation: the so called *internal composition*. For example, considering a transformation from UML class diagrams to Java, two rules can be composed when they both transform UML classes to Java classes with different mapping details. In [14], Wagelaar presents sophisticated internal composition techniques for ATL and QVT [9] in order to improve the design of model transformations. Since these approaches focus on internal composition only, they do not discuss the computation of the transitive transformation from two given transformations.

In [3], the compositionality of model transformations is addressed. By compositionality the authors do not mean *sequential composition* as meant in this paper, but they are interested in the *spatial composition* when mapping a model to its semantic domain. Compositionality is guaranteed by a transformation T if the execution of T produces a set of semantic expressions (instances of the semantic domain) such that their composition represents the semantics of the whole model.

In summary, to our best knowledge no comparable approach to ours exists in the field of model-driven engineering for composing two transformations into the transitive transformation.

Composition in Model Management. In the area of data engineering, model management [2] has gained much interest during the last decade. Model management stands for the idea of dealing with evolution in data engineering by using models (*i.e.,* schemas and mappings between them) and operators for producing new models out of existing ones. They define schema operators, such as *diff* and *merge*, as well as mapping operators, such as *inverse* and *compose*. The goal of the *compose* operator is similar to our model transformation composition approach. However, its realization is quite different (cf. [1] and [15]). First, in data engineering, only relational and hierarchical schemas are considered in contrast to object-oriented meta-models, which are the basis for the composition approach of this paper. Second, in data engineering, pre-defined relational operators (*e.g., project, select,* and *join*) are used for describing mappings between schemas. In contrast, our approach is built on graph transformations, which is a significantly different paradigm for describing mappings between object-oriented meta-models.

7 Conclusion and Future Work

In this paper, we provide a mechanism for composing individual rules from a transformation chain. This composition allows for the creation of a new transformation involving only the initial and target meta-models. Although some assumptions must be made on the syntax of rules, the composition procedure is general enough in the sense that it is independent from the input model. The presented approach is based on the syntactic composition of the rules. Extending the procedure to the transformation level requires to take into account the semantics of the chain of transformations.

The main benefits of our approach are: (1) it is possible to reduce the complexity of transformation chains by eliminating unnecessary transformation steps, (2) if there is traceability from m_1 to m_2 and from m_2 to m_3, we are able to provide traceability from m_1 to m_3, and (3) our approach seems to be perfectly suited in metamodel evolution scenarios where the target metamodel evolves. If there is already an instance migration transformation from the initial target metamodel version to the new target metamodel version, this migration transformation may be composed with the transformation between the source and the initial target metamodel in order to ensure transformation co-evolution.

For future work, a number of open issues still remain. In the presented example, we have only considered the core part of ATL which is comparable to the core of other M2M transformation approaches, such as QVT-Relations [9]. In particular, we did not focus on transformations requiring an explicit rule scheduler (*e.g.*, with a control flow). Also, several other features of ATL should be supported, such as OCL queries and *called rules* (rules that are not automatically executed by the transformation engine but that have to be explicitly invoked in the transformation). Furthermore, our example only considers simple attribute value assignments in the rules. However, before considering more complex attribute manipulations in the composition, one should first think of how to map them to graph transformations in order to provide a theoretical basis for extending the composition procedure. Moreover, dealing with arbitrary OCL expressions when composing transformations is challenging and should certainly form a composition topic on its own. Finally, we have to provide tool support for transforming the composed transformations, expressed as graph transformations, back to ATL transformations. In this context, we have planed to migrate our current prototype to a bi-directional model transformation formalism.

References

1. Bernstein, P.A., Green, T.J., Melnik, S., Nash, A.: Implementing mapping composition. VLDB J. 17(2), 333–353 (2008)
2. Bernstein, P.A., Melnik, S.: Model management 2.0: manipulating richer mappings. In: Int. Conf. on Management of Data (2007)
3. Bisztray, D., Heckel, R., Ehrig, H.: Compositionality of model transformations. In: ENTCS, vol. 236, pp. 5–19 (2009)
4. Ehrig, H., Ehrig, K., Prange, U., Taentzer, G.: Fundamentals of Algebraic Graph Transformation. In: EATCS, Springer, Heidelberg (2006)
5. Fabro, M.D.D., Albert, P., Bézivin, J., Jouault, F.: Achieving rule interoperability using chains of model transformations. In: Int. Conf. on Theory and Practice of Model Transformations (2009)
6. Jouault, F., Kurtev, I.: Transforming models with ATL. In: Model Transformation in Practice Workshop (2006)
7. Kühne, T., Mezei, G., Syriani, E., Vangheluwe, H., Wimmer, M.: Explicit transformation modeling. In: MoDELS 2009 Workshops (2010)
8. Mens, T., Van Gorp, P.: A taxonomy of model transformation. In: GraMoT 2005, Tallinn (Estonia). ENTCS, vol. 152, pp. 125–142 (March 2006)
9. Object Management Group. Meta Object Facility 2.0 Query/View/Transformation Specification (April 2008)
10. Oldevik, J.: Transformation composition modelling framework. In: Int. Conf. on Distributed Applications and Interoperable Systems (2005)
11. Pons, C., Giandini, R., Perez, G., Baum, G.: An algebraic approach for composing model transformations in QVT. In: Int. Workshop on Software Language Engineering (2008)
12. Rivera, J.E., Ruiz-Gonzalez, D., Lopez-Romero, F., Bautista, J., Vallecillo, A.: Orchestrating ATL model transformations. In: MtATL Workshop (2009)
13. Vanhooff, B., Baelen, S.V., Hovsepyan, A., Joosen, W., Berbers, Y.: Towards a transformation chain modeling language. In: Vassiliadis, S., Wong, S., Hämäläinen, T.D. (eds.) SAMOS 2006. LNCS, vol. 4017, pp. 39–48. Springer, Heidelberg (2006)
14. Wagelaar, D.: Composition techniques for rule-based model transformation languages. In: Int. Conf. on Theory and Practice of Model Transformations (2008)
15. Yu, C., Popa, L.: Semantic adaptation of schema mappings when schemas evolve. In: Int. Conf. on Very Large Data Bases (2005)

The 3rd International Workshop on Non-functional System Properties in Domain Specific Modeling Languages (NFPinDSML2010)

Marko Bošković[1], Daniela Cancila[2], Claus Pahl[3], and Bernhard Schätz[4]

[1] SCIS, Athabasca University, Canada
marko.boskovic@athabascau.ca
[2] Atego, Paris Office, France
daniela.cancila@atego.com
[3] School of Computing, Dublin City University, Ireland
claus.pahl@computing.dcu.ie
[4] fortiss GmbH, Germany
schaetz@fortiss.org

Abstract. The NFPinDSML2010 is the 3rd issue in the series of workshops discussing a challenging issue: principles and methods of integrating estimation and evaluation of Non-functional System Properties (NFP), in Model-driven Engineering (MDE) with Domain Specific Modeling Languages (DSML). Particularly, NFPinDSML2010 topic was integration of certification and compliance in MDE.

1 Introduction

In software engineering meeting non-functional system requirements (NFR), such as safety, reliability, timeliness and so on, has been recognized as important as meeting functional. Model Driven Engineering (MDE) is emerging as a major paradigm for engineering software systems, and generally, advocates use of models and transformations in all phases of software engineering process.

In MDE, models are typically specified in Domain Specific Modeling Languages (DSMLs), languages dedicated to engineering systems of particular domain. In order to provide support for evaluating meeting of non-functional system properties, DSMLs need to be complemented by formal languages for estimation and evaluation languages. Similarly to DSMLs, for particular NFPs exist standardized languages. Due to large variety of DSMLs and NFPs that need to be estimated and evaluated, and used formalisms, there is an need for exploring principles of their synergies. NFPinDSML is a workshop that discusses such topic. Particularly, NFPinDSML2010 has explored integration of certification and compliance in MDE.

2 The Workshop Program

NFPinDSML2010 has consisted of two invited talks, one paper presentation session, and one interactive panel session with panelists from the domains of certification and compliance.

2.1 The Morning Workshop Part

The morning workshop part consisted of two sessions. The first session was an invited talk by Prof. Richard Paige from the University of York, United Kingdom. In his talk, he he has introduced a model-driven perspective that goes beyond software engineering and provides support for organizational problem solving. Particularly, for complex and very-long term strategic decisions of large organizations. His initial results show that MDE techniques appear as very useful in supporting strategic decision making. However, there is still a need for thorough exploration.

The paper presentation session consisted of three presentations. Mauro Luigi Drago from the Politecnico di Milano, Italy, has presented $QVTR^2$ language. $QVTR^2$ is an extended QVT-Relations language, and facilitates keeping information about the design rationale in declarative transformations. For keeping the design rationale, $QVTR^2$ borrows variability modeling from the domain of Software Product Lines, and keeps alternatives as variation points of the transformation. With such a support, various techniques can be used to evaluate candidate solutions. Particularly, he was demonstrating performance optimization transformation.

Thomas Kuhn from the Fraunhofer Institute of Experimental Software Engineering, Keiserslautern, Germany, was the second presenter. He has introduced an approach for integration of Component Fault Tree analysis into the UML. Fault Tree Analysis is one of the major techniques for safety engineering. Embedding such formalism in standard languages for software development helps in automating software analysis and can significantly reduce the cost and effort for performing one. Thomas and his colleagues have extended the UML component diagrams with concepts for Component Fault Three modeling in the form of UML Profile.

The final presenter was Dominik Sojer from the Technical University Munich, Germany. Dominik's work was, similarly to Thomas' a safety engineering domain. He introduced an approach for propagation, transformation and refinement of safety requirements. The outcome of his work is a set of algorithms that support previously mentioned operations on safety requirements. These algorithms are implemented as FTOS tool for model driven development of fault-tolerant embedded systems.

The presentation session was ended with a mini panel. In the mini panel, the presenters were asked to discuss about potential of synergies of their work. All participants have seen a big potential in combining approaches for various analysis purposes. However, a deeper and more thorougher discussion is still needed.

2.2 The Afternoon Workshop Part

The afternoon workshop part consisted of a second invited talk and a highly interactive panel with three experienced researchers from the domains of certification and compliance.

Prof. Daniel Amyot from the University of Ottawa, Canada, was the second invited speaker and he has presented the use of User Requirements Notation (URN) for analyzing compliance. URN is a language for elicitation, modeling, analysis, specification and validation of requirements, standardized by ITU-T. In his talk he introduced the main elements of URN, and how these elements have been used for compliance in the health care domain. In final remarks of his talk, he outlines that URN appears as a competitive DSML for business process modeling and analysis. Furthermore, its capabilities also show as very valuable in measurement and monitoring of processes, compliances, and NFPs. URN also demonstrates a good potential for modeling process evolution.

The final session was an interactive panel session. The invited panelists were **Prof. Ketil Stolen** from SINTEF and Department of Informatics at the University of Oslo, Norway, **Dr. Mario Trapp** from the Fraunhofer Institute of Experimental Software Engineering, Keiserslautern, Germany, and **Prof. Daniel Amyot** from the University of Ottawa, Canada. **Ketil's** major area of research is security and enforcement of policies within trust management. He pointed out two major issues in dealing with compliance and security. One of them is difficulties in capturing natural language in some formalism, which is necessary for reasoning on policies and security. The second concern are modeling languages themselves. Particularly broadly used languages like UML which have a trace and not a trace set execution semantics. Such languages restrict enforcement of policies and security analysis. **Mario Trap's** background is safety critical and embedded systems. He has emphasized integration of standards in software engineering processes as one of the major concerns. Finally, **Daniel's** position was from the compliance perspective. In his talk, he pointed out that compliance also depends from the maturity of organization. Mature organization, usually have compliance integrated in the software engineering process, while not so mature ones do not. Furthermore, he concurred to Ketil on difficulties in capturing laws in some formalization because of their freeness to the interpretation. Finally, he concluded that languages should be small in order to have a simple learning curve. Ideally, lawyers should be modelers, but that implementation of that vision is still in infant phase.

3 Final Remarks

NFPinDSML2010 was the third successful edition in the series of workshops dealing with integration of NFP assurance and domain specific modeling languages. It gathered researchers discussing certification and compliance. All papers have been published at the CEUR workshop proceedings (http://www.CEUR-WS/Vol-642/). The workshop has also been well attended, having overall more than 35 participants.

The workshop is followed by a special issue of the Springer Computer Science — Research and Development (CSRD) journal. This is the second special issue on this topic. Two special issues in three years, and the attention that the workshop attracts clearly demonstrates its need. Furthermore, the number of research issues that have been identified during the previous three editions give a very promising future to this workshop.

Acknowledgments. This research was in part supported by Alberta Innovates – Technology Futures through the New Faculty Award program.

Integration of Component Fault Trees into the UML

Rasmus Adler[1], Dominik Domis[2], Kai Höfig[2], Sören Kemmann[1], Thomas Kuhn[1], Jean-Pascal Schwinn[3], and Mario Trapp[1]

[1] Fraunhofer IESE
{rasmus.adler,soeren.kemmann,thomas.kuhn,mario.trapp}@iese.fraunhofer.de
http://www.iese.fraunhofer.de

[2] University of Kaiserslautern, Computer Science Department
{dominik.domis,kai.hoefig}@cs.uni-kl.de
http://agse3.informatik.uni-kl.de

[3] Siemens AG, Corporate Research and Technologies
jean-pascal.schwinn@siemens.com

Abstract. Efficient safety analyses of complex software intensive embedded systems are still a challenging task. This article illustrates how model-driven development principles can be used in safety engineering to reduce cost and effort. To this end, the article shows how well accepted safety engineering approaches can be shifted to the level of model-driven development by integrating safety models into functional development models. Namely, we illustrate how UML profiles, model transformations, and techniques for multi language development can be used to seamlessly integrate component fault trees into the UML.

1 Introduction

Embedded systems are of crucial importance to our society. We recognize our dependence in the moments when these systems fail. Headlines in newspapers about plane crashes or car accidents show the tight coupling of advantages and dangerous disadvantages of these systems. Therefore, embedded systems development comes with a large responsibility. Particularly the development of safety critical systems is constrained by a series of legislative and normative regulations making safety to one of the most important non-functional properties of embedded systems. One of the main requirements is a sophisticated safety analysis of the system. Particularly in the case of software-intensive embedded systems, their complexity is rapidly increasing and extended analysis techniques are required that scale to the increasing system complexity. Model driven development is currently one of the key approaches to cope with increasing development complexity in general. Applying similar concepts to safety engineering is a promising approach to extend the advantages of model driven development to safety engineering activities. First, it makes safety engineering as a standalone subtask of system development more efficient. Second, and even more importantly, this is an essential step towards a holistic development approach closing the gap between functional development and safety engineering. This paper illustrates application of model driven design principles to safety analysis techniques in order to enable efficient analysis of complex systems. In contrast to other approaches, it is not our goal to extend existing development approaches with additional safety properties. Instead, we shift full-fledged, established, and well-accepted safety engineering approaches to the level of model-driven development and integrate them seamlessly to functional development. Safety meta models are seamlessly integrated into functional meta models, yielding tailored languages for the design of safety critical embedded sytems. In this paper, we use fault trees as an established analysis approach and illustrate their integration into a model-driven design approach. As a starting point we use component fault trees, which extend standard fault trees with the concept of modularity. In order to shift this approach to the model driven development level, we define a domain specific modeling language and according analysis and transformation algorithms. Since safety and particularly certification bodies are usually very conservative, it is very important support proven-in-use tools for performing analyses. Through model transformations, we generate exchange formats for proven tools like FaultTree+ [11]. Regarding first applications in industry, the advantages of model-driven development can be successfully extended to safety engineering. The combination of modularization, reuse, and automation can tremendously increase the efficiency of safety analyses of large systems. The remainder of this paper is structured as following: First, we present related work. Second, we introduce component fault trees. Third, we present a more formaldefinition of CFTs based on a generic meta-model for components. Based on, we explain our multi language integration for integrating CFTs into architectural design models. Afterwards, a short case study regarding worst case executon time analysis is given that uses integrated safety and architecture models. Finally, we summarize our approach and discuss its benefits for industrial usage.

2 Related Work

Many approaches exist that try to integrate safety analyses and design models in order to reduce effort by automatically transforming the integrated model into a classical safety analysis such as fault trees. These approaches are divided into Semantic Enriching, Fault Injection, and Failure Logic Modeling.

Semantic Enriching annotates additional safety-relevant semantic information to design models such as the role of a class in a fault tolerance mechanism, the safety requirements of the annotated entity, or failure modes and their likelihood of occurrence.

The assumption for approaches belonging to this category is that adding *semantic* information to entities of the system model is sufficient for the deduction of a safety analysis model and requires less effort, than modeling safety behavior manually. In UML models, stereotypes, tagged values, and constraints are used for this purpose, usually. In [9], such annotations are used to mainly identify redundancy mechanisms. They concentrate on recurring safety analysis model constructs and automatically construct parts of the safety analysis model at a high level. The annotations presented in [6] can be applied to all elements of the design model. The used annotations are generically defined to cover the whole design space and to allow a detailed deduction of the safety analysis model. This coverage and the high detail of the safety analysis model is in this approach achieved at the expense of a large number of different annotations.

The advantage of Semantic Enriching is that safety-relevant information is specified in a language that is intuitive to design engineers and programmers and within the same model as the analyzed system. It supports consistency of design safety analysis model and increases communication between developers and safety engineers. However, the high level of detail needed for safety analysis is a drawback. Another drawback is that annotations do not support widely used semantics of fault trees. This makes them difficult to apply, they are time-consuming, error prone and unfamiliar for safety engineers and certification bodies.

Fault Injection requires a formal or an executable design model. Undesired behavior is modeled along with the system model and model checkers or simulations are used for finding inconsistencies between models and safety requirements. This enables a high degree of automation and ensures strong correctness of results. Using model checking for fault injection was invented by Liggesmeyer in [16]. More examples may be found in [3], [12] and [5]. The drawback this approach the need for formal models. Furthermore, it does not solve the problem of finding appropriate failure modes or support humans to think about conceptual faults that were explicitly specified.

The approach presented in this paper belongs to the third category: **Failure Logic Modeling** (FLM) modularly defines the failure propagation of system modules in parallel to its data-flow similar to standard safety analysis. The disadvantage of FLM is that the annotation is still a manual task and very similar to a manual safety analysis. However, in our opinion this is also its advantage against Semantic Enriching and Fault Injection. The used development model is not constrained to be executable, as in fault injection, and the advantages of semantic enrichment that come from combination of system models and safety analysis models may be achieved without the drawback of applying a complicated and unfamiliar set of annotations. Examples of Failure Logic Modeling can be found in [19], [10] an [18]. The most similar approach to this paper are the Hierarchically Performed Hazard Operation and Propagation Studies (HiP-HOPS), which annotate subsystems in Matlab/Simulink with propositional formulas, which are mathematically equivalent to fault trees [18]. The approach has already been integrated into EAST-ADL [4], which extends the UML/SysML.

In contrast to the approaches discussed before, we propose an approach that uses model-based concepts to integrate fault tree models with UML models. This way, safety becomes an integral part of design models, and still remains analyzable with existing and prooven tools.

3 Introduction to CFTs

Fault tree analysis is a deductive, top-down method that analyzes the causes of a hazardous failure of a complex system. Fault trees offer thus a breakdown with regard to the hierarchy of failure influences. The root of the tree is called TOP EVENT and the leaves are called BASIC EVENTS. The decomposition of the top event into the basic events is defined by the remaining nodes which are logical operators. However, this kind of hierarchical decomposition is not sufficient when dealing with complex technical systems. In the functional design, the complexity of these systems is typically handled by an appropriate component concept that allows the decomposition into manageable components. To facilitate this architectural decomposition also for the fault tree analysis, the concept of component fault trees (CFTs) has been proposed in [14].

CFTs feature a decomposition approach that is used in a similar way in modern software design notations: subcomponents appear as "black boxes" on the next-higher level and are connected to the environment via their interface. The output interface is given by so-called OUTPUT EVENTS and the input interface is given by so-called INPUT EVENTS. Further, a CFT comprises so-called BASIC EVENTS that represents internal faults. The CFT relates every output event to its internally caused basic events and its relevant input events. This decomposition is modeled with logical operators as it is done in the decomposition of a top event to a set of basic events in a common fault tree. Similar to a component, a CFT can be instantiated several times in other CFTs. In their environment, these instantiations are called "subcomponent" or "CFT instances". These instances can be composed by connecting input and output events. In- and output events of a CFT appear as subcomponent events when they are instantiated on the next-higher hierarchy level. The CFT graph as a whole is defined by its edge connections and the mappings from subcomponents to the corresponding CFT model describing their "internals". The complete CFT can be evaluated qualitatively and quantitatively like a classical fault tree (see [13] for a formal specification of CFTs, [14] for a description of the BDD-based and compositional evaluation algorithm used for CFTs; UWG3, a tool for modelling and evaluation of CFTs, can be found at [8]).

In the following, we exemplify the modeling of CFTs with the running example of this article. It is a system for charging the battery of a car with an electric power train. This system *charging* has to fulfill the safety requirement that the car must not start-up when the male connector is plugged, since otherwise the charging cable may crack and electrocute somebody. For detecting the plugging of the male connector, the system comprises a hardware component *ProximitySensor*, a hardware component *VoltageSensor*, and a software component *PlugDetection*.

The hardware components send respectively a signal to the component *PlugDetection* that indicates whether the male connector is plugged or not. The component *ProximitySensor* outputs the boolean signal *proximity* that is supposed to be *true* when the connector is plugged and *false* when the connector is unplugged. The component *VoltageSensor* outputs a signal *voltage* that is

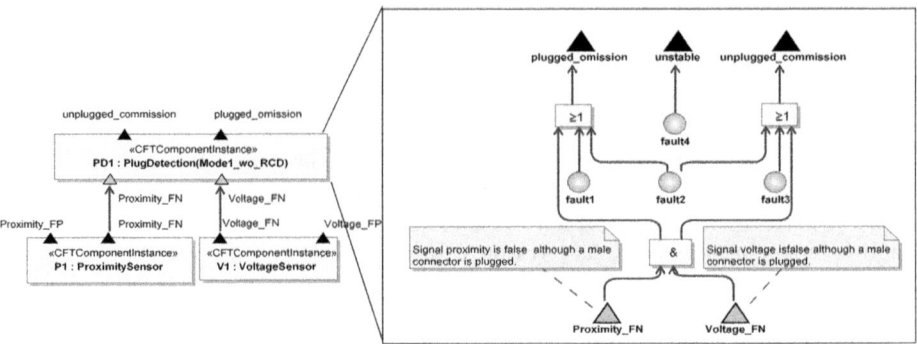

Fig. 1. Example for a component fault tree (CFT)

supposed to be *true* when the plug connection is energized and *false* otherwise. If both signals are *false* then the component *PlugDetection* sets its Boolean output signal plugged to *true* else it sets signal plugged to *false*. In this way, the component minimizes the risk of violating the safety requirement due to an undetected plugged connector.

Figure 1 shows the CFT *PlugDetection* that refers to the detection of a plugged connector based on the signals *proximity* and *voltage*. The CFT comprises three OUTPUT EVENTS (top triangles), two input events (bottom triangles) and four basic events (circles). The event *plugged_omission* refers to the common failure mode OMISSION, i.e., an unexpected absence of a signal when it is required. The event *unplugged_commission* refers to the common failure mode COMMISSION, i.e., an unintended provision of a signal when not required, and the third output event *unstable* refers to a rapidly changing signal. The input event *Proximity_FN* captures a false negative value of signal *proximity*, i.e., the value is *false* although a connector is plugged. Accordingly, the input event *voltage_FN* refers to a false negative value of signal *voltage*. A false negative value of both input signals leads to an undetected plugging of the connector. Hence, the CFT defines that the conjunction of the input events causes both output events. As the outputs events can also be caused by internal faults of the component *PlugDetection*, the CFT comprises the basic events that refer to these internal faults. It has three basic events in order to distinguish between different kinds of faults. Basic event *fault_1* refers for the class of faults that causes only a omission of signal plugged. Basic event *fault_2* refers to faults that cause an omission and a commision of signal plugged. Accordingly, it is connected to both OR gates. Basic event *fault_3* refers to faults that cause an comission of signal plugged and basic event *fault_4* causes an unstable signal. Please note that the identifiers *fault_1 fault_2 fault_3* and *fault_4* are anonymized due to NDA reasons. In practice the names should be expressive and semantically meaningful.

The CFT *ProximitySensor* that describes the failure behavior of the proximity sensor comprises an output event *Proximity_FN* that refers to a false negative value of the measured signal *proximity*. The CFT *VoltageSensor* that describes the failure behavior of the voltage sensor comprises an output event *Voltage_FN* that refers to a false negative value of the measured signal *voltage*. As illustrated in Figure 1, instances of the CFTs *ProximitySensor* and *PlugDetection* are composed by connecting output event *Proximity_FN* with input event *Proximity_FN* in order to define the overall CFT graph of the system. Instances of CFTs *VoltageSensor* and *PlugDetection* are composed by connecting output event *Voltage_FN* with input event *Voltage_FN*. This means that the fault trees belonging to output events *Proximity_FN* and *Voltage_FN* are adhered to the fault trees belonging to output events *plugged_omission* and *unplugged_comission*.

4 Towards Model-Based CFTs

Component fault trees enable developers to formally specify failure-propagation of their systems and enable formal analysis techniques. CFTs are on the most abstract level hierarchical components with parts and connections between them. We therefore define CFTs based on a generic meta-model for component based software development that resembles the most important principles of component based development CBD (cf. Figure 2).

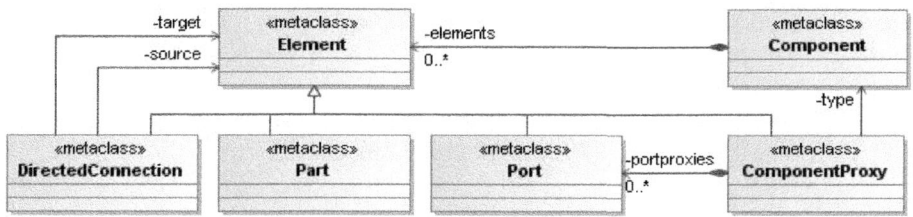

Fig. 2. Component Meta model

The meta model consists of COMPONENTS, which define component types, COMPONENT PROXIES, which represent component instances, PORTS, and DIRECTED CONNECTIONS. All are well known concepts in CBD. Components consist of ELEMENTS, which may be COMPONENT PROXIES, CONNECTIONS, or generic PARTS. Generic PARTS are abstract placeholders for more specialized language constructs therefore and need to be specialized by more concrete meta models.

CFTs are defined based on this abstract meta model (cf. Figure 3). They define specialized types of components, CFTCOMPONENT, and specializes generic ports to INPUT- and OUTPUT EVENT PORTS. GATES and EVENTS are specializations of the abstract element PART. GATES combine events with each other. Two predefined gate types are common to all calculation backends, these are the predefined AND and OR gates. EVENTS represent faults, which are the core of fault trees. After identifying faults and their propagation logic, the next step is the definition of counter-measures to mitigate or tolerate the faults. Because classic (C)FTs do not support the modelling of measures, in practice the workaround is to model a failing measure as a basic event and relate it to the fault or the fault-subtree with an AND-GATE. The semantic of this would be that a fault propagates, whenever the fault occurs AND the counter-measure fails, too. The disadvantage is that one cannot distinguish original faults from failing countermeasures. Having a meta-modelled DSML it is straight forward to add a modelling element called MEASURE. This makes it not only possible to distinguish faults from measures graphically, but also to use the extended semantic information for additional analyses. One analysis could be to reason, whether every fault is covered by at least one measure. Figure 3 shows the complete meta model of Component Fault Trees, which is the abstract syntax of the CFT language.

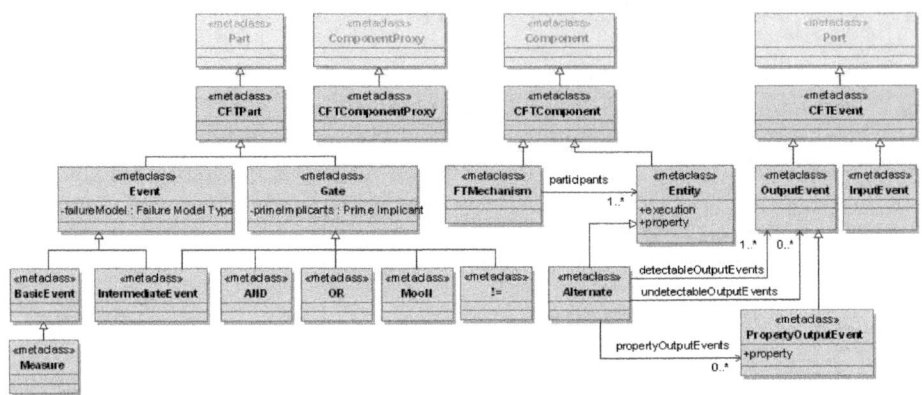

Fig. 3. CFT Meta model

New domain specific languages need to be integrated with existing tool chains. For this reason, the concrete syntax of CFTs is realized as a UML profile. This enables the use of UML modeling tools for developing component fault trees, and it enables us to inherit the UML profiling mechanism for vendor specific language adaptations. For this reason, the meta model has been converted to a UML profil.

UML based modeling enables rapid integration of application specific extensions to fault trees. Common extensions are application specific gate types. They provide special gates that are relevant to specific domains; these are valuable, and therefore may not be hidden by a modeling framework. Introducing application specific gates yielded a challenge for us: a DSML based approach yields a huge advantage for fault tree modeling on the one hand, on the other hand, there was demand for supporting several back-ends with vendor specific language extensions. While some gate types such as m-out-of-n-gates cannot be directly transformed to the back-end language of other tools, other can't. Analytical expressiveness of different back-ends is therefore not necessarily equal

Therefore we decided to apply the aforementioned profile based approach together with tailored transformation rules for each tool. This way, different backends may be connected to the DSML; transformations are specific to a tool and an application domain; adding tool specific transformation rules to support new gate types is therefore feasible. Integration of specialized gate types into the DSML is supported through profile specialization. By creating a profile that specializes the generic CFT profile, new stereotypes representing application specific gates may be exposed to users. Similar to other gate types, new gate types in specialized profiles must specialize the stereotype Gate.

This way, a graphical frontend language for component fault trees was created that provides a common interface to heterogeneous vendor specific tools. Our approach enables rapid integration and use of different tools with the same model without disabling tool specific extensions.

5 UML Profiling as DSML Design

Even though CFTs have been implemented as UML profile, they are an isolated UML-based language. While this language has its own benefits as a common tool frontend, even higher value may be generated by integrating several modeling languages for system development.

System development yields a large number of different artefacts. Systems consist for example of hardware units, software, mechanical parts. Additionally, non functional properties, such as safety constraints and worst case execution times need to be integrated. When different modeling languages are used, the same information needs to be replicated in multiple modeling languages. For example, consider a System that is modelled by two DSMLs: the Architecture DSL for defining software architectures, and the CFT DSML for creating component fault trees. Even if both languages are implemented as UML profiles, are integrated into the same tools, and even if both languages cover different aspects of the developed system, it is likely that information needs to be replicated manually between both languages. This is because different language elements are used by both languages. With each additional language, the number of new language elements increase.

Language integration solves this issue. Integrating (domain specific) modeling languages with each other is however still a challenging and uncommon topic, In the following, we will therefore document language integration using the example languages Architecture DSML and CFT DSML. Therefore, we first need to briefly introduce the Architecture DSML:

Architecture DSML only very basic concepts of software architectures, which are COMPONENTS, PORTS, and RELATIONS. Relations are specialized into generalizations, aggregarions, compositions, and directed/non-directed relations. Component types may consist of component proxies that represent instances of types.

When integrating both languages, the following properties must hold: both languages must remain useable. The presentation of either language must not be changed. Existing model transformations and validations must remain functional as well as extension mechanisms. In our example, this implies that after integrating both langauges, tool specific transformations and adaptations of the CFT language must still be possible. We distinguish between two approaches for language integration: referencing and harmonization. Referncing provides a loose integration between two modeling languages without needing to adapt meta models. It is therefore suitable for integrating languages that are implemented in different tools that must not be changed, or for langauges that are built on mostly different meta models. Hermonization provides a much tighther integration between two languages, but requires access to meta models, and requires both languages to be implemented in the same tool(s). This is used preferrably for UML based languages.

In both cases, we define a meta language to be a tuple l_{Name} that consists of a name $Name$, a set of Meta Classes M, and a set of relations R. Meta classes $m \in M$ define a tuple that consists of a name $Name$ as well, and a set of attributes $a \in A$. Operations are not considered here. For this paper, we consider a subset of properties of attributes: $P_{isReadOnly}$, $P_{isDerived}$, $V_{opposite}$ represent the properties isReadOnly, isDerived, and opposite of each attribute. Other properties are handled equally. isReadOnly and isDerived are predicates, opposite is a property that is empty or holds another attribute a. The set of relations R consists of Generalizations R_{Gen}, Aggregations R_{Aggr}, Associations R_{Assoc}. Properties are handled equally to properties of attributes; a thorough description is ommitted here for space reasons.

Referencing defines mapping functions between two models m_{CFT} and m_{Arch} that conform to meta models $meta_{CFT}$ and $meta_{Arch}$. here, a set of functions F defines mappings from $meta_{CFT}$ to $meta_{Arch}$. Each function $f \in F$ maps a part from the CFT DSML to the architecture DSML. The set of functions $f^{-1} \in F^{-1}$ define mappings back from m_{Arch} to m_{CFT}. When more than two languages are to be integrated through referencing, it is feasible to define a common intermediate meta model, and a common model m_{shared} that stores all information that is to be shared amongst languages.

Mappings do not need to be complete. All aspects that are not covered by mapping functions are silently ignored. Referncing is therefore a well suited approach for integrating meta models that have only very little in common, e.g. UML and Simulink. Integration between two languages enables using of UML for modeling software architectures, and Simulink for defining detailed behavior of components.

Referencing may be implemented with various tool-chains and modeling languages. Its flexibility is an advantage. Additionally, the approach scales very well, because only relevant parts of language meta models need to be considered. Drawbacks of referencing is its overhead. Depending on the implementation, the whole set of functions must be executed to synchronize both languages. A concrete realization of a referencing based approach was published in [15], which illustrates this concept of language integration in greater detail.

Language harmonization provides a much tighter integration between DSMLs. This is achieved through meta model integration. Therefore, it is necessary that both languages are built on a common meta model. here, we assume MOF or UML based DSMLs. Harmonization of both DSMLs will be performed as following:

- Definition of the harmonized meta model or profile M_{Common}.
- Harmonization of meta classes/stereotypes from M_{CFT} and M_{Arch}. For every pair of meta classes m_{CFT} and m_{Arch} that are similar in originating meta models, a new meta class m_{Common} is created that generalizes m_{CFT} and m_{Arch} is created. If m_{CFT} and m_{Arch} are stereotypes, their meta classes are set to the union of meta classes of m_{CFT} and m_{Arch}. Additionally, a new meta class h that specializes e and f is created.
- Harmonization of class attributes for hermonized meta classes m_{CFT} and m_{Arch}. Every attribute a of meta class m_{CFT}, for which $a \in m_{CFT}$ and $a \in m_{Arch}$ holds is moved to m_{Common}, iff meta properties of a can be harmonized (see below). Attribute remains in m_{CFT} or m_{Arch} otherwise, or need to be harmonized manually by language developers.
- Harmonization of regular associations R_{Assoc}: Regular relations are handled like attributes, therefore, the rules for attributes apply here as well.
- Harmonization of generalizations R_{Gen}: Generalization relations g between two elements $m_{CFT}^1 \in M_{CFT}$, $m_{CFT}^2 \in M_{CFT}$ are added as new generalization relations g' between elements $m_{Common}^1 \in M_{Common}$ and $m_{Common}^2 \in M_{Common}$.
- Harmonization of aggregations a: Aggregation relations are handled like attributes.

For the harmonization of attributes, additional meta properties need to be checked to ensure proper harmonization. These properties are the following:

- *defaultValue* defines the default value of a property. Here, a suitable new default value must be found if default values from both harmonized elements $m_{CFT} \in M_{CFT}$ and $m_{Arch} \in M_{Arch}$ differ from each other. If no default value is found, no default value is assumed for $m_{Common} \in M_{Common}$.
- *isComposite* defines whether a property is contained in its owner or not. If the value of this property differs in source elements $m_{CFT} \in M_{CFT}$ and $m_{Arch} \in M_{Arch}$, a creative decision is to be made by language developers to avoid meta modeling conflicts. this may yield the decision of keeping both properties seperated, because they obviously follow different (static) language semantics, or to decide for one value for $m_{Common} \in M_{Common}$.
- *isDerived* defines whether a property value may be derived from other properties. If the value of this property differs in source elements $m_{CFT} \in M_{CFT}$ and $m_{Arch} \in M_{Arch}$, *isDerviced* needs to be set to false in $m_{Common} \in M_{Common}$, because its value needs to be set manually and cannot be calculated.
- *isReadOnly* defines whether a property may be modified. If $m_{CFT} \in M_{CFT}$ and $m_{Arch} \in M_{Arch}$ differ, the value for $m_{Common} \in M_{Common}$ is false. This may open unexpected privileges that were not given by original meta models, which is necessary in this case.
- *opposite* defines an opposite value for an attribute. If values from both originating meta models differ, again a creative decision is necessary, because there is no automated way for harmonization.

– The *name* property is typically the same and kept during harmonization, the type is set to the harmonized input type that was created during the second step of our approach.

The outlined algorithm does not cover all properties of meta models that need to be harmonized. however, its extension to missing properties is streaightforward. Figure 4 illustrates meta model harmonzation graphically with a subset of both languages. In the example, harmonization of component language elements of the two DSMLs is documented.

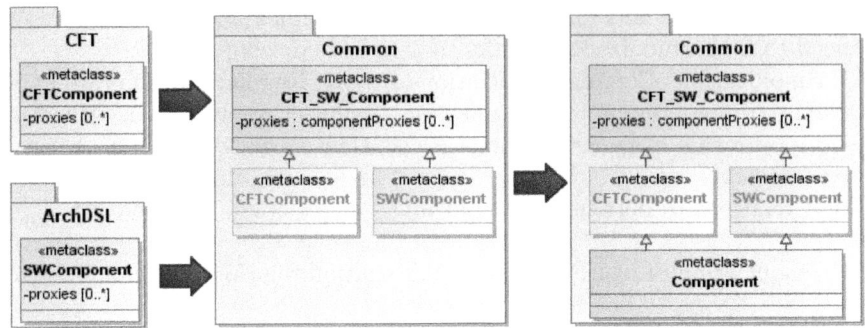

Fig. 4. Meta model harmonization example

The algorithm that was outlined above ensures a conforming integration of two DSMLs. The following properties hold after two langauges have been integrated:

– If two language elements e and f were distinct in the originating meta models M and N, there are two distinct language elements e' and f' in the combined meta model O.
– All language elements e' in the integrated meta model O have at least all properties of their originating language elements e from each originating meta model.
– All language elements e' in the integrated meta model O are compatible to their source type (i.e. also have the type) e from their originating meta model M.

This guarantees that existing profiles, model transformations, validations, and model checkers may still be used with the integrated meta model, which is our definition of compatibility. Integration on the other hand guarantees the following:

– If two language elements e and f were similar in both originating meta models M and N, they are represented by only one element g' in the resulting meta model O. This applies to language elements, relations, and attributes.
– Attributes with conflicting types from originating meta models are not harmonized.

– Attributes with conflicting default values are given a new default value that conform to the integrated meta model.

These definitions may be extended to integrated meta models that originate from more than two meta models. Meta model harmonization, as outlined above, is not a new technique. Both, the UML and the MOF apply this technique to merge language packages that define subsets of their respective meta models. Package merging of one package with another creates the union of both packages, which spans meta classes, attributes, and relations. Current implementation of package merging is ambiguous in some cases. For example, when two attributes with different default values or types are being merged. The authors of [7] therefore propose different semantics for package merging. For our appropach, we fall back to explicit decitions of language developers, since these cases often imply domain knowledge and often cannot be solved through generic rules.

Language-specific presentations ensure that in each view only properties that are of relevance to the currently used DSML are visible. For example, the safety engineer that models with CFTs only perceives CFT related properties of the Component modeling elements, software architects only perceive UML related properties. Realization of views is tool specific - in our case, we used the DSL engine of MagicDraw [17] to realize these views. Meta model harmonization also has implications on the semantics of modeling languages. When a component with an associated CFT is generalized, the sub-components inherit the CFT of the parent component. Therefore, they may add new failure analysis, for example for new ports that are introduced by specialized components. A thorough analysis of these implications for all possible integration scenarios is considered to be future work.

6 Case-Study: Considering Worst Case Execution Times

In this section, we highlight an approach that exploits the benefits of DSML-based fault tree modeling and language integration by combining safety views and worst case execution times (WCETs) of components to automatically deduce probabilistic execution times of fault tolerance mechanisms. Those generated probabilistic execution times are hard to deduce manually and require a seamlessly integrated safety analysis and architecture model that is capable to reflect the structure of the system model with its entities and connections. The results of the methodology are used for subsequent safety analyses and provide input for approaches dealing with probabilistic worst case execution times, e.g., as presented in [2] and [1].

To automatically deduce probabilistic execution times for fault tolerance mechanisms that have a certain amount of timing overhead for redundantly executable elements, we use the meta-model as depicted in figure 3. It addresses CFTCOMPONENTS and OUTPUTEVENTS and enriches the system model by modeling the semantics of fault tolerance mechanisms generically. A FTMECHANISM identifies the component holding the fault tolerance mechanism, that typically consists of some redundant ALTERNATES and additional ENTITIES for, e.g., checkpointing and orchestration. To later on reflect the WCET for an entire FTMECHANISM, ENTITIES get assigned a WCET as a PROPERTY and, if they are not a redundant ALTERNATE, an EXECUTION behavior that describes whether the ENTITY is executed before or after certain ALTERNATES. The EXECPATTERN allows modeling the overall behavior of the FTMECHANISM by defining all combinations of executed ALTERNATES that are capable to produce a correct result (so called *runs*). Since the probability for a certain run to occur depend on failures of redundant ALTERNATES, two types of OUTPUTEVENTS are assigned to this model element: failures that can be detected within the mechanism (DETECTABLEOUTPUTEVENTS) and failures that cannot be detected within the mechanism (UNDETECTABLEOUTPUTEVENTS). A third class of assigned OUTPUTEVENTS affect the PROPERTY of an ALTERNATE by extending the WCET, e.g., due to additional hardware failures like an overheated CPU that slows down the calculation, what is generally uncovered by WCET analyses.

To demonstrate how approaches that encompass entities of safety analysis models and entities of system development model benefit from the seamless integration of both models, we extend the example as provided in section 3 and use the DSML-based fault tree language to apply the above presented annotations for the automated generation of probabilistic worst case execution times. The generated results provide then probabilities for different WCETs if the addressed entities of the safety analysis model are quantified.

The system is here extended by an additional component *PlugDetection2* (PD2), that is developed design diversely and executed in parallel to PD1. Both plug detection mechanisms report their result to a component called *Decider* (D). This component is able to detect the OUTPUTEVENT *unstable* of PD1 and then selects the output of component PD2 to tolerate the fault. The OUTPUTEVENT *unstable* of PD1 is tagged as an DETECTABLEOUTPUTEVENT, both other output events are tagged as UNDETECTABLEOUTPUTEVENTS. This system builds a FTMECHANISM with PD1 and PD2 as ALTERNATES and D as an additional ENTITY. Following the semantic, the system produces acceptable output if PD1 produces an acceptable output ($run_1 = (PD1)$) and if PD1 fails detected and PD2 produces an acceptable output ($run_2 = (\overline{PD1}, PD2)$). Both so-called *runs* build the EXECPATTERN tag of the FTMECHANISM stereotype. The component D is always executed once, its EXECUTION tag is set to *once*.

Since the component PD2 is developed design diversely, it has a different WCET of 4ms compared to PD1 with a WCET of 3ms and the component D produces an additional WCET overhead of 2ms compared to the system without the fault tolerant redundant element PD2 and D. The overall WCET for this system is 6ms compared to the WCET of 3ms for the system without redundancy and the decider D.

To demonstrate the benfits of language integration, we assume an additional late failure mode of PD2. The CFT for PD2 is similar to the CFT of PD1, but PD2 does not produce an *unstable* OUTPUTEVENT, but produces an additional timing failure *late+1* of one millisecond instead, triggered by the internal event *PD2.fault4*. This OUTPUTEVENT is tagged as an PROPERTYOUTPUTEVENT.

After the system is semantically enriched encompassing the entities of the mechanism, corresponding failure modes and the semantics, we are able to generate WCETs as depicted in table 1. The first row with an overall WCET of 5ms corresponds to the run where only PD1 and D are executed. Since PD1 and PD2 are executed in parallel, the WCET for PD2 does not influence the overall WCET if PD1 computes no detectable failure, because the WCET of PD1 is smaller than the WCET of PD2. The second row represents the WCET for a detectable failure in PD1, and no additional timing failure in PD2, what extends the WCET in this case to 6ms. The last row represents the overall WCET for an additional timing failure in PB2. The likelihood for a specific WCET can be calculated using ordinary fault tree logic by calculating the probability for the corresponding Boolean formula. The mathematical model to generate those different WCETs is not described here, since it would exceed the limitations of this paper. We are able to generate similar results for various numbers of additional ENTITY components, PROPERTYOUTPUTEVENTS and parallel or sequentially executed VARIANTS, by generating WCETs for all combinations of runs and additional timing failures.

Table 1. Generated WCETs and corresponding Boolean formulae

Run	overall WCET	Boolean Formula
$(PD1)$	5ms	not(PD1.unstable)
$(\overline{PD1}, PD2)$	6ms	PD1.unstable
$(\overline{PD1}, PD2)$	7ms	PD1.unstable AND PD2.late+1

This approach benefits from the seamless integration of the DSML-based Fault Tree Language by providing a sophisticated access to the failure models of participants of fault tolerance mechanisms, what simplifies the process of identifying the relevant failure events for this approach. The influence of failure models on non functional properties like execution times can be educed dynamically within one coherent model instead of dealing with static probabilistic values, what would be error prone for repeated events or common cause failures. The results of the previously described approach can be directly used and integrated into the existing safety analysis model by inserting new failure modes for every row as depicted in table 1 to the CFT for the FTMECHANISM component. Thereby, they can be used for subsequent safety analyses and allow a trade-off between increased safety and additional time overhead for fault tolerance mechanisms.

7 Conclusion

From a safety point of view, safety analyses are indispensable for ensuring the safety of embedded systems. Particularly for complex, software intensive systems, safety analysis is very time consuming and error-prone. Our approaches have shown in practical application our method of applying the principles of model driven engineering to safety analyses reduces required effort for safety analysis and to increase their quality at the same time. Integration of safety analysis models amd functional development models leads to higher potential for reuse as well as automated generation and consistency checks of safety models.

From a DSML point of view, integration of safety models has shown that multi language integration enables integration of non-functional models and functional development models. The harmonization of the modeling language based on profiles as well as model transformations enable the integrated use of accepted modeling environments and proven-in-use analysis tools.

Our approach has been implemented and evaluated in context of a cooperation project between Fraunhofer IESE and Siemens-CT. Implementation of the modeling language based on UML profiling mechanisms with language integration was five times more efficient than traditional development approaches (a team that developed a standalone CFT modeler using a traditional development approach required more than five times the effort that was consumed by anothe team that was developing the DSML-based modeler). Besides this speed-up factor, another important advantage is the flexibility of our approach. CFT extensions may be easily modified and extended, which enables fast tailoring to organization-specific and even project-specific requirements, which has been a crucial advantage over inflexible off-the-shelf solutions.

References

1. Bernat, G., Burns, A., Newby, M.: Probabilistic timing analysis: An approach using copulas. J. Embedded Comput. 1, 179–194 (2005)
2. Bernat, G., Colin, A., Petters, S.: pWCET: A tool for probabilistic worst-case execution time analysis of real-time systems. Technical report (2003)
3. Bozzano, M.: ESACS: An integrated methodology for design and safety analysis of complex systems. In: Proc. of European Safety and Reliability Conf. ESREL, pp. 237–245 (2003)
4. Cuenot, P., Chen, D., Gérard, S., Lönn, H., Reiser, M.-O., Servat, D., Kolagari, R.T., Törngren, M., Weber, M.: Towards improving dependability of automotive systems by using the east-adl architecture description language, pp. 39–65 (2007)
5. Damm, W., Votintseva, A., Metzner, A., Josko, B., Peikenkamp, T., Bde, E.: Boosting Re-use of Embedded Automotive Applications Through Rich Components. In: Proceedings, FIT 2005 - Foundations of Interface Technologies (2005)
6. de Miguel, M.A., Briones, J.F., Silva, J.P., Alonso, A.: Integration of safety analysis in model-driven software development. Software, IET 2(3), 260–280 (2008)
7. Dingel, J., Diskin, Z., Zito, A.: Understanding and improving UML package merge. Software and Systems Modeling 7(4), 443–467 (2008)
8. Essarel homepage, http://www.essarel.de/index.html (last accessed on 2010/08/02)
9. Ganesh, P., Dugan, J.: Automatic Synthesis of Dynamic Fault Trees from UML SystemModels. In: 13th International Symposium on Software Reliability Engineering (ISSRE) (2002)

10. Grunske, L.: Towards an Integration of Standard Component-Based Safety Evaluation Techniques with SaveCCM. In: Proc. Conf.Quality of Software Architectures QoSA, vol. 4214 (2006)
11. Isograph homepage, http://www.isograph-software.com/ftpover.htm (last accessed on 2010/08/02)
12. Joshi, A., Heimdahl, M., Steven, M., Whalen, M.: Model-Based Safety Analysis (2006) NASA
13. Kaiser, B., Liggesmeyer, P., Mäckel, O.: A new component concept for fault trees. In: Proceedings of the 8th Australian Workshop on Safety Critical Systems and Software (SCS 2003), Adelaide, pp. 37–46 (2003)
14. Kaiser, B., Zocher, A.: Bdd complexity reduction by component fault trees. In: Proceedings of the European Safety and Reliability Conference (ESREL 2005), Adelaide, pp. 1011–1019. Balkema Publishers, Rotterdam (2005)
15. Kuhn, T., Kemmann, S., Trapp, M., Schaefer, C.: Multi-language development of embedded systems. In: 9th OOPSLA DSM Workshop, Orlando, USA (2009)
16. Liggesmeyer, P., Rothfelder, M.: Improving system reliability with automatic fault tree generation. In: Twenty-Eighth Annual International Symposium on Fault-Tolerant Computing. Digest of Papers, pp. 90–99, 23-25 (1998)
17. Magicdraw homepage, http://www.nomagic.com/ (last accessed on 2010/08/02)
18. Papadopoulos, Y., Maruhn, M.: Model-Based Automated Synthesis of Fault Trees from Matlab.Simulink Models. In: International Conference on Dependable Systems and Networks (2001)
19. Rugina, A.: System Dependability Evaluation using AADL (Architecture Analysis and Design Language) (2005) LAAS-CNRS

QVTR²: A Rational and Performance-Aware Extension to the Relations Language[*]

Mauro Luigi Drago, Carlo Ghezzi, and Raffaela Mirandola

Politecnico di Milano
DeepSE Group - Dipartimento di Elettronica e Informazione
Piazza Leonardo Da Vinci, 32 - 20133 Milano, Italy
{drago,ghezzi,mirandola}@elet.polimi.it
http://deepse.dei.polimi.it

Abstract. Model transformations glue together models in an MDE process and represent the rationale behind it. It is however likely that in a design/development process different solutions (or alternatives) for the same problem are available. When alternatives are encountered, engineers need to make a choice by relying on past experience and on quality metrics. Several languages exist to specify transformations, but all of them bury deep inside source code rational information about performance and alternatives, and none of them is capable of providing feedback to select between the different solutions. In this paper we present QVT-Relations Rational (QVTR²), an extension to the Relations language to help engineers in keeping information about the design rationale in declarative transformations, and to guide them in the alternatives selection process by using performance engineering techniques to evaluate candidate solutions. We demonstrate the effectiveness of our approach by using our QVTR² prototype engine on a modified version of the common UML-to-RDBMS example transformation, and by guiding the engineer in the selection of the most reasonable and performing solution.

---

[*] This research was partially founded by the European Commission, IDEAS-ERC Project 227977-SMScom and EU FP7 Q-ImPrESS project.

Tenth International Workshop on OCL and Textual Modelling

Jordi Cabot[1], Tony Clark[2], Manuel Clavel[3], and Martin Gogolla[4]

[1] École des Mines de Nantes, France
jordi.cabot@inria.fr
[2] Middlesex University, UK
t.n.clark@mdx.ac.uk
[3] IMDEA Software Institute and Universidad Complutense de Madrid, Spain
manuel.clavel@software.imdea.org
[4] University of Bremen, Germany
gogolla@informatik.uni-bremen.de

Abstract. This paper reports on the 10th OCL Workshop held at the MODELS conference in 2010. The workshop's motivation was to bring together researchers and practitioners in textual modelling standards, such as OCL, to report advances in the field, to share results, to identify common areas and potential for integration, and to identify common tools for developing textual modelling languages, with a view to advancing the state-of-the art. The workshop included sessions with paper presentations and a final discussion session.

1 Introduction

Modelling started out with UML and its precursors as a graphical notation. However, graphical notations were found to have limitations in terms of specifying detailed aspects of a system design and in terms of processing and managing models. Limitations in using graphical languages include: specifying detailed behaviour; linking models to other traditional languages; making models executable; model transformation; extensions to modelling languages; model management. Many of these limitations have been addressed in recent years by proposals for textual modelling languages (e.g. there is a growing number of tools to textually define UML models) that either integrate with or replace graphical notations for modelling. Typical examples of such languages are OCL, textual MOF, Epsilon, Alloy, etc.

The current textual modelling landscape offers many interesting topics for research and experimentation including (but not limited to): new and/or successful applications; mappings to other languages/formalisms; new algorithms; evaluation strategies and optimizations for validation, verification and testing, model transformation and code generation, metamodeling/DSLs, and query and constraint specifications; alternative graphical/textual notations; evolution, transformation and simplification of expressions; libraries, templates and patterns; complexity results, quality models and benchmarks for comparing and evaluating tools and algorithms; case studies on industrial applications; experience reports; empirical studies about the benefits and drawbacks; and innovative tools.

The papers presented in the workshop covered many of the aforementioned topic of interests. All submitted papers were reviewed by three industrial or academic members from the Program Committee.

2 Workshop Papers

In this section we summarize the contents of the papers presented in the workshop, except for those whose full version is published in this volume: namely, *Integrating OCL and Textual Modelling Languages* by Florian Heidenreich, Jendrik Johannes, Mirko Seifert, Michael Thiele, Christian Wende and Claas Wilke, and *A Specification-based Test Case Generation Method for UML/OCL* by Achim D. Brucker, Matthias P. Krieger, Delphine Longuet and Burkhart Wolff.

2.1 Re-engineering Eclipse MDT/OCL for Xtext by Edward Willink

The current tooling used for the Eclipse OCL project uses an LALR parser generator. Enhancing the tooling to support editing motivated a migration to exploit the inherently model-driven characteristics of Xtext. This paper summarizes the experiences of that migration, identifies the many benefits and discusses a few changes in implementation approach that were required.

2.2 A Feature Model for an IDE4OCL by Joanna Chimiak-Opoka and Birgit Demuth

An Integrated OCL Development Environment (IDE4OCL) can significantly improve the pragmatics and practice of OCL. This paper presents a feature model for the IDE4OCL vision. The earlier work identified domain concepts, tool-level interactions with IDE4OCL, and use cases for OCL developers including a set of predefined features. In the second step described in this paper, the OCL community was asked for their feedback on the proposal. The results provide a valuable insight in the needs of OCL usage both in usual and advanced OCL applications.

2.3 MySQL-OCL: A Stored Procedure-Based MySQL Code Generator for OCL by Marina Egea, Carolina Dania and Manuel Clavel

This paper introduces a MySQL code generator for a significant subset of OCL expressions which is based on the use of stored procedures for mapping OCL iterators. The paper discusses the class of OCL expressions covered by the definition (which includes, possibly nested, iterator expressions) as well as some extensions needed to cover the full OCL language. The paper also discusses the efficiency of the generated MySQL code.

2.4 Navigating across Non-Navigable Ecore References via OCL by Martin Hanysz, Tobias Hoppe, Axel Uhl, Andreas Seibel, Holger Giese, Philipp Berger and Stephan Hildebrandt

The Eclipse Modeling Framework (EMF) and its meta-meta model Ecore support uni-directional and bi-directional references. It is quite common that references are defined uni-directionally only because of saving storage space or separating meta models, which is problematic when implementing Object Constraint Language (OCL) constraints that require navigation against the direction of uni-directional references. This paper presents an approach that overcomes the aforementioned issue by providing navigation across non-navigable Ecore references via OCL. Different alternative solutions are discussed. This paper also briefly describes the realization that was outcome of a project in cooperation with the SAP AG.

2.5 Towards a Conceptual Framework Supporting Model Compilability by Dan Chiorean and Vladiela Petrascu

The ever-growing use of modeling languages today is largely due to a maturation of model-based development technologies. However, there is enough room for improving language specifications and consequently, the efficiency of their usage. The state of facts in specifying Well Formedness Rules is among the most important issues calling for improvements. To solve it, there is the need of a rigorous conceptual framework supporting the specification of modeling languages' static semantics. This would stand as a basis for ensuring model compilability, a mandatory requirement in a model-driven context. This paper aims to provide core ideas that contribute to the creation of such a framework. The approach is testing-oriented and promotes the use of OCL specification patterns.

2.6 Verified Visualisation of Textual Modelling Languages by Fintan Fairmichael and Joseph Kiniry

This paper details a formal relationship between the textual and graphical forms of a high-level modelling language called the Business Object Notation (BON). It describes the semantics of the graphical and textual representations and the relationship that holds between them. It also formally defines a view on an underlying model as an extraction function, and models difference as a means of tracking changes as a model evolves. This theoretical foundation provides a means by which tools guarantee consistency between textual and graphical notations, as well showing how to efficiently perform model updates, reason about model views, and interpret properties between modelling perspectives.

2.7 Support for Bidirectional Model-to-Text Transformations by Anthony Anjorin, Marius Lauder, Michael Schlereth and Andy Schurr

In recent years, model-driven approaches and processes have established themselves as pragmatic and feasible solutions with tangible advantages.

Transformations play a central role in any model-driven solution. This paper identifies important areas and scenarios for bidirectional model-to-text transformations that are not, or only partially supported, by currently existing solutions. Based on the requirements of a real-world case study, it introduces a new concept that has been inspired by a successful bidirectional model-to-model transformation approach: Triple Graph Grammars.

2.8 An Overview of F-OML: An F-Logic Based Object Modeling Language by Mira Balaban and Michael Kifer

F-OML is an F-Logic based Object Modeling Language. It can be used for *extending* UML diagrams, *reasoning* about them, *testing* UML models, and defining their *syntax* (meta-modeling) and *semantics*. F-OML is layered on top of an elegant formal language of *guarded path expressions*, called *PathLP*, inspired by F-logic. This paper informally describes the main constructs of PathLP and F-OML, provides examples that demonstrate the four modes of F-OML usage, analyzes how language features in F-OML contribute to its expressiveness, and provides a brief comparison with OCL.

2.9 On the Need of User-Defined Libraries in OCL by Thomas Baar

User-defined libraries are widely used to share implementation code among different projects. In contrast to this, the *specification language* OCL merely offers the OCL Standard Library for reuse in different projects. There is no standardized way to import user-defined OCL constraints into another project. This paper argues for the need of a standardized mechanism to make reuse of OCL specifications within a different context possible.

2.10 Evolution of the OCL OMG Specification by Mariano Belaunde - Invited Presentation

The OCL language has reached a good acceptance in the model-driven community and a variety of commercial or academic tools support the language since many years. However, maintenance of OMG OCL specification is painful for various reasons. This paper describes the process for maintaining the specification and explains some of the reasons the evolution of OCL requires a big amount of work. It also describes major issues that the revision and finalization task forces need to solve and the major changes introduced in the specification. Finally some perspectives on future evolution of OCL standard are provided.

3 Final Discussion

The workshop concluded with a discussion of features that the workshop participants would like to see in a future version of OCL. The key points are as follows:

User Defined Parameterized Types. OCL contains types such as Set(T). However there is no way for the user to define such types which would be useful to capture polymorphic structures.

Functions. OCL contains many features that are similar to functional languages such as ML and Scheme. Iterators involve processing that is traditionally performed by anonymous functions in FP; however iterators are limited in comparison. Adding anonymous functions (closures) to OCL would remove the limitations and make OCL much more expressive.

Overloading. Operators in OCL cannot be overloaded with respect to the type of the operands. Providing a mechanism for defining operator overloading and dynamic dispatch would make OCL more expressive.

Stereotypes. OCL cannot access or define stereotypes in UML. Since stereotypes are part of UML that needs to be constrained using OCL, this situation should be addressed.

Implicit Collection Operations. OCL inserts implicit asSet and collect operations when multiple links are traversed. The point was raised that this can cause confusion (as can the difference between '−>' and '.') and makes tooling difficult. No consensus was reached on this, but the proposal was made to force the operations to be given explicitly or to introduce different versions of these operations. It would help if tooling gave smart typing advice as expressions were typed.

Equality. OCL provides a single equality operations whereas many languages provide both *identity* and *structural equivalence*. These should be added to OCL.

Reflection. OCL should have better support for reflection. It should be able to reason about its own meta-definition.

Syntax. OCL should have a concrete to abstraction syntax mapping.

Types. The standard definition of OCL should include a type construction algorithm.

Frame Condition. It is often the case that a specification needs to define a state change and also require that *everything else stays the same*. Currently OCL requires all state in scope to be explicitly referenced in a state change. It would be useful to have a frame condition such as **modifies only:** and to leave all other state in scope unchanged.

Tool Checking. For OCL versions > 2.2, each chapter should be defined by a tool checked model. It should be possible to have a clear separation between an OCL core with no casting and an upper-layer with appropriate syntax for casting. The specification should define a mapping from the upper layer to the lower layer, and tools must implement this.

A Specification-Based Test Case Generation Method for UML/OCL

Achim D. Brucker[1], Matthias P. Krieger[2,3], Delphine Longuet[2,3], and Burkhart Wolff[2,3]

[1] SAP Research, Vincenz-Priessnitz-Str. 1, 76131 Karlsruhe, Germany
achim.brucker@sap.com
[2] Univ. Paris-Sud, LRI UMR8623, Orsay F-91405*
[3] CNRS, Orsay F-91405
{krieger,longuet,wolff}@lri.fr

Abstract. Automated test data generation is an important method for the verification and validation of UML/OCL specifications. In this paper, we present an extension of DNF-based test case generation methods to class models and recursive query operations on them. A key feature of our approach is an implicit representation of object graphs avoiding a representation based on object-id's; thus, our approach avoids the generation of isomorphic object graphs by using a concise and still human-readable symbolic representation.

Keywords: OCL, UML, test case generation, specification-based testing.

1 Introduction

Automated test data generation is an important application domain for OCL specifications. Instead of verifying concrete code via a Hoare-Calculus for a specific programming language against OCL method contracts—a technique developed in detail for OCL in [9, 11]—test generation can be a more light-weighted (but logically less safe) formal method to reveal errors both in specification and implementations. A particular advantage of black-box testing is that implementations may consist of arbitrary mixtures of (dirty) programming languages.

In this paper, we will adapt existing specification-based testing techniques to UML/OCL, i. e., an object-oriented specification formalism centered around the concept of an object-graph as state, state-transitions described by class-models and state-charts (which we will ignore here), and a type system based on subtyping and inheritance. The work presented here is based on the previous work on a formal UML/OCL semantics [7, 11] and attempts to develop, in contrast to prior works such as [4], a *comprehensive* test-generation method for the complete language and for realistic test-scenarios. Overall, our contribution consists in:

1. the extension of specification-based test generation methods to the world of object-oriented specifications,

---

* This work was partially supported by the Digiteo Foundation.

2. a *deductive*, theorem-prover based test data generation from OCL specifications including language features such as recursive query-operations, and
3. a particular representation of object-graph classes by our novel concept of an *alias closure*; rather than representing the explicit object graphs we represent the object identity by an equivalence relation.

This paper is written with hindsight to the HOL-TESTGEN system [10], into which we will implement the technique presented here in a future step. This implies that our technique must fit to the underlying logical framework Isabelle/HOL (an embedding of UML/OCL has been presented in [11]), and that it can be organized into the generation phases of HOL-TESTGEN.

2 A Gentle Introduction to a Formal OCL 2.2 Semantics

In this section, we briefly present a formal semantics for OCL 2.2 [20], see [7] for details. With respect to the syntax, we use the mathematical notation of HOL-OCL [8] which allows for a concise presentation of OCL constraints.

2.1 Higher-Order Logic

Higher-order Logic (HOL) [12] is a classical logic with equality enriched by total parametrically polymorphic higher-order functions. It is more expressive than first-order logic, e. g., induction schemes can be expressed inside the logic. Pragmatically, HOL can be viewed as a typed functional programming language like Haskell extended by logical quantifiers.

HOL is based on the typed λ-calculus, i. e., the *terms* of HOL are λ-expressions. Types of terms may be built from *type variables* (like α, β, ...), optionally annotated by Haskell-like *type classes* as in $\alpha :: order$ or $\alpha :: bot$) or *type constructors* (like bool or nat). Type constructors may have arguments (as in α list or α set). The type constructor for the function space $\Rightarrow$ is written infix: $\alpha \Rightarrow \beta$; multiple applications like $\alpha_1 \Rightarrow (\ldots \Rightarrow (\alpha_n \Rightarrow \alpha_{n+1})\ldots)$ have the alternative syntax $[\alpha_1, \ldots, \alpha_n] \Rightarrow \alpha_{n+1}$. HOL is centered around the extensional logical equality $\_ = \_$ with type $[\alpha, \alpha] \Rightarrow bool$, where bool is the fundamental logical type. We use infix notation: instead of $(\_ = \_) E_1 E_2$ we write $E_1 = E_2$. The logical connectives $\_ \wedge \_$, $\_ \vee \_$, $\_ \Rightarrow \_$ of HOL have type $[bool, bool] \Rightarrow bool$, $\neg\_$ has type $bool \Rightarrow bool$. The quantifiers $\forall \_.\_$ and $\exists \_.\_$ have type $[\alpha \Rightarrow bool] \Rightarrow bool$. The quantifiers may range over types of higher order, i. e., functions or sets.

The type discipline rules out paradoxes such as Russel's paradox in untyped set theory. Sets of type α set can be defined isomorphic to functions of type $\alpha \Rightarrow bool$; the definition of the elementhood $\_ \in \_$, the set comprehension $\{\_.\_\}$, $\_ \cup \_$ and $\_ \cap \_$ is then standard.

2.2 Valid Transitions and Evaluations

We recall that OCL expressions form a typed assertion language whose syntactic elements are composed of (a) operators on built-in data structures such as Boolean or collection types like Set or Bag, (b) operators of the user-defined data-model such as attribute accessors, type-casts and tests, and (c) user-defined, potentially recursive, side-effect-free method calls.

The topmost goal of the formal semantics for OCL expressions is to define the notion of a *valid transition* over states of a system; even concepts like *object invariants* can be derived from this notion. Let σ be a pre-state and σ' a post-state and let ϕ be a Boolean OCL expression, then we write

$$(\sigma, \sigma') \vDash \phi$$

for "the transition from σ to σ' is valid in ϕ." A formula ϕ is valid if and only if its evaluation in the transition $\tau = (\sigma, \sigma')$ yields true. As all types in HOL-OCL are extended by the special element $\bot$ denoting undefinedness, we define formally:

$$\tau \vDash \phi \equiv \left(I[\![\phi]\!]\, \tau = \lfloor \text{true} \rfloor \right).$$

In OCL, the evaluation of all expressions can result in an undefinedness element called invalid which we will write $\bot$ for short. The test for definedness (not _.oclIsInvalid()) will be written ∂ _ and is defined by $\partial X \equiv \text{not}\ (X \triangleq \bot)$. Here, _ $\triangleq$ _ denotes the strong equality, which is a reflexive, symmetric and transitive congruence relation; therefore, the strong equality allows for substituting equals with equals in any OCL expression, even if the expressions are undefined. In contrast, the standard equality in OCL, i.e. _ $\doteq$ _, is *strict*, which means $x \doteq \bot$ is strongly equal to $\bot \doteq x$ which is strongly equal to $\bot$.

Since all operators of the assertion language depend on the context τ and results can be $\bot$, all expressions can be viewed as *evaluations* from τ to a type $\alpha_\bot$. All types of expressions are of a form captured by the type abbreviation:

$$V(\alpha) = \sigma \times \sigma \Rightarrow \alpha_\bot,$$

where $\sigma \times \sigma$ stands for the type of a pair of system states (i.e., the type of τ).

2.3 Semantics of Object Invariants and Operation Contracts

The OCL semantics [20, Annex A] uses different interpretation functions for invariants and pre-conditions; instead, we achieve their semantic effect by a syntactic transformation _$_{\text{pre}}$ which replaces all accessor functions _.i by their counterparts _.i@pre. For example, $(self.\text{i} > 5)_{\text{pre}}$ is just $(self.\text{i@pre} > 5)$. The operation _.allInstances() is also substituted by its @pre counterpart. Thus, we can re-formulate the semantics of the two OCL top-level constructs, invariant specification and method specification, as follows:

$$I[\![\text{context}\ c : C\ \text{inv}\ n : \phi(c)]\!]\tau \equiv$$
$$\tau \vDash (C.\text{allInstances()->forall}(x|\phi(x))) \land \qquad (1)$$
$$\tau \vDash (C.\text{allInstances()->forall}(x|\phi(x)))_{\text{pre}}$$

The standard forbids expressions containing @pre constructs in invariants or preconditions syntactically; thus, mixed forms cannot arise. Since operations have strict semantics in OCL, we have to distinguish for a specification of an *op* with the arguments $a_1, \ldots, a_n$ the two cases where all arguments are defined (and *self* is non-null), or not. In the former case, a method call can be replaced by a *result* that satisfies the contract, in the latter case the argument is $\bot$:

$$I[\![\text{context } C :: op(a_1, \ldots, a_n) : T$$
$$\textbf{pre } \phi(self, a_1, \ldots, a_n)$$
$$\textbf{post } \psi(self, a_1, \ldots, a_n, result)]\!]\tau \equiv \forall s, x_1, \ldots, x_n.$$
$$\Delta(s, x_1, \ldots, x_n) \wedge \tau \vDash \phi(s, x_1, \ldots, x_n)_{\text{pre}} \quad (2)$$
$$\longrightarrow \tau \vDash \psi(s, x_1, \ldots, x_n, s.op(x_1, \ldots, x_n))$$
$$\wedge \neg\Delta(s, x_1, \ldots, x_n) \longrightarrow \tau \vDash s.op(x_1, \ldots, x_n) \triangleq \bot$$

where $\Delta(s, x_1, \ldots, x_n)$ is an abbreviation for $\tau \vDash s \not\equiv \texttt{null} \wedge \tau \vDash \partial s \wedge \tau \vDash \partial x_1 \wedge \ldots \tau \vDash \partial x_n$. This definition captures the two cases: if the arguments of an operation are defined and, moreover, *self* is not `null`, the result of a method call must satisfy the specification; otherwise the operation will be strict and return invalid $\bot$. By these definitions an OCL specification, i.e., a sequence of invariant declarations and operation contracts, can be transformed into a set of (logically conjoined) statements which is called the *context* Γ_τ. The *theory* of an OCL specification is the set of all valid transitions $\tau \vDash \phi$ that can be derived from Γ_τ. For the logical connectives of OCL, a conventional Gentzen-style calculus for pairs of the form $\Gamma_\tau \vdash \phi$ can be developed that allows for inferring valid transitions from Γ_τ by deduction (cf. [11]). Due to the inclusion of arithmetic, any calculus for OCL is necessarily incomplete. It is straight-forward to extend our notion of context to multi-transition contexts such as:

$$\Gamma \equiv \{(\sigma, \sigma') \vDash \phi, (\sigma', \sigma'') \vDash \psi\}$$

such that we can reason over systems executing several transitions.

2.4 Strict Operations and Their Role in Reasoning

The OCL standard [20] defines most operations as strict, not just the special case of the strict equality $x \doteq y$ mentioned earlier. Overall, we have the rule

$$f(x_1, \ldots, \bot, \ldots, x_n) \triangleq \bot. \quad (3)$$

A notable exception from this rule are the logical connectives, which are a three-valued strong Kleene-logic; e.g., $\bot$ and `false` $\triangleq$ `false` and analogously $\bot$ or `true` $\triangleq$ `true`. Overall, using a three-valued logic is a burden if a simple compilation of OCL to standard automated theorem provers is envisaged. Looking at the wealth of tools (that are specialized for two-valued logics) like Kodkod [22] or Z3 [17], this is perceived as a major drawback of OCL by many.

The methodology of OCL (in particular the strictness of most operations and the fact that most OCL expressions, e.g., invariants, are, by definition, defined) enforces that a reduction to a two-valued representation is always possible; it suffices to apply the case-distinction:

$$\tau \vDash \phi(\bot) \vee (\tau \vDash \partial E \wedge \tau \vDash \phi(E)) \tag{4}$$

exhaustively to all sub-expressions E (the $\tau \vDash \phi(\bot)$-parts will either reduce quickly due to Fact 3 to $\tau \vDash \bot$ which is just false or again be subject to Fact 4). The result are formulae of the form: $\tau \vDash \partial E_1 \wedge \cdots \wedge \tau \vDash \partial E_n \wedge \tau \vDash \phi$ or just $\Delta_\phi \wedge \tau \vDash \phi$ for short. In this form—called Δ-long-form—all implicit definednesses in a valid OCL-formula are made explicit. We call the process of constructing a Δ-long-form Δ-saturation. We do not distinguish between $\{\tau \vDash E_1 \wedge \tau \vDash E_2\} \cup \Gamma$ and $\{\tau \vDash E_1, \tau \vDash E_2\} \cup \Gamma$.

This process can be optimized: if we have, for example, as consequence of an invariant $\tau \vDash f(a) \doteq b$ in our context Γ (meaning that it holds and, thus, evaluates to true), we can infer that $\tau \vDash \partial f(a)$ and $\tau \vDash \partial b$. From there, we can further infer $\tau \vDash \partial a$ (if f is strict). The same holds for the common connective $\tau \vDash X$ and Y (but not for _ or _). Once that the implicit knowledge on definedness is established, rules of the following form can be applied:

$$\tau \vDash \text{not } X = \neg \tau \vDash X \qquad \text{if } \tau \vDash \partial X$$
$$\tau \vDash X \text{ or } Y = \tau \vDash X \vee \tau \vDash Y \qquad \text{if } \tau \vDash \partial X \text{ and } \tau \vDash \partial Y$$
$$\tau \vDash X \text{ and } Y = \tau \vDash X \wedge \tau \vDash Y \qquad \text{if } \tau \vDash \partial X \text{ and } \tau \vDash \partial Y$$
$$\tau \vDash X \doteq Y = \tau \vDash X \stackrel{\Delta}{=} Y \qquad \text{if } \tau \vDash \partial X \text{ and } \tau \vDash \partial Y$$

By applying this form of equations to Γ and ϕ, we transform them into sets of judgments of the form $\tau \vDash \phi$, i.e., perfect two-valued statements that can be treated by conventional SMT solvers like Z3 (provided that we add an appropriate background theory that axiomatizes the basic operations of the OCL language).

3 Running Example: Linked Lists

In this section, we present a small UML/OCL specification that will serve as a running example for our test case generation technique. We will also discuss the translation of OCL into HOL and discuss the implicit invariants of this example.

3.1 Singly-Linked Lists

Fig. 1 illustrates our running example of a singly-linked list: the list stores integers as data and links between nodes are modeled by an association. As a node does not necessarily need to have a successor, the association end next has multiplicity 0..1. An invariant of the class states that the integers are stored in a descending order in the list. We specify an operation insert that adds an integer to the list. The postcondition of the insert operation states that the set of integers stored in the list in the post-state is the set of stored integers in the pre-state extended by the argument. For defining the set of integers stored in the list, we separately specify the recursive query operation contents().

```
context Node                                  |        Node         |
inv: next <> null implies i > next.i          | i:Integer           |
                                              | contents():Set(Integer)
context Node::contents():Set(Integer)         | insert(x:Integer)   |
  post: result = if next = null                   0..1 /\ next
                 then Set{i}
                 else next.contents()->including(i)

context Node::insert(x:Integer)
  post: contents() = contents@pre()->including(x)
```

Fig. 1. A Singly-linked list specified in OCL (excerpt)

In the following, we will describe how to build Γ_τ from this OCL specification via the semantic definitions. We will add to Γ_τ semantic presentations of the specification which are already in a "massaged format" suitable for test case generation later. Since the transition is not changing in the rest of this paper, we will assume one global transition τ (understood to be relative to the specification of this example); we will drop the index and abbreviate $\tau \vDash \phi$ to just $\vDash \phi$. In our test case generation approach, we assume that all diagrammatic constraints over the class model are represented as OCL expressions (for details, see [15]). For example, associations are usually represented by collection-valued class attributes together with OCL constraints expressing the multiplicity.

3.2 Translating Invariants into Recursive HOL-Predicates

The example in Fig. 1 only includes one explicit invariant. The multiplicity constraints in the class model constitute invariants semantically. For our example, the multiplicity constraints could be expressed as follows in OCL:

```
inv: (next = null or next <> null) and i <> null
```

In the following, we will assume that attributes and arguments that have a basic datatype (e.g., Integer) have a multiplicity of 1..1, i.e., they cannot be null. Thus we can simplify the invariant representing the multiplicity constraints to:

```
inv: (next = null or next <> null)
```

This simplification improves the readability of the formulae in this paper and is not a fundamental restriction of our approach.

For our purposes it will be convenient to convert invariants to recursive predicates and add them to Γ, paving the way for the exploration of input parameters by simply unfolding them rather than making them, based on Fact 1, lengthy arguments over .allInstances(). Of course, not any recursive predicate is consistent; however *these* recursive predicates can be derived from the invariants by using a greatest fixed-point construction and proving that the body of the invariant is monotone—the reader interested in the details is referred to HOL-OCL [9] where this is done automatically (albeit for OCL 2.0, i.e., without null):

$$\forall \; \text{self}. \quad \vDash \partial \; \text{self} \land \vDash \text{self} \not\doteq \text{null} \longrightarrow \quad \vDash \text{inv}_{\text{Node}}(\text{self})$$
$$\Longleftrightarrow \vDash \text{self.next} \doteq \text{null} \lor (\vDash \text{self.next} \not\doteq \text{null}$$
$$\land \vDash \text{self.i} > \text{self.next.i} \land \vDash \text{inv}_{\text{Node}}(\text{self.next}))$$

Additionally to this recursive predicate, we add to Γ the fact that any defined non-null object will satisfy this invariant:

$$\forall \; \text{self}. \quad \vDash \partial \; \text{self} \land \vDash \text{self} \not\doteq \text{null} \longrightarrow \quad \vDash \text{inv}_{\text{Node}}(\text{self})$$

Our recursive definitions are a conjunction of the explicit invariant and the multiplicity constraints of our example; we used Δ-short form in order not to clutter up our presentation too much, i.e., facts like $\vDash \partial \; \text{self.i}$ were omitted. The invariant $\text{inv}_{\text{Node}}\text{@pre}$ expresses well-formedness in a pre-state:

$$\forall \; \text{self}. \quad \vDash \partial \; \text{self} \land \vDash \text{self} \not\doteq \text{null}$$
$$\longrightarrow \quad \vDash \text{inv}_{\text{Node}}\text{@pre}(\text{self}) \Longleftrightarrow \vDash \text{self.next@pre} \doteq \text{null}$$
$$\lor (\vDash \text{self.next@pre} \not\doteq \text{null} \land \vDash \text{inv}_{\text{Node}}\text{@pre}(\text{self.next@pre})$$
$$\land \vDash \text{self.i@pre} > \text{self.next@pre.i@pre})$$

3.3 Translating Contracts into HOL

Given the fact that $\vDash (\text{true})_{pre}$ just collapses to true, the formulae that we add to Γ is the straight-forward simplification of the semantics rule Fact 2:

$$\forall \; \text{self}. \quad \Delta(\text{self}) \longrightarrow \quad \vDash \text{self.contents}() \triangleq$$
$$\text{if self.next} \doteq \text{null then Set}\{i\}$$
$$\text{else self.next.contents}() \text{->including}(i)$$
$$\land \; \neg \Delta(\text{self}) \longrightarrow \quad \vDash \text{self.contents}() \triangleq \bot$$

where $\Delta(\text{self})$ is a short-cut for $\vDash \partial \; \text{self} \land \vDash \text{self} \not\doteq \text{null}$. The variant for $\text{contents@pre}()$ looks as follows:

$$\forall \; \text{self}. \quad \Delta(\text{self}) \longrightarrow \quad \vDash \text{self.contents@pre}() \triangleq$$
$$\text{if self.next@pre} \doteq \text{null then Set}\{i\}$$
$$\text{else self.next@pre.contents@pre}() \text{->including}(i)$$
$$\land \; \neg \Delta(\text{self}) \longrightarrow \quad \vDash \text{self.contents@pre}() \triangleq \bot$$

4 Test Generation

In the specification-based testing, we are interested in testing the formula ϕ—called *test specification*—in the statement:

$$\Gamma \vdash \phi$$

instead of proving it (the $\vdash$ is interpreted as implication). We are interested in test specifications which contain calls to operations $s.\text{op}(a_1, \ldots, a_n)$; the core of the technique consists in selecting arguments consistent with the specification Γ

and the semantic rules for the operations of OCL, executing the implementation of op and checking if the result validates ϕ. We follow the classical approach of transforming the test specification into a disjunctive normal form (DNF), extended by invariant-handling and the treatment of recursive definitions, which corresponds to partitioning the input space of the operation(s).

Another class of case distinctions arises from *aliasing*; i.e., the fact that two object references can designate the same object, i.e., `s.next.next` is in fact identical to `s` due to a cycle in the object graph. Aliasing is a crucial phenomenon in object-oriented systems. It is likely that a system behaves differently depending on the aliasing relationships among the objects it handles. Therefore we will add further case distinctions to the specification under analysis that distinguish different aliasing relationships. We will refer to this transformation as *alias closure*.

4.1 Test Specifications: Getting Started

Depending on the specific test purposes, there are various ways to test a system: a test could be concerned with the normal behavior of operations, which will be the default considered here, or with exceptional behavior (what happens if the precondition is not satisfied?), or with operation sequences, e.g., $(\sigma, \sigma') \models \phi \wedge (\sigma', \sigma'') \models \psi$. It is even conceivable to express in test specifications the sharing of pre-state and post-state or different parameters; in our specification, the implementation of `insert` can have a copying semantics (all object-contents in the list were copied to freshly generated objects) as well as a sharing semantics.

Since OCL expressions cannot have side-effects, properties of non-query operations like `insert` cannot be expressed inside OCL. We therefore suggest to present the test specification directly in HOL. Thus, following Fact 2, we have for the case of a "normal behavior unit test":

$$\Delta(\mathtt{s},\mathtt{x}) \longrightarrow \models \mathtt{s.contents()} \doteq \mathtt{s.contents@pre()->including(x)}$$
$$\wedge \; \neg\Delta(\mathtt{s},\mathtt{x}) \longrightarrow \models \mathtt{s.insert(x)} \triangleq \bot$$

where s is a free variable for which we look for solutions that meet all possible constraints (arising from the context Γ, but also locally in ϕ). Since $(\Delta \longrightarrow A) \wedge (\neg\Delta \longrightarrow B)$ is equivalent to $(\Delta \wedge A) \vee (\neg\Delta \wedge B)$ and the latter is closer to a DNF, we rewrite our test specification and have:

$$\Delta(\mathtt{s},\mathtt{x}) \wedge \models \mathtt{s.contents()} \doteq \mathtt{s.contents@pre()->including(x)}$$
$$\vee \; \neg\Delta(\mathtt{s},\mathtt{x}) \wedge \models \mathtt{s.insert(x)} \triangleq \bot$$

which boils down to:

$$\Delta(\mathtt{s},\mathtt{x}) \wedge \models \mathtt{s.contents()} \doteq \mathtt{s.contents@pre()->including(x)}$$
$$\vee \models \mathtt{s} \doteq \mathtt{null} \wedge \models \mathtt{s.insert(x)} \triangleq \bot$$
$$\vee \models \mathtt{x} \doteq \bot \wedge \models \mathtt{s.insert(x)} \triangleq \bot$$

Here, we can already apply unit propagation in clauses and extract the two test cases: $\models \mathtt{null.insert(x)} \triangleq \bot$ and $\models \mathtt{s.insert(\bot)} \triangleq \bot$ which essentially test the corner-cases imposed by the semantics of OCL.

4.2 Test Hypotheses

The test cases $\vDash$ `null.insert(x)` $\triangleq \bot$ and $\vDash$ `s.insert(`$\bot$`)` $\triangleq \bot$ give also some deeper insight into testing. Test cases are *classes* of concrete tests, i.e., the ground instances (e.g., $\vDash$ `null.insert(0)` $\triangleq \bot$ or $\vDash$ `null.insert(1)` $\triangleq \bot$) of these formulae. Overall, a *test case* for an operation *op* in a DNF is a conjoint:

$$\vDash \phi_1(x_1, \ldots, x_n) \wedge \cdots \wedge \vDash \phi_n(x_1, \ldots, x_n)$$

where at least one ϕ_i depends on *op*. In test cases, we can partition the clauses into two groups: in *oracles* O, i.e., those $\vDash \phi_i(x_1, \ldots, x_n)$ that depend on *op*, and in *constraints* C, i.e., all others. Constructing a test boils down to finding a solution, i.e., a ground substitution for $x_1, \ldots, x_n$ that satisfies all constraints in C, while the test proceeds by executing the implementation of *op* for this solution and check if the oracles evaluate to true.

Logically, this means that we made the assumption "if there is an input vector $(x_1, \ldots, x_n)$ satisfying all constraints, and if this input passes the oracle execution, the oracles will pass for all inputs satisfying the constraints." This type of assumption underlying a test is called a *uniformity hypothesis* written:

$$(\exists x_1, \ldots, x_n.\ C(x_1, \ldots, x_n) \wedge O(x_1, \ldots, x_n))$$
$$\longrightarrow (\forall x_1, \ldots, x_n.\ C(x_1, \ldots, x_n) \longrightarrow O(x_1, \ldots, x_n))$$

While this is the most fundamental testing hypothesis, there are other useful ones that help to establish case distinctions used in specification-based tests. A notable other well-known form of a testing hypothesis is the *regularity hypothesis*:

$$(\forall x_1, \ldots, x_n.|x_1, \ldots, x_n| < k \wedge\ C(x_1, \ldots, x_n) \longrightarrow O(x_1, \ldots, x_n))$$
$$\longrightarrow (\forall x_1, \ldots, x_n.\ C(x_1, \ldots, x_n) \longrightarrow O(x_1, \ldots, x_n))$$

or in other words: whenever we tested all data up to a given complexity measure (like size of collections) k, we assume that the execution of *op* satisfies the specification. In the context of OCL testing, there is a similar form of regularity hypothesis: here, we will implicitly argue over the bound k on the number of different objects in a state that has been used for the tests.

4.3 Unfolding

For generating a set of test cases, we start with the test specification given above, restricted to the part where s is defined and not `null`.

$$\Delta(\text{s,x}) \wedge\ \vDash \text{s.contents()} \doteq \text{s.contents@pre()->including(x)}$$

This test specification does not show any explicit case distinctions. Rather, the case distinctions are hidden in the recursive specification of `contents()`.

The invariants over the different arguments of the operation (including s) must be taken into account for the generation of relevant test cases. In our example, only ordered lists can occur in pre-states and post-states of the `insert` operation.

A Specification-Based Test Case Generation Method for UML/OCL   343

Adding these invariants as constraints over the pre-states or post-states reduces the number of test cases derived from the test specification by removing as many non-satisfiable clauses as possible before the test data selection. Because of the facts contained in Γ, we obtain:

$$\forall\ \texttt{self}.\ \vDash \partial\ \texttt{self}\ \wedge\ \vDash\ \texttt{self}\ \neq\ \texttt{null}\ \longrightarrow\ \vDash\ \text{inv}_{\text{Node}}(\texttt{self})$$

These invariants can be inserted at any time during the unfolding process.

For instance, we can already insert the invariant for the pre-states and post-states of the `insert` operation, knowing that `s` is defined and not `null`:

$$\Delta(s,x)\ \wedge\ \vDash\ \text{inv}_{\text{Node}}\texttt{@pre}(s)\ \wedge\ \vDash\ \text{inv}_{\text{Node}}(s)$$
$$\wedge\ \vDash\ \texttt{s.contents()}\ \dot{=}\ \texttt{s.contents@pre()->including(x)}$$

To enrich this condition with explicit case distinctions, we unfold the operation calls and invariants by replacing them with their specification: an operation call will be replaced with its contract and an invariant with its definition, which is allowed here since we have $\Delta(s,x)$. For the sake of readability, we do not replace the `contents` operation calls directly with their contract but rather conjoin the contract with the existing formulae. We obtain the following conditions:

```
Δ(s,x)
∧ (⊨ s.next@pre ≐ null
   ∨ (⊨ s.next@pre ≠ null
      ∧ ⊨ s.i@pre > s.next@pre.i@pre ∧ ⊨ inv_Node@pre(s.next@pre)))
∧ (⊨ s.next ≐ null
   ∨ (⊨ s.next ≠ null ∧ ⊨ s.i > s.next.i ∧ ⊨ inv_Node(s.next)))
∧ ⊨ s.contents() ≐ s.contents@pre()->including(x)
∧ ⊨ s.contents() ≜ if s.next ≐ null then Set{s.i}
                   else s.next.contents()->including(s.i)
∧ ⊨ s.contents@pre() ≜
    if s.next@pre ≐ null then Set{s.i@pre}
    else s.next@pre.contents@pre()->including(s.i@pre)
```

A second refinement step could be performed by unfolding the invariants and the operation calls a second time: we could insert the invariant definitions again and instantiate the operation contract for the `contents` operation with `s.next` (correspondingly for the pre-state).

The unfolding process and invariant insertion can be stopped at any time, once the refinement is sufficient according to the tester's needs. Then, the DNF of the obtained formula is generated to enumerate the different test cases coming from case distinction. The DNF obtained for the previous formula is the following, leading to four clauses distinguishing whether `s.next` and `s.next@pre` are `null`.

```
(Δ(s,x)
∧ ⊨ s.next ≐ null
∧ ⊨ s.next@pre ≐ null
∧ ⊨ s.contents() ≐ s.contents@pre()->including(x)
∧ ⊨ s.contents() ≜ Set{s.i}
∧ ⊨ s.contents@pre() ≜ Set{s.i@pre})
```

$\vee$ $(\Delta(s,x)$
    $\wedge \vDash$ s.next $\neq$ null $\wedge \vDash$ s.i > s.next.i $\wedge \vDash$ inv$_{\text{Node}}$(s.next)
    $\wedge \vDash$ s.next@pre $\doteq$ null
    $\wedge \vDash$ s.contents() $\doteq$ s.contents@pre()->including(x)
    $\wedge \vDash$ s.contents() $\triangleq$ s.next.contents()->including(s.i)
    $\wedge \vDash$ s.contents@pre() $\triangleq$ Set{s.i@pre})
$\vee$ $(\Delta(s,x)$
    $\wedge \vDash$ s.next $\doteq$ null
    $\wedge \vDash$ s.next@pre $\neq$ null $\wedge \vDash$ s.i@pre > s.next@pre.i@pre
    $\wedge \vDash$ inv$_{\text{Node}}$@pre(s.next@pre)
    $\wedge \vDash$ s.contents() $\doteq$ s.contents@pre()->including(x)
    $\wedge \vDash$ s.contents() $\triangleq$ Set{s.i}
    $\wedge \vDash$ s.contents@pre() $\triangleq$ s.next@pre.contents@pre()
                                                    ->including(s.i@pre))
$\vee$ $(\Delta(s,x)$
    $\wedge \vDash$ s.next $\neq$ null $\wedge \vDash$ s.i > s.next.i $\wedge \vDash$ inv$_{\text{Node}}$(s.next)
    $\wedge \vDash$ s.next@pre $\neq$ null $\wedge \vDash$ s.i@pre > s.next@pre.i@pre
    $\wedge \vDash$ inv$_{\text{Node}}$@pre(s.next@pre)
    $\wedge \vDash$ s.contents() $\doteq$ s.contents@pre()->including(x)
    $\wedge \vDash$ s.contents() $\triangleq$ s.next.contents()->including(s.i)
    $\wedge \vDash$ s.contents@pre() $\triangleq$ s.next@pre.contents@pre()
                                                    ->including(s.i@pre))

The first case boils down (due to constant propagation and set reasoning) to:

$\Delta(s,x) \wedge \vDash$ s.next $\doteq$ null $\wedge \vDash$ s.next@pre $\doteq$ null
$\wedge \vDash$ s.i $\triangleq$ s.i@pre $\wedge \vDash$ s.i $\triangleq$ x

All other cases are not yet "ground" enough and contain application redexes like $\vDash$ inv$_{\text{Node}}$(s.next) for further invariant unfolding. The derivation

$\Delta(s,x)$
$\wedge \vDash$ s.next $\neq$ null $\wedge \vDash$ s.i > s.next.i $\wedge \vDash$ inv$_{\text{Node}}$(s.next)
$\wedge \vDash$ s.next@pre $\doteq$ null
$\wedge \vDash$ s.next.contents()->including(s.i) $\doteq$ Set{s.i@pre}
                                                    ->including(x)

for the second case expands to:

$(\Delta(s,x)$
$\wedge \vDash$ s.next $\neq$ null $\wedge \vDash$ s.i > s.next.i $\wedge \vDash$ s.next.next $\doteq$ null
$\wedge \vDash$ s.next@pre $\doteq$ null
$\wedge \vDash$ s.next.contents()->including(s.i) $\doteq$ Set{s.i@pre}
                                                    ->including(x))
$\vee$ $(\Delta(s,x)$
$\wedge \vDash$ s.next $\neq$ null $\wedge \vDash$ s.i > s.next.i
$\wedge \vDash$ s.next.i > s.next.next.i $\wedge \vDash$ s.next.next $\neq$ null
$\wedge \vDash$ inv$_{\text{Node}}$(s.next.next)
$\wedge \vDash$ s.next@pre $\doteq$ null
$\wedge \vDash$ s.next.contents()->including(s.i) $\doteq$ Set{s.i@pre}
                                                    ->including(x))

While the second sub-case is unsatisfiable since it asserts that the insertion increases the list length by two, the first sub-case reduces to:

$$\Delta(s,x)$$
```
∧ ⊨ s.next ≠ null  ∧ ⊨ s.i > s.next.i  ∧ ⊨ s.next.next ≐ null
∧ ⊨ s.next@pre ≐ null
∧ ⊨ Set{s.next.i}->including(s.i) ≐ Set{s.i@pre}
                                           ->including(x)
```

which, due to set reasoning, corresponds to a test case in which the inserted element x is not already in the list. The test cases still containing an occurrence of the invariance predicate correspond to the class of "yet to be tested" test cases.

4.4 Alias Closure

Unfolding and invariant insertion represent only a first step of the exploration of the specification by case distinction. There is another implicit case distinction that needs to be considered, since the two references s and s.next could actually refer to the same object, due to a cycle in the object graph. We should then distinguish the cases where s.next $\triangleq$ s and where s.next $\not\triangleq$ s. In the same way, we should distinguish the cases s.next@pre $\triangleq$ s and s.next@pre $\not\triangleq$ s.

To handle these four cases in the test case generation, we add the following tautology, called *alias distinction*, to the unfolding of our test specification:

```
  (⊨ s.next ≜ s ∨ ⊨ s.next ≇ s)
∧ (⊨ s.next@pre ≜ s ∨ ⊨ s.next@pre ≇ s)
```

In the cases s.next $\triangleq$ s and s.next@pre $\triangleq$ s, the invariants evaluate to false due to the strict inequality, thus only the cases s.next $\not\triangleq$ s and s.next@pre $\not\triangleq$ s remain. Computing the DNF in our example leads to almost the same formula as in the previous subsection, where ⊨ s.next $\not\triangleq$ s ∧ ⊨ s.next@pre $\not\triangleq$ s is added to each conjoint.

In the general case, the alias closure of a formula is the conjoint of the tautologies p $\triangleq$ q ∨ p $\not\triangleq$ q for all the references p and q occurring in the formula (all other reference pairs are not relevant for case-splitting; so when we decided to unfold the invariants to a certain depth, we also made a decision on the maximum path-sizes and finally the maximum number of nodes in a state). Formally, let Path(φ) be the set of path-expressions (references) occurring in a formula φ. We define AliasClosure(φ) as the set of formulae

$$\{ \, p \triangleq q \vee p \not\triangleq q \mid p, q \in \text{Path}(\varphi) \wedge p \text{ non-identical to } q \, \}$$

This produces all possible objects graphs, instead of only tree-like structures.

4.5 Generating Test Object-Graphs from Test Cases

Finally, ground instantiations of the underlying object model (i.e., in our example, instances of singly-linked lists) need to generated. For example, a concrete state-pair $\tau = (\sigma, \sigma')$ that can be given for test case

Table 1. Sample set of resulting test cases

List in pre-state	Inserted element	List in post-state
3	3	3
5	9	9 → 5
6 → 1	1	6 → 1
6 → 3	5	6 → 5 → 3
8 → 5 → 1	5	8 → 5 → 1
7 → 6 → 5	9	9 → 7 → 6 → 5

$\Delta(s,x) \land \vDash$ s.next $\neq$ null $\land \vDash$ s.i > s.next.i
$\land \vDash$ s.next.next $\doteq$ null $\land \vDash$ s.next@pre $\doteq$ null
$\land \vDash$ Set{s.next.i}->including(s.i) $\doteq$ Set{s.i@pre}
                                               ->including(x)

and the ground instance s.insert(2) of the operation call insert() is:

σ = { $oid_0 \mapsto (\!|$ i = 3, next = null $|\!)$ }
σ' = { $oid_0 \mapsto (\!|$ i = 3, next = $oid_1 |\!)$, $oid_1 \mapsto (\!|$ i = 2, next = null$|\!)$ }

which describes the requirement that inserting 2 into the list that only contains the element 3 should result in the sorted singly-linked list that contains the elements 3 and 2. Table 1 shows a sample set of test cases resulting from an unfolding of the test specification up to a list length of 3. For every list length there are two test cases: one for the case that the inserted element is already in the list and one for the case of an actual insertion.

5 Integrating the Technique in HOL-TESTGEN

HOL-TESTGEN [10] is a specification and test case generation environment extending the interactive theorem prover Isabelle/HOL [18]. The HOL-TESTGEN method is two-staged: first, the original formula is partitioned into test cases by transformation into a normal form called test theorem. Second, the test cases are analyzed for ground instances (the test data) satisfying the constraints of the test cases. Particular emphasis is put on the control of explicit test hypotheses. Finally, HOL-TESTGEN supports the generation of test drivers that allow for validating that an implementation fulfills its abstract specification. As such, developing UML/OCL support for HOL-TESTGEN, including its integration into a formal model-driven development toolchain, e. g., [6], enables the validation that an implementation fulfills the test specifications given in UML/OCL.

Extending HOL-TESTGEN with support for OCL creates certain challenges: the unfolding of OCL invariants introduces a new kind of splitting rule that needs to be supported efficiently by the splitter algorithm of HOL-TESTGEN. Moreover, HOL-TESTGEN does not yet support conjoint clauses that have no reference to the program under test (resulting in a failure during test data form computation). This is motivated by the fact that we cannot generate test drivers for such conjoint clauses. In the future, the generated test drivers could either silently drop such test cases or, following the OCL semantics, test for a deadlock.

6 Related and Future Work

6.1 Related Work

While there are several works that discuss specification-based test case generation based on UML/OCL models, none of them supports the three-valuedness of OCL. The most closely related works [1, 2, 4, 24] are all inspired by the seminal work of Dick and Faivre [13] and, thus, share the idea of using symbolic DNF computation for partitioning the input space. Moreover, there are works using sequence diagrams as an input for test case generation, e. g., [16], or pairwise testing of OCL contracts, e. g., [19]. Finally, Gogolla et al. [14] apply random-testing strategies for analyzing properties of OCL specifications.

For program-based tests, there are two test data generators that apply symbolic techniques: Korat [5] and Java Pathfinder [23]. Korat [5] generates from preconditions and a bound on the number of nodes of data structures, an input partitioning by a combination of symbolic execution and (simple) constraint solving. The idea of integrating a symbolic state deeply inside the execution environment, i. e., inside a Java virtual machine (JVM) as suggested in JPF-SE [3] (a successor of Java Pathfinder [23]), substantially improved the approach and inspired systems such as Pex [21] (a model-based testing tools for the .net).

6.2 Future Work

HOL-TESTGEN's generation strategies are geared towards inductively generated data (such as enumeration types, or lists and sets). In this paper, we have shown how *co*-inductively generated data such as object graphs can be tackled. The described translation is a pre-computation step, but it remains to provide new tactical infra-structure to implement the unfolding strategies and the alias closure. The concrete model-generation for the resulting specification is a standard-game for SMT-based model-construction generators in HOL-TESTGEN.

References

[1] van Aertryck, L., Jensen, T.: UML-CASTING: Test synthesis from UML models using constraint resolution. In: Jézéquel, J.M. (ed.) AFADL 2003 (2003)
[2] Aichernig, B.K., Pari Salas, P.A.: Test case generation by OCL mutation and constraint solving. In: QSIC 2005, pp. 64–71. IEEE Computer Society, Los Alamitos (2005)
[3] Anand, S., Păsăreanu, C.S., Visser, W.: JPF–SE: A Symbolic Execution Extension to Java PathFinder. In: Grumberg, O., Huth, M. (eds.) TACAS 2007. LNCS, vol. 4424, pp. 134–138. Springer, Heidelberg (2007)
[4] Benattou, M., Bruel, J.M., Hameurlain, N.: Generating test data from OCL specication. In: WITUML (2002)

[5] Boyapati, C., Khurshid, S., Marinov, D.: Korat: automated testing based on Java predicates. In: ISSTA, pp. 123–133 (2002)
[6] Brucker, A.D., Doser, J., Wolff, B.: An MDA framework supporting OCL. Electronic Communications of the EASST 5 (2006)
[7] Brucker, A.D., Krieger, M.P., Wolff, B.: Extending OCL with null-references. In: Ghosh, S. (ed.) MODELS 2009. LNCS, vol. 6002, pp. 261–275. Springer, Heidelberg (2010)
[8] Brucker, A.D., Wolff, B.: HOL-OCL: A Formal Proof Environment for UML/OCL. In: Fiadeiro, J.L., Inverardi, P. (eds.) FASE 2008. LNCS, vol. 4961, pp. 97–100. Springer, Heidelberg (2008)
[9] Brucker, A.D., Wolff, B.: An extensible encoding of object-oriented data models in HOL. Journal of Automated Reasoning 41, 219–249 (2008)
[10] Brucker, A.D., Wolff, B.: HOL-TestGen: an interactive test-case generation framework. In: Chechik, M., Wirsing, M. (eds.) FASE 2009. LNCS, vol. 5503, pp. 417–420. Springer, Heidelberg (2009)
[11] Brucker, A.D., Wolff, B.: Semantics, calculi, and analysis for object-oriented specifications. Acta Informatica 46(4), 255–284 (2009)
[12] Church, A.: A formulation of the simple theory of types. Journal of Symbolic Logic 5(2), 56–68 (1940)
[13] Dick, J., Faivre, A.: Automating the generation and sequencing of test cases from model-based specifications. In: Larsen, P.G., Woodcock, J.C.P. (eds.) FME 1993. LNCS, vol. 670, pp. 268–284. Springer, Heidelberg (1993)
[14] Gogolla, M., Hamann, L., Kuhlmann, M.: Proving and visualizing OCL invariant independence by automatically generated test cases. In: Fraser, G., Gargantini, A. (eds.) TAP 2010. LNCS, vol. 6143, pp. 38–54. Springer, Heidelberg (2010)
[15] Gogolla, M., Richters, M.: Expressing UML class diagrams properties with OCL. In: Clark, A., Warmer, J. (eds.) Object Modeling with the OCL. LNCS, vol. 2263, pp. 85–114. Springer, Heidelberg (2002)
[16] Li, B.L., shu Li, Z., Qing, L., Chen, Y.H.: Test case automate generation from UML sequence diagram and OCL expression. In: Computational Intelligence and Security, pp. 1048–1052. IEEE Computer Society, Los Alamitos (2007)
[17] de Moura, L., Bjørner, N.S.: Z3: An efficient SMT solver. In: Ramakrishnan, C.R., Rehof, J. (eds.) TACAS 2008. LNCS, vol. 4963, pp. 337–340. Springer, Heidelberg (2008)
[18] Nipkow, T., Paulson, L.C., Wenzel, M.: Isabelle/HOL—A Proof Assistant for Higher-Order Logic. LNCS, vol. 2283. Springer, Heidelberg (2002)
[19] Noikajana, S., Suwannasart, T.: An improved test case generation method for Web service testing from WSDL-S and OCL with pair-wise testing technique, pp. 115–123. IEEE Computer Society, Los Alamitos (2009)
[20] Object Management Group: UML 2.2 OCL specification (2010), Available as OMG document formal/2010-02-01
[21] Tillmann, N., de Halleux, J.: Pex–white box test generation for.NET. In: Beckert, B., Hähnle, R. (eds.) TAP 2008. LNCS, vol. 4966, pp. 134–153. Springer, Heidelberg (2008)
[22] Torlak, E., Jackson, D.: Kodkod: A relational model finder. In: Grumberg, O., Huth, M. (eds.) TACAS 2007. LNCS, vol. 4424, pp. 632–647. Springer, Heidelberg (2007)
[23] Visser, W., Havelund, K., Brat, G.P., Park, S., Lerda, F.: Model checking programs. Autom. Softw. Eng. 10(2), 203–232 (2003)
[24] Weissleder, S., Schlingloff, B.H.: Quality of automatically generated test cases based on OCL expressions. In: ICST, pp. 517–520. IEEE Computer Society, Los Alamitos (2008)

Integrating OCL and Textual Modelling Languages

Florian Heidenreich, Jendrik Johannes, Sven Karol, Mirko Seifert,
Michael Thiele, Christian Wende, and Claas Wilke

Institut für Software- und Multimediatechnik
Technische Universität Dresden
D-01062, Dresden, Germany
{florian.heidenreich,jendrik.johannes,sven.karol,mirko.seifert,
michael.thiele,c.wende,claas.wilke}@tu-dresden.de

Abstract. In the past years, many OCL tools achieved a transition of OCL from a language meant to constrain UML models to a universal constraint language applied to various modelling and metamodelling languages. However, OCL users still experience a discrepancy between the now highly extensible parsing and evaluation backend of OCL tools and the lack of appropriate frontend tooling like advanced OCL editors that adapt to the different application scenarios.

We argue that this has to be addressed both at a technical and methodological level. Therefore, this paper provides an overview of the technical foundations to provide an integrated OCL tooling frontend and backend for arbitrary textual modelling languages and contributes a stepwise process for such an integration. We distinguish two kinds of integration: *external* definition of OCL constraints and *embedded* definition of OCL constraints. Due to the textual notation of OCL the second kind provides particularly deep integration with textual modelling languages. We apply our approach in two case studies and discuss the benefits and limitations of the approach in general and both integration kinds in particular.

1 Introduction and Motivation

The Object Constraint Language (OCL) [1] has originally been developed to constrain models defined with the Unified Modeling Language (UML) [2]. Its standardised textual syntax and formal semantics promoted the implementation and adoption of OCL by different tool vendors which in turn supported practical adoption of OCL in combination with UML. Beyond its application to UML, OCL advanced to a constraint language applicable for various modelling languages. This includes support for modelling [3,4,5,6,7,8] and metamodelling languages [9,10] like the Meta-Object Facility (MOF) [11] or Ecore [12]. The request for language-independent reuse of OCL led to extensible and adaptive approaches for OCL parsing and evaluation [7,10,13,14].

Today, we experience a discrepancy between the technical facilities and their application in practice. While the Eclipse Modeling Framework (EMF) [12] is equipped with an extensible OCL parser and evaluator [10], EMF (meta)models that use OCL constraints for well-formedness rules or integrate it as a constraint language are hard to find. We argue that one reason for this observation is a lack of adequate end-user tooling. While parsers and evaluation engines [10,13] already provide means to apply OCL on various languages, OCL users still experience a lack of adequate tooling to write constraints in the first place [15]. Advanced OCL editors that provide name resolution, code navigation, auto indentation, code macros, code completion, or debugging are highly required. However, their implementation faces a special challenge, which results from the manifold applications of OCL. All the above mentioned editor functions are based on a structural and semantic evaluation of OCL expressions that are strongly influenced by the language OCL is combined with or applied to.

Our goal is to provide such advanced editing functionality for OCL in combination with arbitrary textual (meta)modelling languages. Achieving this goal does not just require an appropriate technical infrastructure, but in particular a systematic process to apply such infrastructure to corporately customise the OCL backend and frontend for different application scenarios. In this paper we provide an overview of the technical foundations to integrate OCL with arbitrary textual modelling languages and contribute a stepwise process for such integration. There, we distinguish two kinds of integration: *external* definition of OCL constraints and *embedded* definition of OCL constraints. We evaluate the benefits and limitations of both types of integration on exemplary case studies.

This paper is structured as follows: In Sect. 2 we motivate OCL integration using a simple example language, which will later be used to explain the general integration process in Sect. 3. Here, we systematically present the steps needed to derive a customised tooling frontend and backend to efficiently apply OCL in combination with arbitrary textual modelling languages. To show the genericity of the approach, its application to Ecore is presented in Sect. 4. In Sect. 5, we report on lessons learnt during application and elaborate current limitations of our integration technique. Related work is investigated in Sect. 6 and Sect. 7 concludes our contributions.

2 Running Example—The Forms Language

To demonstrate the integration of OCL into a textual modelling language, we integrate OCL with the *Forms Language*[1]—a language to model simple forms in a textual manner. Such form models can be transformed into PDF or HTML forms or interpreted by an Eclipse-based wizard providing the form's fields. The Forms language was designed using EMFText [16].

Figure 1 shows a pizza order form specified in the Forms language. The Form consists of two Groups containing multiple Items to enter the order information. As shown, Items can have different types like FreeText, Number or Choice. Although the model is fully specified, no integrity checks can be performed.

---

[1] http://www.emftext.org/language/forms/

```
FORM "Pizza Order"
  GROUP "Your Personal Pizza"
    ITEM "dough" "Select your dough" :
      CHOICE ( "american", "italian", "cheesy crust" )
    ITEM "topping" "Select your topping" :
      CHOICE multiple ( "ham", "salami", "ananas", "onions",
         "mushrooms", "tuna" )
    ITEM "extraCheese" "Do you want extra cheese?" :
      DECISION ( "yes", "no" )
    ITEM "amount" "How many pizzas do you want?" : NUMBER
  GROUP "Your Order"
    ITEM "name" "Enter your name" : FREETEXT
    ITEM "dateOfBirth" "Enter your date of birth" : DATE
    ITEM "telephoneNo" "Enter your telephone number" : FREETEXT
```

Fig. 1. Example Pizza Order Form Specification

```
package PizzaOrder

context YourPersonalPizza
inv noTunaWithSalami: self.topping->includes(ChoiceTopping::tuna)
    implies self.topping->excludes(ChoiceTopping::salami)

context YourOrder
inv correctTelephoneNo: let digits = self.telephoneNo.characters() in
    digits->first() = '+' and
    digits->subSequence(2, digits->size())->forAll(not toInteger().oclIsInvalid())

endpackage
```

Fig. 2. Example Pizza Order with External Constraints

To overcome this limitation, we like to extend the Forms language with support for specifying constraints on instances of form models (i.e., completed forms). To formulate such constraints we want to use OCL. In principle using OCL in this context can be achieved by embedding OCL directly into form definitions or by employing external OCL constraints that refer to the form of interest.

Before we actually start the discussion of the integration process, we first want to sketch the desired result of this process. Figure 2 shows an excerpt of an OCL file defining integrity constraints ensuring that undesired compositions of pizza toppings are not allowed. Furthermore, the entered telephone number of a pizza order form is checked for correctness. This is one possible style of integration—the external use of OCL.

Figure 3 shows the same constraints embedded into the pizza order form. This second integration example corresponds to the second style of integration—the embedding of OCL. As can be seen, packages and contexts of OCL constraints have not to be declared as they can be derived implicitly from the given specification. Besides the advantage of having shorter specifications, OCL is now specified in the same document as the constrained model. This improves the

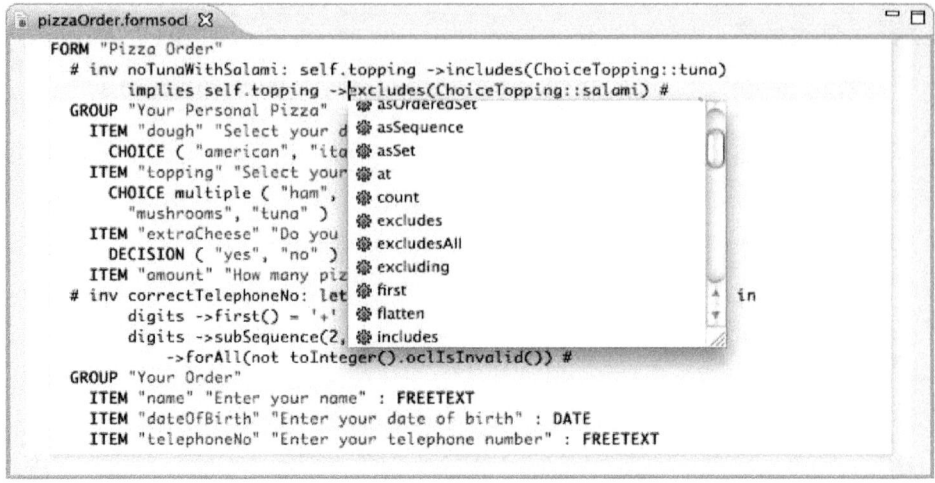

Fig. 3. Example Pizza Order with Embedded Constraints

readability and comprehensibility of constraints since the developer does not need to switch between multiple views to understand constraints and their contexts. Furthermore, if model elements are modified, the constraints' context is modified implicitly and no invalid states of constraints referring to non-existing model elements can occur.

3 Integrating OCL with Textual Modelling Languages

In the previous section we have shown that either the external or embedded definition of OCL constraints can be used to enrich the Forms language. In the following we present an integration process applicable for both approaches and textual modelling languages in general.

3.1 OCL Integration Process

We have developed an integration process to use OCL with different modelling languages. The process is built around small specifications out of which all necessary artefacts are created. The process itself is tool independent and thus is not bound to the tools used in our case studies. The presented process consists of the five steps depicted in Fig. 4. We used Ecore for metamodel definition and *EMFText* [16] for textual syntax specification. *DresdenOCL* [17] was used for OCL parsing and evaluation. Although the use of other tools should be possible we did not evaluate further tools. Static semantics integration was realised using an attribute grammar based on the *Scala* [18] library *Kiama* [19].

During *Metamodel Integration* (1), the metamodels of OCL and the textual modelling language are combined. The resulting metamodel (`FormsOCL.ecore`) is used by the EMF code generator to generate a Java metamodel implementation.

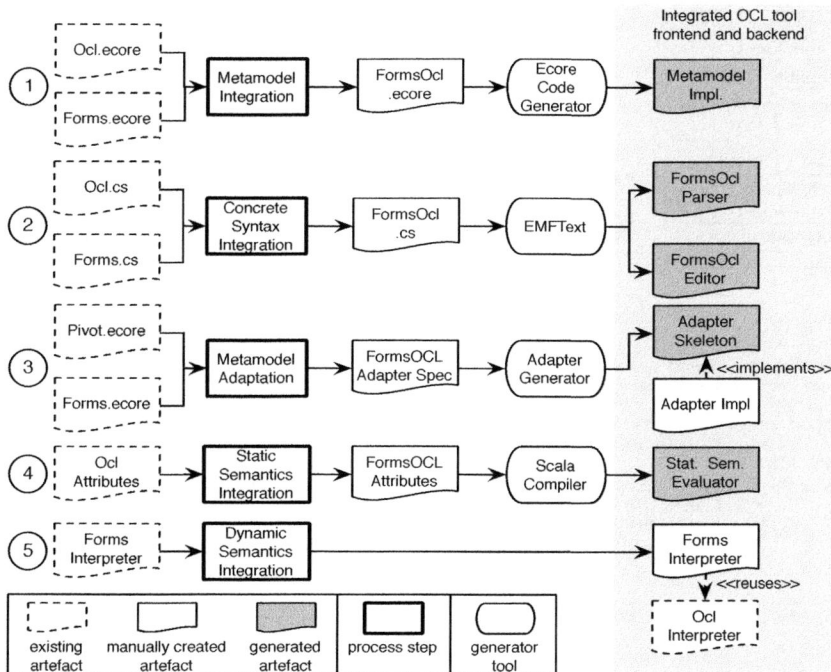

Fig. 4. The Generative OCL Integration Process (on the example of Forms language)

Next, during *Concrete Syntax Integration* (2) the textual syntax of both languages is integrated and used for the generation of a textual parser/editor using EMFText. Since only an embedded OCL integration requires a new parser/editor, these first two steps are only required for embedded OCL definitions. The step *Metamodel Adaptation* (3) is required for both approaches. The creation of a Pivot Model representation of the DSL's model enables DresdenOCL to parse OCL constraints that refer to DSL model elements. *Static Semantics Integration* (4) results in a combined static semantic analysis for integrated languages of step (2). The additional attributes are only necessary with the embedded approach as the static semantic analysis has to be extended to refer to DSL model elements in that case. For external OCL definitions the metamodel adaptation from step (3) is sufficient to allow semantic analysis of constraints defined on DSL model elements. The last step (5), the *Dynamic Semantics Integration* is necessary to evaluate integrated OCL constraints. Since evaluation is required for all OCL integrations, both approaches require this step.

3.2 Integration Steps

After presenting the integration process as a whole, we now dive into detailed descriptions of the individual steps using the Forms language integration as example for explanation where necessary. We will particularly highlight the problems that are accompanied with each step and how we solved them.

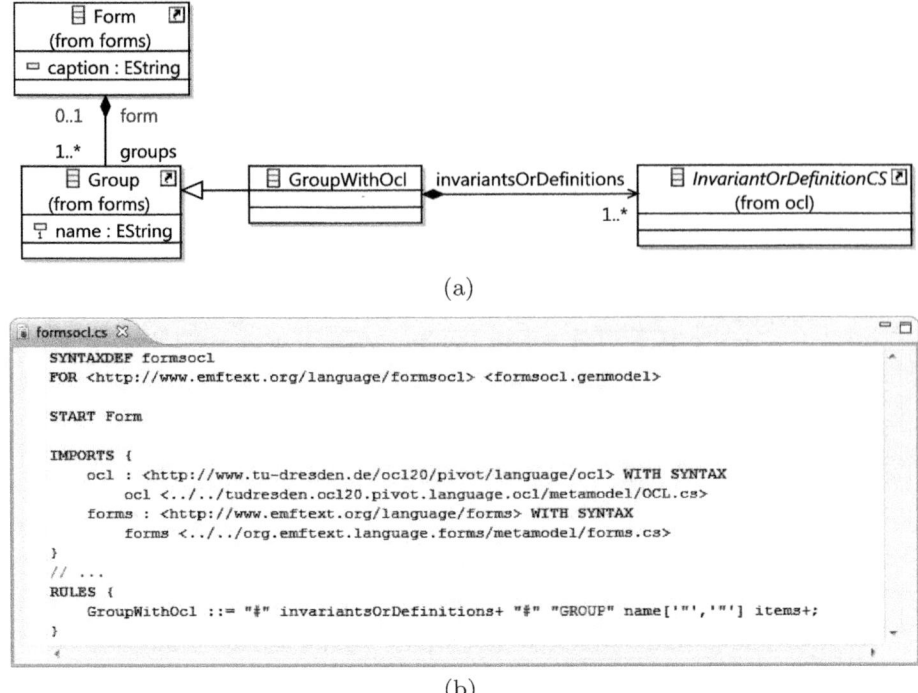

Fig. 5. (a) Metamodel and (b) Syntax Integration

(1) Metamodel Integration (for embedded integration only). We used Ecore metamodels to describe the abstract syntax of languages. To create an integrated language, one has to create a new Ecore metamodel that imports both the metamodel of OCL and of the language to integrate with. As Ecore is an implementation of Essential MOF [11], which in turn promotes a plain object-oriented metamodelling language, the options for metamodel integration are delegation and inheritance. Thus, one can either subclass one or more metaclasses or add references to metaclasses of the involved modelling languages. By creating subclasses the integrated metamodel will allow to reference new types (i.e., to store new kinds of objects in existing references). This can be used to allow elements of the OCL metamodel (e.g., invariants or expressions) in places where the embedding language did not do so before. Alternatively, one can "frame" the embedding language by introducing a new root metaclass that points to this language as well as to OCL metaclasses.

To extend the Forms language, a new metaclass called `GroupWithOcl` that extends `Group` and has a reference to multiple `DefinitionOrInvariants` is created (cf. Fig. 5(a)). By subclassing `Group`, Forms can reference either `Groups`—as before—or reference groups with OCL expressions.

Conceptually, metamodel extension by inheritance and delegation was sufficient to embed OCL in the Forms language. This is due to the fact, that we reused large portions of OCL (invariants and expressions) as a whole. In other cases of language integration, dedicated metamodel extension facilities may be more appropriate (cf. Sect. 5).

(2) Syntactic Integration (for embedded integration only). After the abstract syntax integration, the textual syntax of the integrated language needs to be specified. In EMFText, textual syntax is defined by specifying one EBNF-like grammar rule for each metaclass (cf. [16] for details). The integrated syntax can import the existing rule sets of the textual modelling language and OCL to reuse them. For the new metclasses, new rules have to be specified. In the case of the Forms language, a new rule for metaclass `GroupWithOcl` was required, which is shown in Fig. 5(b). EMFText puts the existing and new rules into relation by considering the inheritance and reference relations between the corresponding metaclasses that were established in Step (1).

In general the integration of the textual OCL syntax and other textual modelling languages is not as easy as observed for the Forms language. Context-free grammars are not closed under composition, which is why adaptations of either the embedding language or of OCL itself can be required. Such adaptations can be performed by overriding imported syntax rules.

Moreover, even if the syntax definition of OCL and the embedding language are theoretically compatible w.r.t. composition, we experienced problems with EMFText and its underlying parser technology. Parsers generated by EMFText use a scanner to split the input document into tokens, which then control the derivation of a syntax tree. If tokens of OCL conflict with tokens of the embedding language, no parser can be generated. For the Forms language, prioritising tokens was sufficient to resolve conflicts, but for more complex host languages, the situation can be more difficult.

(3) Metamodel Adaptation (for both integration styles). OCL can not be parsed, typed and evaluated in the context of a language without reasoning on the elements of the language's metamodel. As mentioned above, we use DresdenOCL for parsing and evaluation. DresdenOCL was designed to be independent of a concrete target metamodel. That is, it can be connected to arbitrary metamodels as long as they contain concepts that can be mapped to the basic concepts of object-oriented languages like types, namespaces, properties and (optionally) operations. DresdenOCL works on standardised interfaces (a *Pivot Model* [8]) which define these concepts and all operations necessary for DresdenOCL to reason on them (e.g., to get all operations defined on a type). For each modelling language that shall be connected to DresdenOCL, an adapter has to be created that maps the concepts of the language's metamodel to the pivot model concepts. To allow OCL evaluation on forms we provided a pivot model adapter for the forms metamodel. It adapts `Groups` as `Types` since they contain typed `Items` that can be adapted to `Propertys` of their `Groups`. This allows the definition of OCL constraints on `Groups` using their `Item`'s values for integrity checks. The `Types` of `Items` are adapted to `Types` as well. For instance, the `FreeText` type is adapted to `String`, `Choices` are adapted to `Enumerations`. The enclosing `Form` is adapted to a `Namespace`. Since a language's adaptation to the pivot model contains parts

that are similar for all adapters, DresdenOCL provides an adapter generator that allows adapter skeleton code generation for Ecore-based metamodels [20, Chapter 8].

(4) Semantic Analysis Adaptation (for embedded integration only). The adaptation of semantics analysis is required for the integration of OCL with modelling languages both by the backend and frontend of an OCL tool. Features like name resolution, type inference and checking enable advanced editor functions like code completion and sophisticated error reporting and are also required for static and dynamic OCL evaluation. In the current EMFText-based DresdenOCL parser, an attribute grammar [21] is used to implement the static semantics of OCL. The attribute grammar rules are specified with Scala using the library Kiama [19].

The semantic analysis is integrated in the tooling frontend by helper classes generated from EMFText that call the attribute grammar during reference resolving. E.g., the `self` variable must be bound to the type of its context to allow code completion for property and operation calls. Since OCL itself is not modified by the integration and type bindings to the integrated language are realised by the pivot model, large parts of the attribute grammar can be reused for every OCL integration. Nevertheless, many of the reused resolving operations require context information given by the concrete language concepts OCL constraints are embedded in. Context computation has to be modified for every embedded OCL integration. Therefore, a new attribute grammar specifying the context computation is mixed into the OCL attribute grammar exploiting the *mixin composition* capabilities of the Scala language [18, Chapter 27].

(5) Dynamic Semantics Integration (for both integration styles). After integrating OCL into a DSL it should be possible to evaluate OCL constraints on DSL-based models. Thus, an OCL evaluation tool has to be integrated as the last step of the process. In general, two different approaches exist to evaluate OCL constraints: the *interpretative* and the *generative approach* [22]. The first one interprets OCL constraints whereas the second one generates check code that has to be integrated into the modelling language's interpreter implementation (e.g., a Java program). DresdenOCL allows both approaches. Using the template-based OCL-to-Java code generator [23], an adaptation to the implementation language can be achieved by modifying these templates. They describe a transformation of OCL expressions into the implementation language and the instrumentation of the constraint evaluation into the implementation code.

In addition, DresdenOCL provides an OCL interpreter [13], which can be used with various runtime objects (e.g., Java objects, XML nodes or even SWT-based widgets). In the case of the interpreter of the Forms language, runtime objects are SWT widgets, which are embedded into a wizard dialog. The evaluation of OCL constraints is triggered when the user hits a *next* or a *finish* button. Figure 6 shows a screenshot from a wizard page that belongs to the pizza order example. As can be seen, the pizza topping constraint has been violated and, thus, an error message is displayed.

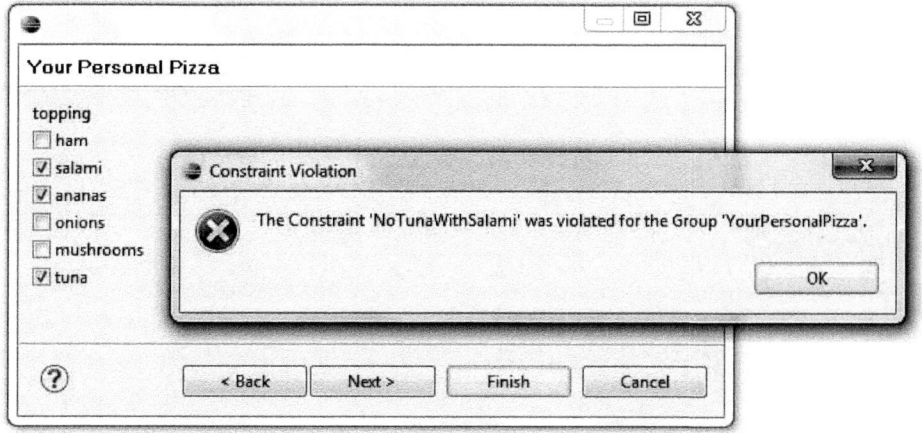

Fig. 6. Form Interpretation with Constraint Violation

4 eOCL - Integrating OCL into Textual Ecore

In addition to the integration of OCL into the Forms language, we implemented an integration of OCL into a textual variant of the Ecore metamodelling language that was developed with EMFText.[2] The aim of this integration is to lower the barrier of using OCL in metamodelling. Although OCL is well suited to define constraints for metamodels [9,10], there seems to be still little usage of OCL in metamodelling in general. For instance, in the AtlanMod metamodel Zoo [24]—a collection of around 300 metamodels—no OCL constraints are delivered with any of the metamodels. We believe that this is to a high degree a tooling issue, since many people that create metamodels are also familiar with OCL. We address this issue with our integration of Ecore and OCL, named eOCL, that allows to describe both a metamodel and OCL well-formedness rules defined on this metamodel using an integrated textual syntax as shown in Fig. 8. The respective metamodel integration is shown in Fig. 7 and similar to the extension performed for the Forms language.

This complex case study showed that the above introduced integration steps were sufficient for the integration of OCL into a more complex textual modelling language than the Forms language. The major difference between the OCL integration into the Forms language and textual Ecore is related to dynamic semantics integration. For the Forms language, we integrated the DresdenOCL interpreter to evaluate the OCL constraints. For Ecore, a generative integration is more applicable since Ecore models are typically used for Java code generation. The desired Ecore/OCL integration generates check code for all OCL constraints and instruments the Java code generated from Ecore for runtime evaluation of this check code.

---

[2] http://www.emftext.org/language/textecore/

EAnnotation
(from ecore)
source : EString
OclAnnotation
invariantsOrDefinitions
1..*
InvariantExpCS
(from ocl)

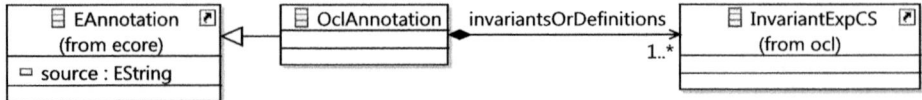

Fig. 7. Metamodel Integration of Ecore and OCL

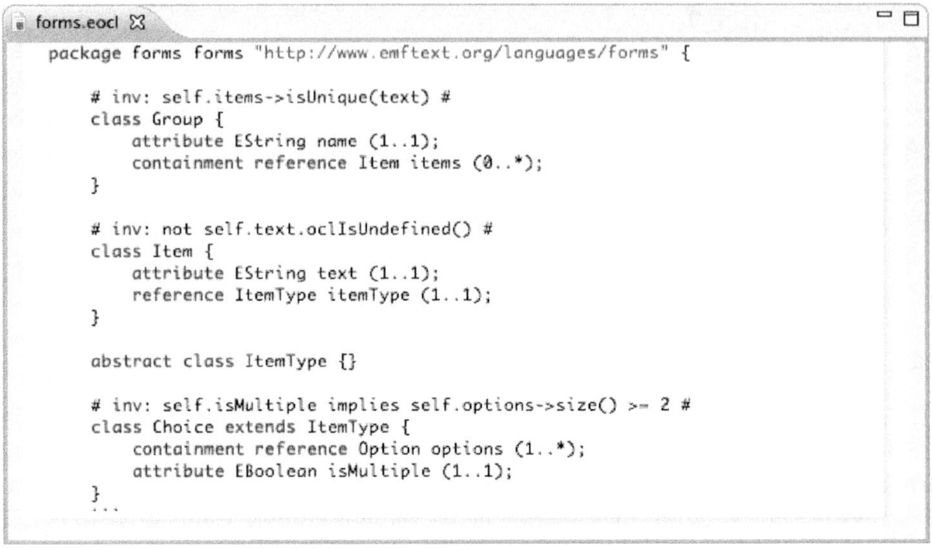

forms.eocl
package forms forms "http://www.emftext.org/languages/forms" {
# inv: self.items->isUnique(text) #
class Group {
attribute EString name (1..1);
containment reference Item items (0..*);
}
# inv: not self.text.oclIsUndefined() #
class Item {
attribute EString text (1..1);
reference ItemType itemType (1..1);
}
abstract class ItemType {}
# inv: self.isMultiple implies self.options->size() >= 2 #
class Choice extends ItemType {
containment reference Option options (1..*);
attribute EBoolean isMultiple (1..1);
}
...

Fig. 8. Forms Language Specification in eOCL

Besides the variation of the OCL evaluation technique, the same integration steps had to be performed for the Forms language and textual Ecore and similar problems were experienced.

5 Discussion

In this section we conclude the limitations of the introduced process w.r.t. its application to the different case studies, motivate potential solutions for future work.

Metamodel Integration. Our integration approach applied inheritance and delegation for the composition of the languages to integrate. This approach was sufficient for OCL integration as we reused the OCL (invariants and expressions) as a whole and worked with compatible metamodels. However, module composition with inheritance is discussed controversially for object orientation [25,26] and language engineering [27]. It breaks the principle of information hiding between modules, since inherited properties can be accessed and altered in arbitrary ways. Furthermore, structural conflicts of combined metamodels (e.g., equally named attributes in classes to integrate) can not be handled appropriately. In future work we therefore plan to combine our suggestions for modular language engineering [27] with the approach presented in this paper.

Syntax Integration. The problems experienced w.r.t. the syntactic integration of OCL in both case studies are originated from the fact that context-free grammars are not closed under composition. Syntactic ambiguities and token overlaps occur for languages that use token definitions in their concrete syntax that are used in OCL as well (e.g., numeric literals, string literals, or operators like +, -, *). In our case studies manual adaptations of the integrated syntax w.r.t. token prioritisation and reuse were sufficient to handle such conflicts. However, a more general solution for this problem could be the application of grammarware approaches that are less restricted w.r.t. syntactic overlaps. In [28], we used lexer states [29] for syntactic embedding and grammar inheritance [30] to create a generic composition system for context-free grammars that can be applied to mainstream parser generators (e.g., JavaCC [31]). Other approaches for modular language definitions are Parsing Expression Grammars (PEGs) [32,33]) and delegating compiler objects [34]. Beyond that, scannerless parsers [35] and context-aware scanning [36] are common approaches to overcome the problem of overlapping token definitions.

Metamodel Adaptation. The implementation of a pivot model adapter to integrate arbitrary languages with OCL is the standard mechanism to couple the backend of DresdenOCL to arbitrary languages. Equivalent mechanisms can be found for other OCL tools [7,10]. Future work has to investigate how we can extend the presented approach to enable completely specification-driven adapter generation. As pivot model adaptation can be considered a concrete technique for metamodel integration we also plan to examine the applicability of our modular language engineering approach [27] in this context.

Semantics Analysis. In Sect. 3.2 we illustrated how the OCL attribute grammar can be reused for multiple OCL integrations using mixin composition. Unfortunately, the current design requires some boilerplate code that is required to integrate the mixin configuration into the EMFText-generated parser. Actually, five classes and two Eclipse extension points are necessary for each language integration. For the Forms/OCL integration these classes contain about 80 lines of code. We plan to improve the language integration process by generating most of this infrastructural code.

Dynamic Semantics Integration. To reuse the same OCL interpreter for various languages it is necessary to adapt model instance objects. In [13] we presented an approach to address this issue. Furthermore, the invocation of OCL interpretation has to be included manually into the tooling for the language OCL is integrated with (e.g., the invocation of OCL interpretation when the finish button in an SWT form is pressed). Currently, we do not see how the proposed process could be improved in this regard.

Generative approaches for semantics integration share the same limitations. The generation of OCL check code can be reused for different integrations if their code generation relies on the same target language. However, code instrumentation or the adaptation of code generation to a new target language still requires manual effort.

6 Related Work

Integrating OCL with different languages has been investigated in various scenarios before. For example, in [3] a report on the integration of OCL with Triple Graph Grammars (TGGs) [37] can be found. The integration of OCL and the RAISE Specification Language (RSL) has been investigated in [4]. OCL has been integrated with Fujaba [5], business rules [6] and a profile for the railway domain [38]. While [3] and [5] embed OCL in graphical languages, the host language was textual in [4] and [38]. In [6] OCL was not embedded into another language, but rather integration was performed by transforming OCL to SQL. In addition, the integration of arbitrary textual languages into graphical languages has been presented in [39]. The diversity of the approaches to integrate OCL with other languages shows the necessity for general guidelines on how to achieve such integration.

As a first step to ease the application of OCL to arbitrary languages, the adaptation of the query and navigation facilities of OCL has been evaluated in [40]. This adaptation is part of the overall process to integrate OCL with other languages as described in this paper. However, we restricted ourselves to the integration of textual modelling languages and OCL. The semantical aspects of this integration, which have been the main subject of the works mentioned above can not be answered here as these highly depend on the host language. Nonetheless, we tried to provide some best practises to achieve practical language integration. For the integration of visual languages with OCL, one may consult [41,42], where a graphical variant of OCL—Visual OCL—is proposed.

Integrating OCL with Ecore, which served as a case study in this paper, has recently been performed by the Eclipse MDT OCL project.[3] Here, the OCLinEcore Editor was released—a very similar approach to integrate OCL and Ecore more tightly. However, while the result of this integration is close to ours, no general procedure to accomplish such a coupling is available. In contrast, the goal of this paper is to outline the steps that are necessary to perform such an integration for arbitrary textual languages.

Other constraint languages, besides OCL have also been subject to integration with modelling languages. For example, the Epsilon Validation Language (EVL) [43], which is part of the Epsilon tool suite, is based on OCL and extends the language with guarded constraints (i.e., constraints which are evaluated only for certain model elements), constraint dependencies and constraint composition (i.e., to compose complex constraints from sequences of simpler constraints).

---

[3] http://www.eclipse.org/modeling/mdt/?project=ocl

From the perspective of integration, EVL is loosely coupled with its target languages. While this enables to reuse constraints across multiple metamodels—given these metamodels share concepts with equal names—it implies that no static checks are applied to the constraints. For example, the binding of constraints to concrete metaclasses or features they navigate on is not achieved at development time as we do in both integration styles.

7 Conclusion

In this paper we presented a tool-supported process to integrate OCL with arbitrary textual modelling languages. Our five step process supports two integration kinds: *external* definition of OCL constraints that point into a textual model and *embedded* definition of OCL constraints that are directly defined inside a textual model. Only two of the five steps are required for the first integration kind, while performing all steps yields support for both kinds. We showed the applicability of the full process on two examples: an integration of OCL into a textual modelling language for forms and an integration of OCL into a textual variant of Ecore.

The embedded integration is specific to textual modelling languages and takes advantage of the fact that both the modelling language and OCL have a textual notation. It provides integrated end-user tooling that is directly generated from the specifications defined during the process using EMF, EMFText and DresdenOCL. Such a generative approach to develop integrated tooling is required to increase the willingness of tool vendors to integrate OCL into new textual modelling languages as well as the acceptance of OCL by end-users through the deeper integration of OCL tooling. In the future we plan to extend the generative component of the tool support for our process—in particular by providing adapter generators for the semantic analysis adaptation.

Acknowledgement

This research has been co-funded by the European Commission within the 6th Framework Programme project MODELPLEX #034081, the 7th Framework Programme project MOST #216691 and by the German Ministry of Education and Research within the projects feasiPLe and CoolSoftware.

References

1. Object Management Group Object Constraint Language. Version 2.2 (February 2010)
2. Object Management Group Unified Modeling Language: Superstructure Version 2.2. Final Adopted Specification formal/2009-02-02 (February 2009)
3. Dang, D.H., Gogolla, M.: On Integrating OCL and Triple Graph Grammars. In: Chaudron, M.R.V. (ed.) MODELS 2008. LNCS, vol. 5421, pp. 124–137. Springer, Heidelberg (2009)
4. Debnath, N., Funes, A., Dasso, A., Montejano, G., Riesco, D., Uzal, R.: Integrating OCL Expressions into RSL Specifications. In: IEEE Int'l Conf. on Electro/Information Technology (EIT 2007), May 2007, pp. 182–186 (2007)

5. Stölzel, M., Zschaler, S., Geiger, L.: Integrating OCL and Model Transformations in Fujaba. ECEASST 5 (2006)
6. Demuth, B., Hußmann, H., Loecher, S.: OCL as a Specification Language for Business Rules in Database Applications. In: Gogolla, M., Kobryn, C. (eds.) UML 2001. LNCS, vol. 2185, pp. 104–117. Springer, Heidelberg (2001)
7. Akehurst, D., Patrascoiu, O.: OCL 2.0 - Implementing the Standard for Multiple Metamodels. Electron. Notes Theor. Comput. Sci. 102, 21–41 (2004)
8. Bräuer, M., Demuth, B.: Model-Level Integration of the OCL Standard Library Using a Pivot Model with Generics Support. In: Ocl4All: Modelling Systems with OCL Workshop at MoDELS 2007, Berlin, Germany, Technische Universität Berlin (October 2007)
9. Loecher, S., Ocke, S.: A Metamodel-based OCL-compiler for UML and MOF. Electron. Notes Theor. Comput. Sci. 102, 43–61 (2004)
10. Eclipse Model Development Tools, http://www.eclipse.org/modeling/mdt/
11. Object Management Group Meta-Object Facility (MOF) Core Specification. Version 2.0 (January 2006)
12. Steinberg, D., Budinsky, F., Paternostro, M., Merks, E.: Eclipse Modeling Framework, 2nd edn. Pearson Education, London (2008)
13. Wilke, C., Thiele, M., Wende, C.: Extending Variability for OCL Interpretation. In: Petriu, D.C., Rouquette, N., Haugen, Ø. (eds.) MODELS 2010. LNCS, vol. 6394, pp. 361–375. Springer, Heidelberg (2010)
14. Kolovos, D., Paige, R., Polack, F.: Detecting and Repairing Inconsistencies across Heterogeneous Models. In: 2008 Int'l Conf. on Software Testing, Verification, and Validation, pp. 356–364. IEEE Computer Society, Los Alamitos (2008)
15. Chimiak-Opoka, J., Demuth, B., Silingas, D., Rouquette, N.: Requirements Analysis for an Integrated OCL Development Environment. In: OCL 2009 Workshop - The Pragmatics Of OCL And Other Textual Specification Languages (2009)
16. Heidenreich, F., Johannes, J., Karol, S., Seifert, M., Wende, C.: Derivation and Refinement of Textual Syntax for Models. In: Paige, R.F., Hartman, A., Rensink, A. (eds.) ECMDA-FA 2009. LNCS, vol. 5562, pp. 114–129. Springer, Heidelberg (2009)
17. TU Dresden: Software Technology Group DresdenOCL (2010), http://dresden-ocl.sourceforge.net/
18. Odersky, M., Spoon, L., Venners, B.: Programming in Scala, 1st edn. Artima Press, Mountain View (2008)
19. Kiama - A Scala library for language processing (2010), http://code.google.com/p/kiama/
20. Wilke, C., Thiele, M.: DresdenOCL - Manual for Installation, Use and Development. Technische Universität Dresden, Dresden, Germany (2011)
21. Knuth, D.: Semantics of context-free languages. Theory of Computing Systems 2(2), 127–145 (1968)
22. Demuth, B., Wilke, C.: Model and Object Verification by Using Dresden OCL. In: Proceedings of the Russian-German Workshop Innovation Information Technologies: Theory and Practice, Ufa, Russia, July 25-31. Ufa State Aviation Technical University, Ufa (2009)
23. Wilke, C.: Java Code Generation for Dresden OCL2 for Eclipse. Großer Beleg (minor thesis), Technische Universität Dresden, Dresden, Germany (February 2009)
24. AtlanMod Metamodel Zoo, http://www.emn.fr/z-info/atlanmod/index.php/Zoos

25. Bracha, G., Lindstrom, G.: Modularity Meets Inheritance. In: Int'l Conf. on Computer Languages, IEEE Computer Society, pp. 282–290. IEEE Computer Society, Los Alamitos (1992)
26. Taivalsaari, A.: On the Notion of Inheritance. ACM Computing Surveys 28(3), 438–479 (1996)
27. Wende, C., Thieme, N., Zschaler, S.: A Role-based Approach Towards Modular Language Engineering. In: van den Brand, M., Gašević, D., Gray, J. (eds.) SLE 2009. LNCS, vol. 5969, pp. 254–273. Springer, Heidelberg (2010)
28. Karol, S., Zschaler, S.: Providing Mainstream Parser Generators with Modular Language Definition Support. Technical Report TUD-FI10-01 - Januar 2010, Technische Universität Dresden (January 2010)
29. Clark, C.: Newlines and Lexer States. SIGPLAN Notices 35(4), 18–24 (2000)
30. Aksit, M., Mostert, R., Haverkort, B.: Compiler Generation Based on Grammar Inheritance. Technical report, University of Twente (July 1990)
31. The Java Compiler Compiler, https://javacc.dev.java.net/
32. Ford, B.: Parsing Expression Grammars: A Recognition-Based Syntactic Foundation. In: 31st Symposium on Principles of Programming Languages (POPL 2004), pp. 111–122. ACM, New York (2004)
33. Grimm, R.: Better Extensibility through Modular Syntax. In: 2006 Conf. on Programming Language Design and Implementation (PLDI 2006), pp. 38–51. ACM, New York (2006)
34. Bosch, J.: Delegating Compiler Objects: Modularity and Reusability in Language Engineering. Nordic J. of Computing 4(1), 66–92 (1997)
35. Heering, J., Hendriks, P.R.H., Klint, P., Rekers, J.: The Syntax Definition Formalism SDF – Reference Manual. SIGPLAN Notices 24(11), 43–75 (1989)
36. Wyk, E.R.V., Schwerdfeger, A.C.: Context-Aware Scanning For Parsing Extensible Languages. In: 6th Int'l Conf. on Generative Programming and Component Engineering (GPCE 2007), pp. 63–72. ACM, New York (2007)
37. Schürr, A.: Specification of Graph Translators with Triple Graph Grammars. In: Mayr, E.W., Schmidt, G., Tinhofer, G. (eds.) WG 1994. LNCS, vol. 903. Springer, Heidelberg (1995)
38. Berkenkötter, K.: OCL-based Validation of a Railway Domain Profile. In: Auletta, V. (ed.) MoDELS 2006. LNCS, vol. 4364, pp. 159–168. Springer, Heidelberg (2007)
39. Scheidgen, M.: Textual Modelling Embedded into Graphical Modelling. In: Schieferdecker, I., Hartman, A. (eds.) ECMDA-FA 2008. LNCS, vol. 5095, pp. 153–168. Springer, Heidelberg (2008)
40. Kolovos, D.S., Paige, R.F., Polack, F.: Aligning OCL with Domain-Specific Languages to Support Instance-Level Model Queries. ECEASST 5 (2006)
41. Kent, S.: Constraint Diagrams: Visualizing Assertions in Object-Oriented Models. In: OOPSLA, pp. 327–341 (1997)
42. Bottoni, P., Koch, M., Parisi-Presicce, F., Taentzer, G.: A Visualization of OCL Using Collaborations. In: Gogolla, M., Kobryn, C. (eds.) UML 2001. LNCS, vol. 2185, pp. 257–271. Springer, Heidelberg (2001)
43. Kolovos, D.S., Rose, L., Page, R.F.: The Epsilon Book, http://www.eclipse.org/gmt/epsilon/doc/book/

Quality of Service-Oriented Software Systems (QUASOSS 2010)

Heiko Koziolek[1], Steffen Becker[2], Jens Happe[3], and Paul Pettersson[4]

[1] Industrial Software Systems, ABB Corporate Research Ladenburg, Germany
heiko.koziolek@de.abb.com
[2] University of Paderborn, Germany
steffen.becker@upb.de
[3] SAP Research, Karlsruhe, Germany
jens.happe@sap.com
[4] Mälardalen University, Sweden
paul.pettersson@mdh.se

Abstract. The 2nd International Workshop on the Quality of Service-Oriented Software Systems (QUASOSS 2010) brought together researchers and practitioners to assess current approaches for analyzing the quality of service-oriented software systems. Due to the current maturation of model-driven methods for service-oriented systems, the declared goal of QUASOSS 2010 was to assess the state-of-the-art, report on successful or unsuccessful application of these methods, and to identify a research roadmap for future approaches. QUASOSS 2010 was attended by 25 participants. It featured a keynote by Prof. Dorina Petriu, 6 paper presentations, and a panel discussion.

1 Introduction

Service-oriented software systems are beginning to pervade many areas of the IT world and promise to deal with dynamically changing environments and strict quality-of-service requirements. Currently, platforms for software-as-a-service (SaaS) applications are emerging, which help to implement service-oriented systems on cloud infrastructures. Cloud-based environments have to offer strict service level agreements to be competitive (e.g. Windows Azure and Amazon EC2 guarantee 99.95% uptime).

Methods for assessing service level agreements regarding extra-functional properties are often based on modeling approaches, which help to reduce the complexity of the problem, focus on specific attributes, and rely on sound mathematical foundations. Models can be used during all life-cycles stages, such as design, implementation, runtime, and system evolution to assess the quality of a system. Here, the term quality refers to extra-functional properties, such as reliability, maintainability, performance, security, usability, sustainability, etc.

The 2nd International Workshop on the Quality of Service-Oriented Software Systems (QUASOSS 2010) brought together researchers and practitioners to assess current approaches for analyzing the quality of service-oriented software systems. Due to the current maturation of model-driven methods for service-oriented systems, the declared goal of QUASOSS 2010 was to assess the state-of-the-art, report on successful or unsuccessful application of these methods, and to identify a research roadmap for future approaches.

The program committee accepted 6 papers that cover a variety of topics, including performance modeling, performance measurements, trade-off analyses between quality attributes, and monitoring service-oriented system at runtime. Approx. 25 participants attended the workshop. Besides a keynote and the paper presentations, the workshop featured a discussion session, where all participants provided their views on what would a good modeling language for the evaluating and improving the quality of software of service-oriented software systems.

The remainder of this summary is structured as follows: Section 2 provides an overview of the keynote speech as well as the paper presentations and Section 3 summarizes the workshop discussions.

2 Workshop Contributions

2.1 Keynote

The keynote speech was given by Prof. Dorina Petriu from Carleton University, Ottawa, Canada. Her talk was entitled "Model-based Performance Analysis of Service-Oriented Systems" . The talk focused on performance analysis of UML models of service-oriented systems, starting early in the development process and continuing throughout the software life-cycle. In order to conduct quantitative performance analysis, an UML model extended with performance annotations is transformed into a performance model (such as queueing networks, Petri nets, stochastic process algebra, etc.), which can be solved with existing performance analysis tools. The "UML Profile for Modeling and Analysis of Real-Time and Embedded systems (MARTE)" can be used for adding performance annotations to a given UML model.

The talk discussed at first the kind of performance annotations that need to be added to UML models and the principles for transforming annotated software models into performance models. Such a transformation must bridge a large semantic gap between the source and target model for two main reasons: performance models concentrate on resource usage and abstract away many details of the original software model, and the performance model requires platform information which is not contained in the software application model.

Finally, the talk highlighted other research challenges, such as a) merging performance modeling and measurements; b) applying variability modeling to service-oriented systems, and c) use of SOA patterns for evaluating and improving the performance of service-oriented systems.

2.2 Paper Presentations

6 papers were presented at the workshop, for the full workshop proceedings see [1]. A synopsis of each presentation is given below, extended versions of the papers [6] and [3] are included in this workshop reader.

- *Using quality of service bounds for effective multi-objective software architecture optimization [6]*
  Qais Noorshams, Anne Martens, Ralf Reussner
  The authors proposed an extension to a method for automatic quality improvement of service-oriented architectures using meta-heuristics. The extension takes bounds into account to optimize the meta-heuristic search process.
- *An integrated tool for trade-off analysis of quality-of-service attributes [4]*
  Leo Hatvani, Anton Jansen, Cristina Seceleanu, Paul Pettersson
  This paper presented a tool based on the Analytical Hierachy Process method and the results from a architecture-based quality prediction tool for determining the tradeoffs between performance, reliability, and maintainability of a service-oriented system.
- *Using software performance curves for dependable and cost-efficient service hosting [7]* **Dennis Westermann, Christof Momm**
  The authors introduced the idea of Software Performance Curves and described how they can be derived by a service provider hosting a multi-tenant system.
- *Performance-driven stepwise refinement of component-based architectures [5]*
  Lucia Kapova, Barbora Buhnova
  Refining the concept of quality-related "completions" for prediction models, the authors proposed a method to a identify and resolve conflicts between multiple applicable completions.
- *Model-based dynamic QoS-driven service composition [2]*
  Antinisca Di Marco, Antonino Sabetta
  This paper proposed a model-based framework, called Smart, that automatically constructs complex services with guaranteed QoS.
- *Usage profile and platform independent automated validation of service behavior specifications [3]* **Henning Groenda**
  The author showed how model-based testing can be applied to validate a quality specification's accuracy and how the attachment of validation settings to specifications can ease validity assessments.

3 Discussion Summary

After the paper presentations of the QUASOSS workshop, the participants joined for a 90-minute discussion session on the topic: "What is the best modeling language for quality of service in service-oriented systems?". Many researchers have proposed modeling languages for service-oriented systems during the last decade, yet a consensus on an industry standard has not been reached.

Some participants pointed out that the UML modeling language is the de-facto standard for modeling and should also be used for modeling service-oriented systems. There are UML profiles for modeling service-oriented systems (i.e., Service oriented architecture Modeling Language, SoaML) and QoS properties (i.e., Modeling and Analysis of Real Time Systems, MARTE), which could be used especially for the modeling tasks discussed during the workshop.

The benefits of using UML were then briefly discussed. Reusing and extending an existing industry standard provides the opportunity to reuse and annotate existing models and thus save time and efforts for modeling. Rich tool support exists for creating UML models and there are even some performance or reliability prediction tools based on model transformations from UML. Domain-specific features or particularities of any QoS prediction approach can be integrated into the UML using the standard mechanism of profiles.

However, some participants also pointed out the drawbacks of the UML. The complexity of UML and the MARTE profile with several thousand pages of specification scares many developers from developing more formal models. The semantics of many concepts are not formally defined, thus different tool vendors have different implementations of the standard.

The MARTE profile is currently hardly used in industry. This partially stems from the fact that MARTE has been released only one year ago. However, its predecessor, the SPT profile, released eight years ago was also not broadly adopted in industry, thus hinting at some deeper underlying issues. Special tool support for these profiles has always been a concern. For example entering the complicated performance annotations should be assisted in structured manner, whereas current tools simply rely on free text fields that easily lend themselves to user input errors.

Other participants favored domain-specific modeling languages, such as service modeling languages or components models that can be used to model service-oriented systems. There are already several component model supporting the specification of extra-functional properties, which could be used to analyze service-oriented systems. Applying quality-oriented component models for service-oriented systems might be even simpler than for component-based systems, because the degree of freedom for deploying a service is usually not present for service-oriented systems.

Some members of the discussion group pointed out that the question of the best modeling language is related to the question of the best programming language, which was debated often in former times. Modeling languages shift the level of abstraction higher, in the same manner as higher-level programming languages raised the abstraction level from assembly code.

The vision for modeling and analyzing QoS properties in service-oriented systems was sketched by the workshop participants as follows:

- **Interoperable tooling:** more emphasis should be put on the interoperability of modeling tools. Any new modeling language should provide semi-automatic conversion or migration tools.
- **Domain focus:** there is a need for domain-specific modeling languages for QoS properties which focus on restricted aspects and are therefore easy to learn.
- **Tool support for QoS annotations:** QoS modeling tools should provide special support for creating QoS annotations (e.g., if text-based, there should be automatic syntax checking, syntax highlighting, auto-completion, etc.).
- **Modeling languages for runtime analysis:** very expressive modeling languages might not allow live QoS analyses during service operation, because

they might require long simulation runs. Thus, there should be specially restricted languages, whose instances can be used for quick analysis and system reconfiguration during runtime.
- **Future UML standards:** future UML standards or profiles should focus on a smaller number of concepts and define these more formally. There is the need for involving strong industry partners in any standardization efforts so that the specification are applied and resource for tool development are given.

Acknowledgment

The QUASOSS organizers would like to thank all participants of the workshop for their lively discussions, the program committee members for their insightful reviews, and especially our keynote speaker Prof. Dorina Petriu for her valuable contribution. The workshop was supported by the European Union Projects Q-ImPrESS and SLA@SOI.

References

1. QUASOSS 2010: Proceedings of the 2nd International Workshop on the Quality of Service-Oriented Software Systems. ACM, New York (2010), http://portal.acm.org/citation.cfm?id=1858263
2. Di Marco, A., Sabetta, A.: Model-based dynamic qos-driven service composition. In: Proceedings of the 2nd International Workshop on the Quality of Service-Oriented Software Systems, QUASOSS 2010, pp. 5:1–5:6. ACM, New York (2010), http://doi.acm.org/10.1145/1858263.1858270
3. Groenda, H.: Usage profile and platform independent automated validation of service behavior specifications. In: Proceedings of the 2nd International Workshop on the Quality of Service-Oriented Software Systems, QUASOSS 2010, pp. 6:1–6:6. ACM, New York (2010), http://doi.acm.org/10.1145/1858263.1858271
4. Hatvani, L., Jansen, A., Seceleanu, C., Pettersson, P.: An integrated tool for trade-off analysis of quality-of-service attributes. In: Proceedings of the 2nd International Workshop on the Quality of Service-Oriented Software Systems, QUASOSS 2010, pp. 2:1–2:6. ACM, New York (2010), http://doi.acm.org/10.1145/1858263.1858266
5. Kapova, L., Buhnova, B.: Performance-driven stepwise refinement of component-based architectures. In: Proceedings of the 2nd International Workshop on the Quality of Service-Oriented Software Systems, QUASOSS 2010, pp. 4:1–4:7. ACM, New York (2010), http://doi.acm.org/10.1145/1858263.1858269
6. Noorshams, Q., Martens, A., Reussner, R.: Using quality of service bounds for effective multi-objective software architecture optimization. In: Proceedings of the 2nd International Workshop on the Quality of Service-Oriented Software Systems, QUASOSS 2010, pp. 1:1–1:6. ACM, New York (2010), http://doi.acm.org/10.1145/1858263.1858265
7. Westermann, D., Momm, C.: Using software performance curves for dependable and cost-efficient service hosting. In: Proceedings of the 2nd International Workshop on the Quality of Service-Oriented Software Systems, QUASOSS 2010, pp. 3:1–3:6. ACM, New York (2010), http://doi.acm.org/10.1145/1858263.1858267

An Accuracy Information Annotation Model for Validated Service Behavior Specifications

Henning Groenda

FZI Forschungszentrum Informatik
Haid-und-Neu-Straße 10-14, 76131 Karlsruhe, Germany
groenda@fzi.de

Abstract. Assessing providable service levels based on model-driven prediction approaches requires valid service behavior specifications. Such specifications must be suitable for the requested usage profile and available hardware to make correct predictions and decisions on providable service levels. Assessing the precision of given parameterized performance specifications is often done manually in an ad-hoc way based on the experience of the performance engineer. In this paper, we show how the accuracy of a specification can be assessed and stated and how validation settings of model-based testing can ease precision assessments. The applicability of the approach is shown on a case study. We demonstrate how our approach allows accuracy statements and can be used in combination with usage profile and platform independent performance validations, as well as point out how accuracy assessments are eased.

1 Introduction

Service providers can use model-driven performance prediction approaches to assess providable service levels before they offer a service level agreement (SLA). The prediction approaches allow reasoning about the resource usage within the provider's environment as well as achievable performance metrics for its clients. The more advanced approaches use parameterized models to allow specification reuse when influencing parameters change. Depending on the change itself and the generality of the specification, this can reduce the need of re-executing or re-testing the service itself or its required services. Additionally, it allows faster responses to SLA requests if the specifications can be reused.

The overall quality of the predictions depends on the used prediction technique and the quality of the specifications themselves. Some, e.g. the usage profile, are directly linked with SLAs, whereas hardware environment and deployment depend on the service provider. The overall quality depends on how closely specified and real performance match. Behavior specifications are in most cases abstractions of an implementation's behavior. On the one hand, this allows a significant reduction of the time required for a prediction compared to an execution of the implementation. On the other hand, validating these specifications and knowing the deviation due to their abstraction level is crucial for the correct interpretation of the prediction results.

So far, research has focused on the performance prediction quality of the approaches under the assumption that specifications are as accurate as possible. Most of these specifications were tailored by performance engineers to match an implementation's behavior. If re-engineering approaches, e.g. [9], are used to create specifications there is no guarantee on the quality of the specification and additional validation is required. This is commonly a manual ad-hoc process requiring specialist knowledge and high human effort. The resulting specifications generally don't contain information about their accuracy and the preconditions on their (input) parameters. This is fine if the specification is not reused or the person using the specification knows these assumption. However, this is very unlikely in multi-party scenarios common to service-oriented environments.

This paper introduces a model for stating the accuracy of service behavior specifications. Additionally, it shows its use in combination with a model-based testing techniques to validate parameterized performance specifications. These specifications constitute a basis for compositional performance prediction approaches and thereby also SLA management. The contributions of this paper are i) an annotation model for attaching accuracy information to service behavior specifications, and ii) an automated validation process for usage profile and hardware environment independent performance specifications.

The application of both is shown on a case study, which demonstrates necessary user interactions, achievable validation results, and how the validity assessment process is eased by the approach.

This paper is structured as follows: Section 2 discusses related work. Section 3 shows the Accuracy Information Annotation Model used to annotate specifications with quality information. Section 4 provides details on the validation process and its features. Section 5 show the practical application of the presented approach on a case study in which an implementation of the Fibonacci algorithm is validated. Assumptions and limitations are discussed in section 6. Finally, Section 7 concludes the paper and provides an outlook on future work.

2 Related Work

Performance behavior specification languages for components and services are still a maturing field. An overview about existing languages is provided in the survey by Becker et al. [5]. The older languages were based on fixed execution times (or distributions thereof) while newer ones allowed to take additional parameters into account. These parameters and the languages supporting them are discussed in [8] in detail. The quality of predictions based on such specifications highly depends on the quality of these specifications. Adding parametric dependencies to the specifications and the trend towards more detailed specifications made the validation of these specifications more complex and at the same time more important. Our approach supports all types of parameters available in current performance specifications and is exemplary applied to the Palladio Componen Model (PCM) [18] specifications, which support all of these parameters.

Reverse engineering approaches for behavior specifications provide the possibility to synthesize behavior specifications from implementations. Two of these constructive approaches are presented below:

The approach of Meyerhöfer [13] uses profiling techniques and black box tests to synthesize behavior specifications. The resulting measurements are stored in a performance repository. The repository is used to query run- and response times in form of statistical estimators, e.g. minimum or maximum, or distribution function. If the number of runtime-equivalent continuous subdomains for each input parameter of a service is known the boundaries between subdomains and values for each subdomain can be estimated by the approach. The specification can have the abstraction level of statistical estimators and distribution functions for the resource demand.

The approach of Krogmann [10] uses a combination of genetic programming and static and runtime Bytecode analysis to create behavior specifications. It significantly reduces the effort necessary to synthesize a specification based on source code. However, it does not ensure that the quality of the specification is below a certain threshold. The dependencies identified by the approach can also be quite complex and a manual adjustment of the abstraction worthwhile.

Runtime behavior verification of implementations is addressed in worst-case execution time (WCET) analyses. Harmon and Klefstad conducted a survey [7] and identified that state-of-the-art analyses are still restricted to a per-method base and often additional information on loop bounds is required for the algorithms. Return-value dependencies within a method are also not supported in general. Several service performance, load, and stress testing tools, e.g. JMeter [3], HP LoadRunner [17], iTKO LISA [14], OpenSTA [1], or PushToTest [2], are available. These tools run predefined service calls on a running service implementation and measure the end-to-end performance or identify bottlenecks. The aim is to determine client-side metrics like response time or throughput. The context of hardware environment and usage scenarios are fixed for the measurements. This leads to meaningful results for the measured context but does not allow inferences for other contexts.

There are also approaches for the automated generation of functional test case inputs, e.g. [4]. This approach uses WSDL-based service descriptions to generate test cases. Different generation strategies allow to generate test cases to cover all operations, messages, and XSD-based messages contained in such a description. The test output must be specified by a developer in order to execute the test cases. The focus is on identifying unexpected functional behavior of a service and not its execution time.

Extra-functional behavior and component testing is also considered by Hamlet [6]. The article presents a compositional testing theory based on subdomain or partition testing. Component test points and their (input and output) propagation are considered to represent the best test criteria or cases. Focus is put on functional behavior but extra-functional behavior is covered as well. The theoretical approach requires full knowledge about data-dependencies and has difficulties in finding fix points for loops / iterations. The specifications are not compositional and systems must be assembled for testing. Furthermore, Hamlet points out that theoretical comparisons between random and subdomain testing have not shown a conclusive advantage either way in detecting failures. The approach presented in this paper does not require knowledge on data-dependencies and calculated functions. It allows validating specifications which are composable. Validation is done using random testing.

The performance modeling standard UML-MARTE (Modeling and Analysis of Real-Time Embedded, Systems) [16] which was developed based on UML-SPT (UML Profile for Schedulability, Performance, and Time Specification) [15], allows to express Quality of Service (QoS) requirements, characteristics, and measurement-based performance models. It is allowed to state required, assumed, estimated, and measured values [15, p.154]. Additionally, statistical properties like minimum, maximum, average, mean, and percentiles can be modeled. MARTE augmented this by attributes for measurement sources, precision, and time expressions [16, p.47,p.439]. The precision is represented by a floating point number between 0 and 1 and its semantic is described as follows:

> Degree of refinement in the performance of a measurement operation, or the degree of perfection in the instruments and methods used to obtain a result. Precision is characterized in terms of a Real value, which is the standard deviation of the measurement.

The approach presented in this paper allows stronger and more precise statements about the precision of a specification and allows to state for which parameter values of a parameterized specification this precision hold.

3 Accuracy Information Model

In this section, we will present details on the annotation model, which enables attaching accuracy information to service behavior specifications. Tool support for model instances is provided by using the Eclipse Modeling Framework (EMF). The Accuracy Information Annotation Model (AIAM) stores quality information in a QualityRepository (see fig. 1). It consists of two parts, one to store the stipulated quality annotations (QualityAnnotation) and one to store specifications of the validation(TBValidationQuality. The quality annotations references the specification of the validations which were instantiated and did not allow to reject the stipulated quality annotations. If any instantiation and test allowed a rejection this reference must not exist. Each part is presented in the following in an own chapter.

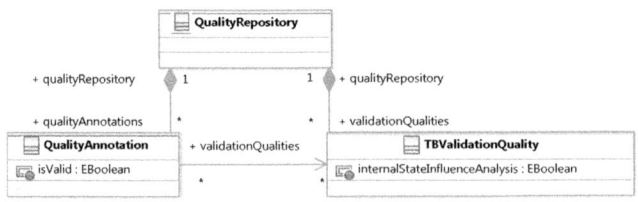

Fig. 1. Quality Repository

An Accuracy Information Annotation Model 373

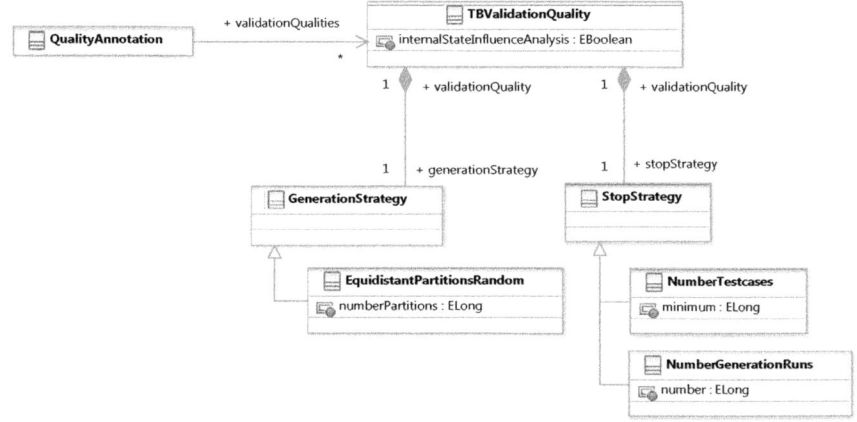

Fig. 2. Quality Annotation

3.1 Validation Quality

The quality of the validation allows estimations on the thoroughness of the validation as well as remaining classes of inconsistencies between a specification and the stipulated quality. The quality of test-based validations depends on the used test case generation method and the criteria when sufficient test cases have been generated. How this information is stored in the model elements (see fig. 2) is explained in the following.

TBValidationQuality bundles the information for test-based validations. It references the used test case generation strategy and generation stop strategy.

All available generation strategies are subclasses of GenerationStrategy. A subclass contains the parameters used for the generation strategy, e.g. the number of partitions for the EquidistandtPartitionsRandomStrategy. The strategy itself is implemented in the validation framework and selected based on the type of the class instance.

All available generation stop strategies are subclasses of StopStrategy. Each class contains the parameters for a strategy. Examples are the minimum number of overall executed test cases for the NumberTestcases strategy or the number of test case generation rounds for the NumberGenerationRuns strategy. Multiple test cases can be generated in a generation round, e.g. one for each service input parameter partition. The strategy itself is implemented in the validation framework and selected based on the type of the class instance.

3.2 Quality Annotation

The stipulated quality annotations are modeled with Quality Annotation. It consists of four parts: The stipulated precision, the input parameter partitions for which the specification is precise, the specification for which the quality annotations are stipulated, and information on the influence of internal state on the accuracy of the specification. These parts are depicted in figs. 3 and 4 and described in the following.

The quality annotations consist of a generic part and one specific for a specification language. The parts necessary for the specification language Palladio Component Model (PCM) are shown with gray background in the figures and provide an example how the annotations are used.

Figure 3 shows the parts for the stipulated precision and the information on the influence of internal state on the accuracy of the specification.

The information on the influence of internal state on the accuracy of the specification is modeled by InternalStateInfluenceAnalysisAggregation. It is based on repetitions of validation runs on the same service instance. If the internal state changes between the repetitions the influence can lead to deviations in the measurements. In order to provide an impression of the potential impact the maximum measured deviation is stored as percent value. The deviations are aggregated for each validation run. The specification of the validation run leading to the deviations is referenced by validationQualitites, the maximum deviation in a parameter in CallParameterDeviation and the maximum deviation in number of calls in NumberOfCallsDeviation. The parameter for which the deviation was measured is referenced by ParameterReference, the required element for which the deviation, in number of calls to it, was measured is referenced by requiredElement.

A RequiredElement is an element required by a component. The elements are ordered hierarchically (childREs and parentRE). For the PCM (PCMRE), the hierarchy has 4 levels. The topmost one is a categorization of requested categories (PCMRECategory), e.g. calls to (Hardware) Resources, Infrastructure Components or Business Components. The next lower level are interfaces (PCMREInterface). Interfaces can be required multiple times, each in a different role (PCMRERole). The lowest level is the call signature (PCMRESignature), identifying an atomar service operation invocation. A consistent use of the hierarchy levels is ensured by OCL constraints on the subclasses of PCMRE. The hierarchies of other specification languages can be modeled analogously.

The information on the stipulated precision is referenced by stipulatedRE Precisions. The precision for each required element is stored in REPrecision. A default precision for the number of calls to the element (defaultPrecision NumberOfCalls) as well as the precision for parameters of the calls (default PrecisionCallParameter) can be set. These default are applied to the type of required element as long as no new definition on a lower hierarchy level overrides the default.

The precision itself is modeled by ValidationPrecision (see fig. 4). One alternative is that the precision is not validated (NoValidationPrecision) which can be used for example to state that call parameters are not validated for infrastructure components. A second alternative is that the measured and specified values are equal (EqualsValidationPrecision). This can be used for example to state that the number of calls to external components are validated. The last alternative is that the deviation must not exceed a relative threshold if an absolute threshold is exceeded (LimitedDeviationValidationPrecision). This allows handling situations in which small absolute deviations lead to big relative deviations but which may have only a small performance impact. The thresholds are set by absolute and

An Accuracy Information Annotation Model 375

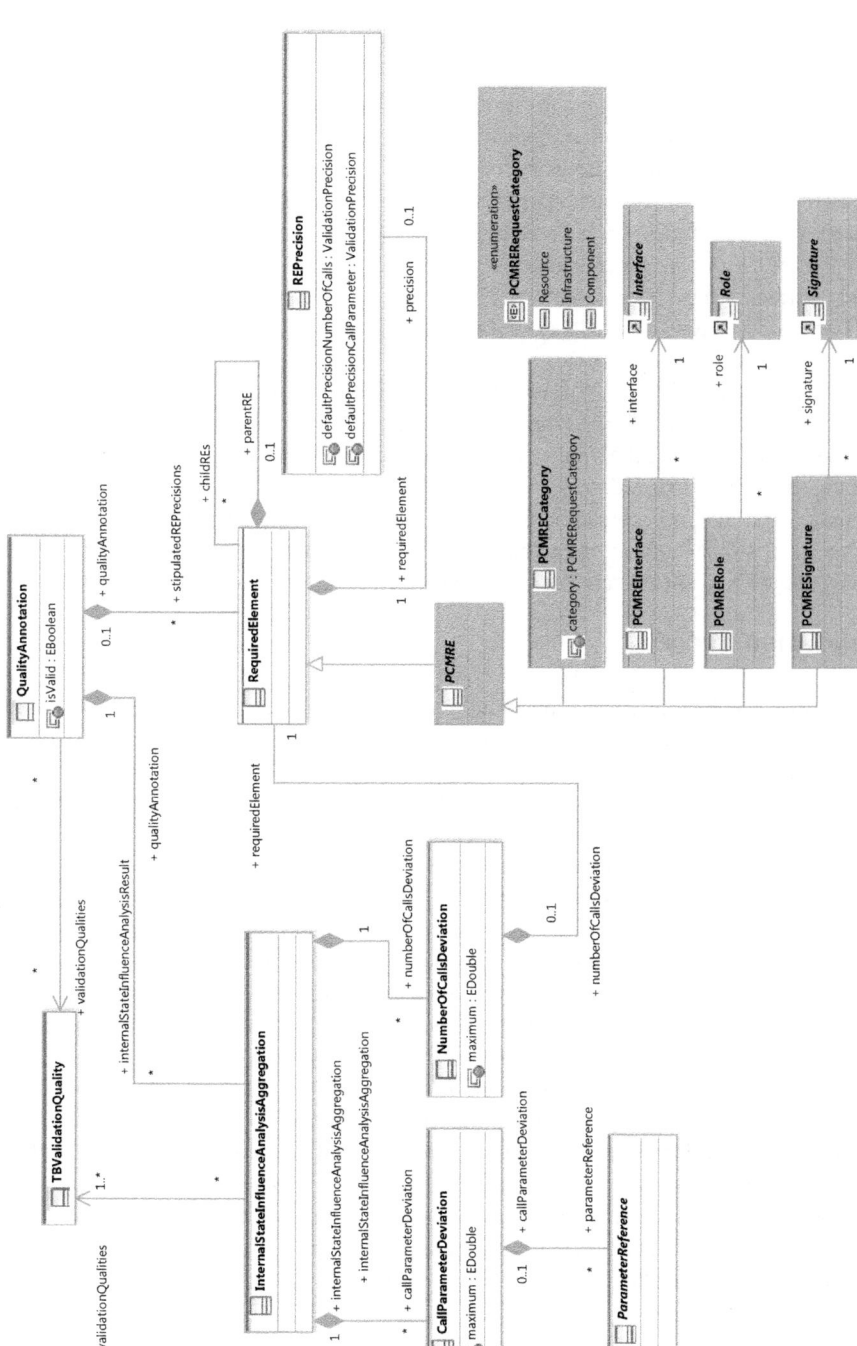

Fig. 3. Stipulated Precision and Internal State Influence Analysis (Classes with Gray Background are PCM-specific)

relative. This can be used for example to state that a certain deviation in the number of calls to infrastructure components is allowed.

Figure 4 shows the parts for the input parameter partitions for which the stipulated precision should hold and the specification for which the quality annotations are stipulated.

The input parameter partitions are modeled by `ParameterPartition`. This is due to the fact that the abstract description of the service's behavior often only holds for certain ranges. It additionally allows to focus the validation effort. The parameter partitions must be subclassed for each specification language, e.g. the PCM. For the PCM, each parameter (`parameterReference`) can have several performance characterisations (`CharacterisedPCMParameterPartition`). The ranges or intervals for each of these characterisations are stored in `CharacterisedPCMParameterPartitionRange` or `CharacterisedParameterPartitionInterval`.

The control flow specification of the service for which the quality annotations are stipulated is modeled by `ServiceSpecification`. In order check if the specification has not been changed since the annotation has been created and validated a checksum of the specification can be stored in `checksum`. The `ServiceSpecification` must be subclassed for each possible specification of a specification language. In case of the PCM, this means that there is one subclass, `PCMServiceSpecification`, which references the service specification used in the PCM (`ResourceDemandingSEFF`).

4 Validation Process

In this section, we introduce our automated validation process for usage profile and hardware environment independent performance validations of service behavior specifications which uses the AIAM.

The validation works with parameterized models. Parameters influencing the behavior of a service can depend on input parameters of the service call, on returned parameters from required services, or on the service configuration. We use model-based testing techniques to validate such parameterized performance specifications. The process is exemplary realized for validating Palladio Component Model [18] specifications against implementations. Our approach uses hardware environment independent specifications which allow inferring the performance in other environments. Resource load is measured in Java Bytecode instructions which is combined with benchmarks to calculate the performance for a specific platform. This step is supported by tools, e.g. ByCounter [11]. Using such specifications in the validation process allows avoiding any side effects of the instrumentation on the measurements.

The steps of the validation process itself are depicted in figure 5 and explained in the following. Prerequisites are deployment instructions, an AIAM instance, a service behavior specification, a service specification including its required and provided interfaces, and a mapping model linking the parameterized behavior specification and the implementation. It is checked if the specified parameters are valid with respect to the AIAM instance.

In step `deploy`, the service is deployed in the test environment. This step might require manual interaction.

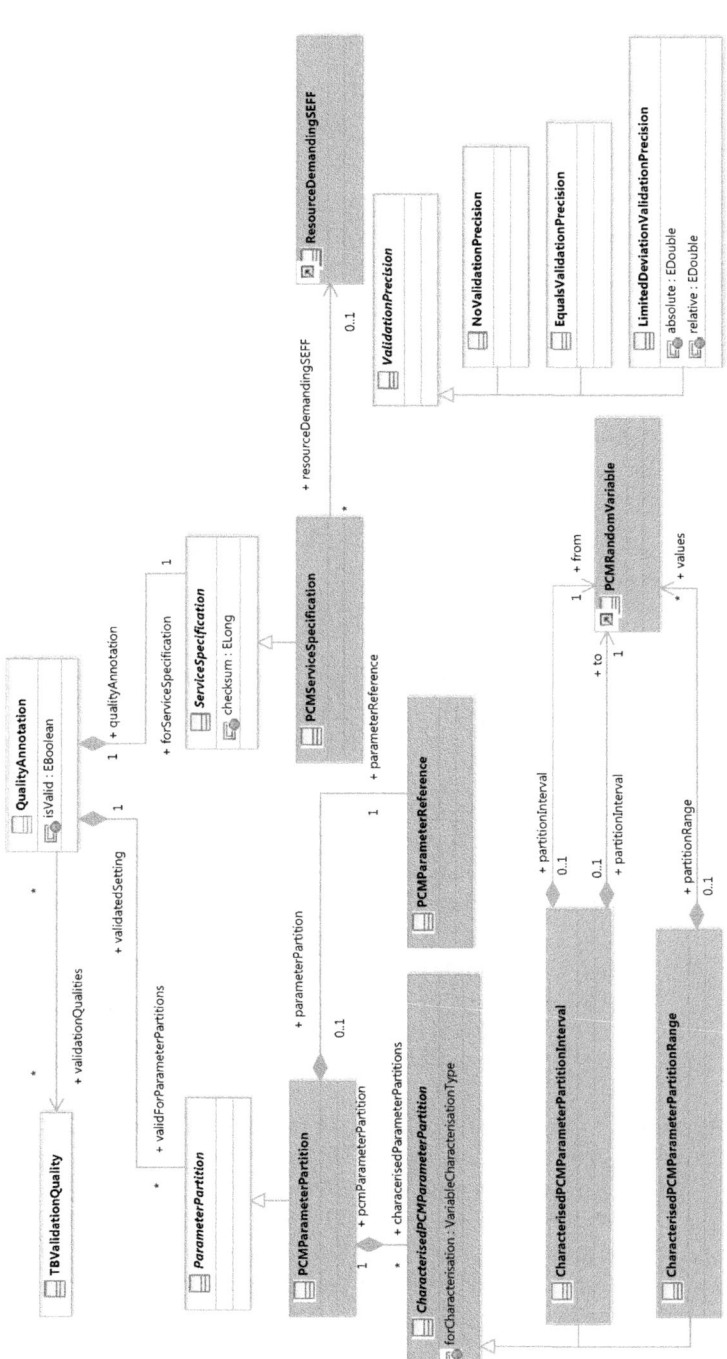

Fig. 4. Specification and Validated Parameter Partitions (Classes with Gray Background are PCM-specific)

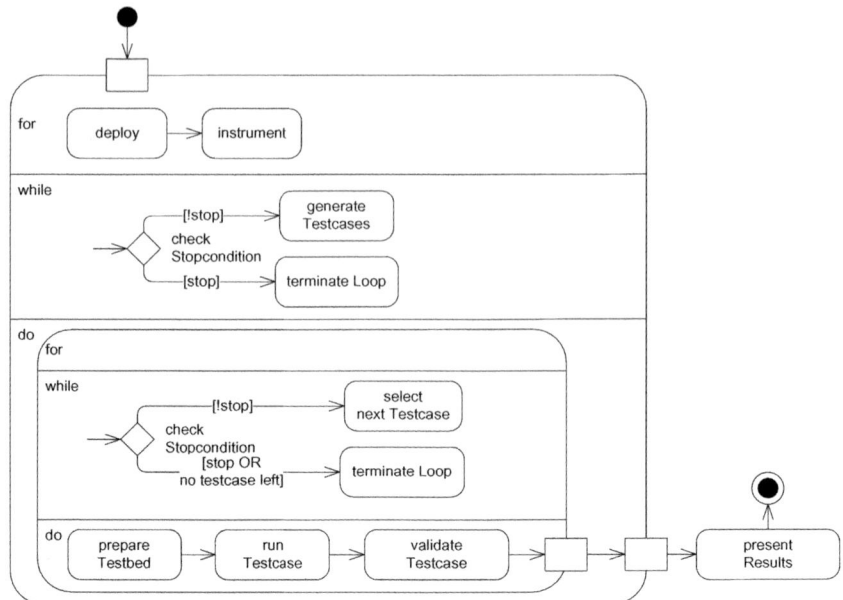

Fig. 5. Activity Diagram of the Service Behavior Validation Process

In step `instrument`, the service under test is automatically instrumented for measurements. If the service behavior specification contains different sections, e.g. internal processing, external calls, loops, or branches, each section is instrumented separately. The instrumentation measures for each section the resource demand in Bytecodes instructions as well as calls to required services (including the used parameters). The ByCounter approach [12] is used for this instrumentation.

In the steps `check Stopcondition`, the `StopCondition` in the AIAM model instance is checked and decided whether new tests should be run or parts of the validation have finished.

In the steps `terminate Loop`, the current active loop is successfully terminated.

In step `generate Testcases`, new test cases are generated based on the selected `GenerationStrategy` in the AIAM model instance.

In step `select next Testcase`, the next testcase which has not been run yet is selected.

In step `prepare Testbed`, the mock-ups for required components in the testbed are prepared according to the behavior stated in the specification.

In step `run Testcase`, the test case itself is executed.

In step `validate Testcase`, specified and measured service behavior are compared with respect to the stipulated precision in the AIAM instance.

In step `present Results`, the results of the validation are presented to the user and the quality annotation in the AIAM instance is updated accordingly.

5 Case Study

In this section, a case study shows the applicability of the overall approach. First, we introduce the service and its structure. We continue with the specification under scrutiny and its link to the service implementation. Finally, we show how the validation is configured and what the outcome of the validation is.

Figure 6(a) shows the static structure of a component implementing a simple service. It depicts a screenshot of the workbench for PCM models. The interface IFibonacciAlgorithm provides the operation fibonacci. This operation returns the Fibonacci number given its index in the Fibonacci sequence. The modeling notation does not differentiate between the primitive data types int and long. Input and output parameters are integers, hence int is used.

The interface is provided by the component FibonacciAlgorithm. The implementation of the component is realized in the class FibonacciAlgorithm and depicted in figure 7. A deployed instance of the component is provided as a service.

The service behavior specification for the implementation is shown in figure 6(b). The service does not call other services and issues only CPU resource demands. The resource demand is combined in PCM to an InternalAction and stated in the number of executed Java Bytecode instructions. The numbers can depend on the value of the input parameter rounds, e.g. the times LLOAD is requested.

The implementation and specification are linked via two models. The first is an abstract view on the source code in form of an Generalized Abstract Syntax Tree (GAST, see figure 8). The elements of this GAST are then linked with a second model to the action of the PCM. In this example, the InternalAction (figure 6(b)) starts and ends at the Block Statement _-iKpQ0YUEd-iYb1IWQK_sg within the fibonacci Method. These links allow to map the resource demands of a running service instance to the specification. They can additionally be also used to check if all source code is covered by the specification.

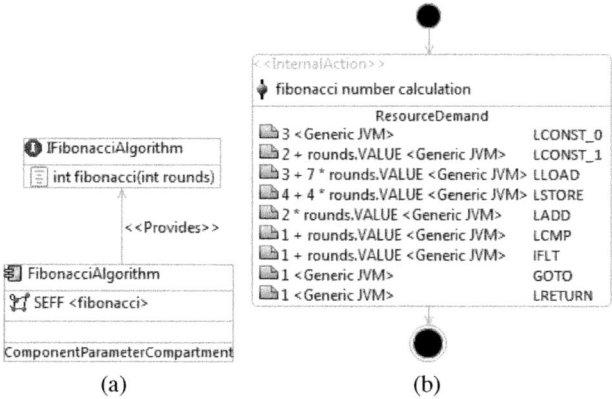

Fig. 6. Example specification overview: (a) shows the component implementing the service and (b) shows the Resource Demanding SEFF for operation fibonacci

```
 1  public class FibonacciAlgorithm {

 3    /**Calculates a Fibonacci number given the number of rounds
          the algorithm should run.
 4     * @param rounds Number of calculation rounds.
 5     * @return Fibonacci number.
 6     */
 7    public long fibonacci(long rounds) {
 8      long i1 = 0;
 9      long i2 = 1;
10      long i3 = 0;
11      // normalized loop
12      for (
13          long i = 0;
14          i < rounds;
15          i++) {
16        i3 = i1 + i2;
17        i2 = i1;
18        i1 = i3;
19      }
20      return i3;
21    }
22  }
```

Fig. 7. Validated Implementation

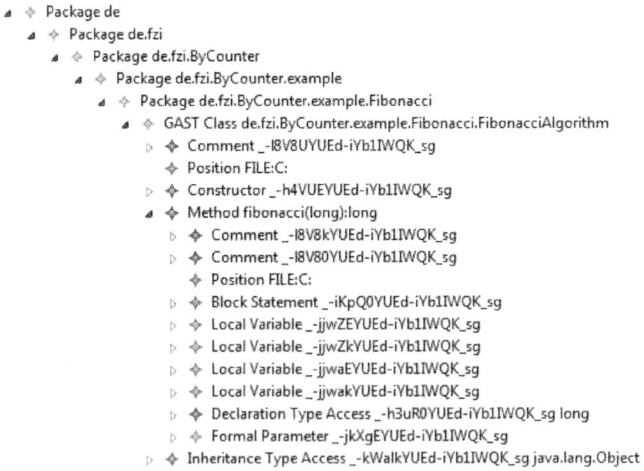

- ▲ ◆ Package de
  - ▲ ◆ Package de.fzi
    - ▲ ◆ Package de.fzi.ByCounter
      - ▲ ◆ Package de.fzi.ByCounter.example
        - ▲ ◆ Package de.fzi.ByCounter.example.Fibonacci
          - ▲ ◆ GAST Class de.fzi.ByCounter.example.Fibonacci.FibonacciAlgorithm
            - ▷ ◆ Comment _-I8V8UYUEd-iYb1IWQK_sg
            - ◆ Position FILE:C:
            - ▷ ◆ Constructor _-h4VUEYUEd-iYb1IWQK_sg
            - ▲ ◆ Method fibonacci(long):long
              - ▷ ◆ Comment _-I8V8kYUEd-iYb1IWQK_sg
              - ▷ ◆ Comment _-I8V80YUEd-iYb1IWQK_sg
              - ◆ Position FILE:C:
              - ▷ ◆ Block Statement _-iKpQ0YUEd-iYb1IWQK_sg
              - ▷ ◆ Local Variable _-jjwZEYUEd-iYb1IWQK_sg
              - ▷ ◆ Local Variable _-jjwZkYUEd-iYb1IWQK_sg
              - ▷ ◆ Local Variable _-jjwaEYUEd-iYb1IWQK_sg
              - ▷ ◆ Local Variable _-jjwakYUEd-iYb1IWQK_sg
              - ▷ ◆ Declaration Type Access _-h3uR0YUEd-iYb1IWQK_sg long
              - ▷ ◆ Formal Parameter _-jkXgEYUEd-iYb1IWQK_sg
            - ▷ ◆ Inheritance Type Access _-kWalkYUEd-iYb1IWQK_sg java.lang.Object

Fig. 8. GAST of Example

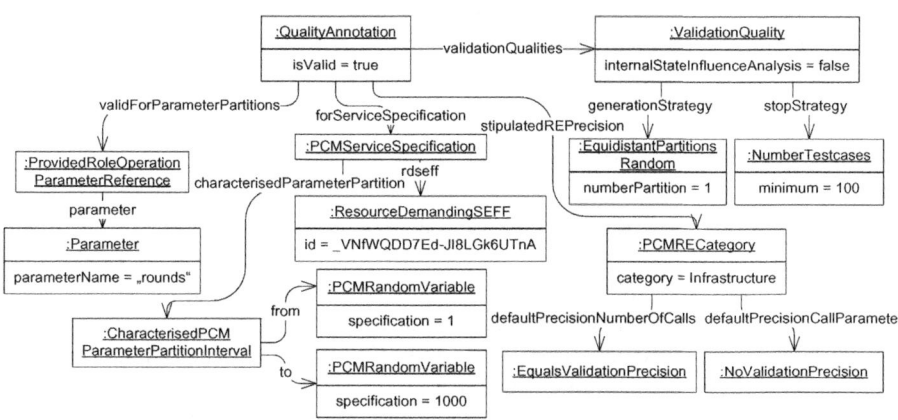

Fig. 9. Example AIAM Instance

The quality of the validation is stated in the AIAM instance shown in figure 9. We want to validate the specification shown in figure 6(b) within the range from 0 to 1000 of the parameter rounds. We want to have an exact matching specification to be sure we can trust predictions based on the specification. Hence, we do not allow the provided specification to deviate from measured Bytecode demands (which are infrastructure calls in PCM). We decide to consider the whole parameter range as one partition and base the validation on 100 test cases. Internal state influence analysis is not requested.

Running the automated validation process, none of the 100 test cases allows rejecting the hypothesis that the specification is valid. Hence, it is considered valid.

6 Assumptions and Limitations

The approach is intended for business services. Real-time performance guarantees or specific optimizations for High Performance Computing, e.g. hardware-specific memory and data structures, are not addressed.

The validation of specifications is currently limited to resource demand to processors. Hard disk and network resource demands are not validated yet.

Internal state analysis of services between calls has not been tested yet. Currently, test cases are executed once and the influence of previous calls is not analyzed. However, repeated executions of identical test cases would allow drawing conclusions on the size of the effect. Such state dependencies are currently also not considered in advanced parameterized performance specifications.

Specification on the abstraction level of Bytecode instructions and link models to the source code implementation is assumed. These artifacts can be synthesized using reverse engineering approaches. Manual fine-tuning, optimization and corrections can be applied to these artifacts without endangering the use of the presented validation process.

Validating a PCM specification on the abstraction level of how often a Bytecode instructions is issued does not guarantee to include all possible effects for a performance prediction but provides reasonably prediction results. This is outweight by the advantage that warm-up and instruction caching effects as well as hardware environment independency can be addressed this way.

7 Conclusion and Future Work

The paper pointed out how the quality of specifications can be expressed and linked to these specifications using the Accuracy Information Annotation Model (AIAM). It additionally introduced a validation process using AIAM instances as a basis for model-based validation of the specifications. The applicability of the fully automated process was shown on case study containing a usage profile and platform independent PCM specification. It demonstrated that user interaction is not necessary beyond providing the specification, implementation, link models between both, and the supposed quality statements. The case study demonstrates that specifications containing resource demand dependencies beyond statistical estimators and distribution functions, e.g. linear functions, can be validated. In contrast to the testing theory by Hamlet [6] or functional testing approaches like WS-TAXI [4], the presented validation process does not require any statements about the implementation other than the specification and its mapping to the implementation. The process furthermore supports multiple parametric dependencies and is not limited to a per-method base as WCET approaches. It provides the advantage of ensuring explicitly stated quality thresholds for specifications and thereby complements current specification synthesis techniques.

The presented quality statements allow users to check if the precision of the specifications is high enough for their intended purpose. This also prevents unnecessary revalidation of specifications. Prediction approaches can additionally use the quality information for error propagation and prediction quality estimations. Thus, the presented process fosters the use of compositional prediction approach by sustaining trust in the prediction results even if usage profile and hardware independent specifications are used. The case study also showed that cumbersome manual work for choosing appropriate instrumentation points, instrumentation, test case execution, and test case evaluation is not necessary with this approach. Hence, performance engineers can focus their effort on the specification and choosing the appropriate performance abstractions.

We plan to extend the validation to the use of required services within a behavior specifications. Additionally, we plan to provide more and extended testing strategies.

Acknowledgements

Support for this work has been provided by the German Federal Ministry of Education and Research (BMBF), grant No. 01BS0822. The author is thankful for this support.

References

1. Opensta website, http://www.opensta.org/
2. Pushtotest website, http://www.pushtotest.com/

3. Apache. Jmeter website, http://jakarta.apache.org/jmeter/
4. Bartolini, C., Bertolino, A., Marchetti, E., Polini, A.: Ws-taxi: A wsdl-based testing tool for web services. In: ICST 2009, pp. 326–335 (2009)
5. Becker, S., Grunske, L., Mirandola, R., Overhage, S.: Performance Prediction of Component-Based Systems – A Survey from an Engineering Perspective. In: Reussner, R., Stafford, J.A., Ren, X.-M. (eds.) Architecting Systems with Trustworthy Components. LNCS, vol. 3938, pp. 169–192. Springer, Heidelberg (2006)
6. Hamlet, D.: Retracted and replaced: Software component composition: a subdomain-based testing foundation. Software Testing, Verification and Reliability 17(4), 243–269 (2007)
7. Harmon, T., Klefstad, R.: A survey of worst-case execution time analysis for real-time java. In: IPDPS 2007, pp. 1–8 (March 2007)
8. Koziolek, H.: Parameter dependencies for reusable performance specifications of software components. PhD thesis, Universität Oldenburg (2008)
9. Krogmann, K., Kuperberg, M., Reussner, R.: Reverse Engineering of Parametric Behavioural Service Performance Models from Black-Box Components. In: MSI 2008, pp. 57–71. GITO Verlag (September 2008)
10. Krogmann, K., Kuperberg, M., Reussner, R.: Using Genetic Search for Reverse Engineering of Parametric Behaviour Models for Performance Prediction. In: IEEE TSE (2010) (accepted for publication, to appear)
11. Kuperberg, M.: FOBIC: A Platform-Independent Performance Metric based on Dynamic Java Bytecode Counts. In: Dependability Metrics Workshop 2008, pp. 7–11. Department of Computer Science, University of Mannheim (May 2009)
12. Kuperberg, M., Krogmann, M., Reussner, R.: ByCounter: Portable Runtime Counting of Bytecode Instructions and Method Invocations. In: Bytecode Workshop at ETAPS 2008 (2008)
13. Meyerhöfer, M.B.: Measurement and management of software components for performance prediction. PhD thesis, University of Erlangen (July 2007)
14. Michelsen, J.: Merging open source and testing strategies. junit and lisa: The perfect match. Technical report, Interactive TKO, Inc. (iTKO) (December 2007)
15. Object Management Group. UML Profile for Schedulability, Performance, and Time, v1.1 (January 2005), http://www.omg.org/cgi-bin/doc?formal/2005-01-02
16. Object Management Group. UML Profile for MARTE: Modeling and Analysis of Real-Time Embedded Systems (November 2009), http://www.omg.org/spec/MARTE/1.0
17. L.P. Hp loadrunner software data sheet. Technical Report 4AA1-2118ENW, Hewlett-Packard Development Company (November 2008)
18. Reussner, R., Becker, S., Happe, J., Koziolek, H., Krogmann, K., Kuperberg, M.: The palladio component model. Technical report, University of Karlsruhe (TH), Germany (May 2007)

Focussing Multi-Objective Software Architecture Optimization Using Quality of Service Bounds

Anne Koziolek, Qais Noorshams, and Ralf Reussner

Karlsruhe Institute of Technology, Karlsruhe, Germany
{koziolek,noorshams,reussner}@kit.edu
http://sdq.ipd.kit.edu/

Abstract. Quantitative prediction of non-functional properties, such as performance, reliability, and costs, of software architectures supports systematic software engineering. Even though there usually is a rough idea on bounds for quality of service, the exact required values may be unclear and subject to trade-offs. Designing architectures that exhibit such good trade-off between multiple quality attributes is hard. Even with a given functional design, many degrees of freedom in the software architecture (e.g. component deployment or server configuration) span a large design space. Automated approaches search the design space with multi-objective metaheuristics such as evolutionary algorithms. However, as quality prediction for a single architecture is computationally expensive, these approaches are time consuming. In this work, we enhance an automated improvement approach to take into account bounds for quality of service in order to focus the search on interesting regions of the objective space, while still allowing trade-offs after the search. We compare two different constraint handling techniques to consider the bounds. To validate our approach, we applied both techniques to an architecture model of a component-based business information system. We compared both techniques to an unbounded search in 4 scenarios. Every scenario was examined with 10 optimization runs, each investigating around 1600 architectural candidates. The results indicate that the integration of quality of service bounds during the optimization process can improve the quality of the solutions found, however, the effect depends on the scenario, i.e. the problem and the quality requirements. The best results were achieved for costs requirements: The approach was able to decrease the time needed to find good solutions in the interesting regions of the objective space by 25% on average.

Keywords: Optimization, Performance, Quality Attribute Prediction, Reliability, Software Architecture.

1 Introduction

The design of software architecture is crucial to exhibit good quality of service (cf. [3]), e.g. performance and reliability. Model-driven, quantitative architecture evaluation approaches help the software architect to reason about the architecture and predict its quality attributes and costs. However, even though there usually is a rough idea of requirements for the non-functional properties, the exact required values may be unclear and subject to trade-offs. For example, the decision of how much response time of the system is acceptable may depend on the costs to achieve this response time and is subject to negotiation between stakeholders. Still, they may agree on bounds specifying the worst acceptable values of the quality attributes, e.g. the mean response time of the system should not exceed 15 seconds. A system that violates any bounds is declared infeasible, i.e. useless for the stakeholders.

Designing architectures that provide optimal trade-offs between multiple quality attributes is difficult. Even with a given functional design, many degrees of freedom in the software architecture (e.g. component deployment or server configuration) still span a large design space. Automated approaches support the software architect to improve their architectural designs and find good trade-offs between quality attributes. They search the design space with multi-objective metaheuristics such as evolutionary algorithms to find many Pareto-optimal candidates. However, as quality prediction for a single architecture is computationally expensive, these approaches are time consuming since many possible candidates need to be evaluated.

In this work, we present an approach to include bound estimations on quality of service requirements into an automated improvement approach to make the search for optimal trade-offs focus on interesting regions of the objective space. We extend the PerOpteryx approach [15] by two aspects: First, we translate requirements specified with the *Quality of service Modeling Language (QML)* [12] into constraints in an optimization problem. Second, we use two constraint handling strategies [10,11] to focus the search on the feasible space.

The contribution of this paper is a novel approach that, to the best of our knowledge, is the first to combine multi-criteria architecture optimization and quality of service bounds so that the search can focus on feasible regions of the search space. With this extension, the time needed to find valuable solutions for the software architects can be reduced. We have implemented the approach in the PerOpteryx tool. Using this tool, we demonstrate the benefits of our approach in a case study.

This paper extends a previous publication [19] by providing (1) the integration of a second constraint handling technique [11] and (2) more sound evaluation including the second technique, using more optimization runs and four different quality requirement scenarios. The evaluation leads to results with higher statistical significance and a more differentiated interpretation of the approaches' effects. We found that the constraint handling is beneficial in scenarios with strict quality bounds (i.e., where many candidates are infeasible). In these scenarios, our extension was able to find solutions in the interesting regions of the objective space in average 25.6% faster than the old, unconstrained approach.

This paper is structured as follows: Section 2 presents related work to our approach. Section 3 gives background on the architecture evaluation approach Palladio that we use in this work. Section 4 then presents our architecture optimization process, which makes use of the specified bounds to focus the search on the feasible architecture candidates. A case study in Section 5 shows the feasibility of our work by applying the process to an example architecture and comparing the effect of the requirements consideration. Finally, Section 6 concludes.

2 Related Work

Our approach is based on performance prediction [2], reliability prediction [13], multi-objective metaheuristic optimization [8], and constraint handling in evolutionary algorithms [9,5]. A survey of constraint handling techniques is omitted here for brevity, but can be found in [18].

In summary, several other approaches to automatically improve software architectures for one or several quality properties have been proposed. Most approaches improve architectures by either applying predefined improvement rules, or by applying metaheuristic search techniques. All approaches except one do not support trade-off between quality attributes after the search. In addition, none of the approaches allows specifying quality requirements for quality attributes that should be optimized, thus, they do not allow to focus on interesting regions of the objective space.

Xu et al. [20] present a semi-automated approach to improve performance. Based on a layered queueing network (LQN) model, performance problems (e.g., bottlenecks, long paths) are identified in a first step. Then, mitigation rules are applied. The search stops as soon as specified response time or throughput requirements are met. The approach is limited to performance only.

The ArchE framework (McGregor et al. [16]) assists the software architect during the design to create architectures that meet quality requirements. It provides the evaluation tools for modifiability or performance analysis, and stepwise suggests modifiability improvements depending on the yet unsatisfied requirements. The search stops as soon as specified requirements are met.

Canfora et al. [7] optimize service composition costs using evolutionary algorithms while satisfying service level agreement (SLA) constraints. They implement constraint handling with dynamic penalty functions.

Menascé et al. [17] generate service-oriented architectures that satisfy quality requirements, using service selection and architectural patterns. They model the degree of requirement satisfaction as utility functions. Then, a weighted overall system utility is optimized in a single-objective problem using random-restart hill-climbing. Thus, preferences for quality attributes and importance of requirements have to be specified in advance.

Aleti et al.[1] present a generic framework to optimize architectural models with evolutionary algorithms for multiple arbitrary quality properties, thus enabling trade-off after the search. In addition, the framework allows to specify constraints for the search problem, for example available memory consumption. However, the constraint handling is relatively simple: Infeasible candidates are just discarded. Quality requirements are mentioned, but not included in the optimization.

3 Palladio Component Model

Generally, our concepts can be used for different software architecture models. To a certain extent, service-oriented architectures can be regarded as a specialization of component-based software architectures. As a consequence, we focus the scope of our work on component-based software architectures.

We apply our approach to the Palladio Component Model (PCM) [4], a modelling language for component-based software architectures with an UML-like syntax. The PCM enables the explicit definition of the i) components , ii) architecture, iii) allocation, and iv) usage of a system in respective artefacts, which comprise a PCM instance (cf. Figure 1):

1. *Component specifications* contain an abstract, parametric description of components. Furthermore, the behaviour of the components is specified using a syntax similar to UML activity diagrams.
2. An *assembly model* defines the software architecture.
3. The resource environment and the allocation of components to resources are specified in an *allocation model*.
4. The *usage model* specifies *usage scenarios*. For each user, one of the scenarios applies defining the frequency and the sequence of interactions with the system, i.e. which system functionalities are used with an *entry level system call*.

Using model transformations, the PCM instance can be analysed or simulated to predict performance (response time and throughput) [4], reliability (probability of failure on demand (POFOD)) [6], and costs [15] of a system.

Figure 2 illustrates an example PCM instance of the so-called business reporting system (BRS) using annotated UML. The BRS provides statistical reports about business processes and is loosely based on a real system. The system consists of 9 components and is allocated to 4 servers. The behaviour description (incl. CPU demands) of one component is illustrated here by an activity diagram. Having only one usage scenario, a user interacts with the system every 5s

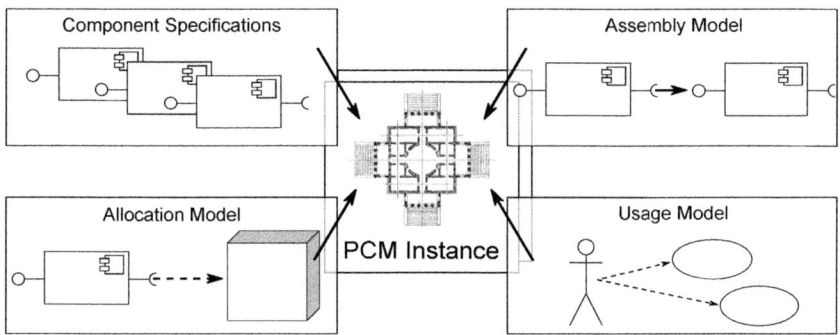

Fig. 1. Artefacts of a PCM instance

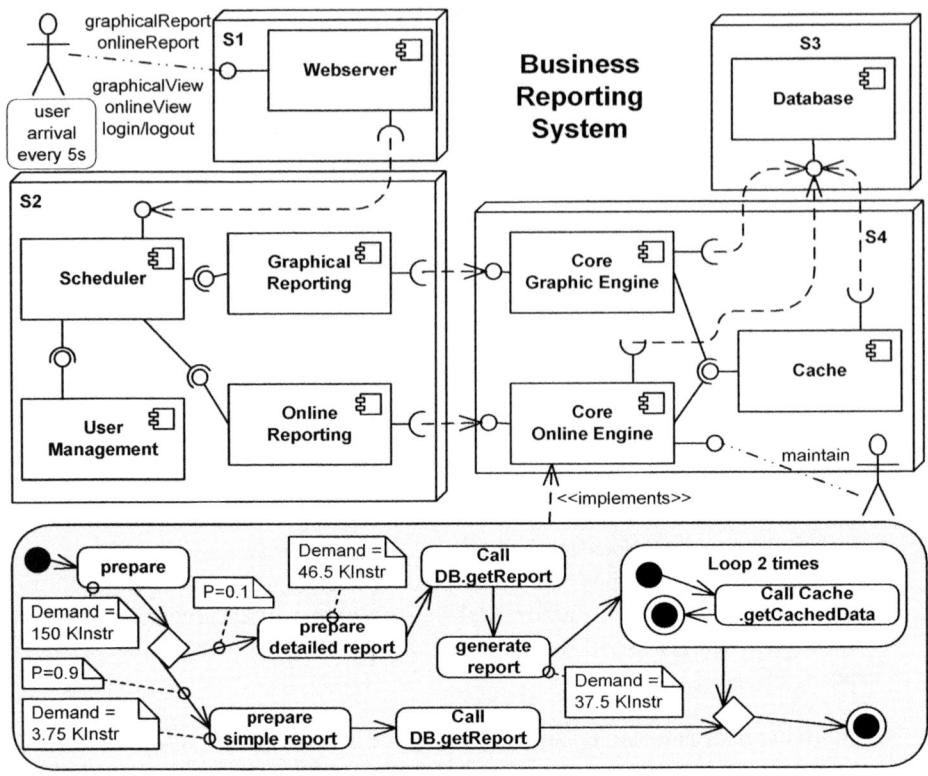

Fig. 2. PCM instance of the BRS (more detail in [15])

requesting a sequence of reports and views. User requests take different paths through the system based on passed parameters, expressed here as probabilities.

4 Finding Satisfactory Architectures

The goal of our work is to optimize component-based software architectures. To achieve this, we use metaheuristic techniques, particularly the multi-objective evolutionary algorithm (MOEA) NSGA-II developed by Deb et al. [10]. A disadvantage of a MOEA is that it may spend too much time exploring uninteresting regions of the objective space. Integrating quality requirements into the search aims at improving this algorithm due to the following advantages identified by Branke [5]:

1. Focus – MOEAs are approximate and non-deterministic. Quality requirements can be used to focus the search and identify particularly interesting alternatives.
2. Speed – Focusing the search avoids wasting computational effort on irrelevant regions of the search space.

3. Gradient – With increasing number of objectives, MOEAs are unable to determine the most promising search direction (*gradient*). Quality requirements provide additional information ensuring optimization progress.

4.1 Constraint Handling

To integrate requirements into this process, we extended the Opt4J framework [14], which implements basic NSGA-II without constraint handling, by the *constrained tournament* method (a.k.a. constrained NSGA-II) [10] and the *goal attainment* method [11], both described briefly below.

Requirements are transformed into constraints. If a solution violates any constraint, it is infeasible, i.e. useless for the user. Otherwise, it is feasible, thus a possible candidate to solve the problem. In their *constrained tournament* method (C), Deb et al. [10] handle constraints by modifying the dominance relation during the mating and the environmental selection of NSGA-II. Infeasible solutions are ranked according to their degree of infeasibility and declared inferior to feasible solutions.

In their *goal attainment* method (G), Fonseca et al. [11] define a goal value for each objective and aim at satisfying all goals by prioritizing objectives not fulfilling goals. Figuratively speaking, the Pareto-based comparison of two solutions is modified, such that before applying Pareto-dominance, the solutions are mapped on the goal value in the objectives that already fulfil the goal. Consequently, the objectives not fulfilling the goal have the impact on which solution dominates the other. Objectives for which no requirements exists are assigned a goal value of $+\infty$ when minimizing or $-\infty$ when maximizing.

We chose these two methods for constraint handling because of the following advantages: First, they explicitly distinguish between feasible and infeasible solutions and declare all feasible solutions superior to infeasible solutions as opposed to e.g. methods based on penalty functions. Second, no additional parameters are required (an advantage because many other methods are sensitive to parameter changes). Finally, they neither require a specific number of constraints nor assume a relation between objectives and/or constraints.

The difference of both methods is how solutions that violate the same constraints are treated: The constrained tournament technique uses a distance measure and favours solutions that are closer to the required values. In contrast, the goal attainment method uses standard Pareto-dominance if two solutions satisfy the same objectives.

4.2 Process

Figure 3 illustrates the optimization process as a whole with four main steps:

1. The system to be optimized is modelled with the PCM. Additionally, the degrees of freedom, i.e. the possibilities to influence the non-functional properties of a system without changing its functional properties, are specified. In a component-based context, the degrees of freedom of a system can be

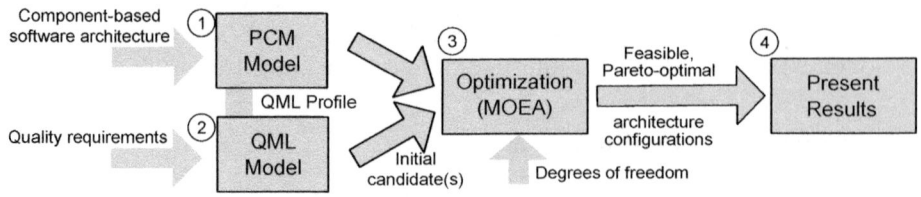

Fig. 3. Process Overview

e.g. component selection, component deployment, and hardware configuration (cf. [15]), but this list is extendable to more and custom degrees of freedom.
2. Quality attributes (e.g. mean response time mrt) and quality requirements of the system (e.g. $mrt<$ 5sec) are modelled using QML as described in [19]. Requirements are attached to a PCM usage scenario using a QML profile.
3. With our tool PerOpteryx, the models are used to optimize the system. The optimization starts with one or more *initial candidates*, i.e. predefined system configurations, which can also be created randomly. Optimizing quality attributes and minimizing costs is pursued using NSGA-II with consideration of the requirements, using either *constrained tournament* or *goal-attainment*.
4. As solving multi-objective optimization problems results in a set of solutions rather than one single solution [9], the set of feasible *Pareto-optimal*[1] architecture configurations with respect to the quality requirements is presented. Finally, the software architect makes the trade-off decision and chooses one of the solutions.

5 Case Study

This section describes a case study demonstrating the benefit of the consideration of requirements during the optimization process. The goal of this case study is to evaluate the benefits of the two constraint handling methods in different quality requirement scenarios.

5.1 Setup

The system under study is the business reporting system (BRS) described in Section 3. The software architect has to choose a candidate that minimizes mean response time, probability of failure on demand (POFOD), and costs.

As degrees of freedom, the components can be allocated to up to nine different servers. Three different webserver implementations with different costs, performance and reliability can be chosen. Additionally, each of the nine servers has a continuously variable CPU rate between 0.75 GHz and 3 GHz. The costs

---
[1] A solution x is *Pareto-optimal* if no other solution y is better than x w.r.t. all considered attributes (cf. [9]).

Table 1. Quality Bound Scenarios

Scenario	costs	POFOD	mean response time
(S_1) Weak requirements	3000	0.00175	5.0 sec
(S_2) Medium requirements	2000	0.0015	3.0 sec
(S_3) Strict requirements	1500	0.0015	2.5 sec
(S_4) Only costs requirements	1000	∞	∞

of the servers depend on the processing rate and the costs model is derived from Intel's CPU price list. A power function is fitted to the data resulting in a costs model of $costs = \sum_i costs(i) = \sum_i 0.7665\, p_i^{6.2539}$ [monetary units (MU)] with the processing rate of each server p_i [GHz]. The coefficient of determination is $R^2 = 0.965$. Compared to [19], we used more realistic reliability values: the servers have a mean time to failure (MTTF) of 43800 hours and a mean time to repair (MTTR) of 3 hours. We get 19 (9+1+9) degree of freedom instances that can be independently varied.

To study the effects of different quality requirement values on the results, we ran the optimization for four different levels of requirements (weak, i.e., only few candidates are excluded from the Pareto front, to strict, i.e., many candidates are excluded). Table 1 shows the four different scenarios. The requirements are modelled with our metamodel of QML [19]. For each scenario $s \in \{1, 2, 3, 4\}$, we optimized the system once for each constraint handling technique $c \in \{C, G\}$, resulting in 8 optimization settings S_s^c, $1 \leq s \leq 4$. As a baseline, we optimized the system without constraint handling (setting S_0).

For each of the 9 settings, the system is optimized using PEROPTERYX. For statistical validity, we ran the optimization 10 times for every setting (runs r, $0 \leq r \leq 9$), so that in total, 90 runs $^r S_s^c$ have been performed. To exclude disturbing effects from differently generated random start populations, we randomly generated 10 start populations with 20 candidates each, and used these 10 start populations to run every setting (so that the rth run of any setting A starts with the same start population as the rth run of any setting B). Each optimization was stopped after 200 iterations.

5.2 Evaluation Measures

To compare the performance of the different settings, quality indicators have been suggested in the literature. Due to the trade-off nature of multi-objective optimization, there is no single quality indicator that objectively assesses an optimization run's performance [21]. The coverage metric $\mathcal{C}(A, B)$ [22] is a useful measure to compare two optimization runs A and B's results independent of the scaling of the objectives. However, the metric may be misleading if the Pareto fronts overlap each other with varying distances to the true optimal Pareto front. Additionally, both directions $\mathcal{C}(A, B)$ and $\mathcal{C}(B, A)$ have to be considered to assess the difference of the fronts. To overcome both problems, we (1) measure size of the dominated space $\mathcal{S}(A)$ [22] to assess the quality of each Pareto front A separately and (2) modify the coverage metric $\mathcal{C}(A, B)$ to make it symmetric.

Additionally, we include the quality bounds in the coverage metric, resulting in the following definition: Let A and B be *feasible, non-dominated sets*[2] and $Q \subseteq A \cup B$ be the feasible, non-dominated set of $A \cup B$. The coverage metric $\mathcal{C}^*$ is defined as $\mathcal{C}^*(A,B) := \frac{|A \cap Q|}{|Q|}$ ($\in [0,1]$). If $\mathcal{C}^*(A,B) > 0.5$ then A is considered better than B because A has a higher contribution to Q than B.

The size of the dominated space $\mathcal{S}(A)$ measures the volume (in the three dimensional case) of the objective space weakly dominated by a Pareto front A. For minimisation problems, this measure requires a reference point to define the upper bounds of this volume. Here, we use the quality of service bounds and thus measure the size of the *feasible* space covered by A: $\mathcal{S}^*(A)$. For setting (4), which does not define upper bounds for response time and POFOD, we use the maximum values in all evaluated candidates of all runs as the upper bounds. Because the scale of the objectives are very different (POFOD ranges from 0, ..., 1, costs from 500 to 3500), and different upper bounds are used in the different settings, we normalize the objective values before determining the volume and, as a result, we cannot compare the absolute volumes across different settings.

We analyse the coverage $\mathcal{C}^*$ of optimization runs with constraint handling over the basic optimization S_0 and compare the size of the dominated space $\mathcal{S}^*$. We study the effect of the constraint handling separately for each scenario $1 \leq s \leq 4$. To study the development of the optimization runs, we plot the coverage measure over the course of the optimization, i.e. determine it for each iteration $0 \leq i \leq 200$, written as $\mathcal{C}^*(A(i))$ for a run A. Similarly, we compare the size of the dominated feasible space over the course of the optimization runs. The size of the feasible space dominated by the basic approach is determined anew for each scenario $1 \leq s \leq 4$ with respect to the quality bounds of this scenario. Then, for each scenario s and each method $c \in \{C, G\}$, we aggregate the measures $\mathcal{C}^*(^rS_s^c, ^rS_0(i))$, $\mathcal{S}^*(^rS_s^c(i))$, and $\mathcal{S}^*(^rS_0(i))$ over all 10 runs r to account for the indeterministic nature of the optimization.

5.3 Results

Figure 4 illustrates the result of the optimization run $^0S_3^C$ with medium constraints using the constrained tournament method C. 7 Pareto-optimal candidates that satisfy all three bounds were found and are marked with triangles.

We present the results in the following by scenario. Figures 5 and 6 show the coverage measure and the size measure for scenario 1. The coverage measure is around 0.5 in average over most of the iterations for both constraint handling methods C and G. With both measures, thus, no improvement towards the basic approach is visible. The size of the dominated feasible space grows similarly for all approaches, too.

Figures 7 and 8 show the coverage measure and the size measure for scenario 2. For both the coverage measure and the size measure, the runs with constraint handling start well (coverage > 0.5 and size larger than size of basic approach). However, the basic approach catches up: At iteration 200, all approaches perform

---

[2] In a non-dominated set, the elements are pairwise non-dominated (cf. [9]).

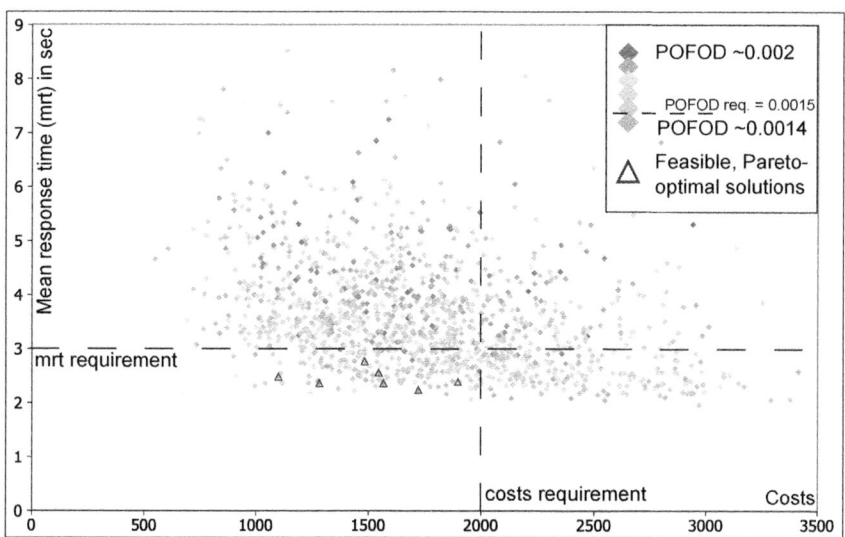

Fig. 4. Result of an optimization run $^0S_3^C$ with medium requirements $s = 3$ and the constrained tournament method $c = C$

equally well (G has a slightly better coverage, C a slightly larger dominated space, so none performs better than the other).

Figures 9 and 10 show the coverage measure and the size measure for scenario 3 with strict quality requirements. Here, we see an improvement of the search: The coverage measure of method C is higher that 0.5 during all iterations, and the size measure is significantly larger than for the basic approach, too. Method G does not perform as well, even has a coverage < 0.5 at the beginning while still having a better size measure than the basic approach.

Finally, figures 11 and 12 show the results for the common case of a budget-only limitation. While both constraint handling method do not perform well in the first 75 iterations, they catch up and provide better results in the last iterations, both regarding coverage and size measure.

To summarise, we observe that the quality bounds have almost no effect in lowly constrained scenarios 1 and 2. In scenario 3, the constrained tournament method C performs well in both coverage and even more so regarding the size of the dominated feasible space. The goal attainment method is less successful. In scenario 4, both constraint handling methods perform well. We conclude that using quality bounds to focus the search is only effective if a large portion of the search space are excluded by the quality bounds, such as given in scenarios 3 and 4. In the two first scenarios, fewer solutions on the Pareto-front are infeasible, so that the constraint handling is seldom used and thus cannot steer the search well. Because it is not necessarily known in advance whether given requirements are strict or lax, the constraint handling methods should always be used, as they do not worsen the performance of the search.

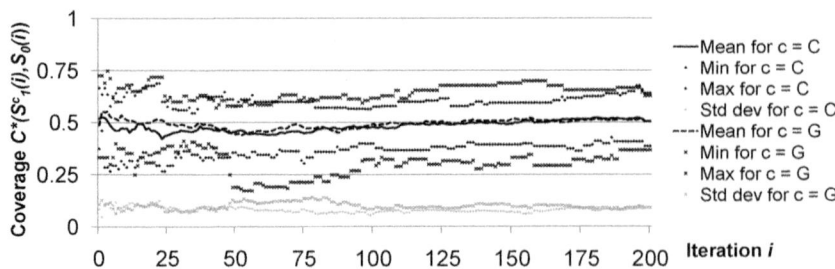

Fig. 5. Coverage measure $\mathcal{C}^*({}^rS_1^c, {}^rS_0(i))$ in scenario 1, aggregated over runs r

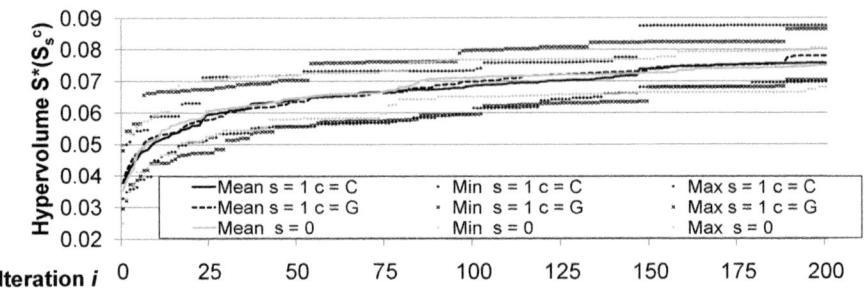

Fig. 6. Size of the dominated space $\mathcal{S}^*({}^rS_1^c(i))$ in scenario 1, compared to the basic scenario $\mathcal{S}({}^rS_0(i))$, aggregated over runs r

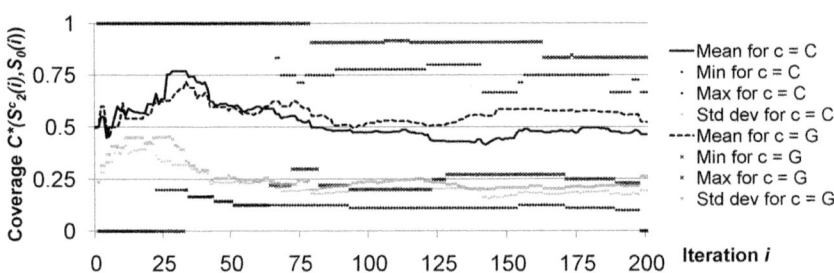

Fig. 7. Coverage measure $\mathcal{C}^*({}^rS_2^c, {}^rS_0(i))$ in scenario 2, aggregated over runs r

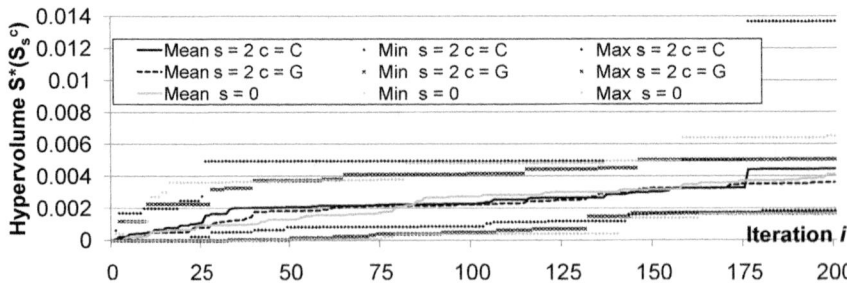

Fig. 8. Size of the dominated space $\mathcal{S}^*({}^rS_2^c(i))$ in scenario 2, compared to the basic scenario $\mathcal{S}({}^rS_0(i))$, aggregated over runs r

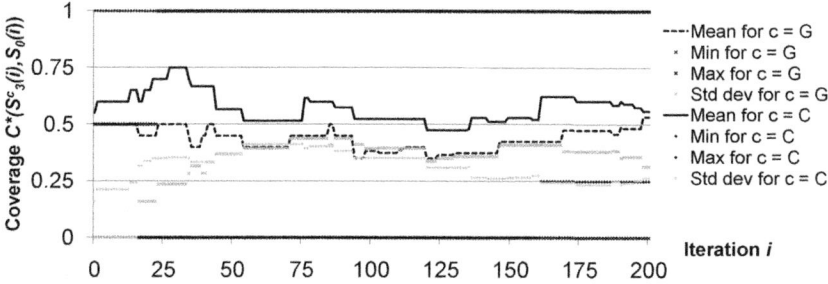

Fig. 9. Coverage measure $\mathcal{C}^*(^rS_3^c, {}^rS_0(i))$ in scenario 3, aggregated over runs r

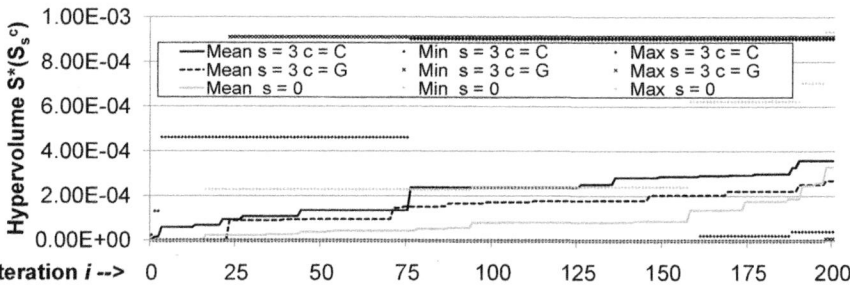

Fig. 10. Size of the dominated space $\mathcal{S}^*(^rS_3^c(i))$ in scenario 3, compared to the basic scenario $\mathcal{S}(^rS_0(i))$, aggregated over runs r

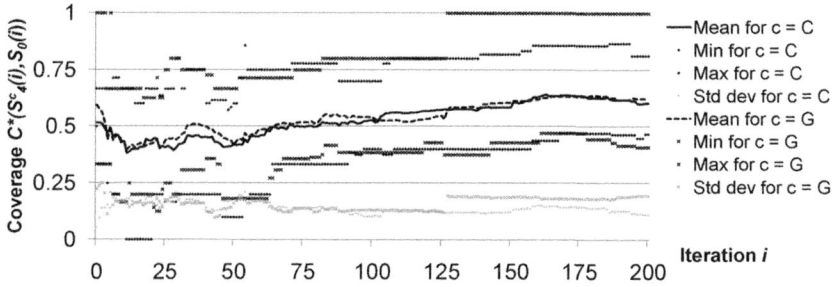

Fig. 11. Coverage measure $\mathcal{C}^*(^rS_4^c, {}^rS_0(i))$ in scenario 4, aggregated over runs r

Furthermore, we examined after how many iterations type runs with constraint handling find solutions equivalent to the final result of basic approach runs based on both quality indicators $\mathcal{C}^*$ and $\mathcal{S}^*$. For both indicators, we first find the smallest j for $\mathcal{C}^*(^rS_s^c(j), {}^rS_0(200)) = 0.5$ or $\mathcal{S}^*(^rS_s^c(j)) > \mathcal{S}^*(^rS_0(200))$, then we find the smallest i for $\mathcal{C}^*(S_0(i), S_0(200)) = 0.5$ or $\mathcal{S}^*(^rS_0(i)) > \mathcal{S}^*(^rS_0(200))$. In other words, we compare the runs with constraint handling with the earliest iteration of basic approach runs where there is no change in solutions w.r.t. the final iteration. We measure the relative time saving $t = \frac{i-j}{\max(j,i)}$. As an example, we compare $^2S_s^c$ and $^2S_0$ regarding the coverage $\mathcal{C}^*$. $^2S_s^c$ has an equivalent

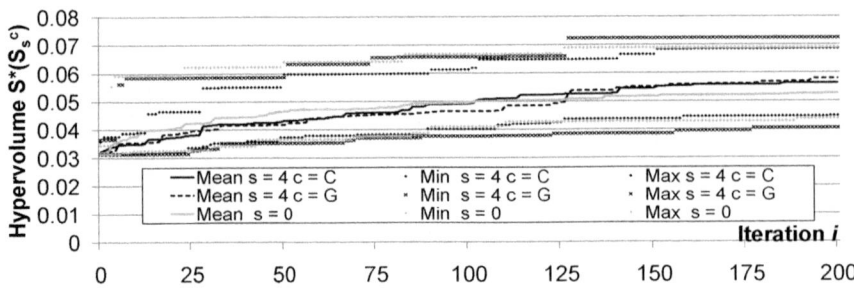

Fig. 12. Size of the dominated space $\mathcal{S}^*(^rS_4^c(i))$ in scenario 4, compared to the basic scenario $\mathcal{S}(^rS_0(i))$, aggregated over runs r

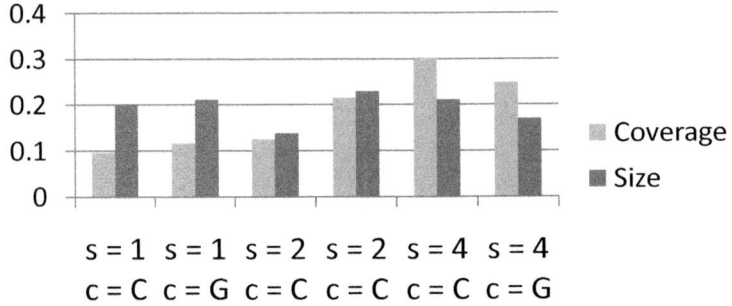

Fig. 13. Time Savings

solution set than $^2S_s^c(200)$ after 171 iterations. $^2S_0$ has the last changes in the solution set in iteration 192. Thus, the run with constraint handling found equivalent results $\frac{192-171}{192} = 10.9\%$ faster.

Figure 13 shows the relative time savings for scenarios 1, 2, and 4. In scenario 3, too few solutions were feasible and Pareto-optimal at the end, so that a sensible assessment of the time saving is not possible. We observe that for all scenarios, the constraint handling methods can find an equivalent front faster than the basic approach. The average time saving is 11.1% with respect to $\mathcal{C}^*$ and 11.8% with respect to $\mathcal{S}^*$, and with the most time saving in scenario 4 with the constrained tournament method (30.3% for $\mathcal{C}^*$ and 21.0% for $\mathcal{S}^*$, average 25.6%).

In further experiments [18], we have also studied to add lower bounds indicating that a quality values is good enough so that further improvement does not bring additional benefit, i.e. that other quality properties should not be traded off for more improvement of this value. However, we found that including such lower bounds does not significantly improve the optimization performance, neither in isolation nor in combination with upper bounds as presented in this work. Note that while we assume minimisation problems in this work, maximization problems can be inverted and handled as well, so that minimal allowed values are translated to upper bounds in our approach.

6 Conclusion

This paper presents a novel extension of multi-criteria architecture optimization to consider bounds for quality requirements so that the search can focus on feasible regions of the search space.

We translate the quality requirements modelled in QML to constraints in an optimization problem. Then, we use existing constraint handling strategies to make the search focus on the feasible space. We compared the performance of two constraint handling strategies, namely constrained tournament methods and the goal attainment method, in several scenarios in a case study. We found that constraint handling, especially the constrained tournament method, improves the efficiency of the search if strict requirements are used, i.e. if a significant portion of the objective space is defined to be infeasible. Additionally, we found that the constrained tournament method was superior to the goal attainment method in our setting.

With this extension, software architects can reduce the time needed to find valuable solutions. Our extension found solutions in the interesting regions of the objective space in average between 15% and 30% faster than the old, unconstrained approach for scenario 4 with strict requirements.

The application of this approach can be interesting in different phases of the software architecture design process. First, the approach can be applied after a first phase of creating an architecture with focus on functional requirements (definition of components and interfaces). This architecture can be used as an input for the optimization to improve the non-functional properties. Second, the optimization could already be used to support decisions during the architectural design: When making a more high level decision, the optimization can be used to assess the potential of the different alternatives. Finally, by modelling more high level decisions as transformations, these decisions could be included in the optimization process as degrees of freedom, thus letting the optimization explore different combinations of decisions.

As future work, we could investigate the effect of constraint handling if other metaheuristic optimization approaches than NSGA-II are used. Additionally, we plan to integrate quality attribute tactics into the search, to allow the search to improve a given candidate using domain knowledge, e.g. by balancing the load on the used servers to improve response time. In combination with bounds, tactics could be used to more directedly steer the search towards feasible regions, which could be especially beneficial in highly constrained problems.

Acknowledgments. The authors would like to thank the anonymous reviewers for their valuable feedback.

References

1. Aleti, A., Björnander, S., Grunske, L., Meedeniya, I.: Archeopterix: An extendable tool for architecture optimization of AADL models. In: Proc. of ICSE 2009 Workshop on Model-Based Methodologies for Pervasive and Embedded Software (MOMPES), pp. 61–71. IEEE Computer Society, Los Alamitos (2009)

2. Balsamo, S., Di Marco, A., Inverardi, P., Simeoni, M.: Model-Based Performance Prediction in Software Development: A Survey. IEEE Transactions on Software Engineering 30(5), 295–310 (2004)
3. Bass, L., Clements, P., Kazman, R.: Software Architecture in Practice, 2nd edn. Addison-Wesley, Reading (2003)
4. Becker, S., Koziolek, H., Reussner, R.: The Palladio component model for model-driven performance prediction. Journal of Systems and Software 82, 3–22 (2009)
5. Branke, J.: Consideration of partial user preferences in evolutionary multiobjective optimization. In: Multiobjective Optimization: Interactive and Evolutionary Approaches, pp. 157–178. Springer, Heidelberg (2008)
6. Brosch, F., Koziolek, H., Buhnova, B., Reussner, R.: Parameterized Reliability Prediction for Component-based Software Architectures. In: Heineman, G.T., Kofron, J., Plasil, F. (eds.) QoSA 2010. LNCS, vol. 6093, pp. 36–51. Springer, Heidelberg (2010)
7. Canfora, G., Penta, M.D., Esposito, R., Villani, M.L.: An approach for QoS-aware service composition based on genetic algorithms. In: Proc. of Genetic and Evolutionary Computation Conference (GECCO), pp. 1069–1075. ACM, New York (2005)
8. Coello Coello, C.A., Dhaenens, C., Jourdan, L.: Multi-objective combinatorial optimization: Problematic and context. In: Advances in Multi-Objective Nature Inspired Computing. SCI, vol. 272, pp. 1–21. Springer, Heidelberg (2010)
9. Deb, K.: Multi-Objective Optimization using Evolutionary Algorithms. John Wiley & Sons, Chichester (2001)
10. Deb, K., Pratap, A., Agarwal, S., Meyarivan, T.: A fast and elitist multiobjective genetic algorithm: NSGA-II. IEEE Transactions on Evolutionary Computation 6(2), 182–197 (2002)
11. Fonseca, C.M., Fleming, P.J.: Genetic algorithms for multiobjective optimization: Formulation, discussion and generalization. In: ICGA, pp. 416–423. Morgan Kaufmann, San Francisco (1993)
12. Frølund, S., Koistinen, J.: QML: A Language for Quality of Service Specification. Tech. Report HPL-98-10, Hewlett-Packard Laboratories (1998)
13. Gokhale, S.S.: Architecture-based software reliability analysis: Overview and limitations. IEEE Trans. on Dependable and Secure Computing 4(1), 32–40 (2007)
14. Lukasiewycz, M., Glaß, M., Reimann, F., Helwig, S.: Opt4J - The Optimization Framework for Java (2010), http://www.opt4j.org
15. Martens, A., Koziolek, H., Becker, S., Reussner, R.: Automatically improve software architecture models for performance, reliability, and cost using evolutionary algorithms. In: Proceedings of the First Joint WOSP/SIPEW International Conference on Performance Engineering (WOSP/SIPEW), pp. 105–116. ACM, New York (2010)
16. McGregor, J.D., Bachmann, F., Bass, L., Bianco, P., Klein, M.: Using arche in the classroom: One experience. Tech. Rep. CMU/SEI-2007-TN-001, Software Engineering Institute, Carnegie Mellon University (2007)
17. Menascé, D.A., Ewing, J.M., Gomaa, H., Malex, S., Sousa, J.P.: A framework for utility-based service oriented esign in SASSY. In: Proceedings of the First Joint WOSP/SIPEW International Conference on Performance Engineering (WOSP/SIPEW), pp. 27–36. ACM, New York (2010)

18. Noorshams, Q.: Focusing the Optimization of Software Architecture Models Using Non-Functional Requirements. Master's thesis, Karlsruhe Institute of Technology, Germany (2010)
19. Noorshams, Q., Martens, A., Reussner, R.: Using quality of service bounds for effective multi-objective software architecture optimization. In: QUASOSS 2010: Proceedings of the 2nd International Workshop on the Quality of Service-Oriented Software Systems, pp. 1:1–1:6. ACM, New York (2010)
20. Xu, J.: Rule-based automatic software performance diagnosis and improvement. Performance Evaluation 67(8), 585–611 (2010); special Issue on Software and Performance
21. Zitzler, E., Knowles, J.D., Thiele, L.: Quality Assessment of Pareto Set Approximations. In: Branke, J., Deb, K., Miettinen, K., Słowiński, R. (eds.) Multiobjective Optimization. LNCS, vol. 5252, pp. 373–404. Springer, Heidelberg (2008)
22. Zitzler, E., Thiele, L.: Multiobjective evolutionary algorithms: a comparative case study and the strength pareto approach. IEEE Trans. Evolutionary Computation 3(4), 257–271 (1999)

First International Workshop on Model Based Engineering for Robotics (RoSym'10)

Laurent Rioux[1], Davide Brugali[2], and Sébastien Gérard[3]

[1] Decision Technologies and Mathematics Lab., Thales Research & Technology, Campus Polytechnique, 1, avenue Augustin Fresnel 91767 Palaiseau cedex France
laurent.rioux@thalesgroup.com
[2] Dept. Computer Science and Mathematics, Università degli Studi di Bergamo, v.le Marconi, 5, 24044 Dalmine, Italy
brugali@unibg.it
[3] CEA LIST, Laboratoire d'Ingénierie dirigée par les modèles pour les Systèmes Embarqués (LISE), Point Courrier 94, Gif-sur-Yvette, F-91191 France
sebastien.gerard@cea.fr

The main objectives of this workshop are to organize common discussions within Model-base Engineering (MBE) and Robotics experts on how MBE can help robotics people and to share issues that robotics people have encountered with MBE. Current engineering approaches for robotic systems have indeed been demonstrated to be insufficient to bypass following constraints that robotics embedded systems are currently facing:

- the problem space is huge: as uncertainty of the environment and the number and type of resources available to the robot increase, the definition of the best matching between current situation and correct robot resource exploitation becomes overwhelming even for the most skilled robot engineer,
- the solution space is huge: in order to enhance robustness of complex robotic systems, existing cognitive methods and techniques need to exploit robotic-specific resources adequately. This means that the robotic system engineer should master highly heterogeneous technologies in order to integrate them in a consistent and effective way.

One ideal process for developing robotic software components is to enable the design and implementation of highly complex and robust robotic systems to involve in less effort as possible. Robotics systems are complex and embedded ones; thanks to MBE that has already demonstrated its efficiency on complex and embedded systems. We expect MBE to be a real promising solution for the development process of robotics software and systems.

Potentially, new MBE techniques have to be developed for robotics which can also be applicable to other domains. Since robotics is a very challenging domain, we are confident that new techniques may possibly open new way for Model Based Engineering.

Integrating Ontological Domain Knowledge into a Robotic DSL

Gaëlle Lortal[1], Saadia Dhouib[2], and Sébastien Gérard[2]

[1] Decision Technologies and Mathematics Lab., Thales Research & Technology, Campus Polytechnique, 1, avenue Augustin Fresnel 91767 Palaiseau cedex France
gaelle.lortal@thalesgroup.com
[2] CEA LIST, Laboratoire d'Ingénierie dirigée par les modèles pour les Systèmes Embarqués (LISE), Point Courrier 94, Gif-sur-Yvette, F-91191 France
saadia.dhouib@cea.fr, sebastien.gerard@cea.fr

Abstract. Coming from the Artificial Intelligence (AI) and Semantic Web (SW) circles, ontologies are used mainly to represent domains. The Model Driven Engineering (MDE) field gave birth to Domain Specific Languages to represent a particular technical domain. Abstracting from their uses, we consider as many others researchers that ontologies and models are closer than their original fields could get to think. Furthermore, their building or development are facing the same problems. They are costly and need experts' interviews in order to grasp specific knowledge and structure it. Likewise, ontologies and DSL can benefit from each other domains in reusing construction methodologies and even reusing knowledge modelled in another format. In this paper we first present the ontologies and DSL definition we use and some methodologies of development enabling the reuse of knowledge (as alignment, fusion). We then present how we propose to reuse the knowledge of a robotic ontology to develop robotic DSLs within the PROTEUS[1] project in order to inject ready-made domain information to the DSL.

1 Introduction

Following (Caplat, 2008), (Guizzardi, 2007), and (Gasevic, 2005), we consider ontologies and models/metamodels as highly close. To use both technologies with the best interests and find the connection points, we compare them on several criteria. The key connection points to use ontologies and models are about the abstraction levels that they represent (and then the necessary abstraction level to bind them) and more the applications and tools that are available for both technologies (and then check which are reusable or interchangeable).

Observing DSLs and ontologies, the first noteworthy remark is on the building/development methodology that is identical. An ontology as a DSL can be built/developed through inquiry, domain survey and modelling. Then we postulate that for the same objective, we should find the same concepts represented (with different formats) and then that we can find equivalent items from the DSL to the ontology.

---

[1] The PROTEUS project is a three-years funded by the French National Research Agency.

In order to check such hypothesis, we built in parallel, from the same use-cases and experts interviews robotic ontology and robotic DSL in the scope of the PROTEUS ANR Project. One of the DSLs is built from the PROTEUS ontology knowledge and the others from scratch. Here is only presented the development methodology of a Robotic Architecture DSL whose requirements are ontology based.

In this paper, we first present a definition of ontology and DSL and their application. In section 3, we then present our analysis grid and in the last section, we present how we propose to reuse the knowledge of a robotic ontology to develop robotic DSLs within the PROTEUS project in order to inject ready-made domain information to the DSL.

2 Ontology, DSL: Some Definitions

We first present a short state of the Art on ontologies and DSLs within the view adopted in the PROTEUS project. In the first part, we describe ontology as a structure of the data and in the second part, we describe the DSL (Domain Specific Language as a language designed for, and intended to be useful for, a specific kind of concern.

2.1 Ontology

The ontology is one of the favourite tools of the Semantic Web (SW). The SW proposes different tools using normalized data or which helps structuring Web data and associating "semantics" to data. A syntactic layer is added to the data available on the Web and is claimed to be the semantic enrichment. It's this layer which aims at enabling a mutual machine-machine or man-machine understanding.

Ontology is defined by (Gruber, 1993) as an explicit specification of a conceptualization. In (Gruber and Lytras, 2004), Thomas Gruber refines its definition of this type of Knowledge Base (KB) taking into account the necessary cooperation of experts of the domain to come to an agreement on the semantics, the ontological commitment: *"Every ontology is a treaty – a social agreement – among people with some common motive in sharing"* (p. 5). The process of negotiation is oriented toward the objective of the conceptualization more than towards its structure. T. Gruber strongly emphasizes the idea of a viewpoint carried by the ontology:

"The ontology is a representation artefact (a specification), distinct from the world it models, and that it is a designed artefact, built for a purpose. [...] I would try to emphasize that we design ontologies." (Gruber et Lytras, 2004, p. 1)

(Lassila and McGuinness, 2001) identify more or less formal ontologies and (Uschold and Grüninger, 1996) organize them according to their uses:

- For human communication (not ambiguous ontology but informal);
- For computer systems interoperability (exchange format);
- For system design (formal encoding and metadata).

We can define a formal ontology as a modelling of knowledge of the World. The knowledge is organized on a network of concepts. An ontology, then, consist in a set of definitions of basic categories (things, relations, properties) which enables to describe the things of the domain of interest, their properties and the relations the things maintain among each others. Then, hierarchical relations (*isa* relations) or horizontal relations among concepts or instances are rigorously defined. The concept properties can have values in finite and predefined intervals and the strictly defined axioms impose logical constraints enabling the control of logical inferences applicable on data (properties inheritance, transitive or inverse properties...). Via these inferences, new knowledge can be discovered. Despite this mechanism, domain experts and knowledge engineers should be involved in the ontology building.

Ontologies are used in several domains. In SW, each element is tagged. The tag is understood by software systems which enables their interoperability (as for Web Services). These tags, normalized and understandable by Human and Software agents, give semantics to the Web. In Artificial Intelligence (AI), the ontologies can be used to mime human behaviours, as for example, human language with linguistic ontologies. In system design (Architecture, Engineering) the ontologies used are formal and propose a complex and rigid modelling of knowledge usable by software agents.

The challenges on ontologies are improvements on knowledge sharing on the Web, systems interoperability, Man-Machine/Machine-machine communication and then step in ontology building (Buitelaar *et al.*, 2005) and update (Cimiano and Völker, 2005), use and reuse of ontologies (annotation (Handschuh and Staab, 2003), fusion/merging/alignment (Noy and Musen, 1999)) and ontology language development (RDF (Brickley *et al.*, 2004), OWL (McGuinness *et al.*, 2004), Topic Maps (Biezunski *et al.*, 1999) etc.).

T. Gruber considers that ontologies are always mixes of informal and formal parts. The ontologies that are said to be semi-formal are mainly informal and he finally concludes that "*all practical ontologies are semiformal*".

2.2 Domain Specific Language

According to (Bezivin, 2004), initially, the objects technologies were supposed to be an integration technology as it was theoretically possible to take into account homogeneously, processes, rules, functions, etc., through objects. Nowadays, we return to less hegemonic vision where the different programming and management paradigms coexist and models are no more considered only as documentary or guiding means for a human activity of programming, but that they can be used to feed tools for software automatic production. The MDE is an integrated vision through DSL based on different paradigms. Indeed, Metamodels and Models are used to ease the whole software lifecycle management, i.e. the code generation but also, integration and interoperability, documentation generation and the automation of software applications deployment. The different levels of Models are represented by M0 - data level/instances, M1 - model level, M2 - metamodel level, M3 - meta-meta-level.

A Domain Specific Language is a formal language, and then a grammar, tailored to a specific application domain. It is then a metamodel at a notation level. Constructs and abstractions of the domain are offered within the language increasing its expressiveness in comparison to General Purpose Languages (GPL). A DSL (or its graphical representation, the DSML - Domain Specific Modelling Language -) is a textual representation of a domain and enables the specification of a M1 - model in accordance with a defined metamodel (M2). The DSL enables to build and read a model. It adds symbols, represents the concepts of a metamodel and enables to handle them.

A model is an abstraction of the reality (as a Data-Base) and therefore is only a specific viewpoint on the reality.

The metamodel (MM) is a self defining model and also underlies model(s) (whether explicitly or not). The MM establishes the concepts which are useful in a specific Domain of interest and the rules of use together. I.e. it defines the relations among the concepts in a distorted view of the situation which is to say according to a certain viewpoint of the domain.

A large collection of M2 standard metamodels exists to represent specific domains (as well as UML profiles). They are sometimes coupled with specific tools enabling to tackle specific principles or methodology. The OMG proposes the MOF meta-meta language on which generic meta-languages (UML) as well as specific meta-languages are built (OMG, 2006). MOF enables to develop Domain languages (DSL) and UML enables to develop Profiles (as MARTE for Modelling and Analysis of Real-Time and Embedded Systems). Other metamodel implementations are available for BPMN (Business Process Model and Notation) or Information Management Metamodel (IMM) systems (SysML) for example[2].

The semantics of the Models is not straightforwardly available. It is more inherent to the use of the model (in reading it, transforming it, edit it, modify it...). I.e. the semantics are in the interpretation of a model and the rules applied to transform it (any rules of decoding/recoding). The rules enable to enrich, filter, add, specialize (and even « retro-engineered") information of the model to generate another model. A semi-automated way for interpreting models is available through transformation languages as QVT (Query, Views, Transformation, (QVT, 2008)) or ATL (ATL, 2010) (Lemesle, 1998, and Bezivin, 2004). However, some constraint expression languages express semantics as they constrain the interpretation of the information. It is the case for the OMG standard OCL (Object Constraints Language) or through a verification tool as PRAXIS (Blanc, 2008).

Even if DSL has for main requirement the proven consistency of the model, it appears that the same fundamental questions are posed in the two domains. What to model, how to model it, how to reconcile user needs and system requirements? But also, what does semantics means? What is granularity and what is viewpoint? How concepts evolve? Then we pose a number of criteria to compare ontologies and DSL. We present them on the next section.

3 Ontology/DSL Comparison

In order to fix the gain of using an ontology in comparison to building a DSL, we ordered our observation on a comparison grid between ontology and DSL. We present this grid here (Tab. 1) as well as other works on the ontology/DSL fusion or reuse.

The main comparison criteria are the design domain, the building methodology, the application domain and the technologies and tools. Another comparison grid could be seen in the challenges described by (Walter *et al.*, 2009) regarding 5 challenges, tooling, language interoperability, formal semantics, learning curve and domain analysis (p.1).

---

[2] The Catalog of OMG Modelling and Metadata Specifications is available at: `http://www.omg.org/technology/documents/modeling_spec_catalog.htm`

3.1 Design Domain and Domain Design

Ontology and DSLs are modelling means to represent a domain. They are used by designers of application in engineering field for the DSL and a more Artificial Intelligence and Knowledge Engineering fields for the Ontology. They are meeting the needs of structuring data and information for application use.

3.2 Building Methodology

According to (Tairas *et al.,* 2009), the ontology building methodology has clearer guidelines than the DSL development methodology.

Some useful guidelines for ontology have been published by ((Biebow and Szulman, 1999), (Noy and Mc Guiness, 2001), (Gomez-Perez *et al.,* 2003)). These building methodologies are usually supported by a tool (respectively, TERMINAE, PROTÉGÉ, ONTOWEB). Though, they are based on more informal principles of user needs/requirement gathering as described in RUP (Kruchten, 2001), (Passing, 2006)), or in Object Oriented Design Methodologies in general.

The basic iterative steps to build/develop an ontology/DSL are usually:

1) Need and requirement phase: Find what are the users need (from experts, domain documents, definition of the use of the model, explanation of the business processes of the users, and eventually, what's reusable);
2) Design phase: It's a knowledge capture and structuring phase where the data collected is organized and structured to be useful within the model;
3) Evaluation: the obtained model is evaluated to check whether it satisfies the specification requirements.

For the DSL, the evaluation is based not only on the design result but also on the DSL support tools developed in an 4) Implementation phase, where the necessary tools for executable DSLs are developed (i.e. compiler or an application generator that translates DSL constructs in an existing language for example).

This 4th phase is considered as differential in DSL vs. ontologies. The ontology support tools are not considered as part of the ontology design process. However, an ontology is not solely a KB; when it is used, it comes with a set of supporting tools as editors, reasoners, etc.

The building of ontology and developing of DSL both consider as highly useful to reuse existing works. Then in the requirement phase, reusable DSLs or ontologies are envisaged. Several integration methodologies have been developed in the both fields. (Pinto and Martins, 2000), describe several types of integration reusing an existing ontology to build a new one.

1) Integration enables to easily collate large ontologies and to reconcile several knowledge sources in keeping their autonomy;
2) Merging integration enables to create a unique and consistent ontology;
3) Alignment/Mapping integration is done by creating links among ontologies which often have a complementary coverage of a broader domain.

(Mernick *et al*, 2005) identify three patterns of design based on an existing language:

- Piggyback domain-specific features on part of an existing language;
- Specialisation by restricting an existing language;
- Extension: by extending an existing language with new features.

Here are two ways of considering the reuse of existing data but that can be equally used in any type of models.

3.3 Application Domain

As for their origin, ontology and DSL are models used for different application. We mainly recover ontologies in AI application (Classification, Knowledge Base, Dictionaries, and Natural Language Generation) or Web application (Automatic Annotation, Web-Services Orchestration). DSL are found in engineering fields as Systems modelling, Code Generation, Functional and non-functional verification, Simulations…

As their applications are different, their design goals are different. They mainly differ on the automation, security and robustness level they should provide when encapsulated in the final application.

3.4 Technologies and Tools

A lot of applications are affiliated to DSL and ontologies but in two main different ways. We then consider some Specification tools or Meta-tools, used to design/build the (Meta-)models, vs. end-use tools.

The specification tools are on the order of Design tool: Editor, Modeller, Ontology GUI, ontology editor, development framework, model composition tool, development graphical environment, inference engine or Consistency tools: Model checker, reasoning engines… The end-use tools are on the order of an orchestration engine based on an ontology, a Web GUI adapting to the concept of the user, the simulation engine playing a model… They are not specifically based on an ontology or a model and it is on these technologies that we can test the coverage and the semantics abilities of DSL and ontologies modelling the same domain for example.

3.5 Rationale for the Use of Ontology in the Design Process of DSLs

Several works have used ontologies for their semantic or structural complementarity with DSLs (with the limitations underlined in the previous section). Two main types of ontologies are referred; (1) the ontology as the *explicit specification of a conceptualization* (Morin *et al.*, 2009), (Walter, 2009) and (2) the Ontology as the metaphysical study of the nature of being and existence (Kurtev, 2007). (Kurtev, 2007) is designing a meta-language (OGML) based on the metaphysical principles of Ontology. It results in a high-level DSL close to the formal ontology metamodels. (Morin *et al.*, 2009) and (Walter, 2009) are combining the ontologies with DSL at a meta-level to extend the coverage of a DSL (Walter and Ebert, 2009) or to integrate a variability viewpoint straightforwardly in a DSML (Morin *et al.*, 2009). In the PROTEUS project, the ontology as (2) is firstly used to represent the domain, i.e. inferring information from a KB that complements with the Architecture DSL and then to develop the DSLs, i.e. as a representation of experts' knowledge.

Table 1. Ontology/DSL Comparison grid

Comparison criteria	Ontology	DSL
Design Domain	Knowledge Engineering	Engineering in general (Computer science engineering, System engineering, Electronics - for example: real time embedded systems, robotic systems, avionics systems-)
Building / Development Methodology	Ontology Building • User need and requirements capture • Reuse possibilities • Domain knowledge and structuring relations • Evaluation	DSL development • User need and requirements capture • Reuse possibilities • Domain knowledge and structuring relations • Implementation of executable DSL tools (i.e. a compiler or translator, …) • Evaluation
Application Domains	Classification, Automatic Annotation, Web-Services Orchestration, Knowledge Base, Dictionaries, Natural Language Generation, …	Systems modelling, Code Generation, Functional and non-functional verification, Simulations, …
Technologies and Tools	Ontology GUI, inference engine, ontology editor, reasoning engines, …	DSL development framework (AMMA, Eclipse GMT,…), Modeler, model composition tool, DSL development graphical environment (DSL Toolkit Microsoft, Papyrus,…), Code generator, Model checker, transformation languages (ATL,…),…
Format	RDF, OWL, Topic Maps,…	MOF, EMF, EMOF, CMOF, SMOF,…

4 On the Use of Ontology for the Development of the PROTEUS DSLs

4.1 The Proteus Project

In (PROTEUS, 2009), the robotic market is described as existing and going on growing at a fast pace. It is then of utmost importance to help French industries have their share of it. The PROTEUS project (Plateforme pour la Robotique Organisant les Transferts Entre Utilisateurs et Scientifiques meaning Robotic Platform to facilitate transfer between Industries and academics) goal is to create a portal for the French robotic community. Such a portal, to be of use, will be constituted of many parts and one key point is a toolset, the technological part of the platform.

The PROTEUS platform will enable to gain new skills in order to create or improve new products, new process or new services by providing easier way to collaborate inside a community. The software created through the project will include components and architecture description allowing its users to create complex systems where they should be able to assess and validate generic software technologies. Moreover, the link to real robots will allow these generic technologies to be inserted in hardware.

The shared infrastructure provided will take into account the definition of the so called standardized robot architecture for some specific domain as well as generic capabilities through the use of formal representations associated with generator tools. The platform should enable the community to use real robots operated by end-users in order to directly assess its achievements (e.g. cognition and control algorithms) onto real industrial robots. The software-oriented considerations are taken into account through tools facilitating knowledge transfer, executable environments creation, and methodologies to make these enabling resources easily exploitable by diverse and numerous adopters of the community. The work to be done on this axis will be to provide a minimal formal language to support the description of scenarios and model integration facilities (model means here an external component, either stand alone components or library of components that that provides access point and capability to be externally sequenced) and open simulation architecture.

The robotic fields considered are restricted to mainly aerial and terrestrial robotic as well as considerations on humanoid robotic.

4.2 The PROTEUS Robotic Ontology

The robotics ontology within PROTEUS is seen as a tool for modelling and analyzing robotic systems. Development, test and validation of embedded systems like mobile robots involve different knowledge domains. A robot's physical structure and control software are designed in order to fulfil a given type of missions. Testing the robot's functionalities needs a model of a robot as well as a model of its nominal environment. Ontologies can be used to do this modelling and validate it (PROTEUS, 2009).

The ontology has been built from the knowledge of robotics experts involved in different sub-domain of the field. Their expertise concerns the following domains: command, control, perception, navigation, localization, traffic control, optimization, mission planning to simulation. To share their knowledge and models it, the experts have been brought together in *modelling meetings*. Their exchanges were supported by the description of scenario representing the use of their field within the autonomous systems domain.

From these modelling meetings the requirements of the Robotic ontology in PROTEUS were described. The Robotic ontology should be able to model the mechanical and electronic component models, as well as control architectures, consistency detection systems and simulators, database of components, control tasks or complete subsystems. The ontology should help modelling different versions of a given robot and follows its evolution. As it comes to model the robot's behaviour, its ability to perform the missions for which it was designed; there is also a need for modelling its environment and its mission in urban area (PROTEUS, 2009).

The resulting OWL DL ontology (in its primary version) consists of 205 concepts linked with 73 relations (OWL properties). A screenshot of this ontology is presented in Fig.1. The ontology is organized around a kernel ontology describing the main concepts of the field and extended with several sub-domain ontologies describing the following topics: Robotic Components, Information, Mission, Environment, and Simulation.

This first version of the robotic ontology has been validated by the industrial users involved in the PROTEUS project but extensions' refinement is planned for the follow-up of the PROTEUS project.

In the PROTEUS project, the ontology is used not only to represent the domain and to develop the Robotic Architecture DSL as presented in this paper, but also to validate DSLs manually developed on Communication and Algorithm.

And then it is also plan to use this ontology:

1) To normalize the robotic domain;
2) To support inference at run-time;
3) To automatically transform Ontology in DSL.

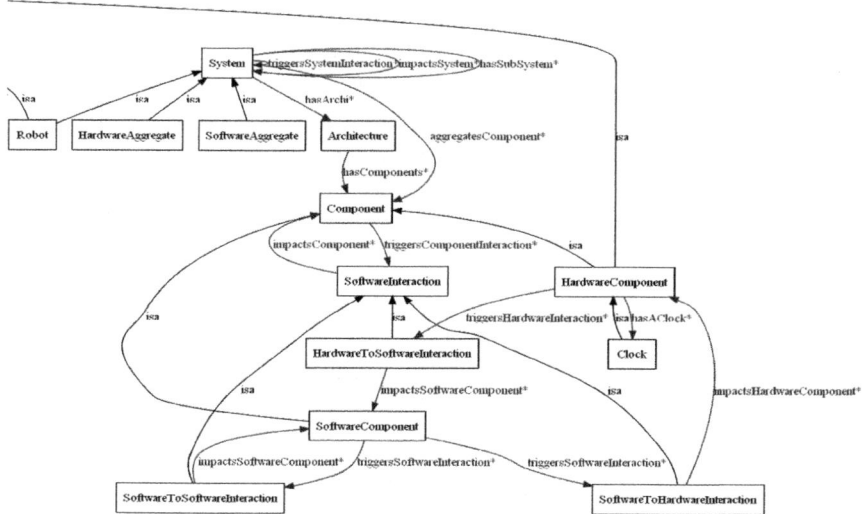

Fig. 1. Screenshot of a part of the kernel ontology

4.3 From PROTEUS Ontology to PROTEUS DSLs

4.3.1 Rationale of the Ontology Use in the Architecture DSL Design Process

The methodology we followed in PROTEUS is described in Fig.2. We show the DSL design process that integrates the ontology. The design process consists in four steps:

1. The requirements of the DSL are gathered from both following sources: in the one hand from the ontology and in the other hand from the state-of-the-art on DSL for robotics systems.
2. Building the domain model of the DSL: The purpose of the domain model is to describe formally the concepts of the domain. The domain model will be described by the means of one or more class diagrams, as well as in the form of textual descriptions.
3. Domain model verification: this step is intended to verify that the aforementioned domain model is covering all the requirements expressed in the first step.
4. UML/textual representation: An alternative for the specification of a DSL is the use of UML, which is a widely known modelling language that has a lot of support tools (Giachetti *et al.*, 2009). Another alternative is a textual representation of the DSL.

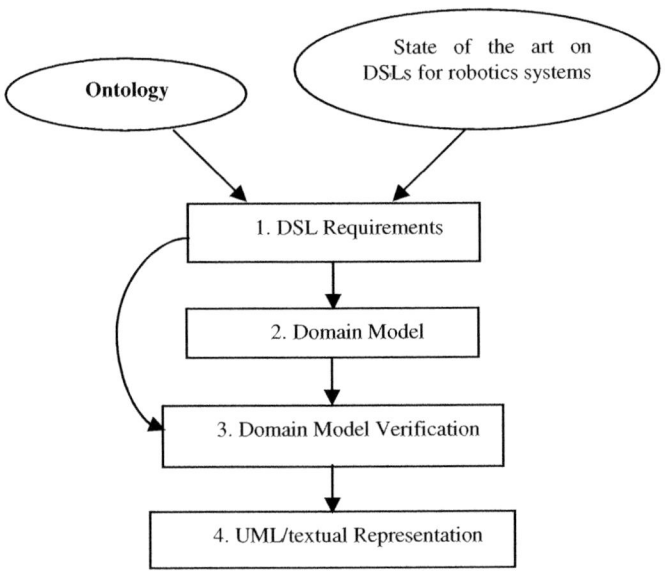

Fig. 2. Integrating the ontology in the design process of the DSL

The ontology is involved in the steps 1 and 2 of the DSL design process. Indeed, the first requirement of the DSL is to correspond to domain concepts defined in the ontology. The other requirements, coming from the ontology, are derived from this one. From the ontology, we extract all the concepts that are specific to the domain. Those concepts are then filtered to retain only the relevant ones for the DSL. On the other hand, if some concepts are missing in the ontology, they are added to the domain model of the DSL.

Table 2. Mapping the ontology to the DSL domain model

Ontology (OWL)	Domain model (UML class diagram)
Concept	Class
subClassOf	Generalization
Property	Association
Property:IsA	Inheritance
Property:HasA	Composition
Cardinality	Multiplicity

The table 2 shows the transition from the ontology, written in OWL DL language, to the DSL domain model specified as a UML class diagram. OMG also proposes the ODM (Ontology Definition Metamodel) which defines a set of QVT mappings from UML to OWL (IBM *et al.*, 2009). Only the automatic transformation from UML to OWL is implemented, the transformation from OWL to UML is not implemented yet. So we have not taken advantage of the ODM project to make the transition from OWL to UML.

4.3.2 Architecture DSL Development on Robotic Ontology Based Requirements

One of the objectives of the PROTEUS project is to provide domain specific languages (and related tools like editors, consistency checkers, etc ...) suitable to specify missions, environments and robot behaviours that have been specified by robotics experts involved in the project. The discussions under the PROTEUS project have lead to the decision of defining three DSLs:

1. The "Architecture DSL" which will ease the definition of specific robotic architectures (reactive, deliberative, hybrid) and specific components that form those architectures (sensors, actuators, planners).
2. The "Control & Communication DSL" that will control the robotic components and will ease the definition of communication mechanisms between components (sending/receiving of events and data).
3. The "Algorithms DSL" that will ease the definition of algorithms which are to be used, triggered with the "Control & Communication DSL" for implementing behaviours in the different components of an architecture described with the "Architecture DSL".

To assist the development of the PROTEUS DSLs, we have used the ontology presented in section 3.2 to build the domain model of the DSLs. In this section, we only present the case of the "Architecture DSL".

The main entry of the design process of PROTEUS DSLs is the ontology presented in section 3.2. As stated before, the ontology is organized around a kernel ontology and extended with several sub-domain ontologies describing the following topics: Robotic Components, Information, Mission, Environment and Simulation.

From this ontology, relevant concepts related to robotic architecture are extracted. In table 3, we list some of those relevant concepts:

Table 3. Subset of concepts extracted from the PROTEUS ontology

Concept	Ontology Source	Concept	Ontology Source
Component	kernel	WeaponHardware	components
SoftwareComponent	Kernel	PowerHardware	components
HardwareComponent	Kernel	SensorHardware	components
Environment	kernel	EnvironmentParameterSensor	components
ActuatorHardware	components	ImageSensor	components
PhysicDevice	components	LocalizationSensor	components
MotorizationHardware	components	ObjectDetectionSensor	components
PrehensionHardware	components	ObjectTrackingSensor	components

From the set of concepts that we have associated to the domain model of the "Architecture DSL", we have eliminated some concepts that are not relevant for the definition of the DSL. For example, the concept "Architecture" is too general and is useless for the specification of a robotic architecture.

On the other hand, we have noticed that there are some missing concepts that have to be added to the domain model of the DSL. For example, concepts such as "ComputingHardware" and "StorageHardware" are not contained in the first version of this ontology and are compulsory for an Architecture DSL.

5 Conclusion

In this article, we have presented a methodology for reusing ontologies in the development process of domain specific languages. The methodology is used in the case of the PROTEUS project and has lead to the definition of the specification requirements for the Robotic Architecture DSL of PROTEUS. The algorithm DSL and the control/communication DSL will be developed from scratch but a comparison methodology will be set up for validation on the ontology.

As an ontology is used more to classify things of the World and DSL are more used to build engineering artefacts, another work to be done is to handle an ontology guided approach to delimitate the borders of these three DSLs from the ontology. Is there tracks in the ontology model of the design viewpoint of the architect? Is it possible to delimitate the scope of the architecture viewpoint? Isn't a DSL an engineering viewpoint on a larger domain in itself?

Acknowledgements

We want to thanks Sébastien Madélénat, Jérôme Le Noir and Florian Noyrit for their fruitful discussions and enlightened comments (we remain responsible for what is written in this paper).

References

ATL (2010), http://www.eclipse.org/atl/

Bézivin, J.: Sur les principes de base de l'ingénierie des modèles. RTSI-L'Objet 10(4), 145–157 (2004), http://atlanmod.emn.fr/www/papers/LObjet2004.pdf

Biébow, B., Szulman, S.: TERMINAE: A linguistics-based tool for the building of a domain ontology. In: Fensel, D., Studer, R. (eds.) EKAW 1999. LNCS (LNAI), vol. 1621, pp. 49–66. Springer, Heidelberg (1999)

Biezunski, M., Bryan, M., et Newcomb, S.R.: Topic Maps, specification ISO/IEC 13250, December 3 (1999)

Blanc, X., Mougenot, A., Mounier, I., Mens, T.: Detecting model inconsistency through operation-based model construction. In: Robby (ed.) Proc. Int'l Conf. Software Engineering (ICSE 2008), vol. 1, pp. 511–520. ACM, New York (2008)

Brickley, D., et Guha, R.V.: RDF Vocabulary Description Language 1.0: RDF Schema (2004), http://www.w3.org/TR/rdf-schema/

Buitelaar, P., Cimiano, P., Magnini, B. (eds.): Ontology Learning from Text: Methods, Evaluation and Applications. Frontiers in Artificial Intelligence and Applications Series, vol. 123. IOS Press, Amsterdam (2005)

Caplat, G.: Modèles et métamodèles, presses polytechniques et universitaires romandes, INSA Lyon, p. 197 (2008)

Cimiano, P., Völker, J.: Text2Onto, A framework for Ontology Learning and Data-Driven Change Discovery. In: Montoyo, A., Muñoz, R., Métais, E. (eds.) NLDB 2005. LNCS, vol. 3513, pp. 227–238. Springer, Heidelberg (2005)

Falbo, R.A., Menezes, C.S., Rocha, A.R.C.: A Systematic Approach for Building Ontologies. In: Coelho, H. (ed.) IBERAMIA 1998. LNCS (LNAI), vol. 1484, pp. 349–360. Springer, Heidelberg (1998)

Gašević, D.O., Djurić, D.O., Devedžić, V.B.: Bridging MDA and OWl Ontologies. Journal of Web Engineering 4(2), 118–143 (2005)

Giachetti, G., Marín, B., Pastor, O.: Using UML as a Domain-Specific Modeling Language: A Proposal for Automatic Generation of UML Profiles. In: van Eck, P., Gordijn, J., Wieringa, R. (eds.) CAiSE 2009. LNCS, vol. 5565, pp. 110–124. Springer, Heidelberg (2009), doi:10.1007/978-3-642-02144-2_13

Gómez-Pérez, A., Manzano-Macho, D., Alfonseca, E., Núñez, R., Blacoe, I., Staab, S., Corcho, O., Ding, Y., Paralic, J., et Troncy, R.: Ontoweb, Deliverable 1.5: A survey of ontology learning methods and techniques, IST Project IST-2000-29243 OntoWeb (June 2003)

Gruber, T.: A translation approach to portable ontologies. Knowledge Acquisition 5(2), 199–220 (1993)

Gruber, T., et Lytras, M.D.: Interview for the AIS Special Interest Group on Semantic Web and Information Systems, vol. 1(3) (2004)

Gruber, T.R.: Toward principles for the design of ontologies used for knowledge sharing. International Journal of Human-computer Studies 43(5-6), 623–965 (1995)

Guizzardi, G.: On Ontology, ontologies, Conceptualizations, Modeling Languages, and (Meta) Models. In: Vasilecas, O., Edler, J., Caplinskas, A. (eds.) Frontiers in Artificial Intelligence and Applications, Databases and Information Systems IV, pp. 971–978. IOS Press, Amsterdam (2007)

Handschuh, S., Staab, S.: Annotation for the Semantic Web. In: Frontiers in Artificial Intelligence and Applications, vol. 96, p. 240. IOS Press, Amsterdam (2003)

International Business Machines, Object Management Group, and Sandpiper Software. Ontology definition metamodel (ODM). OMG Document ad/2003-02-23 (2009), http://www.omg.org/

Kruchten, P.: The Rational Unified Process. In: Booch, Jacobson, Rumbaugh (eds.). Object Technology Series, pages 332. Addison-Wesley, Reading (2003)

Kurtev, I.: Metamodels: Definitions of Structures or Ontological Commitments? In: Workshop on TOWERS of Models. Collocated with TOOLS Europe 2007, pp. 53–65 (2007), http://www.cs.york.ac.uk/ftpdir/reports/2007/YCS/416/YCS-2007-416.pdf

Lassila, O., et McGuinness, D.: The Role of Frame-Based Representation on the Semantic Web. Linköping Electronic Articles in Computer and Information Science 6, 005 (2001), http://www.ida.liu.se/ext/epa/ej/etai/2001/018/01018-etaibody.pdf

Lemesle, R.: Transformation rules based on meta-modeling. In: EDOC 1998, San Diego, November 3-5 (1998), http://atlanmod.emn.fr/www/papers/EDOC98-lemesle.pdf

McGuinness, D.L., et Van Harmelen, F.: OWL Web Ontology Language Overview, W3C Recommendation, February 10 (2004), http://www.w3.org/TR/2004/REC-owl-features-20040210/

Mernik, M., Heering, J., Sloane, A.M.: When and how to develop domain-specific languages. ACM Computing Surveys 37(4), 316–344 (2005)

Morin, B., Perrouin, G., Lahire, P., Barais, O., Vanwormhoudt, G., Jézéquel, J.-M.: Weaving Variability into Domain Metamodels. In: Schürr, A., Selic, B. (eds.) MODELS 2009. LNCS, vol. 5795, pp. 690–705. Springer, Heidelberg (2009), http://www.irisa.fr/triskell/publis/2009/Morin09c.pdf

Noy, N., McGuinness, D.: Ontology Development 101: A Guide to Creating Your 1st Ontology (2001), http://protege.stanford.edu/publications/ontology_development/ontology101-noy-mcguinness.html

Noy, N., Musen, M.A.: PROMPT: Algorithm and Tool for Automated Ontology Merging and Alignment. In: AAAI/IAAI 2000, pp. 450–455 (2000)

OMG, Meta Object Facility (MOF) Core Specification Version 2.0 (2006), http://www.omg.org/mof/

Passing, J.: Requirements Engineering in the Rational Unified Process, Seminar Requirements Engineering, Summer term, Hasso Plattner Insitute for Software Systems Engineering, 16 pages (2006)

Pinto, H.S., Martins, J.P.: Reusing Ontologies. In: AAAI 2000 Spring Symposium on Bringing Knowledge to Business Processes, pp. 77–84. AAAI Press, Menlo Park (2000), http://www.aaai.org/Papers/Symposia/Spring/2000/SS-00-03/SS00-03-012.pdf

PROTEUS Consortium, PROTEUS- - Platform proposal to ANR, ARPEGE call, 152 pages (2009)

QVT (OMG-QVT 2.0, 2008), http://www.omg.org/spec/QVT/index.htm

Tairas, R., Mernik, M., Gray, J.: Using Ontologies in the Domain Analysis of Domain-Specific Languages. In: Chaudron, M.R.V. (ed.) MODELS 2008. LNCS, vol. 5421, pp. 332–342. Springer, Heidelberg (2009)

Uschold, M., et Grüninger, M.: Ontologies: Principles, Methods and 16 applications. Knowledge Engineering Review 11(2), 93–136 (1996)

Walter, T., Ebert, J.: Combining DSLs and Ontologies Using Metamodel Integration. In: Taha, W.M. (ed.) DSL 2009. LNCS, vol. 5658, pp. 148–169. Springer, Heidelberg (2009)

Walter, T., Silva Parreiras, F., Staab, S.: *OntoDSL*: An Ontology-Based Framework for Domain-Specific Languages. In: Schürr, A., Selic, B. (eds.) MODELS 2009. LNCS, vol. 5795, pp. 408–422. Springer, Heidelberg (2009)

Weisemöller, I., Schürr, A.: A Comparison of Standard Compliant Ways to Define Domain Specific Languages. In: Giese, H. (ed.) MODELS 2008. LNCS, vol. 5002, pp. 47–58. Springer, Heidelberg (2008)

Author Index

Adler, Rasmus 312
Albayrak, Sahin 209
Amaral, Vasco 274
Amyot, Daniel 110
Aranega, Vincent 259
Asztalos, Mark 293

Bagheri, Ebrahim 110
Baresi, Luciano 90
Becker, Steffen 364
Bencomo, Nelly 204
Bergmayr, Alexander 4
Bézivin, Jean 145
Blair, Gordon 204
Blumendorf, Marco 209
Bošković, Marko 110, 308
Brandsteidl, Marion 40
Broman, David 140
Brosch, Petra 184
Brucker, Achim D. 334
Brugali, Davide 400

Cabot, Jordi 329
Cancila, Daniela 308
Cazzola, Walter 105
Cellier, François E. 140
Cichos, Harald 244
Clark, Tony 329
Clarke, Peter J. 35
Clavel, Manuel 329
Czarnecki, Krzysztof 165

Dekeyser, Jean-Luc 259
Deridder, Dirk 180
Dhouib, Saadia 401
Diskin, Zinovy 165
Domis, Dominik 312
Drago, Mauro Luigi 328

Elvesæter, Brian 1
Espinoza, Huascar 70
Etien, Anne 259

Fleurey, Franck 204
Fritzson, Peter 75, 140

Gašević, Dragan 110
Gérard, Sébastien 70, 400, 401
Ghezzi, Carlo 328
Giese, Holger 224
Gogolla, Martin 329
Gray, Jeff 105
Groenda, Henning 369

Happe, Jens 364
Hardebolle, Cécile 274
Hatala, Marek 110
Heidenreich, Florian 349
Heinze, Thomas S. 244
Helle, Philipp 75
Höfig, Kai 312
Huemer, Christian 40

Jeanneret, Cédric 204
Johannes, Jendrik 349

Kappel, Gerti 150, 184
Kargl, Horst 184
Karol, Sven 349
Kemmann, Sören 312
Kerzhner, Aleksandr A. 279
Kessentini, Marouane 293
Kienzle, Jörg 105, 125
Koziolek, Anne 384
Koziolek, Heiko 364
Kramer, Max E. 125
Krieger, Matthias P. 334
Kuhn, Thomas 312
Kusel, A. 150

Langer, Philip 184
Lee, Edward A. 140
Lehmann, Grzegorz 209
Lengyel, László 274
Longuet, Delphine 334
Lortal, Gaëlle 401
Lúcio, Levi 239

Maoz, Shahar 194
Mirandola, Raffaela 328
Morzenti, Angelo 90
Motta, Alfredo 90

Author Index

Mottu, Jean-Marie 259
Mussbacher, Gunter 110

Noorshams, Qais 384

Ober, Ileana 70
Ober, Iulian 70

Pahl, Claus 308
Paredis, Christiaan J.J. 75, 279
Pettersson, Paul 364
Pierantonio, Alfonso 180

Retschitzegger, W. 150
Reussner, Ralf 384
Ringert, Jan Oliver 194
Rioux, Laurent 400
Rossi, Matteo 90
Rumpe, Bernhard 194

Schamai, Wladimir 75
Schätz, Bernhard 1, 180, 308
Schoenboeck, J. 150
Schwinger, W. 150
Schwinn, Jean-Pascal 312
Seibel, Andreas 224
Seidl, Martina 35, 184

Seifert, Mirko 349
Sien, Ven Yu 55
Soley, Richard M. 145
Stein, Dominik 105
Syriani, Eugene 293

Tamzalit, Dalila 180
Thiele, Michael 349
Trapp, Mario 312
Trollmann, Frank 209
Trubiani, Catia 19

Vallecillo, Antonio 145
Van Baelen, Stefan 70
Vangheluwe, Hans 274
Vieira, Elisangela 239
Vogel, Thomas 224

Weigert, Thomas 70
Weißleder, Stephan 239
Wende, Christian 349
Wieland, Konrad 40, 184
Wilke, Claas 349
Wimmer, Manuel 150, 184, 293
Wolff, Burkhart 334

Xiong, Yingfei 165

GPSR Compliance

The European Union's (EU) General Product Safety Regulation (GPSR) is a set of rules that requires consumer products to be safe and our obligations to ensure this.

If you have any concerns about our products, you can contact us on ProductSafety@springernature.com

In case Publisher is established outside the EU, the EU authorized representative is:

Springer Nature Customer Service Center GmbH
Europaplatz 3
69115 Heidelberg, Germany

Batch number: 09478804

Printed by Printforce, the Netherlands